NOT JUST
BLACK AND WHITE

NOT JUST
BLACK AND WHITE

Historical and Contemporary Perspectives on
Immigration, Race, and Ethnicity
in the United States

WITHDRAWN

Nancy Foner and George M. Fredrickson
Editors

Russell Sage Foundation, New York

Library of Congress Cataloging-in-Publication Data

Not just black and white : historical and contemporary perspectives on immigration, race, and ethnicity in the United States / Nancy Foner and George M. Fredrickson, editors.
    p. cm.
    Includes bibliographical references and index.
    ISBN 0-87154-259-5 (cloth)   ISBN 0-87154-270-6 (paperback)
    1. United States—Emigration and immigration. 2. United States—Race relations.
3. Immigrants—United States. 4. Ethnicity—United States. 5. United States—Ethnic
relations. I. Foner, Nancy, 1945– II. Fredrickson, George M., 1934–

JV6465.N67 2004
304.8'73—dc22   2003066830

The paper used in this publication meets the minimum requirements of American National Standard for Information Sciences—Permanence of Paper for Printed Library Materials. ANSI Z39.48–1992.

Text design by Genna Patacsil.

RUSSELL SAGE FOUNDATION
112 East 64th Street, New York, New York 10021
10 9 8 7 6 5 4 3 2 1

For John Higham, 1920–2003

Contents

Contributors

NANCY FONER is Distinguished Professor of Sociology at Hunter College and the Graduate Center of the City University of New York.

GEORGE M. FREDRICKSON is Edgar E. Robinson Professor of History Emeritus and former codirector of the Research Institute for the Comparative Study of Race and Ethnicity, Stanford University.

RICHARD ALBA is Distinguished Professor of Sociology and Public Policy at the University at Albany, State University of New York.

JAMES BARRETT is professor of history at the University of Illinois, Urbana-Champaign.

ALBERT M. CAMARILLO is professor of history and Miriam and Peter Haas Centennial Professor in Public Service at Stanford University.

STEPHEN CORNELL is professor of sociology and director of the Udall Center for Studies in Public Policy at the University of Arizona.

NANCY DENTON is associate professor of sociology and associate director of the Center for Social and Demographic Analysis at the University at Albany, State University of New York.

YEN LE ESPIRITU is professor of ethnic studies at the University of California, San Diego.

NEIL FOLEY is associate professor of history and American studies at the University of Texas.

STEVEN J. GOLD is professor of sociology at Michigan State University.

DOUGLAS HARTMANN is associate professor of sociology at the University of Minnesota.

VICTORIA HATTAM is associate professor of political science at the New School for Social Research.

JOHN HIGHAM was the John Martin Vincent Professor Emeritus of History at Johns Hopkins University (died 2003).

JOSÉ ITZIGSOHN is associate professor of sociology and ethnic studies at Brown University.

GERALD JAYNES is professor of economics at Yale University.

PHILIP KASINITZ is professor of sociology at the Graduate Center and Hunter College of the City University of New York.

ERIKA LEE is associate professor of history at the University of Minnesota.

JOHN LIE is Class of 1959 Professor and Dean of International and Area Studies at the University of California, Berkeley.

JOEL PERLMANN is senior scholar at the Levy Economics Institute of Bard College and research professor at Bard College.

KENNETH PREWITT is Carnegie Professor of Public Affairs at Columbia University.

DAVID ROEDIGER teaches history and Afro-American studies at the University of Illinois, Urbana-Champaign.

JOE W. TROTTER is Mellon Professor and chair of the Department of History at Carnegie Mellon University, Pittsburgh.

MARY C. WATERS is Harvard College Professor and chair of the Department of Sociology at Harvard University.

Acknowledgments

This volume has its origins in a series of workshops sponsored by the Social Science Research Council's Committee on International Migration, which brought together a distinguished group of social scientists and historians to reflect on the relationship between immigration, race, and ethnicity in the United States from the end of the nineteenth century to the present. The first workshop of the Working Group on Immigration, Race, and Ethnicity in Historical Perspective was held in February 2001 in Savannah, Georgia; the second took place a year later, in March 2002, at the Kennolyn Conference Center, Soquel, California.

Many people contributed to the success of the workshops. In the very beginning, at a planning meeting at Stanford, Albert Camarillo, Philip Kasinitz, Rudolph Vecoli, and Roger Waldinger provided helpful ideas and suggestions. At the workshops themselves a number of people served as commentators and discussants. Stanley Licberson offered valuable reflections and questions at the Savannah meeting; in California, Richard Delgado, Gary Gerstle, Jennifer Hochschild, Leland Saito, Jean Stefancic, and Roger Waldinger gave excellent commentaries on the papers. The presentations by Jonathan Hanson and George Sánchez provided insights that we and many of the authors in this volume have found extremely useful. We benefited from the comments of Charles Hirschman, chair of the SSRC Committee on International Migration, who attended the California meeting. We are also grateful to Kenneth Prewitt for his special presentation at the California workshop, which provided the basis for his chapter in this volume.

We owe a special debt to Josh DeWind, director of the International Migration Program at the SSRC. At every stage in planning and developing the workshops, he played an important role. From the very start, when the workshops were only an idea, until much later, when we began to organize this volume, he served as a much-valued intellectual sounding board and a source of ideas and good advice. His commitment to and enthusiasm for the project, and his own expertise in the immigration field, were critical ingredients in making the workshops a success—and this volume possible. Also at the SSRC, program assistants Veda Truesdale and Cynthia Chang helped with the often complicated arrangements for the workshops; Cynthia eased our burden by dealing with many of the administrative chores involved in getting the manuscript ready for publication. In the last stages, Jennifer Holdaway (program officer) and Elisabeth Roesch (program assistant) also provided assistance.

At the Russell Sage Foundation, we are grateful to Suzanne Nichols for shepherding the manuscript through the publication process with expertise and good humor. Thanks as well to Eric Wanner, president of the foundation, for his support of the volume. We are also grateful to the three anonymous reviewers for providing useful suggestions that we believe have made this a better book.

Finally, our appreciation to all of the authors in the volume for their commitment to the project, their responsiveness to requests for revisions from us and from the reviewers, and, of course, the quality of their contributions. One of the most active and influential contributors was John Higham, long the nation's most prominent historian of immigration and ethnicity. Professor Higham died at the age of eighty-two just after finishing the revisions of his brilliant essay "The Amplitude of Ethnic History: An American Story." This volume is dedicated to his memory.

Nancy Foner and George M. Fredrickson

Introduction

Immigration, Race, and Ethnicity in the United States: Social Constructions and Social Relations in Historical and Contemporary Perspective

The United States has seen two massive waves of immigration since the late nineteenth century: 27.6 million immigrants arrived between 1881 and 1930, and then, after a hiatus of more than three decades due to restrictive laws, depression, and war, more than 25 million came between 1965 and 2000, a flow that continues virtually unabated into the twenty-first century (Gerstle and Mollenkopf 2001, 1–9). The two great waves differ in how the race and ethnicity of the majority of the new arrivals have been perceived, but the contrast is not as sharp as is commonly believed. In the late nineteenth and early twentieth centuries, most immigrants came from southern and eastern Europe. They were regarded as white under the law and came to think of themselves in the same way, but in the popular discourse of old-stock Americans they could be, and often were, considered racially "other." Whether they were a genetically inferior subcategory of whites or an "in-between" people who did not quite qualify as white, they were considered different in ways that went beyond acquired cultural characteristics. The bulk of the immigrants in the new wave of the past forty years have been from Latin America, the Caribbean, and Asia, and most of these are classified as nonwhite or as "people of color," both by themselves and by other Americans. In the last two decades alone, the percentage of Asians and Hispanics in the United States has doubled, with Asians representing 3.6 percent of the nation's population and Hispanics 12.5 percent at the time of the 2000 census.

How we perceive the race or ethnicity of immigrants and the significance we attach to these categorizations cannot be considered apart from the color line that has existed in American society since the colonial period. When Europeans founded a new society in what was to become the United States, they appropriated the land of the indigenous peoples and imported slaves from Africa to work on their plantations and farms, thus creating a society in which privilege and pigmentation were closely correlated. With the arrival in large numbers of immigrants who differed significantly in culture or phenotype from the Americans who were descended from the original (mostly British) colonists, difficult questions arose as to where they might fit in the preexisting racial order.

This book brings together a distinguished group of social scientists (mostly sociologists and political scientists) with a roughly equal number of prominent historians to consider the relationship between immigration, race, and ethnicity in the United States since the late nineteenth century. Several core questions frame the volume: How and with what consequences have the racial and ethnic identities of various groups been formed and transformed in the context of immigration in the past and the present? What have been the relationships between immigrant communities and existing or indigenous racial minorities, especially African Americans? How have the various racial and ethnic minorities related to each other?

Broadly conceived, the first three parts of the volume are concerned with the construction of race and ethnicity. Part I begins with a focus on general conceptual and historical issues; part II looks at the role of state policy, and part III considers the concept of panethnicity in relation to whites, Latinos, and Asian Americans. The chapters in part IV explore some of the important socioeconomic trends that have affected the development of ethno-racial identities and relations; finally, part V looks at the nature of intergroup relations in the past and present, in particular relations between immigrants and African Americans.

Some of the contributors take a "then and now" approach—they systematically compare immigrant experiences and interactions with other racial or ethnic groups in the two great periods of mass immigration. The essays in this volume suggest that systematic comparisons of then and now come more naturally to social and behavioral scientists (see especially part IV) than they do to historians. The latter are generally more interested in telling the story of how we got from then to now and analyzing the causes of the main developments. The tendency of social scientists to make theoretical generalizations and of historians to tell stories and emphasize particulars and ambiguities is evident to varying degrees in some of the essays. Yet we are even more struck by the cross-fertilization that is manifested here—that is, by the willingness of historians and social scientists to learn from each other. The more conventionally social scientific contributions are generally informed by a firm knowledge of the historical scholarship on race and ethnicity, and most of the essays by historians make substantial use of theories and concepts derived from the social sciences.

THE CONSTRUCTION OF RACE AND ETHNICITY IN THE UNITED STATES

Terminology is crucial to our enterprise, and we must therefore begin with an effort to determine what we mean by the key concepts of immigration, race, and ethnicity as used in this volume. "Immigration" is the least problematic of the terms, referring in this case to the quantifiable *voluntary* movement of people from elsewhere to the United States with the intention of residing there permanently, or at least for an extended period. "Race," however, is a much more problematic concept. Geneticists tell us that the way we generally use the term is devoid of scientific validity. Race is a socially, culturally, and historically "constructed" category that usually has a close connection to "racism" as an ideology or attitude (Fredrickson 2002). It refers to the belief that socially significant differences between human groups or communities that differ in visible physical characteristics or putative ancestry are innate and unchangeable. When two or more such groups coexist in the same society, there is a strong tendency on the part of the more powerful group to use race as a criterion to justify a dominant and privileged position for itself. As Kwame Anthony Appiah (1990) has pointed out, it is logically possible to be a racial essentialist without endorsing a hierarchy of races. He calls such a viewpoint "racialism." It is much more common, however, for such a sense of deep, unalterable difference to be accompanied by the notion that "we" are superior to "them" and need to be protected from the real or imagined threats to our privileged group position that might arise if "they" were to gain in resources and rights. Here we have "racism" in the full and unambiguous sense of the term.

The concept of race entered American history in the seventeenth century, when the colonists began to identify themselves as "white" in distinction from the Indians whose land they were appropriating and the blacks they were enslaving. By the time of the first census in 1790, the distinctive and subordinate statuses of blacks and Indians were well established, and for reasons having to do with representation and taxation, racial taxonomy—along with classifications by gender and age—had become central to the enumeration and characterization of the American population (see Prewitt, this volume). This sense of race as white entitlement was also applied to immigration in 1790 when the first law passed by Congress to regulate the access of immigrants to citizenship limited the right of naturalization to "free, white, person[s]." In 1857, in the notorious *Dred Scott* decision, the Supreme Court declared that people of African descent born in the United States, whether free or slave, could not be considered citizens—that, in other words, they could not take advantage of the birthright citizenship available to all native-born whites. After the Civil War the Fourteenth Amendment extended birthright citizenship and the right of naturalization to blacks, but Indians born in the United States were not granted automatic citizenship until 1924, the Chinese remained ineligible for naturalization until 1943, and only in 1952 was naturalization extended to all Asians.

The formal exclusion of Asian immigrants, beginning with the ban on most Chinese in 1882, established a precedent for using race as a criterion for entering the United States that was eventually applied (albeit implicitly) to southern and eastern Europeans (see Lee, this volume). Immigrants from Europe were at all times legally white, although old-stock Americans from time to time expressed doubts as to whether some groups fully deserved this status. A different kind of racial hierarchy, one based on the notion that Europeans could be subdivided into superior Aryans or Nordics and inferior Mediterraneans and Slavs (primarily on the basis of head shape), influenced nativist advocates of immigration restriction in the early twentieth century and helped justify the discriminatory quota system put into effect in 1924. The belief, cited by Erika Lee in her essay on "gatekeeping," that Poles and other Slavic peoples of eastern Europe were actually part Asian shows how the ideas of white supremacists about the color-coded "great races" and the ideas of nativists concerning the "little races" of Europe could be synthesized. In a similar fashion, the popular designation of Italian immigrants as "Guineas" conveyed the belief that they were part African in ancestry. The immigration policy in the United States between the 1920s and the abolition in 1965 of the quota system for Europeans and the remaining special bars to Asian immigration was clearly based on racial constructions.

Our other key term, "ethnicity," can be distinguished from "race," but not as easily or as unambiguously as scholars have sometimes maintained. Kenneth Prewitt shows in his essay that the census never officially racialized immigrants from Europe but rather classified them by nation of origin. It did, however, place Asians in a distinct racial category, and in 1930 it did the same for Mexicans. But after protests from the Mexican government, Mexicans were reclassified as white between 1940 and 1970, when the ethnic category "Hispanic" was introduced. In this context, "ethnic" referred to a multiracial group that shared a common cultural background or origin. Thus, without denying the reality or significance of race, the U.S. government for the first time endorsed people's right to consider cultural affinities more important than phenotypical characteristics in affirming their membership in a category regarded by the census takers as equivalent in importance to age and gender.

In his contribution to this volume, John Higham argues that ethnicity is "an analytically sharper" category than race. This may be true in the sense that ethnicity undoubtedly strikes many of us as having a substance and tangibility that race lacks. But the term itself is of relatively recent coinage, and disagreements persist on what "ethnicity" really means. One of the editors of this volume recalls that in the late 1960s, when he first taught the course that was later to be entitled "Race and Ethnicity in the American Experience," he called it "Race and Nationality in American History," thus making the association that was then common between national origin as a source of diversity and group identity in American society that could be clearly distinguished from the color consciousness associated with race. As the term "ethnicity" took hold, it was conventionally asserted that it referred to a group with common cultural characteristics as opposed to one associated with physical traits. But in the first essay in this volume, Stephen Cornell and Douglas Hartmann revert to Max Weber's classic conception by associating ethnicity with ancestry or descent rather than with culture per se. They argue that ethnicity as well as race is based on "primordialist claims." Could one become Irish American, it might be asked, by converting to Catholicism and marrying a person of Irish descent? Or for that matter, would one cease to be ethnically Irish by marrying out and forsaking the religious identity usually associated with the group? To what extent does Jewish ethnicity depend on Judaism, and to what extent does it depend on having Jewish ancestors? Does a Gentile convert become Jewish in an ethnic as well as a religious sense? Does a person who was born a Jew and becomes nonreligious or converts to another religion cease to be a Jew? Pondering such questions makes one aware that Cornell and Hartmann are right to question the reduction of ethnicity to alterable cultural characteristics such as religious belief. Their conception recalls the ethnic essentialism of Horace Kallen, the inventor of "cultural pluralism," who contended that ethnic identity does not depend on cultural choice but on the one thing an individual can never change—the identity of his or her grandfather. For Cornell and Hartmann, the differences between the two assertions of group difference arise primarily from who is doing the asserting and for what purpose. Race, they argue, is a construction that is imposed on a group against its will and that serves to rationalize oppression and discrimination. Ethnic consciousness, on the other hand, is a self-construction that comes from the group itself and is embraced by it for its own purposes.

A further understanding of the difference between race and ethnicity in the American context can be derived from Victoria Hattam's examination of how the term "ethnic group" was first used in the United States. Those who have claimed that ethnicity did not come into existence as a social science concept until World War II, or even later, have looked only for the noun and have ignored the longer history of the adjective. Hattam traces the concept of the "ethnic group" in American discourse back to the efforts of Jewish intellectuals in the period around the First World War to resist being assimilated into the melting pot while avoiding racialization. Very much aware of the American color line, Jewish thinkers like the philosopher Horace Kallen and the educator Isaac Berkson strove to legitimize difference without running the risk of being put on the wrong side of the great racial divide. Hattam contends that the recent construction of Hispanic ethnicity may serve similar purposes for some of its architects. Ethnicizers, we take her to be saying, want to validate their difference from the dominant culture in a way that avoids being designated a nonwhite race. In America at least, the concept of ethnicity would seem to be understandable only in the context of differences defined as racial and efforts to avoid racialization.

Hattam uncovers an interesting difference between Kallen and Berkson that brings us back to the issues raised by Cornell and Hartmann. As indicated earlier, Kallen believed that ethnicity is inevitably a product of one's ancestry. But Berkson took explicit exception to this viewpoint and made it his project (anticipating the social scientists criticized by Cornell and Hartmann) to root ethnic consciousness entirely in culture by de-essentializing it and making it purely voluntary. A strictly cultural ethnicity as advocated by Berkson remains theoretically possible, although as Cornell and Hartmann rightly point out, it is not what people normally understand ethnic identity to mean. Some communities that might be defined as ethnic (if we broaden the definition a bit) do not depend on having common ancestors but rather on a simple willingness to share the culture and embrace vicariously the collective memories of the group. When Abraham Lincoln (1992, 145–46) proclaimed in 1856 that one could venerate the Founding Fathers even if one's ancestors were in Ireland or Germany at the time of the American Revolution, he expounded a notion of American nationality that does not depend on ancestry or kinship. Religious groups that form bounded cultural communities that function in many ways like ethnicities do not depend on ancestry. (The Mormons would be a good example except that they believe in universal immortality and thus consider themselves responsible for converting their ancestors to the faith.) Recent newspaper accounts of a woman with no Mexican or Latino ancestry whatsoever who became a leader in a Chicano community of northern California suggest that ethnic communities may differ in their willingness to incorporate outsiders. But for the purpose of realistic social analysis, we cannot afford to ignore either the Cornell-Hartmann view of ethnicity as a form of primordialism or the Berkson-Hattam view that it is a construction based on cultural distinctiveness. It could be said perhaps that putative ancestry or descent is usually what determines membership in an ethnic group, but that the primary indicator or sign of that membership is cultural rather than physical or genetic. The performance of ethnicity as group culture may be at least as important as real or imagined "blood ties" with the other members of the group.

It is at this point that John Higham's enlargement of the concept of ethnicity and his hope that it could replace race as a central theme of American history needs to be taken into account. For Higham, all groups of people whose identity and solidarity are based on shared historical memories and cultural commitments that distinguish them from other groups in the society deserve to be considered ethnic. Although he does not say so explicitly, it does not appear that common descent is a sine qua non of ethnic membership. To extend the concept beyond immigrants to old-stock Americans normally identified with regions, such as the nineteenth-century New Englanders and post–Civil War southerners, he implicitly rejects the ancestry test. Yankees could and did become loyal southerners by embracing a southern view of the world, and New England Brahmins were receptive to the incorporation of new blood so long as it met certain cultural and intellectual standards. (Think of the great Harvard philosophers of the turn of the century: the Scotch-Irish New Yorker William James, the Californian Josiah Royce, and the Spaniard George Santayana.) In Higham's scheme, everyone is ethnic but in different ways. Dividing the ethnicities into those of settlers, immigrants, and captives, he devotes much of his attention to the settlers, because he believes that the ethnic character of their experience has been ignored. The voluntary immigrants have been much studied, and Higham sees little need to focus on them. The mistake, he suggests, has been to consider them the only Americans with ethnicity. His third category—captives—includes Native Americans and involuntary immigrants from Africa. The Puerto Rican experience, which he considers in some detail, constitutes for him a hybrid of captivity and immigration. If he had included Mexican Americans as part of his survey, he might have found another hybrid case, one that involves both the captivity resulting from conquest in the midnineteenth century and the later immigration from what remained of Mexico.

Higham's effort to extend the concept of ethnicity to white people who are not immigrants or the descendants of immigrants and to those whose incorporation into the society has been by force rather than consent is a bold effort to make ethnicity central to all of American history and to replace the emphasis on race, which he believes has outlived its usefulness. Extending it to groups of "settlers" with collective memories and myths of origin is a fresh and potentially fruitful insight. But, following Cornell and Hartmann's distinction between race and ethnicity, it could well be argued that race remains the appropriate characterization when we are referring to the identities of populations resulting from forced incorporation. Also, groups like Puerto Ricans and Chicanos may indeed represent mixed cases, but might it not be useful to think of their hybridity as one of race and ethnicity? Moreover, Higham's typology has no apparent place for voluntary immigrants of color, such as the Chinese and Japanese of the nineteenth and early twentieth centuries, who were treated quite differently from the generic immigrants he describes.

Several of the essays in this volume go beyond race and ethnicity to confront the relatively new concept of panethnicity, which is what happens when a number of previously discrete ethnic groups seek to join together in reaction to the dominant group's tendency to homogenize them for the purpose of discriminating against them. From the Cornell-Hartmann perspective, panethnicity might be theorized as what happens when a "race" tries to make itself an ethnicity by embracing and reconstructing a previously imposed identity.

The most obvious recent example of panethnicity as a response to racialization is the development of an Asian American identity movement, as described and analyzed in this volume by Yen Le Espiritu. Without the construction by whites of a threatening "Mongolian" or "yellow" race that had to be barred from citizenship or kept out of the country, it is doubtful that Chinese, Japanese, Koreans, and Vietnamese (all from homelands with a history of mutual animosity) would have found much common ground in America. But Espiritu also posits an international basis for Asian American panethnicity. The disruptive effects of American expansionism in the Far East, she contends, created a basis for solidarity among the peoples who were uprooted and forced across the Pacific. But this clearly applies to some groups better than others—most obviously to Filipinos and Vietnamese, less clearly or not in the same way to Japanese, Chinese, and Koreans, and scarcely at all to Asian Indians. Espiritu acknowledges that differences in class status and educational attainments among Asian groups, and consequently in their ability to take advantage of American opportunities, make panethnic solidarity difficult to achieve. Asian Indians, Japanese, and Filipinos are among the most successful ethnic groups in American society, while the Hmong and Cambodians are among the least. Such examples of Asian American diversity "confirm the plural and ambivalent nature of panethnicity." It is striking and paradoxical that a major success of the Asian American movement was a campaign to force the U.S. Census Bureau to allow people of Asian ancestry to identify themselves by national origin or subgroup rather than simply as Asians.

Hispanic or Latino panethnicity, as discussed in the essays by José Itzigsohn and Neil Foley, seems to have somewhat different implications. If Asian American panethnicity takes a previously denigrated racial category and valorizes it, the Latino version has, at least in some of its formulations, sought to avoid racialization. It appears from both of their accounts, as well as from Victoria Hattam's brief discussion of Hispanic ethnic identity, that maintaining distance from blacks and avoiding an unambiguous designation as nonwhites has at times been a motivating force in efforts to unify people of Latin American origin or derivation in the United States. In Foley's formulation, Latinos in Texas have tried to straddle the color line. Penalized in the civil rights era by their legal categorization as white, Tejanos affirmed racial difference to the extent that it could justify legal action against discrimination but not to the point of accepting equivalence with African Americans as a racial minority. According to Itzigsohn, cooperating Latino groups in the Northeast have often revealed a strong resistance to any association with blackness. Latino pan-ancestry has thus challenged the white-black binary of American race relations. As we have seen, the post-1970 census categories of "non-Hispanic whites" and Hispanics who "may be of any race" constitute the Census Bureau's first acknowledgment of an ethnic category that is distinguished from race.

But what is the actual basis of Latino panethnicity, and how strong a bond does it create? It is not devotion to the Spanish language, Itzigsohn reports, because many second- and third-generation Latinos speak only English. Not only is the Latino community variable in skin color, but there are also substantial cultural differences, although some Spanish heritage, if not necessarily language, would seem to be the common denominator. As with Asian Americans, different Latino groups have greatly differing socioeconomic profiles. The contrast between predominantly white and middle-class Cubans and poor people of black, Indian, or mixed race from parts of Central America and the Caribbean suggest the limits of pan-Latino solidarity. One version of Latino panethnicity especially favored by Mexican American activists features, in addition to culture, identity as a "brown" or mestizo people. Phenotypically distinctive Latinos, like Asians, have long been racialized—in practice if not in law—on the basis of pigmentation, especially in the Southwest. Affirmation of "brownness" has become a way to affirm an antiracist racial solidarity while at the same time remaining nonblack.

It would seem that Latinos, like Asians, are strongly attached to their more specific ethnic or national identities and come together only in situations where cooperation enables them to exert political influence to the common advantage of the participating nationalities. To the extent that the white or Anglo majority, nationally or locally, treats either Asians or Latinos as a single group and acts in ways that affect all or most of those so designated, panethnic identities and movements tend to emerge. Their function would seem to be primarily political rather than cultural, and reactive more than self-generating.

Has there also been a white panethnicity? David Roediger and James Barrett confront this issue in their essay on the role of the Irish in racializing the "new immigrants" of the period 1890 to 1930. What they call "an oppressive white panethnicity" emerged when Irish gang members tried to enlist Poles and Lithuanians in violence against blacks in the Chicago race riot of 1919. Another more benign form emerged when the Irish sought to cooperate with other European immigrant nationalities in opposing nativism and immigration restriction. The "others" for this panethnicity were Anglo-Americans, not blacks. But Irish Americans could also manifest disdainful and bigoted attitudes toward Italians, Poles, and other immigrant nationalities and even seek identification with old-stock Americans. Catholicism was another path to the broadening of group sympathies and affiliations, as was the labor movement. But Roediger and Barrett give the general impression that the Irish remained intensely loyal to their narrower ethnic affiliation and embraced more inclusive identities in a more or less opportunistic or situational fashion. Even more than in the case of Asians and Latinos, panethnicity based squarely on whiteness was a function of specific relationships with people of color, especially blacks, and did not connote any deep cultural affinity or sense of kinship among those designated as white. It might even be asked whether panethnicity of this sort is a form of ethnicity at all. If a distinction between race and ethnicity is to be maintained, we might simply call it "white racism" and leave it at that. The one thing that "white panethnicity" might have in common with the arguably better grounded panethnicities of Latinos and Asians is the fact that it constitutes a political project and cannot be understood except in the context of interactions and power relationships with other ethnic or racial groups.

How does America's principal non-immigrant minority, African Americans, fit into this mosaic? As we have seen, the special position of blacks has been an essential element in how ethnic or racial groups of immigrant origin define themselves and their position in American society. Has a history of special disadvantage—slavery, Jim Crow, ghettoization, and, most recently, massive incarceration—made the black experience different in kind from that of other minorities? Several of the essays in this book suggest that it has. Richard Alba and Nancy Denton show that blacks have been, and still are, more residentially segregated than the other groups. Joel Perlmann and Mary Waters demonstrate that they have been persistently less likely to marry outside the group than other racial and ethnic minorities. And according to Philip Kasinitz, "most evidence would seem to argue that the African American experience remains poles apart from that of other groups in the United States." Blacks are the quintessentially racialized Americans. There would be no African American identity had it not been for a history of massive oppression and stigmatization.

How, if at all, do the concepts of ethnicity and panethnicity apply to blacks? Cornell and Hartmann use their way of distinguishing race and ethnicity to offer a partial answer to this question. Accepting the categorization imposed on them by whites, African Americans, they argue, turned it into a positive sense of "peoplehood." "They thereby reconstructed themselves as an ethnic group, becoming both race and ethnic group at once." It might seem curious, however, that blacks themselves seem to have been loath to describe the rise of group consciousness in these terms. Sociologists of the 1970s who wrote about the rise of black power and consciousness described it as a process of "ethnogenesis" (for example, see Taylor 1979), but we know of no African American public intellectuals who have embraced "ethnicity" as a model for their group self-consciousness. The reason for this reluctance to abandon race in favor of ethnicity can perhaps be found in Joe Trotter's historical account of scholarly comparisons of black migration to the North and immigration from abroad. The notion, popular in the 1950s and 1960s, that black migrants were simply the "last immigrants" and could be expected to advance in northern urban society the way European newcomers had done earlier came under sharp attack in the 1970s for underestimating white racism and the obstacles it presented to black equality and opportunity. To embrace the notion that blacks were—or were in the process of becoming—an ethnicity seems premature to those who see racism as a persistent problem for blacks that requires special race-conscious responses.

Nevertheless, it is hard to avoid the conclusion that American society as a whole would be better off if blacks could characterize themselves and be characterized by others as an ethnic group rather than a race. The combination of group memory, consciousness of common descent, and shared culture already constitutes a strong basis for black self-respect and, if racism could be truly overcome, would invite the respect of other Americans. But such an ethnicity might have one drawback. A normal degree of ethnic specificity might limit membership in the group to descendants of those who were enslaved in the southern United States, thereby excluding black immigrants from Africa and the Caribbean, who have had somewhat different group memories, cultural traditions, and historical experiences. But a black panethnicity is already being constructed around the concepts of "the Black Diaspora" and the "Black Atlantic." Panethnicities, as we have seen, are difficult to construct, but this one might have a brighter future than most.

SOCIAL RELATIONS

If many essays in this volume focus on the construction of race and ethnicity in the context of the changing character of immigration, others are concerned with social relationships between immigrants and established residents who are defined as racially or ethnically distinct. Indeed, there is a dialectical interplay between social constructions and interethnic or racial relations. Certainly, these relations are shaped by the way race and ethnicity are constructed in specific times and places; at the same time, day-to-day social relations—in communities, neighborhoods, organizations, and families—can play a role in altering the boundaries between ethno-racial groups and thus the very way in which the groups are defined and conceived. (In discussing the interactions among such groups, not all contributors have found it necessary to insist on the distinction between race and ethnicity that is stressed in the more theoretical and historical essays. The use of composite terms like "ethno-racial" becomes justified when what is being considered is simply the consciousness of members of one descent group or "people" that its differences from other groups—however they may be defined—create a basis for solidarity that is deep-seated, significant, and capable of transcending or overwhelming other actual or potential identities, such as those based on class, gender, or religion.)

In probing the dynamics of interethnic or racial relations, there is a risk, as John Lie cautions, of slipping into an essentialism that presumes the organic solidarity of ethno-racial groups and categories. Ethno-racial groups, he reminds us, are abstractions; groups do not interact, but people who are seen to "belong" to these groups do, and they have a variety of identities and allegiances that come into play in social relations and interactions. As Lie argues, we cannot assume the primacy of ethno-racial identities; what he calls, in an analytic nod to Marx, "ethnicity for itself" does not exist in all times and places. This said, the fact is that people's race and ethnicity—in terms of how they are identified by others and how they identify themselves—have a powerful influence on a wide range of social relations in the United States, both today and in the past.

One of the main concerns of this book is to explore how immigration affects interethnic or racial relations and the contexts in which they develop as well as the very nature of these relations and their consequences. This of course is a vast topic, and the volume was not designed to cover all groups and all contingencies in either the past or the present. The essays in parts IV and V offer analyses of some of the important social trends and forces that have shaped, and continue to shape, ethno-racial relations—

residential segregation, intermarriage, and second-generation patterns of assimilation—as well as case studies, with both a historical and contemporary dimension, of the character of relations between African Americans and immigrants, in particular Asian and Hispanic groups.

Segregation, Strain, and Conflict

In actuality, relationships between immigrants and long-established minorities are often a complex tangle of conflict and cooperation, distancing and intermingling, tension and accommodation, yet for analytic purposes it is helpful to look at these opposing tendencies separately.

On one side, there are the trends toward, and instances of, segregation, strain, and conflict, which, as a number of the chapters note, have received considerable—some would say undue—attention. As we have already noted, Alba and Denton's analysis of immigrant residential patterns at the beginning and end of the twentieth century points to the persistence of black-white segregation; people of African ancestry, native and immigrant alike, continue to be highly segregated from the white majority—much more so than Asians and lighter-skinned Latinos. Rates of out-marriage with whites show the same trend (Perlmann and Waters, this volume). Looking back in time, Alba and Denton point out that black-white residential segregation actually worsened in many nonsouthern cities in the second and third decades of the twentieth century—just when European immigrants and their children were moving away from ethnic enclaves and becoming less segregated from majority neighborhoods. In 1910 the newer European immigrants were often more segregated from native whites than were blacks; by 1920, in the early stages of the Great Migration of African Americans from the South, there was a reversal of this pattern, which has persisted into the current era. Although residential segregation certainly does not preclude interactions in other settings, certainly it limits opportunities for contact in neighborhoods and a host of neighborhood institutions, from schools to social clubs and churches.

There is also the fact that, whatever their race or ethnicity, many immigrants continue, in time-honored fashion, to cluster in ethnic neighborhoods, partly by choice but also owing to constraints, including poverty and discrimination. Admittedly, as Alba and Denton point out, such neighborhoods usually have not been ethnically exclusive. As they also note, residential space is less determining of strong ties than a century ago now that immigrants are less likely to work within walking distance of their homes and can maintain connections to kin and co-ethnics through telephones, automobiles, and computers. Nonetheless, with the heavy concentration of co-ethnics in many neighborhoods—and often in workplaces as well—many immigrants carry out most, sometimes virtually all, of their day-to-day interactions with people from their home countries and communities and are thereby isolated from people in other groups. In his memoir, Nancy Foner's father, who grew up in an early-twentieth-century Jewish neighborhood in Brooklyn, remembers that it was not until he was in high school (and his parents had been in the United States for twenty years) that a non-Jewish person—the Russian (non-Jewish) pitcher on his brother's baseball team—came to his house. "Our neighborhood," he reports, "was so Jewish that it wasn't until we were practically adults that we were really aware of the larger culture around us" (Foner 2002, 6). No doubt, there are many similar stories today.

In this urban Jewish neighborhood a century ago there were no African Americans, Hispanics, or Asians—indeed, their number was tiny in all the northeastern and midwestern cities experiencing massive immigration at that time. As Albert Camarillo notes in his chapter, intergroup relations in the early decades of the twentieth century in the nation's largest cities were largely defined by contact between native-born whites and European immigrants (and their offspring): "The patterns in the final decades of the century were earmarked, by contrast, more by interactions between nonwhite groups in cities, especially urban areas where minorities were beginning to form majorities. . . . Consequently relations among and between people of color increasingly define a new racial frontier in intergroup relations in the American metropolis and in many metropolitan suburbs." Today African Americans are a significant proportion of the population in the cities where contemporary immigrants commonly settle, and a growing number of neighborhoods are a mix of blacks and Hispanics, and sometimes Asians and whites as well (Alba et al. 1995). Even in these multi-hued neighborhoods, however, newcomers and established residents may have quite limited contact. In his study of a multiethnic Queens neighborhood with a mix of Latino and Asian immigrants, African Americans, and whites, Michael Jones-Correa (1998, 32) speaks of communities that overlap but do not touch. In Houston apartment complexes, Nestor Rodriguez (1999, 430), writes, Latino immigrants and African Americans share a common settlement place but, besides casual encounters, live culturally and socially apart. Even in the county park, African American youth can be found on the basketball court while Latinos are on the soccer fields.

Social interactions in multiethnic workplaces and schools throughout urban America are also often characterized by ethnic separation as people gravitate toward those who share common cultural understandings, customs, and language and avoid those with whom they feel less comfortable or who they fear will reject them. Even if they work side by side with people in different groups, workers often eat lunch and take breaks with "their own kind." Thus, Alex Stepick and his colleagues (2003) report that in the Miami apparel factory they studied virtually everyone sat in well-established spots in the cafeteria during lunch, talking only with those in their own ethnic group. In the New York nursing home studied by one of the editors of this volume, the small groups of nursing aides who socialized at meals and breaks were generally composed of co-ethnics; the women who lent each other a hand on the job were generally of the same ethnic background; and even the small groups of two or three who walked to the subway regularly after work each day were ethnically homogeneous (Foner 1994, 140–41). In many schools immigrants and native minorities sit next to each other in class, but informal social groups and extracurricular clubs and organizations are divided along ethno-racial lines (see, for example, Fass 1989 on New York City high schools in the 1930s and 1940s, and Olsen 1997 on a multicultural high school in contemporary California).

If maintaining distance from blacks is involved in contemporary pan-Latino identities, it is also true, as a number of historians have written, that in the past southern and eastern European immigrants and their children claimed membership in the racial majority by similarly setting themselves apart from blacks (see, for example, Guterl 2001; Jacobson 1998; Roediger 1994). Of relevance here is that distancing strategies—in particular the desire of immigrants in various groups to distinguish themselves from African Americans—can accentuate separation and exacerbate strains. Interestingly, immigrants who share a common African ancestry with or are closest in phenotype to African Americans—West Indians and dark-skinned Hispanics and South Asians—are the most active in drawing the divide as a way to avoid being mistaken for African Americans, especially poor African Americans. And it is among those who have the least success in doing this and the most frequent interaction with African Americans in inner-city neighborhoods—West Indians—that relationships with African Americans are especially difficult and strained (see Foner 2001; Vickerman 1999).

As for actual conflict, we do not have to embrace what John Lie calls the conflict thesis—the view that conflict and discord characterize interethnic relations—to acknowledge that conflict occurs between immigrant minorities and African Americans. A broad range of locally specific circumstances determine the particular focuses, intensities, durations, forms of expression, and resolutions of individual conflicts. Yet what Ewa Morawska (2001, 84) calls basic hostility-generating factors can be identified for native blacks, including shared perceptions of numerical, residential, economic, or political encroachment by immigrants and competition with them in one or more arenas, combined with the belief that other groups have made their gains undeservedly and at the cost of blacks' progress.

Already there are signs of escalating tensions between Hispanics and African Americans in many areas. Nationally, Hispanics, according to 2002 census figures, have surpassed blacks as the largest minority, and in a number of places Hispanic groups have numerically overtaken and begun to challenge African Americans' newly won accession to positions of power and control. Moreover, Hispanics often make challenges for inclusion on grounds similar to those that African Americans have used before, such as past exclusion and discrimination. In general, competition for political influence, jobs, housing, and other resources is at the root of African American–Hispanic conflicts, although negative stereotypes and factors such as language divisions also usually come into play.

In his chapter, Neil Foley notes that in cities in Texas and elsewhere in the Southwest where Hispanics have recently outnumbered African Americans, the two groups are in direct competition for representation on school boards and city councils and in other local arenas of power. South Central Los Angeles is another area where black-to-brown residential succession has been taking place in many neighborhoods (Johnson, Farrell, and Guinn 1999). In Compton, the lower-income Los Angeles community that Albert Camarillo describes here in detail, African Americans finally achieved power after a long struggle, only to see their position contested by a growing Latino population that is almost exclusively of Mexican origin. Some black leaders have rejected the legitimacy of Latinos' calls for affirmative action, arguing that it was created to redress the wrongs of slavery, not to benefit immigrants, and that Latinos are latecomers who did not engage in civil rights struggles. For their part, Latinos complain of lack of access to municipal jobs and leadership positions in local government as well as African American school officials' and teachers' biases against Latinos and insensitivity to Latino students' special language needs (see also Johnson et al. 1999; McLain and Tauber 2001; Mindiola, Niemann, and Rodriguez 2002). There is a different twist to African American–Latino strains in Miami, where a large and established black minority now find themselves living in a city dominated demographically, politically, and economically by Latinos. Tensions between Miami's African Americans and Cubans, in the words of Guillermo Grenier and Max Castro (2001, 155), "are seething constantly and fuming periodically"—with the two communities divided by space, class, political party, ideology, and language. African Americans regard Cubans as their "new masters" who, among other things, give preferential governmental treatment to Hispanics and are indifferent to African American concerns.

The other arena of conflict discussed in this volume, that between Asians and African Americans, is based in the dynamics of merchant-customer relations. "Entrepreneurially-induced" conflicts (Johnson et al. 1999), as Steven Gold shows in his essay, have a long history and have involved various groups of immigrant merchants and inner-city minority residents over the past century. In the 1930s and 1940s conflicts between Jewish business owners and African American customers were in the news; now it is strains between Koreans and inner-city blacks. Among the factors involved today that are mentioned by Gold and Lie in their respective chapters are language and cultural barriers, co-ethnic hiring, and political efforts by urban African Americans to demand economic empowerment and social dignity. And as Gold notes, group-specific, local, and contextual issues contribute to and shape the contours of particular conflicts. Gold argues, however, that at base, patterns of racial, ethnic, and economic inequality and boundary maintenance in American society are to blame—and that as long as these endure at least some fraction of entrepreneurs and customers are likely to be embroiled in conflicts.

Cooperation, Accommodation, and Tolerance

Interethnic and racial relations, of course, are not all about conflict, and several of the chapters warn against overlooking the many instances of cooperation, accommodation, and tolerance. Indeed, Lie contends that undue emphasis on and media attention to violent outbreaks can fan the flames of dissension and heighten ethnic-based identities and group mobilization. Peaceful coexistence is often the rule between immigrants and African Americans, and even if some members of the groups are in conflict, others may live in harmony. It is thus wrong, Lie argues, to assume, for example, that merchant-customer tensions between some Koreans and African Americans imply that all of them are inevitably at loggerheads.

As for merchant-customer conflicts themselves, Gold makes it clear that the vast majority of interactions between immigrant entrepreneurs and their customers are conflict-free. Among other things, owners and customers realize their mutual dependence and generally make an effort to maintain civil relations. Even when immigrant businesses have been attacked or looted, they have often just been accessible targets in times of social disorder rather than the focus of public outrage.

In residential communities like Compton, Camarillo argues, an exclusive focus on African American–Latino conflict misses the many examples of cooperation and coalition building. While Compton's leaders were struggling over issues of political representation and access to institutional resources, black and Latina mothers were supporting each other across ethno-racial group lines in their day-to-day interactions—looking after each other's children and working together on projects to keep the streets clean.

Although ethnic distancing and segregation are often the rule in multiethnic schools and workplaces, we need to be sensitive as well to the friendships that develop in classrooms and playgrounds among African American, immigrant, and white students (see Goode, Schneider, and Blanc 1992) and to the patterns of cooperation and personal friendship that emerge on the job (Stepick et al. 2003). In her chapter, Hattam mentions the class-based political and labor coalitions of African Americans and "white ethnics" in the 1930s and 1940s. In the present era African Americans and immigrant minorities may come together in political alliances on certain issues and electoral campaigns; the structure of the local political system and political traditions play a key role in determining whether and how such alliances develop (see McKeever 2001; Mollenkopf 1999; Rodriguez 1999; Sanjek 1998). And if immigrants resort to distancing strategies to differentiate themselves from African Americans, this does not mean that distancing characterizes all of their relations; on some occasions they may identify and align with native blacks, the case of West Indians being especially noteworthy in this regard. Indeed, the longer West Indians live in the United States, and thus the longer they are exposed to the same kind of racial discrimination that African Americans experience, the more they identify with African Americans (see Vickerman 1999, 2001).

Moreover, much of the action today, in terms of day-to-day cooperation, coalition building, and culture creation, is taking place among members of the second generation, who are growing up in multiethnic neighborhoods and cities with no clear racial majority. In New York, Philip Kasinitz, John Mollenkopf, and Mary Waters (2002) report that second-generation youth have more contact with each other and native minorities than with native whites and that new cultural hybrids are emerging in the interaction between the various first- and second-generation immigrant groups and native minorities: African American young people dance to Jamaican dance hall music, and Dominican and Haitian second-generation boys are enmeshed in a street culture that is in large part African American and Puerto Rican. Members of the second generation are learning to be "New Yorkers" in colleges, labor unions, and offices, where they interact with each other, native minorities, and native whites. Indeed, to the second generation the very definition of "New Yorkers" could include "immigrant groups, native minority groups, or . . . Italians, Irish, Jews, or the like" (Kasinitz, Mollenkopf, and Waters 2002, 1034). Beyond (and including) New York, an added dynamic is that in post–civil rights America what Kasinitz in his chapter calls African American–inspired models of racial difference and racial politics are more salient for nonblack nonwhites than in the past. For example, one study he cites reports that Asian American professionals feel moderate levels of kinship with African Americans and Latinos because these minority communities provide role models in fighting racism. Indeed, Kasinitz suggests that one difference from the past is that an earlier second generation fought for inclusion *despite* being members of previously racialized and excluded groups, while the current second generation at least has the option of fighting for inclusion *because* they are members (or resemble members) of previously excluded groups.

Although there is plenty of evidence of anti-immigrant feeling today on the part of non-Hispanic whites and strains with new Asian and Hispanic arrivals, particularly in communities where whites have long been a dominant presence, several chapters in the volume note trends in the current period that bode well for relations between whites, Asians, and Latinos and present a more optimistic scenario regarding black-white relations. In that most intimate of arenas, the family, significant numbers of second-generation Asians and Hispanics have non-Hispanic white spouses or partners, and their children are being raised in mixed-origin homes. In what Perlmann and Waters describe as a "very strong hypothesis" predicting intermarriage patterns, the fourth- and fifth-generation descendants of the Hispanic and Asian immigrants of our time will be almost all of mixed origin, and almost all will also be the descendants of non-Asians and non-Hispanics. In this scenario, clearly the very conceptions of racial and ethnic categories will undergo a sea change, and a key question, once again, concerns how blacks will fit in, since black-white intermarriages, though rising in frequency, are still relatively rare.

The residence patterns outlined in the chapter by Alba and Denton also suggest the potential for growing intermingling with non-Hispanic whites for many second-generation Hispanics and Asians. Despite continued large-scale immigration in the 1980s and 1990s, Asians and Hispanics remain only moderately segregated from non-Hispanic whites. For both Asians and Latinos, the most powerful determinant of residential location is socioeconomic position—the greater their income and the higher their educational status, the larger the percentage of non-Hispanic whites in their neighborhood. Living in the same neighborhood, as we have noted, does not tell us about the quality of interaction, yet as Alba and Denton suggest, even if immigrants keep to their own kind, their children in suburban communities are likely to develop ties with whites and members of other groups in schools, playgroups, and other local arenas.

And while the evidence shows that blacks remain more isolated from whites than Asians and Hispanics, Gerald Jaynes's conceptual scheme suggests that class can trump race in structuring intergroup relations so that middle-class blacks today often can avoid stigmatization by whites in everyday interactions by making their class position clear. In Jaynes's account, the growth of the black middle class in post–civil rights America and the mass immigration of people of color who occupy diverse class positions have made race a less reliable guide for identifying the dependent poor. Without evidence to the contrary, middle-class Americans generally assume that blacks and other people of color belong to the "underclass." For Jaynes, this presumption—or calculated prejudgment—is now rebuttable by better-off and better-educated blacks (and other minorities); once they avoid being seen as belonging to the "underclass," their relations with middle-class whites "are likely to be equalitarian." This analysis fits in with other predictions that foresee increased intermingling among the black and white middle and upper-middle classes based on common class and occupational status, school ties, contacts at work, and other social connections. Whatever the future of intergroup relations, Jaynes's chapter makes clear that class is an integral part of the process that must be considered in understanding the ever-changing nature of ethno-racial relations, boundaries, and identities.

FUTURE RESEARCH

As immigration continues to change the United States, it is reshaping the way Americans think about race and ethnicity—the very definitions of groups and categories, the boundaries between them, and the identities that develop—as well as the nature of relations among people in different ethno-racial groups. This is not a new process. We might say that it has been part of the fabric of American society since the very beginning, yet as this book makes clear, there are many new dimensions in the current era. In bringing together historians and social scientists, the chapters in this volume, taken together, chart trends and changes since the end of the nineteenth century, make comparisons between the present and last great immigration periods, and bring out the particularities and ambiguities of specific times, groups, and places at the same time as they identify broad general processes and patterns. In many ways this is a beginning book, and the essays raise questions pertaining to the past, present, and future that suggest a host of directions for additional research.

We still have a lot to learn about the reformulation of group boundaries and identities in the context of immigration. We also have yet to determine whether—and in what ways—the experiences of European immigrants and their descendants in the past are a guide to what is happening today and to what may happen in the years ahead among new arrivals and their children. In their chapter, Steven Cornell and Douglas Hartmann lay out some crucial questions: Which groups have the freedom to construct themselves, and why? Which groups find themselves caught in inescapable categories constructed by others, and why? Which groups are moving from one situation to another? Why and how are they doing so? Which groups get combined together, and which are seen as separate and distinct?

And as Victoria Hattam, Erika Lee, and Kenneth Prewitt lead us to ask, what is the role of the state? State policy—including immigration policy itself—both reflects and shapes the construction of race and ethnicity. Building on Lee's historical analysis, we can ask whether, and how, gatekeeping regulations that decide who can or cannot legally enter the country will continue to influence, and be influenced by, notions of racial and ethnic difference. Also looking ahead, there is the potentially transformative role of the new multiple-race option in the census, used for the first time in 2000. Prewitt's analysis makes it clear that state measurement systems have an independent effect on racial discourse and on which groups people see themselves as belonging to— yet we can only speculate at this point about the impact of the new multiple-race option. Among the possibilities he mentions are continuing pressures from advocacy groups to expand the number of primary groups in the racial classification system. How this process unfolds is a critical topic for study. So is the continuing "active, self-conscious politics of sorting and classifying" as different groups seek to position themselves in terms of the racial taxonomy and how they wish to be counted.

Panethnicity is clearly influenced by state classification systems, yet panethnic identities are not simply imposed from above. They are also actively created by individuals and groups as a basis for forging alliances and asserting solidarity. Following Itzigsohn, one challenge for the future is to investigate whether and in what ways people adopt a panethnic identity, the meanings they attribute to it, the political projects constructed around it, and the sites in which these identities and projects are constructed. There is also the question of how panethnic identities—and indeed, racial and ethnic identities generally—vary by national origin, class, phenotype, gender, sexuality, immigrant status, and generation. As Philip Kasinitz notes, many of the second generation who are seen as nonwhite feel they are not "American," or not "American enough," yet they are also not immigrants culturally. Among the questions he raises: Will the children of Koreans and Chinese become "Asian American"? Will the children of Peruvians, Colombians, and Dominicans become "Hispanic"? And building on Perlmann and Waters's analysis, how does intermarriage fit into the picture? How, among other things, are the children of various types of "mixed marriages" identifying themselves—and how are they identified by others (see, for example, Williams-Leon and Nakashima 2001)?

With regard to intermarriage, Perlmann and Waters call for studies that take into account the role of national origin, class background, and phenotype to help clarify how the experiences of contemporary Asians and Hispanics compare to those of Europeans in the past. The role of gender also needs to be included in any full-scale analysis of immigration, race, and ethnicity. Why, for example, are Asian American women today more likely to marry whites than their male counterparts, while the reverse pattern is found among African Americans (see Jacobs and Labov 2002)? How does this compare to gender patterns in the past? And what are the implications for ethno-racial identities and relations? In general, do the ethno-racial identities of the contemporary second generation differ by gender? Was this true among the second generation of earlier eras, and if so, in what ways? Gender also comes into play in interethnic relations; Camarillo's study raises the question of how common it is to find the kind of bridge building and cooperation that he reports among African American and Latina women in Compton. By contrast, for instance, Tatcho Mindiola, Yolanda Flores

Niemann, and Nestor Rodriguez (2002) found in their Houston study that black and Hispanic women were more hostile to each other's groups than their male counterparts.

Camarillo's study also highlights the need to explore the differences among local communities, cities, and regions—specifically, to assess how the construction of race, ethnicity, and intergroup relations has been shaped over time by the unique characteristics of particular places and their distinctive immigration flows. To be "Hispanic" or "Latino" means something quite different in New York City, with its large Spanish-speaking Caribbean population, than in Los Angeles, where Latinos are mostly of Mexican and Central American origin, or in Miami, where Cubans dominate, just as one hundred years ago being Jewish was very different in New York City than in small midwestern and southern cities. Following Roediger and Barrett, we can also examine the host groups in different places from whom immigrants learn about race, both in the past and in the present, and of course what in particular they learn.

We need to compare not only the meaning and content of ethno-racial identities in different communities, cities, and regions but also the nature of political mobilization and the conflicts that develop along ethno-racial lines. Will Latinos displace African Americans from positions of power in areas where they outnumber African Americans? Are the conflicts in Compton a harbinger of things to come elsewhere? And what countervailing forces come into play that can bring different groups together, as well as tear them apart, in particular urban contexts? Additional insights can come from comparing relations between immigrants and established residents in previous historical periods and also, following Joe Trotter's lead, from considering the experiences of African American migrants as they settled in northern cities in the industrial era.

Our focus has been on relations between immigrant minorities and African Americans, yet relations between immigrants and native whites also require further study. Tensions are often rife today in many formerly all-, or nearly all-, white communities receiving large numbers of nonwhite immigrants. To mention one example, at the beginning of 2003 the small city of Lewiston, Maine, which had experienced an influx of over one thousand Somali immigrants, was the site of demonstrations after the mayor issued a public letter asking the Somali elders to stop the inflow. In what ways does this response parallel (or differ from) reactions in the same city to Irish and French Canadian immigration in earlier eras? Or to contemporary Latino and Asian immigration into virtually all-white communities elsewhere in the country? Detailed studies by historians of the complex dynamics of interethnic relations in communities in the past and over time can help us understand the elements involved in both creating and reducing (or preventing) conflicts then as well as now—just as on-the-ground ethnographic studies can tease out the countervailing forces for conflict and cooperation that operate today.

And finally, we come back to an underlying issue that is at the heart of any discussion of immigration and race in America: how today's Latino, Caribbean, and Asian immigration will affect the future of the color line. The essays in this volume offer different prognoses—Kasinitz pointing to evidence that the central cleavage will be black-nonblack; Prewitt suggesting that "white" may become the catchall category for most new immigrants; and Jaynes predicting that as the number of poor Asians and Latinos grows, the tradition of "confounding poverty and dependency with being African American" will die. Whatever the outcome, one thing is clear: immigration will continue to alter the construction of race and ethnicity in the United States and the contour of intergroup relations. The frameworks and analyses in this volume, with their attention to contemporary and historical scholarship, theories, and concepts, provide new insights and ways of thinking about immigration, race, and ethnicity that, in the end, are fundamental to our understanding of what American society is, has been, and will be.

REFERENCES

Alba, Richard, Nancy Denton, Shu-yin Leung, and John R. Logan. 1995. "Neighborhood Change Under Conditions of Mass Immigration: The New York City Region, 1970–1990." *International Migration Review* 29(3): 625–56.

Appiah, Kwame Anthony. 1990. "Racisms." In *Anatomy of Racism*, edited by David Theo Goldberg. Minneapolis: University of Minnesota Press.

Fass, Paula. 1989. *Outsider In: Minorities and the Transformation of American Education*. New York: Oxford University Press.

Foner, Moe. 2002. *Not for Bread Alone: A Memoir*. Ithaca, N.Y.: Cornell University Press.

Foner, Nancy. 1994. *The Caregiving Dilemma: Work in an American Nursing Home*. Berkeley: University of California Press.

———. 2001. "West Indian Migration to New York: An Overview." In *Islands in the City: West Indian Migration to New York*, edited by Nancy Foner. Berkeley: University of California Press.

Fredrickson, George M. 2002. *Racism: A Short History*. Princeton, N.J.: Princeton University Press.

Gerstle, Gary, and John Mollenkopf. 2001. "Introduction: The Political Incorporation of Immigrants, Then and Now." In *E Pluribus Unum: Contemporary and Historical Perspectives on Immigrant Political Incorporation*, edited by Gary Gerstle and John Mollenkopf. New York: Russell Sage Foundation.

Goode, Judith G., Jo Anne Schneider, and Suzanne Blanc. 1992. "Transcending Boundaries and Closing Ranks: How Schools Shape Interactions." In *Structuring Diversity: Ethnographic Perspectives on the New Immigration*, edited by Louise Lamphere. Chicago: University of Chicago Press.

Grenier, Guillermo, and Max Castro. 2001. "Blacks and Cubans in Miami: The Negative Consequences of the Cuban Enclave on Ethnic Relations." In *Governing American Cities*, edited by Michael Jones-Correa. New York: Russell Sage Foundation.

Guterl, Matthew Pratt. 2001. *The Color of Race in America, 1900–1940*. Cambridge, Mass.: Harvard University Press.

Jacobs, Jerry A., and Teresa G. Labov. 2002. "Gender Differentials in Intermarriage Among Sixteen Race and Ethnic Groups." *Sociological Forum* 17(4): 621–46.

Jacobson, Matthew Frye. 1998. *Whiteness of a Different Color: European Immigrants and the Alchemy of Race*. Cambridge, Mass.: Harvard University Press.

Johnson, James H., Walter C. Farrell Jr., and Chandra Guinn. 1999. "Immigration Reform and the Browning of America: Tension, Conflicts, and Community Instability in Metropolitan Los Angeles." In *The Handbook of International Migration*, edited by Charles Hirschman, Philip Kasinitz, and Josh DeWind. New York: Russell Sage Foundation.

Jones-Correa, Michael. 1998. *Between Two Nations: The Political Predicament of Latinos in New York City*. Ithaca, N.Y.: Cornell University Press.

Kasinitz, Philip, John Mollenkopf, and Mary C. Waters. 2002. "Becoming American/Becoming New Yorkers: The Experience of Assimilation in a Majority Minority City." *International Migration Review* 36(4): 1020–36.

Lincoln, Abraham. 1992. Speech at Chicago, Illinois, July 10, 1856. In *Lincoln: Selected Speeches and Writings*. New York: Vintage/New American Library.

McKeever, Matthew. 2001. "Interethnic Politics in the Consensus City." In *Governing American Cities*, edited by Michael Jones-Correa. New York: Russell Sage Foundation.

McLain, Paula D., and Steven C. Tauber. 2001. "Racial Minority Group Relations in a Multiracial Society." In *Governing American Cities*, edited by Michael Jones-Correa. New York: Russell Sage Foundation.

Mindiola, Tatcho, Yolanda Flores Neimann, and Nestor Rodriguez. 2002. *Black and Brown: Relations and Stereotypes*. Austin: University of Texas Press.

Mollenkopf, John Hull. 1999. "Urban Political Conflicts and Alliances: New York and Los Angeles Compared." In *The Handbook of International Migration*, edited by Charles Hirschman, Philip Kasinitz, and Josh DeWind. New York: Russell Sage Foundation.

Morawska, Ewa. 2001. "Immigrant-Black Dissensions in American Cities: An Argument for Multiple Explanations." In *Problem of the Century: Racial Stratification in the United States*, edited by Elijah Anderson and Douglas S. Massey. New York: Russell Sage Foundation.

Olsen, Laurie. 1997. *Made in America: Immigrant Students in Public Schools*. New York: New Press.

Rodriguez, Nestor. 1999. "U.S. Immigration and Changing Relations Between African Americans and Latinos." In *The Handbook of International Migration*, edited by Charles Hirschman, Philip Kasinitz, and Josh DeWind. New York: Russell Sage Foundation.

Roediger, David. 1994. *Toward the Abolition of Whiteness*. London: Verso.

Sanjek, Roger. 1998. *The Future of Us All: Race and Neighborhood Politics in New York City*. Ithaca, N.Y.: Cornell University Press.

Stepick, Alex, Guillermo Grenier, Max Castro, and Marvin Dunn. 2003. *This Land Is Our Land: Immigrants and Power in Miami*. Berkeley: University of California Press.

Taylor, Ronald L. 1979. "Black Ethnicity and Persistence of Ethnogenesis." *American Journal of Sociology* 84(6): 1401–23.

Vickerman, Milton. 1999. *Crosscurrents: West Indians and Race in America*. New York: Oxford University Press.

———. 2001. "Jamaicans: Balancing Race and Ethnicity." In *New Immigrants in New York*, revised and updated edition, edited by Nancy Foner. New York: Columbia University Press.

Williams-Leon, Teresa, and Cynthia L. Nakashima, eds. 2001. *The Sum of Our Parts: Mixed Heritage Asian Americans*. Philadelphia: Temple University Press.

Part I

Historical and Theoretical Perspectives on Race and Ethnicity

Stephen Cornell and Douglas Hartmann

Chapter 1

Conceptual Confusions and Divides: Race, Ethnicity, and the Study of Immigration

First, a story—a brief anecdote that captures, symbolically at least, the core issue that motivates this chapter. The year was 2000. The place: an academic conference on race, ethnicity, and immigration in the United States. Scholars on a panel on Asian American studies were making a set of formal presentations on the contribution of the field to the study of U.S. immigration. For the most part, the presentations framed Asian immigration in terms of, among other things, a broad critique of American racial categories and the processes by which those categories have been constructed and applied.

At the conclusion of the presentations, a member of the audience—a senior scholar with a significant record of research on ethnicity in American life—commented that this was all very interesting, but, he asked, with some frustration, What about the Poles? What about the Germans? What about the Jews? What did all of this have to offer in trying to understand *their* experience, in trying to understand what happened to *them*?

At one level, the questioner—and others in the audience who echoed these sentiments—might be dismissed as merely wanting something the panelists had no obligation to provide or even to consider in light of their own particular interests. Or perhaps the question was simply an effort to clarify differences within the universe of American immigrant processes and populations.

We think the questioner's reaction to the panel points to something more. His question illustrates a deep conceptual divide in the study of intergroup relations in the United States. The questioner seemed to detect—and to be frustrated by—a disjunction in the larger discussion of immigration and intergroup relations. Immigration has long been a topic of analytical interest in the United States. It could hardly be otherwise: surely immigration has been among the most important formative processes in the shaping of American society. Its enormous and changing effects continuously ripple—or noisily rumble—through the American economy, American social life, and American cultural development.

Yet it sometimes seems as if the people who study immigration or race or ethnicity—or all of these together—inhabit two different intellectual worlds. They not only study different groups and times—in the exchange described here the panelists were concerned largely with Asian Americans in the latter part of the twentieth century, the questioner largely with European Americans half a century or more before—but also bring to the study of these groups different assumptions and conceptual tools. Until quite recently, for example, few students of European immigration to the United

States paid much attention to today's racial categories, much less to their contingent and changing nature.[1] And most of those who have been concerned with racial categories in recent years have paid relatively little attention to the kinds of local community processes and analyses that long preoccupied earlier students of immigration.[2] There was a sense at this particular conference of two groups of scholars who, though united in their concern with immigration, were divided in their intellectual interests, assumptions, and approaches and were thus speaking past each other. Indeed, the panelists in this particular case, perhaps doubting the likelihood of a productive exchange, did not directly address the questioner's remarks, and the opportunity for engagement across the conceptual divide was lost.

That divide is the topic of this chapter. We are interested in its genealogy, its consequences, the possibilities of building bridges across it, and how such bridges might inform and advance the study of immigration. We are concerned with lost opportunities and with what these two groups might usefully learn from each other. Ultimately, we are concerned with how to turn this conceptual divide into a site not only of connection and dialogue but of theoretical creativity and empirical insight that will substantively advance the study of immigration and intergroup relations. We also are concerned with the conceptual confusions that often complicate discussions of race and ethnicity and hinder more productive intellectual exchange.

It would be presumptuous of us to claim that we alone can close such a divide or clear up such confusions in the space of this chapter—or, perhaps, anywhere else. But we hope that in exploring how studies of race and ethnicity do and do not converge, we can suggest some useful avenues of advance while illuminating the issues themselves and providing a vantage point for considering the more empirical work presented in this book.

IMMIGRATION AND INTERGROUP RELATIONS

Migration is a common human activity as old perhaps as any other. It is the mechanism by which human beings originally peopled the globe, and one of the ways they have responded to opportunity or crisis—or just plain restlessness—ever since. Of course not all migrations are voluntary. The trans-Atlantic slave trade is perhaps the most prominent instance of coerced migration, but it is hardly an isolated one. States, for example, have used migration variously as a weapon in war, as a tool for the management of labor shortages, and as a means to resolve intergroup conflict (see, among others, Burawoy 1976; McGarry 1998).

As a broad human phenomenon, migration has changed over time. In the last century and a half it has become increasingly frequent, involved unprecedented numbers of persons, covered distances that once were unfathomable to most people, and been subject to patterns of movement—such as circular migration—that once were much less common. But wherever and however it happens, migration precipitates change: in those who move, in the societies they leave, and in the societies that receive them.

This is readily apparent in the United States, where highly variable but more or less continuous immigration has led to extraordinary changes, reorganizing politics, redistributing resources, transforming groups, and challenging national identity. The pattern of urban politics through much of U.S. history, for example, is incomprehensible without paying attention to immigration and internal migration, and the same could be said of, among other things, the historical fortunes of black Americans.[3] The very notion of "whiteness," which found such resonance and controversy within the academy in the 1990s, has little meaning without the category "nonwhite" or its variants. This category itself was born of immigration, first by northern Europeans into the lands of indigenous Americans, then by others into lands that had become dominated by earlier arrivals. Students of race and ethnicity cannot help but be students of immigration too—at least in the United States. Oscar Handlin went so far as to write, in his classic study *The Uprooted: The Epic Story of the Great Migration That Made the American People* (1951, 3): "Once I thought to write a history of immigrants in America. Then I discovered that the immigrants *were* American history."

Even the concepts of race and ethnicity, as realized in American history and life, are largely products of immigration. A distinguishing feature of both concepts is their preoccupation with difference, that is, with the classification of human beings into groups and with the bases of such classifications. Classification—both formal and informal—is set in motion by contact and mixing, and immigration inherently involves both. In the United States group classification not only has helped sustain race and ethnicity as organizing concepts in social, economic, and political life but also has shaped the ways those concepts have been transformed, applied, and experienced over time.

A full genealogical study of the origin and evolution of these terms, in either popular or scholarly usage, has yet to be written, and this obviously is not the place to undertake so imposing a task.[4] But at least two points need to be made. First, in American history and culture it is largely the language of race that has provided the terms of social differentiation. Werner Sollors (1986) observes that the modern concept of ethnicity did not make its way into the scholarly lexicon or public usage until well into the twentieth century, having seldom been heard until the 1940s. When Robert Park, the Progressive Era Chicago sociologist who provided much of the conceptual framework for modern studies of ethnicity in the United States, suggested that there is a recurrent trajectory in intergroup relations, he called it a "race relations cycle" (1926/1950), despite the fact that the great exception to his model of eventual accommodation and assimilation was the group occupying the core of the American racial classification system—African Americans. According to David Roediger (2002), when ethnicity finally did begin to emerge as a distinct analytical term, it did so in the context of larger debates about nationality and immigration—and race.

Second, the meanings of these terms and the relationships between them have been plagued by inconsistency, ambiguity, and confusion. "Race" and "ethnicity" sometimes have been treated as referring to the same things, sometimes as referring to very different things, sometimes as referring to subcategories of each other—and their meanings have changed over time. In immigration studies, for example, this variability sometimes has resulted in debates over which of the two terms is more appropriate to the analysis (see, for example, Gjerde 1999; Sánchez 1999; Foner 2000; Portes 1997), while a common approach in the more general study of intergroup relations has been to subsume one to the other. Thus, for example, Michael Omi and Howard Winant (1994) privilege race over ethnicity, while David Hollinger (1995), Joane Nagel (1994), and Ashley Doane (1997) treat ethnicity as the broader and more useful category.

In the absence of any ultimate authority to adjudicate such definitional disputes, social science has tended either to rely on the sometimes idiosyncratic definitional preferences of individual scholars or, more commonly, to accept uncritically a convention that says race has to do with physical difference and ethnicity has to do with cultural difference.[5] For reasons noted later in the chapter, we find this convention inadequate.[6]

PREVAILING CONCEPTIONS AND THEIR PROBLEMS

Race and ethnicity seem to have something in common, but what is it? They also seem not to have everything in common, but what are the differences between them?

Leaving commonalities aside for the time being, we see two dimensions of difference. First, race and ethnicity generally have been used to refer to different, if sometimes overlapping, empirical phenomena. Second, they have stimulated very different, if in some ways complementary, analytical approaches.

We take up the empirical issues in this and the following section. We then turn to the analytical approaches that have come to be associated with each of these concepts over the last half-century or so. In subsequent sections, we explore ways to bring these analytical approaches together and suggest what such a synthesis might offer to the study of immigration.

Four tendencies characterized much of the empirical treatment of race and ethnicity during the last four decades of the twentieth century. The first was a tendency to reduce race and ethnicity to characteristics of individual persons, rather like age or sex, and then to focus the inquiry largely on how these characteristics, in effect, sort persons into different positions in stratification systems. The second, already noted, was a tendency to see race as a social construction based on physiological difference and ethnicity as a social construction based largely on cultural difference. "Races" became physically distinct groups; "ethnic groups" became culturally distinct groups. The third was a tendency to subsume one concept under the other: either to treat race as one of the factors—along with language, provenance, customs, and so on—that support or make up ethnic identity or categorization (ethnicity is everything) or to treat ethnic phenomena, such as the rise or fall in the salience of ethnic identities, as by-products of tension and change within racial relations (race is everything). The fourth was a tendency to see an instrumentalist, interest-based logic as determining racial and ethnic categorization and group formation (see, for example, Steinberg 1981; Olzak 1992; Roosens 1989). Not all empirical work displayed these tendencies, either singly or in combination, and they often were only implicit, but they were broadly apparent in much of the study of intergroup relations in late-twentieth-century social science.

There are several problems with these largely complementary tendencies. First, treating race and ethnicity as primarily characteristics (however constructed) of individual persons leaves the power, salience, and meaning of racial and ethnic categories unexplained. It examines measurable, individual-level outcomes of racialization and ethnicization but tends to ignore the processes themselves, their deeper societal roots, and their less easily measured consequences.

This has changed to some degree in the last two decades as scholars in history, legal studies, cultural studies, and sociology have paid growing attention to race as—in many societies and certainly in the United States—both a foundational principle of social order and a comprehensive system of meanings that informs and shapes action (see, for example, Essed and Goldberg 2002). In this sense race and even ethnicity can be seen as part of a society's "deep structure," by which we mean, in part, culture: that set of deeply embedded, taken-for-granted understandings through which, often uncon-sciously, much of social process moves and social outcomes are constructed. This ap-proach, while still embracing the daily experience of inequality, grants to ethnicity and race a greater independence, power, and significance than traditional approaches have done, and it suggests that, analytically, race and ethnicity should be treated not so much as subfields within stratification or social psychology but as central and independently consequential social phenomena or forces and as key organizing concepts in the study of societies.

Second, the instrumentalist assumption that particular racial and ethnic categories and identities are prominent because they are useful reduces them to by-products of circumstantial dynamics, precipitates of material conditions. Yet these categories often appear to carry enormous and remarkably durable moral or emotional power. At var-ious times and in various places, they have generated both ecstasies of self-glorification and paroxysms of lethal violence. Many of these categories and identities also survive substantial changes in material conditions; if they are merely products of circumstances, the coupling between the two often seems peculiarly loose. And finally, circumstances frequently throw up multiple possibilities for collective identification. A black, female textile worker, for example, has several alternative bases on which to organize self-concept and action—or on which to be conceived and acted upon. Why do race and ethnicity so often gain pride of place? In short, circumstances alone often seem incapa-ble of explaining the power and persistence of these phenomena. Circumstances may at times account for the emergence of specific categories and identities, but they are much less able to account for the durability of race and ethnicity or for what people actually do in their names. Missing from much of the analysis of these phenomena has been an adequate account of why race and ethnicity, under hugely variable and discontinuous circumstances, have retained their apparent privilege and power as bases of identity, social organization, and collective action and as the grounds on which many groups, in effect, *choose* to interpret and pursue their interests.

Third, the focus on culture as the basis of ethnicity has turned ethnicity into an analytically clumsy concept. Much depends on how we define culture, but it seems safe to say that most societies generate numerous groups that share cultural distinctions of one kind or another. Many of those groups defy our commonsense conception of eth-nic groups: for example, the professoriate, the working class, New Age enthusiasts, Deadheads, firefighters, upper-middle-class teenagers, and so on. How are these groups different from ethnic groups? And if, given their cultural distinctiveness, these *are* ethnic groups, then most of us are members of far more ethnic groups than we ever realized. Furthermore, even within commonly perceived ethnic groups, the degree and nature of shared culture not only vary but change over time. If shared culture is the basis of ethnicity, at what point does a group cease to be an ethnic group? Acculturation pro ceeds apace in many cases, yet numerous acculturated groups—indistinguishable be-haviorally from the mainstream of the society of which they are a part—continue to see themselves and to be seen as ethnic. Are some more ethnic than others? All of which begs a larger question: if culture is not the distinguishing feature of ethnicity, what is?

Finally, the tendency to subsume one of these concepts within the other has ob-scured both their differences and their commonalities and reduced their analytical util-ity. It either promotes a split into separate fields of study or collapses the study of one into the study of the other.

DISENTANGLING RACE AND ETHNICITY AS
EMPIRICAL PHENOMENA

Dissatisfied with the common distinction between race and ethnicity—the conventional conception of race as a matter of physical difference and of ethnicity as a matter of cultural difference—how would we modify it? Yes, these phenomena have something in common; no, they are not the same. Empirically, we see the following key points.

First, at the heart of both race and ethnicity as social categories or common usages lies the assumption that human origins are uniquely powerful in determining differences between social groups. Race focuses on genes as the critical dimension of origins: it is genetics and their manifestations in human bodies—especially through skin color or other visible physiological features—that are given power in racial conceptions. Ethnicity, in contrast, while still turning to origins as the imputed basis of difference, focuses on descent and homeland: it is kinship and provenance that are given power in ethnic conceptions.[7]

Second, by focusing on origins, both claim, in effect, to be "natural" categories—in some sense ordained by the circumstances of birth—and each typically is accompanied by a language or idiom of essentialism or primordiality. It is this claimed primordiality that most importantly distinguishes race and ethnicity from most other bases of social organization, identity, and collective action.

Third—and paradoxically, given their essentialist pretenses—both are characterized by empirically traceable processes of social construction. In the case of race, the construction process tends to focus on comprehensive categories within the organization of society as a whole; in the case of ethnicity, it focuses on localized identities. In neither case does construction depend on some objective determination of facts. Races and ethnic groups are based on presumption: what matters is not the actual extent of, for example, genetic or kinship links among persons, which may be entirely fictive; what matters is that people think there are such links, and furthermore, that they think those links are important. It is processes of social construction that make race and ethnicity "real."

Fourth, though it would be easy to overstate the case, these construction processes typically take somewhat different forms, driven by differently situated and empowered groups. Race is largely the product of the assignment to others of biological difference: powerful groups, wishing to draw a boundary between themselves and others, define those others as racially distinct. The critical issue for race is who *they* are and how *they* are fundamentally different from *us*. By sorting people into particular "races," more powerful groups specify the position of the less powerful and thereby maintain their own power, status, and authority.[8]

In contrast, ethnicity is largely (although not exclusively) a product of self-assertions of collective identity and blood ties, based on descent or homeland: the community claims such an identity for itself, asserting its own distinctiveness or peoplehood. The critical issue for ethnicity is who *we* are. Power differentials typically play a lesser role in the process, although those who assert a particular ethnic identity may find themselves in conflict with racial or other classification schemes within which they are being assigned a very different identity.[9]

Fifth, race is more exclusive and less flexible than ethnicity. In most systems, categorization in one race precludes categorization in another, and categorical entry and exit are difficult. In the United States, for example, the racial system has had an underlying exclusivity originating in black-white relations. Racially, you could not be both white and something else; by virtue of being something else, you were necessarily not white. Ethnicity, on the other hand, is more tolerant of split categorizations and multiplicity, and categorical entry and exit are easier.

Sixth, race typically implies differential valuation on moral, aptitudinal, or other grounds—in other words, differential merit or ability—and is skeptical of the possibilities of change in group characteristics or group position. The typical racial dichotomy opposes the civilized or worthy or capable to the uncivilized or unworthy or incapable, and its biological essentialism suggests permanence in such descriptors. Ethnicity is celebratory and typically ethnocentric, but it is less inclined to link origins with inherent worth and less dependent for its vitality on assertions of fundamental differences. Ethnicity tends to be more optimistic about change, through either pluralism or assimilation.

In summary, both race and ethnicity are constructed social categories based on primordialist claims regarding differences between persons. The critical distinctions between the two terms have to do with the claimed nature of those differences (genes versus kinship or provenance), with who typically is making the claims (outsiders versus insiders), with the moral implications of those claims (more significant in the case of race versus less significant in the case of ethnicity), and with the role of power in the construction process (racial constructions are more power-dependent; ethnic constructions are less so).

It should also be clear from this discussion that a single population could be at the same time, in our terms, both a race and an ethnic group, or at least it could have both racial and ethnic characteristics (see figure 1.1). An example would be early Irish immigrants to the United States, who, some historians claim, were assigned a nonwhite racial status but at the same time claimed for themselves a distinctive identity based on common provenance and kinship, broadly conceived.[10] Also, a group could move from one category to another. For example, Europeans and Euro-Americans placed Africans in a single, physically distinct category, thereby "creating" a race, and assigned them a racial identity that—for Europeans at least—took social precedence over the diverse group boundaries that actually organized African lives. Enslaved and thrown into the New World, large numbers of these Africans found their lives radically reorganized along racial lines. Over time, however, the experience of racial categorization persuaded some of them to think and act on the basis of the assigned distinction. Abandoning less inclusive identities and adopting the racial boundary as their own, they began also to attach their own meanings to that boundary and asserted their own conception of themselves, a conception in which kinship and common provenance became part of the idiom of peoplehood and, in conjunction with other things, the basis of a claim to a distinctive identity and culture. They thereby constructed themselves as an ethnic group, becoming both race and ethnic group at once.

TWO ANALYTICAL APPROACHES TO THE STUDY OF INTERGROUP RELATIONS

Race and ethnicity not only have referred in common social science usage to different, if somehow related, empirical phenomena; they also have generated different analytical approaches to the study of intergroup relations—different lenses through which such relations are approached and analyzed. We can think of these as an "ethnicity" ap-

FIGURE 1.1   Ethnic Groups and Races

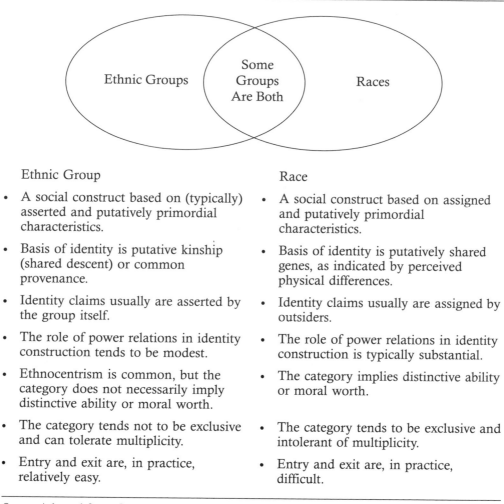

Ethnic Group

• A social construct based on (typically) asserted and putatively primordial characteristics.

• Basis of identity is putative kinship (shared descent) or common provenance.

• Identity claims usually are asserted by the group itself.

• The role of power relations in identity construction tends to be modest.

• Ethnocentrism is common, but the category does not necessarily imply distinctive ability or moral worth.

• The category tends not to be exclusive and can tolerate multiplicity.

• Entry and exit are, in practice, relatively easy.

Race

• A social construct based on assigned and putatively primordial characteristics.

• Basis of identity is putatively shared genes, as indicated by perceived physical differences.

• Identity claims usually are assigned by outsiders.

• The role of power relations in identity construction is typically substantial.

• The category implies distinctive ability or moral worth.

• The category tends to be exclusive and intolerant of multiplicity.

• Entry and exit are, in practice, difficult.

Source: Adapted from Cornell and Hartmann (1998, 35). Copyright © 1998 by Pine Forge Press. Reprinted by permission of Sage Publications, Inc.

proach and a "race" approach. This overstates the case somewhat; some works would be difficult to classify as falling wholly into either approach, and the line between the two is often fuzzy. But as we suggested with our opening anecdote, there is a conceptual and analytical divide within the broad field of intergroup relations. What follows, though admittedly formalistic and a generalization, is our attempt to characterize that divide.

The Ethnicity Approach

This approach dominated much of twentieth-century American social science in the fields of both intergroup relations and urban studies, and it remains important in studies of immigration today. Its central characteristics include the following:

- It has historical and empirical roots in studies of immigration and settlement, especially in cities.

- The primary unit of analysis is groups or communities within a larger population, with national borders typically constraining the reach of the research.

- It conceives ethnicity as a property of groups and communities indicated by cultural patterns, behaviors, and expressed identity (who "we" are or are not).

- It is empirically concerned with individual or community experience, community social organization, and individual assimilation (or the lack of it), as measured by language use, family structure, intermarriage, labor market integration, and the like.

- Its orientation is implicitly comparative, although the empirical work often takes the form of community studies with the experiences or fortunes of group members as the primary objects of research.

- Categorical and group boundaries are seen as mutable but are not typically objects of critical inquiry in and of themselves.

- If there is a political focus in such studies, it tends to be largely on the pursuit of community interests and on conflict over societal resources.

- Its central problematic is assimilation and mobility, and it has expectations of eventual societal integration.

The Race Approach

This approach came to prominence in the 1980s and 1990s and now dominates the study of intergroup relations in the United States. Among its central characteristics:

- It has historical and empirical roots in the study of slavery, black-white relations, and colonialism around the world.

- The primary unit of analysis is the social system, and it often conceives the system as transnational or even global.

- It conceives race as an organizing principle that is deeply embedded in culture and social structure and has profoundly shaped both intergroup relationships and society as a whole.

- It is empirically concerned with stratification systems, with the sociocultural construction of difference and the reproduction of racial categories and hierarchies, and, to a lesser degree, with the study of attitudes.

- Its orientation is less comparative and more systemic or relational, focusing on social processes (such as migration, globalization, and development) that reflect or create racialized categories and structures.

- Categorical and group boundaries are conceived as constructed, contested, and as critical objects of inquiry in their own right.

- It typically has a more explicit political focus on the contested construction of categories and on the assignment of persons to those categories—and on the maintenance of power and privilege that goes along with both.

- Its central problematic is power, and it assumes that conflict and inequality are endemic aspects of the social order.

While admittedly schematic, we think this summary captures something of importance that was captured as well, in microcosm, in the interaction anecdotally described in the introduction to this chapter. "What about the Poles?" was an ethnicity-approach question caught in a race-approach discussion.

But once we laid it out, another aspect of this summary immediately struck us: these two analytical approaches are far more complementary than contradictory. Strengths in one seem to correspond to weaknesses in the other. Where the race paradigm emphasizes systemic phenomena and effects but tends to ignore localized processes of group formation and agency, the ethnicity paradigm does the reverse. Where the ethnicity paradigm is concerned largely with group social organization, culture, and change but tends to ignore system-level categories, assumptions, and change, the race paradigm does the opposite. One emphasizes the evolution and experience of particular racial or ethnic communities, while the other emphasizes the racialization of societal structures, including culture, within which community evolution and experience proceed. One seems concerned more with what happens in individual lives while the other is concerned more with what happens in the life of society. The ethnicity paradigm is more likely to be concerned with subordinate group conceptions—for example, with how subordinate groups conceive themselves and what they are trying to do—while the race paradigm is more likely to be concerned with where the repertoire of available self-concepts comes from, with societywide conceptions of categories and boundaries, and with how large-scale structures shape action. The community orientation of the ethnicity approach offers us a window on the localized processes of group formation and the felt power of ethnic identity, while the systemic orientation of the race approach offers us a more subtle and complex analysis of power, one that can generate critical insights not only into contemporary social relations and processes within and between nation-states but into the context in which ethnic assertions occur and take their form.

Such complementarities suggest an opportunity for constructive engagement between these two approaches, an engagement with potential benefits for the study of immigration. They suggest a way of thinking about immigration that recognizes the social formations we generally refer to as ethnicity and race as distinct, if related, empirical phenomena, but that then joins the respective strengths of these analytical approaches to produce a more comprehensive and integrated picture of the intergroup relations at the core of the immigration experience and of the broader significance of immigration itself.

TOWARD A SYNTHESIS

Of course, complementarity does not necessarily translate into compatibility. In this case at least, we need some broader theoretical framework or conceptual vision within which to integrate these different empirical phenomena and the analytic orientations and insights that have grown up around them. We believe the commonalities and overlaps between race and ethnicity as discussed here suggest such a framework or vision: the substantial—if often ignored or minimized—set of shared empirical characteristics that, for all the confusion it presents, makes pairing them seem almost natural and inevitable. We refer to their common primordialist claims and their substantially similar sociostructural dynamics of construction and reproduction.

As we have argued, racial and ethnic phenomena are distinguished, respectively, by their appeals to perceived, systematic, physical difference (broadly: genes) and to perceived, shared descent or common provenance (broadly: kinship). Although clearly these claims are not the same, both identify origins as privileged and somehow fundamental. Both rely on a rhetoric of primordialism to generate the deeply felt experience and social power of the categories, and it is this appeal to origins that not only unifies race and ethnicity but helps account for their surprising power and persistence in the modern world. Where so much of social life appears to be mere by-product of historical contingencies, vast social forces, and instrumental action, the appeal to origins generates an emotional attachment and experiential resonance that seems to many to be natural and authentic, beyond the contingencies of history and human agency. Race and ethnicity are what we have called "constructed primordialities" (Cornell and Hartmann 1998, 89)—social products given power by their (sometimes only implicit) essentialist appeals.[11]

Many questions remain as to why and how categories that are so obviously socially constructed and historically contingent come to be felt and understood as somehow beyond history and agency.[12] Certainly this paradox calls for more substantial exploration, but what is important for present purposes is the simple fact that these categories are so often expressed and experienced this way. This, we believe, is what makes them so consequential, and it binds them conceptually to each other.

They are bound to each other as well by substantially similar processes of boundary construction (compare Barth 1969). We argued earlier that race and ethnicity are distinguished not only by the nature of the claims each term represents but by the claimants themselves, by who the driving force typically is in the process of social construction. Ethnic categories, in this scheme, are largely the product of subordinate or minority group agency and activity, while racial categories typically are imposed by a dominant group on a less powerful one, with self-categorization as an unspoken by-product of this process. But "largely" and "typically" are critical terms in this distinction, for in practice these construction processes are inevitably interactive. As Joane Nagel (1994) has pointed out in a discussion focused largely on ethnicity, ethnic and racial categories are always products *both* of the actions and intent of the actors who inhabit these categories *and* of the external forces and social others they encounter. Our point is that the drivers in racial constructions tend to be dominant groups who are categorizing others, while the drivers in ethnic constructions tend to be minority populations categorizing themselves. But in each case these are more likely than not to be contested processes in which both human actors and impersonal conditions construct group boundaries for inclusionary and exclusionary purposes.

This fact underlines the need for synthesis. Not only do race and ethnicity share a constructed primordiality; they also require and would benefit from a more comprehensive analytical strategy, one that draws on the respective strengths of both analytical approaches to capture the complexities of category, group, and boundary formation and of intergroup dynamics. Such a strategy would draw on the ethnicity paradigm's concern with group formation, felt experience, and the power of constructed primordiality as a basis of community and action. It would draw on the race paradigm's concern with the impact of social structure (including not only patterns of power but what we referred to earlier as "deep" structure or foundational cultural assumptions), with social context, and with the consequences of structure and context in shaping life experience. From the study of race it also would draw a more nuanced analysis of power and of the impacts of the social forces, such as expanding capitalism, globalism, and transnationalism, that increasingly drive the movement and mixing of populations all over the world. In other words, putting race and ethnicity together is not just a disciplinary convention—it is a necessary analytical move.

ILLUSTRATIONS AND ELABORATIONS

We believe the parameters and benefits of such a synthesis are apparent in the study of what is commonly known as panethnicity. Panethnicity typically begins as what is commonly thought of as race, as a category developed by dominant populations to describe those they perceive as fundamentally different from themselves. In the history of the United States and its precursor colonies, for example, the various indigenous peoples of North America were combined as "Indians"; slave populations of multiple African origins became "Negroes" or "blacks"; and immigrants from hugely diverse Asian societies became "Orientals" or "Asians." Those who constructed such categories were not necessarily oblivious to the differences among the peoples they thus combined, but they tended to see differences within the category as of minimal significance next to perceived differences between the category and themselves. From the point of view of racial categorizers, the fact that others are not like "us" is far more important than the fact that they are not like each other.

It is here that both primordiality and differential worth—two of the key characteristics of racial classifications—exert their profound influence. Racial categorization is about the supposedly incomparable power of biological origins to shape human characteristics and about the differential worth of the human results.

But while the terrain of panethnic group formation has been—in the United States at least—first and foremost a racial terrain, it cannot be adequately understood within only a racial paradigm. It also has to be addressed from within the categorized population—that is, from a perspective that is conventionally understood in ethnic terms. Categories have consequences, and one of the likely consequences of social organization through racial categories is that the categories become bases of identification on the part of the categorized groups. Over time they begin to use the category not so much at first to define boundaries (one of the purposes of the category's originators) but to contest the meanings and the differential worth assigned to the category (the originators' other purpose), and then, once new meanings are in hand, to contest the uses to which the boundaries are put.

Earlier we offered the example of African Americans who seized the racial identity imposed on them by the dominant society and made it the basis of their own ethnic assertions. Another example can be found in the evolution of American Indian identity, known to some scholars as "pan-Indianism" (for example, Thomas 1968; Hertzberg 1971). As usual, the "panethnic" identity begins as a racial phenomenon, a European category that embraces multiple peoples held to be commonly different from Europeans, and is used to support their differential treatment. Again, the category becomes in time a basis not only of dominant-group assignment but of subordinate-group assertion, as people from an assortment of Indian nations begin to claim an American

Indian identity as their own, attach their own meanings to the category, and organize and act within it (Cornell 1988, 1990; Nagel 1996).[13]

These processes of adoption of the category as a basis of identity, assertion of new meanings to be attached to the category, and use of the category for political purposes are classically ethnic processes involving a claiming not of who "they" are but of who "we" are. They remain primordialist but resist both differential worth and its presumed genetic basis. And they move forward, typically, through the kinds of community processes and perceptions that the ethnicity paradigm outlined in these pages has long addressed.

Of course not all panethnic categorizations lead in this direction. Some groups, and for a variety of reasons, resist racial classification. One of the most interesting recent explorations of these dynamics—albeit using both different terms and a different framework from ours—is Mary Waters's (1999) examination of West Indian immigrants to New York City. These immigrants enter a racialized system in which they are assigned a black identity. But they soon discover that this assignment to a black American category has heavy costs in discrimination and downward mobility. One response has been to struggle to preserve and assert West Indian identities against the negative consequences of racial assignment. In a reversal of the assimilationist model that has long dominated American thinking about immigration, these immigrants and their children find that the more they assimilate to the racial category black, the more barriers to mobility they encounter.[14] This conflict over boundaries and meanings is made even clearer by class distinctions. As Waters notes, less well-off and mobile immigrants, sharing social worlds for the most part with similarly disadvantaged black Americans, tend to accept the categorizations of the larger society so as not to be perceived by other blacks as "acting white." Waters (1999, 324) writes that "the more socially mobile the individual, the more he or she clings to ethnic identity as a hedge against racial identity" (see also Foner 2001). From our point of view, the critical point has less to do with whether these identities are ethnic or racial than with the conflict between immigrant assertions of who—for various purposes—they want to be and the assignments being made by the society at large.

As this suggests, various groups in American life have found themselves embedded in consequential intergroup dynamics, but not all have responded in the same ways.[15] One group, however, generally has been thought to escape much of this process, or at least to have been more the organizer than the object of it: whites. As the dominant racial population in American life, whites also have dominated processes of racial classification, yet their own identity has been largely unspecified. To be white has been to occupy the unspoken, taken-for-granted, benchmark category—the "hidden ethnicity," as Ashley Doane (1997) calls it—against which racial and ethnic "others" are classified. Some whites may assert particular ethnic identities, such as Italian American or Polish American, at different times, and some—such as the Irish—may have struggled early on to be classified racially as whites, but once within the dominant classification, no further assertions have been necessary. The seat of power need not describe itself.

In recent decades, however, as the privileges of whiteness have been challenged, and as whites increasingly have been subjected to unaccustomed processes of racialization and objectification, their identities and worth being defined by others, this has changed.[16] Certain whites have been driven to take up the tasks of ethnic assertion, claiming an explicitly white identity, struggling to control the meanings attached to that category, and defending the traditional entitlements of whiteness. In the process they are transforming racial whiteness into white ethnicity.

This has two results. First, it contributes to the ongoing transformation and blurring of the analytical boundary between ethnicity and race. Second, it further reveals the constructedness of yet another category of identity and belonging: nation. In the United States at least, the conventional distinctions between race and ethnicity seem to turn on the naturalized or taken-for-granted category of "the nation." If being white means being American and being "ethnic" indicates the possibility of becoming American, being "racial" signals an identity that is problematic and somehow less American. In American life, ethnicity has indicated a sort of belonging-in-progress, while race has indicated not really belonging at all.[17]

What we are most interested in, however, is not whether whites—or any other group—are best understood through the paradigm of race or through the paradigm of ethnicity. Our interest instead is in the boundaries that they are asserting and contesting, the meanings and identities that are contained within these boundaries, and the broader implications of such boundary making and meaning making.

Immigration is deeply embedded in these activities. First, it is a vehicle of contact and mixing that sets in motion the very processes of boundary construction that we have been talking about. Second, it tends to give those processes a certain urgency. When it happens on a substantial scale, as it often has in the history of the United States, immigration is a disruptive force. Not only does it cause rupture in quotidian social relations through its impacts on labor markets, residential space, and the like, but it also causes rupture in received notions of nationhood. Who qualifies for American nationhood, and whose nation is it?

IMPLICATIONS FOR THE STUDY OF IMMIGRATION

Are immigrants, then, racial outsiders whose fates will be determined by powerful, external others? Or are they ethnic agents free to choose their own identities and futures? Surely they are both. To try to force them into one category or the other is to lose an appreciation for the complexity of the immigration experience. A comprehensive study of immigration and of its intersections with race and ethnicity requires both the localized focus of the ethnicity paradigm and its understanding of the felt power of primordialist claims at the group level and the comprehensive penetrations of the race paradigm and its understanding of the hegemonic structure and power of primordialist claims and assumptions at the system level. We have tried to suggest that this can best be accomplished by de-emphasizing the "is it race or is it ethnicity?" debate and concentrating instead on the construction of group boundaries and identities within the context of American nationalism.

So, to return to our beginning: what about the Poles? We see this question as an opportunity for productive exchange rather than as the challenge it might appear to be if race and ethnicity are understood as separate phenomena to be differently addressed. Scholars of Asian immigration to the United States might use such an opportunity to explain the changing historical forces that have precipitated a succession of migrations of Asian populations who were very different in origin, class composition, and cultural orientation; the categorical schemes—including racial ones—and structural barriers these different migrations encountered when they arrived; and the consequent shape of their communities and the patterns of their integration, tracing an analytical strategy with potent comparative power for scholars of European immigration to the United States.

Meanwhile, the latter group of scholars might point to the ways in which European immigrants struggled with—and sometimes took advantage of—the different but related categorical schemes they encountered on American shores, launching transformations not only in their own communities but in those schemes, transformations that eventually had consequences for later arrivals, including Asian ones. And both sets of scholars might conceive American immigration as a long, ongoing, historical process that, while hardly seamless, has continually reorganized communities, categories, American society, and the very idea of the American nation, with racialization happening here, ethnogenesis happening there, sometimes both happening at once, in recurrent cycles of reproduction and transformation.

There is nothing particularly radical or innovative in these suggestions. Rather, they form a framework for facilitating interaction, communication, and exchange about immigration and its consequences in the racial and ethnic landscape—a way to elucidate general commonalities and particular differences. The key, as always, is the questions to be asked: Which groups have the freedom to construct themselves? Which groups find themselves caught in inescapable categories constructed by others? Which groups are moving from one situation to the other? How do both our definitions of groups and the groups themselves change when populations are moving to a society in which both ethnicity and race are prominent categories? Who gets combined together, and who is seen as separate and distinct? How do racialization and ethnogenesis progress, and how do they affect each other? And what is happening to an America that has relied for much of its national self-concept on the racialization of others when immigration presents it with so many claims by groups that insist on being, in effect, *American ethnics*— that is, on sharing a broad American commonality while retaining a narrower ethnic identity and rejecting the racial categorizations that have been fundamental to the American way of dealing with immigration?

This is an approach to the study of immigration that is less concerned with individual outcomes than with the recurrent reconstitution of intergroup relations and the social order itself. Among other things, it is concerned with how that order can accommodate one set of identity claims ("we are Americans, but we are also a people in our own right") without organizing power and privilege through another set of such claims ("you are racially 'other'"). It is an approach that can help us better understand not only present immigration and its consequences in American life but also past immigration and its role in producing the social worlds of the present.

NOTES

1. The last decade and a half, however, has seen a burst of such work; see, for example, Barrett and Roediger (1997), Ignatiev (1995), Jacobson (1998), Roediger (1991, 1994), Rogin (1996), and Waters (1990).

2. Again, there are exceptions, including some of those cited in note 1; see also Hartigan (1999).

3. The literature is vast, but see, for example, Kasinitz (1992), Katznelson (1973), Erie (1988), Foner (2001), Waldinger (1996), Waters (1999), and Waters and Eschbach (1995).

4. Elements of such a discussion, however, can be found in Russell Kazal's (1995) treatment of the evolution of the concept of assimilation in American ethnic history.

5. This distinction is widespread. For example, a popular reader in the field (Yetman 1999, 3) states: "Whereas an *ethnic group* is distinguished by *cultural* characteristics, *race* refers to a social category that is defined on the basis of *physical* characteristics" (emphasis in original).

College texts likewise often follow the same convention. See the discussion in Cornell and Hartmann (1998, 16–18).

6. We should make a third point as well. Race and ethnicity are far from the only sources of group formation and collective identity in the modern world. Class, religion, language, gender, and sexuality also have organized much of personal and social life, a topic explored in depth by scholars working on intersectionality (for example, Hondagneu-Sotelo 1994; Lowe 1996). But race and ethnicity have been particularly powerful in American society and in the immigrant experience. Among the reasons for this are the inequalities attached to race and ethnicity and the power of appeals to blood and kin as sources of authenticity in the modern world (see Cornell and Hartmann 1998, 91–94)—points to which we return later. Indeed, this may explain why some groups not traditionally conceived as racial or ethnic turn to the language of race and ethnicity in search of recognition and mobilizational power (see, for example, Cohen 1994).

7. Although this idea of presumed kinship and/or provenance as defining features of ethnicity departs from recent conventions in sociology and related disciplines that rely instead on supposed "cultural differences," it cleaves to a long-standing tradition. See, for example, Weber (1968), Schermerhorn (1978), Horowitz (1985), and the discussion in Cornell and Hartmann (1998). This tradition has nearly disappeared from sociological work on ethnicity in the United States, but it remains vibrant within anthropology and in studies of ethnicity elsewhere.

8. This is readily apparent in the United States, where a central mechanism in the maintenance of white privilege is the construction of racial categories to which "others" can be assigned. This is one of the central insights of critical studies of whiteness.

9. Following John Ogbu (1990), we might say that the difference between race and ethnicity is rather like the difference between involuntary and voluntary migration.

10. See Ignatiev (1995), but also the critical discussions in Arnesen (2001) and Kolchin (2002).

11. On constructed primordiality, see Appadurai (1990) and Griswold (1994); cf. Gil-White (1999).

12. The examples are legion. See, among numerous others, Hanson (1989, 1991), Malkki (1995), and Conzen and others (1992); see again the discussion of authenticity in Cornell and Hartmann (1998, 91–94).

13. See also Yen Le Espiritu's (1992) treatment of a comparable process among Asian Americans.

14. This is an excellent example of what Alejandro Portes and Min Zhou (1993) call segmented assimilation.

15. Some of the other ways in which groups experience and respond to these dynamics are explored in detail in later sections of this book.

16. For some useful discussions, see Winant (1997) and Hartigan (1999).

17. A similar argument is made by Amy Kaplan (1993), while historical treatments of these issues are given by, among others, John Higham (1955) and, more recently, Gary Gerstle (2001). For materials employing some similar ideas in the case of Great Britain, see Cohen (1994).

REFERENCES

Appadurai, Arjun. 1990. "Disjuncture and Difference in the Global Cultural Economy." *Public Culture* 2: 1–24.

Arnesen, Eric. 2001. "Whiteness and the Historians' Imagination." *International Labor and Working-class History* 60 (Fall): 3–32.

Barrett, James R., and David Rocdiger. 1997. "Inbetween Peoples: Race, Nationality, and the 'New Immigrant' Working Class." *Journal of American Ethnic History* 16(3): 3–44.

Barth, Fredrik. 1969. "Introduction." In *Ethnic Groups and Boundaries: The Social Organization of Culture Difference*, edited by Fredrik Barth. Boston: Little, Brown.

Burawoy, Michael. 1976. "The Functions and Reproduction of Migrant Labor: Comparative Material from Southern Africa and the United States." *American Journal of Sociology* 81(5, March): 1050–87.

Cohen, Robin. 1994. *Frontiers of Identity: The British and the Others*. London: Longman.

Conzen, Kathleen N., David A. Gerber, Eva Morawska, George E. Pozzetta, and Rudolph J. Vecoli. 1992. "The Invention of Ethnicity: A Perspective from the USA." *Journal of American Ethnic History* 12(September): 3–41.

Cornell, Stephen. 1988. *The Return of the Native: American Indian Political Resurgence*. New York: Oxford University Press.

————. 1990. "Land, Labor, and Group Formation: Blacks and Indians in the United States." *Ethnic and Racial Studies* 13: 368–88.

Cornell, Stephen, and Douglas Hartmann. 1998. *Ethnicity and Race: Making Identities in a Changing World*. Thousand Oaks, Calif.: Pine Forge Press.

Doane, Ashley W., Jr. 1997. "Dominant Group Ethnic Identity in the United States: The Role of 'Hidden Ethnicity' in Intergroup Relations." *Sociological Quarterly* 28(3): 375–97.

Erie, Steven P. 1988. *Rainbow's End: Irish-Americans and the Dilemmas of Urban Machine Politics, 1840–1985*. Berkeley: University of California Press.

Espiritu, Yen Le. 1992. *Asian American Panethnicity: Bridging Institutions and Identities*. Philadelphia: Temple University Press.

Essed, Philomena, and David Theo Goldberg, eds. 2002. *Race Critical Theories: Text and Context*. Oxford: Blackwell.

Foner, Nancy. 2000. "Anthropology and the Study of Immigration." In *Immigration Research for a New Century*, edited by Nancy Foner, Rubén G. Rumbaut, and Steven J. Gold. New York: Russell Sage Foundation.

————, ed. 2001. *Islands in the City: West Indian Migration to New York*. Berkeley: University of California Press.

Gerstle, Gary. 2001. *American Crucible: Race and Nation in the Twentieth Century*. Princeton, N.J.: Princeton University Press.

Gil-White, Francisco J. 1999. "How Thick Is Blood? The Plot Thickens . . .: If Ethnic Actors Are Primordialists, What Remains of the Circumstantialist/Primordialist Controversy?" *Ethnic and Racial Studies* 22(5): 789–820.

Gjerde, Jon. 1999. "New Growth on Old Vines—the State of the Field: The Social History of Immigration to and Ethnicity in the United States." *Journal of American Ethnic History* 18(4): 40–65.

Griswold, Wendy. 1994. *Cultures and Societies in a Changing World*. Thousand Oaks, Calif.: Pine Forge Press.

Handlin, Oscar. 1951. *The Uprooted: The Epic Story of the Great Migration That Made the American People*. Boston: Little, Brown.

Hanson, Allen. 1989. "The Making of the Maori: Culture Invention and Its Logic." *American Anthropologist* 91: 890–902.

————. 1991. "Reply to Langdon, Levine, and Linnekin." *American Anthropologist* 93: 449–50.

Hartigan, John, Jr. 1999. *Racial Situations: Class Predicaments of Whiteness in Detroit*. Princeton, N.J.: Princeton University Press.

Hertzberg, Hazel W. 1971. *The Search for an American Indian Identity*. Syracuse, N.Y.: Syracuse University Press.

Higham, John. 1955. *Strangers in the Land: Patterns of American Nativism, 1860–1925*. New Brunswick, N.J.: Rutgers University Press.

Hollinger, David A. 1995. *Postethnic America: Beyond Multiculturalism*. New York: Basic Books.

Hondagneu-Sotelo, Pierrette. 1994. *Gendered Transitions: Mexican Experiences of Immigration*. Berkeley: University of California Press.

Horowitz, Donald L. 1985. *Ethnic Groups in Conflict*. Berkeley: University of California Press.

Ignatiev, Noel. 1995. *How the Irish Became White*. New York: Routledge.

Jacobson, Matthew Frye. 1998. *Whiteness of a Different Color: European Immigrants and the Alchemy of Race*. Cambridge, Mass.: Harvard University Press.

Kaplan, Amy. 1993. "'Left Alone in America': The Absence of Empire in the Study of American Culture." In *Cultures of United States Imperialism*, edited by Amy Kaplan and Donald A. Pease. Durham, N.C.: Duke University Press.

Kasinitz, Philip. 1992. *Caribbean New York: Black Immigrants and the Politics of Race*. Ithaca, N.Y.: Cornell University Press.

Katznelson, Ira. 1973. *Black Men, White Cities: Race, Politics, and Migration in the United States, 1900–1930 and Britain, 1948–1968*. London and New York: Oxford University Press for Institute of Race Relations.

Kazal, Russell A. 1995. "Revisiting Assimilation: The Rise, Fall, and Reappraisal of a Concept in American Ethnic History." *American Historical Review* 100(2, April): 437–71.

Kolchin, Peter. 2002. "Whiteness Studies: The New History of Race in America." *Journal of American History* 89(1, June): 154–73.

Lowe, Lisa. 1996. *Immigrant Acts: On Asian-American Cultural Politics*. Durham, N.C.: Duke University Press.

Malkki, Liisa H. 1995. *Purity and Exile: Violence, Memory, and National Cosmology Among Hutu Refugees in Tanzania*. Chicago: University of Chicago Press.

McGarry, John. 1998. "'Demographic Engineering': The State-Directed Movement of Ethnic Groups as a Technique of Conflict Regulation." *Ethnic and Racial Studies* 21(4, July): 613–38.

Nagel, Joane. 1994. "Constructing Ethnicity: Creating and Re-creating Ethnic Identity and Culture." *Social Problems* 41(1): 152–76.

———. 1996. *American Indian Ethnic Renewal: Red Power and the Resurgence of Identity and Culture*. New York: Oxford University Press.

Ogbu, John U. 1990. "Minority Status and Literacy in Comparative Perspective." *Daedalus* 119(2, Spring): 141–68.

Olzak, Susan. 1992. *The Dynamics of Ethnic Competition and Conflict*. Stanford, Calif.: Stanford University Press.

Omi, Michael, and Howard Winant. 1994. *Racial Formation in the United States: From the 1960s to the 1990s*. 2nd ed. New York: Routledge.

Park, Robert E. 1950. "Our Racial Frontier on the Pacific." In *Race and Culture*. Glencoe, Ill.: Free Press. (Orig. pub. 1926.)

Portes, Alejandro. 1997. "Immigration Theory for a New Century: Some Problems and Opportunities." *International Migration Review* 31(4): 799–825.

Portes, Alejandro, and Min Zhou. 1993. "The New Second Generation: Segmented Assimilation and Its Variants." *Annals of the American Academy of Political Science* 530: 74–96.

Roediger, David R. 1991. *The Wages of Whiteness: Race and the Making of the American Working Class*. London: Verso.

———. 1994. "Whiteness and Ethnicity in the History of 'White Ethnics' in the United States." In *Towards the Abolition of Whiteness: Essays on Race, Politics, and Working Class History*. London: Verso.

———. 2002. "The Problem with 'White Ethnic' History: New Immigrants and Racial Inbetween-ness." Unpublished paper. University of Illinois, Champaign-Urbana.

Rogin, Michael. 1996. *Blackface, White Noise: Jewish Immigrants in the Hollywood Melting Pot*. Berkeley: University of California Press.

Roosens, Eugeen E. 1989. *Creating Ethnicity: The Process of Ethnogenesis*. Newbury Park, Calif.: Sage Publications.

Sánchez, George. 1999. "Race, Nation, and Culture in Recent Immigration Studies." *Journal of American Ethnic History* 18(4): 66–84.

Schermerhorn, Richard. 1978. *Comparative Ethnic Relations: A Framework for Theory and Research*. Chicago: University of Chicago Press.

Sollors, Werner. 1986. *Beyond Ethnicity: Consent and Descent in American Culture*. New York: Oxford University Press.

Steinberg, Stephen. 1981. *The Ethnic Myth: Race, Ethnicity, and Class in America*. Boston: Beacon Press.

Thomas, Robert K. 1968. "Pan-Indianism." In *The American Indian Today*, edited by Stuart Levine and Nancy O. Lurie. Baltimore: Penguin.

Waldinger, Roger. 1996. *Still the Promised City? African-Americans and New Immigrants in Postindustrial New York*. Cambridge, Mass.: Harvard University Press.

Waters, Mary C. 1990. *Ethnic Options: Choosing Identities in America*. Berkeley: University of California Press.

———. 1999. *Black Identities: West Indian Immigrant Dreams and American Realities*. New York and Cambridge, Mass.: Russell Sage Foundation and Harvard University Press.

Waters, Mary C., and Karl Eschbach. 1995. "Immigration and Ethnic and Racial Inequality in the United States." *Annual Review of Sociology* 21: 419–46.

Weber, Max. 1968. *Economy and Society,* edited by Guenther Roth and Claus Wittich. Berkeley: University of California Press.

Winant, Howard. 1997. "From Behind Blue Eyes: Whiteness and Contemporary U.S. Racial Politics." In *Off White: Readings on Race, Power, and Society*, edited by Michelle Fine, Lois Weis, Linda C. Powell, and L. Mun Wong. New York: Routledge.

Yetman, Norman, ed. 1999. *Majority and Minority: The Dynamics of Race and Ethnicity in American Life*. 6th ed. Boston: Allyn and Bacon.

Victoria Hattam

Chapter 2

Ethnicity: An American Genealogy

One cannot go very far when reading popular or academic accounts of American culture and politics without quickly encountering numerous references to ethnic groups and races. Yet the particular meanings of the words "race" and "ethnicity" and the boundary between them usually remain quite vague; most often the two are positioned as a family resemblance rather than a stark opposition. Moreover, the term "ethnic" is a rather permissive one, referring variously to religious, linguistic, cultural, and other subnational identifications as important nodes of difference within the American polity. Despite the permissiveness of the term "ethnic" and its ambiguous positioning vis-à-vis "race," I want to suggest that the two are *not* simply used interchangeably in the United States. Rather, the terms "race" and "ethnicity" obtain much of their meaning from the *relational dynamic* between them, a dynamic that was set in place this century during the teens and twenties when a number of New York intellectuals began to refer to ethnic groups as distinct social formations. By examining both the social context of these early ethnicity essays and by attending more closely to the relational dynamics between these two terms *within* texts, we can begin to identify some of the key parameters of ethnic identification in the United States. American ethnicity, as we will see, has always been anchored by repeated comparisons with race through which the early ethnicity theorists sought to fix race in order to unfix ethnicity.

In the first quarter of the twentieth century, questions of group difference and national belonging came to a head when extensive immigration from southern and eastern Europe and the migration of African Americans from the South coincided with both World War 1 and the international Zionist movement. It was out of this context that several New York intellectuals, many of them Jews, began to distinguish ethnic groups *from* races and to ponder the basis of ethnic solidarity. Between 1914 and 1924, Horace Kallen, Edward Sapir, Julius Draschler, and Isaac Berkson, for example, all wrote books and essays in which they referred with some regularity to ethnic groups and loyalties. Moreover, their uses of the term "ethnic" seem remarkably familiar, since they were embedded in discussions of group identity, American pluralism, and racial difference.[1]

Before analyzing the social context and textual workings of these early invocations of the term "ethnic," two qualifications are in order. First, the point of reconstructing a genealogy of the term "ethnic" is not to insist on a linear continuity from the 1920s to the present. Indeed, ethnic and racial politics have changed in critical ways over the last seventy-five years, and I believe that it is precisely the boundary, or distinction, between race and ethnicity set in place in the teens and twenties that is being called into question in many quarters today. If we are interested in reworking notions of race and ethnicity now, and especially for those interested in building a broad-based antiracist coalition, we would do well to attend to the ground on which the current cultural and political battles are being waged. Specifically, I want to urge that we attend more closely to the terms we use, and to their social and political associations, so that we can more self-consciously shape the changes at hand.

A second provisional note concerns Werner Sollors's (1989, xiii) claim that the word "ethnicity" did not appear until 1941, with the publication of W. Lloyd Warner and Paul S. Lunt's *The Social Life of a Modern Community*.[2] The difference in timing between Sollors's and my account hinges on the fact that Sollors is especially concerned with identifying the appearance of "ethnicity" the noun rather than the adjectival form "ethnic." I am not sure what is at stake in this distinction for Sollors, but I would suggest that most of the key features of the new social category of ethnicity were already manifest in the texts published between 1914 and 1924. To be sure, discussions of ethnic difference in the teens and twenties remained a minor strand within American culture and politics; the dominant discourse was not yet infused with references to ethnic groups and loyalties but called instead for the Americanization of immigrants via their assimilation into mainstream American life. Even though only a minor strain, there is much to be gained by examining these early ethnicity essays. Because the term "ethnic" was not yet in general circulation, these authors could not presume any commonsense understanding of the word. As a consequence, these early ethnicity theorists go to some lengths to elaborate the social phenomena they are describing and to specify in considerable detail exactly what they take the term "ethnic" to mean. More important still, if one begins the analysis of ethnicity in the 1940s, as Sollors does, or in the 1970s, as do those focusing on the ethnic revival, one is more likely to overlook the constitutive relationship between ethnicity and race, since by those later periods the dynamic relationship between the two terms no longer needed to be specified. In the teens and twenties the meaning could not yet be taken for granted and so was spelled out in no uncertain terms.

The chapter proceeds in three parts. Part one briefly maps the social context out of which the term "ethnic" emerged. Part two provides a close textual reading of three early ethnicity essays in which we can see the dynamic relation between race and ethnicity at work. I conclude by discussing the long-term implications of American constructions of ethnicity for American immigrant and racial politics in subsequent decades.

PROGRESSIVE ERA IMMIGRATION: NEGOTIATING RACE AND WAR

From 1880 through 1924, New York City was the principal port of entry, and the ultimate destination, for almost one-quarter of the new immigrants entering the United States.[3] If we measure immigration as a percentage of the resident population, this second wave of immigration spanning the years 1880 through 1924 was the largest influx of immigrants in American history, and New York City remained the destination of choice of most of the new arrivals. In the first three decades of the twentieth century, almost two million immigrants settled in New York, so that by 1900, 84 percent of the city's households headed by whites were immigrants themselves or the children of immigrants (Rosenwaike 1972, 95). But it was not just a question of numbers. Whereas midnineteenth-century immigrants had originated primarily in Germany and Ireland,

Progressive Era immigration stemmed largely from Russia, Austria-Hungary, and Italy. This shift from western to southern and eastern Europe marked an important change in the religious and class composition of the new arrivals and was considered by many to signal an important change in the racial composition as well.[4] By 1935 New York City was approximately 50 percent Catholic, 30 percent Jewish, and 17 percent Protestant. Thus, in the first three decades of the twentieth century, New York's old native stock became a distinct religious minority, thereby fueling fears of national and racial degeneration. Hence popular treatises anxiously bemoaning the declining hegemonic status of the white race proliferated.[5]

It is also important to remember that European immigration intersected the Great Migration of African Americans from the South to the North and West. Although there was some migration out of the South in the two decades following the Civil War, the big push came between 1890 and 1930. From 1890 to 1910, the African American population of New York almost tripled, and from 1920 to 1930 it more than doubled again—from 152,467 to 327,706 (Osofsky 1970, 18). By the early 1920s, several contemporary commentators were remarking on the arrival of African Americans in the city as they tried to assess the significance of the Great Migration.[6] By 1930 there were more African Americans living in New York City than the African American populations of Birmingham, Memphis, and St. Louis combined. In 1930 African Americans, concentrated principally in Harlem, made up 12 percent of Manhattan's population (see Osofsky 1970, 19, 128).[7]

The intersection of southern and eastern European immigration, African American migration, and World War I put two questions in play: How were new immigrants going to position themselves, and be positioned by others, in relation to questions of race *and* nation? Or put differently, how were immigrants going to negotiate both their loyalty to the nation and their place in the American racial hierarchy? The heightened state of war put considerable pressure on immigrants to assimilate, a pressure evident in both Teddy Roosevelt's (1915/1991) and Woodrow Wilson's (1915/1991) declarations that there was no place for "hyphenated Americans" in times of war when all new immigrants needed to become "100 percent American." These presidential appeals for immigrant assimilation were buttressed at the local level by an extensive campaign of Americanization in which numerous organizations both public and private worked relentlessly toward immigrant incorporation (Higham 1963, ch. 9; King 2000; McClymer 1978). Moreover, as whiteness scholars have shown, assimilation meant much more than simply identifying as an American citizen; it also entailed accommodation to American cultural norms, including aspirations to white racial identification. Becoming American, many have argued, meant becoming white as well.[8]

However, when reexamining early ethnicity essays, I was struck by the fact that many authors adamantly opposed assimilation and began to articulate an alternative vision of immigrants' place in American culture and politics. Randolph Bourne, Horace Kallen, John Dewey, Norman Hapgood, Isaac Berkson, Julius Draschler, and others argued that preserving the plurality of American cultural affiliations was central to maintaining a vibrant democratic life. The health of American democracy, cultural pluralists argued, was dependent on maintaining immigrant difference as a balwark against the homogenizing effects of industrialization. This argument was put most elegantly by Randolph Bourne (1916) in his "Transnational America" essay, but notions of hyphenated loyalties were somehow in the air, as many intellectuals began to advocate anti-assimilationist positions in which multiple loyalties could be sustained without compromising loyalty to America (Du Bois 1897/1970; 1903/1969; Schechter 1906, 5; Bentley 1908/1935, chs. 22 and 23; Berkson 1920b; Dewey 1940; Moore 1981, ch. 4).

But arguments for hyphenation and plurality were not yet arguments for ethnicity; not all cultural pluralists wrote in terms of ethnic groups and loyalties. Rather, it was a particular subset of New York intellectuals who began to refer to *ethnic* groups in the decade between 1914 and 1924—namely, those engaged in debates over American Zionism. Jewish immigrants had to navigate issues of group loyalty and national belonging somewhat differently from other immigrants, since it was by no means clear what word to place on the left side of the hyphen. No term provided an easy sign for Jews to unite behind. Nationality was problematic, since they had no shared territorial origin; their diasporic origins made standard arguments for hyphenated national identity untenable. The emerging Zionist movement could perhaps diminish national differences by creating a national homeland to be from, but not all Jews embraced these nationalist aspirations, and even those who did could not yet count on them being fulfilled.

At times some intellectuals have tried to hyphenate religion with nation. But the term "Jewish-American" never gained much currency, no doubt in part because Jews themselves remained divided as to their religious orientations and commitments, but perhaps also because of the long-standing liberal commitment to keeping religious identifications out of the public domain (Kallen 1915b). Moreover, for many, religious belief alone did not encompass the full extent of their Jewishness, which many began to locate variously in claims of history, community practices, and group consciousness. Or as some put it, Jewish identity was tied to Jewish culture rather than to religion or nation. Exactly what was meant by "culture" was not always clear, though most often it seemed to boil down to a Boasian view of group consciousness and social practices that could never simply be reduced to race or nation.[9]

The flourishing of American Zionism in the teens and twenties brought these long-standing arguments over what it meant to be both Jewish and American to a head. Zionism did not settle questions of Jewish identity; rather, it raised them anew as pro- and anti-Zionists argued over the purposes of the new homeland. Questions of territory, nationality, religion, and culture all were advanced with new vigor as American Jews debated the basis of their collective solidarity both within the American nation and in the world at large and the role of Zionism in furthering these ends.[10] An important site for this debate over Jewish identity can be found within the pages of the *Menorah Journal*, a bimonthly publication intended for, as the masthead declared, "the study and advancement of Jewish culture and ideals." Not all who wrote for the *Journal* were Jews, nor were all the contributors Zionists, and even those who were often disagreed over what they understood Zionism to be. The *Menorah Journal* by no means advanced a particular party line, but despite their differences, almost all contributors took questions of Jewish solidarity and how to sustain it as the starting point for their essays. The *Journal* became an important venue for debates over how best to negotiate being both an American and a Jew. It is precisely from within these discussions of Jewish solidarity that several key intellectuals began to refer to ethnic groups and loyalties and to specify their relationship to race.

AMERICAN JEWS AND AMERICAN ETHNICITY: THE *MENORAH JOURNAL*, 1915 TO 1961

The *Menorah Journal* was the official publication of the menorah movement, which began in the fall of 1906 when a small group of students, Horace Kallen among them, established the first menorah society at Harvard University (Intercollegiate Menorah

Association 1914, ch. 2). The *Journal* was published continuously from 1915 through 1961, although the heyday remained the interwar decades from 1915 through 1945. The *Journal* was a quite remarkable publication that contained essays from a spectacular array of American luminaries. Mary Antin, Louis Brandeis, Felix Frankfurter, Roscoe Pound, Charles Beard, Bertrand Russell, Edward Sapir, Alfred L. Kroeber, Horace Kallen, Randolph Bourne, Isaac Berkson, Lewis Mumford, Norman Hapgood, G. Stanley Hall, Alvin Johnson, Hannah Arendt, John Dewey, and Charles W. Eliot all had essays published in the *Journal* between the wars. Moreover, almost all of the leading Zionists of the period wrote essays as well: Theodor Herzl, Richard Gotteil, Chaim Weizmann, Schmarya Levin, Jacob De Haas, Jacob Schiff, Martin Buber, Julian Mack, and Mordecai Kaplan all contributed articles in the interwar years. Finally, it is worth noting that the *Journal* was very broadly conceived, with considerable space being devoted to poetry, drama, and art. Not all of the artistic and literary contributors became famous in their own right, but certainly figures such as Pablo Picasso, Marc Chagall, Camille Pissarro, Max Weber (the painter), Thomas Mann, Israel Zangwill, and Lionel Trilling matched the prominence of the *Journal*'s social commentators. Indeed, the *Menorah Journal* provides a fascinating and much neglected counterpoint to the New Negro movement; both seem to have provided broad-ranging forums for renegotiating ethnic and racial identities in the interwar years.

Numerous essays published in the *Journal* began to specify the particularity of Jewish identity by carving out a new category of ethnicity; the new category, however, was not created de novo but was continually elaborated through repeated comparisons with competing identifications, especially that of race. As I began to track references to ethnic groups and loyalties in these early essays, I began to see that the newly emerging term "ethnic" took much of its meaning from these relational dynamics; in some important sense, *one was an ethnic in the United Sates because one's difference was not configured in racial terms.* Comparisons with nationality also were extremely important in setting the parameters of the category of ethnicity, but owing to space constraints I focus here on the relational dynamics with race. To illustrate this dynamic at work, I examine two early ethnicity essays published in the *Menorah Journal*—one by Alfred Kroeber and the other by Isaac Berkson. I might have selected any number of essays from the pages of the *Journal*; almost all engaged questions of Jewish identity, and most did so, either directly or indirectly, by contrasting ethnic solidarity with other forms of collectivity. To be sure, the specifics of the arguments varied, but the general point stands: ethnic identity was specified by contrasting it in numerous ways with race and nation. Thus, Kroeber and Berkson provide rather typical explorations of Jewish solidarity, additional variants of which can be found throughout the pages of the *Menorah Journal*.

Alfred Kroeber was Franz Boas's first Ph.D. student at Columbia University. He went on to a distinguished career in the Department of Anthropology at the University of California at Berkeley and also embarked on a second career as a psychoanalyst. Ultimately, however, he made anthropology his principal vocation and was one of the last anthropologists to produce original work across all the fields in anthropology. Kroeber's *Menorah Journal* essay is just one piece in a very broad-ranging corpus of research. Unlike almost all the other ethnicity theorists, Kroeber was neither an immigrant nor a Jew. Although born in the United States, Kroeber nevertheless grew up in a largely German immigrant household; his father's first language was German, the family spoke German at home, and Kroeber was even schooled in German by a tutor until the age of seven (Kroeber 1970).

Kroeber's *Menorah Journal* essay, "Are the Jews a Race?," is a classic Boasian exploration of the relationship between culture and race. Kroeber (1917, 290) begins with a quite extensive discussion of what he considers race to be:

> All members of a race are born with certain common features and traits which they cannot lose. Nor can the race become divested, except in small degrees and after lapse of ages, of its special qualities. It may dilute and wash itself out by intermixture with other races. It can be supplanted by a new and higher type. But for all practical purposes, it is unalterable.
>
> . . . It is among those rare things in the world which may be broken and destroyed, but which cannot be bent.

Right from the outset, Kroeber presents race as something "unalterable," as something enduring and unbending. Or as he puts it a little later in the essay:

> Heredity is the great conservative factor, the forever steadying fly-wheel of race. And if heredity means anything, it means permanence, repetition of the same, generation after generation.
>
> What is individual in us may therefore be distinctive; but what we owe to race is inevitable, fixed before our birth, and ineradicable. What human minds acquire, they receive from education, from environment. What human minds inherit from their race is instinctive and unalterable. The leopard cannot change his spots. (291)

It is important to note that this effort to fix race as permanent and unchanging marks a quite dramatic change from nineteenth-century Lamarckian notions of race in which it was assumed that acquired characteristics can become heritable traits. Lamarckian assumptions thus presumed a much more plastic notion of race in which one's racial makeup was presumed to change with changes in environmental conditions.[11] The incessant effort to fix race, evident in many of these early ethnicity essays, speaks to the importance of contrasting race with ethnicity. But it was difficult to position ethnicity against a moving target, hence the ethnicity theorists' anxious efforts to specify race.

Kroeber ends his discussion of race asking, "By these tests, are the Jews a race?" At first, his position seems confused: in the opening pages of the essay, he carefully specifies Jewish racial location, only to go on in the remainder of the essay to argue explicitly that Jews are not a race. What are we to make of these apparently contradictory arguments? Why, and in what ways, are Jews simultaneously raced and not raced for Kroeber? It is worth looking carefully here, since Kroeber discusses the relationship between Jewish identity and race at length and thus gives us a chance to see how ethnic identification was specified by *distinguishing* it from race. At the outset, Kroeber (1917, 291) takes some care to specify the racial status of the Jews as members of the Mediterranean race along with Phoenicians, Arabs, Syrians, Egyptians, Greeks, Italians, Spaniards, and all "the nations that fringe the shores of the Mediterranean Sea." Thus, Kroeber unambiguously places Jews within what he further specifies as "one of the main branches of the Caucasian stock" (1917, 291). But as the essay progresses it becomes clear that these racial classifications of Mediterranean and/or Caucasian are of little or no consequence for Kroeber, since they do not distinguish Jews from all the other groups along the shores of the Mediterranean and as such cannot explain what makes Jews Jews. In Kroeber's hands, race becomes a set of distant background conditions that have little bearing on his immediate intellectual preoccupation, namely, how to understand and find a means of sustaining Jewish solidarity in the early twentieth century.

In short, although Jews are, for Kroeber, members of the Mediterranean race, this is not what makes them Jews, not what makes them cohere as a distinct group. Addressing questions of *Jewish particularity* requires a quite different set of arguments, all of which begin from the assumption that whatever it is that makes Jews cohere as a group, it is not race. The second half of the essay shifts the focus from racial classification per se to a critique of race-based views of Jewish identity. Here Kroeber's (1917, 291) argument hinges on the national variability of Jews: "If the Jew were everywhere the same, if he formed, physically, a true race, then the Polish Jew should be long-headed like his fellow Jew of Africa. But the Polish Jew resembles, instead, the Polish Gentile, and is short-headed!" Kroeber speculates briefly on the cause of the national variability of Jews and suggests that it might be due to either environment or intermarriage. But his principal purpose is to establish that "whatever the cause, the fact remains that throughout the civilized world the Jew, *in his body*, is essentially the same with the Gentile of the same country," and hence ought not to be considered a separate race (1917, 292, emphasis added).

Note how Kroeber equates race with both bodily form and stability of type over time and place. Malleability and change, in and of themselves, are taken as evidence that the collective identification must be of a nonracial kind. There is nothing logical or inevitable about the chains of equivalence that Kroeber creates here; one can readily imagine a line of argument that used Progressive Era immigration and the problems it raised for the extant racial taxonomy as an opening for deconstructing the racial taxonomy itself. That is, since southern and eastern European immigrants did not fit easily into the existing racial categories, one possible response would have been to use this disjuncture as a means of reexamining the category of race. But this is not the line of argument pursued by Kroeber, nor by any of the early ethnicity theorists. Instead, a new social category emerged, the category of ethnicity, which absorbed the residual classificatory problems resulting from the recent immigration. As a consequence, the disruptive potential of Progressive Era immigration in terms of the extant racial taxonomy was muted by the invention of ethnicity. The invention of ethnicity thus helped the older black-white binary remain intact.

Kroeber concludes his essay by posing two questions: "What traits have the Jews in common?" and "If the Jew is not a race—what is he?" Like many fellow contributors to the *Journal*, Kroeber specifies Jewish particularity by contrasting its "social" basis with hereditary notions of race. He puts the comparison as follows:

> There is no doubt a "typical Jew" in character and temperament, but he is the product of social conditions, not of heredity and race. . . . As a matter of fact, the "typical," or Ghetto-made Jew is not at all typical of Judaism in its wider historical aspect. It is only short-sightedness that projects him into a past in which he never existed. (Kroeber 1917, 293)

Note how Kroeber again equates historical continuity with biological fixity and hence with race, while the more malleable identities, like those of the Jews, are seen as being tied to social conditions, and thus as changing over both time and place. Kroeber concludes his essay stating:

> If, then, the Jew is not a race, what is he? For over two thousand years he has not formed a nation in the political sense. For nearly as long he has not been a geographical unit. For the same period he has not even possessed the unifying bond of a common

language, except for ritual purposes. Only one thing is common to Jews of the past and present and to all Jews of today—their faith.

The Jew, then, is a group, a caste, in the better sense of the word, held together by religion. Hence the emphasis is justified which the Jew always has laid and still lays on his faith. . . . Their future as Jews, therefore, is clearly and indissolubly bound up with Jewish belief and worship; but their future as human beings is in no sense limited or predestined by any bonds or race, but lies in themselves as individual men, and in their ideals and character. (Kroeber 1917, 294)

For Kroeber, the Jews are not a race, but a social formation—a collectivity bound by religious faith.

Although Kroeber clearly wants to distinguish Jewish identity from race and nation, he does not fully articulate this view of Jewish particularity in terms of ethnicity, nor does he extrapolate from Jews to other immigrant groups to make a more general claim about the importance of subnational identification. Put another way, Kroeber does not generalize in this essay from the Jews to ethnic groups per se; nevertheless, his desire to oppose the social basis of Jewish particularity with race and nation is clear. Jews, Kroeber claims, are "in no sense limited or predestined by" race; being Jewish, for Kroeber, is a cultural and social phenomenon in contradistinction to the supposedly more heritable notions of race.

Other contributors to the *Journal*, however, did make the extension from Jewish particularity to ethnicity quite explicitly.[12] Isaac Berkson provides an especially useful comparison with Kroeber because he clearly sees Jews as the architects, and principal practitioners, of the new social category of ethnicity. Isaac Berkson was born in Brooklyn, New York, in 1891; he received his B.A. from City College of New York, where he also helped establish the City College menorah society and served as its second president. After graduating from City College, Berkson went on to earn master's and Ph.D. degrees in education at Columbia University, where John Dewey served as one of his advisers. Berkson spent most of his professional career working at the intersection of Judaism and education, initially for the Jewish Board of Education and subsequently as executive director of the Central Jewish Institute at 125 East Eighty-fifth Street in New York. The Institute had been deeply influenced by Mordecai M. Kaplan, a key figure in early-twentieth-century Jewish circles, a regular contributor to the *Menorah Journal*, and a fellow graduate of City College and Columbia University.

Berkson extends arguments of Jewish particularity to more general claims about ethnicity in the very first paragraph of his *Menorah Journal* essay, "A Community Theory of American Life," which is worth quoting in full.

The community theory here proposed as a constructive suggestion is really the formulation of a process already shaping itself among some of our immigrant groups. To the writer the suggestion has come from the experience of the Jewish group; and although elements of this plan are discernible among other immigrant nationalities, the Jews have undoubtedly gone furthest in its development. In fact, it may be regarded as the response of the Jewish group to the problem of adjustment. While many among the Jews would differ with this proposal or with some of its elements, the tendency of Jewish institutional development to-day indicates that the community theory, as presented below, is the acceptable mode of adjustment for the Jewish group as an *ethnic entity*. Drawn from Jewish life, it will undoubtedly apply most closely to Jewish life; nevertheless it is hoped that the Jewish experience may form the basis of a theory of adjustment applicable to all groups which desire to maintain their identity in the midst of American democratic life. (Berkson 1920a, 311, emphasis added)

Jews, for Berkson, are the quintessential ethnics because they embody a very particular kind of subnational identification that cannot easily be equated with either race or nation. Berkson further specifies Jewish ethnicity by elaborating his notion of "community" as follows:

> The community theory insists on the value of the ethnic group as a permanent asset in American life. It differs from the "Americanization" and "melting pot" theories in that it refuses to set up as an ideal such a fusion as will lead to the wiping out of all ethnic distinctions. Furthermore, it regards a rich social life as necessary for the development of the culture of the foreign group. In the "federation of nationalities" theory, which is pivoted on the identity of race, the argument is primarily that "we cannot change our grandfathers." The community theory, on the other hand, makes the history of the group, its esthetic, cultural, and religious inheritance, its national self-consciousness, the basic factor. *This change of emphasis from race to culture* brings with it a whole series of implications, arising from the fact that culture is not inherited but must be acquired through some educational process. The difference is crucial. A community of culture possible of demonstration becomes the ground for perpetuating the group, rather than an identity of race, questionable in fact and dubious in significance. (311–12, emphasis added)

Interestingly, Berkson specifically tries to establish ethnicity as a social rather than a heritable identity by critiquing Horace Kallen's classic statement that whatever else we do we cannot change our grandfathers. Berkson replaces Kallen's emphasis on descent with his "community theory" of ethnicity, which more fully distinguishes ethnic solidarity from race and nation.[13] Note how Berkson equates "ethnic distinction," "culture," and "history," on the one hand, and "fusion," "inheritance," and "race," on the other. Inheritance becomes the means of linking race and nation in opposition to the cultural and historical production of ethnicity.

Having marked off ethnicity as social, Berkson is well aware that breaking with notions of ancestry and descent brings with it a set of vulnerabilities as well. The break with heredity means that the survival of ethnic groups is no longer guaranteed, so that Jews come face to face with "the danger of disintegration" and possible "extinction" (Berkson 1920a, 316). Ethnic groups, for Berkson, are not self-reproducing but must be sustained through cultural institutions whose task it is to cultivate a sense of self-conscious identity and history for the group. Educational institutions, Berkson argues, are especially important to this process of group renewal. Perhaps not surprisingly, Berkson spent his entire professional life in just such institutions, working for the Bureau of Jewish Education and the Central Jewish Institute, in New York.

Arguments claiming ethnicity as central to American democracy certainly were not confined to the pages of the *Menorah Journal;* they could be found in a variety of sources in the first quarter of the twentieth century. The *Journal* nevertheless provides a highly concentrated exchange over the nature and meaning of ethnic identification that reveals some of the central parameters of the category-in-formation. It is interesting to read Horace Kallen's classic ethnicity text "Democracy Versus the Melting Pot" (1915a) in light of the *Menorah Journal* debates. Doing so enables one to see Kallen's text in a rather different light.

CULTURAL PLURALISM AND ETHNICITY: REREADING KALLEN

Horace Kallen coined the term "cultural pluralism" in 1906 as a means of defending immigrant difference as central to American democratic life. His theories have undergone something of a renaissance in recent years as several scholars have begun to view his work as one of the precursors to multiculturalism.[14] But not all celebrate Kallen's pluralist vision; John Higham (1975, ch. 10) and Werner Sollors (1986a), in particular, have waged extensive critiques of Kallen's work in which they point out that African Americans are never included in Kallen's pluralist pantheon and that the "influence of the negro" is set aside as "at once too considerable and too recondite . . . for casual mention. It requires separate analysis" (Kallen 1924/1998, 218). Thus, although Kallen is an ardent defender of greater tolerance and plurality in American society, his pluralist vision never challenges the color line.

Even though Sollors and Higham are quite right to point out that African Americans are never included as one of the constituent groups in Kallen's federation of nationalities, they mistakenly equate this omission with the claim that Kallen pays little or no attention to race. Just because Kallen excludes African Americans from his federation of nationalities, it is *not* the case that race plays little or no role in his work. On the contrary, Kallen (1915a, pt. 1, 191–93), like many of his *Menorah Journal* counterparts, frequently refers to "whites," "negroes," and "Anglo Saxons." Why is it, I want to know, that such explicit and numerous racial referents have largely been ignored? Why is Kallen's essay known for its silence on race? The answer, I want to suggest, lies in the quite particular ways in which Kallen deploys racial terms as a means of anchoring ethnicity. That is, both explicit and implicit comparisons between race and ethnicity run throughout the essay, so that the text itself simultaneously invokes and displaces race. It is worth looking in some detail at Kallen's textual deployment of race.

If we look more closely at his essay, we see that Kallen invokes explicitly racial terms in two quite specific contexts—namely, when referring to the colonial period in the United States and to the South, both of which Kallen contrasts with the culture and politics of his own time and place: the Northeast, or more specifically New York City, in 1915. For example, early in the essay Kallen (1915a, 192) writes:

> South of Mason and Dixon's line the cities exhibit a greater homogeneity. Outside of certain regions in Texas the descendants of the native white stock, often degenerate and backward, prevail among whites, but the whites as a whole constitute a relatively weaker proportion of the population. They live among nine million negroes, whose own mode of living tends, by its mere massiveness, to standardize the "mind" of the proletarian South in speech, manner, and the other values of social organization.

Kallen, like many northerners in his day, equates the South with homogenization, degeneration, and backwardness. The southern problem is especially acute, Kallen argues, because southern workers are being homogenized on two fronts. First, southern white workers have to negotiate the same forces of standardization that confront all workers during industrialization, namely, the standardization of work and production. But southern workers also have to "live among nine million negroes," whose very presence, Kallen claims, tends to further "standardize the 'mind' of the proletarian South" (Kallen 1915a, 192). The best prospects for escaping the stifling forces of standardization are to be found, Kallen argues, in the Northeast, where new immigrant communities are providing the basis for resisting both the economic and racial dimensions of homogenization.

Immediately after noting the homogenized character of the South, Kallen turns to the immigration question, which remains his central preoccupation. Once he begins this discussion of immigration in earnest, issues of race gradually disappear. Thus, Kallen simultaneously invokes and displaces race by continually tying race to the past and to the South, then using the image of southern homogeneity as a counterpoint to the more heterogeneous and cosmopolitan social relations in the Northeast. In short, Kallen invokes racial difference precisely to underscore the quite distinct notions of difference that had emerged with the influx of nationalities in recent decades. As a consequence, the *text itself* draws the readers' attention away from race and focuses it on nationality and ethnicity—precisely the themes that the essay is known for today. But it is important to recognize that all the key characteristics of ethnic identification have been conveyed to the reader through repeated comparisons with race. Kallen defines ethnicity against race.

Even as early as 1915, then, Kallen was homogenizing notions of race in order to pluralize notions of ethnicity. The comparison of race and ethnicity that runs throughout Kallen's essay was critical to the process of category formation. Indeed, I have come to see the comparison with race as constitutive of the category of ethnicity itself. One is an ethnic, in the American context, to the extent that one's difference is not configured in racial terms. Ethnicity in the United States is positioned as cultural difference as opposed to the supposedly more bodily differences of race.

CONCLUSION: ETHNIC POLITICS IN A RACIAL POLITY

Since American Zionists and cultural pluralists were by no means the dominant voices in American politics in the teens and twenties, and by the 1930s had receded even further from view, we might well ask, what has been the long-term significance of their conception of ethnicity? Was the new social category of ethnicity carved out in the teens and twenties only a fleeting phenomenon, one that was quickly displaced by class-based identifications as the organizing matrix of American politics in the 1930s, and by race-based politics in the 1960s and 1970s? Perhaps more important, what difference does it make to the prevailing social cleavages and political alliances when we distinguish ethnicity from race rather than view the two as interchangeable terms and subject positions?

Although the Depression and the New Deal certainly led to the subordination of ethnic identifications to those of class, the category of ethnicity did not vanish altogether. After all, we still speak of the New Deal coalition as an alliance of organized labor, African Americans, and ethnic groups in ways that suggest that even though class trumped ethnicity in the 1930s and 1940s, the distinction between racial and ethnic groups was maintained, albeit in a subterranean form. Indeed, if we look inside class-based institutions of the 1930s and 1940s, such as the large industrial unions and the Democratic and Communist parties, we see that many organizations continued to mobilize constituents into distinct ethnic and racial subunits. Class-based coalitions were forged, but the very notion that they were *coalitions* speaks to the persistence of categorical distinctions between ethnic groups and races—a distinction, we have seen, that was set in place in the preceding two decades.[15]

Perhaps the most important impetus for reinvigorating the category of ethnicity came with the third great wave of immigration in the post-1965 era. Without the new immigration, ethnicity might well have waned as a distinct identification, and the social category eventually have fallen into disuse. The arrival of large numbers of immigrants, however, this time principally from Asia and Latin America, and the coincidence of this new immigration with the civil rights and Black Power movements revived distinctions between race and ethnicity. Only now it was Hispanics and/or Latinos, rather than Jews, who were cast quite formally by the federal government as the new ethnics. On May 12, 1977, the Office of Management and Budget promulgated Statistical Policy Directive 15, a brief two-page document stipulating the official categories to be used by *all* federal government agencies when collecting and reporting data on race and ethnicity. In many ways, Directive 15 might be seen as one of the most enduring legacies of the civil rights movement of the 1960s, since the categories stipulated therein quickly migrated to state governments and private-sector organizations that interfaced with federal government agencies. As a consequence, the Directive 15 categories have become the de facto racial and ethnic categories for American society as a whole (*Federal Register* 59[110], June 9, 1994, app.: 29834–5).

The initial impetus for Directive 15 lay in the civil rights legislation of the 1960s and 1970s: the Civil Rights Act of 1964, the Voting Rights Act of 1965, the Fair Housing Act of 1968, the Equal Credit Opportunity Act of 1974, and the Home Mortgage Disclosure Act of 1975 all required that the federal government begin to identify and monitor ethnic and racial discrimination in a variety of policy domains. Doing so, agencies first had to specify the relevant protected groups, which in turn required that ethnic and racial categories be stipulated. Directive 15 was the first effort to standardize ethnic and racial categories across federal government agencies; although revised in 1997 to allow for the multiple-race option, the basic parameters of Directive 15 remain in force today.[16]

It is amazing to see the ways in which our federal statistical system as codified in Directive 15 echoes the views of Kroeber, Berkson, and Kallen on ethnicity and race examined here. Despite its brevity and apparent simplicity, Directive 15 distills America's complex ethnic and racial history into a formal ethnic and racial taxonomy. Simply put, it specifies four racial groups: American Indian or Alaskan Native, Asian or Pacific Islander, black, and white, while Hispanics and/or Latinos are designated as an ethnic group, *not* a race, because of their Spanish origin and culture. As an ethnic group, Hispanics and/or Latinos can be of any race, since their race is not what makes them cohere as a group. The distinction between race and ethnicity contained within Directive 15 is the reason why contemporary accounts of American demographic data usually contain a footnote stating that Hispanics can be of any race, and then go on to differentiate between "non-Hispanic whites" and "Hispanic whites." The assumption is very much the same one articulated by Kroeber and Berkson, namely, that Hispanics may be white but this is not their principal point of identification. Rather, their shared culture, especially their religion and language, is what marks them as a distinct group and has been the source of their quite particular form of discrimination. Even today, then, the federal measurement system continues to distinguish ethnicity from race.

What is at stake in this positioning of ethnicity against race? What difference does it make to prevailing social relations and political alliances in the United States? Elaborating the consequences of our ethno-racial taxonomy is an issue beyond the scope of this chapter—and one that I explore at length elsewhere—but let me at least indicate why I think it matters. Perhaps the most important consequence of distinguishing ethnicity from race has been the fostering of divisions between ethnics and African Americans, making it more difficult to forge enduring coalitions across the race-ethnicity divide. At times alliances have been built, for example, between Jews and African Americans during the civil rights movement, and between Hispanics and/or Latinos and African Americans in the Harold Washington administration in Chicago and the David Dinkins administration in New York. Each of these coalitions, however, has remained vulnerable to enduring division and distrust between ethnics and blacks. This division and distrust, I want to suggest, has been fueled by the long history of defining ethnicity against race.[17] To be sure, categories and identities are not the only sources of division between immigrants and African Americans; many scholars have shown that political institutions and economic conditions continue to pit ethnic and racial groups against each other.[18] But it is a mistake to think of institutions, interests, and identities as competing explanations in which we ought to assign so much variance to each. Rather, what is so powerful about processes of category formation is that they create the very terms, or units of analysis, through which interests are formed and negotiated. That is, interests themselves have no a priori standing in social analysis but are tied to, or dependent on, the terms we use and the identities they engender. Put simply, there is nothing inevitable or natural in the American distinction between ethnicity and race; the distinction itself is the product of a quite particular set of social relations, but once accepted, these categories, and the relational dynamics between them, have shaped the expectations, social cleavages, and political alliances in play.

Finally, I suggested at the outset of this essay that the boundary between race and ethnicity is currently being called into question on many fronts. Indeed, I think that some of the key political battles taking place right now are the struggles *within* various Hispanic and/or Latino and Asian communities over how to position themselves within the American ethnic and racial taxonomy. Exactly how these competing identifications will play out is by no means certain, but preliminary evidence suggests that the very categories we use, and the relations between them, are being quite dramatically reconfigured. Take the 2000 census, for example: 42 percent of Hispanics and/or Latinos did not abide by federal government guidelines and identify as ethnics and then go on to specify their race as well. Rather, 42 percent of Hispanics and/or Latinos checked the "other race" box and then wrote in various terms indicating Hispanic and/or Latino identity. Moreover, the fact that 97 percent of those who checked "other race" were Hispanic and/or Latino suggests that this category holds some particular appeal for Hispanics and/or Latinos. Some have suggested that the disproportionate number of Hispanics and/or Latinos selecting "other race" might be due to problems of question wording, question ordering, or confusion over what exactly is being asked. But rather than assuming ignorance and confusion, we might also consider whether these responses are not better understood as efforts to rework the categories of race and ethnicity. Many Hispanics and/or Latinos, it seems, are racializing their ethnicity and in so doing are calling into question the ethnic and racial divide put in place almost a century ago.[19]

Exactly how the struggle over racial and ethnic identifications will play out within various ethnic and racial communities is unknown; the very categories and the relations between them are up for grabs. But what is clear is that how Hispanics and/or Latinos come to identify is one of the critical factors to watch. Will the majority of Hispanics and/or Latinos continue to accept the designation "ethnic," or will they begin to racialize their identity by positioning themselves as "people of color"?

Of course, questions of ethnic and racial identity are by no means simply voluntarist matters; much will be determined by the attitudes and actions of the dominant white population. How will those in power view Hispanics and/or Latinos in the decades to come? The genealogy presented here suggests both that the terms in contention have very deep roots and that the categories we deploy are of considerable consequence. Whether ethnicity continues to be treated as a distinct social category from that of race will establish quite different sets of social divisions and political alliances for decades to come.

Much of the research for this article was completed while a National Endowment for the Humanities (NEH) Fellow at the Institute for Advanced Study, Princeton, New Jersey, in 2000–2001. I would also like to thank the Social Science Research Council (SSRC) for sponsoring the conferences on which this volume is based. Many colleagues and friends have commented on earlier drafts of this material. I would especially like to thank Talal Asad, Kevin Bruyneel, Cathy Cohen, Josh DeWind, Edmund Fong, Joshua Freeman, Gary Gerstle, Jennifer Hochschild, Richard Locke, Ira Katznelson, Joseph Loundes, Uday Mehta, Mae Ngai, Anne Norton, Ken Prewitt, Adolph Reed, Joan Scott, Carl Schorske, George Shulman, Stephen Skowronek, Bob Vitalis, Michael Walzer, Priscilla Yamin, Aristide Zolberg, and the editors of this volume.

NOTES

1. For numerous references to ethnic groups and loyalties between 1914 and 1924, see Kallen (1915a, 1924/1998), Drachsler (1920a, 1920b), Berkson (1920a, 1920b, 1921), and Sapir (1924). Many other essays in the *Menorah Journal* that did not explicitly use the term "ethnic" nevertheless advanced similar arguments concerning the importance of sustaining the cultural particularity of immigrant groups; see, for example, Kallen (1915b) and Mumford (1922).

2. Sollors (1996) provided a more complete history of ethnicity a few years later in the introduction to *Theories of Ethnicity*, his ethnicity reader. For a somewhat different critique of Sollors's account of the invention of ethnicity, see Conzen and others (1992). Although Kathleen Conzen and her colleagues also see the term "ethnic" as having a much longer history, they pay insufficient attention to differences between notions of nation, nativity, and ethnicity and do not attend to the relationship between ethnic and racial differences.

3. Ira Rosenwaike (1972) remains the principal authority on early-twentieth-century population statistics for New York City. Rosenwaike estimates that for the three decades following the opening of Ellis Island in 1892, between 17.1 and 24.9 percent of immigrants entered the United States through Ellis Island.

4. At the turn of the century, no hard and fast distinction was as yet drawn between language and culture, religion, nationality, and race. Rather, all were seen as part and parcel of a quite different Lamarckian conception of race; see Stocking (1968/1982), Hudson (1996), Lopez (1996), and Hattam (forthcoming, ch. 2).

5. For estimates of the religious composition of the New York City population, see Rosenwaike (1972, 122–30, 153). For classic statements of national and racial degeneration, see Lodge (1891), Grant (1916), and Grant and Davidson (1930).

6. See, for example, Woodson (1918) and the special issue of the *Journal of Negro History* in October 1921 on "The Negro Migration of 1916–1918"; see also Osofsky (1970, 17).

7. Southern migration was further complicated by the arrival of black immigrants principally from the Caribbean. In 1910 there were 11,757 foreign-born blacks in New York City, 30,436 in 1920, and 54,754 in 1930. Although Caribbean immigrants remained a relatively

small percentage of New York City's population, their concentration in Harlem alongside African Americans raised questions about the intersection of immigration and race in the United States; see Cruse (1984, pts. 1 and 2) and Watkins-Owens (1996).

8. The whiteness literature is now enormous, but for influential works, see Baldwin (1984, 10–12), Dyer (1988), Morrison (1989 and 1993), Alba (1990), Roediger (1991 and 1994), Sacks (1994), Ignatiev (1995), Lopez (1996), Rogin (1996), Lipsitz (1998), Jacobson (1998), and Gerstle (2001).

9. Not surprisingly, Boasian views of culture were advanced by Alfred Kroeber (1917), Edward Sapir (1924), and Alexander A. Goldenweiser (1922), all of whom had been students of Franz Boas. For a very useful account of the Menorah movement and its contributors' views of culture, see Korelitz (1997).

10. The period from 1914 through 1921 is often viewed as the high point of American Zionism, when membership grew exponentially from 7,500 in 1914 to 149,000 in 1919. But perhaps as important as the leap in membership figures was the way in which World War I made America the principal organizational home of the international Zionist movement. The declaration of war split the World Zionist Organization Executive apart and led in 1914 to the creation of the Provisional Executive Committee for General Zionist Affairs in New York, which Louis Brandeis chaired until 1921.

11. For an excellent account of Lamarckian notions of race, see Stocking (1968/1982). Lamarckianism was by no means the only strand within nineteenth-century racial discourse; numerous other strands were in play as well. For useful accounts of the complex mix of eighteenth- and nineteenth-century racial thought, see Fredrickson (2002), Gossett (1997), Stocking (1993), and Hudson (1996). Lamarckianism, however, was critical to discussions of race and environmentalism. For a more elaborate discussion of the break with Lamarck and its impact on changing conceptions of race, see Hattam (forthcoming, ch. 2).

12. See the sources cited in note 1.

13. Horace Kallen's (1915a) "Democracy Versus the Melting Pot" remains perhaps the classic ethnicity text from the early twentieth century. Berkson's critique anticipates the descent-based reading of Kallen offered by Sollors (1986b) in recent years. I provide a rather different reading of Kallen's essay in the section that follows.

14. For Kallen's account of how he coined the term "cultural pluralism," see Schmidt (1975). For works reinvigorating Kallen's legacy, see Walzer (1996) and Gerstle (1994).

15. For organization along ethnic and racial lines within both industrial unions and the Communist Party, see Fraser (1993), Freeman (2000), Draper (1957, 188–93), who writes of the importance of "foreign-language federations," and Slayton (2001) for the importance of ethnicity for Democratic Party mobilization. For a fascinating account of this shift from ethnicity to class, and the complexities therein, see Cohen (1990).

16. For the history of Directive 15, see "Standards for the Classification of Federal Data on Race and Ethnicity," *Federal Register* 59 (110), June 9, 1994, 29831–2, and Edmonston, Goldstein, and Lott (1996). For the 1997 revisions to Directive 15, see Office of Management and Budget, "Recommendations From the Interagency Committee for the Review of the Racial and Ethnic Standards to the Office of Management and Budget Concerning Changes to the Standards for the Classification of Federal Data on Race and Ethnicity, Notices," *Federal Register* 62(131), July 9, 1997, 36874–946; Office of Management and Budget, "Revisions to the Standards for the Classification of Federal Data on Race and Ethnicity; Notices," *Federal Register* 62 (210), October 30, 1997, 58782–90; and Prewitt (this volume).

17. For discussions of Latino–African American alliances and divisions during the Harold Washington campaign and administration, see Betancur and Gills (1997) and Bennett

(1993). For the Dinkins administration, see Thompson (1990 and 2003), Mollenkopf (1994), and Hayduk (forthcoming).

18. For elegant examples of interest and institutional analyses of ethnic and racial conflict and division, see Mollenkopf (1999) and Zolberg (1999).

19. For interpretation of "other race" as a data problem, see Edmonston, Goldstein, and Lott (1996, 21). Stanley Lieberson (1985) makes much the same plea as I do—that we might usefully read some so-called data problems as signals of changing identifications. For interesting survey data documenting the complexity of Latino ethnic and racial identification, see Pew Hispanic Center/Kaiser Family Foundation (2002, 24–33) and Tafoya (2003).

REFERENCES

Alba, Richard D. 1990. *Ethnic Identity: The Transformation of White America*. New Haven, Conn.: Yale University Press.

Baldwin, James. 1984. "On Being White . . . and Other Lies." *Essence* (April): 10–12.

Bennett, Larry. 1993. "Harold Washington and the Black Urban Regime." *Urban Affairs Quarterly* 28(3): 423–40.

Bentley, Arthur F. 1935. *The Process of Government*. Bloomington, Ind.: Principia Press. (Orig. pub. 1908.)

Berkson, Isaac B. 1920a. "A Community Theory of American Life." *Menorah Journal* 6(6): 311–21.

———. 1920b. *Theories of Americanization: A Critical Study, with Special Reference to the Jewish Group*. New York: Teachers College.

———. 1921. "The Jewish Right to Live: A Defense of Ethnic Loyalty." *Menorah Journal* 7(1): 41–51.

Betancur, John J., and Douglas C. Gills. 1997. "Black and Latino Political Conflict in Chicago." In *Race and Politics*, edited by James Jennings. New York: Verso.

Bourne, Randolph. 1916. "Transnational America." *Atlantic Monthly* 118(July): 86–97.

Cohen, Lizabeth. 1990. *Making a New Deal: Industrial Workers in Chicago, 1919–1939*. New York: Cambridge University Press.

Conzen, Kathleen Neils, David A. Gerber, Ewa Morawska, George Pozzetta, and Rudolph J. Vecoli. 1992. "The Invention of Ethnicity: A Perspective from the U.S.A." *Journal of American Ethnic History* 12(1): 3–41.

Cruse, Harold. 1984. *The Crisis of the Negro Intellectual*. New York: Quill.

Dewey, John. 1940. *Education Today*. New York: Putnam's Sons.

Drachsler, Julius. 1920a. "Americanization and Race Fusion." *Menorah Journal* 6(3): 131–38.

———. 1920b. *Democracy and Assimilation: The Blending of Immigrant Heritages*. New York: Macmillan.

Draper, Theodore. 1957. *The Roots of American Communism*. New York: Viking Press.

Du Bois, W. E. B. 1969. *Souls of Black Folk*. New York: New American Library. (Orig. pub. 1903.)

———. 1970. "The Conservation of Races." In *W. E. B. Du Bois Speaks: Speeches and Addresses 1890–1919*. New York: Pathfinder. (Orig. pub. 1897.)

Dyer, Richard. 1988. "White." *Screen* 29(4): 44–65.

Edmonston, Barry, Joshua Goldstein, and Juanita Tamayo Lott, eds. 1996. *Spotlight on Heterogeneity: The Federal Standards for Racial and Ethnic Classification*. Washington, D.C.: National Academy Press.

Fraser, Steve. 1993. *Labor Will Rule: Sidney Hillman and the Rise of American Labor*. Ithaca, N.Y.: Cornell University Press.

Fredrickson, George M. 2002. *Racism: A Short History*. Princeton, N.J.: Princeton University Press.

Freeman, Joshua B. 2000. "Racial and Ethnic Categorization by New York City Unions After

World War II." Paper presented to the annual meeting of the American Public Health Association. Boston (November 15).

Gerstle, Gary. 1994. "The Protean Character of American Liberalism." *American Historical Review* 99(4): 1043–73.

———. 2001. *American Crucible: Race and Nation in the Twentieth Century*. Princeton, N.J.: Princeton University Press.

Goldenweiser, Alexander A. 1922. "Concerning Racial Differences." *Menorah Journal* 8(5): 309–16.

Gossett, Thomas F. 1997. *Race: The History of An Idea in America*. New York: Oxford University Press.

Grant, Madison. 1916. *The Passing of the Great Race: Or the Racial Basis of European History*. New York: Charles Scribner's Sons.

Grant, Madison, and Charles Stewart Davidson. 1930. *The Alien in Our Midst: Or 'Selling Our Birthright for a Mess of Industrial Pottage.'* New York: Galton.

Hattam, Victoria. Forthcoming. *Shadows of Pluralism: The Racial Politics of American Ethnicity*. Manuscript in progress.

Hayduk, Ronald. Forthcoming. *Gatekeepers to the Franchise: Election Administration and Voter Participation in New York*. Albany: SUNY Press.

Higham, John. 1963. *Strangers in the Land: Patterns of American Nativism 1860–1925*. New York: Atheneum.

———. 1975. *Send These to Me: Jews and Other Immigrants in Urban America*. New York: Atheneum.

Hudson, Nicholas. 1996. "From 'Nation' to 'Race': The Origin of Racial Classification in Eighteenth-Century Thought." *Eighteenth-Century Studies* 29(3): 247–64.

Ignatiev, Noel. 1995. *How the Irish Became White*. New York: Routledge.

Intercollegiate Menorah Association. 1914. *The Menorah Movement: For the Study and Advancement of Jewish Culture and Ideals, History, Purposes, and Activities*. Ann Arbor, Mich.: Intercollegiate Menorah Association.

Jacobson, Matthew Frye. 1998. *Whiteness of a Different Color: European Immigrants and the Alchemy of Race*. Cambridge, Mass.: Harvard University Press.

Kallen, Horace M. 1915a. "Democracy Versus the Melting Pot: A Study of American Nationality." *The Nation,* February 18, 190–94, and February 25, 217–20.

———. 1915b. "Nationality and the Hyphenated American." *Menorah Journal* 1(2): 79–86.

———. 1998. *Culture and Democracy in the United States*. New Brunswick, N.J.: Transaction Publishers. (Orig. pub. 1924.)

King, Desmond. 2000. *Making Americans: Immigration, Race, and the Origins of the Diverse Democracy*. Cambridge, Mass.: Harvard University Press.

Korelitz, Seth. 1997. "The Menorah Idea: From Religion to Culture, from Race to Ethnicity." *American Jewish History* 88(March): 75–100.

Kroeber, Alfred L. 1917. "Are the Jews a Race?" *Menorah Journal* 3(5): 290–94.

Kroeber, Theodora. 1970. *Alfred Kroeber: A Personal Configuration*. Berkeley: University of California Press.

Lieberson, Stanley. 1985. "Unhyphenated Whites in the United States." *Ethnic and Racial Studies* 8(1): 159–80.

Lipsitz, George. 1998. *The Possessive Investment in Whiteness: How White People Profit from Identity Politics*. Philadelphia: Temple University Press.

Lodge, Henry Cabot. 1891. "Lynch Law and Unrestricted Immigration." *North American Review* CL11: 602–12.

Lopez, Ian F. Haney. 1996. *White by Law: The Legal Construction of Race*. New York: New York University Press.

McClymer, John F. 1978. "The Federal Government and the Americanization Movement." *Prologue* (Spring): 23–41.

Mollenkopf, John Hull. 1994. *A Phoenix in the Ashes*. Princeton, N.J.: Princeton University Press.

————. 1999. "Urban Political Conflicts and Alliances: New York and Los Angles Compared." In *The Handbook of International Migration: The American Experience*, edited by Charles Hirschman, Philip Kasinitz, and Josh DeWind. New York: Russell Sage Foundation.

Moore, Deborah Dash. 1981. *At Home in America: Second Generation New York Jews.* New York: Columbia University Press.

Morrison, Toni. 1989. "Unspeakable Things Unspoken: The Afro-American Presence in American Literature." *Michigan Quarterly Review* 28(1): 1–34.

————. 1993. *Playing in the Dark: Whiteness and the Literary Imagination.* New York: Vintage Books.

Mumford, Lewis. 1922. "Nationalism or Culturalism." *Menorah Journal* 8(3): 129–38.

Osofsky, Gilbert. 1970. *Harlem: The Making of a Ghetto: Negro New York, 1890–1930.* Chicago: Ivan R. Dee.

Pew Hispanic Center/Kaiser Family Foundation. 2002. *National Survey of Latinos: The Latino Electorate.* Washington, D.C.: Pew Hispanic Center and Henry J. Kaiser Family Foundation.

Roediger, David. 1991. *The Wages of Whiteness: The Making of the American Working Class.* New York: Verso.

————. 1994. *Towards the Abolition of Whiteness: Essays on Race, Politics, and Working-Class History.* New York: Verso.

Rogin, Michael. 1996. *Blackface, White Noise: Jewish Immigrants in the Hollywood Melting Pot.* Berkeley: University of California Press.

Roosevelt, Theodore. 1991. "Americanism." In *Immigration and Americanization: Selected Readings*, edited by Philip Davis. New York: Ginn and Co. (Orig. pub. 1915.)

Rosenwaike, Ira. 1972. *Population History of New York City.* Syracuse: Syracuse University Press.

Sacks, Karen Brodkin. 1994. "How Did Jews Become White Folks?" In *Race*, edited by Stephen Gregory and Roger Sanjek. New Brunswick, N.J.: Rutgers University Press.

Sapir, Edward. 1924. "Racial Superiority." *Menorah Journal* 10(3): 200–12.

Schecter, Soloman. 1906. *Zionism: A Statement.* New York: Press of Clarence S. Nathan, Inc.

Schmidt, Sarah. 1975. "A Conversation with Horace M. Kallen: The Zionist Chapter of His Life." *Reconstructionist* 41(November): 28–33.

Slayton, Robert. 2001. *Empire Statesman: The Rise and Redemption of Al Smith.* New York: Free Press.

Sollors, Werner. 1986a. "A Critique of Pure Pluralism." In *Reconstructing American Literary History*, edited by Sacvan Bercovitch. Cambridge, Mass.: Harvard University Press.

————. 1986b. *Beyond Ethnicity: Consent and Descent in American Culture.* New York: Oxford University Press.

————, ed. 1989. *The Invention of Ethnicity.* New York: Oxford University Press.

————, ed. 1996. *Theories of Ethnicity: A Classic Reader.* New York: New York University Press.

Stocking, George W., Jr. 1982. "Lamarckianism in American Social Science, 1890–1915." In George W. Stocking Jr., *Race, Culture, and Evolution: Essays in the History of Anthropology.* Chicago: University of Chicago Press. (Orig. pub. 1968.)

————. 1993. "The Turn-of-the-Century Concept of Race." *Modernism* 1(1): 4–16.

Tafoya, Sonya M. 2003. "Latinos and Racial Identification in California." *California Counts: Population Trends and Profiles* 4(4): 1–15.

Thompson, J Phillip. 1990. "David Dinkins' Victory in New York City: The Decline of the Democratic Party Organization and the Strengthening of Black Politics." *PS: Political Science and Politics* 23(2): 145–48.

————. 2003. *Double Trouble: Overcoming Institutional Racism and Black Nationalism in Urban Politics.* Unpublished paper.

Walzer, Michael. 1996. *What It Means to Be an American.* New York: Marsilio.

Warner, W. Lloyd, and Paul S. Lunt. 1941. *The Social Life of a Modern Community.* New Haven, Conn.: Yale University Press.

Watkins-Owens, Irma. 1996. *Blood Relations: Caribbean Immigrants and the Harlem Community, 1900–1930.* Bloomington: Indiana University Press.

Wilson, Woodrow. 1991. "Americanism." In *Immigration and Americanization: Selected Readings*, edited by Philip Davis. New York: Ginn and Co. (Orig. pub. 1915.)

Woodson, Carter G. 1918. *A Century of Negro Migration*. New York: Russell and Russell.

Zolberg, Aristide R. 1999. "Matters of State: Theorizing Immigration Policy." In *The Handbook of International Migration: The American Experience*, edited by Charles Hirschman, Philip Kasinitz, and Josh DeWind. New York: Russell Sage Foundation.

John Higham

Chapter 3

The Amplitude of Ethnic History: An American Story

Its volume fluctuates, its sources change. Immigration of some kind, however, is one of the constants of American history, called forth by the energies of capitalism and the attractions of regulated freedom. From the outset those energies and attractions have also characterized the country at large. Capitalism, Carl Degler (1959, 1) once observed, came in the first ships. The same westerly breezes carried the seeds of freedom, which have swelled into the most celebrated, though equivocal, feature of American society and institutions.

The resulting congruities between immigrants as a type and migration as a national style have nourished both the history of immigration and the myths of a moving people. But the claim—resounding after World War II in the exciting new field of social history—that all Americans are migrants and immigration is therefore the grand theme of American history, went too far (Handlin 1951).[1] A feature of the largely discredited consensus version of American history, the immigrant analogy was an obstacle to thinking about major divisions among the American people. We are all immigrants, it told us. Now that conflict seems more illuminating than consensus to most students of American history, they search in an uncertain landscape for significant differences, rivalries, and alignments. No longer do history and American studies offer a grand theme. We have replaced it with a grand problem, perceived as more dangerous and lasting than all the other problems of our society. It is the problem of race.

But race, let us remember, is an elusively subjective category. Its meaning shifts from one context to another, from one era to the next. It can breathe affection or reverberate with anger, depending on who is using it. In spite of its vagueness as a concept and unreliability as an identity, race dominates and too often distorts the language of social theory. In observing a steady retreat from racism over the last three-quarters of a century, many are finding that the analytically sharper categories of nation and ethnic group work better than race. They grant people greater agency in defining their collective identity. Races are mostly known by superficial phenotypical markings and implausible assertions of solidarity and preeminence. To a larger degree, ethnic groups and nations create themselves through interactions within the group that differentiate it from outsiders.

Races, nations, and ethnic groups are further molded through descent. But races are very large divisions of humanity, and usually perceived as relatively fixed. Ethnic groups are much smaller, more numerous, and often more restrictively defined as subordinate elements of a larger society. They set themselves apart by customs such as language or religion, and especially by collective memories of a supposedly distinctive origin (Schermerhorn 1978, 12; Bradley 1996, 114–15).

We have many wide-ranging books about race in American history, but no similarly encompassing surveys of ethnicity. This is partly, I think, because ethnicity does not trouble Americans as much as race; it does not typically announce itself as a problem. Also, the sheer complexity of ethnicity in a population recruited from so many sources as ours has been daunting, to say nothing of the endless possibilities for interaction between ethnic groups and the changes within them as they come into contact with one another.

Nevertheless, a means of generalizing about American ethnic groups, and distinguishing among them, lies at hand, surprisingly neglected. It lies in the recognition that all such groups arise from, or must create, a community of memory. Partly real and partly imagined, memory is what binds an ethnic group together, assigning its tasks and maintaining its identity. Memory recalls and fixates a particular origin, from which it projects a continuity of subsequent experience.

In graduate history programs memory used to be treated only as an obstacle to scholarship: a trap for unwary neophytes. Now it is recognized as a force in history and a major source of collective identities and public policies. Today the documentation of memory supplies much of our ethnic history with a vividness that reached burning intensity in the rediscovery of the Holocaust (see, for example, Henretta, Kammen, and Katz 1991; Bodnar 1992; Klinkenborg 1991; Powell 2000). Nevertheless, this recovery of memory has rarely focused on the taproot of ethnic memory, a mythic scene of origins. If memory is at the core of ethnic identities, historians of the making of modern America might do well to take the promptings of memory as seriously as the coercions of race.

I propose that the groups that have survived their initial encounter with the new society forming on the Atlantic littoral were left with a crucial memory of the terms of their incorporation, terms that supplied an initial image of their New World identities. Over time these collective memories have done much to shape a three-tiered hierarchy of ethnic groups. Each tier, or stratum, has had an impact on those that came before, but all of them have persisted in one form or another from the colonial period to the twentieth century. So it will be necessary at the outset to give special attention to the earliest tier, the *settlers*. A second tier emerged soon after in the form of *captives*, that is, people incorporated by conquest. A third tier, the *immigrants*, consisting of voluntary entrants from foreign lands who came in search of a new home, sprang up in the eighteenth century between the other two. Examining the three tiers more largely as ethnic than as racial may offer a fresh perspective on American history.

Those in what became the upper tier entered on the basis of an English claim to possession of the land. I call them "settlers" to stress their sense of entitlement by seizure and descent, although the constitution they gave the country as its founders featured equal rights. The earliest of these settlers date from two British emigrations, one in the mid-seventeenth century, the other extending from that time to the eve of the American Revolution. In the 1630s an organized exodus of English Calvinists who were unwilling to submit to the Church of England colonized a distinctive stretch of the north Atlantic coast that explorers had named New England. They came—men, women, and children—in a single movement that lasted just eleven years, after which the English Revolution kept enemies of the king busy at home. Meanwhile, hundreds of miles to the south in the feeble royal colony of Virginia, disadvantaged younger sons of Anglican aristocrats were receiving princely land grants from the king. But they would have to look elsewhere for people to work their land (Fischer 1989, 14–57, 207–56).

Spun off from opposite sides in England's civil war, these earliest permanent English settlements on the Atlantic mainland could hardly have been more different. The Puritans, an occupationally diverse population from the middling classes, were driven by a Calvinist work ethic and indoctrinated with a Calvinist insistence on literacy and therefore on education. Their religion taught an unshakable right of private judgment in construing scripture, but also the importance of a close-knit local community, morally armed and led by an educated clergy and pious magistracy. Moving westward, the Puritans brought with them a distinctive institutional complex: the compact village gathered closely around the meetinghouse, a school, and the town commons (Miller 1956; Howe 1988; Shain 1994; Hine 1980).

In the nineteenth century their underlying sense of interdependence and common purpose aroused the more God-fearing descendants of the Puritans to the social evils pressing in on them from a sinful world: slavery in the South, Catholic subversion and racial inequality in the North, and everywhere irreligion and intemperance. There was a radical strain in Puritanism that roused its women, its intellectuals, and its saints to expunge this corruption, to purify themselves and their communities. Radical purgation often clashed with the practical organizational skills that more worldly Puritan leaders cultivated to mediate the raging disputes in their churches, and with the entrepreneurial initiatives that structured banks, legally binding trusts, and smoothly functioning factories (Carwardine 1993; Altschuler and Saltzgaber 1983; Hall 1982). From Yankee peddlers and gold seekers, slow to settle down in one place, to the town boosters who sparked the swift growth of midwestern cities, New Englanders were in the forefront of economic development as well as moral reform.

The English colonization of Virginia took a far more conservative direction. It featured aristocratic rather than middle-class leadership, sprawling plantations rather than busy villages, and the established Church of England in place of rebellious conventicles. What made the Virginia pattern a reality was not sensible planning or collective endeavor, as in New England, but a sudden, fortuitous demand—in London and other cities—for tobacco. Instead of the diversified traffic of an industrious population, an exotic and chancy staple crop became the basis of the economy (Morgan 1975).

To secure a deferential labor supply, the impecunious aristocrats adopted a new legal device called indentured servitude. It offered landless, low-skilled youths, especially those trapped in desperate poverty in the tradition-oriented counties of southern England, an escape to America. In return for transportation to the colony, maintenance, and a modest freedom payment on his or her release, a bonded servant contracted to work for four years under a designated master or his assigns.

Stressed though the system was by exploitative landowners and the epidemic diseases that swept away many servants before their term was up, the goal of eventually possessing a bit of land of one's own remained so teasingly alluring that indentured servitude provided the bulk of the white population for all of England's southern colonies throughout the seventeenth century (Galenson 1981). Those who survived their term of service faced new hardships. Free but landless and impoverished, they were less and less able to buy land with access to water. Yet they were also ill prepared for life in the backcountry, and on plantations after 1660 they were increasingly replaced by African slaves (Nash 1984). Such bruising experiences in an unsettled, intensely acquisitive society presumably taught lower-class whites not to depend on any loyalties wider than immediate neighbors or relatives.

The children of these former servants apparently blended with a much larger eighteenth-century migration of a proud and quarrelsome people from the border lands of north Britain—English, Scots, and Protestant Irish. A hardy, mixed population, suffering from greedy landlords, evictions, and the breakdown of the clan system in Scotland, they were ideally suited for clearing land, dispossessing Indians, and relying on subsistence farming and hunting to live in a vast backcountry. Between the opening of the American Revolution, which they ignored, and the admission of Missouri to the Union in 1821, these "men and women of the western waters" occupied five new states south of the Ohio River and west of the Mississippi (Rohrbough 1978, 15–40, 134–217; Bailyn 1986, 44–55).

By 1800 an ethnically mixed population of Scotch-Irish[2] and others from Pennsylvania and the upland South had established itself in southern Ohio and was busy raising corn, cattle, and hogs, some with profitable new techniques. A widening stream of Yankees (as New Englanders were now called) was slowly working its way across upper New York State in a tumult of religious excitement. Around the turn of the century they began to arrive in force in northern Ohio. The scorn of the Yankees for the upland southerners was loud and enduring. Yankee publicists, ignoring completely the strong Pennsylvanian contingent among their predecessors, exaggerated the shiftlessness and backwardness they found in the river counties, while depicting themselves, perhaps truthfully enough, as ambitious, obsessively argumentative, and self-righteous (Swierenga 1989).[3]

Sharp as these regional irritations might be, they turned into ethnic antagonisms only when each group directly threatened what was precious to the other. Eighteenth-century observers, based as often in the middle colonies as in the South, relished a common disparagement of "the saints of New England" (Murrin, n.d., 24–28). But there was as yet no sense of collective confrontation or enmity, for the apparently limitless resources of the West lay open to both North and South. Writing to a French correspondent in 1785, Thomas Jefferson gives us his own ironic summation of the contrasting temperaments, all the while avoiding any ethnic label. Jefferson's table of regional traits presents "the South" and "the North" as opposites, between which Pennsylvania offers a middle ground where "the two characters seem to meet and blend." "In the North," he observes, "they are cool, sober, laborious, persevering, jealous of their own liberties, and just to those of others, interested," and "chicaning." Denizens of the South, by contrast, "are fiery, voluptuary, indolent, unsteady, zealous for their own liberties, but trampling on those of others, generous, candid" (Jefferson 1953, 468).

In the 1820s the issues of slavery in the Louisiana Purchase and regional equity in tariffs exploded into national politics. Jefferson's coolly cosmopolitan contrast now had to give way to some term or phrase that would identify the settlers of the Southeast and the Southwest without alluding divisively to their collective dependence on African slavery. The immense region below the Mason-Dixon Line had been fragmented by its ingathering of miscellaneous white settlers, its dispersed population, its pervasive ethic of personal independence, and its reliance almost entirely on kinship for a sense of common identity (Ford 1988, 5, 338–39, 344). Its people had no distinctive name, and the uncertainty in establishing one is reflected in early attempts dating from 1827 (see Mathews 1951, 1600–2).

The *southerns* will not long pay tribute.
—*Spirit of Seventy-Six*, Frankfort, Kentucky, October 11, 1827

I am a Republican in principle and a *Southron* in feeling.
                    —*Free Press*, Tarboro, North Carolina, November 9, 1828

A Yankee is a Yankee over the globe. . . . The *Southerner*, too, is such over the whole globe.
                    —*Western Monthly* II(1828): 12

The annual migration of the *southerns* is very suggestive.
                    —*Archibald Prentice, A Tour in the United States* (1848)

What brought forth these uncertain claims to a sectional or ethnic identity from the 1820s onward? A fundamental precondition, though not a full explanation, lies in the rising nationalism of the early nineteenth century. Many internal linkages were spreading through the young republic at the same time that it was embarking on a huge expansion outward. Beginning with the adoption of the Constitution, a nation whose people abhorred power at a distance created institutions that reached far beyond local settings: roads, canals, and steamboats; a national court system, federal land policy, and national bank; post offices everywhere; and an enormous interregional market. All of these webs of communication, trade, and authority made regions more vulnerable, more active, and more rivalrous, while simultaneously entangling them in what the antifederalist Patrick Henry had scornfully called "the ropes and chains of consolidation."[4] The boisterous nationalism that followed the War of 1812 was especially destabilizing because it sharpened the incompatibility between the modernizing, nationalizing impulses at work throughout the Union and the South's sense of overwhelming dependence on slavery. A hugely profitable labor system, slavery was inseparable from an ever more archaic and morally degrading scheme of human relations, which the southern states could not summon the will to change (Potter 1968, 34–83).

A second and more concrete factor behind the growing sense of southern vulnerability was the loss of a dominant position in the Union. In the agricultural republic of the eighteenth century, the southern states had taken for granted a dependable alliance with the growing West, enabling the two together to hold back protective tariffs and other regulatory projects of the urbanizing Northeast. Suddenly, in 1819, this Jeffersonian coalition was challenged. Missouri, the first state to emerge from the Louisiana Purchase, petitioned Congress for admission to the Union under a state constitution that would maintain indefinitely its access to slaves. New York Congressman James Tallmadge, a longtime critic of the advantage that the three-fifths clause in the U.S. Constitution gave to slave states in national elections, seized the occasion to propose an amendment terminating slavery in Missouri (Freehling 1990, 144–54).[5]

At this stage slavery itself was not the immediate problem that Tallmadge's amendment disclosed. What was at stake in the extraordinarily bitter debate of 1819–20 was the South's power in the Union. Although a practical compromise gave Missouri the pro-slavery constitution it wanted, a new and more threatening provision of the compromise excluded slavery from all the rest of the Louisiana Purchase north and west of Missouri itself. Worse yet perhaps, from a southern point of view, the debate fractured the traditional alliance of South and West against the East. All eight congressmen from the three new states of the Old Northwest voted with New England for the Tallmadge Amendment (Sydnor 1948, 125–32, 153–56). They did so partly, no doubt, because Yankees, escaping from the rocky soil of New England, were already preeminent in

Ohio. Farther west, frontier populists from Pennsylvania and the border states, calling themselves "the white folks," mobilized to keep slaves and plantation owners out of Illinois.[6] The Tallmadge debates revealed to the white South that its national preeminence was fading. And to people who thought of themselves increasingly as southerners, the outcome indicated that they were becoming an American minority.

A third fundamental factor in building resistance to the North was the formation in the deep South of an active white racial solidarity that reached beyond the bounds of individual states, political parties, localities, and social classes. Roughly speaking, the denser the presence of slaves in an area, the more fervent and widespread was popular support for slavery. The racial divide threatened all whites in the lower South and therefore solidified a sense of equality among them. On lesser whites, slavery conferred autonomy and status by dramatizing their own civic inclusion. Moreover, a fabulous boom in cotton production, set off at the end of the eighteenth century by the industrial revolution, enabled pioneers and small farmers of the upcountry to buy a few slaves, raise cotton themselves alongside the great planters, and fulfill their old dream of independence on the land (Ford 1988; McCurry 1995). They would fight anyone threatening to take that away.

Yet the boundary between the deep South and the Yankee North was a wide zone of transition, and many ties between the sections remained strong. Among southern leaders broadly, therefore, the new sense of northern enmity was slow to harden. It surged during, and sank after, each but the last of the increasingly overwrought political confrontations of the next four decades. In the South's growing assertions of a distinct and separate identity, something was almost always lacking. While behaving as an oppressed minority, southern apologists persistently built their case against the North on constitutional grounds (Freehling 1990). In appealing so confidently to the founding document of American nationality, they revealed the shallowness of southern ethnicity and culture. The South lacked a tangible memory of its origin.

In the nineteenth century, romantic nationalism supplied a language for invoking the soul of a people and proclaiming their destiny. Across eastern Europe this new nationalism awakened oppressed minorities. In America it infused the unforgettable appeals of Daniel Webster and Abraham Lincoln for harmony and an inclusive Union (Howe 1979, 70–71, 86, 234; Remini 1997, 178–87).[7] The South, however, had lost touch with contemporary thought. In responding to New England's huge advantages on the terrain of culture and history, the best that southerners could do was to invent the Cavalier as a literary rival to the Puritan and his successor, the Yankee. According to nineteenth-century mythmakers, the Cavaliers' loyalty to their beleaguered English king had endowed Virginia, and the rest of the South through her, with a social order capped by honor, tradition, dignity, and aristocratic refinement. Focused entirely on maintaining a hierarchical society, this plantation legend—with its patriarchal planters and their submissive belles—was no match at all for the aggressive and dynamic Puritan-Yankee, whom New Englanders were learning in the midnineteenth century to identify with the progress of liberty throughout the Western world (Taylor 1961; Watson 1993; Norton 1986, 3–11, 15, 181–82).[8]

What finally produced a fully ethnic solidarity, overriding differences of region, class, culture, and party, was the Civil War. It was the forge of a people, the making of a deep collective memory. The devastation of their landscape, the unparalleled loss of life on both sides, and the years of suffering and social disorganization left Americans a legacy of hatred: hatred of "rebels" on one side and hatred of racial equality on the other, a legacy that only a second Lincoln might have assuaged.

The war also left the rank and file of southern whites with another burden, Wilbur J. Cash (1941, 113) tells us. They had acquired not only a great body of memories in common with their leaders, "but a deep affection for these captains, a profound trust in them, a pride which was inextricably intertwined with the commoners' pride in themselves" (see also Blight 2001, 54–57). This, according to Cash, was the origin of the "Solid South"—and, one might add, of the stagnation that accompanied it into the midtwentieth century.

By the early nineteenth century, New Englanders had lived together in their isolated region for two centuries without serious intrusion from outsiders. From the outset they felt threatened not only by unpredictable savages—"Children of Hell" in the literal rhetoric of their sermons—but also by the wilderness itself. In the minds of Puritan leaders, it was a realm of natural freedom, tempting the sinful heart to slip from civilized ways into barbarism. A precarious city on a hill, encompassed by an unfathomable wilderness, demanded a mobilization of righteousness that was always a hallmark of the Puritans (Salisbury 1982, 219–25, 234; Calloway 1997; Thomas 1975). A situation more conducive to intense ethnocentric feeling would be difficult to imagine.

Nevertheless, the rule-bound world of Calvin turned out to be readily responsive to the wider uniformities of the Enlightenment. In the eighteenth century a flourishing transatlantic and coastal trade, growing wealth in the larger towns, and above all a widening diffusion of the rationalism of the Enlightenment drove a gradual but inexorable process of secularization. Without surrendering a faith in its religious heritage, New England opened itself to a larger world.

Among orthodox Puritans one common response to worldliness and doctrinal schisms was an insistent call on the present generation to remember their forefathers, the heroic founders of New England, and to be true to their example (Bozeman 1988, 112–14; see also Ward 1973). Memory still served as the linchpin of ethnic solidarity.

Additionally, during and after the American Revolution a trust in divine guidance, together with biblicized memories of escape from England's "House of Bondage," taught New Englanders to read the overall history of America as an extension of their own emergence into the light of freedom (see David Tappan's 1782 Massachusetts election sermon, quoted in Stout 1990, 69–70; see also Berens 1978). This was the fulcrum of Webster's tremendous address at Plymouth on the two-hundredth anniversary of the landing of the Pilgrims, an address that set the mold for the predominance of New England in the study of American history throughout the nineteenth century. New England was the birthplace of the American spirit.[9]

During the middle decades of the nineteenth century, what I have called the radical side of the Puritan heritage was at flood tide in nativism and the antislavery, women's rights, and temperance movements. Less well known but no less significant was the prominence of Yankees in collaborative tasks: business leadership, technology, finance, and education. Since America's industrial revolution started in New England, it is hardly surprising that 51 percent of the top executives in textiles, railroads, and steel during the 1870s were New England–born, and certainly many more sprang from the greater New England that spread across the upper Middle West. A more interesting fact perhaps is that the first great American philanthropist, George Peabody, who started working as a grocer's apprentice in Danvers, Massachusetts, spent millions on cheap and decent housing for the London poor, then millions more on American educational institutions, before he died in 1869 (Gregory and Neu 1962, 197; Rosenberry 1909; Cutri 1963, 179–81). Following in Peabody's footsteps, the outstanding philanthropists of the next generation were mostly Yankees: John D. Rockefeller, Henry Ford, Josephine Shaw Lowell, and George Eastman, to name but a few.

Equally innovative as institution-builders were the Yankee educators like Horace Mann and Henry Barnard, who persuaded reluctant legislators to adopt statewide standards for public schools and to finance state universities (on Mann, see Cremin 1980, 133–43; Schultz 1973). Along with endless appeals to public pride, the Yankee educators employed the quiet arts of compromise and negotiation, which had so often contended against a passion for purity and separateness in the history of New England. Determined to make public schools as inclusive as possible while accepting local supervision by popularly elected boards, the reformers by 1860 had brought the public schools of every midwestern state into centrally regulated systems (Kaestle 1983).

The building of an adequately financed common school system in the North was but one of several midcentury projects for a richer civic life in which descendants of the Puritans played a leading role without separating themselves from other native white Protestants. From the beginning of their outpouring from New England, they had intermarried with old-stock strains from the mid-Atlantic region. Then the arrival in the 1850s of a massive immigration from Germany and Ireland raised their consciousness of an American Protestant identity and of new civic tasks awaiting it.

Prodigies of voluntary organization followed during the Civil War (Bremner 1980). After the war the Protestant community busied itself endlessly in founding more hospitals, libraries, historical societies, and fraternal orders, organizing pioneer celebrations, building grandly imposing churches, and sponsoring large interdenominational projects such as Chautauqua, the Young Men's Christian Association, and the Woman's Christian Temperance Union. At an elite level, intercollegiate athletics and the first socially prominent athletic clubs in the major cities belonged to the same loose, far-flung network of social cohesion.[10]

The moral issues and ethno-cultural conflicts that had engaged Evangelical Protestants and nativists before the Civil War persisted long after. Problems of immigration, strong drink, political corruption, and the regulation of schools repeatedly mobilized Protestant voters. Yet little changed in social relations or political power, and no crisis comparable to that of the 1850s broke until the 1920s. There were, to be sure, boundaries in private life between the major ethno-religious groupings. Moreover, as incoming peoples became more disparate, conflicts over employment grew more bitter, especially in weakly governed areas such as the Mountain West (Licht 1992, 78–79, 95, 133–38; Tsai 1986, 10–32, 56–76).[11]

By the end of the nineteenth century, a generalized racial nationalism was intensifying throughout the Western world. In this country race-conscious intellectuals infused new energies into the outreach programs of a Yankee core population that was extending its authority within an otherwise highly decentralized society (Kelley 1984; Wiebe 1975; Hofstadter 1965). In comparative perspective, we may ask how the United States in the late nineteenth century avoided for the most part a punishing recurrence of the urban violence of the 1850s. Surely part of the answer must be that the Protestant community outside of the South felt secure within the ruling Republican Party, which had inherited from antecedents in New England a propensity for vigorous government and civic rectitude. Against the Republican posture of moral authority and national preeminence, their opponents were legion but continually fractured by their own diversities (Jensen 1971).

Accordingly, the Protestant majority in the late nineteenth and early twentieth centuries depended far more on the vitality and influence of its leadership in politics, culture, business, and philanthropy than it did on the strength of an ethnic boundary. This was indeed the golden age of ethnic Protestantism. Its universities, richly endowed and more or less open to students of diverse antecedents, rivaled the best in Europe. Its art museums and architects attained equal distinction. Its urban planners filled the cities with parks. Its greatest foundations developed international programs of public health and literacy. Its political leadership reached an apogee in Theodore Roosevelt. The growth of Protestant church membership in the major cities culminated about the same time. Winthrop Hudson has rightly called the period from 1890 to 1914 "the halcyon years" of American Protestantism (Hudson 1961, 124–27).[12]

The brilliance of those years, however, obscures a restlessness that was growing behind the spectacular advances of imperialism, progressivism, and a rising socialist movement. A good many young people, born into the genteel respectability of a generalized Protestantism and searching for a more vivid identity, felt adrift (Higham 2001).[13] We might say that they were suffering from excessive assimilation as a consequence of the diffusion of the Puritan-Yankee strain through migration and intermarriage. Inevitably, intermarriage has a dissipating influence on a community of memory because the parents can no longer reinforce one another in the community's perpetuation. In rebellion against their bland, middle-class origins, these self-styled "young intellectuals" of heterogeneous antecedents found one another in New York City's Greenwich Village, proclaimed their own moral freedom, and took to wearing a badge of identity in the form of flannel or corduroy shirts for men and, for women, sandals without corsets. The more intellectually adventurous among them, such as Randolph Bourne, set about redefining America as a pluralistic nation without a legitimately dominant culture (May 1959; Hollinger 1985, 56–73; Brooks 1908; Bourne 1977, 248–64, 301–6; Zurier 1985, 83).

Well before World War I, this new generation launched a literary offensive against the Puritan as the symbol of everything oppressive and stultifying in American culture. Ever since the Civil War, intellectuals had been guardians of the inherited ethnic culture. Now they were its adversaries or critics.

Their voices were enormously amplified by a new generation of publishers, mostly Jewish, who discovered authors far outside the genteel consensus. In a somnolent publishing industry, Ben Huebsch made his mark by sponsoring radical naysayers such as Thorstein Veblen and Theodore Dreiser along with scandalous foreigners like James Joyce and D. H. Lawrence. His fellow pioneer, Alfred Knopf, became famous for translations of great modern European writers. Both men relied for advice on H. L. Mencken, whose tirades against Puritans and Anglo-Saxons made him the great debunker of that first founding of America.[14]

Conquering publishing was relatively easy. Its small private enterprises required little capital. The great universities, however, were harder to crack. From one point of view, they were massive investments by the Protestant upper class. But the increasing number of Jewish candidates for faculty posts could not be systematically excluded, and in the 1920s the newly created social sciences brought into the secularized halls of academe the modern study of race relations. By the 1930s modernism was overwhelming the tired culture of ethnic Protestantism, and the settlers were beginning to share the heights of their society with the immigrants.

To explain the breakdown in the 1920s of what Henry May (1983) has called "Progressive Patriotic Protestantism," at least one further cause should be added to assimilation, generational rebellion, and modernism. This was a hardening of class divisions that developed incongruously in the midst of the early-twentieth-century celebration of democracy. The Protestant Ascendancy, as Joseph Alsop (1992) has styled the northeastern upper class, began sealing itself off from the white middle class through new status-conferring institutions such as genealogical societies, prep schools for the right children, and all sorts of philanthropic projects. These associations offset the anonymity of bureaucratic hierarchies (Kusmer 1979; Larson 1984). But they also withdrew leadership from politics and churches, to which the broad masses had looked for support and guidance. Theodore Roosevelt's unsuccessful rebellion in 1912 stilled the voice of conscience in the Republican Party, and it has never fully returned. Today we may discern only a faint afterglow of the Puritan conscience in the fact that almost all of the states without a death penalty are concentrated in New England and the upper Middle West.[15]

In the nation's ethnic hierarchy, the middle tier consists of those who are known as immigrants or descendants thereof. These are voluntary newcomers freely admitted from foreign lands, plus their children, part of the third generation, and those among their descendants who remain warmly attached to that origin. The arrival of an immigrant group, though often invested with a poignant sense of loss, is characteristically remembered as an active choice and a new beginning.

Perceptions of the immigrants as a distinct social category produced the word "immigrant" in the late eighteenth century. Looking back in 1809, a traveling naturalist, Edward Kendall, reflected that *"Immigrant* is perhaps the only new word of which the circumstances of the United States . . . demanded the addition to the English language" (Mathews 1951, 863). Immigrants had become visible as self-directed, non-English additions to a moving people.[16]

Until the twentieth century, the line between immigrants and settlers was principally one of social rank and recognizable behavior, differentiating relative newcomers from a core population who more easily identified themselves with the founders of the country. A characteristic weakness of territorial roots among both settlers and immigrants has continually blurred distinctions between the two groups in most parts of the country. Except in the white South, where place loomed large in the making of an identity, geographical mobility has been one of the most striking and distinctive features of American life. A propensity to deal with problems by moving on, and therefore by looking ahead rather than dwelling on the gains or losses of the past, has been a feature of American behavior among settlers and immigrants alike at least since the Revolution (Higham 1999, 41–45; Pierson 1973).

As an intermediate stratum, however, the immigrants have had special advantages and problems. From the outset an inescapable difference of power and status separated them from settlers in spite of their need for one another in upholding and advancing a society that has rewarded both. In the first generation, detached from their own country, the immigrants typically lose the psychic comforts of home and find themselves in bewildering settings under uncaring taskmasters. In the long run, however, the immigrants have had a huge advantage over the captives and even over some branches of the settlers. No one forced them to be here, and nobody but "the bosses" were to blame for their deprivations. They knew they had to depend on their families, their fellow workers, and themselves.

Measuring their gains during the first generation by the lower standards of their homeland, they expected improvement, strained for it, and instilled their children with a similarly unbending work ethic. The children, of course, remember their own origin in the strenuous relocation that their parents risked. But by the third or fourth generation, vivid memories of an Old World origin slip away. The field of memory moves to America, to the growth and satisfactions this country has offered and the obstacles it has raised.

Overall, the immigrant experience has been one of continuous though unsteady social ascent—much slower in some ethnic groups than in others, but in all substantial. And with this advancement attachment to distinctive pasts becomes equivocal. Unless the immigrants hold fast to an ethnic church, mosque, or synagogue, only shrinking minorities among them can maintain their formative identities. So far at least, the relentless assimilation they undergo has replenished the settlers and kept in check the numbers of the immigrants, while vastly expanding their power and influence.

Nonetheless, assimilation has sharpened awareness of the differences in role and status between immigrants pressing into the mainstream and settlers desirous of keeping an accustomed precedence. We need to look more closely to understand how easy relations between immigrants and settlers broke down toward the end of the nineteenth century.

By then, immigration from new and often radical sources in southern and eastern Europe was converging heavily on cities across the country. Already in the 1850s the first great wave of emigration from the European mainland had burdened the largest American cities with poverty, crime, and contagion on a new scale. But the railroads and the lure of the vast interior soon dispersed most of that first wave. This time, at the end of the century, the immigrant torrent coincided with ominous class antagonisms reaching into all sections of the country and sharply dividing urban from rural areas. Now as never before systematic immigration restriction gained enduring support among the old settlers in rural America. Simultaneously, in industrial centers, advances in mechanization reduced the need for skilled workers from northwestern Europe and fueled a demand for their low-skilled rivals from southeastern Europe. This massive shift in the labor market split the working class, and that split in turn obstructed the class-based politics that was emerging strongly in western Europe (Goldin 1994; Mink 1986).

A third segment of American society, deeply underprivileged, sprang up through forcible incorporation rather than choice. Admittedly, a captive or conquered group may receive benefits from its submission. If the experience of seizure includes a traditional homeland, the myths that cling to the landed heritage the group brought with it can entail some esteem and even advantage. Indian tribes have had substantial success in their legal challenges to gross violations of their treaty rights. Now also the exemption of reservations from state laws allows tribes in antigambling states to operate profitable casinos. Yet disadvantage usually overwhelms whatever benefits may derive from incorporated homelands. By fostering dependency and painful memories of displacement, these bases may actually add to the impoverishment of the captives.

Puerto Ricans are a special case. Part captive and part immigrant, they have enjoyed as captives great economic benefits in tax exemptions and federal transfer payments but much less of the freedom and initiative of immigrants. Their history in the main is one of a painful, incomplete, but hopeful transition from captivity to migration.

From the mainland, where almost half of all Puerto Ricans now live, they appear to be just another migratory Hispanic people whom the accidents of history have thrust upon us. From an island-based perspective, on the other hand, Puerto Ricans can be seen as captives, acquired by the United States during the Spanish-American War (1898) without either consent or resistance and still unable and unwilling to throw off the connection. Therein lies the problem of a Puerto Rican identity, which is hotly contested because it is both strong and incomplete. The persistent inability of Puerto Ricans to decide whether their native ground lies mostly in preconquest traditions or in their American citizenship creates an assertive but divided identity that has defined the politics of the island. Instead of adhering primarily to the conservative-liberal alignment that drives politics in the states, local political parties in Puerto Rico are based on contrasting approaches to the American imperium.

The strength of a Puerto Rican ethnic identity is widely apparent. It explains the very high turnout at island elections; animates the ubiquitous popularity of the Puerto Rican flag; lingers in the connections of mainland immigrants with the villages of their origin; and flourishes at international sports competitions and other gatherings, especially the annual Puerto Rican Day Parade, which far surpasses the much older St. Patrick's Day Parade in vivacity and attendance. Above all, this collective identity arises from two strong ethnic bonds—the inclusive language of "the Great Puerto Rican Family" and its distinctive place, its island home (Carr 1984, 1–14, 68–69, 243, 267–68, 273–78; Duany 2002, 15–24, 185–207, 279–83; Pérez 2000, 54–55, 139–63).

For four centuries before the Americans came, the inhabitants of this severely over-populated island—a mingling of Spanish, Taíno Indians, and Africans—had lived in abject neglect under a government that held the island chiefly to protect the sea lanes to Cuba. Accordingly, the American invasion met no resistance. Rather, it brought a breeze of hope to an overwhelmingly rural population dependent on a failing sugarcane industry and on the importation of basic foodstuffs they could not afford. "Unemployment and underemployment," a British authority reports, "probably affected over half of the work force; an undernourished and illiterate population, riddled with disease, had a life expectancy of thirty-five" (Berbusse 1966, 47–51, 64–65).[17]

The American administrators promptly set about building roads, hospitals, sanitation systems, and public schools. But their own ethnocentric predilections demanded a public school system that was based on English as the predominant language of instruction, employed American teachers as far as possible, and focused on inculcating Anglo-Saxon values. The arrogance of the project, and the persistence of successive U.S.-appointed governors in pursuing it, was breathtaking. Not until 1947, when Congress finally allowed Puerto Rico to elect governors empowered to appoint the commissioner of education, was Spanish adopted as the language of instruction (Morris 1995, 38–44, 162–64). By then, two generations of sullen children had learned to hate school and missed an adequate Spanish-speaking education. The catastrophic dropout rate of *their* children and grandchildren from the New York City schools of the 1950s and after may be seen as a long-term consequence.

The suffering that Puerto Ricans confronted in a worldwide demographic transition, and amid the extreme inequalities accompanying it, have also afflicted other migratory minorities, but less severely, I suspect. Puerto Ricans underwent all the traumas of modernization compacted within too brief a span of years, partly because of the scantness of alternatives to emigration from their small island, and partly because of their uncontrolled exposure, as nearby U.S. citizens, to mainland markets and conditions.[18]

Pressed continuously by an ever-rising birthrate, Puerto Ricans emigrated seasonally to neighboring Caribbean plantations after the turn of the century but were in no hurry to reach farther (Korrol 1993). Through the 1920s, emigration to the mainland averaged two thousand per year. Then the worldwide depression of the 1930s turned the island into a scene of almost unrelieved misery. Sixty percent of the population was unemployed. Somehow more found the means to leave.

Mass emigration, however, waited for the end of World War II, when cheap air travel between San Juan and New York was inaugurated. This largely coincided with a grandiose governmental program to attract private capital that would transform a sleepy agricultural economy into a dynamic industrial one. The investments that poured in, stimulated by large tax benefits, brought visions of a mainland level of consumption. But they failed to put large numbers of Puerto Ricans to work. Agriculture was deserted, the cities choked in unemployment, and emigration skyrocketed, both literally and figuratively.

Nevertheless, the country was changed. Within twenty-five years, from the 1940s to 1970, Puerto Rico shifted from an agricultural economy with a predominantly rural society to an urban society with capital-intensive (rather than labor-intensive) industries. Vast numbers, uprooted from the countryside, passed on from San Juan to New York. In the 1950s alone, net emigration from Puerto Rico reached nearly half a million. It was one of the most massive exoduses, proportionate to population, in American immigration history (Whalen 2001, 2; Rivera-Batiz and Santiago 1996, 8–19, 43–45).

The destination most in demand was the great "Barrio" that earlier arrivals had established in Spanish Harlem, a deteriorating neighborhood squeezed between Italians to the east and African Americans to the west. It is fondly remembered for a people who were poor but hopeful, a place where block musicians beat out rhythm on tin cans and bongos and a stickball team was also a gang battling for the neighborhood's boundaries. In the late 1950s all this began to be lost. The Barrio became a site for slum clearance, and huge impersonal "projects" devastated Puerto Rican community life (Suro 1998, 140–44; Lapp 1990, ch. 4).

Most of the immigrants continued to cluster wherever they could in and around New York City, but at an increasing disadvantage to other newcomers who were more willing to learn English if, like African Americans, they did not already speak it.

Many Puerto Ricans yearned for their island home, and large numbers went back in the 1960s and 1970s. Most prominently, the returnees were unskilled workers of limited education who had failed to find stable employment. With unemployment on the island increasing sharply during the 1970s and 1980s, the returnees often became circular migrants, moving back and forth between temporary jobs at great cost to family stability (Rivera-Batiz and Santiago 1996, 55–62, 94–100).

Other island-bound Puerto Ricans were a second generation, raised in New York. This group had to contend with resentment from peers who had never left the homeland and now disparaged their "Nuyorican" manners, clothes, and hairstyles, their half-forgotten Spanish and addiction to TV or their rough street English. New York had been traumatic for many of the Nuyoricans, and now Puerto Rican intellectuals were blaming them for contaminating the island's culture. They responded by drawing apart, clustering in areas they could call their own (Pérez 2000, 60–61; Morris 1995, 124–25, Duany 2002, 23–24, 28–37).

In New York, stuck at the bottom of the job market, Puerto Ricans sustained two more shocks in the 1960s and 1970s. Half a million blue-collar jobs disappeared as aging factories closed and the city's economy shifted to post-industrial services. About the same time the Black Power model encouraged growing disorder in the streets, and at home the indocility of teenage children severely tested the traditional strength of the Puerto Rican family (Pérez 2000, 64–65, 82–84; Fitzpatrick 1987, 68–102).

All in all, Puerto Ricans remain a handicapped people. Their island base has one-half of the per capita income of Mississippi, the poorest state in the Union. Rates of suicide, drug addiction, and crime are said to be among the highest in the world. At their base and rallying point on the mainland, New York City, they rank in educational achievement far below African Americans and about on a par with Mexicans, who have arrived more recently. According to a broader study in 1992, Puerto Ricans had the highest poverty rate for individuals in the United States (Fernandez 1996, xi, 2; Foner 2000, 98–104; National Puerto Rican Coalition, cited in Davis 2000, 104).

Still, there is another story, less well known but gaining significance. The island's birthrate has gradually fallen since 1950, bringing down the size of families and helping to raise school achievement. Although emigration to the United States remains substantial, the desperation that drove it in the 1950s and 1960s has abated, and per capita income on the mainland has advanced along with educational attainment.

Most striking is a decline, beginning in the 1990s, of the Puerto Rican presence in New York and several other major cities where the immigrants had flocked to be close to one another. By the 1990s a middle-class avant-garde was looking outward. A more or less deliberate deconcentration was under way. Safe neighborhoods in the secondary cities of accessible states are the destinations of choice for a third generation of Puerto Ricans, now largely middle-class (Rivera-Batiz 1996, 22–49, 64–67, 126–65; Suro 1998, 69–70). Quietly assimilationist in tactics if not in principle, this latest foray in migration seems to repeat an ongoing American refrain.

Memory has worked differently in Puerto Rican and in African American experience. For Puerto Ricans, the formative collective memory fixated on rootedness and therefore on place—their verdant, sun-washed island home. Though captured, they were never conquered and have never risen against their North American masters. For African Americans, memory has been deep and extreme, a source of humiliation in many situations and of anger in others. Nevertheless, in both ethnic groups the clutch of memory has been loosening in recent decades.

The largest of the captured groups, African Americans were imported to substitute for Indians as plantation laborers in the early seventeenth century, then retained within the Anglo-American society instead of being expelled (Crane 1928). Their captivity has extended through recurrent cycles of hope and defeat. Not all of the setbacks are remembered, but each has surely reinforced a memory of repeated failure. This in turn has encouraged either alienation or a crippling sense of inferiority.

The Berkeley anthropologist John Ogbu (1991) is engaged in a long-term study of the school performance of minority groups around the world. He is learning that the relatively weak academic achievement of black students in the United States is replicated by that of "involuntary" minorities in other countries, regardless of IQ, mental ability, linguistic impediments, or even class standing. The pattern that Ogbu and his associates are finding strongly suggests that "voluntary minorities"—that is, immigrants—do better than captives, independently of race or class, because they arrive with hope and usually transmit it to their children.[19]

Some of the defeats that Africans have suffered over the course of their captivity have surely been forgotten or repressed. Memories of an initial capture and sale by other Africans vanished long ago. The travail of slavery in a land of freedom, however, lives on in mournful song and story. From time to time a new vision of release from humiliation and confinement has sprung up—and signaled another failure when it proved unsustainable.

The cycle began with the Civil War itself. The sudden and complete emancipation that came with the war's end in 1865 called forth an unforgettable exhilaration, linked with anxiety and bewilderment. A wrenching decade of struggle followed, ending for blacks in a reign of terror and their enclosure in a new form of peonage (Litwack 1979). Worse yet, toward the end of the nineteenth century a flurry of lynchings and mob outrages, accompanied by systematic segregation of all public facilities, reduced the former slaves in much of the South to a subservience more impersonal, rigorous, and unrelieved than slavery itself.[20] This was perhaps the most demoralizing setback of all, if only because the termination of slavery left the black masses without the paternalistic protection their masters had commonly supplied to dependents (Kolchin 1987, 150–56).

Nevertheless, the struggle went on. In the South the black family was stabilized by the 1870s, and the subsequent tightening of segregation promoted the development of a middle class to supply the services and leadership that black communities required. Churches, schools, and music called forth the strongest commitments (Jenkins 1998; Meier and Rudwick 1976, 173–80; see also Gates 1988).

Advances on a national scale did not resume until the 1920s. By then, automobiles, movies, and chain stores were weakening the parochialism of the white South. Moreover, some of the costs that the South was paying for repression could now be felt in a huge emigration of black manpower to northern cities, dramatizing as it did a glaring contrast of southern poverty with the prosperity of the industrial North. Meanwhile, in leading universities a new generation of social scientists were embarking on a critical study of race relations, while New York intellectuals and black musicians promoted an interracial culture and society in Harlem and Greenwich Village (Grossman 1989; Tolnay and Beck 1995, 213–33; Lewis 1981).

Still, African Americans would require another thirty-five years of confrontation and resistance to achieve a lasting victory for civil rights and social decency—and by then it was too late to avoid a devastating upheaval. The two great civil rights laws of 1964 and 1965 empowered the federal government to punish any public institution practicing discrimination. In the long run this was to make a huge difference in race relations. But it could do nothing directly for lower-class blacks who were jammed into decrepit neighborhoods by race prejudice, poverty, and—equally important but generally overlooked—the overwhelming numbers of their own flight from the South.[21] This ultimate frustration at the moment of a great victory for the black middle class demanded an outlet. One by one, the principal black ghettos of the North exploded in fire and pillage.

A cumulative total of more than one hundred major riots from 1964 to 1968 failed to provoke an organized backlash (Klinkner 1999, 288–316; Higham 1997, 9–30). But the riots did mark a kind of exhaustion of liberal efforts to build a more integrated society. Driving whites out of the civil rights movement, young blacks codified as "Black Power" the aggressive style of Malcolm X. The slogan was taken up in turn by organizers of "Red Power," La Raza, hopeful promoters of Asian solidarity, radical feminists, and gay rights.

Amid this wide encouragement of oppositional cultures and resistive identities, one is aware of a background music. It seems to mingle a patriotic melody of fairness with notes of resentment at entitlements for underlings or privileges for overlords. The music hints withal at a willingness to bend toward one or the other, as each may serve the common good. Quietness, however, has fallen on the song and its audiences. Martin Luther King's triumphant crusade and Rosa Parks's refusal to move remain proud memories, but their vividness as inspiration has gone.

NOTES

1. See also, in literary criticism, Joseph R. Urgo's (1995) insightful work on Willa Cather and, in history, Pierson (1973).

2. An American term for the Protestant Irish, probably coined in Pennsylvania in the eighteenth century. As the largest single component of the new people in the southern backcountry, they became enormously important in the politics of the upland South, from Andrew Jackson onward; see Fischer (1989, 609, 615–19, 642–50) and Miller (1985, 156–68).

3. The traditional picture comes down to us from Flint (1826) via Power (1953). For a corrective, see Hudson (1994) and Meinig (1993, 279–84).

4. Patrick Henry, speaking against the new national Constitution, quoted in Fischer (1989, 780). "Consolidation" was the specter that haunted champions of state rights down through the Civil War and beyond.

5. A North-South compromise in writing the U.S. Constitution allowed each slave to count as three-fifths of a person in apportioning seats in the House of Representatives and the Electoral College. That extra margin could swing close elections, as in Jefferson's victory over John Adams in 1800.

6. Power (1953), although overgeneralized, offers many interesting details. Hudson (1994) is thorough. See Flint (1826) on early Ohio and Simeone (2000).

7. The enormous circulation of Webster's historical speeches is suggested by their frequent inclusion in the 47 million copies of the McGuffey readers that were sold, mostly to public schools, between 1836 and 1870 (Cremin 1980, 69–73).

8. The ideal of honor in the Old South was real enough, as Bertram Wyatt-Brown (1986) has demonstrated, but its significance in sectional conflict remains unpersuasive. See Mark Twain's (1996, 155–65) sketch of two exemplars of the First Families of Virginia in a Missouri town in the midnineteenth century.

9. Webster's first major public oration, given on the two-hundredth anniversary of the landing of the Pilgrims, was a two-hour summation of American history untainted by the South; see Webster (1891, 25–54); see also Vartanian (1971).

10. On the emergence of a grand style in church architecture, see Frisch (1972, 145). On postwar athletic organizations, see Rader (1983, 50–57, 70–80, 108–11, 149–52).

11. On the social separation of Anglo-Protestants from other religious and ethnic groups, see Zunz (1982, 55–59, 68).

12. For statistics, see Christiano (1987). What the modern American university owes to a set of powerful Yankee presidents is reviewed in Turner and Bernard (1988–89).

13. On the tepidness of the generalized Protestantism of the early twentieth century, see Moorhead (1999).

14. Mencken's memoirs are deposited in the Oral History Research Office, Columbia University. See also Horace B. Liveright's exuberant report on the sales of his "Modern Library of Classics" in *The Independent* 108(February 18, 1922): 163.

15. *New York Times*, September 22, 2000, A19. The New England states, led by New Hampshire, also seem to rank favorably in civic engagement by ordinary citizens; see *New York Times*, August 26, 2001, 1, 14.

16. An adjacent entry from Jedidiah Morse's *American Geography* (1789) seems to exclude the English deliberately from the immigrant population in noting the presence of "many immigrants from Scotland, Ireland, Germany, and some few from France." A habit of thinking

of English-born neighbors as more American than the "immigrants" persisted in Willa Cather's recollections of her Nebraska childhood; see King (2000, 12).

17. Constructing a cultural memory of Puerto Ricanness in the nineteenth century and before has been largely the work of folklorists and ethnographic museums since the 1950s. See Duany (2002).

18. The Jones Act of 1917 granted American citizenship to Puerto Ricans. This, together with the swiftness of air travel, made the mainland seem close and very accessible.

19. I am heavily indebted to Ogbu's basic distinction. A case in point: the Japanese Buraku outcasts do less well than the majority of Japanese when attending schools in Japan but are as successful as the majority of Japanese when both groups attend schools in the United States (Ogbu 1991, 5).

20. My own awareness of unbidden subservience came on a Saturday afternoon in the late 1950s on the busy main street of Manteo, North Carolina. As I accompanied my well-behaved eight-year-old daughter to a doctor's office, the black people around us parted, some stepping into the road, to assure us of a lordly untouched passage. This of course was long after the traumatic events of the turn of the century, so acutely described in Ayers (1992), 142-59, Tolnay and Beck (1995), and Williamson (1984).

21. Nicholas Lemann (1991, 6) estimates that five million blacks came north between 1940 and 1970, a number far exceeding the so-called Great Migration of 1910 to 1930.

REFERENCES

Alsop, Joseph W., with Adam Platt. 1992. *I've Seen the Best of It: Memoirs*. New York: W. W. Norton.

Altschuler, Glenn C., and Jan M. Saltzgaber. 1983. *Revivalism, Social Conscience, and Community in the Burned-over District*. Ithaca, N.Y.: Cornell University Press.

Ayers, Edward L. 1992. *The Promise of the New South: Life After Reconstruction*. New York: Oxford University Press.

Bailyn, Bernard. 1986. *Voyagers to the West: A Passage in the Peopling of America on the Eve of the Revolution*. New York: Vintage.

Berbusse, Edward J. 1966. *The United States in Puerto Rico, 1898–1900*. Chapel Hill: University of North Carolina Press.

Berens, John F. 1978. *Providence and Patriotism in Early America, 1640–1815*. Charlottesville: University Press of Virginia.

Blight, David W. 2001. *Race and Reunion: The Civil War in American Memory*. Cambridge, Mass.: Belknap Press of Harvard University Press.

Bodnar, John, ed. 1992. *Remaking America: Public Memory, Commemoration, and Patriotism in the Twentieth Century*. Princeton, N.J.: Princeton University Press.

Bourne, Randolph. 1977. *The Radical Will: Selected Writings, 1911–1918*, edited by Olaf Hansen. New York: Urizen Books.

Bozeman, Theodore Dwight. 1988. *To Live Ancient Lives: The Primitivist Dimension in Puritanism*. Chapel Hill: University of North Carolina Press.

Bradley, Harriet. 1996. *Fractured Identities: Changing Patterns of Inequality*. Cambridge, Mass.: Polity Press.

Bremner, Robert Hamlett. 1980. *The Public Good: Philanthropy and Welfare in the Civil War Era*. New York: Alfred A. Knopf.

Brooks, Van Wyck. 1908. *The Wine of the Puritans*. New York: Norwood Editions.

Calloway, Colin G. 1997. *New Worlds for All: Indians, Europeans, and the Remaking of Early America*. Baltimore: Johns Hopkins University Press.

Carr, Raymond. 1984. *Puerto Rico: A Colonial Experiment*. New York: New York University Press.

Carwardine, Richard J. 1993. *Evangelicals and Politics in Antebellum America*. New Haven, Conn.: Yale University Press.

Cash, Wilbur J. 1941. *The Mind of the South*. New York: Alfred A. Knopf.

Christiano, Kevin J. 1987. *Religious Diversity and Social Change: American Cities, 1890–1906*. New York: Cambridge University Press.

Crane, Verner W. 1928. *The Southern Frontier, 1670–1732*. Durham, N.C.: Duke University Press.

Cremin, Lawrence A. 1980. *American Education: The National Experience, 1783–1876*. New York: Harper & Row.

Cutri, Merle. 1963. *American Philanthropy Abroad: A History*. New Brunswick, N.J.: Rutgers University Press.

Davis, Mike. 2000. *Magical Urbanism: Latinos Reinvent the U.S. City*. London: Verso.

Degler, Carl N. 1959. *Out of Our Past: The Forces That Shaped Modern America*. New York: Harper.

Duany, Jorge. 2002. *The Puerto Rican Nation on the Move: Identities on the Island and in the United States*. Chapel Hill: University of North Carolina Press.

Fernandez, Ronald. 1996. *Disenchanted Island: Puerto Rico and the United States in the Twentieth Century*. Westport, Conn.: Praeger.

Fischer, David Hackett. 1989. *Albion's Seed: Four British Folkways in America*. New York: Oxford University Press.

Fitzpatrick, Joseph P. 1987. *Puerto Rican Americans: The Meaning of Migration to the Mainland*. 2nd ed. Englewood Cliffs, N.J.: Prentice-Hall.

Flint, Timothy. 1826. *Recollections of the Last Ten Years* . . . Boston: Cummings, Hilliard & Co.

Foner, Nancy. 2000. *From Ellis Island to JFK: New York's Two Great Waves of Immigration*. New Haven, Conn., and New York: Yale University Press and Russell Sage Foundation.

Ford, Lacy K., Jr. 1988. *Origins of Southern Radicalism: The South Carolina Upcountry, 1800–1860*. New York: Oxford University Press.

Freehling, William W. 1990. *The Road to Disunion: Secessionists at Bay, 1776–1854*. New York: Oxford University Press.

Frisch, Michael. 1972. *Town into City: Springfield, Massachusetts, and the Meaning of Community, 1840–1880*. Cambridge, Mass.: Harvard University Press.

Galenson, David. 1981. *White Servitude in Colonial America: An Economic Analysis*. Cambridge: Cambridge University Press.

Gates, Henry Louis, Jr. 1988. "The Trope of a New Negro and the Reconstruction of the Image of the Black." *Representations* 24(Fall): 129–55.

Goldin, Claudia. 1994. "The Political Economy of Immigration Restriction in the United States, 1890 to 1921." In *The Regulated Economy: A Historical Approach to Political Economy*, edited by Claudia Goldin and Gary D. Libecap. Chicago: University of Chicago Press.

Gregory, Frances W., and Irene D. Neu. 1962. "The American Industrial Elite in the 1870s: Their Social Origins." In *Men in Business: Essays on the Historical Role of the Entrepreneur*, edited by William Miller. New York: Harper & Row.

Grossman, James R. 1989. *Land of Hope: Chicago, Black Southerners, and the Great Migration*. Chicago: University of Chicago Press.

Hall, Peter Dobkin. 1982. *The Organization of American Culture, 1700–1900: Private Institutions, Elites, and the Origins of American Nationality*. New York: New York University Press.

Handlin, Oscar. 1951. *The Uprooted*. Boston: Little, Brown.

Henretta, James A., Michael G. Kammen, and Stanley N. Katz, eds. 1991. *The Transformation of Early American History: Society, Authority, and Ideology*. New York: Alfred A. Knopf.

Higham, John, ed. 1997. *Civil Rights and Social Wrongs: Black-White Relations Since World War II*. University Park: University of Pennsylvania Press.

———. 1999. "Cultural Responses to Immigration." In *Diversity and Its Discontents: Cultural Conflict and Common Ground in Contemporary American Society*, edited by Neil J. Smelser and Jeffrey C. Alexander. Princeton, N.J.: Princeton University Press.

———. 2001. *Hanging Together: Unity and Diversity in American Culture*, edited by Carl J. Guarneri. New Haven, Conn.: Yale University Press.

Hine, Robert V. 1980. *Community on the American Frontier: Separate but Not Alone*. Norman: University of Oklahoma Press.

Hofstadter, Richard. 1965. *The Paranoid Style in American Politics, and Other Essays*. New York: Alfred A. Knopf.

Hollinger, David A. 1985. *In the American Province: Studies in the History and Historiography of Ideas*. Bloomington: Indiana University Press.

Howe, Daniel Walker. 1979. *The Political Culture of the American Whigs*. Chicago: University of Chicago Press.

———. 1988. "The Impact of Puritanism on American Culture." In *Encyclopedia of the American Religious Experience: Studies of Traditions and Movements*, vol. 2, edited by Peter W. Williams and Charles H. Lippy. New York: Scribner.

Hudson, John C. 1994. *Making the Corn Belt: A Geographical History of Middle-Western Agriculture*. Bloomington: Indiana University Press.

Hudson, Winthrop. 1961. *American Protestantism*. Chicago: University of Chicago Press.

Jefferson, Thomas. 1953. *The Papers of Thomas Jefferson*. Vol. 8. Princeton, N.J.: Princeton University Press.

Jenkins, Wilbert L. 1998. *Seizing the New Day: African-Americans in Post–Civil War Charleston*. Bloomington: Indiana University Press.

Jensen, Richard J. 1971. *The Winning of the Midwest: Social and Political Conflict, 1888–1896*. Chicago: University of Chicago Press.

Kaestle, Carl F. 1983. *Pillars of the Republic: Common Schools and American Society, 1780–1860*. New York: Hill & Wang.

Kelley, Robert. 1984. "Comparing the Incomparable: Politics and Ideas in the United States and the Soviet Union." *Comparative Studies in Society and History* 26(October): 675–80.

King, Desmond. 2000. *Making Americans: Immigration, Race, and the Origins of the Diverse Democracy*. Cambridge, Mass.: Harvard University Press.

Klinkenborg, Verlyn. 1991. *The Last Fine Time*. New York: Alfred A. Knopf.

Klinkner, Philip A., with Rogers M. Smith. 1999. *The Unsteady March: The Rise and Decline of Racial Equality in America*. Chicago: University of Chicago Press.

Kolchin, Peter. 1987. *Unfree Labor: American Slavery and Russian Serfdom*. Cambridge, Mass.: Belknap Press of Harvard University Press.

Korrol, Virginia Sánchez. 1993. "In Their Own Right: A History of Puerto Ricans in the U.S.A." In *Handbook of Hispanic Cultures in the United States*, edited by Nicolas Kanellos and Claudio Esteva-Fabregat. Houston: Arte Publico Press.

Kusmer, Kenneth L. 1979. "The Social History of Cultural Institutions: The Upper-Class Connection." *Journal of Interdisciplinary History* 10(Summer): 137–46.

Lapp, Michael. 1990. "Managing Migration: The Migration Division of Puerto Rico and Puerto Ricans in New York City, 1948–1968." Ph.D. diss., Johns Hopkins University.

Larson, Megali. 1984. "The Production of Experts and the Constitution of Expert Power." In *The Authority of Experts: Studies in History and Theory*, edited by Thomas L. Haskell. Bloomington: Indiana University Press.

Lemann, Nicholas. 1991. *The Promised Land: The Great Black Migration and How It Changed America*. New York: Alfred A. Knopf.

Lewis, David Levering. 1981. *When Harlem Was in Vogue*. New York: Alfred A. Knopf.

Licht, Walter. 1992. *Getting Work: Philadelphia, 1840–1950*. Cambridge, Mass.: Harvard University Press.

Litwack, Leon F. 1979. *Been in the Storm So Long: The Aftermath of Slavery*. New York: Alfred A. Knopf.

Mathews, Mitford M., ed. 1951. *A Dictionary of Americanisms on Historical Principles*. Chicago: University of Chicago Press.

May, Henry F. 1959. *The End of American Innocence: A Study of the First Years of Our Own Time 1912–1917*. New York: Alfred A. Knopf.

———. 1983. "The Religion of the Republic." In *Ideas, Faiths, and Feelings: Essays on American Intellectual and Religious History, 1952–1982* by Henry F. May. New York: Oxford University Press.

McCurry, Stephanie. 1995. *Masters of Small Worlds: Yeoman Households, Gender Relations, and the Political Culture of the Antebellum South Carolina Low Country*. New York: Oxford University Press.

Meier, August, and Elliott Rudwick. 1976. *From Plantation to Ghetto*. 3rd ed. New York: Hill & Wang.

Meinig, D. W. 1993. *The Shaping of America: A Geographical Perspective on Five Hundred Years of History*. New Haven, Conn.: Yale University Press.

Miller, Kerby A. 1985. *Emigrants and Exiles: Ireland and the Irish Exodus to North America*. New York: Oxford University Press.

Miller, Perry. 1956. *Errand into the Wilderness*. Cambridge, Mass.: Belknap Press of Harvard University Press.

Mink, Gwendolyn. 1986. *Old Labor and New Immigrants in American Political Development: Union, Party, and State, 1875–1920*. Ithaca, N.Y.: Cornell University Press.

Moorhead, James. 1999. *World Without End: Mainstream American Protestant Visions of the Last Things, 1880–1925*. Bloomington: Indiana University Press.

Morgan, Edmund S. 1975. *American Slavery, American Freedom: The Ordeal of Colonial Virginia*. New York: W. W. Norton.

Morris, Nancy. 1995. *Puerto Rico: Culture, Politics, and Identity*. Westport, Conn.: Praeger.

Murrin, John M. n.d. "War, Revolution, and Nation-Making: The American Revolution Versus the Civil War." Unpublished paper.

Nash, Gary B. 1984. "Social Development." In *Colonial British America: Essays in the New History of the Early Modern Era*, edited by Jack P. Greene and J. R. Pole. Baltimore: Johns Hopkins University Press.

Norton, Anne. 1986. *Alternative Americas: A Reading of Antebellum Political Culture*. Chicago: University of Chicago Press.

Ogbu, John. 1991. "Immigrant and Involuntary Minorities in Comparative Perspective." In *Minority Status and Schooling: A Comparative Study of Immigrant and Involuntary Minorities*, edited by Margaret A. Gibson and John Ogbu. New York: Garland.

Pérez y González, María E. 2000. *Puerto Ricans in the United States*. Westport, Conn.: Greenwood.

Pierson, George W. 1973. *The Moving American*. New York: Alfred A. Knopf.

Potter, David M. 1968. *The South and the Sectional Conflict*. Baton Rouge: Louisiana State University Press.

Powell, Lawrence N. 2000. *Troubled Memory: Anne Levy, the Holocaust, and David Duke's Louisiana*. Chapel Hill: University of North Carolina Press.

Power, Richard Lyle. 1953. *Planting Corn Belt Culture: The Impress of the Upland Southerner and Yankee in the Old Northwest*. Indianapolis: Indiana Historical Society.

Rader, Benjamin G. 1983. *American Sports: From the Age of Folk Games to the Age of Spectators*. Englewood Cliffs, N.J.: Prentice-Hall.

Remini, Robert V. 1997. *Daniel Webster: The Man and His Time*. New York: W. W. Norton.

Rivera-Batiz, Francisco L., and Carlos E. Santiago. 1996. *Island Paradox: Puerto Rico in the 1990s*. New York: Russell Sage Foundation.

Rohrbough, Malcolm J. 1978. *The Trans-Appalachian Frontier: People, Societies, and Institutions, 1775–1850*. New York: Oxford University Press.

Rosenberry, Lois Kimball Mathews. 1909. *The Expansion of New England . . . to the Mississippi River, 1620–1865*. Boston: Houghton Mifflin.

Salisbury, Neal. 1982. *Manitou and Providence: Indians, Europeans, and the Making of New England, 1500–1643*. New York: Oxford University Press.

Schermerhorn, R. A. 1978. *Comparative Ethnic Relations: A Framework for Theory and Research*. Chicago: University of Chicago Press.

Schultz, Stanley K. 1973. *The Culture Factory: Boston Public Schools, 1789–1860*. New York: Oxford University Press.

Shain, Barry Alan. 1994. *The Myth of American Individualism: The Protestant Origins of American Political Thought*. Princeton, N.J.: Princeton University Press.

Simeone, James. 2000. *Democracy and Slavery in Frontier Illinois: The Bottomland Republic*. De Kalb, Ill.: Northern Illinois University Press.

Stout, Harry S. 1990. "Rhetoric and Reality in the Early Republic: The Case of the Federalist Clergy." In *Religion and American Politics from the Colonial Period to the 1980s*, edited by Mark A. Noll. New York: Oxford University Press.

Suro, Roberto. 1998. *Strangers Among Us: How Latino Immigration Is Transforming America*. New York: Alfred A. Knopf.

Swierenga, Robert P. 1989. "The Settlement of the Old Northwest: Ethnic Pluralism in a Featureless Plain." *Journal of the Early Republic* 9(1): 73–105.

Sydnor, Charles S. 1948. *The Development of Southern Sectionalism, 1819–1848*. Baton Rouge: Louisiana State University Press.

Taylor, William R. 1961. *Cavalier and Yankee: The Old South and American National Character*. New York: Braziller.

Tsai, Shih-shan Henry. 1986. *The Chinese Experience in America*. Bloomington: Indiana University Press.

Thomas, G. E. 1975. "Puritans, Indians, and the Concept of Race." *New England Quarterly* 48(March): 3–27.

Tolnay, Stewart E., and E. M. Beck. 1995. *A Festival of Violence: An Analysis of Southern Lynchings, 1882–1930*. Urbana: University of Illinois Press.

Turner, James, and Paul Bernard. 1988–89. "The Prussian Road to University? German Models and the University of Michigan, 1837–c.1895." *Rackham Reports* (Horace H. Rackham School of Graduate Studies, University of Michigan): 6–52.

Twain, Mark. 1996. *The Tragedy of Pudd'nhead Wilson*. New York: Oxford University Press. (Orig. pub. 1894.)

Urgo, Joseph R. 1995. *Willa Cather and the Myth of American Migration*. Urbana: University of Illinois Press.

Vartanian, Pershing. 1971. "The Puritan as a Symbol in American Thought: A Study of the New England Societies, 1820–1920." Ph.D. diss., University of Michigan.

Ward, Harry M. 1973. "The Search for American Identity: Early Historians of New England." In *Perspectives on Early American History: Essays in Honor of Richard B. Morris*, edited by Alden T. Vaughan and George Athan Billias. New York: Harper & Row.

Watson, Ritchie Devon. 1993. *Yeoman Versus Cavalier: The Old Southwest's Fictional Road to Rebellion*. Baton Rouge: Louisiana State University Press.

Webster, Daniel. 1891. *The Great Speeches and Orations of Daniel Webster*. Boston: Little, Brown.

Whalen, Carmen Teresa. 2001. *From Puerto Rico to Philadelphia: Puerto Rican Workers and Postwar Economies*. Philadelphia: Temple University Press.

Wiebe, Robert H. 1975. *The Segmented Society: An Introduction to the Meaning of America*. New York: Oxford University Press.

Williamson, Joel. 1984. *The Crucible of Race: Black-White Relations in the American South Since Emancipation*. New York: Oxford University Press.

Wyatt-Brown, Bertram. 1986. *Honor and Violence in the Old South*. New York: Oxford University Press.

Zunz, Olivier. 1982. *The Changing Face of Inequality: Urbanization, Industrial Development, and Immigrants in Detroit, 1880–1920*. Chicago: University of Chicago Press.

Zurier, Rebecca. 1985. *Art for the Masses, 1911–1917: A Radical Magazine and Its Graphics*. New Haven, Conn.: Yale University Art Gallery.

Joe W. Trotter

Chapter 4

The Great Migration, African Americans, and Immigrants in the Industrial City

Domestic and international migration are major themes in U.S. history. Yet these processes did not gain substantive scholarly attention until the interwar years of the twentieth century. After a flurry of scholarship before World War II, migration research declined during the cold war years of the 1950s. The United States had placed stiff legislative restrictions on international migration during the mid-1920s. Over the next two decades the number of newcomers dropped precipitously to its lowest level since the 1840s. By the late twentieth century, however, a new round of scholarship had emerged from the confluence of several social, political, legal, and intellectual forces. These forces included the increasing deindustrialization of the nation's urban economy, the growth of a new information-based economy, and the mass migration of Latino and Asian immigrants into the country. The transformation of scholarship also reflected the emergence of the black liberation struggle, the new social history movement, and the resurgence of the feminist movement. Together, these latter developments ushered in new class, race, and gendered perspectives on American society and the dynamics of mass population movements.

Past and present migration research overlaps in its theoretical, methodological, and substantive concerns. Both bodies of scholarship engage several interlocking issues—the forces driving decisions to move from one place to another, the reception that migrants receive in their new homes, and migrant responses to the host society, including their own ethnic resident populations. Nonetheless, the two fields—internal and international migration—are insufficiently joined. As Charles Hirschman, Philip Kasinitz, and Josh DeWind (1999, 20) note, "U.S. internal migration and immigration studies now constitute different 'literatures' and are pursued, for the most part, by different sets of scholars." As a means of helping to bridge these disparate bodies of knowledge, this essay focuses on the experiences of African Americans and immigrants during the industrial era.

Specifically, this essay begins with a review of the literature and concludes with a series of comparative questions. How did scholarship on African Americans and immigrants change from the early twentieth century through the onset of the modern civil rights and Black Power movements? How did these bodies of scholarship overlap or diverge over time? I then ask questions about the comparative premigration, transit, and settlement experiences of the different groups. How did premigration experiences condition decisions to move? How were the different groups received by the predominantly white, Anglo-Saxon, Protestant host society? How were they received by their own U.S.

ethnic or nationality-based communities? Finally, how did migrants respond to their new homes?

Blacks and immigrants have shared certain fundamental experiences across ethnic, nationality, and racial lines. In addition to a problematic relationship with scholarly and popular conceptions of the migrant and immigrant experience, each group has confronted profound dislocations in its communities of origins; the economic pull of American industrial development; varying levels of ethnic and racial hostility in receiving communities; and the tremendous push to create its own relatively autonomous workplace- and community-based modes of resistance and empowerment. Despite such shared experiences, however, inter- and intragroup differences make it exceedingly difficult to generalize about the migration process. None of the groups were monolithic. They were fragmented by significant class, regional, gender, and other differences. Still, compared to other groups, African Americans experienced the most problematic relationship not only with the predominantly white Anglo-Saxon society but with diverse waves of immigrants.

CHANGING PERSPECTIVES ON DOMESTIC AND INTERNATIONAL MIGRATION, 1870 TO 1950

During the early twentieth century, contemporary social science and policy studies set the terms of research on U.S. migration and immigration history. Although interpretations have varied significantly from one group to another and across time, there has been substantial overlap in the theory, research, and interpretation of African American and immigrant life. The first generation of urban migration research emerged in the teeth of white supremacist thinking about race, immigration, and nation-building. By the late nineteenth century, Charles Darwin's notion of human evolution and "civilization" informed popular and scholarly perceptions of people from diverse ethnic and racial backgrounds (Jacobson 1998; Fredrickson 1971; Bay 2000).

Adapting Darwin's ideas to their own ends, white supremacist writers excluded people of African, Asian, and Latino descent from the pale of modern, industrializing society. But Euro-Americans reserved their most vicious stereotypes for African Americans. Turn-of-the-century writers produced a broad range of racist works that denigrated the character of African Americans. Such writings aimed to exclude blacks from the human family. The titles of such books are themselves quite telling: Charles Carroll's *The Negro, A Beast* (1900/2000), Robert Schufeldt's *The Negro, A Menace to American Civilization* (1907), Thomas Dixon's *The Leopard's Spots* (1902/1967) and *The Clansman: An Historical Romance of the Ku Klux Klan* (1905). According to Dixon (Trotter 2001, 334), African Americans were inferior to whites and absolutely nothing could change that fact: "The Ethiopian can not change his skin or the leopard his spots." Moreover, according to Dixon and his cohort, emancipation had removed the discipline of slavery and now blacks were regressing into a state of "heathenism and brutishness" that threatened the republic. The image of the black male as rapist permeated these popular accounts and justified the spread of lynchings and mob violence. At the same time, whites viewed black workers as "lazy" and "irregular" in their work habits (Trotter 2001, 339–40).

Racialist thinking also shaped perceptions of people of Asian and Latino descent. In his writings on Asians in California, for example, Hubert Howe Bancroft (Hune

1989, 18–42) underscored the point: "We want the Asiatic for our low-grade work, and when it is finished we want him to go home and stay there until we want him again." Such racist thinking underlay the creation of the "sojourner" stereotype of Chinese immigrants. In this view, the Chinese came to America with temporary aims. They hoped to work, save money, return to China, and reestablish themselves on their own land. As a result of their presumed transient character and loyalty to their old country ideas and ways of living, the Chinese were also held responsible for any hostility that they experienced in the United States from elites and white workers alike (Hune 1989; Chan 1990, 37–75; Takaki 1993, 191–276).

Even before the United States conquered Mexico and subordinated its indigenous residents in the wake of the Texas Revolution and the Mexican-American War during the 1830s and 1840s, Euro-Americans had already constructed images of Mexicans as a "blood-thirsty" and "sexually depraved" people. Describing Mexicans as a "mixed race" people, Euro-Americans maintained that Mexicans combined the worst characteristics of people of Spanish and Indian heritage. During the late nineteenth and early twentieth centuries, however, as immigration from Mexico escalated, this stereotype gave way to another equally vicious one—the Mexican worker as racially inferior, "docile, indolent, and backward" (Riesler 1976, 128; Gutiérrez 1993; Saragoza 1989–90; Almaguer 1987).

White supremacist ideas affected not only people of African, Asian, and Latino descent but Europeans of so-called inferior stock. The new wave of immigrants from southern, central, and eastern Europe faced the brunt of intraracial stereotyping and denigration of character. Italians, Slavs, Poles, and Russian Jews all confronted white Anglo-Saxon Protestant efforts to create a hierarchy of white "races." In 1916 Madison Grant (1916/1970) published *The Passing of the Great Race*, which attacked people of central and eastern Europe as a threat to the purity of "Nordic" stock. According to Grant, people of Nordic background represented the race of the "white man par excellence" (quoted in Higham 1955, 156). Moreover, as a means of placing distance between themselves and the newcomers, American-born descendants of people from northern and western Europe often equated the new European immigrants with characteristics presumably found mainly among Asians, Latinos, and even African Americans. As James Barrett and David Roediger (1997, 3–4) note in their important essay on the subject, not only were Italians described as the "Chinese of Europe" in some parts of the world, but in the United States they and other south central Europeans became "guinea," a term originally used to describe Africans. Moreover, in racist folklore, the Jews were regularly referred to as "niggers"—inside out.

Against this powerful backdrop of white supremacist views of migration and immigration in American life, the rise of the so-called Chicago School of sociologists at the University of Chicago was salutary. The principal architects of the Chicago School— Robert E. Park, Ernest Burgess, and Roderick McKenzie (1925)—built on the conceptual insights of William I. Thomas and Florian Znaniecki (1918–20). Focusing mainly on immigration from southern, central, and eastern Europe during the late nineteenth and early twentieth century, Robert Park and his colleagues viewed the city as an organism that absorbed recurring waves of new people. While these scholars acknowledged the "push" of changes in the immigrants' Old World way of life, they accented the "pull" of America's industrial might. They also portrayed a painful but ultimately "progressive" process of assimilation into a predominantly white Anglo-Saxon society (Bukowczyk 1996; Bulmer 1984; O'Connor 2001).

The ideas of the Chicago School gained sharp theoretical articulation in Robert Park's race relations cycle theory. Generalizing on the basis of fieldwork on Hawaiians and West Coast Asians, Park cast his theoretical net across a broad range of migrant and immigrant groups, mainly people from southern, central, and eastern Europe. Park's race relations theory included four interrelated phases of interaction between new groups and the host society: contact, competition, accommodation, and assimilation. In his view, the established group (American-born whites of northern and western European background) gained the upper hand and forced the new groups to accept its authority. The new power relationships entailed not only economic and political discrimination but geographical segregation of racial groups within the housing, institutional, and social life of the city. Minority groups would enter the so-called mainstream, but the process would begin gradually with individuals (rather than entire groups) gaining upward mobility and establishing networks for elevating their kinsmen over time (Park, Burgess, and McKenzie 1925).

Park recognized problems in his linear portrait of the assimilation process. At times, he acknowledged, a linear model was inappropriate for explaining the complicated patterns that emerged on the ground of social relations. In a thoughtful critique of Park's ideas, for example, sociologist Rubén G. Rumbaut (1999, 188) notes that Park "explicitly rebutted" the notion of "a unilinear assimilative outcome to race conflict" in a 1937 introduction to a book on interracial marriage in Hawaii. Still, Park and his colleagues helped to popularize the treatment of assimilation as "inexorable." As Park put it, the race relations cycle tended to repeat itself in all social settings, and "eventual assimilation" was "apparently progressive and irreversible" (Park 1934; Park 1950, 150).

The first generation of research on domestic and international migration included not only the work of the Chicago School of sociologists but the scholarship of immigration historians as well. Writing under the influence of Frederick Jackson Turner's "frontier thesis," these scholars focused on the experiences of the older mid-nineteenth-century wave of immigrants from northern and western Europe. In 1891 Turner had argued—"with a poetic lilt," as the historian John Higham (1973, 175) notes—that the European encounter with the rural West "explained the distinctive features of America: above all, its democracy and its amalgamation of many people and sections into a united nation" (Novick 1988, 88–89).

As young scholars who had come to maturity amid dramatic urban-industrial change, immigration historians soon developed different ideas—from Turner and Park—about the place of immigration in U.S. history. The historian Arthur M. Schlesinger made explicit the connection between Turner's frontier thesis and a new generation of immigration studies. In his essay "The Significance of Immigration in American History" (1921), Schlesinger argued that immigration should be viewed as a "dynamic factor in American development," not as a "social problem." Based primarily on the experiences of immigrants from countries like Norway, Sweden, and Germany, historical studies by Theodore Blegen, Marcus Lee Hansen, and Carl Wittke accented the constructive role that immigrants had played in the settlement and development of the West. According to the historian Jon Gjerde (1999), immigration historians, whom he dubbed "ethnic Turnerians," placed greater emphasis on the premigration experiences of migrants than their sociological counterparts, who emphasized the commanding pull of American urban-industrial opportunities. Although these historians shifted the focus from the city to the rural West and from south central to northern and western Europeans, they nonetheless reinforced the Eurocentric bias of the assimilationist model. Their notion of a diverse democracy revolved around people of diverse "European backgrounds" (Gjerde 1999).

The race relations cycle model was exceedingly problematic. It assumed the superiority of northern and western European culture and downplayed the distinctive experiences of a variety of ethnic and racial groups. It also denigrated the culture and forms of resistance that diverse groups brought to the industrial city. Still, within the context of the interwar years, the assimilationist model represented an advance over earlier overtly racist interpretations of urban migration and industrial development. By treating the migration experiences of diverse groups as a complicated social process, the Chicago School and immigration historians modified the restrictive tenets of the social Darwinist model of U.S. urban and social history. In varying degrees, diverse ethnic and racial groups would use the assimilationist idea to fight patterns of racial and class discrimination against their group. Research on African American migration reflected both the advantages and disadvantages of using the assimilationist model to counteract white supremacist ideas.

With the onset of the Great Migration, the Chicago School gave increasing attention to the movement of southern blacks into northern cities. Research on black urban migration had deep roots in W. E. B. Du Bois's *The Philadelphia Negro* (1899/1996), but it was only during World War I and its aftermath that black migration scholarship flourished (Katz and Sugrue 1998; Lewis 1993; Williams 1989). In addition to the U.S. Department of Labor's *Negro Migration in 1916–1917* (1919/1969) and the historian Carter G. Woodson's *A Century of Negro Migration* (1918), important black migration studies continued to emerge through the 1920s and early 1930s. Studies by Emmett J. Scott, Thomas J. Woofter, Charles S. Johnson, Louise V. Kennedy, and Clyde V. Kiser all documented the changing volume, origins, and direction of black population movement during the era of the Great Migration (Trotter 1991).

Black migration studies expressed an optimistic belief that blacks were gradually making the transition from disfranchisement to full participation in American democracy. Woodson (1918, 188) concluded that these migrants "were not lazy, shiftless and desperate as some predicted that they would be." In work for the Chicago Commission on Race Relations, the sociologist Charles S. Johnson (Chicago Commission on Race Relations 1968, 400) argued that southern blacks had "made a satisfactory record" in their move from farm to city. In her book, Louise Kennedy (1930, 10) went a step further and placed the black migration squarely within the context of changes in national and international capitalism. "African American migration," she said, "is linked with the trend from the open country, which has been characteristic of all peoples in recent decades."

Park's ideas received their greatest support in research by the sociologist E. Franklin Frazier. On the one hand, Frazier emphasized African American flight from a feudal "past" to "cities of destruction," where, in his view, their rural traditions and mores were decimated. On the other hand, like his Chicago School mentors, Frazier developed a complex ecological analysis of black life in northern cities. According to Frazier, in Harlem and Chicago, African Americans had sorted themselves out geographically along class and status lines. Unless whites insisted on maintaining artificial racial barriers, upper-class blacks would soon join the white world beyond the predominantly working-class and poor black community. Thus, African Americans seemed poised to make the transition from a "racial caste" to a "racial minority" with prospects for repeating the cycle of contact, competition, accommodation, and assimilation (Park 1939, 3–45, and Park 1950, 81–116).[1]

During the 1930s the race relations cycle theory suffered a setback as African Americans faced the onset of the Great Depression, massive unemployment, and declining rates of out-migration from the South. As these processes took hold, social anthropologists like W. Lloyd Warner and his associates at the University of Chicago persuasively argued that African Americans in the rural South and, to some extent, in the urban North continued to face a castelike system of social stratification. Based on stringent rules of endogamy, this system blocked African American access to mainstream or predominantly white institutions as both producers and consumers of goods and services. In his massive study *An American Dilemma: The Negro and Modern Democracy* (1944), the Swedish economist Gunnar Myrdal reinforced notions of caste and class in his interpretation of African American life, but as we see later in the chapter, the events of World War II and its early aftermath would witness the resurgence of assimilationist ideas. African Americans would also intensify their use of such ideas to justify their full inclusion in the perquisites of citizenship in a democratic society.

Latino and Asian American scholars and activists also embraced theories of integration as weapons in their struggle against exclusion and popular misconceptions about their role in the migration process. A group of Mexican American intellectuals and their Anglo allies—George Sánchez, Carlos Castaneda, Manuel Gamio, Paul S. Taylor, and Carey McWilliams—challenged prevailing portraits of Latino people as unassimilable, indolent, and docile. In his careful survey of the literature on Mexican Americans in the West, the historian David Gutiérrez (1995) forcefully argues that the first generation of Latino scholars used social science scholarship to help free their people from European stereotypes and notions of Anglo superiority. They aimed to advance the cause of full citizenship rights by portraying "ordinary working class Mexican Americans and Mexican immigrants as complex, fully-formed, and fully-functioning human beings" (Gutiérrez 1993, 523). Although a new generation of Chicano activist-scholars would reject the first generation's scholarship as too accommodating to Anglo culture, class, and political imperatives, Gutiérrez (1995, 525) concludes that the first generation's accent on the ability of Mexicans to assimilate to the so-called majority culture was, for the times, "a bold—and inherently political—project of excavation and recovery." To contest the sojourner thesis, several Chinese writers also emphasized ethnic and racial barriers to Chinese mobility and integration into American society (Coolidge 1969; Lasker 1931; Ichihashi 1969).

African Americans and immigrants not only used established social science and historical concepts and methodologies to advance their cause but retained access to their own alternative and highly celebratory nationalist histories. During the interwar years, immigration scholars often commented on the clash of earlier "filiopietistic" and "immigration restrictionist" accounts of the immigrant experience. By the late nineteenth and early twentieth centuries, each group had developed its own strong, achievement-oriented historical accounts. Such studies praised the contributions of particular ethnic groups and their forebears to American and Western culture and democracy. Celebratory immigrant group histories both reflected and stimulated the growth of ethnic historical societies. Some of these societies represented certain northern and western European group responses to notions of Anglo-Saxon superiority: the Scotch-Irish Society (1889), the American Irish Historical Society (1898), the Pennsylvania-German Society (1891), and the American Jewish Historical Society (1892), to name a few. Perhaps more so than either Latinos or Asian Americans, however, African Americans were active in forming their own historical societies: the Negro Historical Society of Philadelphia (1897), the Negro Society for Historical Research (1911), and the Association for the Study of Negro Life and History (1915). Although such histories offered much-needed psychic support and group self-esteem, they nonetheless emphasized the doings of "Great Men" and "Great Women" and downplayed intragroup conflicts and the dynamics of social change. Nonetheless, by establishing records of myriad ethnic and nationality group experiences, early-twentieth-century ethnic historical societies and publications helped to establish a foundation for recovering detailed community histories during the late twentieth century (Saveth 1948, 200–3).[2]

THE TRANSFORMATION OF MIGRATION RESEARCH, 1950 TO 2000

Under the impact of World War II and the cold war years thereafter, the assimilationist model evolved into a virtual article of faith. In his widely acclaimed synthesis on the subject, the historian Oscar Handlin (1951) noted premigration influences but accented the Chicago School's emphasis on contact, conflict, accommodation, and assimilation. He described the process of migration as a wrenching and "uprooting" experience. It unanchored large numbers of people from their familiar rural worlds of family, community, and culture.[3] Despite his view of immigration as an inherently alienating experience, however, Handlin believed that it would result in the newcomers' acquisition of the fruits of American citizenship. "The newcomers were on the way toward being Americans almost before they stepped off the boat, because their own experience of displacement had already introduced them to what was essential in the situation of Americans" (272). With the publication of *The Newcomers* in 1959, Handlin expanded his view of the assimilation process to include African Americans and Puerto Ricans (see also Higham 1975).

Although Handlin produced the signature work of immigration for his times, the growing appeal of the assimilationist model was closely intertwined with popular reactions to the horrors of racism in Nazi Germany. At the core of Germany's Third Reich was a destructive racial ideology that defined Aryans as the master race and targeted Jews, Gypsies, homosexuals, Jehovah's Witnesses, and "genetically diseased" Germans as the prime candidates for annihilation and expropriation of property. By the end of World War II, Germany had forced some six million Jews from all over Europe into concentration camps and gas chambers. At the same time, the German government had imported forced laborers from other parts of Europe, particularly Poland and parts of the Soviet Union, to aid its work of industrial development and imperial expansion across the continent (Friedlander 1995; Hertzberg and Hirt-Maheimer 1998; Poltawska 1999). Coupled with its newly proclaimed role as leader of the free world, it is no wonder that the post–World War II United States would turn to the assimilationist model (Hirschman, Kasinitz, and DeWind 1999).

Despite the popularity of Handlin's important book, there was a growing undercurrent of reaction against integrationist theory. Within less than five years after publication of Handlin's *The Uprooted*, the historian John Higham issued an indirect but compelling challenge to the underpinnings of the assimilationist model. In his pivotal book *Strangers in the Land* (1955), Higham vigorously argued that nativism, a form of white Anglo-Saxon nationalism, constrained the lives of numerous nationality groups as they sought entrée into the American nation.[4] According to Higham, racial and ethnic hostility gained its most powerful manifestations in popular movements against Catholics, political radicals, and people of color. By highlighting patterns of hostility that greeted diverse ethnic groups, including nonwhites as well as people from southern, central, and eastern Europe, Higham helped to give pause to the assimilationist propositions advanced by Handlin just a few years earlier.

The first wave of postwar scholarship on northern black urban communities echoed Higham's emphasis on the role of ethnic hostility and conflict. In studies of New York City, Chicago, Detroit, and Cleveland, historians emphasized the making of racially segregated black communities—the rise of "the ghetto." In these studies, black migration was a "tragic" and exceptional experience. African Americans were not the "last of the immigrants," who would gain a foothold on the occupational ladder and parallel the upward path of white southern, central, and eastern European groups. Although African Americans did not face entirely unique barriers to their progress, compared to other groups they faced a more intense and destructive barrage of social forces—the discriminatory policies of white workers, social welfare officials, the police, and real estate agencies and exceedingly low wages in the industrial economy.[5]

Partly because the ghetto studies offered sparse quantitative evidence to back up their propositions, some scholars gradually produced a series of social-scientific studies that also challenged the "last of the immigrants" thesis (Lieberson 1963; 1980, 383; Taeuber and Taeuber 1965; Thernstrom 1973). In his systematic comparative study of blacks and European immigrants, the historical demographer Stanley Lieberson (1980, 383) concluded: "The [quantitative] data comparing blacks and the new Europeans earlier in this century lead one to a rather clear conclusion. . . . The situation for new Europeans in the United States, bad as it may have been was not as bad as that experienced by blacks at the same time." The social historian Stephen Thernstrom came to the same conclusion based on a similar engagement with existing statistical evidence on the city of Boston between 1880 and 1970. "Until very recently," Thernstrom (1973, 219) concluded, "it seems clear, the problems of black men in a white society were different in kind from those of earlier newcomers." At about the same time increasing numbers of Asian and Latino historians focused attention on anti-immigrant sentiment and efforts to restrict the movement of people across the Pacific and the Rio Grande (Saragoza 1989–90; Gutiérrez 1993; Chan 1990; Hune 1989). Although these scholars expressed increasing dissatisfaction with racial barriers to the upward mobility of people of color, they failed to give sufficient attention to the ways in which poor and working-class members of diverse groups forged strategies to shape their own migration experience and resist their subordination and exploitation in American society.

Under the impact of the Black Power movement of the late 1960s and early 1970s, scholars of black urban history placed poor and working-class blacks at the center of their story. They also turned toward research on the process of black migration itself. Beginning his investigation of black migration from the South to Chicago, James Grossman (1989, 6) documented the Great Migration as a grassroots social movement, replete with its own indigenous leadership and channels of information for decision-making. "This 'dynamic of migration,'" he argued, "not only affected how migrants reacted to what they found; it also informs our understanding of those reactions." Peter Gottlieb (1987, 7) analyzed the southern blacks' migration to Pittsburgh as "a process of self-transformation." Through "seasonal migration and temporary industrial work within the South," he demonstrated that African Americans "prepared themselves for geographic movements further afield." Along with their participation in the emerging industries of the New South, Gottlieb reconstructed the premigration status of blacks in southern agriculture as owners, as tenants, and as farm laborers.

As the Black Power movement revamped our understanding of the Great African

American Migration, it also stimulated and reinforced the transformation of scholarship on a variety of migrant and immigrant groups in the industrial city. Research on domestic migration was by no means limited to African Americans. Large numbers of southern whites, particularly from the Appalachian region and the Dust Bowl Southwest, had moved into the cities of the urban North and West in the 1930s and 1940s (Obermiller, Wagner, and Tucker 2000). The first wave of scholarly observations and writings on the experiences of white migrants mirrored rural stereotypes. During the 1950s and early 1960s, the Berea College professor of economics and sociology Roscoe Giffin described Appalachian migrants to the urban Midwest as people from a predominantly rural, isolated, and premodern culture—one that required massive external intervention to initiate a process of "modernization" (Tucker 2000). A similar image had emerged from the earliest scholarship on the white migrants who moved to West Coast cities in the wake of the Dust Bowl conditions in the American Southwest (Obermiller, Wagner, and Tucker 2000; Berry 2000; Gregory 1989).

In many ways, similar to African American migration, a tragic portrait of southern white migration soon emerged. Not only were Southern white migrants presumably pushed out of the South and Southwest by conditions beyond their control, but they supposedly confronted the new environment with few resources for rebuilding their lives. Beginning during the late 1960s and early 1970s, a new perspective on southern migrants to American cities gradually emerged and prevailed during the 1980s and 1990s. In a series of case studies, James Gregory, Chad Berry, Phillip Obermiller, and William Philliber, to name a few, argued that southern white migration was not the product of a static or "backward" culture but the outcome of historical processes—including the impact of industrialism, socioeconomic and political changes in host cities, and the creative reactions of migrants to their own predicament at both the point of origin and the point of destination. In these studies, southern whites transformed poor urban neighborhoods into tight-knit Appalachian communities, replete with their own taverns, neighborhood social groups, and associations (Obermiller, Wagner, and Tucker 2000; Guy 2000).

Inspired by the new social history and Black Power movements, the Chicano movement helped to transform scholarship on Mexican Americans. Scholars like Rodolfo Acuña, Tomás Almaguer, Richard Griswold del Castillo, and Albert Camarillo challenged stereotypical portraits of Mexicans by documenting the intricacies and complexities of Mexican American culture. These scholars showed how Latinos both confronted and resisted systems of inequality in America. Sucheng Chan, Ronald Takaki, Stanford Lyman, and others accomplished a similar feat for Chinese and Japanese immigrants (Saragoza 1989–90; Gutiérrez 1993; Chan 1990; Hune 1989). In the hands of the latter writers, "sojourning" was not simply a decision to remain separate from American society but represented a way "to *adapt* America and its ways to their own purposes rather than *adopt* it to the exclusion and surrender of their own values" (Chan 1990, 68). Moreover, rather than depicting Chinese workers as victims of contract labor systems—as "coolie laborers"—scholars now more often perceived them as "by and large, free and voluntary" (194).

Responding to new social history and political movements, scholars also reconceptualized European immigration history. Beginning notably with the work of Rudolph Vecoli, immigration historians challenged Handlin's emphasis on cultural breakdown and alienation. In his seminal essay, "Contadini in Chicago: A Critique of *The Uprooted*" (1964), Vecoli helped to usher in a fresh view of immigrants from southern and eastern Europe. According to Vecoli, the peasant village, which Handlin depicted in

The Uprooted, "did not exist in southern Italy" during the late nineteenth and early twentieth centuries. Rather than inhabiting a rural village of "solidarity, communality, and neighborliness," Vecoli concluded, southern Italian immigrants to America had lived in a "rural city" of substantial social change, conflict, hard work, and poor living conditions. Still, according to Vecoli, southern Italian settlement in America was not entirely alienating. The Italian family represented a cohesive institution that enabled immigrants to build forms of solidarity and community in the new American environment. Over the next two decades scholarship on European immigration proliferated.[6] In 1985 the immigration historian John Bodnar substituted Handlin's ubiquitous "uprooted" with "the transplanted" in his influential synthesis on the subject. Bodnar (1985, xx) summarized the central thrust of the new scholarship when he wrote, "Ordinary individuals are rescued from the status of victims; they are not simply manipulated by leaders, their class standing, or their culture, but active participants in an historical drama whose outcome is anything but predictable" (see also Barrett 1992).

Despite the transformation of scholarship on migration and immigration by the mid-1980s, such studies neglected the role of women and gender issues. Across all ethnic and racial groups, scholarship inspired by the new social history and political movements focused mainly on men. Women were treated largely as a minor theme in the larger story. Stimulated by a strong resurgent feminist movement, the challenge to male-dominated scholarship steadily mounted. The first set of books and essays, published during the late 1970s and early 1980s, emphasized the need to include women in the emerging social history emphases on migration, work, and community building from the bottom up. These studies simply included women in the narrative; they failed to probe deeply the meaning of gender as a distinct category of analysis (Faue 1993; Weinberg 1992; Hine 1991; Guerin-Gonzales 1994; Saragoza 1989–90; Gutiérrez 1993; Peffer 1992; Ling 2000; Friday 1994, 530).

During the late 1980s and 1990s, a second set of studies analyzed gender as a dynamic social force along with class, race, and ethnicity. Pioneers in the gendering of migration studies included Darlene Clark Hine, Sharon Harley, Earl Lewis, and Jacquelyn Jones in the African American field; Donna Gabaccia, Judith Smith, and S. J. Kleinberg in the Euro-American field; Sucheng Chan, Evelyn Nakano Glenn, Judy Yung, Valerie Masumoto, and Huping Ling in the Asian field; and Vicki Ruiz, Antonia Castañeda, Peggy Pascoe, and Sarah Deutsch in the Latino field. Rather than simply identifying and locating women in kin, friend, and communal networks, these scholars documented the integral role that women no less than men played in the migration process. They also delineated the ways in which certain push and pull forces undergirding population movements often had different meanings for men and women migrants. Sexual inequality and exploitation, they argued, compounded the migration and settlement experiences of women. Moreover, these scholars insisted that new knowledge about gender and gender relations would require the crafting of new narratives of the migration experience itself (Faue 1993; Weinberg 1992; Hine 1991; Guerin-Gonzales 1994; Saragoza 1989–90; Gutiérrez 1993; Peffer 1992; Ling 2000; Friday 1994, 530).

The call for a more "gendered" history, as opposed to a women's history, would soon catapult research on white male racial identity to the forefront of academic research in history and American studies. Inspired by David Roediger's seminal study *The Wages of Whiteness* (1991), a variety of studies focused on the ways in which recurring groups of immigrants remade themselves into a race-conscious part of the American working class and politics. According to Roediger (and somewhat later, his collaborator James Barrett), the new immigrants were originally "in-between people," neither black nor entirely white. Only after they arrived in America would they gradually become white. Integral to this process was their ability to absorb American notions of social hierarchy, which placed blacks uniformly below whites in the struggle for prestige, power, and resources. In other words, as Barrett and Roediger (1997, 3) put it, most of the new immigrants "did not arrive with conventional United States attitudes regarding 'racial difference,'" but they somehow "got caught up in . . . this racial thing" and became "white" over time. In their view, the process of "becoming American" and "becoming white" were tightly interwoven. A variety of other studies suggested that Latino and Asian immigrants also struggled to define themselves in racial terms as closer to white than black (Foley 1997, 208–10; Lewis 1996; see also Fuchs 1990; Model 1990).[7]

In the meantime, a critical assessment of whiteness studies has gradually been taking shape. Recent reviews raise pointed questions about the precise definition of whiteness; the nature and timing of transitions from "not so white" to white identities; and the relationship between whiteness and other forms of identity. From the outset of their settlement in the United States, European immigrant groups both perceived of themselves as white and were considered to be white by the majority culture. As Nancy Foner (2002, 107–8) relates in an extended response to commentaries on her book *From Ellis Island to JFK* (2000), "Clearly Jews and Italians were, from the very beginning, recognized as whites in terms of legal and political rights; they were allowed to vote in states that restricted the suffrage to whites, and miscegenation laws were never enforced to prevent their marriages to other Europeans." Perhaps most important, some scholars are challenging the narrow national rather than international scope of existing scholarship on the subject. In his recent review of the field, the historian Peter Kolchin (2002, 170–71) concludes that "one of the most striking features of the whiteness studies works is their assumption—sometimes asserted and sometimes unspoken—that the racism they describe is uniquely American and that American whiteness can be understood in isolation, without considering anything abroad."[8] As I suggest in the conclusion to this chapter, an international perspective will enable us to delineate more clearly the specific contours of race-making in U.S. history.

CONCLUSION

During the late twentieth century, a new set of social conditions reshaped patterns of domestic and international migration to American cities. For the first time in U.S. history, most immigrants came from countries in Latin America and Asia. Although a variety of contemporary social scientists and policy experts are now analyzing these recent population movements, we nonetheless need to bring these disparate bodies of scholarship together with research on the industrial era and offer sharp comparative assessments. By bringing together research on African Americans and a variety of white and nonwhite nationality groups during the early twentieth century, this essay suggests a conceptual framework for doing the same for the recent period.

Although migration and immigration research converged considerably in the treatment of certain themes during the industrial era, such scholarship also reveals substantial differences in the inter- and intragroup experiences of internal and international migrants. The most striking contrasts revolved around enslavement, emancipation, and the rise of the Jim Crow system for African Americans; the decline of serfdom and the rapid commercialization of agriculture for southern, central, and eastern Europeans; and U.S. and European imperial expansion for immigrants from Asia and Latin America. Together, these forces undermined the livelihood of growing numbers of rural and semirural people and precipitated the mass movement of diverse ethnic, racial, and nationality groups to urban-industrial America, but the precise timing, magnitude, and nature of these processes varied considerably from group to group.

Chinese immigration to the United States emerged against the background of English penetration of key Chinese port cities and parts of the mainland following the Opium War (1839 to 1842) and another four-year war between 1856 and 1860. The British government not only "opened" China to European and U.S. trade but forced the Chinese people to accept opium imports, pay indemnities for war damages, limit the amount of duties imposed on foreign shippers, and allow the British to occupy the island of Hong Kong as an independent entity. These measures placed hardships on small Chinese landholders, renters, and household manufacturers, precipitated a rise in the number of landless laborers, and led the Chinese government to sign agreements allowing the recruitment of Chinese citizens for labor abroad.

Latino migration and immigration developed against the unique background of shifting U.S.-Mexico relations and rapid social changes in the U.S. economy along the Mexican border. In contrast to other groups discussed in this essay, the Latino population entered the United States through a combination of conquest, immigration, and political settlements. Similar to Native Americans, large numbers of Latino Americans were illegally deprived of the land of their birth. As a result of the Texas Revolution in 1836 and the Mexican-American War of 1846 to 1848, Mexicans in much of the western and southwestern United States became a conquered people. Although the Treaty of Guadalupe Hidalgo, which ended the war, protected the landowning rights of Spanish-speaking people in the region, within a few decades most Mexican residents had lost title to the land through a variety of legal and extralegal acts. In the meantime, changing socioeconomic and political conditions in Mexico (including the revolution of the 1910s and 1920s), on the one hand, and in the southwestern United States, on the other, precipitated increasing migration across the border. During the early twentieth century, U.S. companies and employees regularly looked across the border for contract laborers to work as household, farm, and general laborers in the Southwest. Thus, as historians of Mexican American life repeatedly note, Mexicans were an integral part of the American Southwest before they became immigrants and before they became "illegal aliens."

Upon entering urban-industrial America, migrants faced varying levels of ethnic, racial, and class conflict. Although the National Origins Act of 1924 severely curtailed the number of people coming from southern, central, and eastern European countries, Asian Americans faced the most hostile reception. In a series of federal immigration restriction laws—the Chinese Exclusion Acts of 1882, 1892, 1902, and 1904—Chinese exclusion was made permanent. (It was repealed only in 1943 as a gesture of goodwill in the context of the war with Japan.) At the same time, the so-called "Gentlemen's Agreement" of 1907 between the United States and Japan restricted Japanese labor migration to the United States. To reinforce the ban on Japanese immigration, President Theodore Roosevelt also issued Executive Order 589 prohibiting the secondary movement of Japanese to the mainland from Hawaii, Canada, and Mexico. During the entire period of massive immigration to the United States, from the nineteenth through the midtwentieth centuries, Asians made up less than 1 million of the 40 million immigrants who poured into the country. Most of these came between 1871 and 1910, when an estimated 270,000 Chinese and Japanese entered the country.

Hostility toward Asian immigrants was closely linked to the role of skin color and the status of blacks in American society. Despite emancipation from enslavement and the acquisition of full citizenship rights under the law following the Civil War, African Americans gained little access to land and soon faced the onset of the Jim Crow system. During the late nineteenth and early twentieth centuries, the rapid spread of white supremacist ideas and social practices (institutional segregation, sharecropping, and disfranchisement) undercut the promise of political and economic emancipation for African Americans and fueled the Great Migration of over two million southern blacks to northern and western cities. Industrialists and white workers alike regularly expressed the belief that the new immigrants and black workers were best suited for the most difficult, dirty, and low-paying jobs, but black workers were considered especially apt.

Becoming white and becoming American were tightly interwoven into the fabric of the nation's history, and different immigrant and migrant groups soon learned to distance themselves from blacks. American-born white workers took the bulk of skilled and supervisory jobs; immigrants occupied the majority of semiskilled and so-called unskilled jobs; and blacks were concentrated mainly in the "unskilled," "general labor," and "domestic" categories of work. In the Southwest, Mexican Americans experienced the tensions of being neither black nor white, but they opted to define themselves as white while retaining their sense of identity as Mexicans. Under mounting pressure from the predominantly middle-class League of United Latin American Citizens (formed in 1929), the U.S. Census Bureau defined Mexicans as white during the 1940s and 1950s. For their part, Asian Indians worked hard to hold on to their Caucasian status. In 1917, as noted earlier, the U.S. Supreme Court granted them their wish but still excluded them from immigration on geographical grounds. A few years later, in *U.S. v. Bhagat Singh Thind* (1923), the Supreme Court continued to allow Asian Indians to claim Caucasian status but ruled that they could by no means claim whiteness. Thus, their hopes for full inclusion in U.S. citizenship on the basis of race were dashed.

In addition to important differences among groups, there were also significant cleavages within groups. As indigenous Mexicans and their descendants faced growing difficulties holding on to land in the Southwest, their immigrant counterparts struggled to gain and retain a foothold in the expanding wage labor force of the region. This process produced substantial cleavages and conflict between the increasingly Americanized segments of the Mexican American community and their Mexican-born brothers and sisters. By the same token, although German Jews played an important social welfare role in the lives of new Russian Jews, they often placed distance between themselves and the newcomers. As Jewish newcomers mobilized to demand a greater measure of respect from their host country, many longtime Jewish residents found their demands abrasive and threatening. Such internal cleavages also convulsed the African American community. In the wake of black migration from the deep South during World War I, southern blacks repeatedly complained that their northern black neighbors looked down on them and treated them with disdain.

Within the context of substantial internal and external conflicts, African Americans and immigrants developed their own visions of citizenship, freedom, and industrial democracy and waged vigorous struggles for equal treatment. To counteract diverse forms of discrimination and inequality, they strengthened their internal kin, friend, and communal networks; launched a variety of community-based institutions and movements for social change; and, where possible, forged political alliances with indigenous elites and workers. Although fraught with destructive tensions and social conflicts, these collective efforts pushed the United States toward a more inclusive (though incomplete) social and political agenda over time. The rise of the new industrial unions, the New Deal state, and the gradual growth of the modern civil rights movement all underscored the long-run impact of domestic and international migration on American society. But the full force of these changes would have to await the postwar years and the gradual deindustrialization of the nation's economy.

NOTES

1. Although West Indian immigrants make up a large percentage of New York City's black population, scholars paid little attention to the black immigrant experience until recent times; see Reid (1939), Watkins-Owens (1996), and James (1998).

2. To some extent, the assimilationist model might have provided some scholars from a variety of ethnic and nationality groups with an opportunity to temper some of the most extreme ethnocentric claims of their particular group; see Meier and Rudwick (1986), Hine (1986), and Novick (1988, esp. ch. 14, "Every Group Its Own Historian").

3. In America immigrants would gradually construct new ethnic communities, but such communities would be insufficient to fully counteract physical and psychic alienation from the land of their birth and the land of their choice. As Handlin (1951, 4) put it, his study would "touch upon broken homes, interruptions of a familiar life, separation from known surroundings, the becoming a foreigner and ceasing to belong." These were the processes of alienation, he said, and from the perspective of immigrants, "the history of immigration is a history of alienation and its consequences."

4. While Higham's book did not fit the growing cold war emphasis on consensus and the relative absence of abrasive conflicts in American society, it did not directly challenge the assimilationist paradigm. As Higham (1955, x) put it, "An account of bitterness and strife inevitably catches the people it deals with at one extreme of their temperamental range; a narrative of hatreds tells little about harmony." He also said that cooperation was also important and perhaps even more important than conflict.

5. For a review of this scholarship, see Trotter (1985, 264–82; 1996, 299–319).

6. For a synthesis of this scholarship, see Bodnar (1985).

7. Color consciousness also influenced the development of black ethnicity. As the historian Irma Watkins-Owens (1996, 168) concluded in her study of West Indian immigrants to New York City, "The color issue . . . is mentioned so frequently by dark-skinned Caribbean immigrants and others as a factor in social relations that it appears certain it also heightened ethnic strife."

8. See also Arnesen (2001) and responses to Arnesen's essay by James Barrett and others in *International Labor and Working Class History* 60(Fall): 33–80.

REFERENCES

Almaguer, Tomás. 1987. "Ideological Distortions in Recent Chicano Historiography: The Internal Model and Chicano Historical Interpretation." *Aztlán* 18(1, Spring): 7–27.

Arnesen, Eric. 2001. "Whiteness and the Historians' Imagination." *International Labor and Working Class History* 60(Fall): 3–32.

Barrett, James. 1992. "Americanization from the Bottom Up: Immigration and the Remaking of the Working Class in the United States, 1880–1930." *Journal of American History* 79(3, December): 996–1020.

Barrett, James R., and David Roediger. 1997. "In Between Peoples: Race, Nationality, and the 'New Immigrant' Working Class." *Journal of American Ethnic History* 16(3, Spring): 3–4.

Bay, Mia. 2000. *The White Image in the Black Mind: African American Ideas About White People, 1830–1925.* New York: Oxford University Press.

Berry, Chad. 2000. *Southern Migrants, Northern Exiles.* Urbana: University of Illinois Press.

Bodnar, John. 1985. *The Transplanted: A History of Immigrants in Urban America.* Bloomington: Indiana University Press.

Bukowczyk, John J. 1996. "Introduction, Forum: Thomas and Znaniecki's *The Polish Peasant in Europe and America.*" *Journal of American Ethnic History* 16(1, Fall): 3–15.

Bulmer, Martin. 1984. *The Chicago School of Sociology: Institutionalization, Diversity, and the Rise of Sociological Research.* Chicago: University of Chicago Press.

Carroll, Charles. 2000. *The Negro, A Beast.* Manchester, N.H.: Ayer Company Publisher. (Orig. pub. 1900.)

Chan, Sucheng. 1990. "European and Asian Immigration into the United States in Comparative Perspective, 1820s to 1920s." In *Immigration Reconsidered: History, Sociology, and Politics*, edited by Virginia Yans-McLaughlin. New York: Oxford University Press.

Chicago Commission on Race Relations. 1968. *The Negro in Chicago: A Study of Race Relations and a Race Riot.* New York: Arno Press. (Orig. pub. 1922.)

Coolidge, Mary. 1969. *Chinese Immigration.* Reprint. New York: Arno Press. (Orig. pub. 1909.)

Dixon, Thomas. 1967. *The Leopard's Spots.* New York: Doubleday. (Orig. pub. 1902.)

———. 1905. *The Clansman: An Historical Romance of the Ku Klux Klan.* New York: American News Co.

Du Bois, W. E. B. 1996. *The Philadelphia Negro: A Social Study.* Reprint. Philadelphia: University of Pennsylvania Press. (Orig. pub. 1899.)

Faue, Elizabeth. 1993. "Gender and the Reconstruction of Labor History, An Introduction." *Labor History* 34(2–3, Spring-Summer): 169–77.

Foley, Neil. 1997. *The White Scourge: Mexicans, Blacks, and Poor Whites in Texas Cotton Culture.* Berkeley: University of California Press.

Foner, Nancy. 2000. *From Ellis Island to JFK: New York's Two Great Waves of Immigration.* New Haven, Conn., and New York: Yale University Press and Russell Sage Foundation.

———. 2002. "Response." *Journal of American Ethnic History* 21(4, Summer): 102–19.

Fredrickson, George M. 1971. *The Black Image in the White Mind: The Debate on Afro-American Character and Destiny, 1817–1914.* New York: Harper & Row.

Friday, Chris. 1994. "Asian American Labor and Historical Interpretation." *Labor History* 35(4, Fall): 524–46.

Friedlander, Henry. 1995. *The Origins of Nazi Genocide: From Euthanasia to the Final Solution.* Chapel Hill: University of North Carolina Press.

Fuchs, Lawrence H. 1990. "The Reactions of Black Americans to Immigration." In *Immigration Reconsidered: History, Sociology, and Politics*, edited by Virginia Yans-McLaughlin. New York: Oxford University Press.

Gjerde, Jon. 1999. "The Social History of Immigration to and Ethnicity in the United States." *Journal of American Ethnic History* 18(4, Summer): 40–65.

Gottlieb, Peter. 1987. *Making Their Own Way: Southern Blacks' Migration to Pittsburgh, 1916–30.* Urbana: University of Illinois Press.

Grant, Madison. 1970. *The Passing of the Great Race.* New York: Arno. (Orig. pub. 1916.)

Gregory, James N. 1989. *American Exodus: The Dust Bowl Migration and Okie Culture in California.* New York: Oxford University Press.

Grossman, James. 1989. *Land of Hope: Chicago, Black Southerners, and the Great Migration.* Chicago: University of Chicago Press.

Guerin-Gonzales, Camille. 1994. "Conversing Across Boundaries of Race, Ethnicity, Class, Gender, and Region: Latino and Latina Labor History." *Labor History* 24(4, Fall): 547–63.

Gutiérrez, David G. 1993. "Significance to Whom? Mexican Americans and the History of the American West." *Western Historical Quarterly* 24(4, November): 519–39.

———. 1995. *Walls and Mirrors: Mexican Americans, Mexican Immigrants, and the Politics of Ethnicity.* Berkeley: University of California Press.

Guy, Roger. 2000. "A Common Ground: Urban Adaptation and Appalachian Unity." In *Appala-*

chian Odyssey: Historical Perspectives on the Great Migration, edited by Phillip J. Obermiller, Thomas E. Wagner, and E. Bruce Tucker. Westport, Conn.: Praeger.

Handlin, Oscar. 1951. *The Uprooted: The Epic Story of the Great Migrations That Made the American People.* Boston: Little, Brown.

———. 1959. *The Newcomers.* Garden City, N.Y.: Doubleday.

Hertzberg, Arthur, and Aron Hirt-Maheimer. 1998. *Jews: The Essence and Character of a People.* San Francisco: Harper San Francisco.

Higham, John. 1955. *Strangers in the Land: Patterns of American Nativism, 1860–1925.* New Brunswick, N.J.: Rutgers University Press.

———. 1973. *History: Professional Scholarship in America.* New York: Harper & Row.

———. 1975. *Send These to Me: Jews and Other Immigrants in Urban America.* New York: Atheneum.

Hine, Darlene Clark, ed. 1986. *The State of Afro-American History: Past, Present, and Future.* Baton Rouge: Louisiana State University Press.

———. 1991. "Black Migration to the Urban Midwest: The Gender Dimension, 1915–1945." In *The Great Migration in Historical Perspective: New Dimensions of Race, Class, and Gender,* edited by Joe W. Trotter. Bloomington: Indiana University Press.

Hirschman, Charles, Philip Kasinitz, and Josh DeWind, eds. 1999. *The Handbook of International Migration: The American Experience.* New York: Russell Sage Foundation.

Hune, Sharon. 1989. "Introduction: Pacific Migration Defined by American Historians and Social Theorists Up to the 1960s." In *Asian American Studies: An Annotated Bibliography and Research Guide,* edited by Hyung-chan Kim. New York: Greenwood.

Ichihashi, Yamato. 1969. *Japanese in the United States.* Reprint. New York: Arno Press. (Orig. pub. 1932.)

Jacobson, Matthew Frye. 1998. *Whiteness of a Different Color: European Immigrants and the Alchemy of Race.* Cambridge, Mass.: Harvard University Press.

James, Winston. 1998. *Holding Aloft the Banner of Ethiopia: Caribbean Radicalism in Early Twentieth-Century America.* New York: Verso.

Katz, Michael B., and Thomas J. Sugrue. 1998. *W. E. B. Du Bois, Race, and the City: The Philadelphia Negro and Its Legacy.* Philadelphia: University of Pennsylvania Press.

Kennedy, Louise. 1930. *The Negro Peasant Turns Cityward: Effects of Recent Migrations to Northern Cities.* New York: Columbia University Press.

Kolchin, Peter. 2002. "Whiteness Studies: The New History of Race in America." *Journal of American History* 89(1, June): 154–73.

Lasker, Bruno. 1931. *Filipino Immigration to the Continental United States and to Hawaii.* Chicago: University of Chicago Press.

Lewis, David Levering. 1993. *W. E. B. Du Bois: Biography of a Race, 1868–1919.* New York: Henry Holt and Co.

Lewis, Earl. 1996. "Race." In *Encyclopedia of the United States in the Twentieth Century,* edited by Stanley Kutler. New York: Scribner.

Lieberson, Stanley. 1963. *Ethnic Patterns in American Cities.* New York: Free Press.

———. 1980. *A Piece of the Pie: Blacks and White Immigrants Since 1880.* Berkeley: University of California Press.

Ling, Huping. 2000. "Family and Marriage of Late-Nineteenth- and Early-Twentieth-Century Chinese Immigrant Women." *Journal of American Ethnic History* 19(2, Winter): 43–63.

Meier, August, and Elliott Rudwick. 1986. *Black History and the Historical Profession, 1915–1980.* Urbana: University of Illinois Press.

Model, Suzanne W. 1990. "Work and Family: Blacks and Immigrants from South and East Europe." In *Immigration Reconsidered: History, Sociology, and Politics,* edited by Virginia Yans-McLaughlin. New York: Oxford University Press.

Myrdal, Gunnar. 1944. *An American Dilemma: The Negro and Modern Democracy.* New York: Random House.

Novick, Peter. 1988. *That Noble Dream: The "Objectivity Question" and the American Historical Profession.* Cambridge: Cambridge University Press.

Obermiller, Phillip J., Thomas E. Wagner, and E. Bruce Tucker, ed. 2000. *Appalachian Odyssey: Historical Perspectives on the Great Migration*. Westport, Conn.: Praeger.

O'Connor, Alice. 2001. *Poverty Knowledge: Social Science, Social Policy, and the Poor in Twentieth-Century U.S. History*. Princeton, N.J.: Princeton University Press.

Park, Robert. 1934. "Race Relations and Certain Frontiers." In *Race Relations and Culture Contacts*, edited by E. B. Reuter. New York: McGraw-Hill.

———. 1939. "The Nature of Race Relations." In *Race Relations and the Race Problem*, edited by Edgar Thompson. Durham, N.C.: Duke University Press.

———. 1950. *Race and Culture*. Glencoe, Ill.: Free Press.

Park, Robert E., Ernest W. Burgess, and Roderick D. McKenzie, eds. 1925. *The City*. Chicago: University of Chicago Press.

Peffer, George Anthony. 1992. "From Under the Sojourner's Shadow: A Historiographical Study of Chinese Female Immigration in America, 1852–1882." *Journal of American Ethnic History* 11(3, Spring): 41–67.

Poltawska, Wanda. 1999. "The Human 'Guinea Pigs' of Ravensbruck." In *When Sorry Isn't Enough: The Controversy over Apologies and Reparations*, edited by Roy L. Brooks. New York: New York University Press.

Reid, Ira de Augustine. 1939. *The Negro Immigrant, His Background, Characteristics, and Social Adjustment, 1899–1937*. New York: Columbia University Press.

Riesler, Mark. 1976. *By the Sweat of Their Brow: Mexican Immigrant Labor in the United States, 1900–1940*. Westport, Conn.: Greenwood.

Roediger, David R. 1991. *The Wages of Whiteness: Race and the Making of the American Working Class*. New York: Verso.

Rumbaut, Rubén G. 1999. "Assimilation and Its Discontents: Ironies and Paradoxes." In *The Handbook of International Migration*, edited by Charles Hirschman, Philip Kasinitz, and Josh DeWind. New York: Russell Sage Foundation.

Saragoza, Alex M. 1989–90. "Recent Chicano Historiography: An Interpretive Essay." *Aztlán* 19(1, Spring): 1–77.

Saveth, Edward N. 1948. *American Historians and European Immigrants, 1875–1925*. New York: Columbia University Press.

Schlesinger, Arthur M. 1921. "The Significance of Immigration in American History." *American Journal of Sociology* 27(1, July): 71–85.

Schufeldt, Robert. 1907. *The Negro, A Menace to American Civilization*. Boston: Richard G. Badger, The Gorham Press.

Taeuber, Karl E., and Alma F. Taeuber. 1965. *Negroes in Cities*. Chicago: Aldine.

Takaki, Ronald. 1993. *A Different Mirror: A History of Multicultural America*. Boston: Little, Brown.

Thernstrom, Stephen. 1973. *The Other Bostonians: Poverty and Progress in the American Metropolis, 1880–1970*. Cambridge, Mass.: Harvard University Press.

Thomas, William I., and Florian Znaniecki. 1918–20. *The Polish Peasant in Europe and America: Monograph of an Immigrant Group*. Chicago: University of Chicago Press.

Trotter, Joe W. 1985. *Black Milwaukee: The Making of an Industrial Proletariat, 1915–1945*. Urbana: University of Illinois.

———. 1991. *The Great Migration in Historical Perspective: New Dimensions of Race, Class, and Gender*. Bloomington: Indiana University Press.

———. 1996. "African Americans in the City: The Industrial Era, 1900–1950." In *The New African American Urban History*, edited by Kenneth M. Goings and Raymond A. Mohl. Thousand Oaks, Calif.: Sage Publications.

———. 2001. *The African American Experience*. Boston: Houghton Mifflin.

Tucker, Bruce. 2000. "Transforming Mountain Folk: Roscoe Giffin and the Invention of Urban Appalachia." In *Appalachian Odyssey: Historical Perspectives on the Great Migration*, edited by Phillip J. Obermiller, Thomas E. Wagner, and E. Bruce Tucker. Westport, Conn.: Praeger.

U.S. Department of Labor. 1969. *Negro Migration in 1916–1917*. Reprint. New York: Negro Universities Press. (Orig. pub. 1919.)

Vecoli, Rudolph J. 1964. "Contadini in Chicago: A Critique of *The Uprooted.*" *Journal of American History* 51(3, December): 404–17.

Watkins-Owens, Irma. 1996. *Blood Relations: Caribbean Immigrants and the Harlem Community, 1900–1930.* Bloomington: Indiana University Press.

Weinberg, Sidney Stahl. 1992. "The Treatment of Women in Immigration History: A Call for Change." *Journal of American Ethnic History* 11(4, Summer): 25–46.

Williams, Vernon J., Jr. 1989. *From a Caste to a Minority: Changing Attitudes of American Sociologists Toward Afro-Americans, 1896–1945.* New York: Greenwood.

Woodson, Carter G. 1918. *A Century of Negro Migration.* New York: Russell and Russell.

Gerald Jaynes

Chapter 5

Immigration and the Social Construction of Otherness: "Underclass" Stigma and Intergroup Relations

Clearly, in the United States during the past few decades, intergroup relations have changed significantly. Moreover, it is just as clear that intergroup stratification, although still sharp, is less rigid than before. Minorities have achieved great advances in occupational mobility, incomes, educational attainments, and acceptance in previously prohibited social roles. Unfortunately, Americans' unbridled self-congratulation regarding this progress is tempered by the disproportionate numbers of minorities who remain jobless or hold the lowest-status occupations, live in poverty, are school dropouts, and, regardless of status attainments, still encounter differential treatment in public spaces and in access to important social institutions and organizations. The coexistence of large numbers of poor minorities with new black and tan middle classes is the most visible reminder of U.S. society's racist past, its successes in overcoming that legacy, and the complexities defining contemporary intergroup relations. Any explication of those relations must acknowledge and explain the intensified class divisions within minority groups and the social effects of those class divisions, and it must explain immigration's effects on the rapidly changing demographic landscape that is redefining social status in contemporary America.

This essay examines the fundamental determinants of these complex relations. It argues that intergroup relations in the United States are structured by a broader set of racialized class relations that can be understood by deconstructing the social meaning and function of the concept of the "underclass." All intergroup relations rest on some group's definition of "the other." The essay argues that the underclass, a metaphor for a host of negative traits defining U.S. society's collective definition of "the other," is the foundation on which rests middle-class America's conditions for any individual's exclusion from the polity. Social relations between those included (broadly construed as the middle classes) and those excluded (the underclass) necessarily define a host of other intergroup relations because of the disproportionate numbers of people of color among the excluded.

By intergroup relations I refer to how ethnic groups perceive and treat one another. My primary interest in such relations flows from the fact that they partially structure social stratification. They do so because a society's distribution of social resources generally endows some groups with disproportionate power to affect everyone's opportunities. Because immigration alters a society's demographic landscape, it can affect interethnic perceptions and the construction and treatment of out-groups. However, immigration can either ratify or subvert a host society's existing intergroup relations.

The ultimate outcome hinges on the precise ways in which immigrants are perceived and treated, how immigration affects perceptions and treatment of native-born groups, and whether and how new ethnic-racial categories and alignments are constructed to explain the social reality transformed by demographic change. This process is determined within the context of the host society's traditional discursive practices: how its culture explains and understands intergroup relations, ethnic difference, and social stratification.

Space prohibits addressing each of these topics fully. My strategy is to outline a conceptual model of contemporary intergroup relations that looks at aspects of immigration's role as cause and effect. I theorize that intergroup relations are dominated by interactions between the classical social constructions of class and race. These race-class relations are mediated through behaviors guided by group stereotyping, which is epitomized in public discourse about the underclass, a more recent social construction and America's most recent "middle-class other." This public discourse and the intergroup relations that underlie it (like the signifier "underclass") exhibit greater plasticity and less rigid racial stratification than did analogous social practices of the past. Immigration has important effects on all three of these social constructions. Furthermore, the sheer volume and ethnic diversity of contemporary immigration dictate that future intergroup relations largely depend on the conditions under which immigrants and their progeny are incorporated into American society. The social dynamics undergirding those conditions of incorporation—second-generation "assimilation" versus "decline"—are codeterminate and mutually dependent, with both the racialized class relations and the public discourse defining the "underclass" other.

We begin with some definitions. By prejudice I refer to a cognitive process emanating from humankind's innate capacity to categorize and then to rationalize salient categories (stereotypes) through emotive reasoning. The connection between emotional commitment and stereotyped beliefs is our warrant for labeling prejudice irrational prejudgment. The attitudes of people holding prejudiced beliefs are virtually immune to both counterempirical evidence and reasoned demonstrations that their rationalized beliefs are logically faulty. Such prejudice-based attitudes should be differentiated from "calculated prejudgment"—a cognitive process that is also undergirded by stereotyping from "facts" that are taken to be true. Moreover, the facts on which a calculated prejudgment is based may, as in the case of prejudice, be false, and the reasoning process through which it is derived faulty. However, unlike prejudiced people, a person behaving on the basis of calculated prejudgment (having no emotional commitment to her beliefs) can be convinced to alter her behavior if shown her facts or reasoning are faulty. The distinction underlies a fundamental transformation in America's intergroup relations.

Until recently, whites' behaviors in intergroup settings were commonly driven by widespread social mores condoning discrimination. Furthermore, whites' stereotypes of minority groups reflected a need to rationalize their social prejudices and group privilege. Today intergroup relations are more likely to be driven by the calculated prejudgments of middle-class Americans (of all colors) stereotyping minorities in settings where the situation renders ambiguous the race-class status of participants. Intergroup relations are driven by widespread public condemnation of blatantly prejudiced behavior but also by acceptance of norms condoning avoidance of those social settings presumed to be *contaminated* by the underclass. The transformation improves the possibilities for minority status attainment because, unlike prejudice-based discrimination, discrimination based on calculated prejudgment is rebuttable. Given evidence that they have erred, contemporary discriminators can often be persuaded to alter their behavior. Minorities who can differentiate themselves from the stereotypes gain access to avenues of upward mobility. Those who do not rebut the underclass presumption find their opportunities severely restricted by intergroup relations. In summary:

- Discrimination is acceptable to many Americans if it can be attributed to motives that invoke salient images of the underclass. Social norms requiring unequivocally equal treatment of all races are undercut by justifying the discriminatory treatment of minorities on the basis of a prejudgment that the target displayed underclass behavior.

- In consequence, the character of intergroup relations is determined less by the prejudices of the participants than by the information emitted by the settings within which the relations occur. Absent evidence to the contrary, minorities are presumed to be underclass and avoided (thus, frequently discriminated against). However, the presumption of underclass status is rebuttable. Where the setting itself or the behavior and demeanor of the minority in question strongly precludes the label "underclass," intergroup relations are likely to be equalitarian.

These intergroup relations are not founded on a consciously articulated social norm. However, they accurately describe middle-class Americans' behavior. Moreover, because of their disproportionate control of social resources, this transformation in the behavior of middle-class whites has several important correlatives for society at large, among them:

1. Movement from prejudice to calculated prejudgment has enhanced minorities' ability to improve their status by individual effort.

2. Even within groups, the means of acquiring the social capital necessary to rebut the "underclass" label are sharply differentiated because of class inequalities; such inequalities structure intergenerational poverty and "second-generation decline" among socially isolated native-born and immigrant minority populations, respectively.

3. The experiences and opportunities confronted by contemporary migrants of color are now more comparable to those of white ethnic immigrants of the past.

These new intergroup relations are consequences of several macrosocial processes remaking contemporary America.

INTERGROUP RELATIONS: UNDERCLASS AND SOCIAL STIGMA

In sociohistorical terms, the evolution of contemporary intergroup relations may be traced to three macrosocial events: the civil rights movement, the 1965 Hart-Celler Act opening immigration opportunities to people of color worldwide, and deindustrialization. During the 1970s nascent effects of these three events—a growing black middle class, accelerating immigration of people of color, and drastic reductions in the weekly wages of less-educated workers—determined an array of important social changes and altered Americans' social reality. Slowly, that altered reality forced public discourse and behaviors to adapt. Improved economic and educational opportunities for minorities and increased immigration from outside Europe contributed to a burgeoning middle class of color at the very time when the reductions in poverty tallied during the previous two decades came to a halt. From a historical low about 11 percent in 1973, the U.S. poverty rate increased and then hovered above 12 percent throughout the 1980s. With population growing, the stagnant rate of poverty translated into a large increase in the numbers of poor Americans. Concentrated in the central cities of large urban metropolises and given extended media coverage, the faces of the dependent poor remained disproportionately black, but the immigration of poor people of color from Asia, the Caribbean, and the Americas increased diversity among the poor as well as the general population. Ultimately, both increased visibility of middle-class minorities, and the diverse complexions of the poverty population made race (from the perspective of a black-white paradigm) a less reliable guide for identifying the dependent poor.

As the civil rights movement restructured public norms about the treatment of people of color, middle class–oriented minorities attained unprecedented social status positions. Simultaneously, deindustrialization deepened the social distress of the poor, further differentiating class divisions within minority groups. The latter outcome increased the attention that society gave to negative social behaviors among the poor as stereotyped attributions of poor minorities became more salient (for a discussion of poverty during this period, see Danziger and Gottschalk 1995; for discussions of intergroup relations and stratification, see Jaynes and Williams 1989 and Smelser, Wilson, and Mitchell 2001). Mass immigration of peoples of color occupying diverse class positions reinforces each of these trends. Many Americans find themselves facing a conundrum. Public expectations require equal treatment of minorities, but the highly disapproved and publicized behaviors of inner-city minorities intensify negative stereotypes of all minorities. These behaviors bolster old prejudices, create new fears, and leave many people ambivalent toward norms of equal treatment. Current race relations resolve this conundrum in the following manner: while pure racial prejudice has declined significantly, differential treatment of people of color has been transformed but has failed to decline proportionately. Differential treatment is now more likely to be based on behavior that instantiates calculated prejudgments and is less likely to be a behavioral expression of pure "prejudice."

The major burden of differential treatment falls on the poor minorities who are least able to rebut the presumption that they are underclass. The disproportionate incidence of negative treatment of poor native-born and immigrant minorities is a major means by which social relations structure their inadequate opportunities for social mobility. The differential access to opportunities also sharpens class divisions within minority groups. The explicit means through which this effect is transmitted in everyday social relations is through the social role assumed by the highly publicized and disdained behaviors of some poor minorities. The label "underclass," a social construct currently structuring how Americans understand race and class, defines that social role. Through the highly publicized and disproportionate participation of inner-city minorities in acts of violence, incarceration, poor school performance, teen parenthood, and recycled poverty, images of, discourse about, and social avoidance of those labeled "underclass" has cast a dominating influence over intergroup relations throughout the United States.

As social restrictions on minorities perceived to be underclass become more debilitating, powerful incentives spur those minorities most equipped to do so to adopt assimilative behaviors to avoid the stigma associated with the underclass. Within

groups, assimilative behaviors induced by the prospect of upward mobility strain tensions across classes. Across groups, tensions are also strained as other minorities seek
to avoid association with the most stigmatized group, the black underclass. Public discourse and intergroup relations deteriorate.

Do not misunderstand my argument. Many Americans possess some of the traits
ascribed to the underclass. People of color are disproportionately among them. But
vernacular uses of the term do too much work. No numerically useful group satisfies all
the connotations signified by "underclass." The signifier has no social-scientific value
except where used symbolically to underscore its actual social function. I use "underclass" to denote the social construct that people refer to when they speak of undesirables whom they wish to avoid. My use of the term is similar to Erving Goffman's
(1974, 2) concept of a "virtual social identity." For Goffman, virtual social identity is a
character imputed to an individual embedded within a given situation and observed to
possess personal attributes that lead the attributor to classify him in a certain category.
The attributions and classification may of course be incorrect. In Goffman's terminology, "underclass" is a "virtual" social identity, while the category and attributes that a
person so classified could be proved to truly possess would be her "actual" social identity. Discrepancies between the two are at the heart of contemporary race relations.[1]

Patterns of Underclass Avoidance

Avoidance of the underclass takes several forms and is motivated by a variety of factors
such as income, personal safety, and social status. Each of these factors has a common
element: the avoider makes a prejudgment that he is about to be in contact with a
member of the underclass or is about to be put in a position where such contact is
impending. We have all heard versions of the basic story. A Latino corporate executive
dressed in an expensive suit and hurrying to a midafternoon meeting cannot get a taxi
to stop until he has his white secretary flag one down; taxi drivers explain their refusal
to stop on the high rate of Latino robberies and a fear of driving into predominantly
minority neighborhoods. Blacks graduate from Ivy League colleges with honors, do
graduate work, and sometimes land highly desirable jobs selling financial securities
only to find that they cannot sell to clients without first disguising their racial identity;
until a client can discover how efficient they are, a trace of a black accent over the
phone or the appearance of a black face immediately signals to many buyers that the
salesman must have had an inferior education and be of low ability. One or two black
families of comparable education and income as their new neighbors move into a previously all-white residential neighborhood. Within a few months FOR SALE signs dot
lawns throughout the area; fleeing whites cite fears of black crime and deteriorating
schools. Within a few years the neighborhood is almost completely minority. Reminiscent of the high-scoring Mexican American high school students in California who
were forced to retake advance placement mathematics exams during the 1980s, at a
Connecticut high school with a diversified student body, a guidance counselor protective of *standards* insists that a black student retake an examination meant to place students in honors classes because she is convinced he could not score as high as he did
on his first test.

Even unprovoked acts of violence against minorities are sometimes perpetrated and
then condoned on the basis of arguments appealing to the existence of the underclass.
For example, in the infamous Bensonhurst case, a black youth looking for help after his
car stalled in a white neighborhood in the New York City area was chased into a street

by whites and killed by oncoming traffic. The white youths who chased him explained their actions by stating that they kept all blacks out of the neighborhood because blacks commit crimes. Similar reasoning has led some local police authorities to instruct officers on street patrol, as a matter of policy, to arbitrarily stop and question blacks found in "white" residential neighborhoods. In Philadelphia, police concerned with the growth of Asian gangs took random pictures of Asian teenagers and placed them in a mug book. In hundreds of communities across the land, black, Latino, and Asian youth are routinely stopped and searched for no legal reason. And in instances when the perpetrators of actual crimes have been identified as black (even falsely), local officials have felt justified in giving police officers a blank-check authorization to stop and search residents of predominantly African American neighborhoods.

Not long ago justice in race relations required that like individuals receive equal treatment regardless of race. For example, for several decades a National Opinion Research Center survey asked respondents whether they agreed that all job seekers should have an equal opportunity for any kind of job regardless of race, color, or creed. In 1944 only 44 percent agreed. By the mid-1970s the percentage agreeing with this principle was 97 percent. However, in practice employers routinely reject job applications from minority aspirants because their addresses are in the wrong neighborhoods or some aspect of their self-presentation (speech, dress, walk, or name) is insufficiently distinguishable from a preconceived notion of the underclass. Even among some liberal intellectuals, unequivocal support for the principle that people should be judged on the basis of their individual merits appeared to be under revision. In the complicated work environments of the 1970s and after, new definitions of job discrimination seemed warranted to some analysts. Some experts argued that employers who discount an individual's predicted work performance because of the average performance of the group to which he belongs are not discriminating. Thus, group membership became a proper consideration for making decisions about individuals in the job market (see Schuman, Steeh, and Bobo 1985; Aigner and Cain 1977; Kirschenman and Neckerman 1991; Newman 2000). Each of these examples illustrates the effects of calculated prejudgments in the presence of statistical correlation between race and status. Taxi drivers and police officers practice racial profiling because racial differences in crime statistics encourage them to treat minorities in terms of their perceived ethnicity rather than as individuals. But discrimination based on such calculated prejudgments (by police, for example) also occur because the general public condones it and too few minority youth are connected to people of influence whose complaints about police harassment might do considerable damage to the career of the law enforcement officers engaged in this practice.

Group Stigma and Social Mobility: Then and Now

To be perceived as a member of the underclass (for example, as a chronically dependent welfare recipient or a member of the criminal class) marks one with a stigma. These attributes are so deeply discrediting to their bearers that behavior toward them that would generally draw sharp social opprobrium is widely condoned as a means of avoiding contact with the underclass. A stigma is a moral condition, a means of classifying people outside the circle of a community's norms of mutual obligation and respect. For the ancient Greeks, stigma referred to a physical sign of disgrace or subjugation—for example, a brand of slavery or criminality that marked its bearer as someone to be avoided, especially in public places. The modern definition of stigma is a visible characteristic indicative of some undesirable or discreditable quality, action, or circumstance. This trait cannot be said to strictly define the moral disgrace itself. It merely indicates by empirical association that the bearer may possess disgraceful qualities. The distinction is fully analogous to the recent transformation in intergroup relations. In the past, dark skin was a stigma in the same sense that the ancient Greeks used the word. Such skin color was the target of prejudice. Today it is more accurate to say that dark skin color is a marker that frequently carries the presumption of underclass stigma. However, that presumption or calculated prejudgment is rebuttable. It is the kind of stigma that approximates the experience of upwardly mobile white ethnic immigrants of the early twentieth century. Thus, to an extent not possible in the past, people of color, often presumed to be underclass and therefore unworthy of close social contact, may present evidence that the presumption is unwarranted. They may attempt to demonstrate that their actual social identity differs from the category of "underclass."

The behaviors adopted by law enforcement officers, taxi drivers, educators, and employers represent calculated decisions to screen individuals and to treat negatively those whose salient characteristics screen poorly. In Goffman's (1974, 44) terminology, the screening agent assigns a virtual social identity to the screened agent; the latter may attempt to break up an otherwise coherent picture to cast doubt on the validity of an anticipated virtual identity, perhaps to establish a different one. I am concerned with real-world settings in which social relations are characterized by the interaction of agents screening other agents who (aware they are being screened) take some action to manipulate the information processed by the screener. In an attempt to alter some important decision, they signal to the screener. People in close proximity to standard representations of the underclass (in physical appearance, language patterns, geography) find that their personal destiny is dictated by the degree to which they are able and willing to distance themselves from this underclass. African Americans of all classes, immigrants of color cloistered within stigmatized inner-city neighborhoods, and the newest cohorts of Asian immigrants too poor and frequently too uneducated to live up to the vaunted stereotype of Asian American success learn that even their most mundane intergroup encounters are conditioned by the possibility that they will be categorized as underclass. People of Puerto Rican, Nicaraguan, Mexican, Panamanian, and Salvadoran descent find that they must negotiate U.S. society's relentless capacity to assimilate them under the homogenizing designation "Hispanic." In doing so, they are perpetually challenged to signal against a negative virtual social identity. Hispanic, argues Ilan Stavans (1995, 25), is "a stereotyping machine" whose "synonyms are drug addict, criminal, prison inmate, and unmarried mother." A high school student who emigrated with his parents from South America to Washington's northern Virginia suburbs expresses the problem this way:

> Central Americans—especially Salvadorans—are giving the rest of us the wrong image. Their fathers and mothers have no control over them, so they just do what they want. Now Americans look at all of us like we are in gangs. If I dress funky on the weekends and go into a store, people look at me like I have a gun. (Welsh 1995, C4)

Minorities attempting to improve their social position by gaining access to schools and decent jobs must emit signals that penetrate the screening process and assure the decisionmaker that they are exceptions. Thus, an Ivy League graduate student confides that early in her childhood she deduced that success required that she not merely learn to speak "standard" English but also that she lose her black accent. Her experience is echoed in many similar confessions by black professionals. The native-born black's flight from her ethnic accent serves the same purpose that emphasizing ethnicity does for many black immigrants. Expecting immigrant status to be a negative, as it generally would be for white immigrants, immigrants of color are surprised to find that their immigrant status is a social benefit. Black Caribbean immigrants and many of their children retain audible and visible markers of their Caribbean ethnicity to differentiate themselves from African Americans. By doing so, they signal to employers (presumed to be negatively screening African Americans) that they are "good blacks." This is a flight from the "underclass" label, not a flight from black identity. It is likely to be most pronounced among upwardly mobile blacks of working-class background and among all blacks in settings where class origins are difficult to discern (Cose 1996; Waters 1996, 1999; Kirschenman and Neckerman 1991; Bourgois 1996).

Flight from stereotyped racial identities can offer large monetary payoffs. Minorities labeled "middle-class" and therefore "acceptable" are not subjected to the most damaging discriminations. Because doors are not peremptorily slammed in their faces, they enjoy much better opportunities than do minorities labeled "unacceptable." Why do not all minorities take advantage of these potential opportunities to achieve?

The virtual social identity of "underclass" may be rebutted in one of two ways: the person at risk may trump the impending imputation completely by signaling that she is middle-class; less ambitiously, she may signal that she is not underclass. To signal that one is middle-class when one's social background is not is a very difficult undertaking. It is nearly as difficult, however, to signal that one is not underclass. To signal successfully that one is not a member of the underclass requires possessing the social information and skill to do so. Just as important, one must believe that the payoff from doing so will be sufficient to warrant the effort. Minorities who learn to successfully signal this way are generally of two kinds. There are those who dedicate themselves to imitating all of the indicators of middle-class culture with which they come into contact; such imitators cannot help but appear sycophantic within their own environment. Then there are those with experience in settings (schools and neighborhoods) that are numerically dominated by members of the middle classes who become accustomed to either assimilating or accommodating expectations of conduct and demeanor in middle-class institutions. Minorities from disadvantaged backgrounds have the most limited social experiences from which to draw in their attempts to negotiate middle-class institutions. Such negotiation comes with significant social and psychic costs.

As Joel Perlmann and Roger Waldinger (1999, 913–14) point out, certain costs and benefits of social mobility are shared by all second generations. During earlier historical periods, unusual upward mobility among children of Irish and Italian descent threatened the normal behavioral and role patterns that structured their communities' lines of authority and expectations of individual behavior. Social norms curtailing extravagant dreams of upward mobility among young people provided ethnically identified and resource-poor communities with social cohesion and protection against a brain drain to the middle classes that might have endangered the functioning of these communities' precarious economic and political niches. Aberrant behavior (middle-class striving) often triggered sharp social sanctions against individual deviants. Equivalent sanctions persist among poor blacks and other economically vulnerable groups. One such sanction is the practice of denigrating upwardly mobile group members with pejorative labels. Thus, among Chinese immigrants and Chinese Americans, the American-born are sometimes referred to as "jook sing," a pejorative name that literally denotes the hollow part of a bamboo pole. Applied to a person, it comments on that person's lack of knowledge and failure to follow Chinese cultural traditions. Among Mexican Americans, an analogous term is "vendido"—someone who consciously ignores her own heritage for another one.

Richard Rodriguez (1982, 26–29) was called "pocho," a Chicano expression that might translate into "Uncle Tom." Rodriguez writes of the pain of assimilation as he consciously chose to imitate and become the Anglo other. His namesake, Luis Rodriguez (1993), followed a different path to the middle class. Witnessing to the identity-stripping rites of passage experienced by many poor Latinos in urban school systems, he writes of identity search and rebellion against assimilation in a mold more reminiscent of the youthful Malcolm X or Harlem's Claude Brown. It is valuable to examine the similarities between these accounts of social mobility and those undergone by many white ethnics, but the comparisons are incomplete. What we find in these examples is in one sense a replication of a process of social assimilation and acculturation undergone by millions of white ethnic immigrants who experienced the psychic pain accompanying the loss of ethnic ties due to upward mobility. In Richard Rodriguez's phrase, there is a conscious decision to trade private space for a place at the public table. But the immigrant analogy can presume too much. For example, as with African Americans, the Latino preoccupation with self as both thesis and antithesis of the American identity is too intimately tied to New World origins and too resilient a cultural marker to categorize Latino American identity formation as one more example of assimilation to an American ideal. Proof of this cultural resistance is easily found in contemporary Latino American literature, a legacy of antecedents such as countless Mexican American corrodos and testimonies ranging from Americo Paredes's semifictional (1940) novel *George Washington Gomez* to Piri Thomas's *Down These Mean Streets* (for a discussion of Paredes, see Portales 2000). While immigrants have occupied an important place in Americans' definition of the "other," for each white ethnic group this status has generally been transitory and restricted to specific geographic regions. The otherness of people of color has proven a more salient and lasting basis on which Americans could base the social construction of the other.[2] Moreover, for the most stigmatized groups of color, the possibility that they might rebut a presumption of inferiority has only recently become a feasible strategy for upward mobility. The process by which it occurred is highly instructive.

IMMIGRATION AND THE
DISCOURSE OF RACE RELATIONS

The social scientists who first applied the term "underclass" to the post–World War II American situation intended it as a clinical term to describe fundamental changes occurring in America's racial and class structures.[3] With increasing prevalence, whites were recognizing higher-status blacks and treating them differently from poor blacks. The concept of an underclass formally differentiated two classes of African Americans to emphasize the emergence of newly developing class relations within midtwentieth-century race relations. From a sociological perspective, the clinical approach was correct in regard to the ongoing changes in race and class occurring at differing paces throughout society. But the sociological perspective erred insofar as it failed to recognize linkages between the social functions of America's racial and class structures and the cultural functions of America's discourse on opportunity and poverty. In the greater public discourse the rhetorical functions of "underclass" quickly resonated with the established cultural practices through which Americans traditionally understood and explained social stratification. The unintended consequence of introducing the underclass construct has been that during the past few decades it has performed an important cultural function in the discourse on race and opportunity in America.

Discourse about "the underclass" is the modality through which contemporary Americans articulate how they think and feel about issues related to race, class, and economic opportunity. A metaphor and a powerful symbolic form, "underclass" serves two social functions—one primarily cultural and the other socioeconomic. With respect to its cultural function, "underclass" is a signifier with a multiplicity of referents, each evoking deep cultural meanings reflective of mainstream America's self-definition. Because self-definition reveals a culture's conception of the "other," the social construct of "underclass" also reflects mainstream America's deepest anxieties.

From Tocqueville to Myrdal, observers of American society have universally subscribed to two persisting components of an American identity: the belief that the United States is a middle-class society of equal opportunity and the nagging realization that the conditions of people of color challenge this belief. Poverty, both visible and persistent, undermines the belief in equal opportunity and threatens the very core of the American identity. A triumph of America's Puritan heritage, this abiding self-identification as a middle-class society reveals volumes about Americans' perspectives on poverty and class. A partial explanation of attitudes toward poverty and the poor is that they benefit market institutions and therefore are bolstered by the political activities of business and political elites. But a comprehensive analysis of poverty and social welfare policy cannot rely solely on economic determinism and the claim that capitalism requires punitive incentives for low-wage work in order to function well. A complete discussion of the societal foundations of contemporary attitudes toward the poor must acknowledge the existence of independent cultural and religious effects. In that regard, we need not fully subscribe to Weberian notions of Protestantism and the spirit of capitalism to appreciate the cultural roots of Americans' continuing moral condemnation and niggardly treatment of the poor. Michael Walzer (1965, 215–17) reminds us that the Puritan vision of a middle-class society demanded that citizens follow a "vocational calling." Moreover, the social critique contained within that demand excluded unproductive or parasitic classes from society. Thus, the Puritan idea of a middle-class society embraced a form of republicanism that denounced both aristocracy and beggary—two forms of dependency that are threats to the attainment of a homogenous, classless society.

Designating their republic a middle-class society, Americans defined the "other" in terms of aristocratic wealth, on the one hand, and dependent poverty, on the other. Especially during difficult economic periods when the sanctity of the national identity is threatened by erosion in the middle of the status structure, the two extremes of great wealth and poverty provide convenient targets for anxiety transference. To escape collective anxieties of personal status decline and evidence of societal imperfection, vulnerable members of the middle-class look to the "other." Like natives of Bordeaux learning that California wines have encroached on French exports, Americans find structural explanations of poverty destabilizing to the collective self-image. Full and open discourse on the subject could invite a national identity crisis. With the national identity at stake, public discourse about poverty easily confines itself to a debate whose terms are delimited by the faces of the poor. Class and race correlate so strongly that the salience of racial stratification dominates the national consciousness. Discussions of poverty become embroiled in the politics of racial representation. Invariably, poverty is seen as the problem of the "other." Differentiating and excluding dependent "others"—placing them outside the polity bereft of the rights of citizenship and public respect—is rooted deeply in American culture. The nativist and anti-immigration crusades that peaked during the midnineteenth and early twentieth centuries frequently designated recently arrived immigrants as the disfranchised other, but black Americans were seldom far from the center of the nation's consciousness.

Historically, the social function performed by the "other" was given to various ethnic and racial pejoratives, each of whose level of usage depended on geographic location and the volume of in-migration undertaken by various ethnic groups. Perhaps the most enduring and nationally recognized was the signifier "nigger." However, during the past few decades the social construction of mainstream America's "other" has been mediated through the signifier "underclass." Viewed within the context of America's historical dialogue about opportunity and poverty, "underclass" simultaneously signifies both change and continuity. Uses of the term "underclass" show that the dialogue remains fundamentally structured in negative perceptions of race and gender; its uses also reveal how immigration and changing social reality are forcing the dialogue to reflect the pluralistic identity of the poorest other America and the increasing obsolescence of a black-white paradigm for explaining race relations.

It was during the turbulent quarter-century between 1970 and 1995 (when the nascent effects of the civil rights movement altered immigration policy and deindustrialization became clearer) that the social construct "underclass" emerged as the means by which Americans reconceptualized ideas of race, immigration, and poverty to conform to altered social realities. Initially, the signifier "underclass" responded to only two effects of these macrosocial events: the expanding black middle class and deepening poverty in central cities. Revealingly, two of its earliest uses in the national press, 1973 and 1974 articles in *The Public Interest* and *Time*, respectively, chose "underclass" to dramatize the authors' observations of behavioral differences between a subgroup of the inner-city poor and the working poor and growing black middle classes. The new designation was intended to signify new social conditions more dependent on economic and social position—that is, class.

As a social signifier, "underclass" reflects the new socioeconomic realities while also resonating with cultural traditions. Its designation as a class conveys that the situation of the very bottom, that lowest stratum of society, is influenced by social and market forces beyond the control of individuals. Furthermore, the underclass population can no longer be adequately identified by skin color alone. Yet the prefix "under" maintains continuity with cultural traditions stretching back to the colonial era's paternalist administration of the poor law. "Under" suggests inferiority, subordination, below the proper standard—in short, a subclass beneath all classes, completely outside the bounds of respectable society, lacking in civic virtues and therefore undeserving of basic rights of citizenship; a group (such as dependent welfare mothers) whom contemporary paternalist-oriented social analysts, such as political scientist Lawrence Mead (1986), argue can justifiably be subjected to the authority, guidance, control, and instruction of the polity. The rhetorical functions served by "underclass" in public discourse quickly resonated with established cultural practices.

The psychic and social needs reflected by the signifier are clear in the cover story of the August 29, 1977, issue of *Time*, entitled "The American Underclass: Destitute and Desperate in the Land of Plenty." Subtitled "Minority Within a Minority," the article focused on a subgroup of poor inner-city African Americans and Latinos. The definitive traits of the underclass were social isolation, alienation, poverty, and anomalous cultural values, each of which were said to differentiate them from the rest of American society. The power of the signifier to mobilize negative political action was quickly demonstrated by the demonization of poor single-parent black mothers as cheating welfare queens during the presidential campaigns of 1980 and 1984, the demonization of liberal social policy through the image of convict Willie Horton during the presidential campaign of 1988, and the demonization of "illegal immigrants" and those legal immigrants perceived to be potential public dependents during several political campaigns of the 1990s. Democratic pollster Stanley Greenberg concluded that among white Democratic defectors to the Republican Party during the 1980s, "not being black is what constitutes being middle class" (Edsall and Edsall 1991). Although some of Greenberg's respondents appear to have harbored old-fashioned racial prejudices, his conclusion captures the essence of the cultural symbols under discussion because the kinds of statements made about blacks stressed attributions of parasitic dependency. Today the rubric "underclass" is increasingly used to impute similar attributes to poor native-born Latino and Asian Americans and to immigrants of color. Still strongly identified with black people, "underclass" is becoming a much more democratic construct. Reflecting ideals of self against a pejorative name that symbolizes the antithesis of thrift, honesty, industriousness, sobriety, and civic virtue, "underclass" operates as Mr. Hyde for a middle-class Dr. Jekyll (on policy toward the poor, see Gans 1995; Trattner 1994; Katz 1989).

Segmented Assimilation as "Underclass" Contamination

As metaphor, "underclass" signifies the "other" for a middle-class culture steeped in a belief in the ubiquity of equal opportunity. The metaphor also shapes a central issue in the contemporary discourse on immigration. Among academics and journalists, debate about the future social position of the children of immigrants is a major industry: will the second generation replicate the experience of early-twentieth-century European immigrants and assimilate into the American mainstream, or, to put it bluntly, will they become economic failures?

Some sociologists reach an intermediate position, using the "underclass" concept to synthesize mainstream assimilation and second-generation decline into a process they label "segmented assimilation." Proponents of segmented assimilation accept the assimilation model as the general American experience, but they argue that there are two distinct American cultures into which immigrants may assimilate. More fortunate immigrants settle among and adopt the values, aspirations, and behaviors of America's middle class. Their assimilation of middle-class norms ensures their successful incorporation into the mainstream of American life. Others, less fortunate, settle in inner cities near native-born underclass minorities whose adversarial stance toward middle-class culture is claimed to be largely responsible for their poverty. Segmented assimilationists claim that many children of today's immigrants will adopt this adversarial stance and experience downward assimilation and poverty (see Portes and Zhou 1993; Portes and Rumbaut 1996).

In designating contact with the underclass a primary cause of second-generation economic failure, the segmented assimilation hypothesis imitates public discourse. Mirroring that discourse, it substitutes the black box "culture" for an analysis of the complex interactions between social structure and individual agency that determine people's behaviors and social roles. Similar to that discourse, segmented assimilation defines class in terms of subjects' behaviors and whether they are consistent with middle-class norms rather than in terms of position within a structure of social and institutional relations. It is at best a descriptive hypothesis lacking analytic specificity and is not susceptible to empirical falsification. A critique of the segmented assimilation hypothesis is equivalent to critiquing public discourse on the nature of immigration, race, and opportunity in America.

STRUCTURAL COMPONENTS OF SOCIAL AND CULTURAL ASSIMILATION

Guatemalan migrants, with their two-parent household structure and Herculean attachment to the labor force, captured large sectors of service-sector employment throughout the Houston area during the 1990s (see Suro 1999). How does a diagnosis that imitation of underclass pathology underlies "second-generation decline" explain the disturbing gang violence, teen parenthood, and epidemic school dropout rates among their children? How does segmented assimilation illuminate similar developments among Cambodian migrants settling in cities such as Racine, Wisconsin, and Minneapolis, where the black presence is small? Immigrants do not arrive as cultural blank slates ready to encode an American outlook through acculturation into the mainstream or understream. Migrants bring traditions and social outlooks with which they forge independent ways of being American. The social character of recent urban migrations is no new phenomenon.

Historically, the primary source of protracted urban poverty and social recalcitrance has been migrants from impoverished agrarian backgrounds. Black, Irish, Italian, Mexican, and Puerto Rican rural-to-urban migrants have each produced disproportionate numbers of youths attracted to gang activities and other less flagrant signs of opposition and resistance to the social roles for which society has deemed them fit. In ascertaining the structural forces shaping identity formation within a world that provides too few poor youth with the means to balance private and public respect, it is neither feasible nor important to assign historical priority to any single group. Many groups have contributed to the expressive lifestyles and conspicuous consumption patterns indicative of urban youths' attempts to be somebody through symbolic representations of self patterned by the symbiotic relationship between adolescent angst and the marketing of consumer goods. Latinos represent an obvious example. During their long history in the United States, many joined the middle class, but many also remained poor within the barrios of the Southwest and Northeast. In those barrios, generations of Chicanos and Puerto Rican Americans lived their versions of inner-city poverty well before current explanations of black cultural poverty became a dominant paradigm for explaining every group's failure to escape poverty. The black youths who initiated 1990s fashion trends among American teens adapted their contemporary "gangsta" attire from the Pachuco dress style of midtwentieth-century Chicanos of the urban Southwest, who wore long shirts buttoned down and untucked over trousers worn low on the hips. Both groups of youths announce their unflinchingly oppositional identities to the middle classes, who acknowledge their existence only during periods of social disruption, such as the 1968 school walkout by ten thousand Chicano students in East Los Angeles. The "vatos locos" (crazy street men with nothing to lose but their respect), like the street youth of Chinatowns in eastern cities such as Boston, attract less attention than do their black counterparts, but the lives of these rebels of resentment are similar to those of the poor urban blacks credited with contaminating the Latino and Asian American youth who now are replicating communities of poverty.

Both the preexisting and the continuing pockets of social distress suggest that poverty and the oppositional identities adopted by the alienated children of poor immigrants have little to do with cultural contamination from the black poor. The second generation's socioeconomic attainments frequently mirror similarly situated native-born attainments because both groups face the same opportunity-limiting schools, employment chances, and discriminatory patterns of intergroup relations and have similar access to criminal careers. Attitudes, behaviors, and socioeconomic outcomes are structured (but not solely determined) by specific patterns of social identity formation that are common to children of migrants from impoverished agrarian backgrounds.

The ubiquity of several salient experiences in the social incorporation of diverse groups of urban in-migrants suggests that much of the process we label "acculturation" is structured by the migration process per se. Migrants arrive with cultural capital and cultural baggage. During the negotiation process we term "socialization" and "cultural assimilation," how do social structure and culture interact with individual agency to determine social outcomes? The sociological and historical literatures have shown how migration produces a new set of experiences to which migrants must adjust. Moreover, migrants do so in light of their prior experience. The second generation is always caught between the social and cultural demands of the new and the old. But we know little about the systematic dynamics involved in the formation of identities among these youth. Recurrent and widely reported similar rites of passage among urbanizing peoples of disparate origins and sociocultural backgrounds demonstrate that a significant component of this identity formation is the fruit of common structural conditions; the process of urbanization is not haphazard. In a general sense, there are only a few social identities that youth can assume, although they can be clothed with many different superficial cultural innovations.

This argument explains the many similarities in the past behaviors of children of Irish and Italian immigrants and the behaviors of many minorities of color. However, there are differences in the degree to which minorities of color faced blocked opportunities. In decades past, opportunities for minorities of color were blocked by the omnipresent and sometimes venal discriminations of prejudiced whites seeking to justify and maintain their privileges. Since native-born, middle-class-oriented minorities can now raise their social positions, minority immigrants with middle-class orientations can too. With a major qualification, minority immigrants' current economic opportunities resemble those of the European immigrants coming into the United States during the early part of the twentieth century. The qualification pertains to the present period's different economic structure and its more demanding class prerequisites for success. Unlike the early twentieth century, schooling (competency at twelfth-grade levels) and a middle-class presentation of self are necessary to attain reasonable labor market success. To the extent that children from poor social backgrounds are spatially distributed in close proximity with poor minorities, their ability to attain these skills is obviously compromised. However, much of that compromised condition is due to the social difficulties experienced by all poor people living in such circumstances, not to a cultural contamination from the native-born.

The strong association between skin color and residential segregation from whites suggests that immigrants do not have unfettered opportunity to settle where they wish. Where they reside and work—and consequently, where their children will be schooled and socialized—depends on the socioeconomic status and ethnicities that migrants bring with them. Whether the background status of immigrants is high or low, the structural forces influencing identity formation among similarly situated native groups and children of migrants are likely to affect similar identity choices. Similar outcomes are the likely product of similar positions within the nation's structure of social relations, and this is surely true independent of any cultural contamination through mere association with native-born role models.

CONCLUSION

Second-generation outcomes already evince significant bifurcation: majorities of children of immigrants who arrived with middle-class-oriented social backgrounds appear to be joining the American middle class, while significant numbers of the children of poor and less-educated immigrants exhibit disturbing school dropout rates and continuing poverty. Currently, aggregated statistics dominated by huge influxes of migrants not acculturated to the urban U.S. middle-class culture and exhibiting social characteristics (a migrant work ethic and quiescent behaviors) that subsequent generations will not adopt conceal the magnitude of a festering alienation among the youth of several minority groups. Continuing cohorts of fresh migrants reinforce invidious comparisons between the native-born poor and immigrants. Such comparisons serve as support for the dominant paradigms used to explain poverty and equal opportunity. These invidious comparisons especially illuminate the cultural functioning of the social construction "underclass"—as, for example, when college-educated immigrant entrepreneurs are used to argue that poor native-born populations are lazy or languishing in a pathological culture. The comparisons are just as informative when the native-born are vilified for not competing effectively for low-wage jobs against poor immigrants whose children in fact will not sustain the work ethic of their parents but become more like the natives. These are the intergroup relations that intensify enmities beyond the envy and hostility that can develop from competition for scarce resources.

Elsewhere (Jaynes 2002) I refer to the alienated youths living in contemporary poverty as "the malcontented." Some commentators argue that the most destructive oppositional agencies are confined to a minority of any group and that therefore the negative effects that these malcontented youths have on the progress of their ethnic groups is minimal. One may agree with the factual premise but disagree with the conclusion. The negative effects of these behaviors (crime, teen parenthood, poor school performance) are much larger than might be predicted by their numerical representation in the population. Given the manner in which intergroup relations operate through the underclass paradigm, second-generation poverty and oppositional behaviors among a segment of any group are a catalyst to deepened discrimination against the larger group. The association of poverty and oppositional behavior with any minority group threatens that group with the "underclass" stigma and discriminatory treatment. Already groups previously immune to the underclass stigma are being associated with it more often. What further consequences does a reinvigorated and multiracial conceptualization of the underclass have for society?

Increased ethnic diversity within the underclass portends a profound transformation in American perceptions of race and in its intergroup relations. My own view is that although the cultural tradition confounding poverty and dependency with being African American will die hard, it will die. Two factors account for this prognostication. First, the continuing slide into inner-city poverty of subsequent generations of today's poor agrarian migrants (for example, Central Americans and Southeast Asians) will solidify the salience of the underclass stigma. Thus, intergroup relations in America are destined to retain their complicated character of race-class interaction. Second, as the size of this putative underclass grows, African American faces will become a minority within it and empirical realities will render the unique association of blackness and dependent poverty false. Moreover, the growing presence of middle-class and elite minorities of color (especially blacks) renders African American and black too imprecise to be sustained as synonyms for "underclass." What language practices and specific nomenclatures will develop to make sense of the complicated relationships between minority group class structures and minority-majority relations is too complicated to foretell at this juncture. However, some such language practices are inevitable.

The author wishes to thank participants in the Social Science Research Council's Conference on Immigration and Race, held in March 2002 in San Jose, California, for their helpful comments. Special thanks are given to Nancy Foner, Steven Gold, Jennifer Hochschild, and Roger Waldinger.

NOTES

1. A full treatment of these issues of the "underclass," stigma, and transformed intergroup relations is given in Jaynes (1994).

2. Obviously, this conclusion is highly nuanced and subject to qualification with regard to different groups' varying experiences. My own view is that "racial" versus "ethnic" classification and social experiences form a finite but wide band of differences in degree as opposed to hard and fast differences in kind. On this point, see Cornell and Hartmann (this volume) and Roediger and Barrett (this volume).

3. American usage is attributed to Myrdal (1963); see also Glasgow (1980), Wilson (1987), and Gans (1995).

REFERENCES

Aigner, Dennis J., and Glen G. Cain. 1977. "Statistical Theories of Discrimination in Labor Markets." *Industrial and Labor Relations Review* 30(2): 175–87.
Bourgois, Philippe. 1996. *In Search of Respect.* Cambridge: Cambridge University Press.
Cose, Ellis. 1996. *The Rage of a Privileged Class.* New York: HarperPerennial.
Danziger, Sheldon, and Peter Gottschalk. 1995. *America Unequal.* New York: Russell Sage Foundation.
Edsall, Thomas Byrne, and Mary D. Edsall. 1991. "Race." *The Atlantic Monthly* 267(5, May): 53–86.
Gans, Herbert J. 1995. *The War Against the Poor.* New York: Basic Books.
Glasgow, Douglas G. 1980. *The Black Underclass.* San Francisco: Jossey-Bass.
Goffman, Erving. 1974. *STIGMA: Notes on the Management of Spoiled Identity.* New York: Jason Aronson.
Jaynes, Gerald. 1994. "Race and Class in Black, Tan, and White." Unpublished paper. Yale University, New Haven, Conn.
———. 2002. "Gangsta Rap: Freedom and Identity Among the Malcontents." Unpublished paper. Yale University, New Haven, Conn.
Jaynes, Gerald, and Robin M. Williams, eds. 1989. *A Common Destiny: Blacks and American Society.* Washington, D.C.: National Academy Press.
Katz, Michael. 1989. *The Undeserving Poor.* New York: Pantheon.

Kendis, Kaoru Oguri, and Randall Jay Kendis. 1976. "The Street Boy Identity: An Alternate Strategy of Boston's Chinese-Americans." *Urban Anthropology* 5(1): 1–17.

Kirschenman, Joleen, and Kathryn Neckerman. 1991. "'We'd Love to Hire Them, But . . .': The Meaning of Race for Employers." In *The Urban Underclass*, edited by Christopher Jencks and Paul E. Peterson. Washington, D.C.: Brookings Institution.

Mead, Lawrence M. 1986. *Beyond Entitlement: The Social Obligations of Citizenship.* New York: Free Press.

Myrdal, Gunner. 1963. *Challenge to Affluence.* New York: Pantheon.

Newman, Katherine S. 2000. *No Shame in My Game: The Working Poor in the Inner City.* New York: Vintage.

Perlmann, Joel, and Roger Waldinger. 1999. "Immigrants, Past and Present: A Reconsideration." In *The Handbook of International Immigration: The American Experience,* edited by Charles Hirschman, Philip Kasinitz, and Josh DeWind. New York: Russell Sage Foundation.

Portales, Marco. 2000. *Crowding Out Latinos.* Philadelphia: Temple University Press.

Portes, Alejandro, and Rubén Rumbaut. 1996. *Immigrant America: A Portrait.* Berkeley: University of California Press.

Portes, Alejandro, and Min Zhou. 1993. "The New Second Generation: Segmented Assimilation and Its Variants." *The Annals* 530(November): 74–96.

Rodriguez, Luis J. 1993. *Always Running.* New York: Touchstone.

Rodriguez, Richard. 1982. *Hunger for Memory.* New York: Bantam.

Schuman, Howard, Charlotte Steeh, and Lawrence Bobo. 1985. *Racial Attitudes in America: Trends and Interpretations.* Cambridge, Mass.: Harvard University Press.

Smelser, Neil J., William Julius Wilson, and Faith Mitchell, eds. 2001. *America Becoming.* Washington, D.C.: National Academy Press.

Stavans, Ilan. 1995. *The Hispanic Condition.* New York: HarperCollins.

Suro, Roberto. 1999. *Strangers Among Us.* New York: Vintage.

Thomas, Piri. 1991. *Down These Mean Streets.* New York: Vintage.

Trattner, Walter I. 1994. *From Poor Law to Welfare State.* New York: Free Press.

Walzer, Michael. 1965. *The Revolution of the Saints: A Study in the Origins of Radical Politics.* Cambridge, Mass.: Harvard University Press.

Waters, Mary C. 1996. "Ethnic and Racial Identities of Second-Generation Black Immigrants in New York City." In *The New Second Generation*, edited by Alejandro Portes. New York: Russell Sage Foundation.

———. 1999. "Explaining the Comfort Factor: West Indian Immigrants Confront American Race Relations." In *Immigration and Opportunity: Race, Ethnicity, and Employment in the United States*, edited by Frank D. Bean and Stephanie Bell-Rose. New York: Russell Sage Foundation.

Welsh, Patrick. 1995. "Lure of the Latino Gang." *The Washington Post*, March 26, 1995, pp. C1 and C4.

Wilson, William Julius. 1987. *The Truly Disadvantaged: The Inner City, the Underclass, and Public Policy.* Chicago: University of Chicago Press.

Part II

Immigration, Race, and the State

Erika Lee

Chapter 6

American Gatekeeping: Race and Immigration Law in the Twentieth Century

The twin metaphors of "gates" and "gatekeepers" were first introduced into national conversations about immigrants and race beginning in the late nineteenth century, when Americans called on the federal government to "close the door" against Asian and, later, European and Mexican immigrants.[1] By the end of the twentieth century, the metaphor had become embedded in academic and public discourses on immigration, reflecting a renewed restrictionist mood. A wide range of scholars and journalists wrote about "guarding the gate," the "clamor at the gates," "the gatekeepers," and the "guarded gate" (see, for example, LeMay 1987; 1989; Glazer 1985; Zucker and Zucker 1987). Perhaps the best known and most recent use of the term is the U.S. Immigration and Naturalization Service's (USINS) Operation Gatekeeper, a militarized effort initiated in 1994 to restrict the illegal entry of Mexican immigrants into the United States near San Diego, California.[2] More recently, the calls to establish tighter gatekeeping measures in the wake of the September 11, 2001, terrorist attacks have received much media attention and great public support.

Although journalists, policymakers, and academics use the gatekeeping metaphor widely, there has been little effort to define or trace what American gatekeeping has actually meant in the past and present. Much has been written explaining why and how changing patterns of American nativism have led to immigration restriction and exclusion. Standard chronologies of important immigration laws are also familiar. But we know very little about the consequences of immigration laws or the broader ways in which immigration is controlled.[3] Several questions remain: What effects do immigration policies have at America's gates and within the nation itself? How is gatekeeping related to domestic race relations and state-building? Finally, how have American gatekeeping ideologies, practices, and laws—first established in the pre-1924 period—both changed and remained the same in contemporary times?

This essay examines the racialized roots of American gatekeeping in the late nineteenth century and then traces the evolution of gatekeeping laws and policies over the course of the twentieth and early twenty-first centuries. One central issue is the impact of America's history of racially restrictive immigration laws on the post-1965 era. Scholars have traditionally divided twentieth-century American immigration into three main periods: the period of "open immigration," from the 1880s to the 1920s, when over 22 million immigrants arrived on America's shores; the period of restriction from the 1920s to the 1960s; and the period of liberalization in the post-1965 era, during which time 27 million immigrants entered the country (USINS 2000). Defining these periods are two immigration laws: the 1924 Immigration Act, which perfected the exclusion of Asian immigrants and restricted the entry of southern and eastern European immigrants through a national origins quota system; and the 1965 Immigration Act, which abolished that discriminatory system and instead established preference categories based on family reunification and professional skills.[4]

Conventional interpretations of twentieth-century American immigration invoke stark comparisons, especially between the first period, which ended in the closing of America's gates, and the third period, which began with their reopening. Not only did radical changes in immigration law in 1965 change the entire system of immigration regulation that had been in place since 1924, but the composition of America's primary immigrant groups was also drastically altered. While the vast majority of pre-1924 immigrants came from Europe, the bulk of post-1965 immigrants entered from Asia, Latin America, and the Caribbean.

Overemphasizing the differences between these two laws and periods, however, has created "historical blind spots"; as a result, historians have been discouraged from either reexamining the continuities linking these two periods or reconceptualizing traditional narratives and chronologies of immigration history.[5] In confronting the challenge posed by this volume to address immigration "then and now," it is necessary to question both the standard periodization and the stark comparisons that scholars have conventionally used. Both a closer and a broader examination of these periods first suggest that the pre-1924 period was not "open," nor was immigration "unlimited," as many scholars have described it (see, for example, Barkan and LeMay 1999, xi). Such a characterization ignores the great restrictions placed on Asian immigration during this time period. Consequently, the origins of American gatekeeping should be placed not at 1924 but at 1882, when the Chinese Exclusion Act of May 6, 1882 (22 Stat. 58) first barred an immigrant group based on its race and class.[6] The Exclusion Act codified important racialized definitions and hierarchies of "undesirable" and "excludable" immigrants. It also helped to establish the bureaucratic state machinery to inspect, document, detain, and deport both legal and illegal immigrants. By 1924 racially restrictive immigration laws had become the primary tool used to limit foreign immigration and maintain the existing racial and ethnic status quo within the United States.[7]

Reexamining America's gatekeeping history also suggests a reinterpretation of the 1965 Immigration Act. Scholars have usually identified it as the embodiment of the American civil rights agenda in immigration regulation. The law is indeed monumentally significant, both for its assault on racial bias in immigration law and for the tremendous new immigration it allowed into the country. Nevertheless, important trends from the pre-1924 era persisted after the act was passed. The gates may have been opened to a wider range and a larger number of immigrants after 1965, but the principle of immigration restriction was never repudiated. Moreover, the various gatekeeping systems of categorizing, processing, surveilling, detaining, and deporting immigrants that were first established during the 1882 to 1924 period continue to function—and have even been expanded—in the contemporary era. Finally, despite the act's intent to abolish racial discrimination in immigration, race still plays an especially central role in the debates over immigration and the ways in which the state regulates immigrants at America's gates and within its borders. Such continuities do not warrant that we begin to look at the twentieth century as a single era in which nothing changed. As many of the essays in this volume make clear, post-1965 immigration is fundamentally different from that of previous eras in many ways. Immigration regulation after 1965 also functions in ways distinct from those of earlier periods. Nevertheless, gatekeeping ideologies, politics, and policies survive and are readily resurrected and reinforced whenever they are deemed necessary, such as in the wake of the terrorist attacks of September 11, 2001.

Mirroring Americans' current ambivalence about immigration, the United States now struggles with its dual identity as a nation of immigrants and a gatekeeping nation. It continues to welcome a diverse group of immigrants and refugees and bases much of American national identity on a celebratory narrative of immigration. At the same time, however, not all immigrants are uniformly welcomed into the country. The United States also continues to support and implement immigration policies that target specific groups of immigrants based on race, religion, ethnicity, and other factors.

DEFINING AMERICAN GATEKEEPING

There are two conventional approaches to the study of immigration law. Scholars usually limit their focus to either the key legislative battles leading up to the passage of new laws or the provisions of the laws themselves (see, for example, Bennett 1963; Divine 1957; LeMay 1987; Bernard 1984; Hutchinson 1981). The immigration restrictions written into federal legislation, however, are just one aspect of the nation-state's gatekeeping powers. State laws, and most important, the administrative policies and internal operations of immigration officials, first under the Bureau of Immigration and the Immigration and Naturalization Service, and now under the new Department of Homeland Security, are especially significant but often overlooked—tools used to control immigration at the country's gates and borders and to keep track of immigrants already residing within the country. Understanding American gatekeeping thus requires an examination of what happened after the laws were passed, how the policies were actually carried out, and what the consequences were for immigrant communities, racial formation, and the state and nation as a whole. An analysis of America's history of gatekeeping shifts the focus away from immigration law only and instead examines the law's relationship to society and nation. It encompasses a broad range of immigration and immigrant policies, considering the legal, political, and social processes behind their inception as well as their enforcement and their consequences.[8]

One way in which American gatekeeping has functioned has first involved distinguishing certain immigrants as threatening, unassimilable, and even inferior on the basis of their race, religion, culture, labor, and gender relations and establishing a hierarchy of immigrant desirability to further differentiate some immigrant groups from others. Such categorizations are often based on race and racialization but often involve myriad factors, including class, immigrant status, job skills, political affiliation, and family reunification. The immigrant danger is then contained or managed through a wide range of surveillance and control systems that may limit economic and geographical mobility and access to services and even infringe on political and other rights. Finally, gatekeeping protects the nation from both further immigrant incursions and dangerous immigrants already in the United States by using the power of the state to legalize the modes and processes of exclusion, restriction, surveillance, and deportation.[9] Inextricably related to gatekeeping is the recognition that the state itself is an actor that both influences the society it governs and reshapes the social, political, and economic relationships within society.[10]

Building the ideological and legal gates that restrict immigration has traditionally involved several overlapping concerns, goals, and variables.[11] America's foreign policy agendas have directly shaped refugee policy. Immigrants have been excluded and restricted on the basis of their race, ethnicity, class, gender, sexuality, moral standing, health, and political affiliation, among other factors. Some of these justifications for exclusion and restriction were more important during certain historical periods than others. But they often intersected and overlapped, working both separately and in concert to regulate not only foreign immigration but also race, class, and gender relations within the United States. In turn, gatekeeping became a primary means of exerting social control over immigrant communities and protecting the American nation at large. Immigrant laborers who were considered a threat to American white working-men were summarily excluded on the basis of class. General restriction laws—especially those that targeted immigrants who were suspected of immoral behavior or of being "likely to become public charges"—affected female immigrants disproportionately (Gabaccia 1994, 26). Immigrant disease and sexuality were also monitored, contained, and excluded through immigration policy. Efforts to exclude immigrant groups on the basis of their alleged health menace to the United States constituted what Alan Kraut (1994, 3) has called "medicalized nativism," and the diseases considered most dangerous were explicitly tied to racialized assumptions about specific immigrant groups. Homosexuals were denied entry beginning in 1917 under clauses in general immigration laws related to morality and the barring of "constitutional psychopathic inferiors" (39 Stat. 874).[12] Immigrants were also judged according to their political beliefs. Anarchists were barred beginning in 1903 (32 Stat. 1203, sect. 2). The Internal Security Act of 1950 increased the grounds of exclusion and deportation of aliens with allegedly subversive beliefs, while the Refugee Relief Act of 1953 gave U.S. presidents special powers to admit refugees fleeing Communist countries (see Barkan and LeMay 1999, 132–33).

Race is not the only factor that has influenced immigration regulation in both the past and present, but it is a most important one. Domestic race relations and ongoing fears that certain immigrants (especially immigrants of color) are not as assimilable or desirable as others have played a crucial role in reinforcing the role of race in immigration policies and, in turn, have shaped the very meanings of race and racial identities themselves.[13] Beginning in the late nineteenth century, federal immigration laws became the means to achieve restrictionists' goals and reflected, reinforced, and reproduced the existing racial hierarchy in the country, leaving America's gates open to some and closing them to others. Understanding the racialized origins of American gatekeeping provides a powerful counternarrative to the popular "immigrant paradigm," which celebrates the United States as a "nation of immigrants" and views immigration as a fulfillment of the "promise of American democracy." As many critics have pointed out, this popular conception of the nation ignores the very real power of institutionalized racism in excluding immigrants and other people of color from full and equal participation in the American society, economy, and polity (Sánchez 1999; Gabaccia 1999a; Lowe 1996). Instead of considering some of the traditional questions of immigration history, such as assimilation or cultural retention, a gatekeeping framework shifts our attention to understanding the meanings and consequences of immigration restriction, exclusion, and deportation for both immigrant and non-immigrant communities.

Reconceptualizing the United States as a gatekeeping nation offers an especially suitable framework for Asian and Latino immigrants, two groups that have been among the largest immigrant populations in the twentieth and twenty-first centuries and that have also caused the most debate and inspired new regulation (Hing 1993, 1–6; Perea 1997). European and other immigrants, however, are not entirely free from the impact of gatekeeping laws. Once built, the gates of immigration law and the bureaucratic machinery and procedures established to admit, examine, deny, deport, and naturalize immigrants became extended to all immigrant groups in the twentieth century.

Gatekeeping also served as an important—though often ignored—impetus to American state-building at the end of the nineteenth century and again at the beginning of the twenty-first century.[14] The great migrations of Asian, Europeans, and Mexicans from the 1880s to 1924 coincided with and helped instigate an expansion of the modern administrative state. The regulation, inspection, restriction, exclusion, and deportation of immigrants required the establishment of a state apparatus and bureaucracy to enforce the immigration laws and exercise the state's control over its external geographical borders as well as its internal borders of citizenship and national membership. Gatekeeping was also inextricably tied to the expansion of U.S. imperialism at the end of the nineteenth century. At the same time that the United States began to assert its national sovereignty by closing its gates to unwanted foreigners, it also expanded its influence abroad through military and economic force and extended some of its immigration laws to its new territories. Border enforcement efforts took on imperialistic overtones when the United States sought to induce in or impose on both Canada and Mexico its American immigration priorities (Lee 2003, 179–87).[15] A century later, immigration remains at the center of new state-building efforts and transnational policies. The response to the terrorist attacks in New York City and Washington, D.C., in 2001 has included new gatekeeping initiatives that have been central to the recent reorganization and expansion of the federal government, as seen in the establishment of the Department of Homeland Security in 2003.

Finally, the construction and closing of America's gates to various "alien invasions" has been instrumental in the formation of the nation itself and in articulating a definition of American national identity and belonging.[16] Beginning in the late nineteenth century, Americans learned to define American-ness by excluding, controlling, and containing foreign-ness. Likewise, through the admission and exclusion of foreigners, the United States both asserted its sovereignty and reinforced its identity as a nation. Gatekeeping has—and continues to have—profound influence on immigrant groups, twentieth-century immigration patterns, immigration control, and American national identity.

CHINESE EXCLUSION AND THE ORIGINS OF AMERICAN GATEKEEPING, 1882 TO 1924

Most scholars identify the debates over immigration and race in the 1920s as the most significant period of immigration restriction in the early twentieth century. Described as a period in which nativism "triumphed," the 1920s, and especially the passage of the 1924 Immigration Act, marked watershed changes in the ways in which race and immigration were defined and controlled.[17] These interpretations generally treat the earlier movement to restrict and exclude Asian immigration as distinct from, and even "tangential" to, the later efforts to stem European immigration. Although the significance of the 1924 act should not be overlooked, American gatekeeping in fact originated much earlier in the Chinese exclusion era beginning in the 1880s. Debates over Chinese immigration and the resulting passage and enforcement of the Chinese exclusion laws reshaped immigration, nation-building, and racial formation at the turn of the twentieth century in critical ways that led directly to the developments of the 1920s and beyond.[18]

Passed on May 6, 1882, the Chinese Exclusion Act prohibited the immigration of Chinese laborers for a period of ten years and barred all Chinese immigrants from naturalized citizenship. Demonstrating the class bias in the law, merchants, teachers, students, travelers, and diplomats were exempt from exclusion. The passage of the act marked the triumph of a decades-old anti-Chinese movement that had begun in California but had national appeal by the 1880s. Opposition to Chinese immigration was rooted in charges that Chinese were racially inferior, threats to white workingmen, and unassimilable foreigners whose alien culture, habits, and aberrant gender relations threatened the very fabric of the nation itself. Exclusionists argued that if the Chinese were allowed to immigrate freely as beneficiaries of America's tradition of unrestricted immigration, the United States would soon be under siege from an unwelcomed and dangerous invasion.[19]

Long identified as a "legal watershed" in the history of American immigration (Daniels 1997, 4; Gyory 1998, 258–59), the Exclusion Act was not only the country's first significant restrictive immigration law but also the first to restrict a group of immigrants based on their race and class. Its significance, however, also lies in the fact that Chinese exclusion introduced a gatekeeping ideology, politics, law, and culture that transformed the ways in which Americans viewed and thought about race, immigration, and the United States' identity as a nation of immigration. It first legalized and reinforced the need to restrict, exclude, and deport "undesirable" and excludable immigrants. It established Chinese immigrants—categorized by their race, class, and gender relations as the ultimate category of undesirable immigrants—as the models by which to measure the desirability (and whiteness) of other immigrant groups. Soon after the Chinese were excluded, calls to restrict or exclude other immigrants followed quickly, and the arguments and lessons of Chinese exclusion were resurrected over and over again during the nativist debates over the "new" immigrants from Asia, Mexico, and southern and eastern Europe.

Following the exclusion of Chinese, Americans on the West Coast became increasingly alarmed by new immigration from Asia, particularly from Japan, Korea, and India. Californians portrayed the new immigrants as yet another "Oriental invasion." Like the Chinese before them, these newcomers were also considered to be threats, owing to their race and their alleged challenge to white labor. The new Japanese and Asian Indian immigrant problems, for example, were immediately connected to the old Chinese one. Headlines in San Francisco newspapers warned that the "Japanese [Are] Taking the Place of the Chinese" and called for the gates to be shut against the "Hindu invasion."[20] Opposition to Mexican immigration also centered on an alleged invasion of cheap, unassimilable laborers similar to the Chinese. Major Frederick Russell Burnham (1930, 48) warned that "the whole Pacific Coast would have been Asiatic in blood today except for the Exclusion Acts. Our whole Southwest will be racially Mexican in three generations unless some similar restriction is placed upon them."[21]

Beginning in the 1890s, some of the race- and class-based arguments used against Asians and Mexicans were applied to certain European immigrant groups. Because distinctive physical differences between native white Americans and European immigrants were not readily apparent, nativists "manufactured" racial difference by making direct connections between the "new" European immigrants and the established Asian threat. Both groups, nativists charged, were racially inferior to Anglo-Saxons, and their use as cheap labor threatened native-born Anglo-American workingmen (Higham 1963, 132–33). Italians, for example, were even given the dubious honor of being called the "Chinese of Europe." They were positioned racially in between black and white and described as "yellow," "olive," or "swarthy" (Gabaccia 1999b, 177–79). Nativist Lothrop Stoddard (1930, 227–28) went even further by arguing that eastern Europeans were not only "like the Chinese" but were in fact part Asian. Eastern Europe, he explained, was situated "next door" to Asia and had already been invaded by "Asiatic hordes" over the past two thousand years. As a result, the Slavic peoples were mongrels, "all impregnated with Asiatic Mongol and Turki blood." The old Chinese exclusion rhetoric was one with which Americans were familiar by the 1910s, and such explicit race- and class-based connections to Chinese immigration served as a strong foundation from which to build new nativist arguments on the national level.

Important distinctions in the ways in which Asian, Mexican, and European immigrants were racialized both in immigration debates and in the laws should not be ignored. Southern and eastern European immigrants came in much greater numbers than did the Chinese, and their status as whites secured them the right of naturalized citizenship, while Asians were consistently denied naturalization by law and in the courts. This claim and privilege of whiteness gave European immigrants more access to and opportunities of full participation in the larger American polity, economy, and society. Although they were eventually restricted, they were never excluded, as Asians were. Mexican immigration differed from both southern and eastern European and Asian immigration on a range of issues. First was Mexico's proximity to the United States and the relatively porous U.S.-Mexico border, which facilitated migration to and from the United States. Mexican immigrants were also treated differently: they were even considered somewhat "safe" from mainstream nativism owing to their status as long-term residents and their propensity to be "birds of passage"—returning home after the agricultural season ended and thus not settling in the United States permanently. After 1924, however, Mexicans would be increasingly categorized as "illegal" immigrants, which reflected not only a unique racial identity but also a distinct legal and immigration status (Cardoso 1980, 22; Sánchez 1993, 20); Hoffman 1974, 30–32; Ngai 1999, 91). Despite the important differences surrounding the restriction and exclusion of Asian, European, and Mexican immigrants, the rhetoric and tools of gatekeeping that were first established by Chinese exclusion were instrumental in defining the issues for all groups and set important precedents for twentieth-century immigration. Each group held its own unique position within the hierarchy of race and immigration, but all eventually became subjected to an immigration ideology and law designed to limit their entry into the United States.

By the early twentieth century, the call to "close the gates" was being sounded in relation not only to Chinese immigration but to immigration in general. The solution to these new immigrant "problems," lawmakers agreed, lay in immigration policy, and a succession of federal laws were passed to increase the control and regulation of threatening and inferior immigrants. The Immigration Act of 1917 (39 Stat. 874) required a literacy test for all adult immigrants, tightened restrictions on suspected radicals, and, as a concession to politicians on the West Coast, denied entry to aliens living within a newly created geographical area that Congress called the "Asiatic Barred Zone."[22] The 1921 and 1924 Immigration Acts drastically restricted immigration from southern and eastern Europe and perfected the exclusion of all Asians, except for Filipinos, who, like Mexicans, were exempt from the 1924 act.[23] By the 1930s the cycle that had begun with Chinese exclusion was made complete. Filipinos were excluded in 1934, and both Filipinos and Mexicans faced massive deportation and repatriation programs during the Great Depression (Melendy 1976, 115–16, 119–25; Balderrama and Rodriguez 1995).

The concepts of race and immigration that developed out of Chinese exclusion provided the models by which other immigrant groups were compared and racialized. Enforcement of the Chinese exclusion laws also set in motion major changes in immigration regulation. Some were written into the Chinese Exclusion Act itself; others were instituted as administrative policy by the immigration service. All would become standard means of inspecting, processing, admitting, tracking, punishing, and deporting all immigrants in the United States. First, the Exclusion Act laid the foundation for the creation of the country's first federal immigrant inspectors by authorizing the creation of "Chinese Inspectors" to examine all newly arriving and departing Chinese on behalf of the federal government.[24] Second, the enforcement of the Chinese exclusion laws initiated the federal government's first attempts to identify and record the movements, occupations, and familial relationships of immigrants, returning residents, and native-born citizens. This was accomplished through the Bureau of Immigration's own elaborate tracking system of registration documents, certificates of identity, and voluminous interviews with individuals and their families.[25] In 1924 the federal government instituted a national census of all Chinese students in the country; the fear was that Chinese immigrants had either gained entry through fraudulent claims of student status or were overstaying their visas and not returning to China following their education (NARA 1933). Third, the Exclusion Act introduced "certificates of registration" for departing Chinese laborers, which contained personal data and entitled the holder to "return and re-enter the United States upon producing and . . . delivering the [document] to the collector of customs." These laborers' return certificates are the first reentry documents issued to an immigrant group by the federal government, and they served as the equivalent of passports facilitating reentry into the country. Chinese remained the only immigrant group required to hold such reentry permits (or passports) until 1924, when the new Immigration Act of May 26 of that year (43 Stat. 153) issued—but did not require—reentry permits for other aliens (Marian Smith, USINS historian, personal communication, October 24, 2000). Moreover, in an effort to crack down on illegal entry and residence, the Chinese exclusion laws were amended to require all Chinese already in the country to possess "certificates of residence" and "certificates of identity" that would serve as proof of their legal entry and lawful right to remain in the country. First outlined under the Geary Act (27 Stat. 25, sect. 7) of May 5, 1892, these documents became the precursors to what is commonly known as "green cards." Any Chinese laborer found within the jurisdiction of the United States without a certificate of residence was to be considered in the country unlawfully and vulnerable to arrest and deportation (sect. 2, Act of November 3, 1893, McCreary Amendment [28 Stat. 7]). Other immigrants were not required to hold similar documents proving their lawful residence until 1928, when "immigrant identification cards" were first issued to new immigrants arriving for permanent residence. These were eventually replaced by the "alien registration receipt cards" ("green cards") after 1940.[26] Immigration raids initiated by the immigration service to track down illegal immigrants also became a particularly effective new means of Chinese exclusion enforcement.

Finally, the Chinese Exclusion Act set another precedent by defining illegal immigration as a criminal offense and establishing the country's first border enforcement and deportation policies.[27] Border inspectors, transnational border policies with Canada and Mexico, immigrant surveillance, and immigration raids became institutionalized in response to Chinese illegal immigration along the U.S.-Canada and U.S.-Mexico borders. Although Chinese made up a mere fraction of a much larger migration of illegal immigrants—most of whom were European—they were singled out for government scrutiny (Lee 2003, 165–73). By setting in motion such drastic changes in U.S. immigration regulation, the Chinese exclusion laws forever changed America's relationship to immigration, but once built, the ideological, legal, and administrative gates of immigration policy became extended to all other immigrant groups.

POST-1965: CONTINUITY AND CHANGE IN AMERICAN GATEKEEPING

Like the Chinese Exclusion Act, the 1965 Immigration Act also ushered in a new era of immigration and immigration law. America's emergence as a superpower following World War II forced the country to reconsider its discriminatory immigration policies. The first step had come during the war, when Congress repealed the Chinese exclusion laws and placed Chinese immigration under the 1924 quota system. Passed as a wartime measure to recognize China's new status as a war ally, repeal was largely symbolic. China's quota, for example, was only 105 persons per year (Reimers 1985, 11–15; Riggs 1950). By 1946 Congress had passed bills to grant quotas of 100 to India and the Philippines and allowed for the naturalization of immigrants from those countries as well. Both measures were passed out of concern about shoring up support from Asian allies. In 1945 and in 1947, Congress continued to relax the country's immigration laws with the War Brides Acts, which allowed the spouses of American servicemen to enter the country (Zhao 2002, 78–83). Although such postwar legislation indicates a trend toward liberalization, the 1952 Walter-McCarran Act reinforced the tough restrictions of the 1920s by maintaining the national origins quotas and the near-exclusion of Asian immigrants. Reflecting its cold-war-era origins, the act also established strict security provisions designed to target suspected subversives, but as a precursor to the 1965 law it set up a system of "preferences" for certain skilled labor and for relatives of U.S. citizens and permanent resident aliens.[28]

Motivated by cold war politics and civil rights activism, immigration reform had increased in momentum by the 1960s. At a time when the United States emphasized its virtues of freedom and democracy over the totalitarianism of communism, the unequal treatment of immigrants based on race exposed the hypocrisy in American immigration regulation. Strong leadership came from the White House under President John F. Kennedy, whose 1958 book *A Nation of Immigrants* was an unabashed celebration of America's immigrant heritage and a call for immigration reform. Following Kennedy's assassination, President Lyndon B. Johnson embraced the cause and declared that the national origins framework was "incompatible with our basic American tradition." Enacted as part of the Johnson administration's larger civil rights agenda, the 1965 Immigration and Nationality Act (79 Stat. 911) abolished the national origins quotas and created a new set of preference categories based on family reunification and professional skills (King 2000, 243; Reimers 1985, 81). Cloaked in the rhetoric of liberal and civil rights reform, the 1965 act has been portrayed as representing a "high-water mark in a national consensus of egalitarianism" (Daniels 1991, 338).[29] Political opposition to the reforms were minimal. National newspapers almost unanimously favored abolition of the national origins quota. Traditional opponents such as the American Legion and the Daughters of the American Revolution warned of the "collapse of moral and spiritual values if non-assimilable aliens of dissimilar ethnic background . . . are permitted . . . to overwhelm our country," but they did not actively oppose the bill.[30] Lawmakers predicted that with the reforms the United States—a "nation that was built by the immigrants of all lands"—would now be able to ask potential immigrants, "What can you do for our country?" rather than, "In what country were you born?" (Johnson 1965, 116).

The 1965 Immigration Act's assault on racism and the tremendous new immigration it has allowed into the country represent some of the most important changes in postwar American law and society. With the 1965 act, immigration policy grew beyond its original role of guarding against dangerous foreigners and sought to build on earlier immigration, a legacy that was now seen as a strength of the nation. The act is the second in the trilogy of landmark civil rights laws, including the Civil Rights Act of 1964 and the 1965 Voting Rights Act. The abolition of the 1924 quota system flung open the gates to a multitude of peoples who had been excluded under the old regime, and the exponential growth in immigration has radically altered the racial composition of the United States. Prior to 1965, the peak decade for immigration was 1911 to 1920, when 5,736,000 immigrants entered the country, mostly from Europe. During the 1980s, a record 7,338,000 immigrants came to the United States, followed by 6,943,000 from 1991 to 1997 (USINS 1999). The 2000 census figures reveal that the United States is accepting immigrants at a faster rate than at any other time since the 1850s.[31] Most new immigrants are from Asia and Latin America. In the 1980s more than 80 percent of all immigrants came from one of these two geographic regions (Daniels 2001, 6). Between 1971 and 1996, 5.8 million Asians were admitted into the United States as legal immigrants, and over 1 million Asians have been admitted as refugees since 1975 (Zhou and Gatewood 2000, 10–11). In the 1990s immigrants born in Latin America made up more than half of all immigrants in the United States for the first time.[32] This dramatic change in immigrant composition has resulted in the racial restructuring of American society, and every sector, from politics and education to health care and intermarriage, has been affected.

Despite such immense changes resulting from the new law, the act itself did not totally overturn all vestiges of the early gatekeeping system. Indeed, the conventional focus on the transformation in immigration patterns after 1965 obscures the significant continuities that persisted in immigration regulation. First and foremost, the 1965 act may have opened up the gates to a wider number of immigrants, but it never sought to dismantle the gates altogether or repudiate the principle of gatekeeping. Indeed, the ideological, political, and legal debates over whether the United States should restrict immigration has remained largely moot in the post-1924 period, as both supporters and opponents of immigration recognize the state's right and need to control the number and types of immigrants admitted into the country. As a result, the United States has retained the right to use gates and gatekeepers to control immigration and to document and keep track of immigrants already within the United States.

Second, restrictions based on race were formally rejected, but the act still limited the number of immigrants allowed into the country each year through new hemispheric and national quotas. Persons from the Eastern Hemisphere were allotted 170,000 visas; persons from the Western Hemisphere were allotted 120,000. No one country in the Eastern Hemisphere could have more than 20,000 visas. "Immediate" family members, such as spouses, minor children, and parents of U.S. citizens, were exempt from the numerical limits.[33] Many of the barriers first established in the nineteenth century, including the likely-to-become-a-public-charge clause, physical and mental health requirements, and ideological tests, also remained firmly in place (Daniels 1991, 340–41).

Most notably, although the 1965 law's main intention was to end racial discrimination in immigration law, race played—and continues to play—a most important role in the debates over immigration reform and in subsequent laws, both during the 1960s and in our contemporary period. The 1965 act abolished the national origins quotas, but lawmakers still expressed a desire to facilitate immigration from Europe and to limit— or at the very least discourage—immigration from Asia, Latin America, and Africa. Indeed, although a racial hierarchy was not explicitly written into the new law, as in 1924, it remained deeply imbedded in the 1965 act's design and intent. European immigrants, the last group to be restricted in the pre-1924 period, were the first to be compensated for past discrimination. When Robert Kennedy testified before Congress about the urgent need to eliminate discrimination in immigration, the examples he cited pertained to European immigrants only (Reimers 1985, 69). President Lyndon Johnson stressed the bill's primary intent to redress the wrong done to those "from southern and eastern Europe" (Johnson 1966). And lawmakers predicted that the main beneficiaries of the new law would be immigrants from Italy, Greece, and Poland, countries that had the largest backlogs of persons awaiting visas. No longer considered immigrant "menaces," these European immigrants had come to epitomize instead the nation's newfound celebration of its "immigrant heritage" by the 1960s.[34] Representative Emanuel Celler (D-N.Y.), one of the key sponsors of the bill, described the previously despised Slavs, Poles, and Italians as brave "people of courage who . . . had worked to make America richer . . . and [whose] diverse cultures [made] the bloodstream of America course with greater vigor in the arts, in the sciences, and in the skills of mankind" (quoted in *Congressional Record*, August 24, 1965, 21579). Senator Edward Kennedy added that the new European immigrants would be easily assimilable. They were "familiar with American ways . . . [sharing] our ideals (as quoted in Stern 1974, 77–79). This emphasis on America's newfound identity as a "nation of immigrants" was rooted in the European immigrant paradigm. It signaled the "total integration" of pre-1924 European immigrants into the nation and became a "metaphor for the success of European immigrant assimilation and boot-strap upward mobility" (Trucio-Haynes 1997, 374, 87).

The 1965 act sought to encourage European immigration and maintain the racial and ethnic homogeneity achieved under the older 1924 quota system through the new family reunification preference category. A compromise measure between organized labor, which wanted continued limits on immigration, and those who wanted to abolish the national origins system, family reunification was supposed to privilege new immigration based on existing (that is, European American) population already in the United States. Critics who charged that the new law did not go far enough argued that such "reforms" were not reforms at all but rather maintained the status quo, just under a different system and with the appearance of nondiscrimination. The Japanese American Citizens League recognized as much when it noted that "although the immigration bill eliminated race as a matter of principle, in actual operation immigration will still be controlled by the now discredited national origins system and the general pattern of immigration which exists today will continue for many years yet to come" (Reimers 1985, 76).

At the same time that European immigrants were described in celebratory terms, concerns about a potential increase in immigration from Asian, Latin American, and African countries persisted, revealing continued anxiety about large increases in the admission of immigrants of color. The numerical caps placed on the Western Hemisphere in the 1965 act were designed to placate lawmakers who were wary of large-scale migration from Latin America. By counting immigrants from the Western Hemisphere against an annual quota for the first time, the number of Mexicans allowed to enter the country legally was dramatically reduced. This provision in particular is an apt example of the restrictive, rather than egalitarian, nature of the law (Reimers 1985, 84–85).[35] Lawmakers also dealt with Asian immigration very cautiously. The 1952 act had abolished the Asia-Pacific Triangle, which excluded all immigrants from this manufactured geographic region, but the action was viewed as a symbolic end to discrimination only. New descriptions of Chinese and Japanese immigrants and their American-born children achieving success "American style" in the 1960s marked the introduction of Asian Americans as "model minorities," but this did not translate into support for an increase in new Asian immigration (Peterson 1966, 28).[36] As the debates over the 1965 Immigration Act make clear, lawmakers were repeatedly assured that the number of Asian immigrants would not materially increase with the changes in the law. Representative Celler disputed charges that the bill would allow entry to "hordes" of Africans and Asians or that the bill would allow the United States to become the "dumping ground" for Latin America (Stern 1974, 120–21; Reimers 1985, 81). Asian American Senator Hiram L. Fong from Hawaii declared in Congress that "racial barriers [were] bad for America," but he also assured his colleagues that only a small number of people from Asia would enter the United States under the 1965 Act (King 2000, 244; see Stern 1974, 162–63). As such cautious reforms guiding the 1965 act illustrate, the great new migrations from Asia and Latin America were largely unintentional.[37] Congress wanted to end the explicitly discriminatory national origins quota, but it did not want to totally abandon either immigration restriction in general or the racial and ethnic homogeneity that the earlier system had provided.

It is thus significant that when it became clear that the main immigrant groups to take advantage of the new law came from Asia and Latin America rather than from Europe, lawmakers did not attempt to rescind the laws or reinstate the older system. The major provisions of the 1965 act remain largely intact, and both supporters and opponents of immigration characterize the post-1965 period as one of liberalized immigration in comparison with the pre-1924 period (Daniels 2001, 46, 50, 58; Graham 2001, 157). Instead of an explicitly race-based hierarchy structuring immigration regulation, post-1965 policies give more weight to class and immigrant status in determining current immigration opportunities and treatment in the United States.

Gatekeeping ideologies, politics, and policies based on race, however, have not been totally abolished. Despite some observers' claims that the new nativism is not as racially based as the nativism of the pre-1924 period, the persistence of racialized understandings about which immigrants constitute a "threat" to the country demonstrates otherwise.[38] The state's systematic efforts to regulate the entry of potentially dangerous foreigners applying for admission and to control those already residing in the country also remain central, even in the most humanitarian and liberal immigration policies.[39]

Gatekeeping does not function in the same way as it did in the earlier period. The immigrants, the gates, and the challenges are different, and immigration law and regulation reflect these important new contexts. Groups that had previously been targeted face less scrutiny from government officials. But other immigrants have taken their place, and the role of race in determining which immigrants are targeted follows patterns first established prior to 1924. The existence of a hierarchy of immigrant desirability and the increased importance of administrative rather than legislative regulations in immigration control also remain important continuities linking the two periods together. The cases of illegal immigration from Mexico and the treatment of Muslim and Middle Eastern immigrants after September 11, 2001, are two important examples.

Caused in part by the Western Hemispheric caps in the 1965 act, illegal immigration from Mexico began to increase in the 1970s and became a prominent political issue. Apprehensions intensified as the number of undocumented immigrants steadily rose from 500,000 in 1970 to nearly 1 million seven years later (Gutiérrez 1995, 188). In the midst of a deep national recession, alarmists talked of the "loss of control" over the country's borders, and their rhetoric reflected a larger anxiety and fear about the unprecedented demographic and racial and ethnic changes brought on by the new post-1965 immigration. Racialized metaphors of war like "invasion," "conquest," and "save our state" were commonly deployed to describe illegal immigration from Mexico (Perea 1997, 67, 73). Similar to the case of Chinese illegal immigration during the exclusion era, nativists in the 1970s, 1980s, and 1990s focused their energy and vitriol mostly on one group—illegal immigrants from Mexico—while ignoring illegals from other countries.[40] The U.S. government's efforts to crack down on illegal Mexican immigrants have placed the entire Mexican American community under suspicion, making illegal immigrants, legal residents, and even native-born American citizens of Mexican descent vulnerable to scrutiny and government action.[41]

The ways in which the U.S. government has attempted to control illegal immigration offer additional evidence of the extension of pre-1924 gatekeeping practices, especially the centrality of administrative rather than legislative initiatives. As Lucy Salyer (1995, 121–78) has demonstrated for the pre-1924 period, the Bureau of Immigration evolved into a highly powerful agency that enjoyed great administrative discretion and little interference from the courts in the enforcement of immigration laws. During the Chinese exclusion era, the Bureau of Immigration used this great discretionary power to expand its reach and control over Chinese immigrants and residents to such an extent that Chinese American organizations protested the veritable "reign of terror" imposed by immigration officials on Chinese communities (McKenzie 1928, 42–43, 127). Beginning in the 1980s, the bureau's successor, the U.S. Immigration and Naturalization Service, similarly relied on its own administrative power and internal operations (with the sanction and increased budgets approved by Congress) to control illegal immigration from Mexico. The Immigration Reform and Control Act of 1986 (IRCA) attempted to "get tough with" illegal immigrants and their employers, but lax enforcement and migrant adaptation have made such provisions ineffectual (Daniels 2001, 52–58). Instead, the U.S. government turned to Border Patrol initiatives with military code names like Operation Gatekeeper in San Diego, California, Operation Rio Grande in Brownsville, Texas, Operation Safeguard in Nogales, Arizona, and Operation Hold the Line in El Paso, Texas. From 1993 to 1996, Congress increased funding for the U.S. Border Patrol by 102 percent (Peters 1996). In 2001 the United States spent $2 billion to build walls and manage a twenty-four-hour patrol over the border that included the use of nightscopes, motion sensors, communications equipment, jeeps, a ten-foot-high steel wall, and 9,400 border agents. The U.S. Border Patrol arrested 1 million individuals along the U.S.-Mexico border in the year 2000 alone.[42] With such efforts resulting in the militarization of the U.S.-Mexico border, no other area of immigration control has so literally embodied American gatekeeping in the contemporary period.

In the wake of the terrorist attacks on the United States on September 11, 2001, the core components of American gatekeeping and immigration law have been pushed to the very forefront of U.S. and international policy. Political pundits and lawmakers have argued in hindsight that American gatekeeping efforts did not work well enough.[43] The Federal Bureau of Investigation failed to act on internal reports of suspicious individuals who were later found to be among the hijackers who attacked the World Trade Center and the Pentagon. At least one September 11 hijacker entered the country on a student visa, while others studied at flight schools in the United States despite their lack of student visas.[44] Several of the suspects spent time in Canada, where less stringent immigration laws allow immigrants and refugees to enter with no passports, apply for asylum, and travel freely while their asylum applications are pending. Canada's open doors, critics argued, increased the risk to America's own national security.[45]

Following the attacks, the identification of a new immigrant threat and the solutions that have followed borrow from and extend earlier gatekeeping efforts. In the search for the perpetrators, entire Middle Eastern and Muslim immigrant communities were vulnerable to blanket racializations as "terrorists," "potential terrorists," or accomplices and sympathizers. Within days of the attacks, law enforcement officials had arrested more than 1,200 people, only a handful of whom would be proven to have had any links to terrorism. At the end of November 2001, approximately 600 people were still in custody, held on unrelated immigration violations.[46] Despite U.S. government appeals to prevent racial scapegoating, hate crimes directed against Middle Eastern Americans and those who appeared Middle Eastern rose throughout the nation, resulting in at least one murder: Balbir Singh Sodhi, a South Asian Sikh gas station owner in Mesa, Arizona, was shot to death by a self-proclaimed "patriotic American" who blamed Sodhi for the terrorist attacks.[47] Racialized as the latest immigrant menace, entire ethnic communities found themselves under suspicion.[48] Newspapers reported a "broad consensus" among both supporters and opponents of immigration that additional immigration restriction was needed as a matter of national security (Center for Immigration Studies 2001).[49]

In an effort to manage the new terrorist threat, U.S. authorities implemented drastic changes in immigration policy immediately following the attack and in the three years since then. There has been no formal legislation restricting immigration from countries suspected of being breeding grounds for terrorists, most likely because such an action would greatly insult countries whose cooperation in the U.S.-led war against terrorism is crucial. But other important controls on immigration—and especially on immigrants already within the United States—have been passed as part of other laws. Policymakers first renewed their focus on increased border security, especially along the northern border. In late September 2001, Paul Celluci, the U.S. ambassador to Canada, publicly called for Canada to "harmonize its [refugee] policies with those of the United States." President George W. Bush sketched out a vision of a "North American security perimeter" in which transnational immigration controls would be central. Discussions with Mexico also secured that country's cooperation in improving security over the shared U.S.-Mexico border.[50] As part of the "Patriot Act" passed in the House of Representatives in October 2001, Congress allowed the long-term detention of noncitizens "certified" by the attorney general as terrorist threats.[51]

Similar to earlier gatekeeping efforts, the internal administrative decisions of immigration officials have also been significantly altered to track, control, and detain immigrants suspected of terrorist activity or those deemed a potential threat to national security. Government authorities quietly amended their own administrative rules and procedures to grant them greater control over all foreigners. Beginning in November 2001, federal agents targeted two hundred college campuses nationwide to collect information on Middle Eastern students.[52] In the same month, the Justice Department expanded the power of its officers to detain foreigners even after a federal immigration judge had ordered their release for lack of evidence. The judicial order can now be set aside if the immigration service believes that a foreigner is a "danger to the community or a flight risk." While critics claim that such sweeping legal changes in immigration control have institutionalized racial profiling and the suspension of liberties for immigrants, supporters claim that the change is necessary in the new war against terrorism. Moreover, the Bush administration's proposals command strong public support.[53]

In April 2002, a Justice Department legal ruling set in motion the use of state police to enforce federal immigration laws. Under a proposed federal plan, local police officers would become deputized as agents of the INS with the power to arrest immigrants for overstaying a visa or entering the country illegally.[54] In June 2002, Attorney General John Ashcroft proposed new Justice Department regulations that would require all Muslim men to register with the INS. Such a measure—so similar to the Geary Act of 1892, which required Chinese laborers to register with the federal government—is intended to provide a "vital line of defense" against terrorists, in the words of the attorney general.[55] Seven months later the new rules were being implemented through two registration programs. The first required that all adult males from over twenty-four mostly Muslim countries be fingerprinted, photographed, interviewed, and registered with the federal government.[56] The second registration system, entitled the Student and Exchange Visitor Information System, required all international students and exchange visitors to register with the federal government their names, addresses, majors, course load, graduation date, and so on, and to update that information regularly.[57] During the first five months of the registration, newspapers reported that 82,000 male immigrants and visitors, predominantly Muslims, had been "questioned in immigration offices, airports and border crossings." Officials reported that they had caught and detained eleven suspected terrorists and 9,000 illegal aliens. Moreover, they cited the programs' success in helping them catch more than 800 criminal suspects and deportable convicts and assist in the surveillance of immigrants from countries that are considered breeding grounds for terrorism. More than 13,000 registrants—roughly 16 percent of the total number—faced deportation as of June 2003.[58]

The effects on immigrants have been immediate. According to the government's own statistics, the vast majority of immigrants detained as a result of the registrations had no links to terrorism. Rather, they were immigrants who had overstayed their visas while living, working, and raising their families in the United States for many years without any interference. Immigrants targeted by the government registration programs describe the fear, anger, and confusion that permeate their communities. Administrative snafus have led to countless detentions. Many others claim that they have been illegally denied the right of legal counsel. Those who had lived in the country for many years with outdated visas have been forced to go underground or face deportation. Muslim and Middle Eastern immigrants feel that the policies amount to racial profiling. "Everyone is afraid," said one Egyptian man waiting in front of an INS office in Virginia in April 2003.[59]

Perhaps the most significant change in immigration regulation since September 11, 2001, was the transfer of all immigration services and border enforcement procedures to the newly created Department of Homeland Security on March 1, 2003. Under the new department, the Bureau of Citizenship and Immigration Services processes visa, work, naturalization, and other applications for new immigrants and residents. The Directorate of Border and Transportation Security handles all other security and the enforcement of immigration laws.[60]

Both the transfer of all immigration services to the new Department of Homeland Security and the federal government's treatment of immigrants since September 11, 2001, have been deeply controversial. Long-term proponents of tighter immigration controls praise the new changes in border enforcement and the stricter visa controls and urge more vigilance in the enforcement of immigration laws in the interior of the country.[61] Immigrant rights advocates charge that by placing immigration regulation under the auspices of homeland security, the government is sending the message that all immigration, not just those immigrants who have links to terrorism, should be considered a matter of national security.[62] As further proof of this trend, they point to an April 2003 ruling by Attorney General John Ashcroft involving a Haitian refugee who had entered illegally but had won the right to be released on bail while awaiting a decision on his asylum claim. Mr. Ashcroft reversed the order of release, declaring that illegal immigrants and asylum seekers who had no known links to terrorist groups could still be classified as threats to national security and detained indefinitely because illegal immigration "strain[ed] national security and homeland security resources" like the Coast Guard. Denouncing the ruling as "incongruously" pairing asylum cases with threats to national security, leaders of immigrant rights organizations voiced their opinion that the Justice Department was intent on restricting all immigration and curtailing immigrant rights under the guise of the war on terrorism.[63]

Criticism of the Justice Department's handling of immigrants after the terrorist attacks of September 11, 2001, followed from within the department itself. In June 2003, Glenn A. Fine, the Justice Department's inspector general, filed a highly critical report that concluded that "significant problems" plagued the department's arrest and detention of 762 illegal immigrants, most of them Middle Eastern. FBI officials, particularly in New York City, "made little attempt to distinguish" between immigrants who had possible ties to terrorism and those swept up by chance in the investigation," Fine wrote. Many people with no connection to terrorism were "treated harshly" and forced to languish in jails for weeks or months without being formally charged (Fine 2003).[64] Attorney General John Ashcroft not only vigorously defended his department's position and policies but also asked Congress to grant the authorities even more power in their pursuit of terrorists, including the ability to detain terrorism suspects before trial without bond.[65]

Such sweeping changes in immigration policy are justified as part of America's new war against terrorism. Nevertheless, the effects and consequences of these new policies will be felt by all immigrants—and indeed, all Americans—and the debate over post–September 11 policies will surely endure for years to come. Questions relating to the role of immigration in the United States, America's identity as a nation of immigrants, let alone those relating to the civil liberties of all Americans, remain to be answered.

CONCLUSION

As these recent changes in immigration regulation highlight, American gatekeeping remains as central to national politics and the lives of America's immigrants as it was during the 1880s, when the United States ended its history of unrestricted immigration. Significant differences between the two periods do exist. The exclusion laws prohibiting Asian immigrants and the quota laws restricting southern and eastern Europeans explicitly discriminated on the basis of race and reflected nativism's triumph in the early twentieth century. They also inspired a wide range of surveillance, processing, identification, and deportation measures designed to control immigration at the ports of entry and immigrants within the country. By 1924 gatekeeping had become firmly embedded in the nation's psyche, laws, and state institutions and functions. The primary question facing Americans was not *whether* to close the gates, but *how* to close them more effectively and to a broader range of immigrants. By the 1960s changes in racial thinking, civil rights activism, and domestic and international events had worked together to push the federal government to reform its immigration laws. The racially discriminatory system of regulation was especially targeted for abolition. The resulting 1965 act ushered in a new era.

The United States is once again admitting record numbers of immigrants, especially from Asia and Latin America. Immigration "now" is clearly different from immigration "then." But American gatekeeping has endured as well, especially in the American state's systematic efforts to regulate entry according to a hierarchy of desirability and to control potentially dangerous foreigners already in the country. U.S. immigration regulation has changed in response to different migration patterns, foreign policy agendas, and domestic and international politics. But the principle of gatekeeping is still firmly in place and broadly supported. Guarded gates and gatekeepers have remained central to the nation and to national sovereignty. They are maintained by the state even during times of low nativist political sentiment and are imbedded in some of the nation's most "egalitarian" and "humanitarian" immigration laws. In times of both peace and war, high immigration and low, American gatekeeping has now become fully integrated into the very fabric of American life, with national as well as transnational consequences for both immigrants and the nation at large.

The author thanks the editors and coauthors of this volume, especially Nancy Foner, David Roediger, Yen Le Espiritu, and Doug Hartmann for stimulating conversations, suggestions, and support. In addition, Gary Gerstle provided an especially helpful critique just at the right time.

NOTES

1. The first known use of the gatekeeping metaphor was in California debates over Chinese immigration in 1877 (California State Senate 1878, 275).

2. See "Illegal? Yes. Threat? No," *New York Times Magazine*, January 7, 1996; "Controlling Illegal Immigration—But at a Price," *Christian Science Monitor*, October 4, 1999.

3. On nativism in general, see Higham (1963, 1999), Reimers (1998), Perea (1997), and Sánchez (1997). On the consequences of immigration law, see Salyer (1995) and Ngai (1998, 1999).

4. Higham (1963) and Reimers (1985) remain the standard works on the 1924 and 1965 Immigration Acts, respectively.

5. Among the scholars attempting to see through these blind spots are Catherine Ceniza Choy (2000), who locates the origins of the post-1965 migration of Filipina nurses to the United States during the American occupation of the Philippines at the beginning of the twentieth century, and Mae Ngai (1998, 1999), who studies immigration law and racial formation in the long-ignored 1924 to 1965 period.

6. The year 1875, when the Page Law (18 Stat. 477) was passed on March 3, is arguably another starting point. The act forbade the entry of Chinese, Japanese, and other Asian laborers brought to the United States involuntarily and women brought for the purpose of prostitution. It was a limited beginning, but the law was the first to significantly extend federal authority over immigration; see Peffer (1999, 58–59) and Hutchinson (1981, 66).

7. On the importance of Asian immigration and exclusion to the racialized foundations of modern America, see Lowe (1996, ix), Hing (1993), Palumbo-Liu (1999), Gotanda (1999), and Lee (2003).

8. I utilize a gatekeeping framework to examine the consequences of the Chinese exclusion laws for both the Chinese in America and the nation at large in Lee (2003). Other examples of scholarship that examines immigration policy more broadly include Salyer (1995), Hing (1993), Ngai (1999), and Johnson (1998, 2000).

9. Other scholars have defined similar frameworks explaining the content and meaning of immigration control. Norman and Naomi Zucker (1996, 3) describe contemporary immigration regulation as a "cold war of a different kind" in which "the armies of the north are border patrols and immigration authorities, the weapons restrictive laws, interdictions, 'humane deterrence,' and forced repatriations." José David Saldívar (1997, 96–97) and other border studies scholars describe the U.S.-Mexico border as a "border state" and a "juridical-administrative-therapeutic border machine" that "positions its subjects in ways that dehumanize them." See also Dunn (1996) and Zolberg (1999, 71, 73).

10. On state-building, see, in general, Skocpol (1985, 7, vii) and Skowronek (1982, ix).

11. For a general overview of immigration law in the twentieth century, see Erika Lee (1999). For analysis and primary documents, see Barkan and LeMay (1999, xxii).

12. My thanks to Margot Canaday for the citation related to homosexuals under the 1917 act.

13. On the relationship between immigration regulation and domestic race relations, see Johnson (1998). As Mae Ngai's (1998, 1999) work has shown, immigration policy directly shaped American "racial formation," what Michael Omi and Howard Winant (1994, 55) have explained as the "socio-historical process by which racial categories are created, inhabited, transformed, and destroyed." See also Sánchez (1999), Jacobson (1998, 2000), and Barrett and Roediger (1997).

14. I use Michael Omi and Howard Winant's (1994, 83) definition of the state as being composed of *institutions*, the *policies* they carry out, the *conditions and rules* that support and justify them, and the *social relations* in which they are imbedded. See also Torpey (2000, 1), Palumbo-Liu (1999, 31), Fitzgerald (1996, 96–144), and Zolberg (1999, 71–93).

15. On the relationship between immigration and foreign policy in general, see Jacobson (2000).

16. On the connections between immigration and national identity, see Lowe (1996, ix) and Gerstle (2001).

17. Desmond King (2000, 4–5) argues that the legacy of the 1920s debates and decisions "create[d] a set of fundamental questions about U.S. identity, membership, and citizenship in American political development," including an exclusionary conception of U.S. identity. See also Ngai (1999, 69–71) and Daniels (1991, 265–84).

18. On the Asian exclusion movements being "tangential," see Higham (1963, preface to the second edition and afterword). Reflecting the limited number of studies that examine race, nativism, and immigration law in a comparative framework, existing studies either focus on the anti-Chinese movement and end with the 1882 Chinese Exclusion Act or begin with the debates surrounding European immigration in the 1890s and end with the 1924 Immigration Act. Rarely is there any explanation of how the former influenced the latter. See Gyory (1998), Higham (1963), and King (2000). One helpful exception is Salyer (1995, which demonstrates how the judicial and administrative enforcement of Chinese exclusion shaped general immigration law enforcement as well.

19. On the anti-Chinese movement, see generally Gyory (1998), Saxton (1971), Mink (1986), and Leong (2000).

20. See "Shut the Gates to the Hindu Invasion," *San Francisco Examiner*, June 16, 1910; "The Watchdog States," *San Francisco Post*, May 24, 1910; and *San Francisco Bulletin*, May 4, 1891; as cited in Daniels (1988, 111).

21. On anti-Mexican nativism in general, see Hoffman (1974, 10); Foley (1997, 51).

22. With this zone in place, the United States effectively excluded all immigrants from India, Burma, Siam, the Malay States, Arabia, Afghanistan, part of Russia, and most of the Polynesian Islands.

23. The Quota Act of 1921 (42 Stat. 5, sect. 2) limited European immigration to 3 percent of the number of foreign-born people of each nationality residing in the United States in 1910. The act was designed to limit the immigration of southern and eastern European immigrants, whose populations had been much smaller in 1910. By the same token, the act was designed to favor the immigration of northern and western European immigrants, who had as a group already been a large presence in the United States in 1910. Though the numbers of southern and eastern European immigrants decreased greatly after 1921, nativists pushed for even greater restrictions. The 1924 act (43 Stat. 153) thus reduced the percentage admitted from 3 to 2 percent and moved the census date from 1910 to 1890, when southern and eastern European immigrants had yet to arrive in large numbers. The 1924 Immigration Act closed the door on any further Asian immigration by denying admission to all aliens who were "ineligible for citizenship (that is, those to whom naturalization was denied). See, generally, Higham (1963, 308–24), Ngai (1999), and Divine (1957, 60).

24. This provision preceded the formal establishment of the Bureau of Immigration, which was formed under the Act of August 18, 1894 (28 Stat. 390).

25. See, for example, the Chinese Arrival Files, Port of San Francisco, RG 85, Records of the USINS, National Archives, Pacific Region.

26. The use of "immigrant identification cards" was first begun under U.S. consular regulations on July 1, 1928. The "alien registration receipt cards," commonly known as "green cards," were the product of the Alien Registration Act of June 28, 1940 (54 Stat. 670) and the corresponding INS Alien Registration Program; Marian Smith, personal communication, October 24, 2000; see also Smith (2003).

27. The act declared that any person who secured certificates of identity fraudulently or through impersonation was to be deemed guilty of a misdemeanor, fined $1,000, and imprisoned for up to five years. Any persons who knowingly aided and abetted the landing of "any Chinese person not lawfully entitled to enter the United States" could also be charged with a misdemeanor, fined, and imprisoned for up to one year, sects. 7 and 11, Act of May 6, 1882 (22 Stat. 58). Section 12 of the act declared that "any Chinese person found unlawfully within the United States shall be caused to be removed therefrom to the country from whence he came." These initial forays into federal regulation of immigration would be even further codified and institutionalized seven years later in the Immigration Act of 1891.

28. Liberals generally viewed the McCarren-Walter act as unduly harsh and racist because of its continuation of the national origins system. President Truman in fact vetoed it, but Congress overrode his veto (Reimers 1985, 17–20).

29. Gabriel Chin (1996, 273, 277) goes even further and suggests that the 1965 Immigration Act was revolutionary in its race-neutrality. Drawing from recent interviews with congressional lawmakers, Chin argues that politicians had indeed assumed that post-1965 immigration would largely come from Asia and Latin America.

30. Testimony before Senate Committee on the Judiciary, Subcommittee on Immigration and Naturalization, hearings on S. 500, 1965, 2:709, as cited in Stern (1974, 248, 296).

31. See "Immigration Growth at Highest Rate in 150 Years," *Washington Times*, June 5, 2002.

32. They were 51.7 percent of all immigrants in the United States (see ibid.).

33. In 1976 the Immigration and Nationality Act of 1965 (P.L. 94–571; 90 Stat. 2703) was amended. The new provisions extended to the Western Hemisphere the 20,000-per-country limit and a slightly modified version of the seven-category preference system. In 1978 immigration legislation (P.L. 95 412; 92 907; Immigration and Nationality Act, 79 Stat. 911) was passed to combine the separate hemispheric ceilings into a worldwide ceiling of 290,000 with a single preference system. See King (2000, 243) and Reimers (1985, 81).

34. Matthew Frye Jacobson (1998, 92) has demonstrated how European immigrants had become fully "Caucasian" by the 1960s.

35. For example, the waiting list for applications from Mexican citizens who qualify for immigration as the brothers and sisters of adult citizens under the 1965 act was recently calculated as taking as long as nine years. The applications of those who filed their papers to come to the United States in March 1989 were only being processed in March 1998 (Johnson 1998, 1134).

36. See also "Success Story of One Minority in the United States," *U.S. News & World Report*, December 26, 1966, 73; Robert Lee 1999, 149–53.

37. David Reimers (1985, 81) was the first scholar to make this argument.

38. Historian Roger Daniels (2001, 46, 50, 58) writes that racially based restriction and even nativism is a thing of the past. The "new nativism," he writes, emphasizes issues of class and environment rather than race, ethnicity, or bloodstream. In contrast, Neil Gotanda and George Sánchez argue that contemporary nativism is highly racialized. Gotanda (1997, 253) writes that "nativist movements have *never* been indiscriminately directed against all foreigners—they have been directed against those immigrants that can be racialized. . . . Popular understandings of 'foreignness' suggest that the concept is now infused with a racial character." Likewise, George Sánchez (1997, 373) describes a new racialized hostility toward immigrants and a "new American racism . . . that has no political boundaries or ethnic categorizations."

39. One of the best examples is the way in which race-based nativism conflicted with the humanitarian goals in refugee policies; see Loescher and Scanlan (1986, 113), Hing (1993, 126), Palumbo-Liu (1999, 245), Zucker and Zucker (1987, 1996), and Gee (2001).

40. A large percentage of the new Irish immigrants arriving in America in the 1980s had no proper documentation or overstayed their visas, and the high-profile cases of Chinese "smuggled" into the country by boat along the West and East Coasts point to a dramatic increase in Chinese illegal immigration. See Corcoran (1993, 144), Kwong (1997), Chin (1999), Smith (1997), and Johnson (1998).

41. For the effects of the anti-immigrant mood and government crackdown on Mexican American communities, see Garcia (1995) and Johnson (2000).

42. See "Ambivalence Prevails in Immigration Policy," *New York Times*, May 27, 2001, A14. In contrast, only 11,000 people were arrested for illegally crossing the U.S.-Canada border; see "11,000 Arrested Last Year Trying to Sneak into the U.S.," *National Post* (Ontario, Canada), November 7, 2001.

43. On immigration matters specifically, see the testimony included in Center for Immigration Studies (2001).

44. See "FBI Chief Admits 9/11 Might Have Been Detectable," *New York Times*, May 30, 2002; "Traces of Terror: Immigration Inquiry Finds 'Widespread Failure' at INS in Handling of Hijackers' Student Visas," *New York Times*, May 21, 2002.

45. See "Nation's Open Borders in Spotlight," *Chicago Tribune*, September 26, 2001, 9; "Support for U.S. Security Plans Is Quietly Voiced Across Canada," *New York Times*, October 1, 2001,

B3; Dennis Bueckert, "Canadian Sovereignty Called into Question in Fight Against Terrorism," *Canadian Press Newswire*, October 3, 2001; "Border Painted as Magnet for Terror," *National Post* (Ontario, Canada), October 4, 2001, A1, A15; "Vast U.S.-Canada Border Suddenly Poses a Problem," *New York Times*, October 4, 2001, B1; "Bills Would Tighten U.S.-Canada Border," *Seattle Times*, October 10, 2001, A1.

46. See "Swept Up in Dragnet, Hundreds Sit in Custody and Ask, 'Why?'" *New York Times*, November 25, 2001; "Al Qaeda Link Seen in Only a Handful of 1,200 Detainees," *New York Times*, November 29, 2001.

47. See "Hate Crimes, Next Steps Mounting Tensions," *Boston Globe*, September 17, 2001.

48. See "Attacks and Harassment of Middle-Eastern Americans Rising," *Boston Globe*, September 14, 2001; "Violence and Harassment: Victims of Mistaken Identity, Sikhs Pay a Price for Turbans," *Boston Globe*, September 19, 2001; "Lax U.S. Visa Laws Give Terrorists Easy Entry—Immigrants Difficult to Track as They Blend into Ethnic Communities," *Detroit News*, September 30, 2001.

49. See also "Immigration Scrutiny a 'Dramatic' Shift in Focus," *Miami Herald*, November 16, 2001; "U.S. Informs Mexico on Migration Plan," *New York Times*, November 21, 2001.

50. See "Bordering on Harmonization: Why Canada Faces Pressure," *National Post* (Ontario, Canada), October 1, 2001, A10; "Mexico's Security Advisor Gives Border Cooperation a Thumbs Up," *Arizona Republic*, November 19, 2001.

51. See "House Passes Terrorism Bill Much Like Senate's, but with Five-Year Limit," *New York Times*, October 13, 2001.

52. See "U.S. Has Covered 200 Campuses to Check Up on Mideast Students," *New York Times*, November 12, 2001.

53. See "Bush's New Rules to Fight Terror Transform the Legal Landscape," *New York Times*, November 25, 2001; "U.S. Makes It Easier to Detain Foreigners," *New York Times*, November 28, 2001.

54. See "Ruling Clears Way to Use State Police in Immigration Duty," *New York Times*, April 4, 2002.

55. See "Ashcroft Proposes Fingerprinting Visas' Holders," *New York Times*, June 5, 2002.

56. See "U.S. Plan to Monitor Muslims Meets with Widespread Protest," *New York Times*, January 18, 2003.

57. See "Electronic Tracking System Monitors Foreign Students," *New York Times*, February 17, 2003.

58. The exact number of total registrants seems to be difficult to ascertain. A February 17, 2003, article in the *New York Times* reported that "more than 130,000" were registered, while a June 7, 2003, article in the same newspaper cited a government report claiming a total of 82,000 registrants. See "More Than 13,000 May Face Deportation," *New York Times*, June 7, 2003; "Fearful, Angry or Confused, Muslim Immigrants Register," *New York Times*, April 25, 2003.

59. "Fearful, Angry or Confused, Muslim Immigrants Register," *New York Times*, April 25, 2003.

60. For more on the new Bureau of Citizenship and Immigration Services, visit the bureau's website, "This Is the BCIS," http://uscis.gov/graphics/aboutus/thisisimm/index.htm (accessed June 30, 2003).

61. See Mark Krikorian's testimony before the U.S. House of Representatives Committee on the Judiciary, Subcommittee on Immigration, Border Security, and Claims, Department of

Homeland Security Transition: Bureau of Immigration and Customs Enforcement (Center for Immigration Studies 2003).

62. See, for example, the June 26, 2002, testimony by Bill Ong Hing before the U.S. Senate Judiciary Committee hearings on immigration reform and the reorganization of homeland defense (Immigration Daily 2002).

63. See "Illegal Aliens Can Be Held Indefinitely, Ashcroft Says," *New York Times*, April 26, 2003; "More Illegal Immigrants Can Be Held," *Washington Post*, April 25, 2003.

64. See "U.S. Report Faults the Roundup of Illegal Immigrants After 9/11," *New York Times*, June 3, 2003.

65. See "Ashcroft Seeks More Power to Pursue Terror Suspects," *New York Times*, June 6, 2003.

REFERENCES

Balderrama, Francisco E., and Raymond Rodriguez. 1995. *Decade of Betrayal: Mexican Repatriation in the 1930s.* Albuquerque: University of New Mexico Press.

Barkan, Elliott, and Michael LeMay, eds. 1999. *U.S. Immigration and Naturalization Laws and Issues.* Westport, Conn.: Greenwood.

Barrett, James, and David Roediger. 1997. "Inbetween Peoples: Race, Nationality, and the 'New Immigrant' Working Class." *Journal of American Ethnic History* 16(3): 3–44.

Bennett, Marion T. 1963. *American Immigration Policies: A History.* Washington, D.C.: Public Affairs Press.

Bernard, William S., ed. 1984. *American Immigration Policy: A Reappraisal.* New York: Harper.

Burnham, Frederick Russell. 1930. "The Howl for Cheap Mexican Labor." In *The Alien in Our Midst, or, Selling Our Birthright for a Mess of Pottage,* edited by Madison Grant and Charles Stewart Davison. New York: Galton.

California State Senate. Special Committee on Chinese Immigration. 1878. *Chinese Immigration: Its Social, Moral, and Political Effect.* Sacramento: State Office of Printing.

Cardoso, Lawrence. 1980. *Mexican Emigration to the United States, 1891–1931.* Tucson: University of Arizona Press.

Center for Immigration Studies. 2001. "Immigration and Terrorism: Panel Discussion Transcript" (November 6). http://www.cis.org/articles/2001/terrorpanel.html (accessed February 1, 2003).

———. 2003. "Securing the Homeland Through Immigration Law Enforcement." Statement before Congress of Mark Krikorian, executive director of the Center for Immigration Studies (April 10). http://www.cis.org/articles/2003/msktestimony410/html (accessed June 30, 2003).

Chin, Gabriel J. 1996. "The Civil Rights Revolution Comes to Immigration Law: A New Look at the Immigration and Nationality Act of 1965." *North Carolina Law Review* 75(1, November): 273–345.

Chin, Ko-lin. 1999. *Smuggled Chinese: Clandestine Immigration to the United States.* Philadelphia: Temple University Press.

Choy, Catherine Ceniza. 2000. "Asian American History: Reflections on Imperialism, Immigration, and 'the Body.'" *Amerasia Journal* 26(1): 119–40.

Corcoran, Mary P. 1993. *Irish Illegals: Transients Between Two Societies.* Westport, Conn.: Greenwood.

Daniels, Roger. 1988. *Asian America: Chinese and Japanese in the United States Since 1850.* Seattle: University of Washington Press.

———. 1991. *Coming to America: A History of Immigration and Ethnicity in American Life.* New York: HarperPerennial.

———. 1997. "No Lamps Were Lit for Them: Angel Island and the Historiography of Asian American Immigration." *Journal of American Ethnic History* 17(1): 3–18.

————. 2001. "Two Cheers for Immigration." In *Debating American Immigration, 1882 to the Present*, edited by Roger Daniels and Otis Graham. Lanham, Md.: Rowman & Littlefield.

Divine, Robert A. 1957. *American Immigration Policy, 1924–1952.* New York: Da Capo Press.

Dunn, Timothy J. 1996. *The Militarization of the U.S.-Mexico Border, 1978–1992.* Austin: University of Texas Press for the Center for Mexican American Studies.

Fine, Glenn A. 2003. "The September 11 Detainees: A Review of the Treatment of Aliens Held on Immigration Charges in Connection with the Investigation of the September 11 Attacks" (June 2). http://www.justice.gov/oig/special/03-06/index.htm (accessed November 21, 2003).

Fitzgerald, Keith. 1996. *Face the Nation: Immigration, the State, and the National Identity.* Stanford, Calif.: Stanford University Press.

Foley, Neil. 1997. *The White Scourge: Mexicans, Blacks, and Poor Whites in Texas Cotton Culture.* Berkeley: University of California Press.

Gabaccia, Donna. 1994. *From the Other Side: Women, Gender, and Immigrant Life in the United States, 1820–1990.* Bloomington: Indiana University Press.

————. 1999a. "Is Everywhere Nowhere? Nomads, Nations, and the Immigrant Paradigm of United States History." *Journal of American History* 86(3, June): 1132–33.

————. 1999b. The "'Yellow Peril' and the 'Chinese of Europe': Global Perspectives on Race and Labor, 1815–1930." In *Migration, Migration History, History: Old Paradigms and New Perspectives*, edited by Jan and Leo Lucassen. Bern: Peter Lang.

Garcia, Ruben J. 1995. "Critical Race Theory and Proposition 187: The Racial Politics of Immigration Law." *Chicano-Latino Law Review* 17(Fall): 118–54.

Gee, Harvey. 2001. "The Refugee Burden: A Closer Look at the Refugee Act of 1980." *North Carolina Journal of International Law and Commercial Regulation* 26(Spring): 559–651.

Gerstle, Gary. 2001. *American Crucible: Race and Nation in the Twentieth Century.* Princeton, N.J.: Princeton University Press.

Glazer, Nathan. 1985. *Clamor at the Gates: The New American Immigration.* San Francisco: ICS Press.

Gotanda, Neil. 1997. "Race, Citizenship, and the Search for Political Community Among 'We the People.'" *Oregon Law Review* 76(Summer): 233–59.

————. 1999. "Exclusion and Inclusion: Immigration and American Orientalism." In *Across the Pacific: Asian Americans and Globalization*, edited by Evelyn Hu-DeHart. Philadelphia: Temple University Press.

Graham, Otis L. 2001. "The Unfinished Reform: Regulating Immigration in the National Interest." In *Debating American Immigration, 1882 to the Present*, edited by Roger Daniels and Otis Graham. Lanham, Md.: Rowman & Littlefield.

Gutiérrez, David G. 1995. *Walls and Mirrors: Mexican Americans, Mexican Immigrants, and the Politics of Ethnicity.* Berkeley: University of California Press.

Gyory, Andrew. 1998. *Closing the Gate: Race, Politics, and the Chinese Exclusion Act.* Chapel Hill: University of North Carolina Press.

Higham, John. 1963. *Strangers in the Land: Patterns of American Nativism, 1860–1925.* New York: Atheneum.

————. 1999. "Instead of a Sequel, or, How I Lost My Subject." In *The Handbook of International Migration: The American Experience*, edited by Charles Hirschman, Philip Kasinitz, and Josh DeWind. New York: Russell Sage Foundation.

Hing, Bill Ong. 1993. *Making and Remaking Asian America Through Immigration Policy, 1850–1990.* Stanford, Calif.: Stanford University Press.

Hoffman, Abraham. 1974. *Unwanted Mexican Americans in the Great Depression: Repatriation Pressures, 1929–1939.* Tucson: University of Arizona Press.

Hutchinson, Edward P. 1981. *Legislative History of American Immigration Policy, 1798–1965.* Philadelphia: University of Pennsylvania Press.

Immigration Daily. 2002. "Testimony of Bill Ong Hing Before the U.S. Senate Judiciary Committee Hearings on Immigration Reform and the Reorganization of Homeland Defense" (June 26). Immigration Daily (ILW.COM), http://www.ilw.com/lawyers/immigdaily/congress_ news/2002,0702-senate-hing.shtm (accessed February 1, 2003).

Jacobson, Matthew Frye. 1998. *Whiteness of a Different Color: European Immigrants and the Alchemy of Race.* Cambridge, Mass.: Harvard University Press.

———. 2000. *Barbarian Virtues: The United States Encounters Foreign Peoples at Home and Abroad, 1876–1917.* New York: Hill and Wang.

Johnson, Kevin R. 1998. "Race, the Immigration Laws, and Domestic Race Relations: 'A Magic Mirror' and into the Heart of Darkness." *Indiana Law Journal* 73(Fall): 11–59.

———. 2000. "Race Matters: Immigration Law and Policy Scholarship, Law in the Ivory Tower, and the Legal Indifference of the Race Critique." *University of Illinois Law Review* 2000(2): 525–57.

Johnson, Lyndon B. 1965. "Annual Message to the Congress on the State of the Union" (January 8, 1964). In *Public Papers of the Presidents of the United States, Lyndon B. Johnson: Containing the Public Messages, Speeches, and Statements of the President,* Volume 1, book 1—November 22, 1963 to June 30, 1964. Washington: U.S. Government Printing Office.

———. 1966. "President Lyndon Baines Johnson's Statement at the Signing of the 1965 Immigration and Nationality Bill, Liberty Island, New York" (October 3, 1965). In *Public Papers of the Presidents of the United States, Lyndon B. Johnson: Containing the Public Messages, Speeches, and Statements of the President,* Volume 2, book 2—June 1 to December 31, 1965. Washington: U.S. Government Printing Office.

Kennedy, John F. 1958. *A Nation of Immigrants.* New York: Harper and Row.

King, Desmond. 2000. *Making Americans: Immigration, Race, and the Origins of the Diverse Democracy.* Cambridge, Mass.: Harvard University Press.

Kraut, Alan. 1994. *Silent Travelers: Germs, Genes, and the "Immigrant Menace."* Baltimore: Johns Hopkins University Press.

Kwong, Peter. 1997. *Forbidden Workers: Illegal Chinese Immigrants and American Labor.* New York: New Press.

Lee, Erika. 1999. "Immigrants and Immigration Law: A State of the Field Assessment." *Journal of American Ethnic History* 18(4): 85–114.

———. 2003. *At America's Gates: Chinese Immigration During the Exclusion Era, 1882–1943.* Chapel Hill: University of North Carolina Press.

Lee, Robert G. 1999. *Orientals: Asian Americans in Popular Culture.* Philadelphia: Temple University Press.

LeMay, Michael C. 1987. *From Open Door to Dutch Door: An Analysis of U.S. Immigration Policy Since 1820.* New York: Praeger.

———. 1989. *Gatekeepers: Comparative Immigration Policy.* New York: Praeger.

Leong, Karen J. 2000. "'A Distant and Antagonistic Race': Constructions of Chinese Manhood in the Exclusionist Debates, 1869–1878." In *Across the Great Divide: Cultures of Manhood in the American West,* edited by Laura McCall, Matthew Basso, and Dee Garceau. New York: Routledge.

Loescher, Gil, and John Scanlan. 1986. *Calculated Kindness: Refugees and America's Half Open Door, 1945 to the Present.* New York: Free Press.

Lowe, Lisa. 1996. *Immigrant Acts: On Asian American Cultural Politics.* Durham, N.C.: Duke University Press.

McKenzie, Roderick Duncan. 1928. *Oriental Exclusion: The Effect of American Immigration Laws, Regulations, and Judicial Decisions upon the Chinese and Japanese on the American Pacific Coast.* Chicago: University of Chicago Press.

Melendy, H. Brett. 1976. "The Filipinos in the United States." In *The Asian-American: The Historical Experience,* edited by Norris Hundley. Santa Barbara, Calif.: CLIO Press for the American Bibliography Center.

Mink, Gwendolyn. 1986. *Old Labor and New Immigrants in American Political Development: Union, Party, and State, 1875–1920.* Ithaca, N.Y.: Cornell University Press.

National Archives and Records Administration (NARA). Pacific Alaska Region (Seattle). 1933. "Census of Chinese Students Following the Immigration Act of 1924: Executive Files Retrieved from Immigration and Naturalization Service Including Instructions for Chinese Inspectors, Compiled by M. C. Faris." Center for the Study of the Pacific Northwest, http://www.washington.edu/uwired/outreach/cspn/curaaw/aawdoc05.html (accessed June 30, 2003).

Ngai, Mae. 1998. "Illegal Aliens and Alien Citizens: United States Immigration Policy and Racial Formation, 1924–1945." Ph.D. diss., Columbia University.

———. 1999. "The Architecture of Race in American Immigration Law: A Reexamination of the Immigration Act of 1924." *Journal of American History* 86(1): 67–92.

Omi, Michael, and Howard Winant. 1994. *Racial Formation in the United States From the 1960s to the 1990s.* 2nd ed. New York: Routledge.

Palumbo-Liu, David. 1999. *Asian/American: Historical Crossings of a Racial Frontier.* Stanford, Calif.: Stanford University Press.

Peffer, George Anthony. 1999. *If They Don't Bring Their Women Here: Chinese Female Immigration Before Exclusion.* Urbana: University of Illinois Press.

Perea, Juan. 1997. *Immigrants Out! The New Nativism and the Anti-Immigrant Impulse in the United States.* New York: New York University Press.

Peters, Katherine McIntire. 1996. "Up Against the Wall—Operation Gatekeeper" (October 1). Government Executive Magazine (GovExec.com). http://www.govexec.com/archdoc/1096/1096s1.htm.

Peterson, William. 1966. "Success Story: Japanese-American Style." *New York Times Magazine,* January 9.

Reimers, David. 1985. *Still the Golden Door: The Third World Comes to America.* New York: Columbia University Press.

———. 1998. *Unwelcome Strangers: American Identity and the Turn Against Immigration.* New York: Columbia University Press.

Riggs, Fred. 1950. *Pressure on Congress: A Study of the Repeal of the Chinese Exclusion Act.* New York: King's Crown Press.

Saldívar, José David. 1997. *Border Matters: Remapping American Cultural Studies.* Berkeley: University of California Press.

Salyer, Lucy. 1995. *Laws Harsh as Tigers: Chinese Immigration and the Shaping of Modern Immigration Law.* Chapel Hill: University of North Carolina Press.

Sánchez, George J. 1993. *Becoming Mexican American: Ethnicity, Culture, and Identity in Chicano Los Angeles, 1900–1945.* New York: Oxford University Press.

———. 1997. "Face the Nation: Race, Immigration, and the Rise of the New Nativism in Late Twentieth-Century America." *International Migration Review* 31(4): 1009–30.

———. 1999. "Race, Nation, and Culture in Recent Immigration Studies." *Journal of American Ethnic History* 18(4): 66–84.

Saxton, Alexander. 1971. *Indispensable Enemy: Labor and the Anti-Chinese Movement in California.* Berkeley: University of California Press.

Skocpol, Theda. 1985. "Bringing the State Back In: Strategies of Analysis in Current Research." In *Bringing the State Back In,* edited by Peter B. Evans, Dietrich Rueschemeyer, and Theda Skocpol. Cambridge: Cambridge University Press.

Skowronek, Stephen. 1982. *Building a New American State: The Expansion of National Administrative Capacities, 1877–1920.* Cambridge: Cambridge University Press.

Smith, Marian. 2003. "Why Isn't the Green Card Green?" (last modified March 1, 2003). U.S. Bureau of Citizenship and Immigration Services, http://www.uscis.gov/graphics/aboutus/history/articles/green.htm (accessed July 1, 2003).

Smith, Paul J., ed. 1997. *Human Smuggling: Chinese Migrant Trafficking and the Challenge to America's Immigration Tradition.* Washington, D.C.: Center for Strategic and International Studies.

Stern, William. 1974. "H.R. 2580, The Immigration and Nationality Amendments of 1965—A Case Study." Ph.D. diss., New York University.

Stoddard, Lothrop. 1930. "The Permanent Menace from Europe." In *The Alien in Our Midst, or, Selling Our Birthright for a Mess of Pottage,* edited by Madison Grant and Charles Stewart Davison. New York: Galton.

Torpey, John. 2000. *The Invention of the Passport: Surveillance, Citizenship, and the State*. New York: Cambridge University Press.

Trucio-Haynes, Enid. 1997. "The Legacy of Racially Restrictive Immigration Laws and Policies and the Construction of the American National Identity." *Oregon Law Review* 76(2, Summer): 369–424.

U.S. Immigration and Naturalization Service (USINS). 1999. *Statistical Yearbook of the Immigration and Naturalization Service, 1998*. Washington: U.S. Government Printing Office. http://www.uscis.gov/graphics/shared/aboutus/statistics/ybpage.htm (accessed November 21, 2003).

———. 2000. "Immigration by Region and Selected Country of Last Residence: Fiscal Years 1820–1998." *Statistical Yearbook of the Immigration and Naturalization Service, 1998*. Washington: U.S. Government Printing Office. http://www.uscis.gov/graphics/shared/aboutus/statistics/IMM00yrbk/IMM2000list.htm (accessed November 21, 2003).

Zhao, Xiaojian. 2002. *Remaking Chinese America: Immigration, Family, and Community, 1940–1965*. New Brunswick, N.J.: Rutgers University Press.

Zhou, Min, and James Gatewood. 2000. "Introduction." In *Contemporary Asian America: A Multidisciplinary Reader*, edited by Min Zhou and James V. Gatewood. New York: New York University Press.

Zolberg, Aristide. 1999. "Matters of State: Theorizing Immigration." In *The Handbook of International Migration: The American Experience*, edited by Charles Hirschman, Philip Kasinitz, and Josh DeWind. New York: Russell Sage Foundation.

Zucker, Norman L., and Naomi Flink Zucker. 1987. *The Guarded Gate: The Reality of American Refugee Policy*. New York: Harcourt Brace Jovanovich.

———. 1996. *Desperate Crossings: Seeking Refuge in America*. New York: M. E. Sharpe.

Kenneth Prewitt

Chapter 7

The Census Counts, the Census Classifies

We start with three propositions. In the political and economic life of a nation, it is not simply "how many" but "how many of what" that matters. We count to get a count, but also to classify, to create categories and taxonomies. When the Lord instructs Moses to take a census, it is to learn how many men there are of fighting age. So it has been across the history of census-taking: how many young males, how many taxpayers, how many women of childbearing age, how many noncitizens, and on and on. The constitutional purpose of the U.S. census is, of course, a variant on this principle. Its intention was not (primarily) demographic classification but geographic sorting. At issue was the apportioning of seats in the new Congress based on the distribution of the population across the thirteen new states.

Our second proposition holds that a taxonomy of standing importance in U.S. census-taking, that by race and ethnicity, is more contested than at any time in its long and tortured history. Since the first decennial census in 1790, the race taxonomy has often been modified for political and economic purposes (see Anderson 1988; Nobles 2000; Skerry 2000). But the game has changed in recent decades. There is now an active politics of sorting and classifying, led by those groups that historically were the subject of shifting taxonomies. The struggle is less about being counted than about being counted as something in particular, when the particular is denominated as a race, ethnicity, subnationality, or ancestry group. Groups whose identities are being expressed, or suppressed, or at least their self-appointed leaders, negotiate both within and across groups for a measurement system that will advance their claims on resources and promote their assertions of group identity. The American racial-ethnic taxonomy—including what is racial and what is ethnic about it—is in a phase of unprecedented uncertainty and volatility.[1] The introduction of the multiple-race option in the 2000 census is a prime exhibit, but the uncertainties extend well beyond this change in measurement strategy.

The third proposition helps explain the second. The politics of statistical proportionality took on a new urgency as a result of the civil rights revolution in the 1960s, the emergence of legal concepts such as disparate impact, and the rhetoric of under- (and over-) representation that fueled the rise of diversity as a goal to be embraced in politics, education, business, and the military.[2] Immigrant flows since the 1960s are, of course, rearranging the definitions of diversity and multiculturalism. Disputes about definitions play against an older racial-ethnic taxonomy that is losing its hold in public discourse, with policy implications that are difficult to foresee (Hollinger 1995).

RACIAL MEASUREMENT IN
AMERICAN HISTORY

In the most recent U. S. census, fielded in 2000, race was measured differently than at any time in its politically charged, complicated history. Americans were no longer forced into a limited number of discrete racial groups. They could declare themselves to be multiracial, to be the products of cross-racial unions. This option has upended assumptions that have defined "race" since the Enlightenment, with consequences both political and theoretical. We can best assess the import of this change in measurement policy by situating the 2000 national census in a narrative that starts in 1790, when the United States initiated an unbroken series of decennial census-taking.

The U.S. census is constitutionally mandated, for reasons only briefly sketched here. America's constitution writers in 1787 were less fixed on taxation and conscription, traditional purposes of census-taking, than on fresher problems that faced the new nation. One was how to establish a democratic form of government based on principles of representation, and a second was how to populate the vast, rich western territories without succumbing to the temptations of colonization (considered incompatible with government based on principles of equal citizenship). The decennial census was instrumental to both nation-building tasks. It allowed for allocating political power proportion to population size in the legislative house "closest to the people." And it facilitated the continuous reallocation of power to new states as the population grew in size and pressed into the sparsely populated areas to the west of the original coastal states.

With these basic nation-building tasks agreed to, attention turned to deciding what kind of census to take. Most issues were easily resolved. For example, the census would be managed by the new federal government, not by the states. It would be done on a fixed schedule and with questions uniformly asked in all parts of the country. The results would be presented to the Congress, which would then apply a formula according to which seats in the House of Representatives would be allocated.

But not all issues were quickly resolved. One debate was whether to base representation on population alone or on population plus wealth. After quickly falling into futile argument about how to measure wealth, the framers realized that there was no sound method given the primitive nature of measurement methods at the time. But in an awkward compromise, they agreed that slaves were an easily measured indicator of wealth. The constitutional passage establishing the census stated that the count in each state "shall be determined by adding to the whole Number of free Persons, including those bound to Service for a Term of Years, and excluding Indians not taxed, three-fifths of all other Persons." The "all other Persons" were the slaves, who were to count as three-fifths of a person for purposes of determining the population size of each state. James Madison, who participated in the Constitutional Convention and recorded its deliberation, famously observed that the Constitution "decides with great propriety on the case of our slaves, when it views them in the mixt character of persons and property. This is in fact their true character" (Madison 1953, 214, Federalist Paper 54).

The significance of this decision is best grasped in the context of another and seemingly unrelated debate that took place in preparing for the 1790 census. James Madison wanted a more expansive census schedule than was eventually adopted; he particularly urged the identification of occupations of the adult male population (Anderson 1994). Madison offered what, to him, was a commonsense rationale and one that we take for granted today: "To accommodate our laws to the real situation of our constituents, we ought to be acquainted with that situation." The Senate rejected his proposal, making the argument that separate interests could not in practice and should not in theory be identified in the census. Governing had to have the common good as its focus. It would be incompatible with this obligation to institute a measurement that gave prominence to the differing economic interests of agriculture, commerce, and manufacturing (Cohen 1982/1999, 159–64).

I recount this familiar history as an aid to understanding the deep history of racial measurement in U.S. census-taking. Whereas the nation's founders resisted an occupational classification that, they felt, would violate the eighteenth-century idea of society as a harmonious whole, they hesitated not at all in creating a racial taxonomy. In particular, the native Indian and the African American could and should be measured in order to separate them from the Anglo-Saxon population. That this initially had a civic rationale, because Indians and slaves were assigned a special relation to the apportionment process, does not lessen its importance in establishing a basic demographic principle—distinguishing between Americans on the basis of race.[3]

The 1790 census, of course, was not the only expression of racial distinctions in the early Republic. The Northwest Ordinance had made it relatively easy to become a citizen in the new territories. Hoping to stimulate population movement, the ordinance "naturalized long-term alien inhabitants as U.S. territorial citizens, without any explicit discriminatory qualifications. French inhabitants, Catholics, the irreligious, free blacks, and individual Native Americans all could claim this new kind of national citizenship" (Smith 1997, 98). This liberal view did not prevail when, in 1790, the new Congress debated citizenship criteria. Congress restricted eligibility for naturalization to free white persons. Naturalization in the new Republic, like its census, made no distinctions of religion, language, or national origin but introduced an explicit exclusion based on race.

In this early American history we get to the first of the propositions set forth at the outset of this chapter. There is no end to the ways in which a national measurement system can count and sort a population: by age, gender, religion, occupation, language, ancestry, ethnicity, intelligence, height, weight, hair color, favorite food. These and hundreds of other population differences can, depending on one's theory of society, become taxonomies with which sociologically to describe and/or politically to govern the population. Which taxonomies are chosen?

A choice was made in designing the first census in 1790. This census did not classify by occupation, as already noted, or by religion, though that would have been easy to do. It did classify by age, gender, and race. The reason was simple: for political and economic purposes, it was necessary to count the number of adult, white males— those who could vote, hold office, own property, pay taxes, and, if needed, become military recruits.

To what extent did the measurement system and its taxonomies have an independent effect on the political, economic, and social life of the nation? This question, which takes us deep into counterfactual reasoning, can never be fully answered. But we might ask how different American history would have been if in 1790, and then in every subsequent census, religion but *not* race had become a dominant feature of population classification. Certainly the United States has had a serious politics of religion. These politics first dealt with establishing tolerance among different Protestant Reform sects—Congregationalists, Anglicans, Methodists, Baptists, Quakers, and so on. The principle of separation between church and state was basic to this earliest foray into religious politics. Matters became more complex when the Protestant nation had to extend civic membership to Catholics and Jews, a task not made easy by the strong anti-Catholic and anti-Semitic prejudices that continued into the twentieth century. As we start the twenty-first century, the nation struggles with incorporating Muslims, Hindus, Sikhs, and Buddhists into a "Christian" nation. This long and at times violent politics of religion, not yet over, took place without a state-sanctioned religious taxonomy. In no meaningful way did religion make it into the measurement system, and thus political struggles over how to incorporate, or resist, "alien" religious practices have not been able to focus on growth rates, proportionality, majorities and minorities, and all the other offshoots of measurement.

No such inhibitions prevented the endless and endlessly changing measurement of race and ethnicity, which resulted in a race and ethnic politics that has always had a "how many" as one of its dominant features. As already noted, the starting point was simple and even naive. Sorting the American population of 1790 into European, African, and native Indian was a reflection of the natural order, as then understood. Enlightenment philosophy attributed observed physical and cultural differences to differences in the natural environment, and what could be more apparent than differences in skin color and facial features?[4] This is the early formulation of what was to become midnineteenth-century polygenetic race science, with its assumption not only of racial differences but of the innate superiority of some races over others.[5]

Although there was no questioning whether the African slave population was to occupy its separate category in America's racial taxonomy, the story of the other non-white race, the native Indian, is more complex. The native Indians, though primitive, were also viewed as a Noble Race. In their fierce independence and love of freedom they exhibited characteristics favored by American Enlightenment thinking. Thomas Jefferson wrote in 1803 that the Indians "will in time either incorporate with us as citizens of the United States or remove beyond the Mississippi." He allowed that incorporation "is certainly the termination of their history most happy for themselves."[6] It was simply an unfortunate accident of history that they happened to occupy land that was destined for the great experiment in republican government that America had engaged. In this thinking, Indians, unlike blacks, had a choice. Jefferson was echoed across the nineteenth century by missionaries and some government officials who held that Indians could, if properly educated and "civilized," join the white race.[7]

Of course, this view competed with the equally strong sentiment that the only good Indian was a dead Indian. Settlers on the frontier and the soldiers sent to protect them sustained this stereotype, which justified as necessary not just the relocation of the Indian but wars of extermination. By the beginning of the twentieth century, scientific racism had trumped what remained of the earlier Enlightenment view, and Indians no less than blacks were considered an inferior race not capable of assimilation.

The race story in American history and in census-taking starts, then, as a narrative based on three groups: European, native Indian, and African American. Matters were soon to become more complex. Territorial wars and land purchase in the nineteenth century added numerous other groups. The purchase of the Louisiana territory from France in 1803 added Creoles as well as a French settler population. The purchase of the Russian colony of Alaska in 1867 added the Inuit, the Kodiak, and other Alaskan natives. The Mexican-American War (1846–48) added the nation's first large Mexican population, about eighty thousand people. The Spanish-American War added Puerto Rico and other Caribbean islands and their peoples. When Hawaii was annexed in 1898, its native Pacific Islander population fell under American rule. Although the population increases that resulted from conquest and purchase were relatively small, they added substantially to the country's demographic diversity.

Numerically, the massive flows of immigrants from the Old to the New World more dramatically transformed the nation's demographic base. In the early decades of the nineteenth century, Irish and Germans dominated immigration, but by the end of the century immigrants from southern and eastern Europe were arriving in large numbers that continued until the eve of World War I. Immigrant flows were predominantly but not only European. In the middle of the nineteenth century, Asian workers immigrated to the West Coast, drawn to the mines and railroad work that offered wages unheard of in China and Japan.[8]

The 1850 census was the first to distinguish between native- and foreign-born. New York City was then more than half foreign-born, and there were similarly high proportions of foreign-born in Chicago, Milwaukee, Detroit, St. Louis, and New Orleans. It was this surge of immigration that led the nativist Know-Nothing Party in the years before the Civil War to worry that Romanism would undermine the Protestant Puritanism on which the nation had constructed its moral and political identity. The efforts by nativist political movements to close America's external borders were not successful. To settle and economically exploit the transmontane regions to the west required much more labor than the natural fertility of the Anglo-Saxon base would provide. With industrialization, even more labor was needed. Anti-immigrant forces intent on protecting cultural homogeneity were routinely defeated by railroad and mining interests, which wanted the West settled, by the shipbuilders and shipowners who profited from the Atlantic crossings, and by the urban factory owners in search of a large labor pool willing to work for low wages.

These midnineteenth-century immigration debates echoed earlier views. Writing in 1787, Tench Coxe, later to become a member of Jefferson's administration, caught the general sentiment when he suggested that though immigration was necessary, it should not be too much or of the wrong kind. He wrote: "How far emigration from other countries into this, ought to be encouraged, is a very important question. It is clear, that the present situation of America, renders it necessary to promote the influx of people; and it is equally clear, that we have a right to restrain that influx, whenever it is found likely to prove hurtful to us."[9] Jefferson had taken a similar position in his *Notes on the State of Virginia*, in which he wrote of the "desire of America to produce rapid population by as great importations of foreigners as possible," but then also advised against "encouragement by extraordinary means" (Jefferson 1787/1984, 201). Jefferson's vision of a transcontinental nation required a growing population, but he worried that if not carefully managed, this need could lead to the importation of nonrepublican sentiments into the new nation.

When anti-immigrant forces could not close the external borders, they focused on creating internal borders that would differentially grant civic rights. The census measurement system and its taxonomies were serviceable in this regard, as the government turned to policies of selective incorporation. Discrimination aimed at non-Anglo Europeans carried into the quota-based restrictive immigration policies of the 1920s. Key to these policies was the use of the 1890 census counts, which established quotas based on the proportion of the population from different European countries. This use of 1890 proportions was designed to—and did—limit the flow of immigrants from southern and eastern Europe. The racist arguments, as summarized by Margo Anderson, held that the older immigrants "were skilled, thrifty, hard-working, like native Americans," whereas the more recent immigrants, from southern and eastern Europe, were "un-skilled, ignorant, predominantly Catholic or Jewish, and thus unfamiliar with and perhaps unassimilable to American institutions" (Anderson 1994, 143).[10]

The political efforts to control immigration in the 1920s were focused more on national origin than on race, and despite the newly established immigration controls, there was gradual civic inclusion for all those nationalities and ethnic groups that could trace their origin to Europe. Those denied equal legal protection and civic membership were marked (and measured) as racially different—the Hispanics, Asians, African Americans, and native peoples.[11]

We do not attribute to the census alone the racialization of American politics. But the availability of a racial taxonomy was handmaiden to the politics of exclusion practiced across the nineteenth century and well into the twentieth. In one version or another, the classification of European, African, and Indian in the original census of 1790 persisted, though the categories changed with the times. By 1820 it was necessary to add "free colored persons" to the classification scheme. After the Civil War, there was interest in shades of color, and the census classified people as mulatto, quadroon, and octoroon. But then the classification had to be expanded even more to accommodate Asians. Chinese and Japanese were separately counted in 1890. Filipinos, Koreans, and Hindus (confusing a religion with a race) were counted in 1920. Hawaiian and part Hawaiian appeared on the 1960 census form, as did Aleut and Eskimo. Mexican as a category appeared in 1930, but then was dropped following political pressure from the Mexican government. Mexicans were then counted as white until 1970. At that point they reentered the census, but as part of an ethnic categorization—persons of Hispanic origin.[12] This category was a deliberate effort to count Hispanics without treating them as a race. They were to be considered a cultural-linguistic group. By this reasoning, Hispanics can have a racial identification separate from their ethnicity, and the census expects Hispanics to also select from the primary racial categories.[13]

Starting with the 1790 census, the census counted and classified by race, by national origin, and now also by ethnicity. The taxonomies created by this shifting measurement effort were used administratively to regulate relations among the groups officially established. Discriminatory social policy designed to protect the numerical and political supremacy of Americans of European ancestry needed a taxonomy that assigned everyone to a discrete racial group. The taxonomy identified those whose national origin, race, or ethnicity was cause for exclusion. Of course, not just census data but vital statistics and, eventually, a comprehensive system of administrative record-keeping, both public and private, played a part.

More generally, the census provided a basis for presuming that separate and distinct races constitute the true condition of the American population and can thereby provide the basis for law and public policy. Because there are measurable groups, there are traits that are presumed to be differently distributed across these groups—including, of course, traits such as intelligence, social worth, and moral habits. On this foundation was constructed a race-based legal code and social and economic practices. The key analytic point is that state-sanctioned discrimination was practiced against persons based on their ascribed characteristics—that is, because of the social groupings to which the census and related record-keeping had assigned them.

An issue unresolved across the long history of counting and sorting by race and ethnicity is whether the categories created in state measurement systems have an independent effect on the groups to which people see themselves as belonging. Pierre Bourdieu (1991, 105) has written that "the act of naming" creates social realities. David

Goldberg (1997, 34) has carried this theoretical argument to the census, writing that racial measurement in the census reflects but also reifies: "it reproduces as it creates and cements as it naturalizes." Every scholar who has written about measurement offers a hypothesis. William Petersen (1987, 206–7, 218) observes that the Census Bureau itself quickens the formation of groups out of statistical categories by "granting to their so-called leaders more authority" than they had previously exercised. It does so by convening advisory committees of activists who are "interested not in statistical procedure as such but in how to shape the census count in order to validate their own perception of social reality." But this same author notes that the group-formation of a census long predates the role of advocacy groups when he suggests that immigrants first began to think of themselves as having come from a particular nation (Italy, for instance) rather than a home region (Sicily, for instance) when confronted by "the questions put to them by immigration officials and census schedules."[14]

Melissa Nobles (2000) offers the most elaborate and useful hypothesis on this broad question. Her detailed analysis of both the U.S. and the Brazil case is a sustained argument that racial discourse—how we think, write, and talk about race—does have causal weight in who we believe ourselves to be racially, and further, that this causal weight is enhanced by the census. This insertion of "racial discourse" in the causal chain that connects census measurement to race identity and race politics offers more theoretical traction than many other formulations.

THE CIVIL RIGHTS MOVEMENT AND RACIAL MEASUREMENT

The civil rights laws of the 1960s reversed the historical uses to which racial classification had been put. Where earlier policies had been discriminatory, new policies would now right those wrongs and benefit those groups that were "historically discriminated against." In this task, statistical proportionality became the favored legal and administrative tool. Across every sector of American life it became commonplace to compare the proportion of a racial or ethnic minority group that suffered some disadvantage with the proportion of the white population so disadvantaged. To the traditional definitions of social justice has now been added the explicit measurement of each group's over- or under-representation. This, of course, requires a population denominator, and it is this that the census counts now provide.

The civil rights movement did not initially have statistical proportionality in mind. It promised the end of social policy based on racial groupings. Echoing Enlightenment thinking, it celebrated universality and unity, not diversity. New policy and law were to be color-blind.[15]

But discrimination did not easily give way. And soon the nation was enmeshed in a form of politics far removed from the more familiar emphasis on individual rights. Individual rights now shared political space with group rights. Equal opportunity was translated as proportionate representation. Discrimination was not only to be found in the intentional act of the real estate agent or the employment office but in housing patterns and wage rates. Statistical patterns were evidence of discrimination. Institutional racism entered the political vocabulary, and disparate impact gained an important place in legal reasoning.

Soon groups other than African Americans were bringing their case forward on the basis of statistical proportionality: Hispanics, Asians, native peoples, women, the disabled. In each instance, the census provided the denominator against which to assess who was being given equal treatment and opportunity and who was not.

The census racial classification system that gave rise to statistical proportionality as a juridical and administrative tool had a small number of discrete categories—white, black, and Indian, to which was added Asian and then, in 1980, Hispanic as an ethnic category. By 1990 every resident of America, according to the census, was one of four primary racial groups: white, black or Negro, native Indian or native Alaskan, Asian, plus a residual "other" category. The four primary categories became five when native Hawaiian or Pacific Islander was separated from the Asian category in preparation for the 2000 census. Being of Spanish-Hispanic origin was treated in the census as an ethnic, not a racial, distinction, on the argument that one could be Hispanic and Asian, black, native Indian, and/or white. The census now says that there can be four colors, but not five: black, red, yellow, and white, but not brown.[16] But Hispanics appear to be suggesting otherwise. The census form has had an open-ended "other race" option, and since 1980 a large number of Hispanics, 42 percent in 2000, have used that option to declare their race as Hispanic, thereby creating a "brown" category and implicitly challenging the government's position that "Hispanic" is an ethnic, not racial, descriptor (for more detail, see Grieco and Cassidy 2001).

The more far-reaching change in the 2000 census was, of course, the multiple-race option. A person can now be two or more of the primary racial categories. "Mark one or more" converts six categories into sixty-three, which, when cross-tabulated by the ethnic category of Hispanic, generates the 126 categories of race-ethnicity.[17] This is now policy for the entire federal statistical system. What for two hundred years has been racial classification based on a small number of discrete groupings is no more.

This happened because Americans who viewed themselves as being of more than one racial heritage, along with parents in mixed-race marriages, argued that being forced to choose only one race for themselves or their children was discriminatory. In congressional hearings on introducing the multiple-race option in the 2000 census the advocacy group Project Race testified:

> The reality is that not all Americans fit neatly into one little box. The reality is that multiracial children who wish to embrace all of their heritage should be allowed to do so. They should not be put in the position of denying one of their parents to satisfy arbitrary government requirements (U.S. Congress 1998, 286).

Five categories too sharply differentiated between what are, of course, blurred boundaries. Two hundred years ago the U.S. Senate held that Madison's proposed three-part occupational taxonomy for the census was arbitrary because people could be farmers *and* manufacturers *and* tradesmen. "Mark one or more" did not occur to them as a solution. For the measurement of race, two centuries later, it did occur. Insofar as race equals color, as it does in the minds of many, the multiple-race option transforms a categorical variable into something that resembles a continuous variable, with many shades of color now officially sanctioned.

MULTIPLE-RACE IN CENSUS 2000

The multiple-race option was not heavily used in 2000.[18] Of the 281.4 million people counted, 6.8 million (2.4 percent) reported themselves as being of two or more races. There was, of course, geographic clustering and higher rates of multiple-race identification in younger age groups (Jones and Smith 2001). But the multiple-race characteristic is overall too small to command major public attention. Indeed, media coverage of the multiple-race patterns focused on bridging from the 2000 to the 1990 and earlier census data so as to chart trends and analyze broad changes in the nation's racial demography. There were scattered human interest stories, but initial public attention was muted.

In part this is because the government agencies that enforce nondiscriminatory laws and race-based public policies accommodated the expanding number of racial categories by devising collapsing rules, and thus no major disruptions in political-administrative conditions occurred. For instance, the multiple-race numbers were generally collapsed into one residual category for purposes of redistricting (see Persily 2002).

Also, and of considerable importance, the Office of the Chief Statistician, which managed the process that led to the multiple-race option in federal statistics, opted not for a single multiracial category but for the "mark one or more" option. "Multiracial" would have been its own discrete category, adding but one more to the existing five primary groups. This would have given to the category more sociological traction, and probably more political salience, than the scattering of multiple-race answers across several dozen discrete categories. The question to which we are unlikely ever to have an answer goes to the heart of how categories become groups and groups gain members. Would a catchall multiracial census box rather than the multiple-race option have created a new "identity" in American race politics?[19]

The short-term public and political response to the multiple-race option does not, I suggest, adequately predict what is in store for the United States. I see four trends:

1. Continuing pressure from advocacy groups to expand the number of primary groups in the racial classification system

2. Growing scientific doubts about racial measurement

3. Increasing public discomfort with racial classification

4. Greater difficulties reconciling how race is measured with how the resulting classification is used in lawmaking and public policy

Expanding the Racial Classification System

In the mid-1990s, when changes in racial measurement were under consideration, groups other than those eventually recognized were asking to be separately identified. There was an effort to have persons of Middle Eastern origin reclassified from "white" to an Arab American category, though this effort was quickly dropped when the Patriot Act became law after the terrorist attacks of September 11, 2001. Recalling the internment of Japanese Americans in 1942, facilitated by small-area census data, Arab Americans now understandably shy away from being specially identified in census counts. In the mid-1990s there were also advocacy groups urging that the "white" category be disaggregated so as to reflect their identify in the census numbers. Illustrative were requests to this end by the Celtic Coalition, the National European American Society, and the Society for German-American Studies.

Over time it will be difficult to resist pressures to expand the present categories. On what grounds does the federal statistical system declare that enough is enough? To have gradually moved from three to four, five, and then, radically, sixty-three separately measured race groups (even accepting that the sixty-three will be collapsed to fewer than a dozen for most purposes) is to acknowledge that there is no natural limit. Adding even one more primary group, would take the 63 to 127, which, when cross-tabulated by Hispanic or non-Hispanic, generates 254 race-ethnic categories. If, as is logical, the Hispanic category also allows for "mark one or more," then the resulting ethnic measure becomes three options: Hispanic, non-Hispanic, or mixed. So the racial groupings, even if limited to sixty-three, would be tripled rather than doubled. If one more primary race were added, and the Hispanic ethnicity presented three options, the total becomes 254 multiplied by 3—or 762 discrete race-ethnic groupings, with no end in sight.

Growing Scientific Doubts

The biological significance of race has, of course, been long contested. The crude nineteenth-century race sciences—polygenism, social Darwinism, eugenics—have been thoroughly discredited. Considerable scientific weight now supports the idea that race is biologically meaningless. For most population geneticists and biologists, genetic variation does not correlate in any meaningful way with race or ethnicity or ancestry group. There is, however, a minority view among reputable scientists. This is the suggestion that global migration flows led to variation in DNA that can be traced today in five major geographic-ancestry groups: sub-Saharan Africa, Asians, Pacific Islanders, native Indians in the Western Hemisphere, and Caucasians, the last including Europe, the subcontinent, and the Middle East. Population geneticists will sort out these contending perspectives, but it is not likely that the resolution will be instructive regarding how to take a census. What is certainly the case is that the flawed race science of the nineteenth century, which conflated biology with anthropology, is a nonrepeatable mistake given the scientific standards of the twenty-first century.

At present, administrative requirements in census-taking override science when it comes to racial classification.[20] This will become more difficult. The multiple-race option certainly calls into question the idea of a fixed number of discrete categories. The assumption in census-taking that one's race is what one wants it to be makes it meaningless to talk about a biological base to the race categories, though it does lend support to the position that race or ethnicity can be a social identification. As scientists document their concerns (in part by analyzing census 2000 data), policymakers and the public alike will become more confused.

Increasing Public Discomfort

Although no reliable baseline exists, informed observers and anecdotal evidence suggest that public discomfort with the race item in the 2000 census was unusually high. The Census Bureau might have inadvertently stimulated this reaction. A combination of factors drew sustained public attention to the fact that census undercounts are unevenly distributed across different racial groups—more specifically, that whites tend to be well counted, perhaps in selected subgroups even overcounted, while racial minorities tend to be undercounted.[21]

These racial differentials in census coverage were widely discussed in the media and became the focus of intense partisan debate over the use of dual system estimation to improve census accuracy. Civil rights groups and their spokespersons in Congress often described the 2000 census as the "civil rights issue of the decade."

Moreover, the Census Bureau mounted an extraordinary public effort to reach the hard-to-count minority groups. Paid advertising, community mobilization, partnership programs, and related public messages stressed the importance of census participation among inner-city minorities, immigrant farmworkers, the rural poor, native Indians, and undocumented workers. Because the public face of the census was disproportionately about reaching those who traditionally have been missed in the census, it was easy to think of the census as something for and about race.

Even the census form may have contributed to this public perception. In preparing for the 2000 decennial, issues of respondent burden and form simplification were important to the Census Bureau. The short form was the shortest in census history. For example, a question on marital status as well as several housing items that had been on the 1990 short form were moved in 2000 to the longer form, which was sent to only one in six households.

What remained on the short form? Primarily items for which block-level data are required: age, race, ethnicity, gender, and number of people in the housing unit. These items are used to enforce voting rights laws.[22] The ethnicity and race items were particularly complicated and thereby lengthy, with multiple categories for the Asian and Hispanic categories. On simply inspecting the short form, it would be reasonable to conclude that the primary purpose of the census was to collect racial and ethnic information. Certainly some Americans saw it that way, as reflected in the following email (one of many along these lines) addressed to me as Census Bureau director:

> You and the other lily white clinton liberals have turned the 2000 census into a money grab by minorities. You admitted as much on the evening news when you said that questions pertaining to race still had to be asked because there was a race problem in this country. The race problem exists mainly because of people like you who want to divide the American people along racial lines since this makes them easier to rule.

Public discomfort lends support to political efforts designed to end race-based social policies through litigation and legislative action. The scope of this public discomfort will be tested, at least in California, when the Racial Privacy Initiative is voted on in 2004. This initiative generally prohibits the collection of race, ethnic, or national origins data by any official body of the state government.[23] It is a classic instance of a phenomenon of modern societies seldom discussed in the social science literature. In a policymaking environment saturated with data and information, to not measure something is itself a policy decision. Those who opposed Madison's proposal for an occupational classification in the 1790 census understood this principle, as do the backers of the Racial Privacy Initiative.

Misalignment Between Measurement and Use

Race, along with gender and age, has been included in every decennial since 1790. As noted earlier, the census has mirrored and contributed to the centrality of race in America's political and social history. For the most part, how race was measured aligned with the political purposes to which it was put, whether the issue was excluding certain groups from civic membership, justifying racial superiority, establishing (or dismantling) discriminatory laws, relocating native Indians, applying racial criteria in immigration controls, introducing equal opportunity programs and affirmative action, fighting racial profiling, or ensuring such basic rights as access to the voting booth.

This long linkage of racial measurement and race-focused policies has rested on a comparatively small number of discrete racial categories. However one views this 210–

year history, at least there has been a reasonably close fit with what the policies set out to do and the way in which race was measured.[24] As noted earlier, this has been so particularly with the introduction of statistical proportionality in public policy.

The multiple-race item in the 2000 census and its spread across all federal statistics represents a sharp break in this historical pattern. None of the current race-conscious laws or policies were designed with 126 or 63 or even a dozen categories in mind. Government agencies responsible for administering race-sensitive laws have done the best they can to align their tasks with this new reality. To assess how well this alignment will work, whether it will withstand legal challenge and what future adjustments will be necessary, is not the task here. What is clear is that the racial measurement system is now more complicated and multidimensional than anything preceding it, and there is little prospect of returning to something simpler. The current classification has too many categories for practices using statistical proportionality yet too few to accommodate the pressures of identity politics and the desire for separate recognition. A taxonomy that has both too few and too many categories is inherently unstable.[25]

RECENT IMMIGRANTS AND RACIAL CLASSIFICATION

This instability will play itself out against a large uncertainty: how will recently arrived immigrant groups position themselves, and be positioned, in terms of a racial taxonomy?

The significant shift in immigration policy initiated in 1965 replaced policies that dated to the 1920s, when the population proportions of different national origin groups were used to set immigration quotas that sharply restricted immigration from southern and eastern Europe in favor of northern and western Europe. The midtwentieth-century immigration policy was influenced by heightened civil rights sentiments. Reunification of families and hospitality to political refugees, along with the traditional emphasis on attracting workers with skills needed in the economy, have become the new criteria.

These new criteria led to massive shifts in the regions of the world sending immigrants to the United States. Europe was displaced. In 1850 more than nine of every ten foreign-born were from Europe. Even by 1900 this number had dropped only slightly (86 percent of the foreign-born were European), and in 1960 Europeans were still 75 percent of the foreign-born. The drop-off was then sharp, as Asians and Latinos arrived in large numbers. More than half of the present foreign-born are from Latin America, more than one-quarter are from Asia, and Europeans are fewer than one in five. These patterns show no signs of reversal.

There are, of course, even deeper demographic constants at work here. Industrialization and mass education produce the transition from high fertility and high mortality to low fertility and low mortality. Toward the end point of this transition, fertility rates often drop below replacement level. As this happens, a country must either manage population decline or adopt permissive immigration policies. This, of course, is why "replacement migration" is emerging as a major point of political contention across Europe and in Australia. The United Nations projects negative population growth for thirty-one OECD countries. For example, under current (median) UN projections, in the next half-century Italy's population will drop from 57 million to 41 million, and the Russian federation from 147 million to 121 million. Similar patterns hold in the advanced economies of East Asia. Accompanying these population declines is population aging, which means that the declines are even more dramatic for the working-age cohort. It is this that leads to the often intense politics of replacement migration, which focus on a simple question: will liberal immigration policies be necessary to offset potentially sharp declines in the relative size of a nation's working-age population?

Because the poorer regions yet to complete a demographic transition are Africa, the Middle East, Central and Southeast Asia, and parts of Latin America, replacement migration radically alters the population composition of the receiving countries. To state the obvious, replacement migration brings immigrants who are culturally, linguistically, ethnically, and religiously unlike the native populations of the receiving countries.

The much-remarked-upon diversity in the United States is a direct reflection of these demographic constants. Immigration plus higher than replacement fertility among the foreign-born added nearly 33 million residents between 1990 and 2000, with especially high levels of growth among the working-age cohort.

The U.S. census of 2000 puts two issues in play: an unstable racial taxonomy and public awareness of a new, unprecedented diversity. What will most matter is how, and how quickly, the two issues become intertwined. Policymakers and statisticians who design future censuses will be pressed, on the one hand, by ethnic lobbies, demographers, and indeed common sense to provide data that allow for meaningful generalization about America's diverse groups—but also to accept that the country's growing diversity makes such distinctions less administratively useful or sociologically meaningful.

Measurement decisions will be contested, with outcomes hard to predict. Will the new immigrant groups want to be separately counted so as to separately matter? If so, the nation will deepen the identity politics that came to the fore when statistical proportionality was introduced as an administrative and political tool. Or will the new immigrants hope to blur the boundaries and "assimilate" in ways practiced by Irish and Italian immigrants a century ago? This, of course, would minimize the politics of recognition and could tilt the balance between group rights and individual rights back toward the latter. Of interest in this regard is the large number of recent immigrants who chose "white" as their racial identity in the 2000 census. Of the 28 million foreign-born counted, two-thirds said they were white—a significant increase over 1990, when half the foreign-born population checked "white" as their race. Perhaps "white" will become the catchall category for the new immigrants, who may treat it as a synonym for opportunity and inclusion, as it was for the southern and eastern Europeans a century ago.

Of course, there can also be an increase in the number of hyphenated groups that try to step outside the racial taxonomy. This strategy echoes how American Jews positioned themselves early in the twentieth century, when they resisted being racialized as nonwhite but also refused to become "Anglo" and thereby lose their cultural identity.[26]

What is certain is that there is an active, self-conscious politics of sorting and classifying, led by those groups that, historically, were the subjects of imposed taxonomies. The Census Bureau now has five active race and ethnic advisory committees, representing groups that historically have been discriminated against: African Americans, Asians, Hispanics, native Hawaiians and Pacific Islanders, and native Indians. Will new immigrant groups—from the Middle East or central Asia or even Islamic Africa—find their way into this preexisting structure, or will they argue for their own committees? If so, how many such committees? Today's immigrants arrive at a moment when the nation's racial-ethnic taxonomy is not fixed. They also arrive when it is assumed that categories will not be chosen by distant government agencies but will emerge from advocacy and political pressure.

THE UNCERTAIN FUTURE

The specifics of racial and ethnic measurement will be framed as elements in a larger public debate that will stretch across several decades, in which the country must answer: What are the political and social purposes served by sorting the population by race and ethnicity?[27]

- Is racial-ethnic measurement justified because it helps the state to police and prevent discrimination? If legislative and legal purposes are central, the racial-ethnic taxonomy should be aligned as closely as possible with public policy goals. The proliferation of categories along with the multiple-race option is hardly helpful.

- Is racial-ethnic measurement justified because "diversity" has become a goal in many sectors of society? Diversity is said to enrich the educational experience, increase business efficiency, strengthen the military, and make government more responsive. If achieving diversity becomes the use to which census categories are put, attention will turn to the search for racial-ethnic-ancestry differentiations thought to best define a socially beneficial diversity. Highly aggregated groupings, such as white, Asian, or Hispanic, might then be subdivided into many more detailed groupings. An institution would not meet its diversity goals by selecting only Hispanics of Cuban ancestry or only whites of northern European ancestry.

- Is racial-ethnic measurement justified because it is a demographic marker used to assert identity and to claim recognition? If so, the racial taxonomy, with its multiple-race option, will be further expanded. It will grow to accommodate new groups and distinguish between them—between a Nilotic, Islamic Somalian and a Bantu, Catholic Ugandan, and both from a ninth-generation Ghanaian slave descendent—and then allow for intermarriage among them and the offspring of those unions.

- Is racial-ethnic measurement justified because it is, however crudely, aligned with the persistence of color as a demographic marker—which historically has meant black, brown, red, yellow, and white? If that is its purpose, the census should allow those Hispanics intent on doing so to self-identify as brown. The multiple-race option, then, will be selected by those who want to opt out of the color pentagon.

- Is racial-ethnic measurement justified because (echoes of the late nineteenth and early twentieth centuries) it allows the nation to track the pace at which recent immigrants are assimilating, however differently that concept might be understood today? Certainly one of the most interesting social questions is what assimilation even means in a multicultural society in contrast to the society in which, it was assumed, the majority of the population was "melting" into a common cultural identity. If assimilation metaphors are reintroduced, the census will need a fine-grained account of the various immigrant groups and their rates of intermarriage, naturalization, language acquisition, homeownership, and the like.

- Or is the best racial discourse no racial discourse at all? If so, efforts similar to the California Racial Privacy Initiative will spread and racial-ethnic measurement will disappear from official measurement, perhaps from the census itself. There are thoughtful commentators who believe it not out of the question that the Supreme Court, citing the Fourteenth Amendment, could rule racial classification to be unconstitutional.

The nation's answer to the basic question of what purpose is served by racial and ethnic measurement must, of course, take account of what was achieved by the midcentury civil rights revolution. The problem is that there are variations in the interpretation of this revolution, and these variations move the measurement system in quite different ways.

There is the straightforward account of a largely black-led movement that eventually produced civil rights legislation and a number of legal remedies designed to address the legacy of slavery and the Jim Crow apartheid system. As these remedies became entitlement policies, buttressed with the administrative tool of statistical proportionality and the legal doctrine of disparate impact, other groups—women, the disabled, but especially other people of color—asserted their place in this new politics. In the more worried versions of this account, the increase in the number of protected groups is in part at the expense of African Americans.

A somewhat different account suggests that the 1960s were about issues broader than addressing the legacy of slavery. This was a time when the nation finally acknowledged what had happened to all groups that had been "historically discriminated against." In this narrative, due credit is given to the role of African Americans (and Jews) in the leadership of the civil rights movement that culminated in the 1960s. But this was also a civil rights *moment* that resulted from decades of struggle by native Indians, Hispanics, Asians, and feminists for fair treatment. This civil rights moment in American civic life was not limited to only one among the many groups of color that had experienced discrimination in labor markets, housing, educational opportunity, and the voting booth. Nor could it fail to respond to historical discrimination against women and the disabled.

Further complicating the story is the extent to which civil rights are about present as well as historic discrimination. It is at this point that claims by recent immigrants enter the picture. Sikhs or Laotians or Tunisians could not, of course, have suffered from discrimination in the United States prior to the 1960s. They were not here. But if they are targets of discrimination today—and some certainly are—they have no less claim to the protections and benefits promised by the civil rights policies.

Under any interpretation, "statistical proportionality" is a powerful symbolic rallying point and a strategic political-legal entry point. Discrimination can be measured in terms of which groups are under- and overrepresented. The ratios require a denominator that in the first instance is provided by census counts. However, the scope and detail of what is to be measured shifts if the "redress the legacy of slavery" version gives way to "people of color historically discriminated against," and then shifts again if what is at stake are all those presently vulnerable to discrimination by virtue of national origin, race, ethnicity, gender or sexual orientation.

Not at all clear is how to fit the multiple-race option into any of these versions, for it makes for difficulties in any policies resting on statistical proportionality.

Even greater uncertainties enter the picture as multiculturalism, identity politics, and diversity goals become intertwined with the traditional focus on discrimination. Many defend diversity as the logical extension of a half-century process that steadily broadened civil rights. I suggest, however, that this gravely underestimates the complications that the diversity rationale introduces into our measurement system.

In higher education, claims to diversity invariably start with reference to groups historically discriminated against, but there is always more to the story. The mission statement of the UC-Berkeley Faculty Center for Leadership in Educational Access and Diversity first offers a familiar formulation: "For many students, barriers [to education] derive from historical and current discrimination." But the statement continues: it notes that there are also students for whom "the barriers derive from economic status and inequities in the delivery of quality education and educational opportunities." That is, the white student from a poor family, or whose high school is not so great, should also be served. We move away from the traditional civil rights agenda.

The diversity language is further broadened to encompass how many states, or nations, are represented in the student body, how many religions are practiced on campus, or lifestyles and sexual orientations. To take only one example, the present website of Rutgers University tells us that diversity "encompasses race, ethnicity, culture, social class, national origin, gender, age, religious beliefs, sexual orientation, mental ability and physical ability."

Corporate America echoes this eclectic approach. At Procter & Gamble, "diversity covers the broad range of personal attributes and characteristics such as race, sex, age, cultural heritage, personal background and sexual orientation." At General Motors, which is no less expansive, "diversity includes race and gender as well as the broader aspects of age, education level, family status, language, military status, physical abilities, religion, sexual orientation, union representation, and years of service."

The goal of a diverse labor pool, student body, medical profession, or armed service would, on first glance, seem to find common cause with a much expanded racial-ethnic taxonomy, including the multiple-race option, and probably would also require that dozens of different cultures, language groups, and nationalities represented in the fresh immigrant streams be separately identified and counted. Further reflection, however, leads to a very different conclusion. Taken at face value, diversity makes measurement demands that cannot be satisfied. Diversity is not only about discrete and separable categories but also about their overlapping nature. So understood, categories proliferate endlessly, or at least well beyond the capacity of any measurement system to record.

Two centuries after the census helped launch the nation on a path that steadily strengthened the use of racial and ethnic classification in public life, we hit a barrier. Its name is diversity.

In the last half-century, statistical proportionality has worked its way deeply into public policy and political consciousness, becoming the vocabulary of choice for discussing social justice—not, however, in 2003 before the Supreme Court as it ruled on two affirmative action cases from the University of Michigan.[28] University administrators defended their practice of taking race into account in assembling an entering class but argued this with reference to educational policy and not as a remedy to historic social injustices. Their central argument was that diversity is educationally enriching, something all students benefit from. The Court, up to a point, agreed. It upheld the practice of the University of Michigan Law School in considering an applicant's race because there was careful judgment on a case-by-case basis. But the Court struck down an undergraduate admission program that mechanically awarded a set number of bonus points to every minority applicant. The latter was too close to a quota to find a majority on the Court.

In giving legal sanction to the social goal of diversity but severing it from any attempt to measure it, the Court comes close to treating diversity and its companion term, "critical mass," like another famously immeasurable term—as something you cannot define but know when you see it.

Have we then come to the end of a story that starts in 1790, when the Founders unhesitatingly divided us into racial groups? I believe there are powerful forces bringing that story to an end—though, unfortunately, the disappearance of racial discrimination is not among them. Barring a Supreme Court ruling to the contrary, there will still be a race question on the 2010 census and, less certainly, on the 2020 census. But the combination of scientific doubt, public discomfort, political opposition and legal action, and the displacement of the antidiscrimination vocabulary with the diversity rhetoric point toward a future, perhaps by the 2030 census, when the question will have disappeared.

A version of this chapter was first presented to the conference "The Measure and Mismeasure of Populations," Paris, December 17–18, 2001, organized by le Centre d'Études et de Recherches Internationals (CERI) and l'Institut National d'Études Démographiques (INED), to be published by Palgrave Press in a volume edited by Denis Lacorne and Patrick Simon.

NOTES

1. This is not just true of the United States. For analysis of similar circumstances elsewhere, see Kertzer and Arel (2002).

2. See the useful essays in Skrentny (2001).

3. William Petersen (1987, 201) writes that the distinction between European, Negroes, and Indians in the first half of the nineteenth century "set the contrast among races as the fundamental ethnic characteristic in censuses."

4. Melissa Nobles (2000, 27) writes: "In keeping with Enlightenment thought, eighteenth-century political elites regarded race as a natural, self-evident component of human identity."

5. For the larger context and a theoretical formulation treating the way in which racist ideologies were fostered by Enlightenment thinking and Western colonialism, see Fredrickson (2002).

6. Thomas Jefferson to Governor William Henry Harrison, February 27, 1803, cited in Ellis (1997, 201).

7. Discussed in greater detail in Prewitt (2001), which will appear in a volume published by the University Press of Virginia.

8. For a comprehensive review and analysis of America's immigration history, see Zolberg (2004).

9. Tench Coxe, "An Enquiry into the Best Means of Encouraging Emigration from Abroad, Consistently with the Happiness and Safety of the Original Citizens. Read Before the Society for Political Enquiries, at the house of Dr. Franklin, April 20th, 1787," cited in Zolberg (2004, chapter 2).

10. Anderson describes at some length the sometimes tortured use of national origins census data to achieve the racist outcomes sought by the strong anti-immigrant forces of the 1920s.

11. For an extensive treatment, see Smith (1997).

12. The politics behind this decision were intense, as reflected in U.S. Commission on Civil rights (1974).

13. The long confusion over what is a race and what is an ethnicity in census-taking, in the United States and elsewhere, is usefully discussed in Kertzer and Arel (2002). Note espe-

cially the introductory chapter by the editors and chapter 3 by Calvin Goldscheider, "Ethnic Categorizations in Censuses: Comparative Observations from Israel, Canada, and the United States."

14. For more extended treatment, see the articles collected in Kertzer and Arel 2002.

15. The favored political quotation in this regard is from Senator Hubert Humphrey (D-Minn.), who shepherded the early civil rights bill through the Senate. Exasperated with the skepticism about whether the bill was race-neutral, he asserted: "If . . . in Title VII . . . any language [can be found] which provides that an employer will have to hire on the basis of percentage or quota related to color, . . . I will start eating the pages [of the bill] one after the other"; see Graham (1990).

16. Our twenty-first-century racial pentagon does not match perfectly with the nineteenth-century version. Then "brown" would more likely have been a reference to Pacific Islanders. Today the descriptor, at least in the United States, applies to Mexican Americans and other Hispanics, whose ancestors are Spanish ("white") and native Indian ("red").

17. Sixty-three is the number of separate categories when all combinations of six are summed, using the formula of two to the sixth power minus one.

18. This section draws from Prewitt (2002).

19. In exploring this question, Jennifer Hochschild (2002, 342) cites a passage from the website of the Association of MultiEthnic Americans: "Every person who is multiethnic and multiracial has the same right as any other person to assert a personal identity."

20. As candidly stated by the Executive Office of the President, Office of Management and Budget (1994, 1997), in adopting a directive in 1977 that largely fixed the present racial and ethnic census categories: "These classifications should not be interpreted as being scientific or anthropological in nature. . . . They have been developed in response to needs expressed by both the executive branch and the Congress."

21. Any serious observer of a decennial census, starting in 1790, knows that the final count is only an approximation of the true count and that in all likelihood the true count has always been higher than the reported count. That is, every census has two major coverage errors: persons missed and persons erroneously included. Historically it has been assumed that the one source of error, missed persons, is higher than the other. Censuses have net undercounts. The first systematic measure of the undercount occurred in the early 1940s, when the government initiated mandatory, universal selective service registration as part of the war effort. Though obviously not its intention, this universal registration provided statisticians with two independent counts of males between the ages of twenty-one and thirty-five: the count recorded in the 1940 census and the count of those registered for military service. Comparing these counts provided the first reliable measure of how many persons, at least in this demographic group, had been missed in the census. It was quickly discovered that African American males of draft age had been missed in the census at much higher rates than white males. Thus, the differential undercount first emerges as a racial classification, an artifact of available vital statistics. That is, had there been two independent measures of social isolation (having a phone in 1940, for example) it might have predicted coverage error more accurately than race. And this artifact persists, for the differential undercount has historically been measured by comparing demographic analysis using vital statistics with census counts. Vital statistics have always distinguished black from nonblack, making that population distinction particularly convenient. Now, of course, the undercount is also measured through dual system estimation, which uses questions from the short form. Because the short form includes race and ethnic data (because these traits are needed at the block for administering the Voting Rights Act), the public discussion of differential undercounts continues to be framed around race. This is not incorrect so much as partial, and it is true only because race is a surrogate for variables that if available might be more strongly predictive of

census coverage errors—social isolation, civic indifference, fear of government, irregular housing, immigrant status, illiteracy, and so on. Additional discussion of the census undercount appears in Prewitt (2003).

22. Name, phone number, and household relationships are also on the short form to assist the Census Bureau in its many quality control operations. One other item, whether the unit is owned or rented, has such a high predictive value for census coverage that it was retained for the short form as a factor for constructing poststrata in dual system estimation.

23. The initiative reads as follows: "The state [including all political subdivisions or governmental instrumentalities] shall not classify any individual by race, ethnicity, color or national origin in the operation of public education, public contracting, or public employment."

24. Nobles (2000) has written persuasively to this point.

25. A point nicely argued by Hochschild (2002).

26. For an important treatment, see Hattam (this volume).

27. The array of possible answers listed here borrows from but modifies and extends a similar list posed by Nobles (2000, 77).

28. *Grutter v. Bollinger* (a University of Michigan Law School case) and *Gratz v. Bollinger* (a University of Michigan College of Literature and the Sciences and the Arts case), decided on June 23, 2003.

REFERENCES

Anderson, Margo J. 1988. *The American Census: A Social History*. New Haven, Conn.: Yale University Press, 1988.
———. 1994. "(Only) White Men Have Class: Reflections on Early Nineteenth-Century Occupational Classification Systems." *Work and Occupations* 21(1, February): 10–14.
Bourdieu, Pierre. 1991. *Language and Symbolic Power*. Cambridge, Mass.: Harvard University Press.
Cohen, Patricia Cline. 1999. *A Calculating People: The Spread of Numeracy in Early America*. New York: Routledge. (Orig. pub. in 1982 by the University of Chicago Press.)
Ellis, Joseph. 1997. *American Sphinx: The Character of Thomas Jefferson*. New York: Alfred A. Knopf.
Executive Office of the President. Office of Management and Budget. 1994. "Race and Ethnic Standards for Federal Statistics and Administrative Reporting (as Adopted on May 12, 1977)." *Statistical Policy Directive* 15(59FR, June 9): 29,831–35.
———. 1997. "Revisions to the Standards for the Classification of Federal Data on Race and Ethnicity." *Federal Register* (62FR, October 30): 58,782–90.
Fredrickson, George M. 2002. *Racism: A Short History*. Princeton, N.J.: Princeton University Press.
Goldberg, David T. 1997. *Racial Subjects: Writing on Race in America*. New York: Routledge.
Graham, Hugh D. 1990. *The Civil Rights Era: Origins and Development of National Policy, 1960–1972*. New York: Oxford University Press.
Grieco, Elizabeth M., and Rachel C. Cassidy. 2001. *Overview of Race and Hispanic Origin: A Census 2000 Brief*. C2KBR/01–1. Washington: U.S. Department of Commerce, U.S. Census Bureau (March).
Hochschild, Jennifer. 2002. "Multiple Racial Identifiers in the 2000 Census, And Then What?" In *Counting Races, Recognizing Multiracials*, edited by Joel Perlmann and Mary Waters. New York: Russell Sage Foundation.
Hollinger, David A. 1995. *Postethnic America*. New York: Basic Books.
Jefferson, Thomas. 1984. *Notes on the State of Virginia*. New York: Library Classics of the United States. (Orig. pub. 1787.)

Jones, Nicholas A., and Amy Symens Smith. 2001. *The Two or More Races Population: 2000: A Census 2000 Brief.* C2KBR/01–6. Washington: U.S. Department of Commerce, U.S. Census Bureau (November).

Kertzer, David I., and Dominique Arel, eds. 2002. *Census and Identity: The Politics of Race, Ethnicity, and Languages in National Censuses.* New York: Cambridge University Press.

Madison, James. 1953. *The Forging of American Federalism: Selected Writings,* edited by Saul K. Padover. New York: Harper Torchbooks.

Nobles, Melissa. 2000. *Shades of Citizenship: Race and the Census in Modern Politics.* Stanford, Calif.: Stanford University Press.

Persily, Nathaniel. 2002. "The Legal Implications of a Multiracial Census." In *Counting Races, Recognizing Multiracials,* edited by Joel Perlmann and Mary Waters. New York: Russell Sage Foundation.

Petersen, William. 1987. "Politics and the Measurement of Ethnicity." In *The Politics of Numbers,* edited by William Alonso and Paul Starr. New York: Russell Sage Foundation.

Prewitt, Kenneth. 2001. "A Nation Imagined, a Nation Measured: The Jeffersonian Legacy." Lecture delivered at "Thomas Jefferson's West," Thomas Jefferson Memorial Foundation Distinguished Lecture Series. University of Virginia (October).

———. 2002. "Race in the 2000 Census: A Turning Point." In *Counting Races, Recognizing Multiracials,* edited by Joel Perlmann and Mary Waters. New York: Russell Sage Foundation.

———. 2003. *Politics and Science in Census-Taking.* Washington, D.C.: The Population Reference Bureau, and New York: Russell Sage Foundation.

Skerry, Peter. 2000. *Counting on the Census? Race, Group Identity, and the Evasion of Politics.* Washington, D.C.: Brookings Institution.

Skrentny, John David. 2001. *Color Lines: Affirmative Action, Immigration, and Civil Rights Options for America.* Chicago: University of Chicago Press.

Smith, Rogers. 1997. *Civic Ideas: Conflicting Visions of Citizenship in U.S. History.* New Haven, Conn.: Yale University Press.

U.S. Commission on Civil Rights. 1974. *Counting the Forgotten: The 1970 Census Count of Persons of Spanish Speaking Background in the United States.* Report of the U.S. Commission on Civil Rights. Washington: U.S. Government Printing Office.

U.S. Congress. House of Representatives. Committee on Government Reform and Oversight. 1998. "Federal Measures of Race and Ethnicity and the Implications for the 2000 Census." Hearings before the Subcommittee on Government Management, Information, and Technology, April 23, May 22, and July 25, 1997. Serial no. 105–57. Washington: U.S. Government Printing Office.

Zolberg, Aristide. 2004. *A Nation by Design.* Cambridge, Mass.: Harvard University Press.

Part III

Panethnicity

David Roediger and James Barrett

Chapter 8

Making New Immigrants "Inbetween": Irish
Hosts and White Panethnicity, 1890 to 1930

Part of the impulse that generated this collaborative volume is a healthy perception that
the longer history of U.S. immigration might deepen our knowledge of more recent
migrations. But contemporary immigration and interdisciplinary scholarship also cause
historians to ask different and sharper questions about the immigrant past. This essay is
structured around issues largely absent from older historical scholarship and poses
questions insistently raised by recent immigration. One such question concerns how
immigrants come to be classified racially. The recent works of Gary Okihiro (1994),
Neil Foley (2000), Charles A. Gallagher (forthcoming), and Mia Tuan (1998) have
shown us how to use the urgency of this contemporary concern in this regard to animate scholarly work. When Okihiro poses and effectively explodes the question "Is
yellow black or white?" it is hardly surprising that the historical racialization of European immigrants also comes to be studied with more sophistication. Similarly, the
sharply posed questions of how, and from whom, contemporary immigrants learn
about life and race in the United States are being studied by scholars as different as
Flore Zéphir (2001), Rubén Rumbaut, and Alejandro Portes (Portes and Rumbaut
2001), causing historians of older migrations to address similar issues (see also Janine
Kim 1999; Clare Jean Kim 1999; Portes and Zhou 1993).[1] Considering the roles of Irish
Americans in the racialization of so-called new immigrants from southern and eastern
Europe in the late nineteenth and early twentieth centuries, however, suggests that the
complexities of contemporary racial categorization and racial learning have historical
precedents.
    A century ago the great photographer-reformer Jacob Riis (1890/1996, 73–75) de-
scribed Irish Americans as permeating all of New York City's social relations. None of
the more recent immigrant groups escaped the Irishman, who as "the cosmopolitan
immigrant . . . shared his lodging with perfect impartiality with the Italian [and] the
Greek," objecting "equally to all of them." Riis saw Irish American influence as pervasive, but this essay chooses limits. The basic one is set by its interest in the ways in
which Irish Americans taught the U.S. racial system and judged the level of civilization
of new immigrants. Sections particularly take up the teaching and judging that occurred
in street fights, politics, churches, workplaces, unions, and schools. These venues do not
exhaust the places in which new immigrants encountered Irish American influence. In
addition to the stock characters of machine politician, schoolteacher, priest, maid, nun,
cop, bartender, and union boss, there were the boardinghouse keeper, landlord, social
worker, fireman, baseball manager, crime boss, and even film censor (Riis 1890/1996,

75, 73; Ware 1935/1994, 31; Kimeldorf 1999, 89; Miller 1985, 499–502; Hayden 2001, 55–63, 78–80; Burgos 2002; Montgomery 1980, 212–16; Diner 1983, 96–97; Curran 1989, 48–52; Walsh 1996, 35–46, 96–279; Brown and McKeown 1997, 134–40; Laurie 1973, 71–88). So prominent were Irish American prizefighters that boxing journalism and history feature frequent references to Jewish Americans "passing" as Irish. One observer reckoned in 1913 that a *majority* of New York City boxers were passing in this way. Jim Flynn, Jack Dempsey's nemesis, was reportedly born as Andrea Chiariglione (Glanz 1976, 102–3; Blessing 1980, 539; Rischin 1962, 263; on Flynn, see La Sorte 1985, 155).

Despite such evidence, we think in terms of new immigrants learning new values, including U.S.-style racism, from something as large and amorphous as the "host society." Such a view is not wrong. The ideology and law of the nation, the mass-marketed culture, and the employment decisions of faraway corporate heads all mattered greatly in shaping the lives and learning of new immigrants to the Unites States from the 1890s through the 1920s. But the host society was also embodied in the lived contacts that immigrants had with those who were longer established in U.S. cities. The historian of Greenwich Village, Caroline Ware (1935/1994, 129), concurred: "The Irish were very much of the Italians' world, occupying the same houses, the same jobs, and the same streets." The Irish neighborhood "was the 'America' to which the immigrant Italians came." For many new immigrants, as Michael Novak (1972, 55) wrote, the "first face of America" was Irish American. This essay asks why new immigrants consistently saw Irish American faces and what they saw in those faces. In particular it considers what Irish Americans taught regarding the racial order and regarding the possibilities of new immigrants joining in a panethnic alliance as whites.

If, as we have argued, along with Robert Orsi (1992) and John Higham (1974, 169), immigrants from southern and eastern Europe were "inbetween people"—neither fully white nor nonwhite—in certain U.S. places and times, Irish Americans contributed as much to sustaining and structuring such inbetween-ness before the 1930s as they did toward resolving it. Gary Gerstle's (2001, 256) remarks regarding Irish Americans' propensity "to join Protestants in determining the pace and character of eastern and southern Europeans' assimilation" might reverse the perception of new immigrants themselves, who perhaps saw the Protestants as traveling in the wake of the Irish Americans (see Barrett and Roediger 2002a).

THE DEMOGRAPHICS OF IRISH HOSTING

Both demographics and a history of confronting U.S. nativism positioned the Irish to host new immigrants. Between 1860 and 1920, there were never less than one million Irish-born people in the United States, and during the height of the new immigration (1890 to 1920), the second-generation Irish American population hovered between 2.92 and 3.38 million (Blessing 1980, 528, 527–45). The census did not separately enumerate the large third-generation Irish American population. The absolute and relative statistics on Irish immigration to the United States, beginning when the famine decade accelerated both the numbers of migrants generally and the numbers of Catholic Irish among them, are summarized in table 8.1.

Such statistics underpinned the subtle social processes through which Irish Americans came to instruct and judge new immigrants. Of course, relatively early arrival and the size of the Irish immigration mattered, but so too did the continuity of immigration. When "new immigration" from eastern and southern Europe cut Irish American

TABLE 8.1   Irish Immigration to the United States, 1841 to 1920

Period	Number	Percentage of Total Arrivals
1841 to 1850	780,719	45.6%
1851 to 1860	914,119	35.2
1861 to 1870	435,778	18.8
1871 to 1880	436,871	15.5
1881 to 1890	655,482	12.5
1891 to 1900	388,416	10.5
1901 to 1910	339,065	3.9
1911 to 1920	148,181	2.5

Source: USINS (1976, 62–64).

proportions of total immigration, the absolute numbers of Irish American immigrants remained substantial. These later immigrants tended to come more often than previously from the Irish-speaking West. Kerby Miller (1985, 526) has well demonstrated that the West was misimagined as "wild" and is better thought of as an "almost schizophrenic" combination of "strikingly novel social processes [and] others which remained obdurately conservative." To Irish American elites, newcomers presented a threat to group respectability. Especially if poor, drunken, or religiously emotive, the newcomer needed education and reform. Among other things, she or he needed to know the U.S. racial order. Irish American greenhorn folklore reflects first encounters with African Americans and suggests the importance of such education. The arrival of these later immigrants and the conflicts they engendered caution us against a monolithic view of Irish Americans, who were in fact divided themselves along regional and class lines. The "wild" greenhorn prepared Irish American parishes and reformers to educate other newcomers and to judge their levels of civilization (see Hayden 2001, 83–84).

Other demographic realities also conditioned Irish hosting. Although slightly smaller than the German American population, Irish Americans were more concentrated in cities, reaching a 90 percent urbanization rate by the 1920s (Blessing 1980, 539). Their numbers were often small in New York's Jewish and Italian neighborhoods by that point, having been "driven out" (Riis 1890/1996, 73) by the newcomers, and they seldom lived alongside African Americans. But they tended to be spread throughout the city, "From Battery Park to Washington Heights" (Henderson 1976, 73). As on the West Side of Chicago or in lower Manhattan's West Village, they often inhabited neighborhoods adjacent to those with heavy Jewish and Italian concentrations. More important, Irish control of political machines and city jobs meant that the face of authority— the cop, the ward boss, the teacher, or the truant officer—even in densely populated "new immigrant" neighborhoods, was often Irish (Henderson 1976, 73–75; see also McGreevy 1996, 37; King 2000, 102). They had the second-lowest remigration rate of the twenty-five ethnic groups studied by Thomas Archdeacon (1983, 139–41)— about 64 percent of the German American rate in the early twentieth century. With naturalization rates about equal to those of the Germans, the Irish were far less divided by religion, widely dispersed throughout the metropolis, and thus perfectly positioned to dominate politics in the cities in which new immigrants settled.[2]

The gender ratios within Irish American immigration further set it apart and shaped its relations with other groups. Between 1899 and 1924, of the major ethnic groups coming to the United States, only the Irish had a majority of women (53.6 percent) among their immigrant population. For Germans, the figure was 42.5 percent. This stream of female immigrants raised the possibility that Irish women and new immigrant men would marry each other, cementing and consecrating white pan-ethnicity. William Ripley (1908, 745–59), a liberal popularizer of racial theory in the early twentieth century, fixed specifically on the "Irish woman" as a party to intermarriage in a 1908 article. "Our Boston foreign colony," he calculated, "[had] a surplus of fifteen hundred Irish females," who were such good "mixers" that "the Irish or Irish American woman bids fair to be a potent physical mediator between the other peoples of the earth." Although Ripley allowed that mixed marriages were "relatively infrequent," he thought that they might "constitute a beginning of racial intermixture." In Boston "the most frequent form of intermarriage perhaps is between Jewish men and Irish or Irish-American women." Ripley further noted "the growing intermarriage between the Irish and the Italians" (see also Archdeacon 1983, 139–40; Diner 1983, 8–9, 30–34). Studies support Ripley's cautions regarding the paucity of actual intermarriage of Irish immigrant women (or men) with new immigrants. Immigrants tended to marry within their ethnicity and, when outside of it, with the British-born (themselves possibly Irish) and with Germans. As Ripley (1908, 751, 754) observed, "The 'Dago' is looked down upon by the Irish," and that constituted a "serious handicap in the matrimonial race." Pride in one's "own Irish race" also limited intermarriage.[3]

Nonetheless, the impacts of early migration, sex ratios, and intermarriage cannot be ignored. In the large Irish American third generation, rates of out-marriage were high, although the extent to which they anticipated later patterns of intra-Catholic, interethnic marriages uniting Irish Americans with new immigrants remains in need of study. Irish Americans appear to have been far more likely to intermarry with immigrants than German Americans were. In Julius Drachsler's pioneering 1921 study of intermarriage in New York City, Irish American women were shown to have out-married with a far greater variety of other ethnicities than any of the other fifty-six groups studied. Moreover, intermarriage even in relatively small numbers had high public visibility, dating back to the unions of Irish women with African and Chinese men in the nineteenth century. In the early 1920s the movie, play, and novel *Abie's Irish Rose* (Nichols 1927, 75–79, 95–98, 101–6) captured the imagination of a wide segment of the U.S. public by sympathetically telling the story of the love between a Jewish man and an Irish American woman. The father of Rose is Patrick Murphy, a contractor who migrated from County Kerry. He condescends to a black employee but is confronted on his racism and anti-Semitism by a remarkable Irish priest. As a youth in New York, Patrick engaged in street fighting against Jews, and later his favorite funny story is "the one of how the Jews got their names." More generally, as Riv-Ellen Prell (1999, 72–77) has written, "Melting pot marriages were ubiquitous in music, film, and theatre," with Irish-Jewish marriages particularly captivating ragtime composers and occurring in twenty-one other films between 1921 and 1930. Such popular culture continued to foreground the available Irish American woman as a possible vehicle for both comedy and the assimilation of new immigrants (see Glanz 1976, 105–6; Curran 1989, 36).[4]

Intermarriages did not simply gauge trends in Irish American acceptance of or opposition to new immigrants. Like the fictional one in *Abie's Irish Rose*, mixed marriages generally were relationships in which the issues of whether the Irish and new immigrants could mix and the identities that the children would carry continued to be contested. Oral histories show couples and relatives arguing the case over decades, with the supposed barbarity of new immigrant *men* often at issue (Stave and Sutherland 1994, 185–87, 190).[5]

Irish Americans were in a different situation from new immigrants with regard to possible marriage partners—and for that matter, with regard to acceptance as citizens, neighbors, and friends. Emory Bogardus's (1928) massive 1924 college student–based "distance" study, included in his *Immigration and Race Attitudes*, featured here as table 8.2, indexes such acceptance.

The data show acceptance of the Irish Americans on every measure. With the Ku Klux Klan's membership, campaigns against Catholics, and efforts to raise legal obstacles to interreligious marriage and restrict immigration reaching a crescendo, Bogardus's findings suggest that Irish Americans, unlike new immigrant groups, were no longer set dramatically apart, at least among educated respondents.

The trend toward such acceptance had long been identifiable, even among nativists. Francis Amasa Walker, the longtime leader of the Census Bureau, developed influential statistics on the threats to "American stock" largely by calculating immigration and birthrates of the suspect Irish versus those of Anglo-Saxons. In the quarter-century after 1870, Walker fretted. Over time, however, the focus of his anxiety switched to the new immigrants. He not only dropped his concern about the Irish but also promoted them as members of the dominant race (see Anderson 1988; Mink 1986, 126; Gossett 1997, 302–4, 440–41; on E. L. Godkin's echoing of Walker's views, see Gossett 1997, 298). In 1891 the patrician Henry Cabot Lodge, the first political science doctorate from Harvard, used dictionaries of national biographies to enumerate the "racial" contribution to U.S. greatness in an article in *The Century*. The "distribution of ability" tables showed 10,376 contributors from the "English race," 1,439 from the "Scotch-Irish," and just over 100 from the Irish (along with six Italians, three Greeks, and one able Pole). Lodge overstressed the point of Irish inferiority in a tortured digression concerning how little "Irish blood" allegedly flowed in Scotch-Irish veins. Within a decade, Lodge would write congenially of a "kinship between English-speaking natives and Celtic immigrants" (Jacobson 2000, 192; see also Higham 1974, 96, 141–42, 323). The context in which Lodge changed—he had a political career in Massachusetts, a state with a huge Irish American electorate that included many first-generation migrants who had used their "whiteness" to qualify for naturalization—shows how Irish Americans took advantage of the ways in which what Evelyn Nakano Glenn (2002) has called "unequal freedom" structured race and political power in the United States.

Dramatic use of cultural citizenship and political power, as well as upward economic mobility, helped to secure Irish acceptance as white Americans in the face of racial as well as religious nativism. Job discrimination had been a fact of life. The years between the 1840s and 1880s had seen widespread portrayals of Irish Americans as apelike, dependent and akin to blacks or Chinese. As late as 1881 the historian Edward A. Freeman opined on a lecture tour that the "best remedy for whatever is amiss in America would be if every Irishman should kill a nigger and be hanged for it" (Gossett 1997, 108–9). When the Knights of Labor flirted with solidarity with African Americans in the 1880s, their Irish American leader received abusive mail on the affinities of "low Irish" and blacks (see Ignatiev 1995; Gitelman 1973; Knobel 1986, 82–99; Kenny 2000, 114–18, 158–59, 219).

Progress in gaining status made Irish Americans a model to which new immigrants could consciously turn. In 1911 the *American Monthly Jewish Review* reflected on Irish American history and on what "the Irish have to teach us": "They were treated worse than ever were Jews at any time in the history of the country. But the Irish talked and

TABLE 8.2   Reactions of 1,725 Americans to Forty Different Races

Regarding Race Listed Below	1 To Close Kinship by Marriage	2 To My Club as Personal Chums	3 To My Street as Neighbors	4 To Employment in My Occupation	5 To Citizenship in My Country	6 As Visitors Only to My Country	7 Would Exclude from My Country
English	93.7%	96.7%	97.3%	95.4%	95.9%	1.7%	0.0%
Americans (native white)	90.1	92.4	92.6	92.4	90.5	1.2	0.0
Canadians	86.6	93.4	96.1	95.6	96.1	1.7	0.3
Scots	78.1	89.1	91.3	92.8	93.3	1.7	0.0
Scotch-Irish	72.6	81.7	88.0	89.4	92.0	16.7	0.4
Irish	70.0	83.4	86.1	89.8	91.4	4.0	0.7
French	67.8	85.4	88.1	90.4	92.7	3.8	0.8
Welsh	60.8	72.3	80.0	81.4	86.0	5.4	0.3
Germans	54.1	67.0	78.7	82.6	87.2	6.7	3.1
French-Canadians	49.7	66.4	76.4	79.3	87.0	4.4	0.8
Swedes	45.3	62.1	75.6	78.0	86.3	5.4	1.0
Dutch	44.2	54.7	73.2	76.7	86.1	2.4	0.3
Norwegians	41.0	56.0	65.1	72.0	80.3	8.0	0.3
Danes	35.0	52.2	65.5	71.4	80.1	4.5	0.9
Spaniards	27.6	49.8	55.1	58.0	81.6	8.4	2.0
Finns	16.1	27.4	36.1	50.5	61.2	12.8	2.8
Russians	15.8	27.7	31.0	45.3	56.1	22.1	8.0

Group							
Italians	15.4	25.7	34.7	54.7	71.3	14.5	4.8
Portuguese	11.0	22.0	28.3	47.8	57.7	19.0	3.3
Poles	11.0	11.6	28.3	44.3	58.3	19.7	4.7
Hungarians	10.1	17.5	25.8	43.0	70.7	20.3	7.0
Roumanians	8.8	19.3	23.8	38.3	51.6	22.0	4.6
Armenians	8.5	14.8	27.8	46.2	58.1	17.7	5.0
Czecho-Slovaks	8.2	16.4	21.1	36.0	47.4	26.0	9.5
Indians	8.1	27.7	33.4	54.3	83.0	7.7	1.6
Jews, German	7.8	2.1	25.5	39.8	53.5	25.3	13.8
Bulgarians	6.9	14.6	16.4	19.7	43.1	21.9	7.0
Jews, Russian	6.1	18.0	15.7	30.1	45.3	22.7	13.4
Greeks	5.9	17.7	18.0	35.2	53.2	25.3	11.3
Syrians	4.3	13.8	18.0	31.0	41.1	21.4	9.0
Serbo-Croatians	4.3	10.4	12.0	10.3	30.4	18.6	8.0
Mexicans	2.8	11.5	12.3	77.1	46.1	30.8	15.1
Japanese	2.3	12.1	13.0	27.3	29.3	38.8	2.5
Filipinos	1.6	15.2	19.5	36.7	52.1	28.5	5.5
Negroes	1.4	9.1	11.8	38.7	57.3	17.6	12.7
Turks	1.4	10.0	11.7	19.0	25.3	41.8	23.4
Chinese	1.1	11.8	15.9	27.0	27.3	45.2	22.4
Mulattoes	1.1	9.6	10.6	32.0	47.4	22.7	16.8
Korean	1.1	10.8	11.8	20.1	27.5	34.3	13.8
Hindus	1.1	6.8	13.0	21.4	23.7	47.1	19.1

Source: Bogardus (1928, 25). Bogardus's samples included not just northern European hosts but a large number of southern and eastern Europeans. Indeed, nearly one-quarter of his almost 1,500 white respondents came from those groups (24).

did much. They organized into various leagues, and these instead of trying to . . . crush one another out, joined hands for the common issue" (see Glanz 1976, 92).

Adamovitch, the Polish cop in Nelson Algren's *Never Come Morning* (1987, 127–28), deplores a "low-class Polack" as the "sort of kid [who] kept spoiling things for the high-class Polacks . . . instead of just being good citizens like the Irish." Adamovitch adds: "That was why the Irish ran City Hall and the Police Department and the Board of Education," while all Polish Americans "could do like the Irish . . . was to fight under Irish names at the City Garden." "[T]heir self-confidence is so adamant," the *Daily Jewish Courier* concluded on March 17, 1914, about Chicago's Irish, "that their neighbors are forced to respect them."[6]

RACE, SPACE, AND THE FIGHTING IRISH

But however well positioned they were to encounter and influence new immigrants, Irish Americans taught layered, even contradictory, lessons about the racial order in the United States and about the places of eastern and southern Europeans in it. In streets, schools, political parties, churches, unions, and workplaces, they drew and blurred color lines, courted alliances with fellow "whites" who had recently arrived, and denigrated those same newcomers. Gang violence provides an apt point of entry into how Irish Americans taught contradictory lessons that reinforced the "inbetween" position of new immigrants.[7]

In James T. Farrell's *The Young Manhood of Studs Lonigan*, the title hero and his buddies take inspiration from the grownup Irish American street gang/athletic club Ragen's Colts. During the Chicago race riot of 1919, Fat Malloy tells Studs, Red Kelly, Weary Reilly, Kenny Kilarney, Three Star Hennessey, and other very Irish friends that the Colts are "marching into the black belt and knocking off niggers." The "Fifty-eighth Street guys" pledge to do likewise. For two hours they patrol, singing all the while. Finding only an African American boy, they take his clothes, "[burn] his tail with lighted matches," and urinate on him (Farrell 1934/1993, 217–28).[8]

Ragen's Colts, functioning as the "military arm of the Irish political machine" locally, had considerably more trouble casting themselves as examples for eastern European immigrants during the riots than they did in impressing Studs's buddies (Barrett 1987, 220). Seeing the conflict as between white and black Americans, many of those immigrants sat it out. Finally, the Colts apparently took desperate measures, entering a Polish and Lithuanian area "Back-of-the-Yards" in blackface disguise by night to torch houses. They hoped that deceived victims of the arson would blame blacks and join the racial terror. The club members knew about blacking up, as they put on minstrel shows for the community.[9]

The horrific street theater of Ragen's Colts operated on different levels. On the one hand, it was perversely an act of inclusion. Poles and Lithuanians were to be taken, indeed tricked, into a white alliance. Although the term is most fully and aptly theorized as a later-twentieth-century and often politically progressive phenomenon, the making of panethnicity—in this case, an oppressive white panethnicity—was also at issue in the minstrelized arson. To expect such a trick to work—it largely did not—and to burn down people's houses both bespoke a contempt for eastern Europeans (Pacyga 1991, 219–20). Such patterns of inclusion and of contempt and conflict run through Irish American receptions of new immigrants. The lessons taught by the Colts therefore deserve to be put in context. If the burning of neighborhoods as consciously designed training in racism for new immigrants was rare, the use of force by Irish Americans to draw racial lines was not. Their strong sense that urban space was racially bounded instructed new immigrants.

Irish American youth enforced "deadlines," specific boundaries that served to carve the city up into distinctly racialized spaces. The deployment of such deadlines— the term had found its way into urban slang after a Gilded Age Irish American cop allegedly instituted such lines to forbid entry into New York City business districts by criminals—against blacks was a broader experience on which the street dramas of 1919 rested and through which other immigrant groups learned to map cities racially. The Irish American radical William Z. Foster (1939, 17, 18) remembered his street gang in late-nineteenth-century Philadelphia with nostalgia for its "real proletarian spirit." Nonetheless, he described their central activity as seeing to it that blacks "were dead-lined at Lombard Street . . . and at Broad Street." The offender who ventured into "white Bulldog territory . . . was unmercifully slugged." In Chicago the deadline on the South Side was Wentworth Avenue. When Langston Hughes (1940/1963, 33) crossed it, he learned that Irish gang members "didn't allow niggers in that neighborhood." Irish Americans won a reputation as the "greatest enemy" of black Americans, some-times sharing the title with Poles as the twentieth century wore on (Lightfoot, n.d.; Davis 1927, 20–21; Thrasher 1927/1963, 5–22; Kisseloff 1989, 190, 268, 296; Drake and Cayton 1945, 42–43, 107, 110, 180–81; Radzialowski 1976, 7–8).[10] Indeed, Mat-thew Guterl's *The Color of Race in America* (2001, 97) shows that even radical black nationalists, fascinated by the example of Ireland after 1916 and eager to make anti-imperialist alliances, still clearly identified the Irish Americans as the leading edge of racist direct action in U.S. cities. In Frances E. W. Harper's important 1880s novel *Trial and Triumph* (1888–89/1994, 215–21), the territoriality unfolds within a public school. The teacher sits Annette, a black student, next to "the Irish saloon-keeper's daughter." By lunch, the Irish girl screams her opposition to "eating with niggers." Annette re-sponds by asking whether the Irish didn't eat with pigs before migrating. "Ireland and Africa," Harper wrote, "were not ready for annexation."[11]

However, two complications should stop us short of concluding that Irish Ameri-can gangs simply taught white supremacy. First, Irish American deadlining applied to new immigrants as well as to African Americans. "The Italian boy knew which [Green-wich Village] street it was good for him to walk on," Ware (1994, 52, 131) observed, "and he also knew the consequences of walking on the other side of the park which the Irish had set aside for themselves." In Buffalo in the early twentieth century, Irish Americans forced Italians "to use the back streets" (Yans-McLaughlin 1982, 112–13). Indeed, the "special hatred" that Irish Americans cultivated toward Italian Americans rises almost to the level of a trope in the latter's autobiographies (Yans-McLaughlin 1982, 112–13; Whyte 1943/1993, 195; Stave and Sutherland 1994, 89, 106, 187; La Sorte 1985, 51, 139, 148–52; Carpenter 1927/1970, 119; Bayor 1978, 3–4; *L'Italia*, August 4, 1912, 1).[12]

Irish American hostility reached far beyond Italians and could create solidarities among migrants with little in common except fear of the Irish (Stave and Sutherland 1994, 180–81, 193). In his account of the 1919 riots in Chicago, Dominic Pacyga (1991, 219–20) pointedly remarks that in the incendiarism of the Ragen's Colts the "traditional" enemies of the Poles, the Irish, lit the flames. Contemporaries attributed the "mad lawlessness" of the anti-Greek riot in South Omaha in 1909 to the Irish. Irish anti-Semitism hardly needed U.S. inspirations: there had been riots against the tiny Jewish community in Ireland in the 1880s and 1890s, and the Irish had acted on broader Catholic anti-Semitism (Keogh 1998, 19–25; see also Nelson 2001, 67, 199,

321, n. 39). One Irish American writing home in the 1920s bemoaned Ku Klux Klan hatred of Catholics as detrimental to anti-Jewish unity,[13] and the Coughlinite movement in the 1930s mobilized Irish American Catholics significantly around anti-Semitism and in concert with the far right (Warren 1996; Bayor 1978, 87–108). In American cities Jews clearly knew where Irish Americans had placed deadlines. Confronting young Irish men necessitated "a bit of a detour" (Glanz 1976, 98). It hardly needs emphasizing that such neighborhood patrolling was closely connected to the discouragement of interethnic romances and marriages, suggesting a close relationship between gender, sexuality, and interethnic violence. At times Jews and African Americans allied to protect themselves against Irish American street violence (Gamm 1999, 227–28).[14]

Nor was such Irish American aggression simply based on an insularity that lacked "racial" dimensions and could find its victims anywhere. Certainly in mining camps Irish/Cornish conflict was as rancorous as any hostilities involving new immigrants, but in most cities Irish Americans had learned as a group to get along with those of Anglo-Saxon and other old immigrant ancestries (Dubofsky 1988, 26). Their deadlines circumscribed people of color and new immigrants. Harvey Warren Zorbaugh's (1929, 34–35) pioneering sociological research on Chicago's Near North Side observed that, "while the Irish and Swedish had gotten on well as neighbors, neither could nor would live peaceably with the Sicilian." As Italians "penetrated" the area, Irish youths strove to "run out" the newcomers. In Bridgeport, Connecticut, in 1939, an Irish American store owner learned to tolerate his sister's "bad enough" marriage to a Scotsman, but added that, "if she ever married one of those Southern Europeans, the family would disown her." Cherishing his Irish American business partner, he declared his total distrust of Italians, his disdain for all Slavs, his use for "niggers" only as laborers, and his willingness to shoot himself before working with a Jew. Another Bridgeport resident looked back from 1940 to the good old days of the early twentieth century as a time when "the Irish, the Swedes, and the English" not only coexisted but also shared lives. Though she spoke of the influx of Jews, Poles, and Italians without great alarm, they were not to be approached: "I do not know them, but from their names and their looks I can tell pretty near who they are." Their alleged proximity to "barbarism" and "paganism" justified the low position of new immigrants in social hierarchies constructed by Irish Americans (Stave and Sutherland 1994, 185–90, 117–18). The Italian immigrant auto worker Antonio Margariti, who wrote an autobiography in 1979, lamented as the "worst part" of the his sixty-six years in the United States "the harsh, negative, uncompromising attitudes of the members of the Celtic race who are convinced that we [are] of a lower social order" (La Sorte 1985, xiii–xiv, 139; see also Wilder 2000, 201).

A second objection to casting the Irish Americans simply as hosts who welcomed new immigrants to U.S.-style white supremacy lies in the significant traditions of Irish American *antiracism*. In a city like Chicago, if immigrants heard antiracist arguments, they were likely to come from Irish Americans. Often the Irish spokespeople most welcoming to new immigrants also disavowed prejudice against African Americans. After the race riots, as C. L. R. James (1939/1996, 113) wrote, black and Slavic workers returned to work "as old friends" on the shop floor, where they "put their arms around one another's necks." If somewhat romanticized, James's account retains force. What it omits is the crucial role of Irish American leaders and rank-and-file workers in building a packinghouse union that could work such wonders. Those Irish Americans who preached the necessity of "checkerboard" unionism uniting the races in the yards included the Chicago Federation of Labor head John Fitzpatrick, the Philadelphia tough turned packinghouse organizer William Z. Foster, and even many craft union leaders.

The women's union in the yards dated back to Irish American activists organized in the Maud Gonne Club and supported by the Protestant head resident Mary McDowell. McDowell recalled that the color bar in the union yielded on a "dramatic occasion" in which "an Irish girl at the door called out—'A colored sister asks admission. What shall I do with her?'" The Irish American response was, "Admit her, of course, let all of you give her a hearty welcome!" (*New Majority* [Chicago], November 22, 1919; Keiser 1965, 38–41; Barrett 1987, 138–42, 172–74; 1999, 79–82).[15]

IRISH AMERICAN POLITICS AND "NEW IMMIGRANT" INBETWEEN-NESS

Irish American politicking brought similar contradictions regarding the possibility of new immigrants entering pan-white coalitions. Certainly Irish American political leaders seemed to possess what some theorists call "bridging" cultural capital in great measure. The imperialist poet Rudyard Kipling (Gossett 1997, 438) provided a usefully overstated portrait of the Irish immigrant to the United States as a political animal:

> There came to these shores a poor exile from Erin.
> The dew on his wet robe hung heavy and chill.
> Yet the steamer which brought him scarce out of hearin'
> Ere't was Alderman Mike inthrojucin' a bill.

Finley Peter Dunne's (1976, 178) comic philosopher Mr. Dooley added, "[I]f ye put wan Irishman among twenty thousand Polackers, Bohemians, Rooshians, German an 'Boolgaharians, he'll be the leader iv thim all. I wanst knew a man be th' nam iv O'Donnel that was prisidint iv the . . . Polacker National Society." Meanwhile, the Jewish press invented stories of John C. O'Brien as leader of the Jewish Democratic Club—"may th' saints preserve him" (see also Riis 1890/1996, 73; Roberts 1904, 325–26).

The extent to which the all-powerful and welcoming Irish American political boss was a stereotype nonetheless remains debatable. We do know, from the important work of Steven Erie (1988, 96–98) and others, that the dramatic image of Irish American leaders as literally bringing new immigrants to citizenship (or at least to the polls) in order to secure their support needs to be balanced against the temptations for Irish Americans to distrust new immigrants, to attempt to suppress the new immigrant vote, and even to discourage naturalization. Certainly by the 1920s and 1930s, and elsewhere much earlier, complex interethnic challenges to Irish American political machines contributed to this distrust and complicated efforts at Irish-led panethnic politics (see Bayor 1978, 30–56; Barrett and Roediger 2002b).

In political leadership of antinativist initiatives and in distribution of patronage, Irish Americans contributed to both domestic white panethnic politics and to divisions among whites. Thomas Gossett's (1997, 442) crediting of the Irish Americans (and Germans) with inventing "the process of defense of ethnic minorities" captures an important truth, as does John Higham's (1974, 123–24) remark that politically "Irish leaders . . . championed the interests of their southern and eastern European followers." In the face of nativist attacks, Irish Americans frequently stood up, as in the 1907 coalition of the Ancient Order of Hibernians and the German American Alliance to "oppose all immigration restriction." However, such activity stood in curious relationship to white panethnicity because it arrayed new immigrants with the Irish but against nativist whites. Moreover, Irish American support for new immigrants against nativists was uneven, both among political leaders and religious ones (see Leon 1998).

Some Irish American political leaders participated in drawing racial distinctions among Europeans even as they defended immigrants' rights. Historians have praised Patrick Ford, the editor of the *Irish World and American Industrial Liberator*, for his support of an egalitarian transnational "struggle of oppressed peoples." However, Ford decidedly placed Italian Americans in an inbetween position when addressing immigration to the United States. Italians were undesirable because they were "incongruous" with the nation's strengths—"penniless," "ignorant," criminal, and unable to govern themselves. What Ford's biographer calls the "racial traits" of Italians did not quite justify their exclusion, although Ford supported contract labor laws and bars on the immigration of socialists and anarchists, whom he associated with Italian origins. The "Mongolian," on the other hand, as a "product of a civilization totally different from ours," was inassimilable and to be barred (Rodechko 1976, 264–65; see also Hayden 2001, 82–83; Foner 1976, 6–55; Montgomery 2001, 1267; Eagan 2000, 513, 512–63, n. 74).

A return to the Ragen's Colts example emphasizes how conditional and racially inflected panethnic political alliances could be. Months after the race riot, the Colts led a mass demonstration against the Ku Klux Klan, hanging a hooded figure in effigy. Though much more palatable to our sensibilities, this action also aimed to unite Catholic immigrants behind Irish American leaders and was undertaken in the context of a campaign stretching over nearly a decade to brand Chicago's alternative to Irish leadership, the Thompson machine, as at once an Anglo-Saxon and an "Africa First" regime (Tuttle 1984, 257, 197–202; Guglielmo 2003; Nelli 1970, 229–30). However, especially before the Great Migration brought African Americans massively north, urban, Irish-led panethnic mobilizations did not necessarily invoke whiteness explicitly.

Irish American machines tended to reserve that particular form of cultural citizenship known as the patronage job to their own. They thereby withheld from new immigrants access to employment and influence over city services. A great deal was at stake. By 1898 New York City's Democratic machine controlled an estimated 60,000 jobs worth $90 million. In an 1897 sketch titled "A Polacker on the Red Bridge," Dunne has Mr. Dooley worry over the appointment of a Pole to "the notoriously unstrenuous job of bridgetender" at a point of entry to an Irish neighborhood and lament that the Irish American commissioner of public works has chosen "to re-pose that sacred thrust in th'hands iv a man that no wan' . . . can swear at an' be answered dacintly." Dooley allows, however, that "th' foreign iliments have to get recognition nowadays. They're too strong to be left out" (Dunne 1976, 176–78). Actually, as Erie has shown, those "iliments" were often left out (see also McNickle 1999, 9).

The firm Irish grasp on patronage jobs in three cities with strong machines illustrates the problem facing more recent immigrants. Between 1900 and 1930 the Irish proportion of total local government employment increased from 30 to 41 percent in Albany, from 36.6 to 51.7 percent in New York City, and from 42.4 to 58.3 percent in Jersey City. During that time, the proportion of the Irish workforce holding government jobs increased from 4.6 to 14.8 percent in Albany. The comparable figures for the other two cities were much higher—from 5.1 to 20.8 percent in Jersey City and from 5.8 to 23.6 percent in New York. Such figures occurring in the context of the ongoing "new immigration" suggest that the Irish were slow to share patronage jobs with newcomers (Erie 1988, 88).

While Erie (1988, 103–13, 69–71, 80, 102–6) at times hints that greater sharing of patronage across ethnic lines might have made Irish American machines better able to overcome opposition after 1930, other data in his *Rainbow's End* raise the possibility that there was no easy way out of intra-European competition over the "spoils" of municipal government. In New York City, Albany, and Jersey City, for example, per capita municipal spending rose by an incredible 111.8 percent from 1902 to 1932. To have new immigrant groups working for the cities at the level of wild overrepresentation of the Irish would have had the public sector rivaling the private. To simply reapportion existing jobs would only have dismantled the Irish American machines' bases of supporters, sacrificing what the sociologist Jan Nederveen Pieterse (n.d.) calls "bonding" social capital in order to deploy "bridging" social capital. Irish Americans had generated much of both the former, in part because of extraordinary premigration experience in mass nationalist politics, and the latter, given the timing of their migration and their location in the U.S. social structure, but the two forms of capital could not always be effectively yoked. Under such constraints, what Erie calls "minimalist" politics— dispensing social services as well as "food, loans, and licenses to the newcomers but not city jobs"—made some sense. But such a strategy laid bare the differences between new immigrants, for whom machine-based systems of cultural citizenship did some favors, and Irish Americans, who were systematically favored (McGivigan and Robertson 1996).

TRANSNATIONALITY, RELIGION, AND IRISH HOSTING

Irish Americans' passionate involvement in Irish national liberation struggles and in Roman Catholicism placed them in transnational networks that cut against Daniel Bell's (Winslow 1993, 374) characterization of them as "an isolated mass." The leading theorist of cultural pluralism, Horace Kallen (Sollors 1996, 86), wrote in 1915 that many Irish Americans regarded the United States as "just a center from which to plot freedom for Ireland." Curiously, however, such a stance did not necessarily isolate Irish Americans. Indeed, Kallen continued by observing that Irish nationalism animated struggles "to escape both race and religious prejudice." The historian John Bodnar (1985, 101) adds that Irish American nationalism constituted a "step in the assimilation of immigrant laborers into American working class traditions." The rhetoric of democracy for Ireland intersected with the U.S. revolutionary heritage of struggle against British colonialism.[16] Moreover, the Irish American insistence on addressing Irish freedom within U.S. popular struggles gave inspiration and language to others who would press claims for national liberation beyond their ethnic communities. Their numbers, early arrival, political power, and trade union strength gave the Irish Americans a special chance to carry out direct action on behalf of their national cause. They could actually lead a coalition that would stop shipping in large East Coast ports during the "Irish Patriotic Strike" in 1920. That Ireland conducted a partly successful struggle for independence during and after World War I helped to make it a model. The height of Irish American nationalism overlapped with similar movements among eastern Europeans and Zionism in the same era. Thus, when Chicago's Slavic workers pressed for foreign policy changes, they gravitated toward the Irish Americans as models and allies (McKillen 1995; Doyle 1996, 357–73; Nelson 2001, 26–38; Montgomery 1984, 111–13).

Even so, the Irish freedom movement could not unproblematically contribute to incorporating new immigrants into a white panethnicity any more than street toughs could. In some ways Irish nationalism divided whites. As Gossett (1997, 439) puts it, the Anglophobia of the movement "put a damper on some of the more extravagant claims of [white] racial unity." In terms of building panethnic coalitions between Irish Americans and new immigrants, the common support of national liberation had mixed results. The Irish freedom movement tended to insist on the extraordinary oppression and unexcelled quality of the Irish "race" so as to dissipate panethnicity around internationalism. Enthusiasm for Irish freedom, as Guterl's (2001, 83–84) work shows, "muted claims of whiteness" at times. "Celtic boosterism," Catherine Eagan (2000, 513, 504–18) writes, clashed with "the common cause of the oppressed." While national liberation rhetoric gave a common language to Irish Americans and some new immigrant groups, the nations blocking self-determination were different and sometimes warring. Programmatic unity was difficult in such situations, as groups called for the United States to distance itself not only from empire but also from specific empires. Finally, some dramatic examples of Irish American alliances around a common passion for national liberation involved groups that were not "white." These included the Friends of Indian Freedom and black nationalists involved in the Garvey movement. The Irish American freedom fighters did frequently insist on reasserting their whiteness—for example, in describing their bondage as especially galling because they were the "only white race in slavery" (Guterl 2001, 88). However, their "white but of the people" stance was insufficiently welcoming or consistent to generate stable white panethnic coalitions around nationalist struggles.[17]

Another scene in the *Lonigan* trilogy opens on to discussion of the complex roles of the other great international passion of Irish Americans, the Catholic Church, in structuring and stalling white panethnic unity with new immigrants (Farrell 1934/1993, 375–76, 455–58, 560). In the mid-1920s, Patrick Lonigan, patriarch and "boss painter," runs into Marty O'Brien, an old friend who has fled the neighborhood. O'Brien declares himself "sorry . . . but glad" to be gone. Lonigan acknowledges problems but cautions against gloom: "To be sure, the jigs have got on Washington Avenue, and a lot of Polacks and Wops have come in along the southwestern edge of the parish, but still I wouldn't be so pessimistic. . . . Particularly since Father Gilhooley is going to build the new church."

In the balance of the chapter, the Wops and Polacks disappear, with O'Brien predicting that "kike real-estate bastards" will leave the neighborhood "so full of black clouds of smoke that a white man won't belong in it." The Lonigans soon move, blaming Father Gilhooley for the fact that parish school pupils "are all jigabooes."[18]

The slippage from the hope that a new Catholic church could anchor an Irish American neighborhood against both new immigrants and blacks to the idea that it could anchor a "white's man" neighborhood specifically against blacks typifies a recurring pattern in Farrell's antiracist classic. Racist lore in the novels provides litanies of new immigrant faults, focusing on bodies and habits, connecting them to blacks, but then declaring the latter group to be the "worst" (Farrell 1934/1993, 402). As a "universal" but Irish-led church, U.S. Catholicism could at times challenge such intra-European race thinking (and even antiblack racism) among parishioners. However, its own history, leadership, and bases of support ensured that the generation of a new panethnic Catholic whiteness would be uneven and prolonged and that a Catholic nonracialism stretching across the color line would be more fragile still.[19]

Their past, reputation, numerical strength, religious homogeneity, and urban concentration set the stage for Irish Americans to host new immigrant Catholics. The "devotional revolution" in nineteenth-century Ireland sent the proportion of priests to population from one to three thousand to one to nine hundred in the sixty years after 1840 (Larkin 1972). As poverty produced late marriage and spinsterhood in Ireland, vocations for nuns shot up even faster, moving from one to sixty-five hundred to one to four hundred. Priests and nuns became exports to the United States. Children of Irish immigrants to the United States also found vocations and set up institutions that could train large numbers of Irish American priests and nuns (Diner 1983, 28, 130, 136). With lay immigrants keeping the faith, and with the clerical leaders increasingly Irish American, critics complained by the 1890s of a church that had become "One Holy, Apostolic, and Irish" (Dolan 1992, 303). By 1920 two-thirds of bishops were Irish Americans, with such major centers as New York, Boston, Philadelphia, and Baltimore all Irish-led (Dolan 1992, 302–3; Gleason 1992, 281; Barrett and Roediger 2002b).

However, quarrels over church structure and the conflicting desires of Irish Americans either to reshape new immigrant Catholics or to avoid them altogether complicated matters at the parish level. By the 1890s some Irish Catholics, led by Archbishop John Ireland of St. Paul, articulated an optimistic, assimilative "Americanizing" mission for the Church in which largely Irish hosts would provide leadership not only in diocesan matters but also in geographically based parishes with ethnically diverse memberships. German Americans dramatically challenged such views, arguing for "national" parishes, native-language use, and power-sharing in the hierarchy. The latter position found support in an 1899 papal pronouncement, but the decline of immigration from Germany left a gap in the forces favoring the national autonomy of parishes during the period of massive new immigration of Catholics. The national parish thrived, but alongside "territorially" based ones that tended to be dominated by the Irish.[20]

Significant local and ethnic variations shaped religiously based new immigrant "inbetween-ness." First, the national parish was itself imagined as geographic with distinct boundaries, even if other national groups and even national parishes existed inside those boundaries. Such parishes were bulwarks of an immigrant world that Dominic Pacyga (1996, 56) describes as "socially segregated" but "spatially integrated" where ethnicity was concerned. Moreover, neither at the level of leadership nor that of laity did Irish Americans universally support either mixed congregations or other aspects of Americanization generally. Many joined Farrell's Patrick Lonigan in cherishing the ethnic purity of Irish American parishes. Since the groups seen as most in need of Americanization—Italians were the textbook case—were also cast as the least desirable of immigrants, whether to provide a separate parish, a mixed parish, or a church basement in an Irish American parish remained an open question. The degree of organization among new immigrants influenced such decisions, but it is worth noting that the Irish American hierarchy saw both the most organized and insistent (Poles) and the least (Italians) as "problems." African American congregations were meanwhile shoehorned into the national parish model and Jim-Crowed from mixed parishes (Kenny 2000, 167–71; Kazal 1998, 539–50; McGreevy 1996, 10–22, 34–35, 84–101, 196–97).

While the national parish played prominent real and symbolic roles in the early twentieth century, countervailing tendencies are underappreciated. Indeed, Chicago, at the time Farrell wrote, was committed to ethnically mixed white parishes. In some areas, such as Boston and Pennsylvania's anthracite fields, Irish American priests were so overwhelmingly present compared to parishioners that they presumably shepherded new immigrant flocks. Bill Bailey (1993, 64–65), during his adolescence in New York City, was thus caught in tricky crosscurrents. His Irish American mother sent him to

Father O'Rourke in search of car fare to a job, but the Italian American assistant who answered his knock called him a "bum." Bailey's mother later berated the priest for his weight, dress, and "contempt for poor people, especially the Irish." She invited him to go straight "back to Italy . . . or wherever he came from." O'Rourke appeared and, after apologizing for her manners, took Bailey's mother aside and gave her five dollars rather than fifty cents. "Yes," the Irish prelate said, "the Lord does work in mysterious ways." The mother gave Bailey a lecture "on the merits of having more Irish priests and fewer 'Eye-talians'" (see Sullivan 1985, 205–6; Roberts 1904, 209–10).

The huge numbers of Irish nuns also produced interethnic Catholic contacts. In Detroit the important Immaculate Heart of Mary order, founded by mulattoes, came to be dominated by Irish Americans, ministered to diverse populations, and suppressed public displays of ethnic origins by members. Irish American nuns impressively learned Italian as one Brooklyn parish changed "racially." However, new immigrant children might not always have appreciated such willingness to teach across national lines. One Polish-Lithuanian remembered Irish Americans getting all of the best grades, prizes, and "honorary jobs" (for example, writing on the blackboard) as a result of the prejudice against Poles and Italians of the Irish nuns who taught at his mixed school (Vinyard 1998, 58, 63, 71; Stave and Sutherland 1994, 179–81; Dolan 1992, 497–98; Pacyga 1996, 29; Liptak 1989, 61–89; McGreevy 1996, 35). The Vitullo family, living in Youngstown in the early twentieth century in Carmen Leone's (1998, 10–14) fictionalized family history, accepted going to Mass in an Irish American–dominated church—the liturgy being universal—but "would not even consider" sending a daughter to the Catholic (they said "Irish") school.[21]

Catholic organizations rooted in parishes but also affiliated beyond parish boundaries provided further venues for Irish American hosting and evidence of how inbetween-ness worked. The Knights of Columbus, founded in the early 1880s by Irish Americans, took an Italian's name to symbolize both its American-ness and the universal struggles against paganism and Anglo-Saxondom. Nonetheless, as the official history of the society puts it, the early Knights were "realists on ethnic issues." Second-generation Irish Americans themselves, "they allowed [in Boston] the establishment of the . . . Ansonia Council for Italian Americans." As Ronald Bayor (1978, 4) writes in his history of interethnic relations in New York City, such segmented inclusion did not always work, even in a body named for Columbus: "Italians did not feel that they could achieve equality in such groups as the Knights of Columbus so long as the Irish controlled the organization. Therefore, separate Italian associations, such as the Sons of Italy, were formed." Nonetheless, when racially and religiously based immigration restriction was sharply posed as a national issue between 1917 and 1929, the Knights stood among the defenders of immigrant rights (Kauffman 1982, 262–63, 269–73; 1992, 10, 23).

Emphases on gradual Americanization, respect for autonomy, and defense of civil liberties characterized the best of the Irish-led Church. Indeed, even "conservative" Irish American Catholic leaders promoted a kind of Catholic panethnicity in their defensiveness against "Anglo-Saxon domination of the world." Nor did Catholic hesitancy to oppose immigration restriction necessarily bespeak softness regarding anti–new immigrant racism, since the Church did support procedural challenges to restrictive legislation (Jacobson 1995, 186–88; Leon 1998).

However, tension between Irish American clergy and laity, on the one hand, and Catholic and Jewish new immigrants, on the other, arose so consistently and forcefully—and in such subtle connection to anti–African American prejudice—as to suggest Patrick Lonigan's typicality. Just as Irish Americans functioned as a "common enemy" for new immigrants on the streets, they often did so within the Church, according to Jay Dolan (1992, 303). As John McGreevy (1996, 30–31) shows, Irish American Catholics shared broader U.S. confusions on the "lines between 'race' and what is now considered 'ethnicity.'" But often enough, sharp "racial hatreds" between Irish and new immigrant Catholics were spelled out. In particular, worry that new immigrants were uncivilized, emotional, superstitious, and likely to bring Catholics as a whole into disrepute surfaced in ways reminiscent of the whole society's prejudices against the Latin and Slavic "races." Indeed, Irish Catholic opinion leaders pursued a "morose" interest in new immigrant birthrates, drawing dire conclusions that much resembled Anglo-American panic regarding a coming "race suicide" for their own group (Diner 1983, 63).

Italians, who were far less given to supporting lavish parishes and Catholic schools than other groups, and whose ranks included significant numbers of anticlerical "mangiapreti" (priest eaters) (La Sorte 1985, 150), were singled out for censure by Irish American (and by Italian) clergy. When they were worshiping, Italian Americans could still seem problematic. The "festa" that communally honored patron saints stood, according to Robert Orsi (1985, 57), as both an "embarrassment" and a challenge to "the authority of official Catholicism." The immigration historian Judith Smith (1985, 147) points out that "all aspects of south Italian saint veneration and attitudes towards Catholicism seemed foreign, pagan and sacrilegious to Irish parishioners and priests," although (or because) the Irish had labored hard to distance *themselves* from such practices (on the Italians, see Browne 1946; Tomasi 1975, 44–47; Nelli 1970, 188–92; Vecoli 1969, 220–33; Luconi 2001, 40–41). When protesting Baltimore Poles trapped the Irish American archbishop in his home, he called police and characterized Polish people as often "not far removed from barbarism" (Wolff 1995; on Irish conflicts with Polish Catholics, see Pacyga 1991, 145; 1996, 29; Liptak 1989, 74, 86; McGreevy 1996, 31, 36, 37; Meagher 2001, 338–49). Interethnic tensions were often cast as "race wars" within the Church, even as what Timothy Meagher (2001, 338–49) calls a "pan-Catholic" culture developed under strong Irish American influences. With all these crosscurrents, what McGreevy (1996, 31, 36, 37) called a "Catholic white" identity could fully develop "only in the context of African-Americans moving in large numbers to a particular area."[22]

WORKING OUT RACIAL IDENTITIES

At work and in unions, Irish Americans likewise taught new immigrants about racism, antiracism, and the perils of being caught on the wrong side of the color line. Two classic 1941 novels of U.S. working-class life, Thomas Bell's *Out of This Furnace* and William Attaway's *Blood on the Forge*, suggest a common eagerness on the part of Slavic and African American workers to avoid contact with Irish Americans. A central character in Bell's (1941/1976, 124) account of Slovak American iron and steel workers reflects on a long train of abuses and then offers the consolation that his people migrated to the United States to "find work and save money, not to make friends with the Irish." In *Blood on the Forge* (1941/1987, 122–23), the African American worker Big Mat saves an Irish American foreman by "laying out" an aggressive native-born "hayseed." Suddenly the Irish bosses and hearth workers discover Mat to be "black Irish." His "Irish guts" make him "a whole lot better Irish than a hunky [Slav] or a ginny [Italian]." Mat nonetheless only wants out and flees the adoration to watch dogs fight.

Yet Irish Americans could hardly be ignored at work. By 1900 they were "everywhere and into everything," as David Montgomery (1980, 205) writes. As late as 1880, that had not been the case. At that point half of all Irish immigrant males and about one-third of their sons worked in unskilled jobs. By 1900 only one-seventh of the second-generation Irish male population worked in unskilled jobs, and for Irish-born males the figure was one-quarter. Even among Irish American women, two-thirds of whom worked in unskilled jobs in 1900, the trend toward greater occupational variety and skill was pronounced. While 71 percent of the first-generation women worked in domestic service in 1900, only 25 percent of second-generation Irish American women workers did, while 19 percent of the second generation worked in sales or offices or as professionals. Indeed, the stratification of the whole Irish American population was by 1900 little different from that of native-born urban Protestants (see Montgomery 1980, 208–15, esp. 211; Erie 1988, 63; Miller 1985, 499–503). However, the large numbers of Irish remaining in the unskilled ranks meant that more recent immigrants worked with Irish laborers as well as for Irish skilled workers and foremen.

The increasing numbers of Irish American women professionals reflected a dynamic that had considerable significance for Irish hosting. Given a late average age of marriage, Irish American families claimed young women's labor for a relatively long time and seemed willing to sacrifice for the education of daughters. Even unskilled workers sent a daughter to high school and especially into teacher training. The "steady work" of teaching school became for Irish American women the "most popular" path that those with options "chose for self-support in the second generation" (Diner 1983, 96). By the twentieth century's first decade, Irish Americans were the largest group of New York City schoolteachers, and 1908 statistics show the Irish holding between 24 and 49 percent of the teaching positions in Buffalo, New York; Fall River, Massachusetts; Providence, Rhode Island; Lowell, Massachusetts; and Scranton, Pennsylvania. Thus, according to Andrew Greeley, the school "Hibernicized" new immigrants as much as it Americanized them. The sociologist E. A. Ross (Diner 1983, 97) found Irish teachers to be "swift climbers." Ross reported a conversation with a city school superintendent who suggested that ability to relate to new immigrant communities was cultural capital for such teachers. When there was doubt, the superintendent counseled, the Irish American woman should always get the job: "[S]he will have less trouble in discipline and hits it off better with parents and the neighborhoods." Here again, Irish Americans were potential models. But tensions inevitably emerged. Doc, a key figure in William Foote Whyte's classic 1943 study of Italian American "slum" life, *Street Corner Society*, got the last word in that book. He began it by dissecting the harm done to the self-esteem of Italian American kids in Boston schools: "You don't know how it feels to grow up in a district like this. You go to the first grade—Miss O'Rourke. Second grade—Miss Casey. Third grade—Miss Chalmers. Fourth grade—Miss Mooney." Students, he argued, "feel inferior" knowing that "the Irish or the Yankees" dominate the "good jobs" in teaching (Whyte 1943/1993, 276). Irish American teaching placed the striving middle-class, second-generation daughters of old immigrants in charge and in judgment of new immigrants' children. The judgments could be harsh and wholesale, as when an Irish American teacher in Newark's schools in 1923 wrote the local paper of her experiences with "hordes of aliens" and with their "offspring flooding in our schools [and] changing their character" (Anyon 1997, 49). Moreover, by the 1920s and 1930s, Irish Americans had lost to second-generation eastern European Jewish women, sometimes bitterly, their relative strength teaching in New York City (see DeVault 1990, 85–87; Jenks and Lauck 1926, 358–59; Mageean 1997, 241; Steinberg 1989, 136–37,

164–66; Stave and Sutherland 1994, 222; Glanz 1976, 90; Perlmann 1988b, 56; Greeley 1969, 32; Bayor 1978, 27).[23]

Though pitched sentimentally and humorously, Myra Kelly's popular 1904 novel *Little Citizens* caught much of the drama and the complexity of the encounter of young female Irish American teachers with their new immigrant pupils. Its Irish American heroine, Constance Bailey, regards her Lower East Side New York City students as both "little savages" and as U.S. "citizen[s] in the making." Dirt, "unintelligible dialect," and drink (even for a seven-year-old) bedevil her attempts to "reform" them. Her fellow Irish American, Bridget Diamantstein, is willing to marry a Jewish widower and to raise his children, but only as Catholics. She refuses to let him "bring up the darlin's for black Protestant Jews like himself." Her boss, Tim O'Shea, "had his prejudices—strong and deep," against new immigrants and their children. He regards them as having transformed the "happy hunting grounds of his youth" into a neighborhood "swarming with strange faces." He nurtures "a sullen grudge against the usurping race." But "race" lines also blur. Bailey counts the Irish American Patrick Brennan among the young objects of her reform efforts. She knows also that the young eastern European, Eva Gonorowsky, could "civilize a whole tribe of savages" (Kelly 1904, 3, 184, 194, 141–42, 167).

The tremendous mobility and variety that came to characterize the Irish American occupational structure between 1880 and 1900 would have telling impacts on the possibilities of Irish Americans fostering panethnic whiteness in the early twentieth century. As the fiction of Attaway and Bell suggests, new immigrants often could not ignore the presence of Irish Americans if they wanted to get and keep unskilled jobs. Irish Americans commanded positions as foremen, as bosses in mining and timber camps, as stevedores, as skilled workers hiring helpers, as contractors (outnumbering German Americans by three to one), as politicians, and as politically connected saloonkeepers doling out day labor funded by political machines. Since rendering ethnic judgments was part and parcel of managing workers, Irish Americans' positions ensured that they would make such judgments. Sometimes, as in Kansas City packinghouses where Irish Catholic foremen had a reputation for securing positions for Catholic new immigrants *and* for mistreating them, the judgments were mixed (Stave and Sutherland 1994, 59–60; Horowitz 1997, 90; La Sorte 1985, 81; Montgomery 1980, 211; Roberts 1904, 326; Kazin 1987, 21).

Given the large Irish American population, some continuing immigration of the unskilled from Ireland, and continuing immiseration and discrimination, absolute numbers of the Irish poor remained significant even as the community's overall position improved. Poor and unskilled Irish Americans more regularly came into contact and competition with new immigrants. For example, Bill Bailey's insistence that the Poles and the Irish occupied the "bottom rungs" of the population in his boyhood neighborhood of Hoboken, New Jersey, probably best described a strata of the Irish population in close contact with Poles. If they benefited, as anecdotal evidence suggests they at times did, from wage discrimination specifying higher wages for the Irish American unskilled than for new immigrants, they also might have worried that such differentials would lead to their replacement by the lower paid (Bailey 1993, 18; La Sorte 1985, 65; Montgomery 1987, 74; Gambino 1976, 77; Nelson 2001, 152).

The relatively early immigration of the Irish and their spread throughout the job structure by the time a durable national union movement gained strength put them in a strong position to lead labor organizations, which sometimes came to contain many new immigrants. As Montgomery (1980, 205–13) observes, no major U.S. industry in this period had a labor force with an Irish American majority. Nonetheless, by the early twentieth century the children and grandchildren of Irish immigrants, and sometimes immigrants themselves, had come to dominate the labor leadership. In the first decade of the twentieth century, Irish Americans held nearly half of all international union presidencies in the United States. During that time the unions overwhelmingly organized on craft lines, but with rare exceptions like plumbing, Irish Americans did not dominate crafts numerically. Especially in construction, iron and steel, and longshore, Irish Americans built and led unions by including and excluding workers of other races and ethnicities. They were on the job to learn the new skills associated with the expansion of those industries and then to welcome (or oppose) unskilled new immigrants. Fitzpatrick's and Foster's promotion of amalgamated, egalitarian unionism in packing and steel was one possible response to such a situation (Karson 1956; O'Donnell 1997, 117–41; Kenny 2000, 189). The results could be arresting. At Homestead in the late nineteenth century, Slavs gained admittance to the Irish National Land and Industrial League, where they learned the advantages of labor unity (Krause 1992, 316). Such Irish American openness concentrated on the radical left. Elizabeth Gurley Flynn, the Industrial Workers of the World's (IWW) "rebel girl" organizer, joined her fellow Irish American Bill Haywood in leading initiatives that united new immigrants with some of the old in spectacular early-twentieth-century textile and mining strikes. Flynn's sympathies with new immigrants led her to scoff at the notion of American liberties: "What freedom? Was it to be called 'Greenhorns' and 'Hunkies' and treated as inferiors and intruders?" In the most famous of the textile strikes, at Lawrence in 1912, Flynn learned from Haywood how to reach new immigrant workers, coming to understand that the "foreign-born usually learned English from their children," who left school quickly. The conclusion: "Never reach for a three-syllable word if one or two would do" (Flynn 1955, 131; see also Keiser 1965, 38–41; Barrett 1987, 191–202; 1999, 79–82, 94–96).

At their best, Irish American labor radicals nurtured class-based panethnic alliances including not only new immigrants but also African Americans. Few other sources match labor tales in giving evidence of Irish American hosts constructing transparent lessons about life in the United States. Mary McDowell recounted the story of a meeting at which the Irish American local president asked if there were "grievances" (meaning, against management) to be processed. The "black and white, Polish, Bohemian, Irish, Croatian and Hungarian" crowd sat wordless until a "morbidly shy black girl" complained of a Polish coworker "taunting her on her color." The president had the two girls stand together, and the Pole admitted the teasing, but added, "[S]he called me a Polack." The tension broke in "hearty, good-natured laughter." The Irish American leader drew the appropriate lessons: "Ain't you ashamed of yourselves? Now shake hands and don't bring any more of your personal grievances here" (see Lewis and Foner 1989, 301–2). Haywood (1929, 241–42), Mary White Ovington (Green 1996, 123–25), and the Connecticut socialist organizer Edna Mary Purtell (Stave and Sutherland 1994, 222) told antiracist Irish American stories that were equally didactic and delightful.

However exemplary some Irish American trade union antiracists were, however, they were not the norm. Concentrated in exclusionary craft unions, Irish American labor leaders included some of the staunchest *opponents* of mass unionism. Calvin Winslow's (1993, 373) characterization of Irish Americans as being almost as absent from movements for industrial unionism as they were from socialism needs qualification, some of which is provided in his own excellent work. However, the logic of racial exclusion pervaded many unions that Irish Americans led. When the International Association of Machinists (IAM) sparred against feeble American Federation of Labor (AFL) attempts to avoid full capitulation to white supremacy within its affiliates, the union's leader was an Irish American. Where they could, for example in Boston, Irish American longshoremen struggled for an all-white longshore labor force. E. Franklin Frazier's study of post–World War I longshoremen found Irish American workers bearing the "greatest antagonisms" to blacks, with Italians "assimilating prejudices" (Winslow 1993, 372; Nelson 2001, 33–38; Taillon 1990).[24]

Here again, however, the Irish American hosts taught lessons that were too contradictory to encourage the full development of a panethnic *white* workerist consciousness. The craft unions, in which Irish Americans were so instrumental in building unity with other old immigrants, proved notoriously slow to open up to new immigrants, even as they Jim-Crowed African Americans. In Boston the "white" longshore campaign targeted Italians as well as African Americans for exclusion, leaving Irish Americans in possession of 85 percent of the work, with the rest going to other old immigrant communities, as late as 1915. Even in New York City, where Irish American longshore workers could not control hiring, they kept union leadership, "cream" jobs, and firm enough control of the "longshoreman's rest" area to exclude Italian Americans from it into the 1930s. Language issues could prove especially volatile, as part of the cultural capital that Irish American labor leaders possessed was command of English; hostility to conducting business in other languages easily bled over into a more generalized suspicion of "foreigners" as potential trade unionists (Lieberson 1980, 346–50; Kimeldorf 1999, 25; Nelson 2001, 22, 54; Ware 1935/1994, 52; Montgomery 1984, 309).

In unions and elsewhere, Irish Americans imparted much at once. They taught the color line and how to breach it. They taught that a line might also be drawn to exclude and demean immigrants, and they modeled how such exclusions might be overcome. In part the great size and diverse social locations of Irish America ensured such variety, which also reflected how the broader society saw and taught new immigrants.

However, the powerful positions of Irish Americans in institutions (churches, schools, political machines, unions, and workplaces, for example) whose logics were by turns both inclusive and exclusive also created contradictory teachings regarding race. Their effectiveness in such institutions depended on both a "bonding" cultural capital that networked with other Irish Americans (and, at times, with other "whites") and a "bridging" cultural capital that mobilized, molded, and managed new European immigrants (and, at times, people of color). Clearly the development of racial knowledge by recent immigrants to the United States is equally layered and complex. It is greatly influenced by changes in the law of civil rights, immigration, and naturalization that have undermined but not undone the link between race and citizenship in the United States.

With transnational cultural production and communication technology, the newest immigrants now encounter U.S. racial mythology, language, and convention long before arriving—in print, on the screen, and through music. Like the "new immigrants" of the earlier era, however, they too encounter entrenched "hosts" within and well beyond their own communities. Many of these encounters, it seems, are with other people of color, which raises fascinating questions about the nature of the racial knowledge conveyed. How have such everyday encounters as well as their own efforts to negotiate official systems shaped the thinking of these most recent immigrants? In tackling such complexities, and in studying the varied groups teaching race to today's newcomers, we might ask whether promising new inclusions and terrifying divisions are again being simultaneously created.

———————————

For their comments and suggestions on this and a related paper, we are much in the debt of Kevin Kenny, Ronald Bayor, Nancy Foner, John McGreevy, Peter D'Agostino, George Fredrickson, John Higham, Richard Delgado, Timothy Meagher, David Montgomery, Caroline Waldron Merithew, Rose Holz, Dexter Arnold, Jean Stefancic, Kerby Miller, Rudy Vecoli, Jan Nederveen Pieterse, Gill Stevens, Eric Arnesen, Tricia Kelleher, the Newberry Library Labor History Group, and the University of Illinois History Workshop and Migration Studies Groups.

NOTES

1. The best example of merging the study of recent and earlier migrations is Foner (2000). For an older study that has significantly influenced our own approach, see Higham (1974). See also Barrett (1992).

2. On ethnically mixed neighborhoods in early-twentieth-century Chicago, see Philpott (1978, 135–45). On the relatively small numbers of Irish in New York's predominantly Italian and Jewish neighborhoods by the time of the 1920 census, see Logan (1997, 14–25). Our thanks to Nancy Foner for suggesting this source and to John Logan for providing it.

3. On the difficulties involved in computing intermarriage across national origins historically, see Herr (1980). On the Irish, see Kenny (2000, 229) and Drachsler (1921). Elsewhere, Drachsler (1920, 20, 122–25, 132) finds Irish American intermarriage rates to be moderate and lower than popularly perceived.

4. On intermarriage in the third generation and beyond, and along religious lines, see Herberg (1955), Abramson (1973), Byron (1999, 142–59), Perlmann (1988a, table 9; 2000, table 13), Drachsler (1921, 56), and Steinberg (1989, 68). On the cohabitation and intermarriage between Irish women and black and Chinese men, see Anbinder (2001, 389–90, 314, 320, 263) and Tchen (1996, 128–30).

5. The question of whether mixed marriages involving the Irish led to a relatively greater number of Irish-identified offspring has yielded differing answers; see Alba (1990, 59–61). For the view that Irish identity claims approximated "actual" ancestry, see Hout and Goldstein (1994). (Thanks to Gillian Stevens for this reference.)

6. For the *Daily Jewish Courier*, see Chicago Foreign Language Press Survey (CFLPS), microfilm, University of Illinois at Urbana-Champaign, reel 32, IC; see also *Lietuva*, October 5, 1915, CFLPS, reel 43, IIIA. Thanks to Todd Michney for the Algren reference.

7. The problem of Irish street gangs, ethnic territoriality, and white racism is more fully developed in Barrett and Roediger (2002b).

8. Farrell's *The Young Manhood of Studs Lonigan* originally appeared in 1934. Interestingly, as Charles Fanning's excellent introduction to the trilogy shows, Farrell's development as a writer was tied to close study of African American forms, which he linked to Irish ones (xiv–xv).

9. On Ragen's Colts and the context for their actions, see Barrett (1987, 219–23), Halpern (1992), Pacyga (1991, 219–27), and Tuttle (1984, 54–55).

10. On the origins of the term "deadline" (or "dead line") as an imaginary marker of restricted access, see Collins (1944, 47–48) and Lewis (1901, 721), as quoted and cited in the Peter Tamony Papers on U.S. slang, Western Historical Manuscripts Collection, University of Missouri at Columbia. For an earlier usage as an imaginary line of demarcation in Civil War military prisons, see Carpenter (1891, 711).

11. Thanks to Tiya Miles for the Harper reference.

12. Thanks to Tom Guglielmo for the *L'Italia* reference. Guglielmo (2003) contains rich evidence on these matters.

13. Thomas "Tot" Waldron to Paddy (his brother), Beloit, Wisc., February 4, 1924, in Kerby Miller's private collection of Irish American transatlantic correspondence, Columbia, Missouri, with thanks to Professor Miller.

14. See also, generally, Dinnerstein (1986, 275–77), Barrett (1992, 1006), Luibheid (1997), Kazal (1998, 536–37), and Broussard (1990), 15.

15. Even the adamant Kate Richards O'Hare, perhaps the most racist among Irish American socialists, for a time moderated her views and befriended black women inmates after spending time in jail; see Foner and Miller (1982, 44–49, 288, 299, 317).

16. "Foreign and American Patriotism," *Sunday Jewish Courier*, March 8, 1914, CFLPS, reel 38, IIIA.

17. McKillen (1995, 175) discusses Irish nationalist connections not only with Asian Indians but also with Puerto Rican, Korean, Chinese, Filipino and Liberian freedom fighters; see also Mishkin (1998, 21–23), Jacobson (1995, 200–43, esp. 226), Nelson (2001, 81), and Walsh (1996, 41).

18. Like most characters and places in his fiction, Farrell based Father Gilhooley and St. Patrick's on his actual experiences—in this case, with Father Michael Gilmartin of St. Anselm's Parish. The new church was completed in late 1925, on the eve of massive racial transformation in Farrell's Washington Park neighborhood, and had become one of the largest African American parishes in Chicago by the late 1920s; see Branch (1996, 15–16), Skerrett (1987, 52), and Fanning (1987, 128–29).

19. On the development of a pan-Catholic identity, see Meagher (2001, 338–49). On the "white" character of this identity amid black populations, see McGreevy (1996).

20. Kenny (2000, 166–71) is superb on these matters, adding nuances for which we do not have space. See also Linkh (1975, 19–31), Liptak (1989, 11, 62), and Gleason (1987, 58–81).

21. Thanks to Thomas Sabatini for the Leone reference. See also *La Tribuna Italiana Transatlantica* (June 18, 1904) in the Chicago Foreign Language Press Survey (Chicago Historical Society) for an Italian American indictment of Irish Catholic arrogance. Thanks to Tom Guglielmo for the last reference.

22. Peter D'Agostino (1997) discounts the "Americanizing" influence of the Irish hierarchy noted by other authors and emphasizes instead the strength of Italian nationalism within the Church and the integrity of Italian Catholic institutions.

23. On nuns and the fostering of female roles as schoolteachers, see Diner (1983, 132), and also see Diner (1983, 14) for the very high relative prevalence of female-headed households among the Irish, another factor in the logic of sacrificing for the education of girls.

24. For Irish American labor leaders' important conservative roles, often in exclusionary unions, see Fink (1974, 162, 197, 327, 373, 384–85, 401–2, 424–25, 442–43, 479–80, 491–92, and 536); see also Gorn (2001, 194, 255, 379, n. 67).

REFERENCES

Abramson, Harold. 1973. *Ethnic Diversity in Catholic America*. New York: John Wiley.

Alba, Richard. 1990. *Ethnic Identity: The Transformation of White America*. New Haven, Conn.: Yale University Press.

Algren, Nelson. 1987. *Never Come Morning*. New York: Four Walls Eight Windows.

Anbinder, Tyler. 2001. *Five Points: The Nineteenth-Century New York City Neighborhood That Invented Tap Dance, Stole Elections, and Became the World's Most Notorious Slum*. New York: Free Press.

Anderson, Margo J. 1988. *The American Census: A Social History*. New Haven, Conn.: Yale University Press.

Anyon, Jean. 1997. *Ghetto Schooling: A Political Economy of Urban Educational Reform*. New York: Teachers College Press, Columbia University.

Archdeacon, Thomas. 1983. *Becoming American: An Ethnic History*. New York: Free Press.

Attaway, William. 1987. *Blood on the Forge*. New York: Monthly Review Press. (Orig. pub. in 1941.)

Bailey, Bill. 1993. *The Kid from Hoboken: An Autobiography*, edited by Lynn Damme. San Francisco: Circus Lithographies.

Barrett, James R. 1987. *Work and Community in the Jungle: Chicago's Packinghouse Workers, 1894–1922*. Urbana: University of Illinois Press.

———. 1992. "Americanization from the Bottom Up: Immigration and the Remaking of the Working Class in the United States, 1880–1930." *Journal of American History* 79(3, December): 996–1020.

———. 1999. *William Z. Foster and the Tragedy of American Radicalism*. Urbana: University of Illinois Press.

Barrett, James, and David Roediger. 2002a. "Inbetween Peoples: Race, Nationality, and the 'New Immigrant' Working Class." In *Colored White: Transcending the Racial Past*, edited by David Roediger. Berkeley: University of California Press.

———. 2002b. "Irish Everywhere: Irish Americans and the 'Americanization' of the 'New Immigrants,' 1880–1930." Paper presented to the "Rewriting Irish Histories" Commonwealth/Neale Fund Conference. University College London (April 4–6).

Bayor, Ronald. 1978. *Neighbors in Conflict: The Irish, Germans, Jews, and Italians of New York City, 1929–1941*. Baltimore: Johns Hopkins University Press.

Bell, Thomas. 1976. *Out of This Furnace*. Pittsburgh: University of Pittsburgh Press. (Orig. pub. in 1941.)

Blessing, Patrick. 1980. "Irish." In *Harvard Encyclopedia of American Ethnic Groups*, edited by Stephen Thernstrom. Cambridge, Mass.: Harvard University Press.

Bodnar, John. 1985. *The Transplanted: A History of Immigrants in Urban America*. Bloomington: Indiana University Press.

Bogardus, Emory S. 1928. *Immigration and Race Attitudes*. Boston: D. C. Heath.

Branch, Edgar M. 1996. *Studs Lonigan's Neighborhood and the Making of James T. Farrell*. Newton, Mass.: Arts End Books.

Broussard, Albert S. 1990. "George Albert Flippin and Race Relations in a Western Rural Community." *Midwest Review* 12(2): 15.

Brown, Dorothy, and Elizabeth McKeown. 1997. *The Poor Belong to Us: Catholic Charities and American Welfare*. Cambridge, Mass.: Harvard University Press.

Browne, Henry J. 1946. "The Italian Problem and the Catholic Church of the United States, 1880–1900." *United States Catholic Historical Society: Historical Records and Studies* 35: 46–72.

Burgos, Adrian. 2002. "Separating the 'Men' from the 'Boys': Privileging Whiteness and Marking Masculinity in Professional Baseball's Labor Conflicts of the Late Nineteenth Century." Unpublished paper, University of Illinois.

Byron, Reginald. 1999. *Irish America*. Oxford: Clarendon.

Carpenter, Horace. 1891. "Plain Living at Johnson's Island." *The Century* 41(March): 711.

Carpenter, Niles. 1970. *Nationality, Color, and Economic Opportunity in the City of Buffalo*. Westport, Conn.: Negro Universities Press, (Orig. pub. in 1927.)

Collins, Ted, ed. 1944. *New York Murders*. New York: Duell, Sloan and Pearce.

Curran, Joseph M. 1989. *Hibernian Green on the Silver Screen: The Irish and American Movies*. New York: Greenwood Press.

D'Agostino, Peter. 1997. "The Scalabrini Fathers, the Italian Emigrant Church, and Ethic Nationalism in America." *Religion and American Culture: A Journal of Interpretation* 7(1, Winter): 121–60.

Davis, Myron. 1927. "Canaryville." Research paper. University of Chicago.

DeVault, Ileen A. 1990. *Sons and Daughters of Labor: Class and Clerical Work in Turn-of-the-Century Pittsburgh*. Ithaca, N.Y.: Cornell University Press.

Diner, Hasia. 1983. *Erin's Daughters in America: Irish Immigrant Women in the Nineteenth Century*. Baltimore: Johns Hopkins University Press.

Dinnerstein, Leonard. 1986. "The Funeral of Rabbi Jacob Joseph." In *Anti-Semitism in American History*, edited by David A. Gerber. Urbana: University of Illinois Press.

Dolan, Jay P. 1992. *The American Catholic Experience: A History from Colonial Times to the Present*. Notre Dame, Ind.: University of Notre Dame Press.

Doyle, Joe. 1996. "Striking for Ireland on the New York Docks." In *The New York Irish*, edited by Ronald H. Bayor and Timothy J. Meagher. Baltimore: Johns Hopkins University Press.

Drachsler, Julius. 1920. *Democracy and Assimilation: The Blending of Immigrant Heritages in America*. New York: Macmillan.

———. 1921. "Intermarriage in New York City: A Statistical Survey of the Amalgamation of European Peoples." Ph.D. diss., Columbia University.

Drake, St. Clair, and Horace R. Cayton. 1945. *Black Metropolis: A Study of Negro Life in a Northern City*. New York: Harcourt, Brace and Co.

Dubofsky, Melvyn. 1988. *We Shall Be All: A History of the Industrial Workers of the World*. Urbana: University of Illinois Press.

Dunne, Finley Peter. 1976. *Mr. Dooley and the Chicago Irish: An Anthology*. New York: Arno Press.

Eagan, Catherine Mary. 2000. "'I Did Imagine . . . We Had Ceased to Be Whitewashed Negroes': The Racial Formation of Irish Identity in Nineteenth-Century Ireland and America." Ph.D. diss., Boston College.

Erie, Steven P. 1988. *Rainbow's End: Irish-Americans and the Dilemmas of Urban Machine Politics, 1840–1945*. Berkeley: University of California Press.

Fanning, Charles. 1987. "The Literary Dimension." In *The Irish in Chicago*, edited by Lawrence McCaffrey, Ellen Skerrett, Michael Funchion, and Charles Fanning. Urbana: University of Illinois Press.

Farrell, James T. 1993. *Studs Lonigan: A Trilogy*. Urbana: University of Illinois Press. (Orig. pub. in 1934.)

Fink, Gary M., ed. 1974. *Biographical Dictionary of American Labor*. Westport, Conn.: Greenwood Press.

Flynn, Elizabeth Gurley. 1955. *The Rebel Girl: An Autobiography*. New York: International Publishers.

Foley, Neil. 2000. "Partly Colored or Other White: Mexican Americans and Their Problem with the Color Line." Paper presented to the Labor and Working Class History Association luncheon lecture, meeting of the Organization of American Historians, St. Louis (April), available at: http:www.lawcha.org/resources/talks/beyondbw.html.

Foner, Eric. 1976. "Class, Ethnicity, and Radicalism in the Gilded Age: The Land League and Irish America." *Marxist Perspectives* 1(Summer): 6–55.

Foner, Nancy. 2000. *From Ellis Island to JFK: New York's Two Great Waves of Immigration*. New Haven, Conn.: Yale University Press.

Foner, Philip S., and Sally M. Miller, eds. 1982. *Kate Richards O'Hare: Selected Writings and Speeches*. Baton Rouge: Louisiana State University Press.

Foster, William Z. 1939. *Pages from a Worker's Life*. New York: International.

Gallagher, Charles A. Forthcoming. "Racial Restructuring: Expanding the Boundaries of Whiteness." In *The Multiracial Movement: The Politics of Color*, edited by Heather Dalmage. Albany: State University of New York Press.

Gambino, Richard. 1976. *Blood of My Blood: The Dilemma of Italian Americans*. Toronto: Guernica.

Gamm, Gerald. 1999. *Urban Exodus: Why the Jews Left Boston and the Catholics Stayed*. Cambridge, Mass.: Harvard University Press.

Gerstle, Gary. 2001. *American Crucible: Race and Nation in the Twentieth Century*. Princeton, N.J.: Princeton University Press.

Gitelman, Howard. 1973. "No Irish Need Apply: Patterns of and Responses to Ethnic Discrimination in the Labor Market." *Labor History* 14(Winter): 56–68.

Glanz, Rudolf. 1976. *Jew and Irish: Historic Group Relations and Immigration*. New York: Rudolf Glanz.

Gleason, Philip. 1987. "Immigrant Assimilation and the Crisis of Americanization." In *Keeping the Faith: American Catholicism Past and Present* by Philip Gleason. Notre Dame, Ind.: University of Notre Dame Press.

———. 1992. *Speaking of Diversity: Language and Ethnicity in Twentieth-Century America*. Baltimore: Johns Hopkins University Press.

Glenn, Evelyn Nakano. 2002. *Unequal Freedom: How Race and Gender Shaped American Citizenship and Labor*. Cambridge, Mass.: Harvard University Press.

Gorn, Elliott J. 2001. *Mother Jones: The Most Dangerous Woman in America*. New York: Hill and Wang.

Gossett, Thomas F. 1997. *Race: The History of an Idea in America*. New York: Oxford University Press.

Greeley, Andrew. 1969. *Why Can't They Be Like Us? Facts and Fallacies About Ethnic Differences and Group Conflicts in America*. New York: E. P. Dutton.

Green, Archie. 1996. *Calf's Head and Union Tales: Labor Yarns at Work and Play*. Urbana: University of Illinois Press.

Guglielmo, Thomas A. 2003. *White on Arrival: Italians, Race, Color, and Power in Chicago, 1890–1945*. New York: Oxford University Press.

Guterl, Matthew. 2001. *The Color of Race in America, 1900–1940*. Cambridge, Mass.: Harvard University Press.

Halpern, Rick. 1992. "Race, Ethnicity, and Union in the Chicago Stockyards, 1917–1922." *International Review of Social History* 37(1): 52–57.

Harper, Frances E. W. 1994. *Trial and Triumph* [1888–89]. Reprinted in *Minnie's Sacrifice, Sowing and Reaping, Trial and Triumph*, edited by Frances Smith Foster. Boston: Beacon Press.

Hayden, Tom. 2001. *Irish On the Inside: In Search of the Soul of Irish America*. London: Verso.

Haywood, William D. 1929. *Bill Haywood's Book: The Autobiography of William D. Haywood*. New York: International Publishers.

Henderson, Thomas. 1976. *Tammany Hall and the New Immigrants: The Progressive Years*. New York: Arno Press.

Herberg, Will. 1955. *Protestant, Catholic, Jew: An Essay on American Religious Sociology*. Garden City, N.Y.: Doubleday.

Herr, David M. 1980. "Intermarriage." In *Harvard Encyclopedia of American Ethnic Groups*, edited by Stephen Thernstrom. Cambridge, Mass.: Harvard University Press.

Higham, John. 1974. *Strangers in the Land: Patterns of American Nativism, 1860–1925*. New York: Atheneum.

Horowitz, Roger. 1997. *"Negro and White, Unite and Fight": A Social History of Industrial Unionism in Meatpacking, 1930–1990*. Urbana: University of Illinois Press.

Hout, Michael, and Joshua R. Goldstein. 1994. "How 4.5 Million Irish Immigrants Became 40 Million Irish Americans: Demographic and Subject Aspects of the Ethnic Composition of White Americans." *American Sociological Review* 59(1, February): 64–82.

Hughes, Langston. 1963. *The Big Sea*. New York: Hill and Wang. (Orig. pub. in 1940.)

Ignatiev, Noel. 1995. *How the Irish Became White*. New York: Routledge.

Jacobson, Matthew Frye. 1995. *Special Sorrows: The Diasporic Imagination of Irish, Polish, and Jewish Immigrants in the United States*. Cambridge, Mass.: Harvard University Press.

————. 2000. *Barbarian Virtues: The United States Encounters Foreign Peoples at Home and Abroad, 1876–1917*. New York: Hill and Wang.

James, C.L.R. 1996. "The 1919 Race Riots in Chicago." In *C.L.R. James on the "Negro Question,"* edited by Scott McLemee. Jackson: University of Mississippi Press. (Orig. pub. in 1939.)

Jenks, Jeremiah W., and W. Jett Lauck. 1926. *The Immigration Problem: A Study of American Immigration Conditions and Needs*. New York: Funk and Wagnalls.

Karson, Marc. 1956. *Labor and Politics*. Carbondale: Southern Illinois University Press.

Kauffman, Christopher J. 1982. *Faith and Fraternalism: The History of the Knights of Columbus, 1882–1982*. New York: Harper & Row.

————. 1992. *Columbianism and the Knights of Columbus*. New York: Simon & Schuster.

Kazal, Russell A. 1998. "Becoming 'Old Stock': The Waning of German-American Identity in Philadelphia, 1900–1930." Ph.D. diss., University of Pennsylvania.

Kazin, Michael. 1987. *Barons of Labor: The San Francisco Building Trades and Union Power in the Progressive Era*. Urbana: University of Illinois Press.

Keiser, John Howard. 1965. "John Fitzpatrick and Progressive Unionism, 1915–1925." Ph.D. diss., Northwestern University.

Kelly, Myra. 1904. *Little Citizens: The Humors of Social Life*. New York: McClure, Phillips.

Kenny, Kevin. 2000. *The American Irish: A History*. Harlow, Eng.: Longman.

Keogh, Dermot. 1998. *Jews in Twentieth-Century Ireland*. Cork: Cork University Press.

Kim, Clare Jean. 1999. "The Racial Triangulation of Asian Americans." *Politics and Society* 27(3, March): 105–38.

Kim, Janine Y. 1999. "Are Asians Black? The Asian-American Civil Rights Agenda and the Contemporary Significance of the Black-White Paradigm." *Yale Law Journal* 108(8, June): 2385–2412.

Kimeldorf, Howard. 1999. *Battling for American Labor: Wobblies, Craft Workers, and the Making of the Union Movement*. Berkeley: University of California Press.

King, Desmond. 2000. *Making Americans: Immigration, Race, and the Origins of the Diverse Democracy*. Cambridge, Mass.: Harvard University Press.

Kisseloff, Jeff. 1989. *You Must Remember This: An Oral History of Manhattan from the 1890s to World War II*. San Diego: Harcourt Brace Jovanovich.

Knobel, Dale T. 1986. *Paddy and the Republic: Ethnicity and Nationality in Antebellum America*. Middletown, Conn.: Wesleyan University Press.

Krause, Paul. 1992. *The Battle for Homestead, 1880–1892: Politics, Culture, and Steel*. Pittsburgh: University of Pittsburgh Press.

Larkin, Emmet. 1972. "The Devotional Revolution in Ireland, 1850–1875." *American Historical Review* 77(3, June): 625–52.

La Sorte, Michael. 1985. *La Merica: Images of Italian Greenhorn Experience*. Philadelphia: Temple University Press.

Laurie, Bruce. 1973. "Five Companies and Gangs in Southwork: The 1840s." In *The Peoples of Philadelphia: A History of Ethnic Groups and Lower-Class Life, 1790–1940*, edited by Allen Davis and Mark Haller. Philadelphia: Temple University Press.

Leon, Sharon. 1998. "Our Immigration Problem: U.S. Catholic Response to U.S. Immigration Restriction, 1915–1930." Unpublished paper. University of Minnesota.

Leone, Carmen. 1998. *Rose Street: A Family History*. Youngstown, Ohio: C. J. Leone.

Lewis, Randolph. 1901. "The Central Office." *Munsey's Magazine* 24(February): 721.

Lewis, Ronald L., and Philip S. Foner, eds. 1989. *Black Workers: A Documentary History from Colonial Times to the Present*. Philadelphia: Temple University Press.

Lieberson, Stanley. 1980. *A Piece of the Pie: Blacks and White Immigrants Since 1880*. Berkeley: University of California Press.

Lightfoot, Claude. n.d. "From Chicago's Ghetto to World Politics: The Life and Struggles of Claude M. Lightfoot." Unpublished paper. Chicago.

Linkh, Richard M. 1975. *American Catholicism and European Immigrants, 1900–1924*. Staten Island, N.Y.: Center for Migration Studies.

Liptak, Delores Ann. 1989. *Immigrants and Their Church*. New York: Macmillan.

Lodge, Henry Cabot. 1891. "The Distribution of Ability in the United States." *The Century: A Popular Quarterly* 42(September): 687–95.

Logan, John. 1997. "The Ethnic Neighborhood, 1920–1970." Working paper. New York: Russell Sage Foundation.

Luconi, Stefano. 2001. *From Paesani to White Ethnics: The Italian Experience in Philadelphia.* Albany: State University of New York Press.

Luibheid, Eithne. 1997. "Irish Immigrants in the United States Racial System." In *Location and Dislocation in Contemporary Irish Society*, edited by Jim MacLaughlin. Notre Dame, Ind.: University of Notre Dame Press.

Mageean, Deirdre. 1997. "Making Sense and Providing Structure: Irish American Women in the Parish Neighborhood." In *Peasant Maids, City Women: From the Countryside to Urban America*, edited by Christiane Harzig. Ithaca, N.Y.: Cornell University Press.

McGivigan, John R., and Thomas J. Robertson. 1996. "The Irish American Worker in Transition, 1877–1914." In *The New York Irish*, edited by Ronald H. Bayor and Timothy J. Meagher. Baltimore: Johns Hopkins University Press.

McGreevy, John T. 1996. *Parish Boundaries: The Catholic Encounter with Race in the Twentieth-Century Urban North.* Chicago: University of Chicago Press.

McKillen, Elizabeth. 1995. *Chicago Labor and the Quest for a Diplomatic Diplomacy, 1914–1924.* Ithaca, N.Y.: Cornell University Press.

McNickle, Chris. 1999. *To Be Mayor of New York: Ethnic Relations in the City.* New York: Columbia University Press.

Meagher, Timothy. 2001. *Inventing Irish America: Generation, Class, and Ethnic Identity in a New England City, 1880–1928.* Notre Dame, Ind.: Notre Dame University Press.

Miller, Kerby. 1985. *Emigrants and Exiles: Ireland and the Irish Exodus to North America.* New York: Oxford University Press.

Mink, Gwendolyn. 1986. *Old Labor and New Immigrants: Union, Party, and State, 1875–1920.* Ithaca, N.Y.: Cornell University Press.

Mishkin, Tracy. 1998. *The Harlem and Irish Renaissances: Language, Identity, and Representation.* Gainesville: University of Florida Press.

Montgomery, David. 1980. "The Irish and the American Labor Movement." In *America and Ireland, 1776–1976: The American Identity and the Irish Connection*, edited by David Noel Doyle and Owen Dudley Edwards. Westport, Conn.: Greenwood Press.

———. 1984. "Immigrants, Industrial Unions, and Social Reconstruction in the United States, 1916–1923." *Labour/Le Travail* 13(Spring): 111–13.

———. 1987. *The Fall of the House of Labor: The Workplace, the State, and American Labor Activism, 1865–1925.* Cambridge: Cambridge University Press.

———. 2001. "Racism, Immigrants, and Political Reform." *Journal of American History* 87(4, March): 1267.

Nelli, Humbert. 1970. *The Italians in Chicago, 1880–1930: A Study in Ethnic Mobility.* New York: Oxford University Press.

Nelson, Bruce. 2001. *Divided We Stand: American Workers and the Struggle for Black Equality.* Princeton, N.J.: Princeton University Press.

Nichols, Anne. 1927. *Abie's Irish Rose: A Novel.* New York: Grosset and Dunlap.

Novak, Michael. 1972. *The Rise of the Unmeltable Ethnics.* New York: Macmillan.

O'Donnell, L. A. 1997. *Irish Voice and Organized Labor: A Biographical Study.* Westport, Conn.: Greenwood Press.

Okihiro, Gary. 1994. "Is Yellow Black or White?" In *Margins and Mainstreams: Asians in American History and Culture* by Gary Okihiro. Seattle: University of Washington Press.

Orsi, Robert. 1985. *The Madonna of 115th Street: Faith and Community in Italian Harlem.* New Haven, Conn.: Yale University Press.

———. 1992. "The Religious Boundaries of an Inbetween People: Street *Feste* and the Problem of the Dark-Skinned 'Other' in Italian Harlem, 1920–1990." *American Quarterly* 44(3, September): 313–47.

Pacyga, Dominic A. 1991. *Polish Immigrants and Industrial Chicago: Workers on the South Side, 1880–1922.* Columbus: Ohio State University Press.

———. 1996. "To Live Amongst Others: Poles and Their Neighbors in Industrial Chicago, 1865–1930." *Journal of American Ethnic History* 16(1, Fall): 55–73.

Perlmann, Joel. 1988a. "The Romance of Assimilation? Studying the Demographic Outcomes of Ethnic Intermarriage in American History." Working paper 230. Annandale-on-Hudson, N.Y.: Bard College, Jerome Levy Economics Institute.

———. 1988b. *Ethnic Differences: Schooling and Social Structure Among the Irish, Italians, Jews, and Blacks in an American City, 1880–1935.* Cambridge: Cambridge University Press.

———. 2000. "Demographic Outcomes of Ethnic Intermarriage in American History: Italian Americans Through Four Generations." Working paper 372. Annandale-on-Hudson, N.Y.: Bard College, Jerome Levy Economics Institute.

Philpott, Thomas Lee. 1978. *The Slum and the Ghetto: Neighborhood Deterioration and Middle-Class Reform, Chicago, 1880–1930.* New York: Oxford University Press.

Pieterse, Jan Nederveen. n.d. "Social Capital and Migration." Unpublished paper. Urbana-Champaign: University of Illinois, Department of Sociology.

Portes, Alejandro, and Rubén Rumbaut. 2001. *Legacies: The Story of the Immigrant Second Generation.* Berkeley: University of California Press.

Portes, Alejandro, and Min Zhou. 1993. "The New Second Generation: Segmented Assimilation and Its Variants." *Annals of the American Academy of Political and Social Sciences* 530: 74–96.

Prell, Riv-Ellen. 1999. *Fighting to Become Americans: Jews, Gender, and the Anxiety of Assimilation.* Boston: Beacon Press.

Radzialowski, Thaddeus. 1976. "The Competition for Jobs and Racial Stereotypes: Poles and Blacks in Chicago." *Polish American Studies* 33(Autumn): 7–8.

Riis, Jacob. 1996. *How the Other Half Lives: Studies Among the Tenements of New York*, edited and with an introduction by David Leviatin. Boston: Bedford Book of St. Martin's Press. (Orig. pub. in 1890.)

Ripley, William Z. 1908. "Races in the United States." *Atlantic Monthly* 102(December): 745–59.

Rischin, Moses. 1962. *The Promised City: New York City Jews, 1870–1913.* Cambridge, Mass.: Harvard University Press.

Roberts, Peter. 1904. *Anthracite Coal Communities: A Study of the Demography of the Social, Educational, and Moral Life of the Anthracite Regions.* New York: Macmillan.

Rodechko, James Paul. 1976. *Patrick Ford and His Search for America: A Case Study of Irish-American Journalism.* New York: Arno Press.

Skerrett, Ellen. 1987. "The Catholic Dimension." In *The Irish in Chicago*, edited by Lawrence McCaffrey, Ellen Skerrett, Michael Funchion, and Charles Fanning. Urbana: University of Illinois Press.

Smith, Judith M. 1985. *Family Connections: A History of Italian and Jewish Immigrant Lives in Providence, Rhode Island, 1900–1940.* Albany: State University of New York Press.

Sollors, Werner. 1996. *Theories of Ethnicity: A Classical Reader.* New York: New York University Press.

Stave, Bruce M., and John F. Sutherland, with Aldo Salerno, eds. 1994. *From the Old Country: An Oral history of European Migration to America.* New York: Twayne.

Steinberg, Stephen. 1989. *The Ethnic Myth: Race, Ethnicity, and Class in America.* Boston: Beacon Press.

Sullivan, Robert E. 1985. "Beneficial Relations: Toward a Social History of the Diocesan Priests of Boston, 1875–1944." In *Studies in Religion and Community*, edited by Robert E. Sullivan and James O'Toole. Boston: n.p.

Taillon, Paul. 1990. "That Word 'White': Racism and Masculinity in the Debate over Black Exclusion in the International Association of Machinists, 1888–1895." Paper presented to the twelfth annual North American Labor History Conference. Wayne State University, Detroit.

Tchen, John Kuo Wei. 1996. "Quimbo Appo's Fear of Fenians: Chinese-Irish-Anglo Relations in

New York City." In *The New York Irish*, edited by Ronald H. Bayor and Timothy J. Meagher. Baltimore: Johns Hopkins University Press.

Thrasher, Frederick. 1963. *The Gang: A Study of 1313 Gangs in Chicago*. Abridged edition. Chicago: University of Chicago Press. (Orig. pub. in 1927.)

Tomasi, Silvano M. 1975. *Piety and Power: The Role of the Italian Parishes in the New York Metropolitan Area, 1880–1930*. New York: Center for Migration Studies.

Tuan, Mia. 1998. *Forever Foreigners or Honorary Whites? The Asian Ethnic Experience Today*. New Brunswick, N.J.: Rutgers University Press.

Tuttle, William M. 1984. *Race Riot: Chicago and the Red Summer of 1919*. New York: Atheneum.

U.S. Immigration and Naturalization Service (USINS). 1976. *Annual Report, 1975*. Washington: U.S. Government Printing Office.

Vecoli, Rudolph. 1969. "Prelates and Peasants: Italian Immigrants and the Catholic Church." *Journal of Social History* 2(Spring): 220–33.

Vinyard, JoEllen McNergney. 1998. *For Faith and Fortune: The Education of Catholic Immigrants in Detroit, 1805–1925*. Urbana: University of Illinois Press.

Walsh, Frank. 1996. *Sin and Censorship: The Catholic Church and the Motion Picture Industry*. New Haven, Conn.: Yale University Press.

Walter, Bronwen. 2001. *Outsiders Inside: Whiteness, Place, and Irish Women*. London: Routledge.

Ware, Caroline F. 1994. *Greenwich Village, 1920–1930: A Comment on American Civilization in the Postwar Years*. Berkeley: University of California Press. (Orig. pub. in 1935.)

Warren, Donald. 1996. *Radio Priest: Charles Coughlin, the Father of Hate Radio*. New York: Free Press.

Whyte, William Foote. 1993. *Street Corner Society: The Social Structure of an Italian Slum*. Chicago: University of Chicago Press. (Orig. pub. in 1943.)

Wilder, Craig Steven. 2000. *A Covenant with Color: Race and Social Power in Brooklyn*. New York: Columbia University Press.

Winslow, Calvin. 1993. "On the Waterfront: Black, Italian, and Irish Longshoremen in the New York Harbor Strike of 1919." In *Protest and Survival: Essays for E. P. Thompson*, edited by John Rule and Robert Malcolmson. London: Merlin Press.

Wolff, Robert S. 1995. "'This Is a White Man's City': Schooling, Society, and the Narrative of American History in Baltimore, 1890–1912." Unpublished paper. University of Minnesota.

Yans-McLaughlin, Virginia. 1982. *Family and Community: Italian Immigrants in Buffalo, 1880–1930*. Ithaca, N.Y.: Cornell University Press.

Zéphir, Flore. 2001. *Trends in Ethnic Identification Among Second-Generation Haitian Immigrants in New York City*. Westport, Conn.: Bergin and Garvey.

Zorbaugh, Harvey Warren. 1929. *The Gold Coast and the Slum: A Sociological Study of Chicago's Near North Side*. Chicago: University of Chicago Press.

José Itzigsohn

Chapter 9

The Formation of Latino and Latina Panethnic Identities

This chapter examines the formation of Latino and Latina[1] panethnicities—that is, the emergence of diverse forms of Latino and Latina individual and collective identities, political projects, and social and cultural practices. The broad labeling of immigrants from Latin America and the Caribbean and their children as Latinos and Latinas has generated a great deal of controversy. The Latino and Latina label refers to a diverse group of people from countries with different and sometimes conflicting histories; it includes immigrants and several generations of people born in the United States, middle-class and working-class persons, voluntary immigrants and those who were made part of the United States through the territorial expansion of the country—namely, Puerto Ricans and parts of the Mexican American population (Gimenez 1992; Massey 1993; Melville 1986). Yet processes of group formation entail the creation of boundaries and meanings that bring together diverse individuals. The challenge is to investigate whether and in what ways people adopt a Latino and Latina identity, the meanings they attribute to it, the political projects constructed around it, and the sites in which these identities and projects are constructed.

The emergence of panethnic individual and collective identities in the United States is the result of a process through which ethnic groups are lumped together and racialized. The dynamics of the contemporary system of ethnic and racial classification leads to the internalization of panethnic identities and the formation of panethnic organizations and social practices. The data-gathering methods of the census and its use by government agencies in allocating resources, the mobilization techniques of political parties and lobbies, the organization of charities and nonprofit groups, the marketing techniques of the media—all these categorize and appeal to people as members of large ethno-racial groups, thereby fostering a sense of panethnic identity.

At the same time, Latinos and Latinas adopt and use this label to construct their own personal and collective identities and projects. Hence, we see the rise of social practices and organizations based on Latino and Latina identities and group formation (Dávila 2001; Itzigsohn and Dore-Cabral 2000, 2001; Laó-Montes and Dávila 2001; Oboler 1995; Rodriguez 2000). Although the idea of Latinamericanism and Latin American unity has a long intellectual and political history in Latin America, it has never become a concrete reality there. Paradoxically, it is in the United States that, to a certain extent, this idea comes into fruition. To put it another way: the social and cultural features of contemporary life in the United States create incentives for immigrants and native-born Latinos and Latinas to identify with a panethnic label for instrumental or expressive purposes.

To assert that Latinos and Latinas use the externally created label to develop their own identities and political and cultural projects is only a partial picture. Since different Latino and Latina groups have diverse experiences in the United States, the process of panethnic identity formation varies among and within them, and it is hard to make statements about Latinos and Latinas in general (Logan 2001). The group is far from seamless, and the political and cultural projects organized around that label are as diverse as the people who make up the group. Because Latino and Latina individuals and groups engage in diverse projects of ethno-racial identity formation and collective action, the label "Latinos and Latinas" can be interpreted in very different ways, and at times can be heavily contested. The meaning and purpose of Latino and Latina identities are as varied as the projects that people pursue.

The obvious fault lines around which different interpretations of Latino and Latina identities are constructed are class, race, nation, region, gender, sexuality, immigrant status, and generation. Another fault line closely associated with generation is language. It is a mistake to assume that Latinos and Latinas are united by the use of Spanish, since Latinos and Latinas of the second generation and beyond are English speakers and often do not even speak Spanish. All these fault lines create possibilities for different and often contradictory articulations of meanings and personal and collective projects. Moreover, many immigrants—at least in the first generation—maintain transnational connections with their countries of origin (Itzigsohn et al. 1999; Portes, Guarnizo, and Landolt 1999). Thus, the formation of new identities and solidarities constructed around Latino and Latina identities need not and may not be limited to the boundaries of the United States. The formation of Latino and Latina identities is a process characterized by a constant tension between converging trends that bring different Latino groups together and centrifugal social processes that reinforce old fault lines and divisions between and within Latino and Latina populations. It involves continuous negotiation and conflict over group boundaries and the meanings of identities.

In this chapter, I focus on the emergence of different forms of panethnic identities. This does not mean that Latino and Latina identities always emerge. Often, people who are labeled Latinos and Latinas reject the panethnic identification and choose to identify with ethno-national categories. Yet my argument is that for many Latinos and Latinas the panethnic identity becomes part of a range of options that they can invoke for building individual and collective identities. I explore the various forms of Latino and Latina identity, their different meanings, and the sites in which they emerge. The different cases of Latino and Latina identity formation described in this essay do not constitute a general model of panethnic formation. Instead, I discuss cases that illustrate the many contemporary processes through which Latino and Latina identities and social practices are articulated. In this way I hope to provide a broad view of the different meanings of Latino and Latina identity and the different political and cultural projects around which it is constructed.

This chapter relies on my own research on Dominican Americans in Providence, Rhode Island, and New York (Itzigsohn and Dore-Cabral 2000; 2001), on my ongoing study of the formation of Latino identities, organizations, and practices in Providence, and on the secondary literature on Latino and Latina identities. Establishing the generalizability and limits of these cases remains a task for comparative research.

The early scholarship on Latino and Latina panethnicity has discussed this identity as a situational political one (Calderón 1992; Padilla 1985) or as a secondary ethnic identity that coexists with national identifications (Itzigsohn and Dore-Cabral 2000; Moore 1990; Oboler 1995). Further work has investigated Latino and Latina panethnicity in relation to the U.S. racial classification system (Flores-Gonzalez 1999; Itzigsohn and Dore-Cabral 2000; Rodriguez 2000). The latest work on the subject looks at the different forms, expressions, and meanings of Latino and Latina identities and practices (Laó-Montes 2001a; Itzigsohn and Dore-Cabral 2001). What follows addresses these different sites of identity formation. I begin by examining the formation of Latino and Latina identities in the political realm and then discuss the use of the Latino and Latina label as a racial category. Finally, I explore different institutional sites in which Latino and Latina identities and social and cultural practices emerge.

LATINO AND LATINA AS A
POLITICAL IDENTITY

The emergence of Latino and Latina as a category of identity is the result of the politics of ethnic and racial classification. The term "Hispanic" began to be used officially by American administrations at the end of the 1960s, and it was incorporated as an enumeration category in the 1980 census. The emergence of the term was the result of the visibility acquired by Chicanos and Chicanas and Puerto Ricans during the civil rights struggles. The choice and use of the term by different state bureaucracies was problematic because it erased the particular histories and experiences of each of these groups (Calderón 1992; Oboler 1995). Yet the external process of categorization by state agencies of different national groups under one ethnic label created social practices of classification and incentives that led to the emergence of panethnic identities and organizations. Following a long American tradition, politics is one of the key areas of panethnic group formation.

Felix Padilla (1984; 1985), one of the first scholars to look at this subject, argued that a Latino ethnic consciousness, which he calls "Latinismo," arises out of the interaction of two or more Latino groups in a situation in which those groups share common interests. Latinismo, as he defined it, is a situational identity that emerges in specific political situations and does not necessarily continue after that situation is resolved. A Latino consciousness, in his view, does not replace a national consciousness; rather, it coincides with a national consciousness as long as the circumstances that gave rise to "Latinismo" continue. Moreover, Padilla warned of possible contradictory interests among Latino and Latina groups that have been historically oppressed in the United States, particularly Mexican Americans and Puerto Ricans, on the one hand, and other newer immigrants such as Miami Cubans, on the other, who enjoy a better economic and political situation in this country.

Lopez and Espiritu (1990), in their analysis of the emergence of panethnic identities among different groups in the United States, argued that structural commonalities—including race, class, generation, and geography—are more likely to constitute a basis for the rise of panethnicity than a shared culture. They conclude that since Latinos diverge more along structural lines than Asian Americans or Native Americans, they are less likely to develop panethnic organizations. They add that the rise of panethnic organizations is ultimately the result of political mobilization by middle-class activists.

These works emphasized the conjunctural and transitory character of Latino and Latina identity, the importance of political organizations in promoting panethnicity, and the role of class and common structural position in panethnic political mobilization. These early views follow well-established traditions in the study of ethnic group formation. On the one hand, they echo the arguments of the political construction of ethnicity thesis that ethnic identities arise in those places and times in which ethnicity is recognized as a basis for making political claims (Nagel 1996). On the other hand, they emphasize the role of organizations and activists in framing identity (Blumer 1958).

These early works helped promote and guide the study of the formation of Latino and Latina identities. They rightly point to the critical role of panethnic organizations and their response to the political incentives created by state policies in the process of establishing a panethnic movement and panethnic identities. Yet the continuous growth in the number and diversity of Latino populations, the increasingly multiethnic character of Latino urban populations, and the surge in Latino political organizations during the 1990s confront us with new and different situations (Laó-Montes 2001a; Logan 2001; Marquez 2001). My own argument is that panethnic identities are more than situational and transitory and that they do not depend on the presence of panethnic organizations. Whereas the latter can give an initial push to Latino and Latina panethnic identification, frame it in particular ways, and ensure its continuous relevance, Latino and Latina identities become internalized beyond the presence or action of particular organizations.

My fieldwork provides strong evidence of the depth of internalization of and commitment to Latino and Latina identities. One set of cases comes from my observation of several political campaigns to elect Latino candidates to the Rhode Island legislature. (There are currently two Latinos and Latinas in the Rhode Island legislature and one on the Providence city council. A few others have unsuccessfully run for office.) People from several Latino and Latina nationalities participated in these campaigns, working together to elect Latino and Latina representatives to the state legislature. All the activists involved in the campaigns had strong national identities, and many were also activists in national-based ethnic organizations. Yet all embraced a discourse of Latino and Latina empowerment and a sense of Latino and Latina identity that went beyond the particular campaign for a particular candidate. In canvassing neighborhoods in search of potential voters, I observed the same sense of Latino and Latina identification among Latino and Latina people. Latinos and Latinas did not identify with candidates as Dominican, Colombian, or Puerto Rican (although they took pride in their nationality) but saw themselves as part of a Latino and Latina movement to achieve political representation as Latinos and Latinas. Moreover, grassroots participation in each of the campaigns took the form of "vote Latino," and on election day countless volunteers who scarcely spoke English and had previously shown little interest in American politics worked to get the Latino and Latina candidates elected.

Certainly, there were times when Latino and Latina activists worked with non-Latino and Latina candidates and urged Latinos and Latinas to vote against Latino and Latina candidates. (Indeed, Latinos and Latinas do not vote as a bloc.) Yet these efforts were based not on nationality allegiances but on the particular activists' aspirations, alliances, and ambitions or on personal animosities. Indeed, the call to vote against a Latino and Latina candidate was always based on the argument that although the other candidate was not Latino and Latina, he or she had a track record of defending Latino and Latina interests.

Moreover, confrontations between Latino and Latina politicians often involve candidates belonging to the same national group. Increasingly we see electoral districts in which numerous Latino and Latina candidates from the same nationality compete against each other for political support. This is particularly the case in areas where a certain group is numerically dominant. A paramount example is New York City's Washington Heights city council district, where several Dominican candidates compete for office. One could argue that this was a case of ethnic rather than panethnic politics. Yet Dominican candidates in upper Manhattan, although they run as Dominican or Dominican American, still have to appeal to other Latino and Latina voters and use the Latino and Latina empowerment discourse alongside the Dominican empowerment one in order to get the vote.

One could say that the Latino and Latina empowerment discourse is merely an instrumental political maneuver. My research suggests, however, that it is more than that. For example, a Dominican political party official in New York told me that "the Dominican identity is very important for me, but my political identity is Hispanic." The paradox is that his political activities are focused almost exclusively on the Dominican Republic. He lived in New York for more than thirty years, and during this time he was engaged in Dominican politics as an important member of one of the large Dominican political parties. Moreover, although he argued that "Dominicans here are as Dominican as those who live there," he defines himself politically as Hispanic.

This case suggests that at least for some Dominicans the Latino and Latina identity is part of a set of internalized identities that they deploy in different circumstances of American life.[2] I do not mean to suggest that panethnic identities are not problematic. Politics in Washington Heights is indeed Dominican-based and has a strong nationalist component. Moreover, there is a great deal of tension between different national groups in New York Latino and Latina politics and in everyday social relations as well (Itzigsohn and Dore-Cabral 2001). My point is that the nationalist sentiments and intraethnic conflict coexist with panethnic identification. Panethnicity becomes part of the language of self-identification used by Latinos and Latinas, a part of their range of identity options—an identity that can be invoked or put aside in different moments for different purposes.

A further complexity of Latino and Latina politics is that it also includes a transnational component. Consider the case of a recently elected Dominican state representative in Rhode Island. A successful local small-business person, he ran as a Latino and Latina candidate on a platform promoting youth activities to diminish crime as well as promoting economic development in the southern part of Providence, an area that has been revitalized through the efforts of immigrant entrepreneurs. Having gotten ahead in business and politics, he epitomizes the successful immigration story. Moreover, he is deeply involved in the local political scene, and his legislative agenda is oriented toward addressing the problems of his local constituency. At the same time, he is also a member of the current governing party in the Dominican Republic (the Partido Revolucionario Dominicano—Dominican Revolutionary Party, PRD). Upon his election to the Rhode Island statehouse, he traveled to the Dominican Republic, where he was received by government officials as a Dominican elected official in the United States.

Participation in the politics of the country of origin is often seen as strengthening national identity to the detriment of panethnic identification and involvement in U.S.-based politics. This is often the case, yet the two examples described here suggest that it is not necessarily so. Increasingly, first-generation Latino and Latina activists—as well as a few second-generation activists—are involved in national-ethnic, panethnic, and transnational political activities at the same time. Often, the political organizations that are oriented toward the country of origin also mobilize to support political candidates who compete in U.S. elections. The boundaries between panethnic, national, and transnational are not sealed and are being constantly crossed.

These examples come from Providence and New York, where there are proportionally large Latino and Latina populations but no one dominant Latino nationality. Certainly, these cases are not representative of Latino politics and identity formation everywhere. I would argue that we need to be sensitive to regional and compositional differences (national, class, and generational) in analyzing Latino and Latina political identity. A growing literature describes and analyzes the emergence of Latino and Latina identities and political mobilization in California, where the Mexican American population is in the majority but the Latino and Latina population is increasingly diverse (Saito 1998; Rocco 1997; Rosaldo and Flores 1997; Valle and Torres 2000). This suggest that panethnic political mobilization is taking place all across the country. The particular regional meanings and contents of panethnic identity and mobilization, however, need to be studied through careful comparative empirical research.

The analysis of Latino and Latina as a political identity is further complicated by the fact that the goals of Latino and Latina political projects are by no means a given. Agustín Laó-Montes's (2001b) analysis of Latino social movements in New York City shows a wide diversity of Latino and Latina political projects. The author identifies three different orientations in Latino and Latina politics. First is Latino and Latina Keynesianism, which he defines as the election of Latino and Latina candidates who can in theory channel resources to their communities. This is mainly a middle-class form of political participation and identity formation. Second is Latino and Latina grassroots politics, which he describes as the formation of grassroots organizations to express the demands of poor and working-class Latinos and Latinas. Finally there is Latino and Latina neoconservatism, expressed in arguments that Latinos need to think beyond racial and ethnic discrimination and make full use of the range of opportunities offered by American society (an increasingly popular movement in all panethnic communities that paradoxically receives its legitimation from the sense of panethnic belonging of those who are part of it). In addition, Laó-Montes notes, many Latino and Latina activists are involved as Latinos and Latinas in movements against racial injustice in what he calls the radical democracy movement, which is not ethnic-based.

Understanding the formation of contemporary Latino and Latina political identities also requires us to look beyond the realm of Latino and Latina panethnic politics. Increasingly, mainstream non-Latino and Latina politicians, Democrats and Republicans alike, are appealing to and trying to mobilize the Latino and Latina vote. The idea of Latinos and Latinas as a "wakening sleeping giant" has captured the attention of both political parties. In the 2000 presidential campaign we saw both candidates utter broken sentences in Spanish as a way to demonstrate their concern and pluralism. Both political parties see Latinos and Latinas as a political bloc that can be mobilized and captured for their own purposes. The mainstream political analysis of Latinos and Latinas as a voting bloc that is economically liberal but socially conservative obviously ignores large differences among Latino electorates in different parts of the country (and differences along national, class, gender, and generational lines). Yet these external appeals help to promote the formation of Latino and Latina identifications among people who want to be active Democrats or Republicans as well as among voters who may begin to see themselves in these terms.

In short, Latino and Latina political identities go beyond particular issues that unite Latinos and Latinas, beyond the presence of particular organizations, and beyond middle-class activism. The political field in the United States is organized in such a way that Latino and Latina identities are constantly invoked, used, and reinforced by mainstream political parties, the historical incentives to organize local politics along ethnic lines, and the distribution of resources. Yet the meanings of Latino and Latina identities vary, and the political projects for which they are mobilized differ. The rapid growth of the Latino and Latina population ensures that Latino and Latina politics will increasingly be a feature of urban and national politics. The meanings and goals of Latino and Latina politics, however, will be highly contested, and opposing projects will compete for the support and loyalty of different Latino and Latina people.

LATINO AND LATINA AS A RACIALIZED IDENTITY

Not only are Latinos and Latinas a political conglomerate of ethnic or national origins groups, but they also occupy a position in the American racial classification system. The Latino and Latina label has its origin in the racialization of ethnicity in the United States: peoples from certain national origins are considered foreign and racial "others" in spite of the passing of generations (Oboler 1995; Okihiro 1994).[3] The broad groupings that found their way into the census racial classifications bring together diverse ethnic or national origins groups into panethnic groups that are also considered racial groups. According to the census classification system, Latinos and Latinas can belong to any of the racial groups it identifies and measures; Latinos and Latinas are a pluri-racial and racially mixed panethnic group. Yet in spite of this internal racial diversity, for many Latinos and Latinas the Latino and Latina label has a racial meaning, designating a distinct racial position different from white and black.

In America, then, ethnicity is racialized, and what we are dealing with, in fact, is a pan-ethno-racial group. Yet because of internal racial diversity, Latinos and Latinas have particular experiences with racialization. Latinos and Latinas' encounters with racial classification and marginalization vary widely by national origin and region. Many members of the large Caribbean population on the East Coast are perceived as black, but this is not the case on the West Coast, where Latinos and Latinas are mostly of Mexican and Central American origin. According to Tomas Almaguer (1994), racial formation on the West Coast has historically centered on the racialization of Chicanos, Asians, and Native Americans rather than the black-white dichotomy. Even there, since Latinos and Latinas are a multiracial group, individual encounters with racism vary according to how each person looks compared to the norm of whiteness. Encounters with racism are also interpreted according to the racial worldview that different Latino and Latina groups bring from their country of origin. In other words, Latinos and Latinas' racial identity formation is not likely to follow a single pattern.

Latinos and Latinas often reject an understanding of race in terms of a black-white dichotomy, a choice that is evident in the large number who choose "other" on the census forms.[4] This choice, however, does not mean that Latinos and Latinas do not identify in racial terms. That many Latinos and Latinas equate a Latino and Latina identity with race comes out of a series of studies conducted by the Census Bureau in 1996, in preparation for the 2000 census, to explore the effects of different race and Hispanic origin questions on racial self-identification. The main concern of the Racial and Ethnic Targeted Test (RAETT) was to determine the consequences of including a multiracial category in the census.[5] The findings showed that the answers most sensitive to different patterns of questions were those related to Latinos and Latinas. When "Hispanic" was not a racial identification choice, between 15 and 25 percent of Latinos and Latinas checked off "other race."[6] When the category "Hispanic" was a choice in the racial identity question, 56.4 percent of respondents selected it; fewer than 1 percent chose the "other" category (Hirschman, Alba, and Farley 2000).

The option of including "Hispanic" as a racial category was ultimately abandoned by the Census Bureau because doing so did not have major political backing. Some Latino and Latina organizations provided only lukewarm support for the idea, and others opposed it outright. There were concerns that including a Hispanic category in the racial self-identification question would lead to an underestimation of Latinos and Latinas and/or to a reduction in national self-identification (Hirschman, Alba, and Farley 2000; Rodriguez 2000). These concerns were real, and it is not my intention here to argue over the best way to organize the census. The point is that when offered a Hispanic racial category for self-identification, a considerable number of Latinos and Latinas chose it, indicating that an important segment of the Latino and Latina population understands this identity in racial terms.

The question remains, however, as to the meaning of "Latino and Latina" as a form of racial self-identification. Clara Rodriguez (2000) asks whether Latinos and Latinas are merely trying to distance themselves from racialization as blacks or whether they are defining race in terms of ethnicity and culture. In her analysis of Puerto Rican racial and ethnic identification, Rodriguez argues that when Latinos answer "other" or write in a Hispanic answer to the racial identification question in the census, they are choosing culture and ethnicity as bases for racial identification rather than an intermediate racial category (Rodriguez and Cordero-Guzman 1992).

My own analysis of the racial identities of first-generation Dominicans suggests a more complex picture. In a survey of first-generation Dominicans in Providence and New York, respondents were asked an open-ended question about racial self-identification and two closed-ended questions about whether they were black, white, or other and whether they thought that Americans saw them as black, white, or other.[7] If respondents chose "other," they were asked to specify how they saw themselves or how they believed mainstream America saw them. Table 9.1 shows the large number of categories that Dominicans used for self-racial identification. It also shows the importance of the Hispano and Hispana label as a form of racial self-identification. Hispano and Hispana was not only the most frequently given response to the open-ended and closed-ended self-identification questions but also the second-ranked answer to the question about how mainstream Americans perceive them, indicating that a significant segment of first-generation Dominicans believe that they are seen racially as Hispanos and Hispanas. The survey is not representative, hence the results should be taken with caution.[8] Yet it is important to point out that the results coincide with the RAETT results reported here.[9]

Given the debate on the use of the Hispano and Hispana or Latino and Latina label, it is interesting that only a small number of Dominicans chose the category "Latino and Latina" in answer to any of the three questions. However, ethnographic observation in Providence and New York indicated that most Dominicans use these categories interchangeably. "Latino and Latina" was also used in the political appeals of many organizations. The large number who chose the answer "Hispano and Hispana" reflects, in my view, the strength of the influence of officially institutionalized categories.[10]

In previous work, I have argued that when Dominicans choose the Hispano and Hispana or Latino and Latina label as a form of racial self-identification, it is a way to position themselves in America's racial classification system as nonblack. It is also a way to reconstruct the Dominican Republic's racial category system, with its emphasis

TABLE 9.1   Answers of First-Generation Dominican Immigrants in New York and Providence to Racial Self-Identification Questions

	How Do You Define Yourself Racially?		Are You White, Black, or Other? (Specify)		How Do You Think Mainstream Americans Classify You Racially?	
	Number	Percentage	Number	Percentage	Number	Percentage
Hispano and Hispana	88	21.1%	84	20.1%	123	29.4%
Black	21	5.0	67	16.0	149	35.6
White	12	2.9	46	11.0	26	6.2
Latino and Latina	13	3.1	11	2.6	13	3.1
Indio and India	42	10.0	75	17.9	16	3.8
Dominicano and Dominicana	41	9.8	8	1.9	1	0.2
Indio-hispano and -hispana	11	2.6	4	1.0	1	0.2
Mixto hispano and hispana	2	0.5	5	1.2	1	0.2
Trigueño and Trigueña	11	2.6	18	4.3	8	1.9
Latino-hispano and -hispana	1	0.2	2	0.5	2	0.5
Black-hispano and -hispana	2	0.5	4	1.0	8	1.9
Mestizo and Mestiza	15	3.6	32	7.7	4	1.0
Moreno and Morena	6	1.4	8	1.9	9	2.2
Latino-Americano and -Americana	2	0.5	2	0.5	—	—
Mulato and Mulata	1	0.2	6	1.4	—	—
Hispano-Blanco and -Blanca	2	0.5	1	0.2	2	0.5
Hispano-Trigueño and -Trigueña	2	0.5	—	—	—	—

(*Table continues on p. 206.*)

TABLE 9.1   *Continued*

	How Do You Define Yourself Racially?		Are You White, Black, or Other? (Specify)		How Do You Think Mainstream Americans Classify You Racially?	
	Number	Percentage	Number	Percentage	Number	Percentage
Hispano-Indio-Trigueño	2	0.5	—	—	—	—
Java-India Claro and Clara	1	0.2	5	1.2	1	0.2
Amarillo and amarilla (yellow)	1	0.2	4	1.0	1	0.2
Oscuro and oscura	1	0.2	1	0.2	—	—
Prieto and prieta	—	—	2	0.5	3	0.7
De color	—	—	—	—	1	0.2
Puerto Rican	—	—	—	—	1	0.2
Britanico and Britanica	1	0.2	—	—	—	—
American	2	0.5	—	—	2	0.5
Citizen of the world	1	0.2	—	—	—	—
Human race	4	1.0	—	—	—	—
Buena raza	4	1.0	—	—	—	—
Everybody is equal	10	2.4	4	1.0	2	0.5
Belong to no race	2	0.5	2	0.5	1	0.2
Do not know	16	3.8	5	1.2	28	6.7
Total answers	320	76.7	398	95.2	404	96.7
No answer	98	23.4	20	4.8	14	3.3
Total	418	100	418	100	418	100

Source: Author's compilation.

on intermediate categories (Itzigsohn and Dore-Cabral 2000). One person who argued that his race was "Indio Hispano" explained that in the Dominican Republic, as opposed to the United States, people recognize shades of color, and since he was Hispano, then his race was Indio.[11] Asked what he would be if he was not Hispano, he answered that he would then be black (Itzigsohn and Dore-Cabral 2001).

I would now argue that the meaning of the label "Hispano and Hispana" is more complex in that it also includes an understanding of Hispanos and Hispanas (or Latinos and Latinas) as a separate racial category associated with physical and cultural markers. Consider the comment by a Dominican immigrant I interviewed in Providence:

> I think my children will be Dominican Americans, my grandchildren, I don't know. But you know, we will always be Latinos. You Argentinians look like Italians, you can merge in this country, but look how we look, our skin is different, our color is different, and also our culture is different, and you know how much we value very much our ways. We can never merge, we are going to be like other communities—different, powerful but different. We are going always to be Latinos.

This answer is telling. First, it associates the label "Latino and Latina" with the homogenization that takes place in American society, a process based on the classification of people according to skin color. For this respondent, white Latinos and Latinas might be able to fully assimilate, but nonwhite Latinos and Latinas are going to be forever different. The comment establishes the color line as the barrier to full integration in the United States. Yet this answer also links the label "Latino and Latina" with the preservation of cultural identity, mixing together race, difference, and culture (Itzigsohn and Dore-Cabral 2000).

Nilda Flores-Gonzalez's (1999) study of racial identity among second- and third-generation Latinos and Latinas in Chicago shows a similar adoption of the label "Latino and Latina" as a racial identity. Flores-Gonzalez's interviewees associated national origin and racial belonging; they identified "American" with whiteness and asserted that they belonged to a Latino and Latina race. This racial belonging allowed them to escape the black-white dichotomy and provided them with a language to understand and express their experiences as a racial "other" in the contemporary United States. At the same time, they saw Latino and Latina experiences as closer to those of blacks' than to whites'. Both Latinos and blacks experienced racial discrimination from institutions at the local and federal levels as well as from many others in the mainstream society.

The results of the Census Bureau's RAETT study, on the other hand, show a much greater identification of Latinos and Latinas with whiteness. In the RAETT study, when "Hispanic" was not included among the racial identification choices, between 56 and 68 percent of Latinos and Latinas identified as white. When the Hispanic category was included, the percentage of people who identified as white was reduced to 13.7 percent.[12] This suggests that Latinos and Latinas reject being labeled as black and would rather define themselves as "other" or white (Hirschman, Alba, and Farley 2000).

The RAETT and Flores-Gonzalez studies present contradictory results concerning the racial identification of Latinos and Latinas. These different results may be related to the different foci and methodologies of the studies. Flores-Gonzalez reports the results of forty interviews with second- and third-generation Latinos and Latinas. The respondents included sixteen Mexicans, seven Puerto Ricans, two Guatemalans, and fifteen people of mixed Latino and Latina ancestry (Flores-Gonzalez 1999). The RAETT results, on the other hand, were based on thousands of Latino and Latina respondents, but the study was not nationally representative. This was due to the sampling methodology that targeted areas of residential concentration (excluding Latinos and Latinas who lived in areas of low residential concentration) and to a very large rate of non-response to the mail questionnaire (Hirschman, Alba, and Farley 2000). What is important for the argument developed here is that both studies show two key points. First, many Latinos and Latinas attribute racial meaning to this label. Second, the meanings attributed to the Latino and Latina label as a form of racial self-identification are not monolithic and in fact display enormous complexity.

For the first-generation Dominicans I interviewed, using the Latino and Latina label was a way to reconstruct the intermediate racial categories of the Dominican Republic in the United States. For Flores-Gonzalez's second-generation interviewees, the label reflected their experience of growing up in the United States as a racial other. That Flores-Gonzalez found the Latino and Latina experience interpreted as close to the black experience whereas those in the RAETT surveys seemed to avoid identifying with blackness suggests that at least some Latinos and Latinas equate national origin with race and, at the same time, Americanness with whiteness. Although they reject the black-white dichotomy, they still see the color line as a pervasive boundary in American society.

That many Latinos and Latinas understand this label as a racial identity and believe that they are seen racially as Latinos and Latinas indicates that the American racial classification system currently works beyond the black-white dichotomy. The criteria involved in the formation of racial categories in present-day America are an eclectic mix of phenotype, ancestry, and national origin, bringing together multiethnic and multiracial groups into pan-ethno-racial categories. There is a convergence toward an understanding of "Latino and Latina" (or "Hispano and Hispana") as a racialized identity that is neither black nor white; in fact, "Latino and Latina" is often equated with "brown" as an intermediate racial category. Of course, this racialized identity coexists with and does not erase national identities. Moreover, different national groups can give different meanings to Latino and Latina identity.

Latinos and Latinas from the Caribbean may have a very different understanding of the Latino and Latina label as a racial category than people from Mexico and Central America. Caribbean Latinos and Latinas construct their racial identity vis-à-vis blackness. First-generation Dominicans, for example, reject being associated with blackness because in the Dominican Republic blackness is associated with Haiti and Dominicans construct their national identity in opposition to Haitians. Mexican Americans, on the other hand, particularly those who adopt a Chicano and Chicana identity, build their racial identity around notions of "mestizaje" and Native American origin. These differences may sometimes make it difficult to build a common racial identity among the different Latino and Latina national groups. Yet the work of Flores-Gonzalez suggests that the possibility of a common identity depends on local contexts. For both the Mexican American and Puerto Rican youngsters she interviewed, the frame of reference for understanding the racialization of Latinos and Latinas was the African American experience. Clearly, comparative studies of Latino and Latina groups in several cities and regions are needed to establish the range of meanings of this category and the use that Latinos and Latinas from different nationalities and generations make of it.

INSTITUTIONAL SITES OF LATINO AND LATINA IDENTITY FORMATION

In previous writings, I have argued that Latino and Latina identity is in fact an important, secondary form of identity superimposed onto national identities (Itzigsohn and Dore-Cabral 2001). Here I want to restate this idea in a different way. I would now argue that Latino and Latina identity becomes part of a range of identity options that people can embrace in different contexts and for different purposes. Panethnicity is part of the language of self and collective definition available to people, a language that can be invoked for certain political and cultural projects and abandoned for others. This conception of identity points to the multiple, fragmentary, and contextual character of identities; it also emphasizes that social identities are neither arbitrary nor completely flexible. Individuals and groups attempt to achieve a certain degree of stability and consistency in their identities. Moreover, identities are formed within fields of social action that promote certain forms of identification at the same time as they limit the range of social identities available.

So far I have explored the emergence of Latino and Latina panethnic identities within the political and racial classification fields. In fact, Latino and Latina identities and social practices based on these identities are formed in many different institutional sites. Several institutional locations in the contemporary United States create incentives for the formation of Latino and Latina identities and social and cultural practices (Itzigsohn and Dore-Cabral 2001; Laó-Montes 2001a). Activists, leaders, representatives of the media, and community members acting in numerous institutional sites attempt to frame Latino and Latina identities for instrumental or expressive purposes. I discuss three of these sites and show the negotiations that take place around the creation of this form of peoplehood.

One of the most important contemporary institutional sites for the formation of Latino and Latina identities is the panethnic media. The media have a powerful interest in promoting the convergence of Latino and Latina peoples—creating a market segment to which it appeals and sells. Various media outlets have developed a series of issues, languages, and tastes that define an audience that begins to see itself in panethnic terms (Rodriguez 1999). At the same time, the media have created discourses of identities that are subject to contestation. Arlene Dávila (2001) shows how Hispanic television promotes a particular form of representation of Latinos and Latinas by portraying them as light-skinned and Spanish-speaking. Dávila's work brings out the racial divide within the Latino and Latina population and the often forgotten fault line between Spanish- and English-speaking Latinos and Latinas. The media portrayal she describes is certainly not the only possible representation of Latinos and Latinas in the United States. It is the result, she argues, of the vision of the particular people who control the production and dissemination of media images. Yet this portrayal has a powerful effect on defining Latino and Latina identities in the public sphere.

At the same time, Latino and Latina radio stations, TV programs, and newspapers and magazines provide Latinos and Latinas with a public site for the expression of their cultural identity in everyday life. The media also serve as a vehicle for the construction of community projects and community solidarity. Providence, for example, has three Latino and Latina radio stations that attempt to define the community and compete for listeners: the stations serve as a vehicle for projects of panethnic community formation. They provide a platform for groups attempting to reach the public for political, cultural, or charitable purposes. In doing so, they amplify the reach of these community groups and the effect of their actions. The Spanish radio and press provide political candidates with a base for mobilization and, in general, a means for mobilizing the community on specific issues. The Latino and Latina media also serve to publicize cultural initiatives such as performances of all kinds, celebrations, and festivals. And they help to forge panethnic solidarity through the organization of fund-raisers for people in need of financial assistance. In Providence the Latino and Latina radio and press have been very effective in helping to raise funds for people who need health care that they cannot afford on their own. These campaigns create a sense of community and solidarity, and although focused around specific issues, they remain part of the collective memories that constitute a community. In engaging in these forms of community action, the local Latino and Latina media go way beyond simply creating a market segment and play an important role in promoting community institution building.

Churches are another institutional site for the formation of Latino and Latina identities. Churches are places to meet people and create common religious as well as social and political projects. Churches catering to the Latino and Latina population are attended by people from different nationalities who come together through worship and other church activities. Churches are also often sites of panethnic political mobilization and social activism. Political campaigns of all sorts, such as demands for immigrant legalization or immigrant workers' rights, are often church-based. Church-based communities also often organize mutual help projects, disseminate information on community projects, and recruit volunteers for these projects. In all these ways, churches serve as a site of panethnic community formation.

In the creation of church-based communities we can see both convergence and differentiation. Church communities and activities contribute both to the strengthening of national-based identities and to the expansion of the boundaries of ethnic identity. For example, religious rituals and festivals are in many churches nationally based. In Providence there are celebrations for the Virgen de la Altagracia (associated with the Dominican Republic), the Virgen de Guadalupe (associated with Mexico), and the Virgen de Urqupiña (associated with Bolivia). These celebrations, although they reinforce national religious identities, are also announced and portrayed as Latino and Latina celebrations and bring together people from different nationalities.

Churches can also be a source of community tension. For example, the challenge to the hegemony of the Catholic Church posed by several other Christian denominations is a potential source of conflict among Latinos and Latinas. Yet such conflicts not only reinforce a sense of unity within each particular denomination but also encourage each church to appeal to Latinos and Latinas as a panethnic group so as to expand its sphere of influence and reach. In this way religious competition can lead to both interethnic tension and a strengthened sense of panethnic identity.

Social service agencies are another important site for the formation of Latino and Latina identities. One way in which social policies are implemented in the United States is through the intervention of nonprofit agencies. Historically, many nonprofit agencies have been organized on the basis of ethnicity. Latino and Latina social services agencies raise funds from federal, state, and local governments as well as from charitable organizations such as the United Way as a way to serve the unmet needs of the community. In the process, they reinforce the idea of the existence of a Latino and Latina community and strengthen Latino and Latina identities among their clients.[13] People may not define themselves as Latinos and Latinas, but Latino and Latina service organizations are often their only access to particular benefits or services. In receiving such services, people learn that their membership provides them with access, and thus they may come to see themselves, at least in part, as Latino and Latina. Even if the workers and clients associated with Latino and Latina service organizations do not initially define themselves in panethnic terms, the very presence and actions of these organizations are predicated on the existence of a Latino and Latina group and in fact reinforce Latino and Latina identities.

Whatever the institutional site, the formation of Latino and Latina identities is not a given but the result of negotiation over meanings. Indeed, different understandings of Latino and Latina identities may be present at the same time, as a description of the 2001 celebration of Cesar Chavez Day in Rhode Island illustrates. The mobilization and pressure of the growing local Mexican American community (as part of a national campaign) prompted Rhode Island to establish Cesar Chavez Day in recognition of the late farmworker union leader. The day is not a holiday but is recognized by the state and celebrated with a ceremony in the legislature. For the state, it is an opportunity to show the growing Latino and Latina community that it is being recognized. Although most Latinos and Latinas in Rhode Island are not Chicanos or Mexican Americans, Cesar Chavez is a figure who appeals to many Latinos and Latinas.

The leaders of the local Mexican American community led the organizing committee. The Mexican American community in the state mainly comprises first-generation immigrants, and Cesar Chavez is defined there not only as a Mexican American or Chicano icon but also as a Mexican one. In recognition of the transnational side of the construction of contemporary Latino and Latina identities, the Mexican consul in Boston was invited to speak at the ceremony. Leaders from all the other local Latino and Latina communities participated as well. A few who were acquainted with the history of Cesar Chavez spoke about the organization of workers and the troubles of immigrant workers today. Others simply mentioned that the celebration of Cesar Chavez Day was one more example of the growth and progress of the Latino and Latina community, a growth also exemplified by the increasing number of Latino and Latina small businesses. These speakers transformed Cesar Chavez into a Latino figure in a discourse of community progress through economic development.

The transformation of Chavez from a Chicano farmworker union leader from California into an all-Latino and Latina icon separated from his historical and regional context became clear when a couple of speakers called upon the audience to follow the path of Julio Cesar Chavez, the name of a famous Mexican boxer. This mix up does not mean that people thought the celebration was for the boxer. Rather, it indicates that Cesar Chavez is not a well-known figure for recent immigrants who have little knowledge of civil and labor rights struggles in this country; for many Latinos and Latinas, the name Chavez is more readily associated with the boxer than with the union leader. Even though people may not have known much about Cesar Chavez, they knew that he was a Latino leader and that the celebration was one of Latino and Latina empowerment.

The celebration of Cesar Chavez Day shows the complex and different meanings of Latino and Latina identities. Cesar Chavez was constructed as a local and transnational Mexican American figure, as someone who fought for workers' rights and was related to current union drives to organize immigrants, and as a symbol of pan-Latino empowerment. Identity formation involves a multiplicity of parallel and sometimes competing cultural and political projects. This may be a source of frustration if we are after simple models of identity formation, yet the complex dynamics reflect the lived experience of Latino and Latina people trying to build their lives in the United States.

PANETHNIC FUTURES?

In this chapter, I have examined the multiple meanings and forms of Latino and Latina panethnic identity formation, which brings together a very diverse group of people in complex ways and in different situations. I have emphasized sites and forms of panethnic identity formation, or, to be more precise, pan-ethno-racial identity formation.

Of course, not every Latino and Latina identity embraces this identity. Far from it. Panethnic identity formation is by no means a given; it is a process, and many people choose not to embrace or ally themselves with other Latinos and Latinas.

Every researcher in this field is acquainted with cases of rejection of panethnic identities. The case of Miami Cubans, as Rodolfo Cortina (1990) points out, is special in that they have acquired unprecedented political and economic power that they do not share with other Hispanic groups, thereby reinforcing a focus on their national identity. In general, access to political power or a privileged class position may lead the members of an ethnic group to resist linkages to other ethnic groups that are less powerful or in a lower class position. Yet with the growth of new Latino and Latina groups in Miami, this situation may be changing, and Cubans may be reaching out, at least in some situations.[14]

Conflict between Latino and Latina groups is not limited to the political realm. High school teachers often report strong animosities among Latino and Latina groups based on national belonging. Moreover, most university professors teaching Latino and Latina studies encounter students who reject the panethnic label because it erases their specific culture and identity.[15] Also, there are powerful conflicts between—and within—groups along status and political lines. For example, important segments of Latinos and Latinas along the Mexican-U.S. border take strong stances in favor of keeping the border closed to immigrants, while other Latinos and Latinas show solidarity with newcomers (Vila 2000). Similarly, although most Latinos and Latinas in California voted against anti-immigrant propositions—such as Proposition 187—an important minority supported these proposals.

Nevertheless, there are, I would argue, strong forces in the contemporary United States leading toward a certain degree of convergence among Latinos and Latinas. Numerous institutional forces—for example, the census, political mobilization, and market formation—appeal to Latinos and Latinas as a pan-ethno-racial group and in the process help the very formation of the group they appeal to. Under these conditions, panethnic identities and loyalties are formed and maintained. Panethnicity becomes part of the language of self-identification of Latinos and Latinas, part of a range of identity options that can be used to construct individual and collective identities. Political, social, and cultural organization and mobilization of people along panethnic lines will be a feature of American life in years to come.

Part of becoming American for people of Latin American origin is becoming part of a racialized social order with racialized panethnic categories. An outcome of the civil rights movement has been an increasing interweaving of race and class in the determination of individuals' life chances. At the same time, America's racial classification system has become more complex owing to immigration and interracial marriage. The color line has indeed been bent, yet it has not disappeared as a feature of American life.

At the same time that forces of convergence lead to the creation of a Latino and Latina group, strong differentiating trends within the group persist. Latino and Latina identities can be heavily contested. Different groups attribute different meanings to Latino and Latina identity and build different and sometimes opposing personal and collective projects around it. It is also true that first-generation immigrants continue arriving as second and third generations grow up. Latino and Latina communities are increasingly fractured along class lines. Different regions of the country have different combinations of classes, nationalities, and generations of Latinos and Latinas. Latino and Latina political projects promote different and often conflicting policies.

We live in times of change, and panethnic identities keep changing with the times.

It is hard to predict the future, but it is clear that panethnicity will be a feature of American ethnic and racial identities and relations in the years to come and that there will continue to be diversity in the forms and meanings of panethnic identity and mobilization.

I want to thank Alberto Pulido and the rest of the participants in the ethnic studies faculty seminar at Brown University for their comments on the ideas that are the core of this chapter. The responsibility for the content and its errors is, of course, mine.

NOTES

1. The appropriate label for people of Latin American origin has long been a subject of controversy. I prefer "Latino and Latina," and that is the label I use in this chapter unless I am reporting the comments of others. In fact, in the Northeast—the region where I live—the labels "Latino," "Latina," "Hispano," and "Hispana" are used interchangeably.

2. This point is also emphasized by Laó-Montes (2001b) in his analysis of Latino and Latina social movements in New York City.

3. Racialization is the assignment of racial characteristics and positions to peoples and groups. Race is a social construction, a form of hierarchical classification of people based on different combinations of phenotype, origin, and ancestry. This classification, in turn, is also a base for group formation. Race is global in character, with different systems of racial classification present in different regions of the modern world system. It is also a historical construction: modern forms of racialization are linked to the emergence of Europe as the core of the modern world system and its historical expansion. Furthermore, different racial classification systems have concrete histories, and racial meanings change with the struggles of racialized peoples. Yet it is important to remember that at any particular time and place the existing racial classification system has powerful effects on the lives and experiences of people; social constructions have real consequences for the lives (and deaths) of people.

4. For example, 43.5 percent of Latinos and Latinas chose "other" as their racial identification in the 1990 census (Rodriguez 2000). In the 2000 census, 42.2 percent chose the "some other race category" (U.S. Department of Commerce 2001).

5. As is well known, the final decision was to allow people to mark more than one racial category.

6. The large number of Latinos and Latinas who chose "other" in response to the racial self-identification question was another of the measurement problems that preoccupied the census takers.

7. The survey was conducted between the fall of 1997 and the spring of 1998. In New York City the survey was conducted in the Washington Heights neighborhood of Manhattan, and in Providence the survey was conducted in South Providence and Washington Park. Both are areas of high Dominican residential and business concentration. In New York 259 people were interviewed, of whom 208 were contacted randomly and 51 through referrals. In Providence 159 people were interviewed, with 86 contacted randomly and 73 through referrals. The interviewers were Dominican, and the questions were asked in Spanish. For the purpose of analysis, the data were pooled for a total sample size of 418.

8. Resource limitations prevented citywide surveys. Instead, the majority of the respondents were selected using a three-stage sampling design. In the first stage, we identified the main

areas of Dominican residential concentration within each city. In the second stage, a random sample of blocks was selected in census tracts with a large concentration of Dominicans. These city blocks served as primary sample units (PSUs). In the third stage, a systematic random sample of households was conducted within each block using a fixed sampling fraction, thus ensuring identical probabilities of selection for eligible households (Kish 1965). Slightly more than two-thirds of the sample (70.3 percent) was selected using this method. About one-third of the sample (29.7 percent) was selected through referrals and snowball chains with different points of entry. This subsample was chosen through referrals from community leaders or transnational actors.

9. Another interesting point emerging from the survey is the large percentage of Dominicans who believe that they are perceived as black by mainstream Americans.

10. The use of the label "Hispano and Hispana" as a racial identification choice may also be related to regional ways of talking about race. The same question applied in other parts of the country might well yield different results.

11. The literal meaning of "indio" is Indian, but in the Dominican Republic this term is used as an intermediate racial classification label that designates people with mixed African and European ancestry as nonblack.

12. In the 2000 census, 47.9 percent of those who identified as Hispanic chose to identify as white.

13. It is also true that in places where there is a clear majority of one particular Latino and Latina group, social service agencies are based on national identities, thereby reinforcing national rather than panethnic identities.

14. For example, Florida's Cuban American representative Lincoln Diaz-Balart supported legislation to allow Nicaraguans and Salvadorans to extend their stay in the United States. In this case, panethnic solidarity was based on the fact that members of these two groups, much like Cubans, were refugees from wars against communism. I am indebted to Silvia Pedraza for pointing out the complexity of Cuban American positions vis-à-vis other Latino and Latina groups.

15. An additional site for the formation of panethnic identities, which I have not discussed, is the presence of Latino and Latina studies in universities (Padilla 1997). This is an important site because it produces the new generation of intellectual leaders who will reframe the meanings of Latino and Latina identity and the forms of Latino and Latina social action.

REFERENCES

Almaguer, Tomas. 1994. *Racial Fault Lines: The Historical Origins of White Supremacy in California.* Berkeley: University of California Press.

Blumer, Herbert. 1958. "Race Prejudice as a Sense of Group Position." *Pacific Sociological Review* 1(Spring): 3–7.

Calderón, José. 1992. "'Hispanic' and 'Latino': The Viability of Categories for Panethnic Unity." *Latin American Perspectives* 75(1): 37–44.

Cortina, Rodolfo. 1990. "Cubans in Miami: Ethnic Identification and Behavior." *Latino Studies Journal* 1: 60–73.

Dávila, Arlene. 2001. *Latinos, Inc.: The Marketing and Making of a People.* Berkeley: University of California Press.

Flores-Gonzalez, Nilda. 1999. "The Racialization of Latinos: The Meaning of Latino Identity for the Second Generation." *Latino Studies Journal* 10(3): 3–31.

Gimenez, Martha E. 1992. "U.S. Ethnic Politics: Implications for Latin Americans." *Latin American Perspectives* 19(4): 7–17.

Hirschman, Charles, Richard Alba, and Reynolds Farley. 2000. "The Meaning and Measurement of Race in the U.S. Census: Glimpses into the Future." *Demography* 37(3): 381–93.

Itzigsohn, José, and Carlos Dore-Cabral. 2000. "Competing Identities? Race, Ethnicity, and Panethnicity Among Dominicans in the United States." *Sociological Forum* 15(2): 225–48.

———. 2001. "The Manifold Character of Panethnicity." In *Mambo Montage: The Latinization of New York*, edited by Agustín Laó-Montes and Arlene Dávila. New York: Columbia University Press.

Itzigsohn, José, Carlos Dore-Cabral, Esther Hernández Medina, and Obed Vazquez. 1999. "Mapping Dominican Transnationalism: Narrow and Broad Transnational Practices." *Ethnic and Racial Studies* 22(2): 316–39.

Kish, Leslie. 1965. *Survey Sampling*. New York: J. Wiley.

Laó-Montes, Agustín. 2001a. "Mambo Montage: The Latinization of New York City." In *Mambo Montage: The Latinization of New York*, edited by Agustín Laó-Montes and Arlene Dávila. New York: Columbia University Press.

———. 2001b. "Niuyol: Urban Regime, Latino Social Movements, Ideologies of Latinidad." In *Mambo Montage: The Latinization of New York*, edited by Agustín Laó-Montes and Arlene Dávila. New York: Columbia University Press.

Laó-Montes, Agustín, and Arlene Dávila, eds. 2001. *Mambo Montage. The Latinization of New York*. New York: Columbia University Press.

Logan, John. 2001. "The New Latinos: Who They Are, Where They Are." Albany: State University of New York, Lewis Mumford Center for Comparative Urban and Regional Research.

Lopez, David, and Yen Le Espiritu. 1990. "Panethnicity in the United States: A Theoretical Framework." *Ethnic and Racial Studies* 13(2): 198–224.

Marquez, Benjamin. 2001. "Choosing Issues, Choosing Sides: Constructing Identities in Mexican American Social Movement Organizations." *Ethnic and Racial Studies* 24(2): 218–35.

Massey, Douglas S. 1993. "Latinos, Poverty, and the Underclass: A New Agenda for Research." *Hispanic Journal of Behavioral Sciences* 15(4): 449–75.

Melville, Margarita B. 1986. "Hispanics: Race, Class, or Ethnicity?" *Journal of Ethnic Studies* 16(1): 67–83.

Moore, Joan. 1990. "Hispanic/Latino: Imposed Label or Real Identity?" *Latino Studies Journal* 1: 33–47.

Nagel, Joanne. 1996. *American Indian Ethnic Renewal*. Oxford: Oxford University Press.

Oboler, Suzanne. 1995. *Ethnic Labels, Latino Lives*. Minneapolis: University of Minnesota Press.

Okihiro, Gary. 1994. *Margins and Mainstreams*. Seattle: University of Washington Press.

Padilla, Felix. 1984. "On the Nature of Latino Ethnicity." *Social Science Quarterly* 65(2): 651–64.

———. 1985. *Latino Ethnic Consciousness*. Notre Dame, Ind.: University of Notre Dame Press.

———. 1997. *The Struggle of Latino/Latina University Students*. New York: Routledge.

Portes, Alejandro, Luis E. Guarnizo, and Patricia Landolt. 1999. "Introduction: Pitfalls and Promise of an Emergent Research Field." *Ethnic and Racial Studies* 22(2): 217–37.

Rocco, Raymond. 1997. "Citizenship, Culture, and Community: Restructuring in South East Los Angeles." In *Latino Cultural Citizenship*, edited by William V. Flores and Rina Benmayor. Boston: Beacon Press.

Rodriguez, America. 1999. *Making Latino News: Race, Language, Class*. Thousand Oaks, Calif.: Sage Publications.

Rodriguez, Clara. 2000. *Changing Race: Latinos, the Census, and the History of Ethnicity in the United States*. New York: New York University Press.

Rodriguez, Clara, and Hector Cordero-Guzman. 1992. "Placing Race in Context." *Ethnic and Racial Studies* 15(4): 523–41.

Rosaldo, Renato, and William V. Flores. 1997. "Identity, Conflict, and Evolving Latino Communities: Cultural Citizenship in San Jose." In *Latino Cultural Citizenship*, edited by William V. Flores and Rina Benmayor. Boston: Beacon Press.

Saito, Leland. 1998. *Race and Politics*. Chicago: University of Illinois Press.

U.S. Department of Commerce. U.S. Census Bureau. 2001. *Overview of Race and Hispanic Origin. Census 2000 Brief.* Washington: U.S. Government Printing Office.

Valle, Victor M., and Rodolfo D. Torres. 2000. *Latino Metropolis*. Minneapolis: University of Minnesota Press.

Vila, Pablo. 2000. *Crossing Borders, Reinforcing Borders*. Austin: University of Texas Press.

Yen Le Espiritu

Chapter 10

Asian American Panethnicity: Contemporary National and Transnational Possibilities

In an article published in *Gidra*, an activist Asian American news magazine, Naomi Iwasaki (1999, under "Asian American or Not") writes, "You know, the hardest thing about pan-Asian solidarity is the 'pan' part. It forces us all to step outside of our comfort zones, whether they be constructed by ethnicity, class, home city, identity, whatever." Iwasaki's statement calls attention to the social constructedness of pan-ethnicity—panethnic identities are self-conscious products of political choice and actions, not of inherited phenotypes, bloodlines, or cultural traditions. In my 1992 publication *Asian American Panethnicity: Bridging Institutions and Identities*, I identify the twin roots of Asian American panethnicity—in the racialization of Asian national groups by dominant groups and in Asian Americans' responses to those constructions. Employing a racial formation perspective (Omi and Winant 1986), I argue that the racialist constructions of Asians as homogeneous and interchangeable spawn important alliances and affiliations among ethnic and immigrant groups of Asian origin. Adopting the dominant group's categorization of them, Asian Americans have institutionalized pan-Asianism as their political instrument, thereby enlarging their own capacities to challenge and transform the existing structure of power. In other words, Asian Americans did not just adopt the pan-Asian concept but also transformed it to conform to their political, economic, and ideological needs.

Though powerful, pan-Asianism is not unproblematic: it can mask salient divisions, subsume nondominant groups, and create marginalities, all of which threatens the legitimacy and effectiveness of pan-Asianism and bolsters (however inadvertently) the racist discourses and practices that construct Asians as homogeneous. In the three decades since the emergence of the pan-Asian concept in the late 1960s, Asian American communities have changed in dramatic ways. No longer constrained by race-based exclusion laws, Asian immigrants began arriving in much larger numbers than before. Many of the post-1965 immigrants have little direct experience with the Asian American movement and little reason to think of themselves as Asian American rather than as immigrants, as low-wage workers, or as members of different national and ethnic groups (Espiritu et al. 2000, 131). Moreover, recent immigration has further diversified Asian Americans along cultural, generational, economic, and political lines—all of which have compounded the difficulties of forging pan-Asian identities and institutions.

This chapter reviews the history of Asian American panethnicity in the United States *then to now*, paying particular attention to the ways in which pan-Asian identities and institutions have been transformed by the post-1965 immigration and by changes in the global economy. The first section documents the social, political, and demographic factors that led to the emergence of pan-Asianism in the late 1960s and early 1970s. The second details how the post-1965 immigration has diversified the Asian American population and made it more difficult for groups to imagine shared origins and destinies. The third establishes that the construction of Asian American identities not only is a response to conditions in the United States but also is deeply bound to U.S. colonial and imperialist practices that propel the contemporary migration of Asians to the United States in the first place. The fourth discusses the political importance of cross-group affiliation, not only among Asians but also with other groups across class, ethnic, racial, and national lines. Of the four sections, the third conveys the chapter's central argument: pan-Asianism in the United States has been determined not exclusively by events and population changes in the United States but also by U.S. colonialism and imperialism in Asia. Much of the published work in the field of U.S. immigration studies has remained "America-centric," focusing on the immigrants' "modes of incorporation" and the process of their "becoming American." In contrast, this chapter takes a *critical transnational approach* to the study of Asian Americans, calling attention to the deep historical entanglements of immigration and imperialism.[1]

COMING TOGETHER:
THE EMERGENCE OF PAN-ASIANISM

Arriving in the United States, nineteenth-century immigrants from Asian countries did not think of themselves as "Asians." Coming from specific districts and provinces in different nations, Asian immigrant groups did not even think of themselves as Chinese, Japanese, Korean, and so forth, but rather as people from Toishan, Hoiping, or some other district in Guandong Province in China or from Hiroshima, Yamaguchi, or some other prefecture in Japan. Members of each group considered themselves culturally and politically distinct. Historical enmities between their countries of origin further separated the groups even before their arrival in the United States. However, non-Asians had little understanding or appreciation of these distinctions. For the most part, outsiders accorded to people from Asia certain common characteristics and traits that were essentially supranational. Indeed, the exclusion acts and quotas limiting Asian immigration to the United States relied on racialist constructions of Asians as homogeneous (Lowe 1991, 28).

The development of panethnicity among Asian Americans has a short history. It was not until the late 1960s, with the advent of the Asian American movement, that a pan-Asian consciousness and constituency were first formed. Before the 1960s, Asians in the United States frequently practiced ethnic disidentification: distancing one's group from another group so as not to be mistaken for a member of that group and to avoid suffering the blame for its presumed misdeeds (Hayano 1981, 161, 162; Daniels 1988, 113). For example, in the late nineteenth century, aware of Chinese exclusion, Japanese immigrant leaders did everything possible to distinguish themselves from the Chinese immigrants (Ichioka 1988, 250). In the end Japanese attempts at disidentification failed. With the passage of the 1924 Immigration Act, the Japanese joined the Chinese as a people deemed unworthy of becoming Americans. Less than two decades later, after the bombing of Pearl Harbor, it was the turn of the Chinese to disassociate themselves from the Japanese. Fearful that they would be targets of anti-Japanese activities, many Chinese immigrants took to wearing buttons that proclaimed positively, "I'm Chinese."

Some Chinese immigrants—and also Korean and Filipino migrants—even joined the white persecution with buttons that added, "I hate Japs worse than you do" (Daniels 1988, 205; Takaki 1989, 370–71). These two examples are instructive not only as evidence of ethnic disidentification but also as documentation of the pervasiveness of racial lumping. Precisely because of racial lumping, persons of Asian ancestry found it necessary to disassociate themselves from other Asian groups.

The development of a pan-Asian consciousness and constituency reflected broader societal developments and demographic changes as well as the group's political agenda. Before World War II, pan-Asian unity was not feasible because the predominantly foreign-born Asian population did not share a common language. During the postwar years, owing to immigration restrictions and the growing dominance of the second and even third generations, U.S.-born Asians outnumbered immigrants. By 1960 approximately two-thirds of the Asian population in California had been born in the United States (Ong 1989, 5–8). With English as the common language, persons from different Asian backgrounds were able to communicate with one another (Ling 1984, 73) and in so doing to create a common identity associated with the United States. Also, the breakdown of economic and residential barriers during the postwar period provided the first opportunity for an unprecedented number of Asian Americans to come into intimate, sustained contact with the larger society—and with one another. Formerly homogeneous, the Asian ethnic enclaves started to house mixed-Asian communities, as well as non-Asian groups. Multigroup suburban centers also emerged. Paul Wong (1972, 34) reported that since the early 1960s Asian Americans of diverse national origins had moved into the suburbs outside the major Asian communities such as Berkeley and San Mateo, California. Although a small proportion of the local population, these Asian Americans tended to congregate in pockets; consequently, in some residential blocks a majority of the residents were Asian Americans.

Although broader social struggles and internal demographic changes provided the impetus for the Asian American movement, it was the Asian Americans' politics—explicitly radical, confrontational, and pan-Asian—that shaped the movement's content. Inspired by anticolonial revolutions in Asia and by black and Chicano revolutionary nationalism, college students of Asian ancestry sought to transcend inter-Asian ethnic divisions and to ally themselves with other "Third World" minorities (Blauner 1972, ch. 2; Omatsu 1994). Through pan-Asian organizations, publications, and Asian American studies programs, Asian American activists forged a pan-Asian consciousness by highlighting their shared resistance to Western imperialism and to U.S. racism. The pan-Asian concept enabled diverse Asian American groups to understand their "unequal circumstances and histories as being related" (Lowe 1991, 30). By the mid-1970s, "Asian American" had become a familiar term (Lott 1976, 30). Although first coined by college activists, the pan-Asian concept began to be used extensively by professional and community spokespersons to lobby for the health and welfare of Americans of Asian descent. Commenting on the "literally scores of pan-Asian organizations" in the mid-1970s, William Liu (1976, 6) asserted that "the idea of pan-Asian cooperation [was] viable and ripe for development."

The advent of state-sponsored affirmative action programs provided another material reason for Asian American subgroups to consolidate their efforts. Because the welfare state bureaucracy often treats all Asian Americans as a single administrative unit in distributing economic and political resources, it imposes a pan-Asian structure on persons and communities dependent on government support. As dealings with government bureaucracies increased, political organization along a pan-Asian line became

necessary, not only because numbers confer power but also because the pan-Asian category is the institutionally relevant category in the political and legal system. Administratively treated as a homogeneous group, Asian Americans found it necessary—and
even advantageous—to respond as a group. The pan-Asian strategy has led to some
political victories. For example, Asian American legislators, community leaders, and
organizations united to fight the Census Bureau's proposal to collapse all Asian racial
codes into one summary category for the 1980 and 1990 censuses. Partly in response to
the strength of their political lobbying, the Census Bureau finally conceded to the coalition's demand for a detailed enumeration of Asian subgroups.[2] Indeed, the emergence
of the pan-Asian entity may be one of the most significant political developments in
Asian American affairs.

CHANGING DEMOGRAPHIC AND ECONOMIC CHARACTERISTICS

The post-1965 immigration surge from Asia has transformed Asian America—and thus
the feasibility of pan-Asian ethnicity—in dramatic ways. The share of immigrants to
the United States from Asia as a proportion of total admission grew from a tiny 5
percent in the 1950s to 11 percent in the 1960s and 33 percent in the 1970s, and it has
remained at 35 percent since 1980 (Zhou and Gatewood 2000, 9). In sheer numbers,
the Asian American population grew from a total of 1.4 million in 1970 to 7.3 million
in 1990, to 10.2 million in 2000.[3] According to Zhou and Gatewood (2000, 14), immigration accounted for more than two-thirds of this spectacular population growth. For
the new national origins groups (Indians, Koreans, Vietnamese, Cambodians, Laotians,
and the Hmong), population growth can be attributed almost entirely to immigration
(Zhou and Gatewood 2000, 14). Projections from the Census Bureau suggest that the
Asian American population will increase from 9 million in 1995 to 34 million in 2050,
growing from 3 to 8 percent of the total U.S. population (Smith and Edmonston 1997).
The dramatic growth in the absolute numbers of Asian Americans has been accom-
panied by increasing ethnic, generational, and socioeconomic diversity within Asian
America, all of which has important implications for pan-Asian identities and practices.
As Michael Omi (1993, 205) succinctly states, "The irony is that the term ["Asian
American"] came into vogue at precisely the historical moment when new Asian
groups were entering the U.S. who would render the term problematic."

Ethnic Diversification

Before the post-1965 immigration surge, the Asian American population was composed
mainly of three ethnic groups: Japanese, Chinese, and Filipino. In 1970 Japanese Americans constituted the single largest group (41 percent of the Asian American population), followed by Chinese Americans (30 percent) and Filipino Americans (24 percent). Members of other national origins groups (mostly Koreans) represented less than
5 percent of the Asian American population total (Zhou and Gatewood 2000, 13).
Coming of age in the 1960s, U.S.-born Japanese and Chinese Americans formed the
core force of the Asian American movement on West Coast college campuses and in
the Northeast (Espiritu 1992). In contrast, in 2000 the U.S. census recorded twenty-four
national origins groups, and no single group accounted for more than one-quarter of
the Asian American population. Although Japan has sent very few immigrants to the

United States, the Philippines, China and Taiwan, Korea, India, and Vietnam have been on the list of the top ten sending countries since 1980 (USINS 1997). Reflecting these changing immigration patterns, in 2000 the Japanese American share of the Asian American population fell to only 8 percent, and the five largest Asian American groups were Chinese and Taiwanese (24 percent), Filipino (18 percent), Asian Indian (17 percent), Korean (11 percent), and Vietnamese (11 percent) (Barnes and Bennett 2002).[4] The new Asian American demographics have complicated the delicate pan-Asian alignments created in the 1960s and 1970s among the then-largest Asian American groups: Japanese, Chinese, and, to a lesser extent, Filipino Americans.

Generational Diversification

Between the 1940s and 1960s, when immigration from Asia was restricted, U.S.-born Asian Americans dominated the Asian American population. By the 1970s the foreign-born reemerged as a large majority. In 2000, 7.2 million Asian Pacific Americans—approximately 70 percent of the total Asian American population—were foreign-born (U.S. Department of Commerce 2002). The foreign-born component dominated all Asian American groups except for Japanese Americans; over 60 percent of Filipinos and nearly 80 percent of Vietnamese and other Asians were foreign-born (Zhou and Gatewood 2000, 14). Because of legal exclusion in the past, it is only among the two oldest immigrant groups—the Japanese and Chinese Americans—that a sizable third or fourth generation exists. Among Asian American children under eighteen years of age, more than 90 percent are either foreign-born or children of foreign-born parents (Zhou and Greenwood 2000, 23). Paul Ong and Suzanne Hee (1993) have predicted that the foreign-born segment will still be a majority in the year 2020.

Class Diversification

Post-1965 immigration has also increased the economic diversity of Asian Americans. In contrast to the largely unskilled immigrant population of the pre–World War II period, the new arrivals include not only low-wage service-sector workers but also significant numbers of white-collar professionals. According to the 1990 U.S. census, more than 60 percent of immigrants (age twenty-five or older) from India and Taiwan reported having attained a college degree (three times the proportion of average Americans), but fewer than 5 percent of those from Cambodia and Laos made such a report. Among the employed workers, about 45 percent of immigrants from India and Taiwan held managerial or professional occupations, more than twice the proportion of average American workers, but fewer than 5 percent of those from Laos and only about 10 percent of those from Cambodia had held such a position. Further, immigrants from India, the Philippines, and Taiwan reported a median household income of about $45,000, compared to $30,000 for average American households; those from Cambodia and highland Laos reported a median household income below $20,000. Poverty rates for Asian immigrants ranged from a low of 7 percent for Filipinos, Indians, and Japanese to a high of more than 60 percent for Hmongs and 42 percent for Cambodians, compared to about 10 percent for average American families (Zhou 1999). Given the diversity of economic background, Asian Americans can be found throughout the income spectrum of the United States. In other words, today's Asian Americans join whites in the well-paid, educated, white-collar service sector of the workforce as well as Latino immigrants in lower-paying service and manufacturing jobs (Ong and Hee

1994). Responding to limited job opportunities for highly skilled immigrants, a large number of Asian immigrants have also turned to self-employment (Ong and Hee 1994).

Implications for Panethnicity in Contemporary Asian America

By most accounts, the expanding diversity of Asian Americans has brought into question the very definition of Asian America—and along with it, the feasibility and appropriateness of pan-Asian identities and practices. In a major public policy report on the state of Asian America, editor Paul Ong (2000) suggests that the pan-Asian identity is "fragile," citing as evidence the group's ethnic and economic diversity as well as the growing population of bi- and multiracial Asian Americans who want to acknowledge their combined racial heritage.[5] Similarly, in the introduction to their substantial multi-disciplinary reader on contemporary Asian America, editors Min Zhou and James Gatewood (2000, 27) caution that "differences in class background among the immigrant generation and divergent modes of incorporation of that generation can deter the formation of panethnicity." Comparing the experiences of affluent Chinese immigrants and Cambodian refugees, Aihwa Ong (1996, 751) concludes that the category "Asian American" "must confront the contradictions and instabilities within the imposed solidarity, brought about by the group's internal class, ethnic, and racial stratifications." In Asian American studies, many scholars have critically pointed to the field's privileging of East Asians (the "old" Asian Americans) over South and Southeast Asians (the "new" Asian Americans)—a clear indictment of the suppression of diverse histories, epistemologies, and voices within the pan-Asian framework. For example, in an edited volume on South Asians in Asian America aptly titled *A Part, Yet Apart*, Rajiv Shankar (1998, x) laments that South Asians "find themselves so unnoticed as an entity that they feel as if they are merely a crypto-group, often included but easily marginalized within the house of Asian America."

A CRITICAL TRANSNATIONAL APPROACH TO PAN-ASIAN ETHNICITY

Elsewhere (Espiritu and Ong 1994; Espiritu 1992, 1996), I have discussed at length one of the challenges facing the contemporary Asian American community: how do Asian Americans build pan-Asian solidarity amid increasing diversities? Like other Asian American scholars and activists, I have suggested that if Asian Americans are to build a self-consciously pan-Asian solidarity, they need to take seriously the heterogeneities among their ranks and overcome the narrow dominance of the professional class and that of the two oldest Asian American groups. I still subscribe to this view—that Asian Americans need to tend to the social, political, and economic inequalities that exist within their communities. At the same time, I am concerned that this view narrowly locates the "problems" of pan-Asian ethnicity *not* in the political and economic oppression or violence that produced massive displacements and migrations of Asians in the first place, but in the internal workings of the Asian American community itself. Thus told, the internal diversities within Asian America become "interiorized," and the focus is shifted away from global politics and power and toward identity politics within Asian America.

An example of this interiorization is the evoking of inter-Asian cultural and linguistic differences to explain (away) the difficulty of building pan-Asian alliances. This statement by Min Zhou and James Gatewood (2000, 19) exemplifies this approach:

> The impact of diversity in national origins is straightforward. National origins evoke drastic differences in homeland cultures, such as languages, religions, foodways, and customs. . . . For some national origin groups, such as the Chinese and Asian Indians, internal differences in languages or dialects and religions are quite substantial. It is therefore extremely difficult to group everybody under a pan-Asian umbrella at the individual level, creating an obstacle for panethnic coalitions.

They also posit that cultural differences complicate intergenerational relations and ethnic solidarity. According to Zhou and Gatewood (2000, 20), native-born Asian Americans have assimilated such American values as labor rights, individualism, and civil liberty that set them apart from their foreign-born counterparts. These differences, "intertwined with the *cultural gap* between immigrant and native-born generations," have impeded pan-Asian coalition and collective action (Zhou and Gatewood 2000, 20, emphasis added).

Another example of interiorization is the focus on socioeconomic diversity. Many Asian American scholars have documented the bifurcated distribution of the Asian American population along class lines, pointing to diverse mobility patterns and divergent destinies. To make matters worse, class differences often correlate with ethnicity, generating internal conflicts that assume an ethnic appearance. For example, Chinese, Japanese, Filipinos, Koreans, and Asian Indians have a growing middle class. But many other groups, especially the most recent refugee populations, are struggling in the most underprivileged segment of U.S society (Zhou and Greenwood 2000, 19; Ong and Blumenberg 1994, 113).

Certainly, ethnic, generational, and class diversity pose new obstacles for pan-Asian mobilization. But to begin and stop the analysis here would be to engage in an "America-centric" approach to the question of the relation between race, ethnicity, nation, and migration. From this perspective, the analysis of pan-Asian ethnicity begins when the immigrants arrive on U.S. soil. Thus told, intra-Asian differences—along ethnic, class, and generational lines—become naturalized, unmediated by global politics and power. Departing from this perspective, I resituate the discussion of pan-Asian relations within a critical transnational framework, one that is attentive to global relations, which set the context for immigration and immigrant life. That is, instead of just asking how the massive influx of immigrants from Asia—and the resultant diversification of the population along class, generational, and ethnic lines—has reshaped pan-Asian identities and practices, we also need to ask how the influx of immigrants from Asia—with its specific configurations—came into being in the first place. As I argue later, pan-Asian American "racial formation" has been determined not exclusively by events in the United States but also by U.S. geopolitical interests in Asia and needs for different types and sources of labor—all of which have produced the particular ethnic, generational, and class configurations that have rendered the term "Asian American" problematic for the post-1965 community.

In the United States public discussion on immigration is fundamentally about people who cross borders. The media, elected officials, and the general public often represent border crossers as desperate individuals migrating in search of the "land of opportunity." This representation makes invisible other important border crossers: U.S. colonizers, military, and corporations that invade and forcefully deplete the economic and cultural resources of less-powerful countries. Calling attention to global structures of inequality, recent social theorists have linked migration processes with the global penetration of Western economic systems, technological infrastructures, and popular cultures in non-Western countries (Burawoy 1976; Petras 1978; Portes 1978; Zolberg 1986). Although details vary, these works posit that the internalization of a capitalistic economic system in "Third World" countries has produced imbalances in their internal social and economic structures and subsequently spurred emigration. As Saskia Sassen (1992, 15) argues, "U.S. efforts to open its own and other countries to the flow of capital, goods, services, and information created the conditions that mobilized people for migration." Indeed, all of the nation-states from which the largest number of U.S. immigrants originate—Mexico, China (including Taiwan and Hong Kong), the Philippines, El Salvador, the Dominican Republic, South Korea, Guatemala, Vietnam, Laos, and Cambodia—have had sustained and sometimes intimate social, political, and economic relations with the United States.

A transnational approach that stresses the global structures of inequality is critical for understanding Asian immigration and Asian American lives in the United States. Linking global economic development with global histories of colonialism, Edna Bonacich and Lucie Cheng (1984) argue that the pre–World War II immigration of Asians to the United States has to be understood within the context of the development of capitalism in Europe and the United States and the emergence of imperialism, especially in relation to Asia. From World War II onward, as the world economy became much more globally integrated, Asia was the site for U.S. expansion. As a result, contemporary immigrants from the Philippines, South Vietnam, South Korea, Cambodia, and Laos come from countries that have been deeply disrupted by U.S. colonialism, war, and neocolonial capitalism (Lowe 1996). The "transnational porosity between the United States and Asia" (Kang 1997, 408) means that "there has been an important continuity between the considerable distortion of social relations in Asian countries affected by U.S. imperialist war and occupation and the emigration of Asian labor to the United States" (Lowe 1996, 7).

The history of U.S. imperialism in Asia suggests that Asian American "racial formation" has never been exclusively shaped by events in the United States but has also been influenced by U.S. colonialism, neocolonialism, and militarism in Asia. However, the process of Asian American racial formation has been neither singular nor unified. Owing to the multiple contexts of colonialism and its various extensions within the development of global capitalism, Asians in the United States have experienced different processes of racialization specific to each group's historical and material conditions. It is these historical and material conditions—rather than intrinsic intra-Asian differences—that we need to investigate to understand the uneven formation of panethnicity among Asian Americans. I do not attempt here to delineate the genealogy of the racialization of all Asian groups in the United States; that task is well beyond the scope of this chapter. Instead, I confine my analysis to the experiences of Filipino immigrants and Vietnamese refugees—two groups with very different socioeconomic profiles—to illustrate the importance of a global conceptual framework in the theorizing of Asian American panethnicity.

Filipinos: Colonized Immigrant

In the twenty years following passage of the 1965 Immigration Act, about 40 percent of the documented immigration to the United States has come from Asia. The Philippines has been the largest source, with Filipinos comprising nearly one-quarter of the total Asian immigration. In the 1961 to 1965 period, fewer than 16,000 Filipinos immigrated to the United States, compared to more than 210,000 in the 1981 to 1985 period. Since 1979 over 40,000 Filipinos have been admitted annually, making the Philippines the second-largest source of all immigration, surpassed only by Mexico. Overall, the post-1965 Filipino immigrants constitute a relatively affluent group: in 1990 more than half joined the ranks of managers and professionals; their median household income exceeded that of all Americans and even that of whites; and the percentage of Filipino college graduates was twice that of all Americans. As Zhou and Gatewood (2000) report, many Filipino immigrants to the United States are college graduates with transferable job skills.

Unlike European or other Asian groups, Filipinos come from a homeland that was once a U.S. colony. Therefore, the Filipino American history of immigration and settlement can best be understood within the context of the colonial and postcolonial association between the Philippines and the United States. Since the 1960s the Philippines has sent the largest number of professional immigrants to the United States, the majority of whom are physicians, nurses, and other health-related practitioners (Rumbaut 1991). The overrepresentation of health professionals among contemporary Filipino immigrants is not accidental; it is the result of a U.S.-built economic infrastructure in the Philippines that proved to be ill suited to the needs of the local populace. During the 1960s, responding to the needs of the United States in its ongoing war effort in Vietnam, the Philippines (over)developed medical and nursing programs to provide personnel to care for the military and civilian casualties in Vietnam. This health professional educational infrastructure remained in place after the Vietnam War had ended and has continued to produce a surplus of physicians and nurses, many of whom migrate to the United States (Liu and Cheng 1994). The migration of Filipino health professionals was also a direct response to deliberate recruitment by U.S. hospitals, nursing homes, and health organizations seeking to address their perennial shortage of medical personnel.

In particular, the Philippines has become the major source of foreign-trained nurses in the United States, with at least 25,000 Filipino nurses arriving between 1996 and 1985. In fact, many women in the Philippines study nursing in the hope of securing employment abroad, and many of the nursing programs in the Philippines accordingly orient themselves toward supplying the U.S. market (Ong and Azores 1994). Again, the migration of Filipina nurses has to be understood within the context of U.S. colonialism. In the first book-length study of Filipina nurses in the United States, Catherine Choy (2003) argues that the development of this mobile labor force is inextricably linked to the history of U.S. imperialism and the early-twentieth-century U.S. colonization of the Philippines. The establishment of Americanized professional nursing training in the Philippines during the U.S. colonial period lay the professional, social, and cultural groundwork for a feminized, highly educated, and exportable labor force (Choy 2003, 42). In the early twentieth century, as U.S.-sponsored scholars, Filipina nurse migrants constituted a unique sector of the Philippine intellectual elite. In the midtwentieth century, as exchange visitors to the United States under the auspices of the Exchange Visitor Program, they became Philippine cultural ambassadors in the United States, and then U.S. nursing ambassadors upon their return to the Philippines. Like the early-twentieth-century scholarship programs to the United States, such as the "pensionado" programs, the Exchange Visitor Program reconstructed a global, cultural, and intellectual hierarchy in which U.S. educational, political, and medical institutions—both in the Philippines and in the United States—were deemed superior to those of the Philippines.[6] By the 1960s Filipina nurses entered the United States through two major avenues: the Exchange Visitor Program and the new occupational preference categories of the Immigration Act of 1965.

Vietnamese: The Refugees

Unlike Filipino and most other contemporary immigrants, the Vietnamese were pushed out of their country and forced to leave without adequate preparation and with little control over their final destinations. Because refugees are less likely to be a self-selected labor force than economic migrants, their numbers include many unemployables: young children, the elderly, religious and political leaders, and people in poor mental and physical condition (Portes and Rumbaut 1990). They are also less likely to have acquired readily transferable skills and are more likely to have made investments (in training and education) specific to the country of origin. For example, significant numbers of Southeast Asian military personnel possess skills for which there is no longer a market in the United States. In a discussion of the economic diversity within Asian America, Evelyn Hu-DeHart (1999, 17) refers to Vietnamese and other Southeast Asian Americans as "the Other Asian America": "'traumatized' immigrants who do not arrive with families intact, and do not come armed with social skills and human capital that can be readily adapted to modern American society." Zhou and Gatewood (2000, 16) concur: "Southeast Asian refugees . . . were pushed out of their homelands by force and suffer tremendous postwar trauma and social displacement, compounded by a lack of education and professional skills, which negatively affects their resettlement."

The Vietnamese are the largest of the refugee groups to have settled in the United States since the mid-1970s. Their arrival is primarily the result of U.S. military intervention in Southeast Asia. I will not rehearse here the violent history of U.S. engagement in the Vietnam War, except to point out that the U.S. desire to contain the spread of communism in Southeast Asia rendered Vietnam completely dependent on U.S. financial and material assistance for its military, its administration, and its economy (Viviani 1984, 13). Soon after the withdrawal of U.S. troops from Vietnam in April 1975, the North Vietnamese took over South Vietnam, triggering an exodus of refugees who fled the country by sea, land, and air. Influenced by the pervasive American presence in their countries in the decade before 1975, some 135,000 Southeast Asian refugees—95 percent of whom were Vietnamese—fled to the United States that year. The number of refugees dropped to 15,000 in 1976 and 7,000 in 1977. Starting in 1978, a more heterogeneous second wave of refugees—the "boat people"—started streaming into the United States. Annual arrivals jumped from 20,574 in 1978 to 76,521 in 1979, to 163,799 in 1980. Their exodus was triggered by continued conflict, natural disasters, and deteriorating economic conditions in Vietnam and also by the legacy of thirty years of warfare, which "demolished cities, destroyed farmland, denuded forests, poisoned water sources, and left countless unexploded mines" (Chan 1991, 157). By 1990 Vietnamese Americans numbered over 615,000, constituting almost 10 percent of the nation's Asian American population.

The Vietnam War (as well as the Korean War) was a major direct and indirect contributor to the supply of working-class Asian immigrants. With the exception of the relatively small elite group who left at the fall of Saigon, most of the refugees lacked education, job skills, and measurable economic resources (Zhou 2001). In addition, the post-1978 refugees had suffered terrible tragedies under the new Communist regimes, survived brutal journeys to neighboring countries, and endured prolonged stays in refugee camps where they received little education and/or job training prior to their resettlement in the United States. Once in the United States, almost all of the refugees started out on public assistance (Zhou 2001, 188). Although their economic situation has improved over the years, the Vietnamese are still heavily concentrated in minimum-wage jobs and still disproportionately rely on public assistance to survive. By 1990 the poverty rate of the Vietnamese stood at 25 percent, down from 28 percent in 1980 but still substantially higher than the national average (Zhou 2001).

Using the Filipino and Vietnamese cases as examples, I argue that different circumstances of exit—the product of different types of U.S. engagement in their respective countries—have shaped the size and timing of migration and the socioeconomic composition of different Asian groups and thus have profoundly affected the process of group formation and differentiation in the United States. Given their divergent migration histories and disparate economic backgrounds, Asian groups from different ends of the class spectrum—such as Filipino Americans and Vietnamese Americans—have few material reasons to come together under the pan-Asian umbrella. Moreover, existing evidence indicates that pan-Asian organizations often reproduce these national and ethnic hierarchies as class and organizational hierarchies. In an ethnographic study of an Asian panethnic community agency in northern California, Eileen Otis (2001) reports that national hierarchies with roots in U.S. colonial and neocolonial relations were reproduced in the distribution of staff positions in the agency, with individuals from more economically developed countries—that is, countries that were most closely tied to the United States—obtaining the coveted staff positions. With the exception of one staff member who came to the United States from Vietnam as a child, all of the staff members were from Asian "Tigers" or "developed" East Asian countries. Otis (2001, 362) concludes that "it was no accident that those from countries with the strongest neocolonial ties to the U.S. obtained these positions, since individuals from countries like Hong Kong, Taiwan, and Thailand tend to have more opportunities to develop English language skills."

PAN-ASIAN NATIONAL AND TRANSNATIONAL POSSIBILITIES

As we begin the twenty-first century, the Asian American community is at a crossroads: how is it to build pan-Asian solidarity amid increasing internal diversities and amid an increasingly racially polarized U.S. society? As I have argued here, Asian American panethnicity is a socially constructed identity that emerged in large part from the violence of racism and imperialism to contest and disrupt these structures of inequality and domination. But it is also a contested category, encompassing not only cultural differences but also social, political, and economic inequalities. In the past two decades underrepresented groups within the pan-Asian coalition have decried the dangers of an Asian American cultural and political agenda that erases differences or tokenizes and patronizes its less dominant members (Strobel 1996; Misir 1996; Nguyen 2002). But pan-Asian possibilities also abound. Since panethnic identities are self-conscious products of political choice and actions, I provide here examples of instances where Asian Americans have made conscious choices to organize politically across difference.

The growing population of bi- and multiracial Asian Americans poses an immediate challenge to pan-Asianism. On the other hand, some existing evidence suggests that the growth in the population of multiracial Asians need not spell the end of pan-Asian-ism. For example, in their analyses of Asian American intermarriages from 1980 and 1990 census data, Larry Hajime Shinagawa and Gin Yong Pang (1996, 140–41) report a prominent countertrend toward pan-Asian interethnic marriages, regardless of gender, nativity, region, and generation: "For a span of ten years (1980 to 1990), nationally and for California, the number of Asian interethnic marriages approaches or now exceeds interracial marriages. Meanwhile, interethnic marriages for Asian Pacific men increased from 21.1 percent in 1980 to 64 percent in 1990, and for women from 10.8 percent to 45.5 percent." They attribute this rise to a combination of factors, including the large population increases and concentrations of Asian Americans, their growing similarities in socioeconomic attainment and middle-class orientation, and their growing racial consciousness in an increasingly racially stratified U.S. society.

But what of the multiracial children? According to the 2000 U.S. census, approximately 850,000 people reported that they were Asian and white, and 360,000 reported that they were two or more Asian groups (Barnes and Bennett 2000, table 4). While there exist no comprehensive data on the racial identification of multiracial Asians, the close contact with Asian American advocacy groups maintained by the Hapa Issues Forum (HIF)—a national multiracial Asian American organization—suggests that multiracial Asian and pan-Asian identities need not be mutually exclusive. From its inception, HIF has pursued a double political mission: pushing for recognition of multi-racial Asians as well as for the civil rights agendas of existing Asian American groups. These two goals are most evident in the group's response to the controversy over the classification of multiracials in the 2000 census. Denouncing the government's past attempts to wedge mixed-race Americans into one rigid racial category, most main-stream multiracial groups favored adding a "multiracial" category to the 2000 census. However, most civil rights groups, including many pan-Asian groups, argued that such a category would dilute the numbers of people who identify with a particular race and cause their respective communities to lose hard-won gains in civil rights, education, and electoral arenas (Espiritu 2001, 31). Refusing this "splitting" of their multiple personal and political identities, HIF's board of directors rejected the "stand-alone multiracial" category and endorsed the "check more than one" format, contending that the latter option would allow them to identify as multiracial *and* "still be counted with their Asian American brethren and sisters" (King 2000, 202). In other words, the "check more than one" format would allow the data to be collected in a way that recognized the existence of multiracial Asians and still make it possible to use the data in "the five racial category format to track discrimination against Asian Americans" (King 2000, 202).

Asian American activists have also engaged in *proactive* efforts to draw together Asian Americans of different classes to organize against anti-Asian racism, defined not as random attacks against Asians but as a product of structural oppression and every-day encounters (Kurashige 2000, 15). The activities of the Asian Americans United, a panethnic community-based organization in Philadelphia, provide an example (Kurashige 2000). When large numbers of Southeast Asian immigrants began experiencing problems in Philadelphia with racist violence, educational inequality, and poor housing, a small group of educated East and South Asian American activists responded. Modeling themselves after the militant Yellow Seeds organization in the 1970s, group members insisted on anti-imperialist politics, a critique of racism as institutional and structural, and a focus on activist organizing and politics. They organized a successful rent strike and were part of a victorious legal campaign to institute bilingual education in the local schools. Most important, they sought to build relationships with working-class Southeast Asian communities by creating a youth leadership training program organized around a pan-Asian identity and radical politics. When a violent attack on Southeast Asian youths in that city by a group of white youths led to a fight that left one of the white attackers dead, city police and prosecutors portrayed the attackers as victims and laid the responsibility for the violence at the hands of the Southeast Asians. Although unable to secure full justice in the court cases that ensued, Asian Americans United seized on the incident as a means of educating its constituency about institutionalized racism. The group succeeded in mobilizing parts of the Asian American community around these efforts, and its success enabled it to move from panethnic to interethnic affiliation through an alliance with a Puerto Rican youth group also plagued by hate crimes, police brutality, and prosecutorial racism (Espiritu et al. 2000, 132). This example suggests that class need not be a source of cleavage among Asian Americans, and that the concerns of working-class Asian Americans *can* unite people at the grassroots level with class-conscious members of the intellectual and professional strata (Kurashige 2000).

Given our globalizing world and the resultant demographic changes, the construction of an Asian American identity is no longer situated—if indeed it ever was—only within Asian America but also through relations and struggles with other communities of color. Today working-class immigrants of diverse backgrounds coexist with African American and U.S.-born Latinos in urban communities across the country. This "social geography of race" has produced new social subjects and new coalitions. For example, young Laotian women in northern California joined Chinese and Japanese Americans in panethnic struggles against anti-Asian racism and also against the "neighborhood race effects" of underfunded schools, polluted air and water, and low-wage jobs that they and their families share with their African American, Latino, Arab American, and poor white neighbors (Espiritu et al. 2000; Shah 2002). In the same way, recognizing their common histories of political fragmentation and disfranchisement, Japanese, Chinese, and Mexicans in the San Gabriel Valley of Los Angeles County formed political alliances to work together on the redistricting and reapportionment process in the Valley (Saito 1998, 10).

Finally, given the internationalization and feminization of the labor force in recent decades, some Asian women in the United States *and* in Asia have begun to conceive of themselves as similarly situated racial, gendered, and classed subjects. The dominance of women in contemporary immigration reflects the growth of female-intensive industries in the United States, particularly in services, health care, microelectronics, and apparel manufacturing. To escape the tightening labor market, employers in the United States have opted either to shift labor-intensive processes to less-developed countries or to import migrant labor, especially female, to fill low-wage, insecure assembly and service-sector jobs (Lim 1983, Hossfeld 1994). Women thus have become a rapidly growing segment of the world's migratory and international workforce (Sacks and Scheper-Hughes 1987).

For post-1965 immigrant women from Asia, their politically insecure status as "alien" and their limited English proficiency have interacted with geographical segregation, racist and sexist hiring practices, and institutional barriers to recertification by U.S. professional boards to narrow greatly their occupational choices. Consequently, many Asian immigrant women, instead of gaining access to a better, more modern, and more liberated life in the United States, have been confined to low-paying service jobs and factory assembly-line work, especially in the garment and microelectronics industries. The similarities in the labor conditions for Asian women here and in Asia, brought about by global capitalism, constitute the "situating grounds for a strategic transnational affiliation" (Kang 1997, 415). Moreover, examples abound of collaboration amongst capitalists *across* geopolitical boundaries. In the case of the garment industry, the small Asian immigrant garment factories in New York and Los Angeles are significant and fairly well integrated components in a globalized production process (Kang 1997). In other words, Asian women working in the garment and electronics factories in major cities in the United States are virtually part of the same labor force as those employed in export-processing zones in Asia or Latin America. Such simultaneous, transnational linkages in Asian women's working conditions—the similarities between exploitive labor conditions for Asian women in Asia and Asian American women in the United States—could disrupt the First World–Third World binary and call attention to their shared lives across geopolitical boundaries (Kang 1997, 429). Since this is the case, the focus on women's labor within the global economy provides *one* means for linking Third World women, immigrant women, and U.S. women of color. The racialized feminization of labor gives rise to a "common context of struggle" among Asian women within, outside, and across the borders of the United States and has resulted in the establishment of numerous cross-border and transnational women's organizations, such as Gabriela, the support committee for Maquiladora workers, and Asian Immigrant Women Advocates (Lowe 1996).

These cross-racial and cross-border alliances and the radical mobilization around gender issues underscore the centrality of "unlikely coalitions" in contemporary political organizing. As Angela Davis (1997, 322) points out, we can accomplish important things in the struggle for social justice if we focus on the creation of "unpredictable or unlikely coalitions grounded in political projects." A complex world requires a complex set of alliances. These unlikely coalitions, including pan-Asian coalitions, along with the antiglobal organizations that are seeking to impose workplace and environmental restraints on multinational corporations and capital, could prove a potent force for social change at both the national and global levels.

CONCLUSION

Since the pan-Asian concept was forged in the late 1960s, the Asian American population has become much more variegated. The post-1965 immigration surge from Asia has fragmented Asian America more clearly than in the past along ethnic, generational, and class lines. This increasing diversity has brought into question the very feasibility and appropriateness of pan-Asian identities and practices, challenging Asian Americans to take seriously the social, political, and economic inequalities that exist within their communities. My main contention in this chapter is that we cannot examine Asian American panethnicity solely in terms of racial politics within the framework of the U.S. nation-state. While important, this framework narrowly focuses on identity politics within Asian America, not on the global politics and power that produced massive displacements and migrations of Asians in the first place. Calling for a critical transnational perspective on the study of panethnicity, I argue instead that different circumstances of exit—the product of different types of U.S. engagement in different Asian countries—have shaped the size and timing of migration and the socioeconomic profile of different Asian groups and thus have profoundly affected their group formation and differentiation in the United States. This approach expands the discussion on pan-

Asian ethnicity by viewing it as an integral part not only of Asian American studies or American studies but also of international and transnational studies. In all, the examples cited in this chapter confirm the plural and ambivalent nature of panethnicity: it is a highly contested terrain on which Asian Americans merge and clash over terms of inclusion but also an effective site from which to forge crucial alliances with other groups both within and across the borders of the United States in their ongoing efforts to effect larger social transformation.

I would like to thank Richard Delgado, Jean Stefancic, Nancy Foner, Josh DeWind, and the participants in the "Immigration, Race, and Ethnicity: Then and Now" workshops for their helpful comments on earlier versions of this chapter.

NOTES

1. For an extended discussion of the critical transnational approach to immigration, see Espiritu (2003). Certainly, I am not the first scholar to apply a critical transnational framework to the study of Asian Americans. Oscar Campomanes (1997), Sucheta Mazumdar (1990), Shirley Hune (1989), and others have written persuasively on the importance of conducting Asian American studies through an "international" frame.

2. For a detailed account of the disputes over the classification of Asian Americans in the 1980 and 1990 censuses, please see Espiritu (1992, ch. 5).

3. According to the 2000 census, 10.2 million reported that they were *only* Asian. An additional 1.7 million people reported that they were Asian and at least one other race (Barnes and Bennett 2002, 3).

4. In 1990 the Japanese American share of the Asian American population was 12 percent, and the five largest Asian American groups were Chinese (23 percent), Filipino (19 percent), Asian Indian (11 percent), Korean (11 percent), and Vietnamese (8 percent).

5. According to the 2000 U.S. census, approximately 850,000 people reported that they were Asian and white, and 360,000 reported that they were two or more Asian groups (Barnes and Bennett 2002, table 4). The debate over the classification of multiracials in the 2000 census often posed the interests of multiracial Asian Americans—the right to claim their full heritage—in opposition to the civil rights needs of pan-Asian America—the possible loss of political clout that is tied to numbers (see Espiritu 2001, 31). Refusing this "splitting," Asian American multiracial organizations rejected the "stand-alone multiracial" category and endorsed the "check more than one" format because the latter would allow them to identify as multiracial *and* "still be counted with their Asian American brethren and sisters" (King 2000, 202). This stance suggests that multiracial Asian and pan-Asian identities need not be mutually exclusive.

6. During U.S. colonization of the Philippines, as part of an effort to acculturate Filipinos and augment their devotion to the United States, the territorial government established the pensionados programs, which sent several hundred individuals (predominantly males) to study in U.S. colleges and universities during the first decade of the twentieth century. Many of the participants in this highly selective program were the children of prominent Filipino families whose loyalty the colonial regime hoped to win (Espiritu 1995, 3).

REFERENCES

Barnes, Jessica, and Claudette E. Bennett. 2002. *The Asian Population 2000*. Washington: U.S. Department of Commerce.

Blauner, Robert. 1972. *Racial Oppression in America*. New York: Harper & Row.

Bonacich, Edna, and Lucie Cheng. 1984. "Introduction: A Theoretical Orientation to International Labor Migration." In *Labor Immigration Under Capitalism: Asian Workers in the United States Before World War II*, edited by Lucie Cheng and Edna Bonacich. Berkeley: University of California Press.

Burawoy, Michael. 1976. "The Functions and Reproduction of Migrant Labor: Comparative Material from Southern Africa and the United States." *American Journal of Sociology* 81(5, March): 1050–87.

Campomanes, Oscar. 1997. "New Formations of Asian American Studies and the Questions of U.S. Imperialism." *Positions* 5(2): 523–50.

Chan, Sucheng. 1991. *Asian Americans: An Interpretive History*. Boston: Twayne.

Choy, Catherine Ceniza. 2003. *Empire of Care: Nursing and Migration in Filipino American History*. Durham, N.C.: Duke University Press.

Daniels, Roger. 1988. *Asian America: Chinese and Japanese in the United States Since 1850*. Seattle: University of Washington Press.

Davis, Angela. 1997. "Interview with Lisa Lowe—Angela Davis: Reflections on Race, Class, and Gender in the USA." In *The Politics of Culture in the Shadow of Capital*, edited by Lisa Lowe and David Lloyd. Durham, N.C.: Duke University Press.

Espiritu, Yen Le. 1992. *Asian American Panethnicity: Bridging Institutions and Identities*. Philadelphia: Temple University Press.

———. 1995. *Filipino American Lives*. Philadelphia: Temple University Press.

———. 1996. "Crossroads and Possibilities: Asian Americans on the Eve of the Twenty-first Century." *Amerasia Journal* 22(2): vii–xii.

———. 2001. "Possibilities of a Multiracial Asian America." In *The Sum of Our Parts: Mixed Heritage Asian Americans*, edited by Teresa Williams-Leon and Cynthia L. Nakashima. Philadelphia: Temple University Press.

———. 2003. *Home Bound: Filipino American Lives Across Cultures, Communities, and Countries*. Berkeley: University of California Press.

Espiritu, Yen Le, and Paul Ong. 1994. "Class Constraints on Racial Solidarity Among Asian Americans." In *The New Asian Immigration in Los Angeles and Global Restructuring*, edited by Paul Ong, Edna Bonacich, and Lucie Cheng. Philadelphia: Temple University Press.

Espiritu, Yen Le, Dorothy Fujita Rony, Nazli Kibria, and George Lipsitz. 2000. "The Role of Race and Its Articulations for Asian Pacific Americans." *Journal of Asian American Studies* 3(2): 127–37.

Hayano, David. 1981. "Ethnic Identification and Disidentification: Japanese-American Views of Chinese Americans." *Ethnic Groups* 3(2): 157–71.

Hossfeld, Karen. 1994. "Hiring Immigrant Women: Silicon Valley's 'Simple Formula.'" In *Women of Color in U.S. Society*, edited by Maxine Baca Zinn and Bonnie Thornton Dill. Philadelphia: Temple University Press.

Hu-DeHart, Evelyn. 1999. "Introduction: Asian American Formations in the Age of Globalization." In *Across the Pacific: Asian Americans and Globalization*, edited by Evelyn Hu-DeHart. Philadelphia: Temple University Press.

Hune, Shirley. 1989. "Expanding the International Dimension of Asian American Studies." *Amerasia Journal* 15(2): xix–xxiv.

Ichioka, Yuji. 1988. *The Issei: The World of the First Generation Japanese Americans, 1885–1924*. New York: Free Press.

Iwasaki, Naomi. 1999. "Pan-Asian What?" *Asian American Revolutionay Movement Ezine,* http://www.aamovement.net/narratives/panasian.html (accessed December 4, 2003).

Kang, Laura Hyun Yi. 1997. "Si(gh)ting Asian/American Women as Transnational Labor." *Positions* 5(2): 403–37.

King, Rebecca Chiyoko. 2000. "Racialization, Recognition, and Rights: Lumping and Splitting Multiracial Asian Americans in the 2000 Census." *Journal of Asian American Studies* 3(2): 191–217.

Kurashige, Scott. 2000. "Panethnicity and Community Organizing: Asian Americans United's Campaign Against Anti-Asian Violence." *Journal of Asian American Studies* 3(2): 163–90.

Ling, Susie Hsiuhan. 1984. "The Mountain Movers: Asian American Women's Movement in Los Angeles." M.A. thesis, University of California at Los Angeles.

Lim, Linda Y. C. 1983. "Capitalism, Imperialism, and Patriarchy: The Dilemma of Third-World Women Workers in Multinational Factories." In *Women, Men, and the International Division of Labor*, edited by June Nash and Maria Patricia Fernandez-Kelly. Albany: State University of New York Press.

Liu, John, and Lucie Cheng. 1994. "Pacific Rim Development and the Duality of Post-1965 Asian Immigration to the United States." In *The New Asian Immigration in Los Angeles and Global Restructuring*, edited by Paul Ong, Edna Bonacich, and Lucie Cheng. Philadelphia: Temple University Press.

Liu, William. 1976. "Asian American Research: Views of a Sociologist." *Asian Studies Occasional Report* 2: whole issue.

Lott, Juanita. 1976. "The Asian American Concept: In Quest of Identity." *Bridge* (November): 30–34.

Lowe, Lisa. 1991. "Heterogeneity, Hybridity, Multiplicity: Marking Asian American Differences." *Diaspora* 1(1, Spring): 25–44.

———. 1996. *Immigrant Acts: On Asian American Cultural Politics*. Durham, N.C.: Duke University Press.

Mazumdar, Sucheta. 1990. "Asian American Studies and Asian Studies: Rethinking Roots." In *Asian Americans: Comparative and Global Perspectives*, edited by Shirley Hune et al. Pullman: Washington State University Press.

Misir, Deborah N. 1996. "The Murder of Navroze Mody: Race, Violence, and the Search for Order." *Amerasia Journal* 22(2): 55–76.

Nguyen, Viet Thanh. 2002. *Race and Resistance: Literature and Politics in Asian America*. New York: Oxford University Press.

Omatsu, Glenn. 1994. "'The Four Prisons' and the Movements of Liberation: Asian American Activism from the 1960s to the 1990s." In *The State of Asian America: Activism and Resistance in the 1990s*, edited by Karin Aguilar-San Juan. Boston: South End.

Omi, Michael. 1993. "Out of the Melting Pot and into the Fire: Race Relations Policy." In *The State of Asian Pacific Americans: Policy Issues to the Year 2000*. Los Angeles: LEAP Asian Pacific American Public Policy Institute and UCLA Asian American Studies Center.

Omi, Michael, and Howard Winant. 1986. *Racial Formation in the United States: From the 1960s to the 1980s*. New York: Routledge & Kegan Paul.

Ong, Aihwa. 1996. "Citizenship as Subject Making: New Immigrants Negotiate Racial and Ethnic Boundaries." *Current Anthropology* 25(5): 737–62.

Ong, Paul. 1989. "California's Asian Population: Past Trends and Projections for the Year 2000." Los Angeles: Graduate School of Architecture and Urban Planning.

———. 2000. "The Asian Pacific American Challenge to Race Relations." In *The State of Asian Pacific Americans: Transforming Race Relations*, edited by Paul Ong. Los Angeles: LEAP Asian Pacific American Public Policy Institute and UCLA Asian American Studies Center.

Ong, Paul, and Tania Azores. 1994. "The Migration and Incorporation of Filipino Nurses." In *The New Asian Immigration in Los Angeles and Global Restructuring*, edited by Paul Ong, Edna Bonacich, and Lucie Cheng. Philadelphia: Temple University Press.

Ong, Paul, and Evelyn Blumenberg. 1994. "Welfare and Work Among Southeast Asians." In *The State of Asian Pacific Americans: Economic Diversity, Issues, and Policies*, edited by Paul Ong. Los Angeles: LEAP Asian Pacific American Public Policy Institute and UCLA Asian American Studies Center.

Ong, Paul, and Suzanne J. Hee. 1993. "The Growth of the Asian Pacific American Population." In *The State of Asian Pacific Americans: Policy Issues to the Year 2000*. Los Angeles: LEAP Asian Pacific American Public Policy Institute and UCLA Asian American Studies Center.

———. 1994. "Economic Diversity." In *The State of Asian Pacific Americans: Economic Diversity, Issues, and Policies*, edited by Paul Ong. Los Angeles: LEAP Asian Pacific American Public Policy Institute and UCLA Asian American Studies Center.

Otis, Eileen. 2001. "The Reach and Limits of Asian Panethnic Identity: The Dynamics of Gender, Race, and Class in a Community-Based Organization." *Qualitative Sociology* 24(3, Fall): 349–79.

Petras, James. 1978. *Critical Perspectives of Imperialism and Social Class in the Third World*. New York: Monthly Review Press.

Portes, Alejandro. 1978. "Migration and Underdevelopment." *Politics and Society* 8: 1–48.

Portes, Alejandro, and Rubén Rumbaut. 1990. *Immigrant America: A Portrait*. Berkeley: University of California Press.

Rumbaut, Rubén. 1991. "Passages to America: Perspectives on the New Immigration." In *America at Century's End*, edited by Alan Wolfe. Berkeley and Los Angeles: University of California Press.

Sacks, Karen, and Nancy Scheper-Hughes. 1987. "Introduction." *Women's Studies* 13(3): 175–82.

Saito, Leland. 1998. *Race and Politics: Asian Americans, Latinos, and Whites in a Los Angeles Suburb*. Urbana and Chicago: University of Illinois Press.

Sassen, Saskia. 1992. "Why Migration." *Report on the Americas* 26(1, July): whole issue.

Shah, Bindi. 2002. "Making the 'American' Subject: Culture, Gender, Ethnicity, and the Politics of Citizenship in the Lives of Second-Generation Laotian Girls." Ph.D. diss., University of California at Davis.

Shankar, Rajiv. 1998. "Foreword: South Asian Identity in Asian America." In *A Part, Yet Apart: South Asians in Asian America*, edited by Lavina Dhingra Shankar and Rajini Srikanth. Philadelphia: Temple University Press.

Shinagawa, Larry Hajime, and Gin Yong Pang. 1996. "Asian American Panethnicity and Intermarriage." *Amerasia Journal* 22(2): 127–52.

Smith, James P., and Barry Edmonston, eds. 1997. *The New Americans: Economic, Demographic, and Fiscal Effects of Immigration*. Washington, D.C.: National Academy Press.

Strobel, Leny Mendoza. 1996. "'Born-Again Filipino': Filipino American Identity and Asian American Panethnicity." *Amerasia Journal* 22(2): 31–54.

Takaki, Ronald. 1989. *Strangers from a Different Shore: A History of Asian Americans*. Boston: Little, Brown.

U.S. Department of Commerce. U.S. Census Bureau. 2002. "Coming to America: A Profile of the Nation's Foreign Born (2000 Update)." *Census Briefs: Current Population Survey, February 2002*. Washington: U.S. Census Bureau.

U.S. Immigration and Naturalization Service (USINS). 1997. *Statistical Yearbook of the Immigration and Naturalization Service, 1995*. Washington: U.S. Government Printing Office.

Viviani, Nancy. 1984. *The Long Journey: Vietnamese Migration and Settlement in Australia*. Carlton, Victoria: Melbourne University Press.

Wong, Paul. 1972. "The Emergence of the Asian-American Movement." *Bridge* 2(1): 33–39.

Zhou, Min. 1999. "Coming of Age: The Current Situation of Asian American Children." *Amerasia Journal* 25(1): 1–27.

———. 2001. "Straddling Different Worlds: The Acculturation of Vietnamese Refugee Children." In *Ethnicities: Children of Immigrants in America*, edited by Rubén G. Rumbaut and Alejandro Portes. Berkeley: University of California Press.

Zhou, Min, and James V. Gatewood. 2000. "Introduction: Revisiting Contemporary Asian America." In *Contemporary Asian America: A Multidisciplinary Reader*, edited by Min Zhou and James V. Gatewood. New York: New York University Press.

Zolberg, Aristide. 1986. "International Factors in the Formation of Refugee Movement." *International Migration Review* 20(2, Summer): 151–69.

Part IV

Socioeconomic Profiles and Trends

Richard Alba and Nancy Denton

Chapter 11

Old and New Landscapes of Diversity:
The Residential Patterns of Immigrant Minorities

An analysis of the residential patterns of immigrants to the United States at the beginning and end of the twentieth century of necessity involves comparing the differences in immigrant streams, the racial hierarchy, and places of residence. All three elements changed over the century and interacted with each other to affect immigrants' residential opportunities. At the broadest level, we argue that the trend for immigrants and for the racial hierarchy has been toward greater heterogeneity and toward a loosening of once more rigid structures, while for places of residence, despite greater diversity at the neighborhood level, there has been a hardening of the urban residential structure. These changes, we argue further, have important implications for the sustainability of cultural diversity and of some racial-ethnic boundaries. Our discussion focuses on how the differences in the immigrants' countries of origin, race-ethnicity, and human capital affect their residential location. Similarly, our discussion of the racial hierarchy focuses on how it is applied in the residential setting; we argue that despite continued segregation, particularly of African Americans, the racial residential order is considerably less rigid now, and certain immigrants arguably do as well as non-Hispanic whites, the ethnic-racial majority group.

At first glance, cities would seem to have shown a similar increase in heterogeneity, and residential opportunities for immigrants would thus seem to have been expanded. However, at the neighborhood level these opportunities are now located in a more rigid locational structure, owing to the weight of the history of city settlement and the fact that many immigrant gateway cities occupy fixed and densely built-up areas. In short, the places into which immigrants settle now are increasingly established. Current immigrants do not have the option of inventing or fashioning or building cities, but rather must settle in them and possibly reshape them. That is quite a different process.

Another plane of our discussion examines what we view as three fundamental patterns of immigrant residential incorporation: the spatial-assimilation model, often seen as descriptive of the European American experience but of more limited application today; a pluralistic pattern associated with the establishment and maintenance of spatially defined ethnic communities (of which the ethnic "neighborhood" is a major, but not the exclusive, exemplar); and racialized ghettoization. All three of these templates can be seen in the historical record of immigration: thus, racialized ghettoization applied not only to the West Indian immigrants of the first half of the twentieth century but also to East Asian immigrants. All three are in the mix today, but elements of the patterns may have changed because of the other changes identified here.

THEN

Geographic Distribution of Immigrants

There is little doubt that a comparison of the regional distribution of immigrants then and now reveals two striking differences. First, at the beginning of the twentieth century the concentrations of immigrants strongly favored the Northeast and Midwest, whereas now the two coasts, as well as the Southwest, are the primary immigrant locations. In 1920 over 80 percent of the foreign-born lived in the Northeast and Midwest, while in 1990 fewer than 40 percent lived there and 42 percent lived in the West. Second, the number of immigrants in nonmetropolitan areas was much greater then than now. The declining proportion of the population in agriculture, combined with the industrial and post-industrial economy, means that for the most part immigrants today locate in metropolitan areas, whereas at the turn of the twentieth century a small but sizable proportion were able to locate in small towns and rural areas. The largest cities were home to just under half of the foreign-born in 1920.

Even within the urban United States immigrants went to more places then than now. In 1920 just over 13 percent of the U.S. population was foreign-born, but table 11.1 shows that forty-seven of the sixty-eight cities that had a population of at least 100,000 had foreign-born populations that exceeded that percentage. In addition, more cities had high representations of foreign-born compared to now. New Bedford, Massachusetts, stands at the top of the list, with over 42 percent of its population foreign-born, followed by New York with 36 percent. Fall River and Lowell, Massachusetts; Paterson, New Jersey; Bridgeport, Connecticut; and Boston all had about one-third of their populations foreign-born in 1920. Specific cities were also associated with specific groups. According to James Olson (1994, 115), most eastern European Jews and Italians located in the cities of the Northeast, especially New York. Of the more than four million Italians, for instance, most

> settled in urban centers from Boston to Norfolk; perhaps 15 percent located in cities along the Great Lakes out to Chicago. Invariably they chose to live close to one another. If relatives were living in Lowell, Massachusetts, the immigrant would try to find them, live with them for a while, and take a job in a local textile mill where other family members worked. If an immigrant was the first of his family to come to America, he would usually seek out companions from his own region of Italy.

Eastern European Catholics and the Orthodox, by comparison, were more concentrated in the industrial cities along the Great Lakes. Though there were more than one thousand Polish immigrant colonies, according to Olson (1994), Poles were mostly concentrated in the major industrial cities of the Midwest—in Chicago above all, but also in Detroit, Milwaukee, Buffalo, Cleveland, and Pittsburgh. Pennsylvania was the initial home to the majority of Slovak, Russian, and Ukrainian immigrants. Cleveland was a center for Slovenians, while Bohemians and Croats settled in Chicago.

Urban Immigrant Settlement

While many immigrants settled in rural areas and small towns at the turn of the last century, those arriving in the first decades of the century primarily settled in urban areas, much as they do now. According to Kenneth Jackson (1985, 70), 90 percent of

TABLE 11.1   Top Cities of Immigrant Concentration, 1920

City (Population of 100,000 or More)	Number of Foreign-Born	Percentage of Population
New Bedford, Mass.	51,078	42.1%
New York, N.Y.	2,028,160	36.1
Fall River, Mass.	42,421	35.2
Lowell, Mass.	38,116	33.8
Paterson, N.J.	45,242	33.3
Bridgeport, Conn.	46,782	32.6
Boston, Mass.	242,619	32.4
Cambridge, Mass.	33,296	30.4
Cleveland, Ohio	240,173	30.1
Chicago, Ill.	808,558	29.9
Worcester, Mass.	53,527	29.8
Hartford, Conn.	40,912	29.6
Providence, R.I.	69,895	29.4
San Francisco, Calif.	149,195	29.4
Detroit, Mich.	290,884	29.3
New Haven, Conn.	46,124	28.4
Newark, N.J.	117,549	28.4
Yonkers, N.Y.	25,796	25.8
Seattle, Wash.	80,976	25.7
Jersey City, N.J.	76,294	25.6
Youngstown, Ohio	33,945	25.6
Trenton, N.J.	30,168	25.3
Springfield, Mass.	31,461	24.3
Milwaukee, Wisc.	110,160	24.1
Rochester, N.Y.	71,411	24.1
Buffalo, N.Y.	121,824	24.0
Minneapolis, Minn.	88,248	23.2
Oakland, Calif.	49,895	23.1
San Antonio, Tex.	36,824	22.8
Philadelphia, Penn.	400,744	22.0
St. Paul, Minn.	51,722	22.0
Los Angeles, Calif.	122,131	21.2
Grand Rapids, Mich.	28,427	20.7
Scranton, Penn.	28,587	20.7
Pittsburgh, Penn.	120,792	20.5
Portland, Oreg.	49,778	19.3
Syracuse, N.Y.	32,383	18.9
Omaha, Neb.	35,645	18.6
Akron, Ohio	38,021	18.2
Camden, N.J.	20,354	17.5
Salt Lake City, Utah	19,897	16.8

(*Table continues on p. 240.*)

TABLE 11.1   *Continued*

City (Population of 100,000 or More)	Number of Foreign-Born	Percentage of Population
Spokane, Wash.	17,096	16.4%
Toledo, Ohio	38,296	15.7
Albany, N.Y.	17,695	15.6
Denver, Colo.	38,230	14.9
Wilmington, Del.	16,337	14.8
St. Louis, Mo.	103,626	13.4
Total	6,281,294	—
Percentage of national total	45.1%	13.2
National total	13,920,692	—

Source: Authors' compilation.

new arrivals at Ellis Island in 1910 became urbanites in America, although the European origins of the majority lay in the countryside. So the urban landscape was still the locale in which most immigrants had to make their place. However, there is little doubt that immigrants then faced a very different urban environment in a myriad of ways from that of today. Perhaps most important, cities at the beginning of the twentieth century were overwhelmingly places characterized by growth: growth in population and expansion in geographical space. Neither of these components of growth is present to any degree in many cities at the beginning of the twenty-first century.

During the last decades of the nineteenth century, city after city sought to extend its boundaries through annexations, and as a result, grew steadily larger in both area and population, over and above the population growth provided by immigration (Monkkonen 1988, 5–6). In fact, it can be argued that part of the impetus for annexation was immigration, given the low regard in which the native whites held the new immigrants, to say nothing of the southern blacks who began arriving soon after them (Jackson 1985, 150). This experience of dramatic growth colors, in ways we do not always acknowledge, the ability of immigrants to adapt to life in their new country. To appreciate the importance of annexation, consider that without it none of the largest cities, with the exception of New York, would have reached a population of one million people. The most significant annexations involved the three largest cities: New York, Chicago, and Philadelphia. Philadelphia's mammoth annexation in 1854, whereby it expanded from 2 to 130 square miles and quadrupled its population, is still the largest in U.S. history. Chicago added 133 square miles on the South Side in 1889, at the time gaining a quarter-million residents, a number that quadrupled in the next three decades. New York's consolidation in 1898 saw it grow from 44 to 300 square miles and add almost two million people. The story is similar in many other cities, both large and small (Orum 1995).

All this expansion provided places for the immigrants to live, though often indirectly, as city residents moved to the suburbs, freeing up urban housing. In addition, the expansion, which required the building of better services to the outlying areas— sewers, roads, and so on—along with new housing, frequently provided a source of jobs. Virginia Yans-McLaughlin (1971, 39) writes that many Italian immigrants took outdoor jobs in construction in Buffalo: "Hundreds took positions as excavators, hod carriers, bricklayers, assistants to skilled workers; a few fortunate craftsmen obtained work in the higher ranks of the building trades. . . . Italians labored as street cleaners, garbage collectors, or street maintenance men."

Moreover, cities were undergoing fundamental changes in their social and economic organization that had an impact on the possibilities for immigrant settlement and segregation. By the last two decades of the nineteenth century, many cities were in transition from an early industrial pattern of organization to a mature industrial one, involving greater specialization of land use. Industrial and commercial spaces were increasingly separated from the residential areas of the native white middle class, and the walking city of the midnineteenth century gave way to one in which an increasing proportion of the population made use of emerging systems of mass transportation, such as trolleys and trains. Indeed, the era of the automobile was imminent. In the environs of New York, for example, six major highways (the Long Island Motor Parkway, Bronx River Parkway, Hutchinson River Parkway, Saw Mill River Parkway, Cross County Expressway, and Henry Hudson Parkway), as well as the George Washington Bridge, were built between 1906 and 1934 (Jackson 1985, 166).

The midnineteenth-century walking city imposed some ecological limits on ethnic segregation, and it has often been observed that, as a consequence, the segregation of the Irish and Germans was not as great as that of the southern and eastern European groups, who arrived later. Walking as a primary mode of transportation privileged the city center, which as the zone of concentration for commercial and industrial activities retained its attractiveness for prosperous native whites. In a common pattern of settlement, their large homes dominated broad avenues while immigrant and other workers lived on side streets and in alleys. This pattern has been described as a result also of the rapid construction of housing to accommodate what seemed at the time to be exponentially growing immigrant and native worker populations; much of this construction "filled in" the many "empty" spaces in the patchwork settlement of the early industrial city. According to the analysis by Theodore Hershberg and his colleagues (1981, 467) of midnineteenth-century Philadelphia, "Irish and German immigrants, 18 and 6 percent of the 1850 population, respectively, were dispersed across the face of the city."

The link between places of work and residence was not immediately broken for the immigrants settling at the end of the nineteenth century. Although the development of systems of mass transportation allowed for the deconcentration of the industrial cities, the first effects were to give new force to Robert E. Park's famous dictum that social distances are mirrored in physical ones. Thus, the increasing efficiency of mass transportation such as trolleys drawn along rails by horses permitted some among the native middle classes and among the more successful members of earlier immigrant groups to move away from the city center, although socially exclusive sections remained a prominent feature of downtown areas in many cities. But as of 1880 only about one-seventh of Philadelphia's population could afford to ride to work. Hence, the new immigrants usually settled near places of work in dense concentrations. Social segregation by socioeconomic status and ethnic origin became firmly established as a consequence, and the now-classic social topography of the mature industrial American city of the early twentieth century began to emerge.

Ethnic Segregation

One feature of this topography was the ethnic neighborhood (or colony), known, depending on the group, as "Little Italy," "Corktown," or "Little Warsaw." These were areas not only of population concentration but also of ethnic institutional infrastruc-ture: stores catering to the needs of the ethnic group (for example, specialty foods); mutual aid societies, which were important to the immigrants because they insured immigrants against risks beyond the financial capabilities of individual families (for example, burial expenses); and churches and synagogues. The development of these areas owed something to the ethnic concentrations of the urban labor market (Glazer and Moynihan 1963/1970). Chain migration also played a part as the earlier-arriving immigrants found lodging for their kin and neighbors who came afterward. This con-tributed to a sort of microsegregation as in some of these neighborhoods—the pattern has been particularly noted for Little Italys—concentrations of immigrants from spe-cific towns and regions could be found on certain streets (Foner 2000; Gabaccia 1984; Yans-McLaughlin 1971).

This ethnic neighborhood was not invented in the late nineteenth century, of course. It is prefigured in the Irish slums of the midnineteenth century in larger cities such as Boston and New York. As Oscar Handlin (1972) describes the pattern, Boston's famine-era Irish immigrants clustered in a few neighborhoods, such as the North End, that were near the wharves and mills. Their poverty, to say nothing of very long work-days, kept the great majority from moving far from work sites. These areas quickly became frightful slums as property owners converted existing buildings, which included what had once been elegant mansions, into tenements to house as many families as possible and exploited any available space to put up jerry-rigged sheds and shanties. In the 1840s and 1850s the sewage systems in the congested immigrant areas were primi-tive, and they and the congestion facilitated high rates of mortality from communicable diseases, along with the occasional epidemic, such as the cholera wave of 1849 that claimed mostly Irish victims. The sociability needs of the immigrants were served by numerous grog shops, which were not infrequently located in cellars.

But Boston's Irish slums represent the extreme end of the spectrum of midnine-teenth-century immigrant settlement. The conditions were so deplorable that any native-born American who could afford to live elsewhere did so. The same seems to have been true of other immigrant groups of that era, such as the Germans; Handlin's maps (1972, 92) show them to be distributed throughout the city, with little concentra-tion in the heavily Irish areas.

Segregation seems to have been more pervasive in the late nineteenth and early twentieth centuries. By a standard measure of segregation, the index of dissimilarity, the segregation of some of the southern and eastern European groups from native whites was quite high, considerably higher than that of northern and western European groups at a comparable point in their immigration. The values are all the more remark-able because the areal unit for which they can be calculated—the city ward—is consid-erably larger than the modern census tract; from a mathematical point of view, as the size of the areal unit increases (in population terms), the value of the index is de-pressed. In the Boston of 1880, for example, the population of 363,000 was divided among just twenty-five wards. Yet the index of dissimilarity for Italians (compared to native whites) was .74, while those for Poles and Russians, respectively, were .62 and .54 (Lieberson 1963, 78–79). By contrast, the segregation value for the largest immi-grant group in Boston at that time, the Irish, was just .15, although that for the Ger-mans was .31. Stanley Lieberson believes that the segregation of the Irish and Germans was probably as high during the early phases of their immigration, but his data do not seem supportive. Boston's population of 1850 was divided among just twelve wards, and this would certainly tend to lower the index. But the value for the Irish was .21, well below the segregation level of the "colored" population, .51. In 1880 the segregation value for African Americans had not changed, and thus the southern and eastern Europeans were more segregated from the native white population than they were.

Yet the immigrant neighborhoods were, in the main, not ethnically homogeneous. Thomas Lee Philpott's (1978/1991, 136; see also White, Dymowski, and Wang 1994) study of Chicago tells how a long-term resident who remembered her neighborhood as all-Irish and all-Catholic was confronted with the stark reality of the census numbers between 1920 and 1940. When told that her neighborhood housed more Swedes than Irish, who were only 13 percent of the population, and sheltered twenty-six to thirty-three ethnic groups, she replied, "I really don't remember anything but Irish." The immigrant neighborhoods were often places where one group set the tone, dominating in terms of institutions, stores, and services or simply because they were the most visible and voluble. But close inspection of maps, including those used by the Chicago School to support their thesis that all groups lived separately, reveals that there was a distinction between what Philpott calls the "ghetto" and the "slum." Some immigrants lived in slums, but they were not a majority of the residents, and most did not live in these areas. In contrast, blacks made up a much larger part of the areas they lived in, and few lived outside of these ghettoes (Philpott 1978/1991, 141–42).

Segregation figures, though informative, give only the broad overview of what life was like for urban immigrants at the beginning of the century. In particular, their residential segregation represents the culmination of how they managed to fit themselves into the structure of the city. As Lieberson (1963, 5) noted in his classic study *Ethnic Patterns in American Cities*: "The cities were in existence with their patterns of housing and commercial establishments before each wave of immigrants arrived during the great era of foreign migration to our cities. Into this pattern or structure of the city came each group of immigrants and, whatever else they might do in the city, they had to adapt to its structure and order." In seeking housing, immigrants were subject to a number of constraints beyond the desire to live near their kin or other initial contacts.

First and foremost was their poverty. About Italian neighborhoods in Pittsburgh, John Bodnar, Roger Simon, and Michael Weber (1982, 70) write that, in the eyes of some observers, they were occupied by "throngs of greasy, unkempt Italians standing around in front of crazy little grocery stores, jabbering or smoking, while slovenly women with filthy youngsters sit on steps or parade up and down in the street strewn with old vegetables, filthy water, and rubbish of all kinds." In this respect, there was considerable continuity between the slum neighborhoods of the Irish in the midnineteenth century and those that housed many of the southern and eastern Europeans in the first few decades of the twentieth.

Very low incomes meant also that immigrant areas were usually close to major areas of work. In this respect, there was an important contrast between mill and factory towns, where workers' housing surrounded the place of work and had often been built by the employer, and larger cities, such as New York, where the immigrants of a given group worked at multiple sites and for different employers. But since most of the poor could afford car fare only part of the time and walked the rest of the time (Monkkonen 1988, 160), they had to live not far from work sites and close to shopping areas, schools, and places of worship.

Another constraint not to be slighted was discrimination. References to the low esteem and scientific racism applied to the new immigrants by both the immigrants who preceded them and native-born whites are abundant in the literature (Glazer and Moynihan 1963/1970; Higham 1970; Lieberson 1980; Barrett and Roediger 1997).

These racist views not only affected immigrants' ability to be hired but translated into limitations on where they could settle, since many areas were controlled by the Germans and Irish who had preceded them. Bodnar, Simon, and Weber (1982, 70) note that in Pittsburgh, "Poles, blacks and Italians, among the poorest and least desired immigrants, received the least desirable land—that is, the land with the highest density, that with the oldest and most deteriorated housing, or that located on the most formidable terrain."

A part of this discrimination that is often overlooked is the presence of the Ku Klux Klan in many of the cities where the immigrants settled. Often thought of primarily as a rural group, in reality the Klan was very active in urban areas after its rebirth in 1915. And immigrants (along with Catholics, Jews, and Negroes) were an important target of the Klan, which had a "100 percent American" policy. A particular showcase for its activities was the Midwest, which provided the Klan with one-third of its national membership. As Jackson (1967/1992, 90) notes: "[I]t was not the decaying town that provided the basis of Klan growth. The Midwest contained thirteen of the nation's fifty largest cities, and it was here, where the keynote was growth, change, and social unrest, that the keagles found their finest potential for success."

Chicago provides a good example of the Klan's urban operations. Though most places had only one Klan group, Chicago, because of its size, had many. Several were located near the black ghetto, but "the Klan also established healthy chapters in areas threatened ethnically rather than racially, such as Irving Park, South Shore, Logan Square, Austin, Windsor Park, Hermosa, Garfield, and Morgan Park" (Jackson 1992, 96). Though more active in the city, the Klan was also familiar in suburbs: it was stronger in southern suburbs like Harvey, Blue Island, Chicago Heights, Tinley Park, Joliet, Aurora, Berwyn-Cicero, and Oak Park, and weaker on the North Side but present in Wilmette and Waukegan. The Indiana suburbs were even more Klan-ridden. About 1920 Chicago had at least 40,000, and perhaps as many as 80,000, Klan members. They represented only 2 percent of the total city population in 1923. But in the same year only 15 percent of city residents were adult, white, native Protestant males—those eligible for membership. So 13 percent of the population eligible for membership were members. Put another way, one in ten of the adult, white, native Protestant males with whom the immigrants might come in contact in Chicago were Klan members. "On that basis Chicago ranked high as a national center of klankraft" (Jackson 1992, 125–26). In addition to its strength throughout the Midwest, the Klan also enjoyed success, albeit more modest, in the East, particularly in Pennsylvania but also in New Jersey, Maryland, New England, and New York, where the *New York Times* estimated state membership at 200,000 in 1923 (Jackson 1992, 170–84).

In addition to the negative effects on residential choice implied by poverty, discrimination, and the Ku Klux Klan, immigrants also had their residential choices limited by religious factors. These are well known in the cases of religious Jews (who were a minority among Jewish immigrants), since they could not ride to synagogues on the Sabbath. But religion was also a powerful spatial determinant for the many Catholic immigrants. Since the Council of Trent in the sixteenth century, the Catholic Church had had a geographically based conception of a parish, namely, that it served everyone who lived in its borders. Though the nationality parishes developed by the American Church as a way of meeting the needs of an ethnically diverse immigrant stream were freed from this constraint, it was natural for parishioners to live within walking distance of their church. Even if the emphasis on services in one's own language would seem less important when all the sacraments and the bulk of the service were spoken in

Latin, a language known to few in the pews, the immigrants still needed priests who could minister to their personal and social needs in their mother tongue. And from the pulpit, priests regularly urged parishioners to buy houses in the parish (McGreevy 1996, 19).

Spatial Assimilation

The pattern of spatial assimilation by European immigrant groups can be traced back as far as the Irish Catholic immigration of the midnineteenth century. Settled initially in the most run-down and unhealthy sections of cities, Irish immigrant families began to relocate as soon as they could afford to. The extension of the horse railroad throughout the Boston metropolitan region during the 1850s, with a fare capped by its charter, allowed many Irish immigrants to relocate, and they had "inundat[ed] the outskirts of Boston" by the 1860s (Handlin 1972, 96).

This relocation away from areas of first settlement, which generally began with selected members of the first generation and continued into the second, appears quite portentous in retrospect. It was observed by the early-twentieth-century sociologists of the Chicago School, such as Louis Wirth, and eventually elaborated into an abstract model of "spatial assimilation" by Douglas Massey (1985), who argued for its broad application to the settlement processes of immigrants in a variety of societies. The key element of the model was the search by immigrants and/or their children for residential amenities, such as better housing, cleaner and safer streets, and better schools, as they improved their socioeconomic positions and acculturated to the host society. As long as the discriminatory barriers against them were not so high as to keep them out of the neighborhoods of the majority group, it was inevitable in the long run that many would enter them, since these neighborhoods were the most advantaged in a number of ways.

Accordingly, the southern and eastern Europeans did not remain highly segregated for long. Changes were visible even during the first few decades of the twentieth century, when mass immigration was not quite at its end. The changing ecology of the city undoubtedly played a role in easing segregation. The industrial infrastructure no longer needed to be built in the center of cities, and companies now took advantage of the periphery, where inexpensive land was available, to establish large factory complexes, such as the automobile plants of the Detroit region. Systems of mass transit continued to be developed—for example, the then privately owned Interborough Rapid Transit (IRT) system established lines into the Bronx and Brooklyn in the first decade of the new century—and to service larger and larger proportions of the working population, thus loosening if not breaking the link between places of work and residence.

The opening up of large areas of cities for settlement by the ethnic working classes drew many away from the inner-city enclaves. This did not automatically imply a decline in segregation, since the departing members of a group sometimes moved to a common site of secondary settlement, such as the South Bronx and Grand Concourse areas, where many eastern European Jews settled in the couple of decades following the extension of the subway lines.

The availability of large, almost empty areas for development also made homeownership a realistic prospect for many white ethnics. Much has been written about the aspirations of many immigrants, perhaps especially those of rural origins in Europe, to own their own homes, and some historians have argued that to satisfy this aspiration they sacrificed the mobility prospects of their children, who were frequently required to enter the labor market at the earliest possible age in order to contribute to the family's finances. Noting that their occupational success was not great, Yans-McLaughlin (1971, 43) argues that the Italians in Buffalo "had their own standard of achievement, namely, the acquisition of family property, usually a home. And in this sense by the 1920s Italians and their children in Buffalo had indeed reached the promised land." Data from a variety of cities show higher rates of homeownership among immigrants than native-born whites. For example, in Cleveland in 1890 German immigrants had a homeownership rate of just over 50 percent, and the Irish just over 40 percent, compared to a rate of 30 percent for all native-born whites (Kusmer 1976, 288). In some cities during the early twentieth century, half or more of the immigrant households owned their own homes within a few decades of arrival—in Philadelphia in 1930, according to the data in Lieberson (1963), this was true of 69 percent of Italian families and 59 percent of Russians. This did not happen everywhere, however. In Boston, by contrast, the ownership rates in 1930 were just 31 and 24 percent, respectively.

Residential property ownership, including homeownership, was also a means to upward economic mobility. Despite the fact that tenement building was a risky investment, "in working-class neighborhoods of Manhattan at the turn of the century, Slavs, Poles, Italians, Jews, and other ethnic groups were the primary spurs for local tenement development within their own respective communities" (Day 1999, 32). The building of tenement housing was a multistage process, with immigrants not only participating at each stage but moving from managing the buildings to ownership as their savings increased. That this was an option open to small investors is evident in two facts: control of the land available for tenements was not dominated by the elites, and many tenement owners owned only one building (Day 1999). Tenement construction did not require much design or imagination: "[T]housands of small-scale developers used, for all intents and purposes, one or two patterns to build incrementally the housing infrastructure of New York's burgeoning working-class neighborhoods. In the process, many of these investors amassed modest fortunes and moved up the economic ladder" (Day 1999, 31).

The spatial assimilation associated with homeownership and mobility away from enclaves is evident in the decline of segregation in many cities. This happened even before the end of mass immigration in the mid-1920s. Lieberson's (1980) analysis of seventeen leading nonsouthern cities in the early twentieth century shows that, between 1910 and 1920, the segregation of southern and eastern Europeans declined appreciably in most cases. This was at a time when the segregation of African Americans was increasing in many cities, and initially the segregation of some of the European foreign-born, namely, the Italians and Russians, seems to have been greater when their relative population size is taken into account (Lieberson 1980). But the ordering of isolation appears to have been reversed by the close of immigration.

The steadily rising integration of the European ethnics contrasts also with the barriers confronted by non-European groups, immigrant and non-immigrant alike. In the early twentieth century, Mexicans were still in an early phase of their history as an immigrant group, which was accelerated by the upheaval of the Mexican Revolution, starting in 1910. But the immigrants were arriving in territory in the American Southwest in which the Mexican presence predated that of Anglos. Many cities of the region had begun as Mexican and Spanish pueblos, with buildings grouped around central plazas. The arrival of non-Mexicans typically moved the focal point of growth away from these plazas, which then became the kernels of barrios, as occurred in Los Angeles (Sánchez 1993). Other cities of the Southwest, especially along the border, retained Mexican majorities. The residential segregation of Mexicans was highly variable but was usually less than that of other non-Europeans (Grebler, Moore, and Guzman 1970).

The Chinese, by comparison, suffered extreme isolation. Unlike the Europeans and the Mexicans, they confronted a panoply of legal discriminations: the elimination of further immigration after the Chinese Exclusion Act of 1882; the exclusion from citizenship as a result of the racial requirements in naturalization law; the segregation of their children in separate schools in the public school systems on the West Coast; and a variety of local ordinances and laws in California that penalized their customs and practices. Most important, the great majority of them were also prevented from having normal family lives by the consequences of restrictionist legislation. The cumulative effect was to confine them to isolated enclaves, the Chinatowns of cities such as New York and San Francisco, where lonely bachelor immigrants lived out their final years (Nee and Nee 1973).

Most revealing of the residential dynamics experienced by non-Europeans was the increasing ghettoization of African Americans, which occurred at the same moment as the initial signs of spatial assimilation among European immigrants. In all the cities where they settled, the immigrants found an established black population that was beginning to experience the early stages of the "Great Migration"—migrants from the South who were as different from many of them as were the southern central and eastern Europeans from the white population. However, while in 1910 the newer immigrant groups were often more segregated from native whites than were blacks, by 1920 this pattern was reversed (Lieberson 1963, 127). The pattern of higher segregation of blacks than of immigrants persisted from that time forward as black segregation increased more rapidly than their population growth would have predicted (Lieberson 1980). The areas where African Americans lived increasingly took on the character of ghettos from which they could not escape. A number of racist forces conspired to produce these ghettos: discrimination by renters, sellers, and agents; segregation in most domains of social life; legal devices such as the restrictive covenant; and outright violence, which reached a crescendo in the white-on-black race riots of the immediate post–World War I period (Grossman 1989; Massey and Denton 1993; Farley and Frey 1994). By 1930 blacks were about as segregated as it was possible for any group to be, and the whites who lived in or near their concentrations were rapidly departing. Ironically, some of these whites were immigrants. Thus, when Italians and Jews left Harlem in the 1920s and left empty flats for newly arriving blacks to occupy (Osofsky 1971, 129–30), it was a foreshadowing of what would also occur in Boston (Levine and Harmon 1992), Detroit (Sugrue 1996), and elsewhere.

NOW

Geographic Distribution of Immigrants

One of the most noted features of the new immigration is its high degree of concentration in a small number of states and metropolitan areas (Farley 1996; Frey 1996; Portes and Rumbaut 1996; Waldinger 1989). Of the immigrants who came to the United States during the 1990s, two-thirds ended up in only six states: California, New York, Texas, Florida, Illinois, and New Jersey (in order of share). Concentration within specific metropolitan areas is almost as extreme: more than half of the immigrants of the 1990s settled in and around New York City, Los Angeles, San Francisco, Chicago,

Miami, Houston, and Dallas. The new immigration is overwhelmingly urban and suburban, as opposed to rural, in destination, even though a portion of its largest nationality component, Mexicans, is still engaged in agricultural work. As of 2000, only twenty-five of the nation's large metropolitan areas (population of 500,000 or more) have above-average concentrations of the foreign-born in their populations (see table 11.2). These regions account for nearly three-quarters of all immigrants.

Geographic concentration is an inevitable by-product of immigration, which is guided by social networks. Settlement patterns are determined partly by the need of immigrants, unfamiliar with American society and frequently lacking proficiency in English, for assistance from kin and co-ethnics. Even so, the degree of geographic concentration among new immigrant groups appears to exceed that of older ones at a comparable stage. Moreover, its ethnic impact is undoubtedly enhanced by the exodus of a considerable number of U.S.-born Americans, both white and black, from these metropolitan areas, thus intensifying immigrants' relative presence (Frey 1996). Only immigrant groups with a large professional stratum, such as Asian Indians, appear to be exceptions—understandably so, since for professionals job considerations typically override the tendency to settle in ethnic communities and particular regions. Places of settlement are also initially more dispersed for refugees, whose original destination in the United States is usually determined by government agencies and private sponsorship. But secondary migrations tend to bring about greater ethnic concentration, exemplified by Cubans in Miami and Vietnamese in Orange County, California (Gold 1992; Portes and Rumbaut 1996).

However, the concentration of immigrant groups in a small number of metropolitan areas appears incompatible with the rapid growth of ethnic populations that is projected if immigration remains at the current level. The National Research Council suggests in a middle-of-the-road scenario that by 2020 Latinos and Asians, the two racial-ethnic populations receiving the bulk of the new immigration, will account for nearly one-quarter of the population, which represents almost a doubling of their proportion in thirty years (Smith and Edmonston 1997, 116–17). It seems self-evident that these groups cannot remain concentrated in a few states and metropolitan areas if growth occurs on this scale. The data from the 2000 census provide considerable evidence of the dispersal of Mexican and Asian immigrants, who, for instance, are showing up in larger numbers throughout the South, a region that heretofore has received very little immigration. Moreover, the statistics on regional concentration cited earlier are significantly reduced from those of 1990, when, for instance, more than 80 percent of recent immigrants were found in six states. A rigorous analysis of 2000 census data indicates that racial and ethnic diversity is increasing over time in most parts of the United States, implying that the impact of immigration is not limited to the few metropolitan regions that are currently the main reception areas (Lee, Matthews, and Zelinsky 2001). One future possibility is the emergence of a much larger number of immigrant cultural centers, especially of Spanish speakers (Massey 1995). Other areas of the country might begin to resemble the immigrant concentrations presently found in metropolises like Los Angeles, Miami, and New York. Yet the hypothesis that movement away from areas of original settlement tends to be associated with a ratcheting forward of assimilation, which seems generally borne out in the experiences of European-descent groups, is also plausible in application to new immigrant groups. There is some evidence that suggests a moderate deconcentration by the second generation, which would be consistent with the assimilation hypothesis, but no firm conclusion is warranted as yet (Frey and Liaw 1998).

TABLE 11.2   Top Metropolitan Regions of Immigrant Concentration, 2000

Metropolitan Area	Number of Foreign-Born (In Thousands)	Percentage of Population
Areas of 1,000,000 or more		
Miami-Fort Lauderdale, Fla.	1,558	40.2%
Los Angeles-Anaheim-Riverdale, Calif.	5,068	30.9
San Francisco-Oakland-San Jose, Calif.	1,902	27.0
New York-northern New Jersey-Long Island	5,182	24.4
San Diego, Calif.	606	21.5
Houston-Galveston-Brazoria, Tex.	896	19.2
West Palm Beach-Boca Raton, Fla.	197	17.4
Las Vegas, Nev.	258	16.5
Chicago-Gary, Ind.-Lake County, Ill.	1,467	16.0
Dallas-Fort Worth, Tex.	785	15.0
Sacramento-Yolo, Calif.	260	14.5
Phoenix-Mesa, Ariz.	457	14.1
Seattle-Bellevue-Everett, Wash.	332	13.7
Washington, D.C.-Baltimore, Md.	981	12.9
Boston-Worcester-Lawrence, Mass.	721	12.4
Austin-San Marcos, Tex.	153	12.2
Providence-Fall River, Mass.-Warwick, R.I.	143	12.0
Orlando, Fla.	197	12.0
Areas of 500,000 to 1,000,000		
McAllen-Edinburg-Mission, Tex.	168	29.5
El Paso, Tex.	186	27.4
Fresno, Calif.	193	21.0
Stockton-Lodi, Calif.	110	19.5
Honolulu, Hawaii	168	19.2
Bakersfield, Calif.	112	16.9
Tucson, Ariz.	100	11.9
Percentage of national total	71.4	
National total	31,108	11.1

Source: Alba and Nee (2003, 250–51). Reprinted by permission of the publishers from *Remaking the American Mainstream* by Richard Alba and Victor Nee, Cambridge, Mass.: Harvard University Press, copyright © 2003 by the President and Fellows of Harvard College. Source: "The New Americans," Lewis Mumford Center, University at Albany, SUNY; "Census 2000: Demographic Profiles," U.S. Census Bureau.

The Changing Landscape of Immigrant Settlement

Compared to the cities of arrival for the great majority of immigrants in the early part of the twentieth century, places of contemporary settlement could not be more different. Some of the same names remain prominent as immigrant destinations, particularly New York and Chicago, but they share their dominance now with Los Angeles, San Francisco, Miami, Houston, and other western, southern, and southwestern cities in a way not dreamed of in the early 1900s. Moreover, while immigrants' arrival in the early years of the twentieth century followed the era of great geographic expansion of cities, the contemporary inflow follows an expansion only in the newer cities of the Southwest, which were not important in the beginning of the century. Those going to older cities like New York and Chicago are going to cities whose geographic boundaries have changed hardly at all since the early twentieth century.

Yet even when the place names remain the same, the actual geographical entities to which those names refer have changed radically. For city boundaries no longer encompass them. Though by 1920 elites were starting to escape the cities and suburban development was quite noticeable in most cities, immigrants at the end of the twentieth century are coming to metropolitan areas, a term that includes both the city and the suburbs but emphasizes their separateness at the same time. By 1970, five years after the change in immigration law associated with what is known as "the new immigration," more people in the United States lived in suburbs than in cities (Jackson 1985, 284). In fact, a major part of the analysis of immigrant location at the turn of the twenty-first century involves determining which parts of groups are living in the central city or suburban portions of the metropolitan areas to which they are coming (Alba, Logan, Stults, et al. 1999; Foner 2000).

Population growth remains an important component of the analysis of cities, but it is a more complex phenomenon now than then. In the newer cities of the South and West, the population growth of both central cities and suburbs acts in much the same way, as an engine of growth, as it did in the earlier time period, with immigrants contributing to that growth along with other groups. In the older, established cities of the Northeast and Midwest, however, the best that can be hoped for is population growth in the suburban fringe, and the role of the immigrants is to keep city populations from declining—or from declining as much as they would have in the absence of immigration.

But these changes pale in comparison to the rigidity of the local or neighborhood-level structures into which the new immigrants must fit. As Jackson (1985, 304) has noted, "[D]ecisions made in the past impose powerful restraints on the future. The location of buildings, of streets, and of highway systems imposes a measure of permanence on the form of community." Despite what may objectively be described as a lessening of overt prejudice and discrimination against immigrants and people of color compared to the blatant nature of these barriers in the earlier period, the local landscape in many cities is racially coded. Most neighborhoods in the suburbs were established under the racial premise of suburbs for whites and cities for nonwhites, a function not only of individual prejudice and realtor codes but also of government policies such as urban renewal and the Federal Housing Administration (FHA) mortgage program (Hirsch 1993). The color-coding of the urban landscape that was firmly fixed in the organization of metropolitan space during the two decades following World War II remains predominant, even if it has blurred more than a little (Farley and Frey 1994; Massey and Denton 1993; Lewis Mumford Center 2001a). Post-1965 immigrants, despite arriving after the passage of the civil rights acts, are forced to confront a housing market that is defined by race and has been for the last century. Though it was certainly true that the neighborhood choices of the Italians and Irish were constrained in some cities by their ethnicity, those constraints were never absolute, and they weakened steadily as the socioeconomic position of these groups improved. Racial segregation serves to define not only the residential locations of African Americans but also the social and economic value of their neighborhoods, as well as the services and amenities these provide. At least some immigrants of color confront these constraints as well.

Patterns of Segregation

Within the metropolitan areas where they concentrate, immigrants and the second generation appear to be segregated from the majority population to a substantial extent, but no more so than were the immigrant groups of the early twentieth century. "Segregation," as measured by the most conventional measure, the so-called index of dissimilarity, has a specific technical meaning that must be kept in mind: namely, that the spatial distribution of a group (across units such as census tracts) differs from that of a comparison group, often the majority. Such a difference may be produced by the existence of immigrant residential enclaves, where immigrants and their children are surrounded by fellow ethnics and have limited contact with outsiders, or by a dispersal of immigrants to some parts of a region but not others. In the latter case, immigrants may live mainly in the midst of people who differ ethnically from them. Or both patterns may combine for any group.

The existence of ethnic enclaves is an obvious part of the contemporary story, just as it was for the earlier European and East Asian groups. Even though the automobile makes it possible for an individual to live at some distance from ethnic institutions, such as shopping areas and places of worship, and maintain regular contact with them, many group members live in the midst of co-ethnics out of preference or necessity. But like the neighborhoods that arose from European immigration, the areas in which contemporary immigrant groups concentrate are usually not ethnically exclusive. Sometimes they even include many members of the non-Hispanic white majority—for example, the areas in Bergen County, New Jersey, where many Koreans can be found are still home to a population that is heavily white. Yet in a situation of continuing immigration, the degree of ethnic presence in enclave areas cannot be regarded as having reached its maximum. That is, the percentages of immigrant families among residents appear to have increased between 1990 and 2000 for these areas and are likely to continue to increase (Lewis Mumford Center 2001a).

Nevertheless, most studies find moderate levels of segregation for ethnic populations growing from immigration but measure this only for the largest populations—that is, Asians and Latinos. Analysis of 1990 census data for metropolitan regions throughout the United States found that the average index of dissimilarity between Hispanics and non-Hispanics was .43, which is virtually unchanged from the 1980 index calculated in an equivalent way. That of Asians from non-Asians is also .43, representing in this case a slight increase from the 1980 value (.41). By contrast, the average 1990 value for blacks was .64. Another study comparing average segregation index values between 1990 and 2000 found the same pattern of stable segregation levels, although the segregation of Hispanics—calculated this time from non-Hispanic whites—came out higher, around .51 (Farley and Frey 1994; Massey and Denton 1987; Lewis Mumford Center 2001a). Remarkably, there appears to have been little or no increase during the 1980s and 1990s in the segregation of Asians and Hispanics, even though these populations were growing very rapidly because of immigration. The entry of many recently arrived immigrants into areas of ethnic concentration would tend, in the absence of any countertrend, to increase the value of the index of dissimilarity. Thus, the stability of the index values implies that others are entering areas with relatively few co-ethnics; whether they are newly arrived immigrants or those who, after a period in immigrant enclaves, are moving elsewhere cannot be inferred from aggregate data alone.

In this context, we should recognize that the index values for very large population aggregates can conceal higher levels of segregation for specific immigrant groups. For instance, the 1990 index-of-dissimilarity values for specific immigrant-ethnic groups in the New York and Los Angeles metropolitan regions generally are in the .5 to .7 range, indicating a "high moderate" to "low high" level of segregation; such values in fact are not much below those for African Americans in the same regions. For instance, in Los Angeles, a city that is a mecca without equal for immigration streams from Asia and Central America, the index of dissimiliarity between Mexicans and Anglos (non-Hispanic whites) was .59, and that between Salvadorans (the second-largest Latino group in the region) and Anglos even higher, at .77.[1] The index values were also relatively high for the major Asian groups: for Chinese, .60; for Filipinos, .54; for Koreans, .58; and for Vietnamese, .66. Yet, except for that of the Salvadorans, a group with many members in marginal legal situations (Menjivar 2000), these values do not seem very remarkable by historical standards; analysis of data from the early twentieth century for New York, for example, finds rather similar values for the immigrant groups of that era (Alba, Logan, Zhang, and Stults 1999; see also Lieberson 1963).

Moreover, when the racial-ethnic compositions of the local areas where the typical member of an immigrant group is found are taken into account—as is done with a different type of segregation measure, the indices of isolation and exposure, which belong to the so-called P* family of measures—then the degree of immigrant segregation usually appears more modest. The typical member of such a group lives in a very mixed neighborhood where other immigrant and non-immigrant groups are present. In fact, it is quite common for non-Hispanic white neighbors to outnumber co-ethnic ones. This is especially true for Asians: for instance, though Chinese were in 1990 the second-largest non-Anglo group in the Los Angeles region, the average Chinese Angeleno resided in a census tract that was only 14 percent Chinese, while approximately 40 percent of their neighbors were Anglo. Only for the large Hispanic groups in regions of heavy immigrant concentration—for example, the Mexicans of Chicago or the Los Angeles region and the Cubans of Miami—do co-ethnic neighbors outnumber Anglo ones. Even in these regions, moreover, at least half of a group usually resides outside of its areas of concentration; in 1990 this was the case for 52 percent of New York's Chinese, despite the existence of Chinatown and satellite neighborhoods, and for 55 percent of Los Angeles Mexicans (Logan, Alba, and Zhang 2002; see also Allen and Turner 1997). In these respects, there is a sharp distinction between the typical residential situation of immigrant minorities and that of African Americans, who are more likely to reside in areas where their own group is in the majority and white neighbors are scarce. Correspondingly, black immigrants tend to be more segregated: both West Indian and dark-skinned Latinos are very likely to be channeled into or near black neighborhoods, especially if they reside in cities (Crowder 1999; Crowder and Tedrow 2001; Denton and Massey 1989). The extent to which immigrant minorities reside with co-ethnics in metropolitan regions such as Los Angeles will almost certainly grow in the future as immigration continues. But they are likely to continue to live with non-group members, including whites, in their midst, unless there is a massive flight of whites from areas of immigrant concentration. This seems unlikely, as many of the areas to which immigrants go are global metropolises with concentrations of headquarters complexes and associated professional and high-level service jobs (Sassen 1988; Waldinger 1996; Waldinger and Bozorgmehr 1996). Whites will not abandon them completely.

Immigrant Suburbanization and Ethnic Neighborhoods

In clear contrast to earlier European immigrant groups, which generally first established urban enclaves and only after a generation or more migrated to suburbs, the new immigrants frequently settle in suburbs either immediately upon arrival in the United States or soon after (Alba, Logan, Stults, et al. 1999; Alba, Logan, Zhang, and Stults 1999; Waldinger 1989; cf. Massey 1985). According to 1990 census data, 43 percent of those who arrived during the 1980s and were living in metropolitan areas already resided outside of central cities. The first analyses of the 2000 census show the numbers of suburban Asians and Hispanics soaring, with increases of 84 percent and 72 percent, respectively (Lewis Mumford Center 2001b). The percentages of suburbanites are particularly high among Asian groups. Within the first decade after their arrival in Los Angeles, many Asian immigrant families "buy up" into suburban neighborhoods. In 1990, 58 percent of Filipino households in metropolitan areas of the nation were located in suburbs, up from 49 percent in 1980. The comparable 1990 figure for whites was only modestly higher, 67 percent. The lowest percentage among Asian groups is found for Chinese, who have long-standing urban enclaves, but as of 1990 almost half were located outside of central cities—a noticeable increase from what it was a decade before (38 percent), despite the heavy immigration of ethnic Chinese during the 1980s. Rates of suburbanization are on average lower for Latino groups, although they are near 50 percent for Mexicans and Cubans. Blacks trail behind both Asians and Latinos, though it should be noted that the 1990s were a decade of substantial gain in suburban representation for them (Lewis Mumford Center 2001b).

Will suburbanization have the same meaning for new immigrant groups as it had for older ones, for whom it was usually associated with the maturity of the residential assimilation process? We cannot definitively answer this question at this point in the history of the new immigration, and in any event, we need to recognize that the term "suburbia" now covers such a varied range of residential contexts that a single, unqualified answer is ultimately unlikely. But the existence of extensive suburban ethnic enclaves, such as the Chinese in Monterey Park in Los Angeles, suggests that the contemporary settlement pattern is distinctive (Fong 1994; Horton 1995). The huge Los Angeles barrio is also for the most part outside of the central city. These examples, along with other evidence, suggest that barriers to suburban entry have fallen for freshly arrived immigrants, who may not speak English well. They can now reside in suburbia without detriment to their ability to function in daily life (for example, to shop or participate in communal activities), presumably because they find sufficient numbers of co-ethnics and an ethnic infrastructure in their vicinity. The existence of affluent suburban ethnic concentrations could undermine one of the principal mechanisms that propelled residential assimilation for European ethnics: namely, the search for improved residential amenities, which typically led them away from urban ethnic areas. If the new immigrants are able to establish suburban ethnic communities that already have such qualities as good schools and clean streets, then presumably their motivation to leave these communities is weakened.

Yet a close examination of neighborhoods in Los Angeles and New York as of 1990 indicates that, for most groups, suburban non-ethnic communities are still likely to prove the most desirable for residential amenities apart from those directly linked to ethnicity itself (for example, proximity to ethnic places of worship). Selected results from Los Angeles are presented in table 11.3 (Logan et al. 2002). A comparison of the levels of ethnic concentration in the different types of area (the areas themselves are census tracts) confirms that the distinctions are meaningful. Typically, the level of a group's representation in the population is several times higher in its areas of concentration than elsewhere, though only the Mexicans achieve a majority in their ethnic neighborhoods. Typically also, the non-ethnic neighborhoods display very low percentages of group representation—under 5 percent of the population, except for the Mexicans, who form a huge portion of the Los Angeles population overall. Significantly, the majority of each group, except among the Salvadorans, reside in the non-ethnic type of neighborhood. This usually means residing in a neighborhood where Anglos are the largest group, if not the majority of the population. However, the large percentages of residents not accounted for by Anglos or the group itself indicate that, generally speaking, these neighborhoods are ethnically diverse.

The average income of an area type undoubtedly is highly correlated with many other qualities that make a neighborhood desirable as a place to live, from good schools to a low crime rate. For three of the four groups in Los Angeles, the highest average incomes are found in the suburban neighborhoods with low levels of ethnic concentration. Significantly, this is true for the Chinese, who by 1990 had established some affluent and ethnic suburban areas, notably, Monterey Park. It is also obviously true for the two Latino groups, with the affluence of the suburban non-ethnic areas where Mexicans reside—these are also the areas where the largest number of Mexicans live—standing far apart from the other types. The only exception to these patterns occurs for Filipinos. The suburban areas of Filipino concentration are a bit more affluent than are other suburban areas where they reside. However, these areas of ethnic concentration do not in fact contain very high percentages of Filipinos, who are outnumbered in them by Anglos.

That suburban neighborhoods that are ethnically mixed or dominated by Anglos are likely to prove attractive to the economically successful members of immigrant groups is bolstered also by studies of urban ethnic areas. One study in New York City found that recent immigrants tend to live in neighborhoods with high levels of such social problems as teenage fertility and juvenile detention. Within the city, immigrants' neighborhood options were highly constrained by race and ethnicity (Rosenbaum and Friedman 2001). This is less true in the suburbs, which is not to deny that race and ethnicity also influence options there.

Spatial Assimilation and Contemporary Alternatives

A series of studies have tracked the individual and household influences on residential location, testing the linkages hypothesized in the spatial location model (Alba, Logan, and Stults 2000; Logan and Alba 1993; Logan et al. 1996; Logan et al. 2002; White, Biddlecom, and Guo 1993). The studies have characterized locations in terms of their median household incomes and the contingents of non-Hispanic whites, the majority group, among residents. In critical respects, the findings sustain an analogy between the residential trajectory of contemporary immigrant groups and that of past European groups, despite the obvious differences between the two eras. That is, the findings generally uphold the relationships expected under spatial assimilation, though the impact of race, among immigrants as well as African Americans, is a qualifier of enormous importance.

TABLE 11.3 Ethnic and Non-Ethnic Neighborhoods of Selected Immigrant Groups in the Los Angeles CMSA, 1990

Neighborhood Type	Suburb		Central City	
	Group	Nongroup	Group	Nongroup
Mexicans				
Number of group members	995,188	1,200,877	698,235	842,143
Mean tract percent of group members	70.5%	24.6%	69.8%	29.2%
Mean tract percent non-Hispanic white	12.5	52.2	9.9	34.1
Median tract household income	$27,631	$38,249	$26,223	$29,508
Salvadorans				
Number of group members	12,370	61,276	140,161	60,981
Mean tract percent of group members	6.7%	2.5%	16.0%	3.3%
Mean tract percent non-Hispanic white	8.6	31.9	13.6	30.6
Median tract household income	$24,131	$32,913	$20,570	$30,666
Chinese				
Number of group members	117,186	100,952	28,109	60,934
Mean tract percent of group members	23.4%	3.3%	29.3%	3.1%
Mean tract percent non-Hispanic white	31.6	59.7	10.8	48.8
Median tract household income	$43,601	$49,144	$23,943	$38,394
Filipinos				
Number of group members	50,718	110,060	65,575	68,761
Mean tract percent of group members	13.5%	2.6%	14.0%	2.9%
Mean tract percent non-Hispanic white	34.2	55.0	26.6	45.8
Median tract household income	$45,628	$42,313	$31,144	$35,403

Source: Logan, Alba, and Zhang (2002, tables 1b, 2b).

For Asians and Latinos,[2] the most powerful determinant of residential location is their own socioeconomic position: the greater their income and the higher their educational status, the larger, for instance, the percentage of non-Hispanic whites in the population of the neighborhood where they reside. Homeownership, a measure of household wealth, also makes a difference. Linguistic acculturation is a second-order determinant: the difference it makes is particularly sizable among Latinos and is most pronounced between those who speak only English at home and those who do not speak English well. Bilinguals, who speak a mother tongue but are proficient at English too, are in between. While generational status (that is, nativity) exerts little direct influence once other variables are taken into account, the effects of socioeconomic status and linguistic assimilation imply generational differences in residential situation of the sort consistent with straight-line assimilation.

After socioeconomic standing, residence in a suburb rather than a city is the strongest predictor of the percentage of the majority group in the neighborhoods where Asians and Latinos live. Even in the metropolitan regions that are most affected by the new immigration and therefore have many new immigrants as potential neighbors, this variable still typically adds about ten to twenty percentage points to the non-Hispanic white share of the neighborhood. In cities the other neighbors in mixed areas are typically members of other minority groups (Sanjek 1998). Perhaps the mixed nature of most neighborhoods has little bearing for immigrants, who may find enough co-ethnics in their vicinity to live in comfortably ethnic ways. But it is likely to have a considerable impact on their children, who as they grow up in suburbs are frequently brought together with whites and members of other ethnic groups in schools and play groups.

This is not to say that, in a strict sense, spatial assimilation requires residence in largely white neighborhoods. Certainly, the residential integration of the European American second generation was frequently a matter of entry into ethnically mixed neighborhoods, not those dominated by Protestants of British ancestry. But the entry of many middle-class Asians and Hispanics into the neighborhoods of the majority population is a strong demonstration of spatial assimilation. Could this feature of the contemporary landscape be undermined by the continuing immigration into the metropolitan regions where immigrants and their children are most concentrated? This, combined with the inclination of some natives to move away from these regions, is altering the racial-ethnic composition of neighborhoods in a way that reduces the availability of majority-group members as neighbors for upwardly mobile immigrant households. Still, even in the areas most heavily affected by immigration, middle-income, linguistically assimilated Asian and Latino suburbanites tended, as of 1990 (the latest date for which the relevant analyses are available), to live in areas where non-Hispanic whites predominate. Only in Los Angeles and Miami—the two large regions with the highest proportions of foreign-born in their populations and thus the most highly developed racial-ethnic shifts brought about by immigration (table 11.2)—was this generalization at risk. In other regions of immigrant settlement, such as San Francisco and New York, which have the third- and fourth-highest concentrations of new immigrant groups, the neighborhoods of even modestly affluent Asians and Latinos generally contained non-Hispanic white majorities, which were quite substantial in suburbs. Presumably the same would have been even more true for most other metropolitan regions, where the concentrations of new immigrant groups are necessarily more modest. In such areas, it will be a long time, if ever, before immigration modifies the racial-ethnic composition of neighborhoods to the point that residential integration with whites for middle-class, acculturated Asians and Latinos is unlikely.

Spatial assimilation, however, is not the only master pattern that is detectable in this series of analyses. The concept of "segmented" assimilation, which implies that assimilation can take place in more than one "segment" of American society, is also relevant. One pattern that the concept calls attention to is the incorporation of some groups and individuals as racial minorities, an older reality that is also very much in evidence today. As Alejandro Portes and Min Zhou (1993) have described this pattern in the contemporary setting, the risks of segmented assimilation are associated with nonwhite racial appearance, low social class position or origins, and an inner-city location (see also Zhou and Bankston 1998).

For the communities where immigrants and the second generation reside, race matters. This is true not only for West Indians but also for Latinos. Light-skinned Latinos—that is, those who describe themselves on the census form as "white" (about half of all Latinos in 1990)—are better able to enter neighborhoods with large numbers of non-Hispanic whites and thus have access to more advantaged areas. As we noted earlier, West Indians are as highly segregated from the white majority as African Americans and tend to live near African American ghettos; indeed, they are sometimes the racial pioneers in largely white neighborhoods and then are followed by African Americans. The residential patterns of Latinos who self-describe as "black" (fewer than 5 percent of all Latinos in 1990) tend also to conform to those of African Americans. Thus, they and West Indians live in neighborhoods with greater disadvantages, such as lower median household income, than we would otherwise expect given their socioeconomic characteristics. Latinos who describe themselves as other than black or white are situated in between.

CONCLUSION

That residential patterns exhibit somewhat contradictory qualities is probably inevitable at an early stage in the unfolding of the consequences of large-scale immigration. Indeed, the early results from the 2000 census indicate both that immigrant enclaves grew during the 1990s and that processes of spatial assimilation continue to function. In particular, the stability of the overall segregation levels for Asians and Hispanics implies that, despite the enormous increase of these populations during the 1990s because of immigration, their distribution across different types of neighborhoods held steady. Given the increased sizes of the groups, this implies some increase in the ethnic density of group enclaves, yet at the same time the numbers who live outside these enclaves, often in neighborhoods with many whites but also in some multihued neighborhoods where many groups mix, are rising. Perhaps the most interesting signal of all is the declining racial and ethnic exclusivity of the neighborhoods where whites live: as of 2000 the average white in the metropolitan regions of the nation resides in a census tract where 20 percent of the residents are nonwhite or Hispanic (up from 15 percent in 1990 and 12 percent in 1980) (Lewis Mumford Center 2001a). Given the historic role of the majority's exclusion of minorities from its residential bastions, the increasing diversity in the neighborhoods of whites suggests that the way is open to further spatial assimilation, at least for some fraction of contemporary immigrant minorities.

But even as we underscore the continuities in spatial assimilation, we are aware that, as a totality, the residential picture is more mixed and, in some ways, more elusive in its significance than was true in the past. Immigrant social worlds can no longer be spatially circumscribed by the radius of walking distance, as was the case at the turn of the last century. Space is less determinative of strong ties today. Through telephones, computers, and automobiles, immigrant ethnics are able to maintain connections to kin and co-ethnics who may live at some distance from them, even in their country of origin. Ethnic infrastructures are therefore less dependent on proximity and spatial concentration. Residential integration is not incompatible with participation in ethnically restricted social activities and networks.

Moreover, elements of persisting segregation appear alongside those of integration. The high walls of residential segregation confronting Americans with visible African ancestry, whether native-born or immigrant, are crumbling very slowly. The evidence is convincing that Hispanics who are black are as affected by this segregation as are African Americans. And the other Hispanics who do not have a European appearance are also residentially disadvantaged, though not to the extent that blacks are. New areas of ethnic concentration are developing as a result of the clustering of immigrant groups, and some offer suburban amenities, which make them much more attractive as places to live than the inner-city enclaves typical of immigration a century ago.

The urban landscape today bears the marks of its development by the earlier waves of European immigrants and post–World War II suburban growth. Many places and neighborhoods that were racially defined by private decisions or government policies in the middle of the twentieth century, such as Levittown, remain racially defined half a century later. The almost universal presence of zoning laws, suburban governmental fragmentation, and the increasing number of gated communities tell us that residential segregation remains salient despite fair housing laws and declining personal prejudice. However the residential patterns of new immigrants work out, they will do so within the context of these constraints and those of the immigrants' race as seen by the larger society.

For the foreseeable future, no single pattern of residential incorporation seems likely to emerge as dominant. Thus, the patches of racial and ethnic colorations on future social mappings of U.S. metropolitan regions, produced by racial segregation as well as by the clusterings of group members for cultural and social purposes, will not disappear. But the visibility of those patches should not obscure the spatial assimilation of a good many immigrants and their children.

NOTES

1. Throughout the remainder of this section, the "immigrant" groups to which we refer include the second and later generations as well as the foreign-born.

2. For technical reasons, the Alba-Logan analyses could not be carried out on more specific groups. Because of the limitations of census data, which to preserve confidentiality prevent the analyst from combining individual-level data with small-area characteristics, it is not possible with publicly available data to improve on these aggregate categories.

REFERENCES

Alba, Richard, John Logan, and Brian Stults. 2000. "The Changing Neighborhood Contexts of the Immigrant Metropolis." *Social Forces* 79(2, December): 587–621.

Alba, Richard, John Logan, Brian Stults, Gilbert Marzan, and Wenquan Zhang. 1999. "Immigrant Groups in the Suburbs: A Reexamination of Suburbanization and Spatial Assimilation." *American Sociological Review* 64(3, June): 446–60.

Alba, Richard, John Logan, Wenquan Zhang, and Brian Stults. 1999. "Strangers Next Door:

Immigrant Groups and Suburbs in Los Angeles and New York." In *A Nation Divided: Diversity, Inequality, and Community in American Society*, edited by Phyllis Moen, Henry Walker, and Donna Dempster-McClain. Ithaca, N.Y.: Cornell University Press.

Alba, Richard, and Victor Nee. 2003. *Remaking the American Mainstream*. Cambridge, Mass.: Harvard University Press.

Allen, James, and Eugene Turner. 1997. *The Ethnic Quilt: Population Diversity in Southern California*. Northridge: California State University, Center for Geographic Studies.

Barrett, James, and David Roediger. 1997. "Inbetween Peoples: Race, Nationality, and the 'New Immigrant' Working Class." *Journal of American Ethnic History* 16(3, Spring): 3–44.

Bodnar, John, Roger Simon, and Michael P. Weber. 1982. *Lives of Their Own: Blacks, Italians, and Poles in Pittsburgh, 1900–1960*. Urbana-Champaign: University of Illinois Press.

Crowder, Kyle. 1999. "Residential Segregation of West Indians in the New York/New Jersey Metropolitan Area: The Roles of Race and Ethnicity." *International Migration Review* 33(1, Spring): 79–113.

Crowder, Kyle, and Lucky Tedrow. 2001. "West Indians and the Residential Landscape of New York." In *Islands in the City: West Indian Migration to New York*, edited by Nancy Foner. Berkeley: University of California Press.

Day, Jared. 1999. *Urban Castles: Tenement Housing and Landlord Activism in New York City, 1890–1943*. New York: Columbia University Press.

Denton, Nancy, and Douglas Massey. 1989. "Racial Identity Among Caribbean Hispanics: The Effect of Double Minority Status on Residential Segregation." *American Sociological Review* 54(5, October): 790–808.

Farley, Reynolds. 1996. *The New American Reality: Who We Are, How We Got Here, Where We Are Going*. New York: Russell Sage Foundation.

Farley, Reynolds, and William Frey. 1994. "Changes in the Segregation of Whites from Blacks During the 1980s: Small Steps Towards a More Integrated Society." *American Sociological Review* 59(1, February): 23–45.

Foner, Nancy. 2000. *From Ellis Island to JFK: New York's Two Great Waves of Migration*. New Haven, Conn.: Yale University Press.

Fong, Timothy. 1994. *The First Suburban Chinatown: The Remaking of Monterey Park, California*. Philadelphia: Temple University Press.

Frey, William. 1996. "Immigration, Domestic Migration, and Demographic Balkanization in America: New Evidence for the 1990s." *Population and Development Review* 22(4, December): 741–63.

Frey, William, and Kao-Lee Liaw. 1998. "The Impact of Recent Immigration on Population Redistribution Within the United States." In *The Immigration Debate: Studies of Economic, Demographic, and Fiscal Effects of Immigration*, edited by James Smith and Barry Edmonston. Washington, D.C.: National Academy Press.

Gabaccia, Donna. 1984. *From Sicily to Elizabeth Street: Housing and Social Change Among Italian Immigrants, 1880–1930*. Albany: State University of New York Press.

Glazer, Nathan, and Daniel Patrick Moynihan. 1970. *Beyond the Melting Pot: The Negroes, Puerto Ricans, Jews, Italians, and Irish of New York City*. 2nd ed. Cambridge, Mass.: MIT Press. (Orig. pub. in 1963.)

Gold, Steven. 1992. *Refugee Communities: A Comparative Field Study*. Newbury Park, Calif.: Sage Publications.

Grebler, Leo, Joan Moore, and Ralph Guzman. 1970. *The Mexican-American People: The Nation's Second Largest Minority*. New York: Free Press.

Grossman, James. 1989. *Land of Hope: Chicago, Black Southerners, and the Great Migration*. Chicago: University of Chicago Press.

Handlin, Oscar. 1972. *Boston's Immigrants*. New York: Atheneum.

Hershberg, Theodore, Stephanie Greenberg, Alan Burstein, William Yancey, and Eugene Ericksen. 1981. "A Tale of Three Cities: Blacks, Immigrants, and Opportunity in Philadelphia, 1850–1880, 1930, 1970." In *Philadelphia: Work, Space, Family, and Group Experience in the Nineteenth Century*, edited by Theodore Hershberg. New York: Oxford University Press.

Higham, John. 1970. *Strangers in the Land: Patterns of American Nativism, 1860–1925*. New York: Atheneum.

Hirsch, Arnold. 1993. "With or Without Jim Crow: Black Residential Segregation in the United States." In *Urban Policy in Twentieth-Century America*, edited by Arnold Hirsch and Raymond Mohl. New Brunswick, N.J.: Rutgers University Press.

Horton, John. 1995. *The Politics of Diversity: Immigration, Resistance, and Change in Monterey Park, California*. Philadelphia: Temple University Press.

Jackson, Kenneth. 1985. *Crabgrass Frontier: The Suburbanization of the United States*. New York: Oxford University Press.

———. 1992. *The Ku Klux Klan in the City, 1915–1930*. Chicago: Ivan R. Dee. (Orig. pub. 1967 by Oxford University Press.)

Kusmer, Kenneth L. 1976. *A Ghetto Takes Shape: Black Cleveland, 1870–1930*. Urbana-Champaign: University of Illinois.

Lee, Barrett, Stephen Matthews, and Wilbur Zelinsky. 2001. "The Spatial Contours of Racial and Ethnic Diversity in the United States, 1980–2000." University Park: Pennsylvania State University, Population Research Institute.

Levine, Hillel, and Lawrence Harmon. 1992. *The Death of an American Jewish Community: A Tragedy of Good Intention*. New York: Free Press.

Lewis Mumford Center. 2001a. "Ethnic Diversity Grows, Neighborhood Integration Lags Behind." State University of New York at Albany. http://www.albany.edu/mumford/census.

———. 2001b. "The New Ethnic Enclaves in America's Suburbs." State University of New York at Albany. http://www.albany.edu/mumford/census.

Lieberson, Stanley. 1963. *Ethnic Patterns in American Cities*. Glencoe, Ill.: Free Press.

———. 1980. *A Piece of the Pie: Blacks and White Immigrants Since 1880*. Berkeley: University of California Press.

Lieberson, Stanley, and Mary Waters. 1988. *From Many Strands: Ethnic and Racial Groups in Contemporary America*. New York: Russell Sage Foundation.

Logan, John, and Richard Alba. 1993. "Locational Returns to Human Capital: Minority Access to Suburban Community Resources." *Demography* 30(2, May): 243–68.

Logan, John, Richard Alba, Thomas McNulty, and Brian Fisher. 1996. "Making a Place in the Metropolis: Residential Assimilation and Segregation in City and Suburb." *Demography* 33(4, November): 443–53.

Logan, John, Richard Alba, and Wenquan Zhang. 2002. "Immigrant Enclaves and Ethnic Communities in New York and Los Angeles." *American Sociological Review* 67(2, April): 299–322.

Massey, Douglas. 1985. "Ethnic Residential Segregation: A Theoretical Synthesis and Empirical Review." *Sociology and Social Research* 69(April): 315–50.

———. 1995. "The New Immigration and Ethnicity in the United States." *Population and Development Review* 21(September): 631–52.

Massey, Douglas, and Nancy Denton. 1987. "Trends in Residential Segregation of Blacks, Hispanics, and Asians: 1970–1980." *American Sociological Review* 52(6, December): 802–25.

———. 1993. *American Apartheid*. Cambridge, Mass.: Harvard University Press.

McGreevy, John. 1996. *Parish Boundaries: The Catholic Encounter with Race in the Twentieth-Century Urban North*. Chicago: University of Chicago Press.

Menjivar, Cecilia. 2000. *Fragmented Ties: Salvadoran Immigrant Networks in America*. Berkeley: University of California Press.

Monkkonen, Eric H. 1988. *America Becomes Urban: The Development of U.S. Cities and Towns, 1780–1980*. Berkeley: University of California Press.

Nee, Victor, and Brett de Bary Nee. 1973. *Longtime Californ': A Documentary Study of an American Chinatown*. New York: Pantheon.

Olson, James. 1994. *The Ethnic Dimension in American History*. New York: St. Martin's.

Orum, Anthony. 1995. *City Building in America*. Boulder, Colo.: Westview Press.

Osofsky, Gilbert. 1971. *Harlem: The Making of a Ghetto: Negro New York, 1890–1930*. 2nd ed. New York: Harper Torchbooks.

Philpott, Thomas Lee. 1991. *The Slum and the Ghetto: Immigrants, Blacks, and Reformers in Chicago, 1880–1930*. Belmont, Calif.: Wadsworth. (Orig. pub. 1978.)

Portes, Alejandro, and Rubén Rumbaut. 1996. *Immigrant America: A Portrait*. 2nd ed. Berkeley: University of California Press.

Portes, Alejandro, and Min Zhou. 1993. "The New Second Generation: Segmented Assimilation and Its Variants." *The Annals* 530(November): 74–96.

Rosenbaum, Emily, and Samantha Friedman. 2001. "Differences in the Locational Attainment of Immigrant and Native-Born Households with Children in New York City." *Demography* 38(3, August): 337–48.

Sánchez, George. 1993. *Becoming Mexican American: Ethnicity, Culture, and Identity in Chicano Los Angeles, 1900–1945*. New York: Oxford University Press.

Sanjek, Roger. 1998. *The Future of Us All: Race and Neighborhood Politics in New York City*. Ithaca, N.Y.: Cornell University Press.

Sassen, Saskia. 1988. *The Mobility of Capital and Labor*. Cambridge: Cambridge University Press.

Smith, James, and Barry Edmonston. 1997. *The New Americans: Economic, Demographic, and Fiscal Effects of Immigration*. Washington, D.C.: National Research Council.

Sugrue, Thomas J. 1996. *The Origins of the Urban Crisis: Race and Inequality in Postwar Detroit*. Princeton, N.J.: Princeton University Press.

Waldinger, Roger. 1989. "Immigration and Urban Change." *Annual Review of Sociology* 15(1989): 211–32.

———. 1996. *Still the Promised City? African-Americans and New Immigrants in Postindustrial New York*. Cambridge, Mass.: Harvard University Press.

Waldinger, Roger, and Mehdi Bozorgmehr. 1996. *Ethnic Los Angeles*. New York: Russell Sage Foundation.

White, Michael, Ann Biddlecom, and Shenyang Guo. 1993. "Immigration, Naturalization, and Residential Assimilation Among Asian Americans." *Social Forces* 72(1, September): 93–118.

White, Michael, Robert F. Dymowski, and Shilian Wang. 1994. "Ethnic Neighbors and Ethnic Myths: An Examination of Residential Segregation in 1910." In *After Ellis Island: Newcomers and Natives in the 1910 Census*, edited by Susan Watkins. New York: Russell Sage Foundation.

Yans-McLaughlin, Virginia. 1971. *Family and Community: Italian Immigrants in Buffalo, 1880–1930*. Urbana-Champaign: University of Illinois Press.

Zhou, Min, and Carl Bankston. 1998. *Growing Up American: How Vietnamese Children Adapt to Life in the United States*. New York: Russell Sage Foundation.

Joel Perlmann and Mary C. Waters

Chapter 12

Intermarriage Then and Now: Race, Generation, and the Changing Meaning of Marriage

Intermarriage has a reasonably long pedigree among American social scientists. There are a few longer pedigrees perhaps; still, when Julius Drachsler (1920) studied the prevalence of intermarriage among the marriage partners of New York City, using the records of 1908 to 1912, he was already asking the crucial questions in a study he called *Democracy and Assimilation: The Blending of Immigrant Heritages in America*. Unions between immigrants and natives, among different subgroups of immigrants, and among the children of all these groups were his special concerns—as well as between Jews and Gentiles, and between blacks and various groups of whites. The study may have been largely empirical, but it rested on the clear conceptualization of intermarriage as a measure of present-day ethnic absorption into the mainstream and of further movement in that direction caused by the very fact of the intermarriages themselves. At least since the time Robert K. Merton (1941) elaborated the dynamics of intermarriage, the subject has had a central place in theorizing about movement across structural divisions, and since Milton Gordon's *Assimilation in American Life* (1964), intermarriage has been seen as the final stage in a theory of assimilation. Admittedly, during many of the years after Gordon wrote, "assimilation" itself was a dirty word, yet its status seems to be reviving. In at least one new synthesis (Alba and Nee 2003), it has been reformed and rehabilitated. Whatever the fate of the assimilation concept, and whatever more refined formulations come to capture the process of full ethnic absorption or incorporation into the American mainstream, crossing once-high ethnic divides to find a spouse is routinely taken to be significant.

When we say that the behavior of intermarriage is routinely taken to be significant, we mean that it is significant in two specific ways: as a measure of the lowering of those divides that has already occurred and as an indication that those social divides will decline still further—as a result of intermarriage itself. The second way in which intermarriage is important to the study of race and ethnicity—as an indication that old social divisions will fall still further in the future—is, in terms of the intermarriage studies themselves, typically only an assumption. Still, related kinds of empirical studies, such as those based on the ancestry question in the 1980 and 1990 censuses, offer confirmation of the expectation (for example, by showing that children of mixed ancestry are less tied to an ethnic origin than those of a single ancestry, Lieberson and Waters 1988).

To a very great extent, then, the traditional field of intermarriage studies has been stimulated by the long-term social processes related to the European immigration to the

United States (and related issues such as the religious intermarriage of Protestants, Catholics, and Jews). The question of racial intermarriage has been part of the intellectual agenda since the beginning and is clearly addressed in Drachsler (1920), Merton (1941), Gordon (1964), and Alba and Nee (2003). Nevertheless, black-white intermarriage always had a special place in studies of intermarriage; it was different from intermarriage among European groups for at least two reasons. First, black-white intermarriage was the great exception, the rare intermarriage type, whatever changes or patterns we might discern in its occurrence. One reason it was rare, of course, was that it was illegal in many places as recently as four decades ago. Second, in the big picture, black-white intermarriage was not like immigrant and white-ethnic intermarriage because the very low incidence did not change with the length of time that black families had spent in the United States. In other words, black families had experienced their forced immigration so many generations back that their immigration experience was utterly irrelevant by the twentieth century. We could quibble about exceptions involving West Indians before 1960, but for the great mass of American blacks, these were truly quibbles.

Thus, the current study of intermarriage can draw on two related traditions: one involving racial intermarriage based on two long-resident populations with very low intermarriage rates (blacks and whites), a tradition in which researchers ignore the generational status of the populations; and the other involving immigrants and their offspring, a tradition in which generational status explains a great deal of the behavior. Moreover, race looms large in contemporary discussions of intermarriage for several reasons. Most immigrants today are classified (either by themselves or by others) as nonwhite; most descendants of older European (white) immigrations now cross the old social divides so easily that (to paraphrase Merton's observation) it can hardly be called intermarriage when they do, since there no longer exists a norm that such behavior violates. (Jewish-Gentile intermarriages may still be the strongest partial exception to this broad generalization.) And there are significant changes to study: for the first time black-white intermarriages, while still relatively rare, are increasing steadily (not least because they have been legal throughout the country only since the late 1960s), and marriages between whites and Asians, Native Americans, and Hispanics are quite common.

Our essay opens with a brief consideration of the contemporary intermarriage patterns from two perspectives—as a racial pattern and as patterns involving the descendants of immigrants. We argue that the relative importance we give to generation as opposed to race in explaining intermarriage leads to different expectations or hypotheses about predicted intermarriage patterns. The weak hypothesis we put forward is that at a minimum studies of Asian and Hispanic marriage patterns are not meaningful unless they take into account the generational status of the populations, as did traditional studies of immigrant intermarriage such as those done with European immigrant groups. Specifically, our weak hypothesis is that treating Asian and Hispanic marriage patterns merely as "racial intermarriage," as we might treat black-white intermarriage, is not correct and underestimates the amount of intermarriage that will occur in later generations. Thus, we argue that generation must be included in any study of contemporary immigration.

At the other pole, we describe the very strong hypothesis that generation is the only factor necessary to understand intermarriage and that racial divisions will not matter to intermarriage patterns in later generations. Stated more fully, the very strong hypothesis is that immigrant Asians and Hispanics rarely intermarry with native-born Americans of other origins, but second-generation Asians and Hispanics commonly intermarry with such people. By the third or fourth generation, out-marriage by the descendants of late-twentieth-century Asian and Hispanic immigrants will have become the norm. Thus, fourth- and fifth-generation descendants of the Asian and Hispanic immigrants of our time will be almost all of mixed origin, and almost all will also be the descendants of *non*-Asians or *non*-Hispanics. We can put a metric to these statements: the very strong hypothesis claims that Asian and Hispanic immigrants of today intermarry at least as often as did the "new immigrant" groups of the last wave of Europeans—the southern, central, and eastern Europeans who arrived between 1890 and 1920. In terms of the second generation, the claim would be that the contemporary Asian and Hispanic second generation is intermarrying about as often now as the second generation of southern, central, and eastern Europeans did then. These second-generation rates of out-marriage, of course, would be well above the rates of black out-marriage, and probably well above the rate of Mexican or Chinese out-marriage early in the twentieth century.

The middle hypothesis, falling between the weak and the very strong hypotheses, is that the pattern of European immigrant and ethnic out-marriage serves as a useful model for what the Asian and Hispanic experience of out-marriage will be—more useful, surely, than the black-white intermarriage model. Nevertheless, because of phenotypical characteristics and the weighty role of race in American life, it may well be that some refinement of the European immigrant and ethnic model of marriage patterns, a refinement that takes "race" into account, will be needed to fully capture the experience of the Asians and Hispanics.

The second section of our essay offers a modest beginning in considering the contemporary intermarriage of Mexican Americans within the context of immigration, national origin, and generational status. Also, it implicitly asks whether any other perspective is needed by contrasting the results with new evidence on the history of Italian first- and second-generation intermarriage in the decades following the great immigrations of 1900 to 1915.

Thus, the first two sections of our essay suggest that much about contemporary ethnic-racial intermarriage can be subsumed under the old understandings of how immigrants "assimilate." And in the spirit of this volume, we show how a comparison of two immigrant groups at two different points in time can illuminate historical similarities and continuities that may be difficult to see in the present day. Specifically, the similarities we show between Italians then and Mexicans now call into question some of the more dire predictions that a racialized Latino immigrant group will have trouble assimilating into American society.

By contrast, the third section of our essay argues that there is something quite new about the new intermarriage, something we are only beginning to know how to address. These new developments make historical comparisons more complicated than might be immediately apparent. The new developments we discuss here concern the great changes in the prevalence of cohabitation and out-of-wedlock childbirth. We argue that the decline in the prevalence, permanence, and tie to procreation of marriage in twenty-first-century America should lead to a change in our thinking about interethnic and interracial relationships and their consequences. With the rise in divorce, cohabitation, and out-of-wedlock births, marriage is different now than it was before. In addition, these changes have affected different race and ethnic groups disproportionately. Although we cannot account for these new meanings of marriage in this study, we draw attention to them, both as a caution for those doing historical comparisons like the one we do here and as a challenge to researchers to begin to rethink the measurement and theoretical understanding of intermarriage in light of these great transformations.

IMMIGRANTS AND RACES IN THE STUDY OF CONTEMPORARY INTERMARRIAGE

Five major groupings make up the historian David Hollinger's (1995) ethno-racial pentagon—blacks, whites, Native Americans, Asians, and Hispanics—and there is a temptation to study the "new" divisions in American life in these terms. However, for much social behavior surely at least two of these groupings—Asians and Hispanics—include such a wide range of subgroups as to demand finer divisions. In every one of the five groupings there are of course great differences in income and education, for example, but among Asians and Hispanics these correspond closely to differences in national origin and generational status—that is, to factors related to immigration pure and simple (Waters and Eschbach 1995). Compare affluent and well-educated Cubans and South Americans, for instance, to more disadvantaged groups such as Mexicans and Puerto Ricans, or Japanese and Asian Indians to Cambodians and Laotians. Moreover, while some of these groups first came to the United States in appreciable numbers after 1965, others—Mexicans and Chinese in particular—have a much longer history of moderately large immigration. These national group differences within the two corners of the ethno-racial "pentagon" called Asian and Hispanic mean that any effort to discuss intermarriage among Asians or Hispanics as a whole is bound to be limited in its explanatory power. The census taker has contributed to this limited explanatory power: the last three decennial censuses have merely ascertained whether a person is native-born or not; they have ignored the issue of whether or not the native-born person is in turn the child of immigrants. Consequently, our largest and most authoritative samples have tempted us to ignore generational standing. We know only that a certain native-born person identifies as Chinese in ethnic origin or Asian in racial origin, but the person could be a second- or seventh-generation American.

Studies that do take nationality and generational status into account confirm the importance of both factors. These studies confirm our weak hypothesis—leaving out generation and national origin in contemporary studies of intermarriage is indeed misleading. Not surprisingly, the second generation routinely intermarry more than the first (see, for example, Gilbertson, Fitzpatrick, and Yang 1996; Qian, Blair, and Ruf 2001; see also tables 12.1, 12.2, and 12.3). In these ethno-racial groups, so heavily a product of recent immigration, to ignore generational standing is to focus primarily on first-generation members, who are least likely to intermarry. To interpret a finding of high in-marriage among a group that is primarily first-generation as evidence of a racial pattern of in-marriage is wrong.

Nevertheless, national origin matters a great deal. Greta Gilbertson, Joseph Fitzpatrick, and Lijun Yang (1996) found that among young people in most Hispanic groups in New York City (including, by the way, Mexicans), out-marriage rates of over 50 percent prevailed in the second generation. Yet within this same ethno-racial grouping, second-generation Dominicans and Puerto Ricans were far less likely to out-marry and in fact showed no increase from the first to the second generation in rates of intermarriage. And so in the same city in which 66 percent of second-generation Cubans were marrying non-Hispanics, the same was true for only 19 percent of second-generation Dominicans. Although class background may explain much of this particular contrast, it does not explain why the rate for Mexicans in the city is closer to the Cuban than to the Dominican rate. It may be that Dominicans and Puerto Ricans in New York are more likely to be dark-skinned than the Mexicans and Cubans and thus more likely to identify themselves and to be identified as nonwhite. Although a range of skin colors and racial identities are present within all of these groupings, the selectivity of migration to New York, the patterns of residence and segregation, and the overall positions of these groups differ among them and shape the likelihood of interactions with white and nonwhite New Yorkers.

In a national study, Zhenchao Qian, Sampson Lee Blair, and Stacey Ruf (2001) also found large national origin differences in the prevalence with which another "ethno-racial" group out-married—Asian second-generation members. Japanese and Filipinos were most likely to marry whites, followed by Chinese and Koreans and then by Southeast Asians and Asian Indians, who were the least likely. More generally, in each ethnic group interracial marriage with whites is more frequent than interethnic marriage with other Asian Americans. This observation reminds us first that without a concern for Asian national origins, we cannot study the phenomenon of Asian pan-ethnicity—operationally defined as the odds that members of Asian national groups will marry members of other Asian national groups more often than non-Asian Americans will do so. But while panethnicity can hint at a trend toward the "racialization" of Asian (or Hispanic) groups, the finding that out-marriage beyond the boundaries of Asian panethnicity is more prevalent in each of these Asian groups argues for the strength of countervailing tendencies.

These studies of Asian and Hispanic intermarriage suggest support for our strong hypothesis—that generation and national origin matter today in the way familiar to us from the earlier history of European immigration. The subtheme of panethnicity, while not numerically as important as out-marriage beyond the panethnic fold, nevertheless suggests that there are features of the present situation that are most usefully explained in terms of the racialization of groups.

MEXICANS NOW, ITALIANS THEN

Mexicans Now

The Mexicans are by far the most important of the recent immigrant groups numerically, and their language, class position, and proximity to the home country might all argue for considerable constraints on out-marriage. The group may not be as racialized as Asian groups, or as Dominicans, but Mexicans have certainly been subject to racialized discrimination in this country during the past century. Our purpose here is to describe what can be said about current out-marriage rates in the group by refining the generational focus as much as possible. The crucial questions involve the native-born children of the current decade's immigration. We focus on relatively young people, born between 1966 and 1980, who are married with a spouse also present in the same household. Our data come from the Current Population Survey (CPS) covering the years 1998 to 2001.[1]

We distinguish first of all between two groups of foreign-born Mexicans, separating out those who came to the United States as young children (when they were under ten years of age—the so-called 1.5 generation) from those who came at older ages. And similarly, among the native-born children of Mexican immigrants, we distinguish those who have two parents born in Mexico (native-born of foreign parentage, or NBFP)

TABLE 12.1   Mexican Americans, by Generation and Birth Cohorts

Birth Cohorts	First Generation[a]	1.5 Generation[b]	Second Generation[c] (NBFP)	2.5 Generation[d] (NBMP)	Third Generation or Higher[e]	Mixed Origin
1926 to 1935	39%	0%	26%	13%	22%	33%
1936 to 1945	48	1	11	11	29	50
1946 to 1955	49	3	6	9	34	60
1956 to 1965	53	5	5	7	30	58
1966 to 1975	53	8	9	6	24	40

Source: Current Population Survey, 1998 to 2001. For additional details on sampling and other technical details relating to tables 12.1, 12.2, and 12.3, see Perlmann (2002).
[a]Born in Mexico, immigrated to the United States at age ten or older.
[b]Born in Mexico, immigrated to the United States at age nine or younger.
[c]Born in the United States to two Mexican-born parents.
[d]Born in the United States to one Mexican-born parent and one parent not born in Mexico. (In most cases, this second parent was born in the United States of Mexican parentage or ancestry.)
[e]Born in the United States to U.S.-born parents; some or all Mexican origins claimed for earlier forebears who immigrated to the United States.

from those who have only one parent born there (native-born of mixed parentage, or NBMP). As it turns out, a very high proportion of all children of a Mexican immigrant today are from just such mixed households (in which the other parent is not a Mexican immigrant; see table 12.1). The proportion of these "exceptions," the mixed second generation, varies over the decades (because it is created, in complex ways, from the ebb and flow of Mexican immigration numbers and the period of immigration is very long). Yet even among the young adult group today, the mixed second-generation group makes up no less than 40 percent of all native-born children of a Mexican immigrant.[2]

Since we are especially interested in the second generation, among whom the NBMP are often routinely counted, we pause a moment to consider, for the NBMP, the identity of that parent who was not a Mexican immigrant.[3] Only in about one-quarter of the cases did that parent have no Mexican origins at all. The other three-quarters of these parents were either American-born of Mexican parentage or American-born of American-born parentage but nonetheless claimed some Mexican ancestry in the more distant past. Note also that many of the American-born parents who claimed some Mexican parentage or ancestry may have *also* had some other parentage or ancestry, the result of intermarriages among their forebears. However, the crucial point for us about the American-born parents who claim some Mexican parentage or ancestry is that they are American-born. And since they are American-born, their own children, our NBMP sample members, are not purely members of the second generation. True, these NBMP have a Mexican-immigrant parent on one side of the family, but on the other side of the family the parent is likely to be American-born (and always is American-born if that parent has Mexican parentage or ancestry). Consequently, on this side of the family the NBMP is really at least third-generation and further from immigrant roots, more familiar with American ways, and more likely to out-marry than a child of two Mexican immigrants.

Finally, we can also track those who have some Mexican origins but whose Mexican forebears are at least three generations back. This is a very varied group: they may have four grandparents who immigrated from Mexico, or (at the other extreme) they may have only one Mexican ancestor whose family came in the sixteenth century to lands that were conquered and lost by Mexico in the midnineteenth century. This group is designated "third- or later-generation Mexican." We do not focus on this group to gain a hint of what intermarriage patterns will be in the future among the later generations of today's Mexican immigration. The third- and later-generation descendants of today are the products of a much older immigration and ethnic experience; aside from all the other differences between then and now, the forebears of the current third- and later-generation Mexicans experienced a history of much greater discrimination than is common today. We would expect, then, that the intermarriage patterns of today's third- and later-generation Mexicans provide a very low minimum rate of intermarriage in judging what to expect of the later-generation descendants of the Mexican immigration of our own time. We include this group partly to emphasize the range of generational types and the differences in outcomes for the grouping "Mexican" defined most broadly.

We compare each of these Mexican generational groups to four groups of non-Mexicans: native-born non-Hispanic whites of native parentage; native-born non-Hispanic blacks of native parentage; other Hispanic immigrants (that is, non-Mexicans), and children of at least one other Hispanic immigrant. We are not interested here in studying the intermarriage patterns of these other Hispanics for their own sake. However, when we study the Mexicans, a question about the meaning of out-marriage arises: does out-marriage include a marriage to a person of non-Mexican but Hispanic origin? Another form of ambiguity also arises in connection with the definition of in-marriage. As we have just seen, two categories of people with Mexican roots also may well have non-Mexican roots: the mixed second-generation members and the third, and later-generation members. When a first- or second-generation person with only Mexican roots marries someone who is only part-Mexican—hardly a rare occurrence—do we call that in-marriage or out-marriage? There is no simple right answer to this question; the point is to examine the patterns and their prevalence.

About one-quarter of second-generation Mexican men and women have a spouse who is likely to be only part-Mexican (table 12.2). Relatively few marriages, by contrast, are to a non-Mexican Hispanic. Treating these latter marriages as in-marriage or as out-marriage for Mexicans changes the Mexican intermarriage rate by only 2 percent for men and 3 percent for women. In studying the big picture, then, pan-Hispanic marriage does not matter much for the Mexican pattern. It may well come to matter more, for example as ever-larger numbers of Mexican immigrants come directly, or soon after entry, to regions other than the Southwest, and of course it may matter more for out-marriage patterns among other Hispanics than it does among Mexicans, by far the largest Hispanic group. In fact, one study recently showed that pan-Hispanic marriage is quite important for some non-Mexican groups in New York (Gilbertson et al. 1996).

The crucial group on which to focus, if we wish to understand Mexican out-marriage in the context of the immigration experience, is the "true" second generation—the U.S.-born children of two Mexican-born parents. Note that the groups that are excluded by this focus, but that would fall under the rubric "Hispanic," are vastly more numerous today than those on whom we focus: those born in Mexico (whether first or 1.5 generation), those American-born with only one Mexican-born parent, those of the third or later generations of Mexican ancestry, and all non-Mexican Hispanics. Yet both

TABLE 12.2   Out-Marriage Among Married Adults Born 1966 to 1980, by Various Definitions

Sex, Ethnicity, Generation	Spouse Has No Hispanic Origins[a]	Spouse Has No Mexican Origins[b]	Spouse May Have Part or All Non-Mexican Origins[c]	Unweighted Sample Size
Men				
Mexican first	6%	9%	15%	1,342
Mexican 1.5	9	11	29	191
Mexican second (NBFP)	18	20	45	171
Mexican 2.5 (NBMP)	35	41	73	102
Mexican third and later	28	31	89	505
Other Hispanic	30	91	95	878
NWNP	96	97	98	7,433
NBLKNP	96	98	99	627
Other	94	97	98	1,597
Total	83	88	92	12,846
Women				
Mexican first	4	7	10	1,237
Mexican 1.5	3	8	8	133
Mexican second (NBFP)	8	11	27	247
Mexican 2.5 (NBMP)	24	29	54	149
Mexican third and later	26	30	84	549
Other Hispanic	30	91	94	877
NWNP	97	98	99	7,491
NBLKNP	98	100	100	565
Other	94	97	98	1,598
Total	83	88	92	12,846

Source: For source and definitions of ethnic groupings, see table 12.1.
Note: The odds that a Mexican second generation (NBFP) woman would marry a Hispanic husband were 250 times as great as the odds that a non-Hispanic women would marry a Hispanic husband.
[a]No Hispanic origins: NWNP, NBLKNP, other.
[b]No Mexican origins: same plus other Hispanic.
[c]Part or all non-Mexican origins: same plus Mexican third and later and Mexican 2.5 (NBMP).
NWNP: Non-Hispanic native white of native parentage.
NBLKNP: Non-Hispanic native black of native parentage.

the generational criterion and that of national origin make very good sense in terms of immigration (not racial) theory.

We begin by considering the strictest definition of out-marriage—excluding from out-marriage a union of a "true" second-generation Mexican with any of the other Mexican or Hispanic categories just mentioned. By this definition, second-generation out-marriage is decidedly a minority phenomenon today: 18 to 20 percent of the men and only 8 to 11 percent of the women choosing spouses that meet the definition of out-marriage. However, the figures are much larger (45 percent and 27 percent) when we include the 2.5 generation and the third and later generations—who are surely more assimilated—and also when we include many spouses of mixed-immigrant origins. As expected, the proportions out-marrying in the 1.5 generation are notably lower, and in the 2.5 generation notably higher, than in the true second generation.

What are we to conclude from the relatively low rate of out-marriage observed when the phenomenon is defined most strictly? First of all, we can ask about the implications of these rates for the ethnic origins of the next generation: how many children of "true" second-generation Mexican Americans will be raised in mixed-origin homes? Overall, the out-marriage rate for men and women is about 15.5 percent (11 percent for women and 20 percent for men). Consider then a group of 10,000 "true" second-generation Mexicans: only 1,550 out-marry, while 8,450 in-marry. But whereas those who in-marry form 4,225 couples, those who out-marry form 1,550 couples, because the former draw a spouse from within the group, while the latter draw a spouse from outside the group. Thus, the rate at which mixed-origin *couples* form will always be greater than the rate at which *individuals* out-marry. In this case, the out-marriage rate for individuals is 15.5 percent, while the mixed-origin couples amount to 1,550/(1,550 + 4,225), or 26.8 percent. Finally, and crucially, the ethnic origins of the next generation result from the rate at which couples form, not the rate at which individuals out-marry.[4] Although fewer than one-sixth of individuals out-marry, more than one-quarter of their offspring will be of mixed origin.

We may still ask, how large is the rate of "more than one-quarter"? One answer is that the figures cited here are in fact smaller than those often cited for second-generation out-marriage, because we have excluded from the American-born children of Mexican immigrants those who had only one Mexican immigrant parent (a group nearly as large as those whom we include), and among this excluded group out-marriage rates are more than twice as high as for the "true" second-generation members.

Italians Then

Finally, we suggest yet another way to evaluate the magnitude of out-marriage among "true" second-generation Mexicans today, namely, through a comparison to the historical experience of other groups in the past. We consider here the experience of the Italians, the largest immigrant group to arrive during the last great wave of immigration, especially between 1900 and 1914. Like the Mexicans today, the Italians came as labor migrants, with low skill levels relative to those of the native-born population. Unlike Mexican immigration of today, however, Italian immigration was tightly compressed in a narrow range of years. By contrast, some Mexicans had settled in the Southwest before the British arrived in the East, and more had immigrated over many decades, especially since 1910. Thus, intermarriage patterns may differ in complex ways related to this difference, because the Mexican second generation of our own time may find a spouse of third- and later-generation Mexican origin, whereas comparable choices were not available to the Italian second generation. Also, Italian immigration ended abruptly owing to immigration restriction (followed by depression and war). Thus, many second-generation Italians were choosing their spouse after immigration from Italy had slowed to a trickle. How this demographic pattern affected the marriage market remains to be worked out.[5] Our examination of Italian intermarriage patterns rests on the public use samples of the 1920 and 1960 U.S. censuses (IPUMS 1998). For our purposes, these sources provide information quite comparable to the information on the Mexicans of our own time that we have drawn from the CPS.[6] Also, for the sake of simplicity, our attention here is limited to the behavior of second-generation Italian women. We study first the birth cohort from 1886 to 1900 and observe their out-marriage rates in 1920 and in 1960 (limiting our attention, in the later year, to those in their first marriage).

The out-marriage rates are not identical in the two samples (see table 12.3)—12 percent in the first and 17 percent in the second—but they are close enough for results from two national samples spaced forty years apart. Recall that using the strictest definitions, Mexican second-generation women out-marry at a rate of some 11 percent today. Thus, the 12 to 17 percent range for those Italian women may be slightly higher but is roughly in the same range; the prevalence of Italians in the American population, however, was far smaller then than the proportion of Mexicans in the American population today. In the 1998 to 2001 CPS files, Hispanics were 18 percent of the sampled husbands in the young birth cohort we are studying; in 1920 Italians were fewer than 3 percent of the sampled husbands. These numbers imply that, all else being equal, it was some six times as hard to limit one's choice of a spouse to an Italian at that time than it is to limit one's choice of a spouse to a Hispanic today. The fact that the second-generation Italian women then nevertheless *did* limit their choice to their own kind roughly as often as second-generation Mexican women do today strongly suggests that the constraints *other* than group size that operated against out-marriage were actually greater for Italian women living at that time than are the comparable constraints operating for Mexican women today. At any rate, we should conclude that such constraints are surely *not* appreciably larger today than they were at that time.

Moreover, out-marriage for second-generation Italian women increased sharply over time. The rates remained pretty constant until the birth cohort of 1906 to 1910—women who turned twenty on the eve of the Depression. But thereafter, out-marriage for "true" second-generation Italian women increased markedly, so that for the cohort of women who reached their twentieth birthday during World War II, out-marriage stood at 41 percent. This rise in out-marriage among the later birth cohorts of Italians—who are of the same generational status as the earlier cohorts—is probably *not* explained by some massive shift in American tolerance for diversity generally. However, a tolerance for Italians in particular may have increased as the group became more familiar to other Americans; also, Italians who arrived later may have been somewhat more rapidly upwardly mobile, partly because of the connections to earlier arrivals. And finally, there may have been more residential change during depression and war.

How much of the observed rapid rise in the Italian out-marriage rate over the decades was due to the cessation of large-scale immigration, depression and war, or other factors that are not common to the Mexican second generation of our own era we cannot say. But it is at least noteworthy that the Mexican constraints on out-marriage look smaller, or at least no larger, than those facing Italians in an earlier period and that from constraints of that magnitude Italian second-generation out-marriage rates shot up during the course of a generation. Thus, immigration history suggests that an approach

TABLE 12.3   Out-Marriage Among Birth Cohorts of Italian Women, Circa 1920

Birth Cohorts	Age Twenty in:	Wife's Origin	Out-Marriage Rate	Number in Sample	Odds of Marrying an Italian Husband: Italian Second-Generation Women (NBFP) and Non-Italian Women Compared
1886 to 1900	1906 to 1920	Italian first and 1.5	3%	1,210	
		Italian second (NBFP)	17	293	763
		Italian 2.5 (NBMP)	65	17	
		Not Italian	99	37,371	
1901 to 1905	1921 to 1925	Italian first and 1.5	6	456	
		Italian second (NBFP)	22	448	327
		Italian 2.5 (NBMP)	51	39	
		Not Italian	99	23,298	
1906 to 1910	1926 to 1930	Italian first and 1.5	9	382	
		Italian second (NBFP)	19	871	318
		Italian 2.5 (NBMP)	45	78	
		Not Italian	99	28,601	
1911 to 1915	1931 to 1935	Italian first and 1.5	16	305	
		Italian second (NBFP)	28	1,410	133
		Italian 2.5 (NBMP)	38	181	
		Not Italian	98	34,318	
1916 to 1920	1936 to 1940	Italian first and 1.5	19	135	
		Italian second (NBFP)	37	1,677	74
		Italian 2.5 (NBMP)	51	296	
		Not Italian	98	39,414	
1921 to 1925	1941 to 1945	Italian first and 1.5	23	228	
		Italian second (NBFP)	41	1,659	59
		Italian 2.5 (NBMP)	55	469	
		Not Italian	98	44,228	
1926 to 1930	1946 to 1950	Italian first and 1.5	25	164	
		Italian second (NBFP)	46	1,192	44
		Italian 2.5 (NBMP)	58	492	
		Not Italian	97	43,574	
1931 to 1936	1951 to 1955	Italian first and 1.5	21	129	
		Italian second (NBFP)	55	644	35

TABLE 12.3   *Continued*

Birth Cohorts	Age Twenty in:	Wife's Origin	Out-Marriage Rate	Number in Sample	Odds of Marrying an Italian Husband: Italian Second-Generation Women (NBFP) and Non-Italian Women Compared
		Italian 2.5 (NBMP)	66	468	
		Not Italian	98	40,039	
1936 to 1940	1956 to 1960	Italian first and 1.5	19	75	
		Italian second (NBFP)	69	223	23
		Italian 2.5 (NBMP)	78	249	
		Not Italian	98	32,848	

Source: IPUMS (1998), sample of the 1920 (first cohort only) and 1960 censuses.
Note: First and 1.5: Italian-born.
Second (NBFP): U.S.-born of two Italian parents.
2.5 (NBMP): U.S.-born of an Italian and another parent.

to current-day Mexican out-marriage that takes immigration and generational status into account does not reveal it to be distinctly lower than that of a comparable European group in the past who are now routinely considered European Americans and white. That the Italians were in many senses "racialized" at the time is not so much the point here; rather, it is that the immigration approach to intermarriage makes much sense of the Mexican out-marriage experience today, whereas our analysis shows that ignoring generational standing and national origin in favor of a unified racial classification of "Mexicans" or "Hispanics" would create confusion. Indeed, having applied the refinements of the immigration approach and found that the behavior of Mexicans today falls within recognized bounds of out-marriage for a comparable second-generation group from the past, what can treating them as a unit on the ethno-racial pentagon add? A possible answer is that the importance of racial themes will show up more clearly in the comparison of Mexicans and other Hispanic groups. Recall the finding of Gilbertson and her colleagues (1996) that Dominicans and Puerto Ricans in New York City were far less likely to out-marry than Mexicans of the same generation.

THE CHANGING MEANING OF MARRIAGE

If the Mexican American out-marriage rate today seems similar to historical rates for immigrants, there are nonetheless some ways in which ethnic and racial mingling today may be quite distinct from anything we have known in the past. One change is quite well known, and we note it only in passing: the rate of black-white marriages, while still low, has been rising steadily over a quarter-century. We wish to concentrate instead on the effect of the societal changes of increased rates of cohabitation and out-of-wedlock births as well as long-familiar high divorce rates. As a result of these, a study of marriage in 2000 does not capture the same proportion of people as a study of marriage would have captured in 1900, and the differences do not capture all ethnic or racial groups in the same way. One might object that this sort of gradation of relationships—cohabitation versus marriage—has always been an issue in the study of intermarriage; one need only think of interracial or interfaith dating versus interracial or interfaith marriage. The point here is the profundity of the shift: cohabitation is much more intimate and of much longer duration than dating and much more likely to result in offspring.

Between 1970 and 1990 the proportion of people in cohabitating relationships tripled (McLanahan and Casper 1995), and over the next seven years, 1990 to 1997, it rose another 46 percent (Seltzer 2000, 1249), from 2.9 million to 4.1 million couples. On the other hand, compared to married couples, cohabitators are much more likely to break up. About 29 percent of couples cohabitating and only 9 percent of married couples break up in the first two years (Seltzer 2000, 1252). Nevertheless, Larry Bumpass, James Sweet, and Andrew Cherlin (1991) report that 20 percent of cohabitators persist in their relationship for more than five years and that 12 percent have children together. Debra Blackwell and Daniel Lichter (2000, 276) report that the percentage of persons who had cohabitated before their first marriage was 44 percent in 1980 to 1984. Nearly 40 percent of women age nineteen to twenty-four in 1995 had cohabited (Seltzer 2000, 1250).

The experimentation implied by cohabitation may extend to the crossing of ethnic divisions that the individuals, or their parents, find less threatening than intermarriage. There is far less evidence available on how these changes affect particular ethno-racial groups. David Harris and Hiromi Ono (2001) have studied nineteen- to thirty-year-olds in 226 separate metropolitan areas, which they describe as marriage markets, using the 1990 census data. They find large differences in the degree of cross-racial relationships between married couples and cohabitators. Thus, the percentage of white women's partners who are Asian is twice as high among cohabitators as among the married, and one and a half times as high for Latino partners. Among married Asian women, Harris and Ono find that 68 percent are in-married, 25 percent are married to whites, 4 percent are married to Hispanics, and 2 percent are married to blacks. By contrast, the comparable cohabitation rates for Asian women are 42 percent with Asian men, 45 percent with white men, 6 percent with Hispanics, and 5 percent with blacks. Latino women are also more likely to cohabit with men from racial out-groups than to marry them (39 percent more for white men, 162 percent more for black men, and 38 percent more for Asian men). Finally, 7 percent of black men have white wives, and 15 percent of black men who cohabit do so with white women. Harris and Ono (2001, 11) conclude that "there are substantially higher levels of intimate interracial contact than marriage data imply, and consequently that the social distance between racial groups is less than previous work suggests." Similarly, Blackwell and Lichter (2000) find that cohabitating couples are significantly less racially endogenous than married couples. In 1990 whites were eight times more likely to be endogamous than exogamous within marriage but only five times more likely to be endogamous rather than exogamous in cohabitation; for Asians, the comparable odds were 55 versus 17, for Hispanics 12 versus 9, and for blacks 365 versus 110.

The other key challenge in discussing marital patterns in connection with immigration then and now is that marriage is not merely less durable but quite simply less universal than it was before—especially for some racial-ethnic groups. For instance, in 1990 only 35 percent of black women under the age of thirty-five had ever been married

(Crowder and Tolnay 2000, 792). When rates of cohabitation and divorce are both high, the meaning of ethnic intermarriage becomes problematic at both ends of the process. Connections across ethnic lines may be established in premarital or postmarital cohabitation. In this brave new world, to pay attention only to the "middle stage" of these processes is problematic and is surely more suspect than it was when the field was developed in the early decades of the twentieth century.

The shift to bearing children out of wedlock is just as portentous. At present, one-third of American children are born to women who are not married. This figure varies dramatically by race and ethnicity. In 2000, 22 percent of births among non-Hispanic whites were to unmarried mothers, as were 69 percent of births among non-Hispanic blacks and 43 percent of births among Hispanic mothers (Martin et al. 2002). As the magnitude of the figure suggests, this pattern is not due to urban ghetto lifestyles or to California or northeastern lifestyles. It is remarkably widespread. Most of the children born out of wedlock do not live with their biological father. Of the total number of nonmarital births, 27 percent in the early 1980s were to couples who were cohabitating (Manning and Landale 1996, 63). Although the rates have been increasing rapidly for whites, the figures for blacks deserve special attention in connection with intermarriage because, as already noted, black out-marriage has been and remains distinctly low and at the same time the pattern is shifting somewhat toward greater intermarriage. Black-white intermarriage falls within a context of low levels of black marriage and higher levels of black-white cohabitation than of black-white marriage; these contexts radically complicate the interpretation of the intermarriage rates.

At the same time, the high proportion of blacks born out of wedlock also complicates the interpretation of the multiracial origins of the offspring of black-white unions. Much of a child's ethnic and even racial identity is related to the connection to parents and grandparents. If a child's father is out of the picture, how does that child consider his or her ethnicity at adulthood? Presumably—other things being equal—the father's ethnic origins stand a lower probability of being important to the next generation. But we cannot assume this outcome; the father might not be completely absent, and visible racialized characteristics, especially skin color, might make a difference in identity independent of the father's presence. Also relevant is the question of how the mother and the child define origins and identity while the child is growing up. Generally in multiracial situations, as David Harris has shown, the context in which questions about origins are asked makes a difference. For example, the child might be alone, or the mother may be in the room. Such differences in context also might interact with the nature of the relation between the biological mother and father (Harris and Ono 2002).

In sum, formal marriage and the children born in wedlock provide us with a conservative view of the degree of intermixing—both in terms of interethnic couples and in terms of the production of mixed-ancestry children. How changes in cohabitation, divorce, and childbearing come to affect interethnic comingling and resultant ethnic and racial identity in the next generation are big issues for the future understanding of ethnic blending. In our view, the most important novel features of American ethnic intermarriage are likely to be bound up with these changes. By comparison, differences in formal intermarriage rates between the largest of the immigrant groups of today and the largest immigrant group of the last great wave of immigration seem minor, even if race plays a somewhat different role in the contemporary pattern compared to historical immigrant patterns.

NOTES

1. A fuller report of the details of this empirical work may be read in Perlmann (2002). For a fuller discussion of the mixed nature of second generations discussed in the next paragraph, see Perlmann (2001).

2. First-generation intermarriage rates can also affect these proportions.

3. The information in this paragraph rests on an analysis of a 1979 CPS dataset in which the NBMP in the relevant age range were still children, living in their parents' homes. The relevant ethnic information about each parent of such children is available directly from questions about birthplace, parental birthplaces, and ancestry that were asked of each of the parents. For more detail, see Perlmann (2002).

4. Ethnic origins are also the result of differences in fertility rates across types of couples, but these differences are typically of much smaller magnitude.

5. Another interesting difference between the groups that is often ignored is the fact that the male-to-female sex ratio among the Italian immigrants was much greater than among the Mexican immigrants, creating a greater demand from unattached young immigrant men for second-generation women.

6. Two caveats to this statement must be made. First, in 1960 we cannot distinguish between Italian-born people who came as adults and those who came as children (the first and 1.5 generations, respectively). Second, we cannot distinguish in either census year between the third- and later-generation Italians and those native whites of native parentage with no Italian origins. This second limitation is of minor importance because so few Italian immigrants had arrived early enough in American history for a third generation to be of consequential magnitude when the second-generation cohorts we study were looking for marriage partners.

REFERENCES

Alba, Richard, and Victor Nee. 2003. *Remaking the American Mainstream*. Cambridge, Mass.: Harvard University Press.

Blackwell, Debra L., and Daniel T. Lichter. 2000. "Mate Selection Among Married and Cohabiting Couples." *Journal of Family Issues* 21(3): 275–302.

Bumpass, Larry, James Sweet, and Andrew Cherlin. 1991. "The Role of Cohabitation in Declining Rates of Marriage." *Journal of Marriage and the Family* 53(4): 913–28.

Crowder, Kyle D., and Stewart E. Tolnay. 2000. "A New Marriage Squeeze for Black Women: The Role of Racial Intermarriage by Black Men." *Journal of Marriage and the Family* 62(3): 792–807.

Drachsler, Julius. 1920. *Democracy and Assimilation: The Blending of Immigrant Heritages in America*. New York: Macmillan.

Gilbertson, Greta A., Joseph P. Fitzpatrick, and Lijun Yang. 1996. "Hispanic Intermarriage in New York City: New Evidence from 1991." *International Migration Review* 30(2): 445–59.

Gordon, Milton. 1964. *Assimilation in American Life: The Role of Race, Religion, and National Origins*. New York: Oxford University Press.

Harris, David R., and Hiromi Ono. 2001. "Cohabitation, Marriage and Markets: A New Look at Intimate Interracial Relationships." Ann Arbor, Mich.: University of Michigan. Institute for Social Research.

———. 2002. "Does It Matter How We Measure? Racial Classification and the Characteristics of Multiracial Youth." In *The New Race Question: How the Census Counts Multiracial Individuals*, edited by Joel Perlmann and Mary C. Waters. New York: Russell Sage Foundation and Levy Economics Institute.

Hollinger, David. 1995. *Postethnic America: Beyond Multiculturalism*. New York: Basic Books.

Integrated Public Use Microdata Samples (IPUMS). 1998. "Integrated Public Use Microdata Series." Minneapolis: University of Minnesota, Minnesota Population Center. www.ipums.umn.edu.

Lieberson, Stanley, and Mary C. Waters. 1988. *From Many Strands: Ethnic and Racial Groups in Contemporary America*. New York: Russell Sage Foundation.

Manning, Wendy, and Nancy Landale. 1996. "Racial and Ethnic Differences in the Role of Cohabitation in Premarital Childbearing." *Journal of Marriage and the Family* 58(1): 63–77.

Martin, Joyce A., Brady E. Hamilton, Stephanie J. Ventura, Fay Menacker, and Melissa M. Park. 2002. "Births: Final Data for 2000." Hyattsville, Md.: National Center for Health Statistics.

McLanahan, Sara, and Lynne Casper. 1995. "Growing Diversity and Inequality in the American Family." In *State of the Union: America in the 1990s*, vol. 2, *Social Trends*, edited by Reynolds Farley. New York: Russell Sage Foundation.

Merton, Robert K. 1941. "Intermarriage and the Social Structure: Fact and Theory." *Psychiatry* 4(August): 361–74.

Perlmann, Joel. 2001. "Toward a Population History of the Second Generation: Birth Cohorts of Southern, Central, and Eastern European Origins, 1871–1970." Working paper 333. Annandale-on-Hudson, N.Y.: Bard College, Levy Economics Institute. www.levy.org.

———. 2002. "Mexicans Now, Italians Then: Intermarriage Patterns." Working paper 350. Annandale-on-Hudson, N.Y.: Bard College, Levy Economics Institute. www.levy.org.

Qian, Zhenchao, Sampson Lee Blair, and Stacey D. Ruf. 2001. "Asian American Interracial and Interethnic Marriages: Differences by Education and Nativity." *International Migration Review* 35(134): 557–86.

Seltzer, Judith A. 2000. "Families Formed Outside of Marriage." *Journal of Marriage and the Family* 62(4): 1247–68.

Waters, Mary C., and Karl Eschbach. 1995. "Immigration and Ethnic and Racial Inequality in the United States." *Annual Review of Sociology* 21: 419–46.

Philip Kasinitz

Chapter 13

Race, Assimilation, and "Second Generations," Past and Present

Since the resumption of mass immigration in the late 1960s, the United States has incorporated tens of millions of new immigrants, the large majority of whom are non-European. Being neither unambiguously "white," in the way that term came to be used in late-twentieth-century America, nor African American, most of these newcomers do not fit easily into traditional North American racial categories. Of course, the presence of "nonblack, nonwhite" groups is hardly new. Native Americans, Latinos, and Asians have always been part of the U.S. racial landscape. Yet their presence in such large numbers, the fact that these numbers are now growing much faster than the numbers of whites or blacks, and the fact that they are now present in so many parts of the country, all raise new questions about what sort of a plural or multicultural society the United States is becoming and how North American notions of race are being reformulated.

The answers to these questions may ultimately lie less with immigrants themselves than with their ambivalently American children. It is this second generation (along with what Rubén Rumbaut (1999) has called the "1.5 generation": children born abroad but raised in the United States) who will determine whether and how the patterns of incorporation into U.S. society echo or diverge from those associated with past immigrants. As these young people become independent actors in the labor force and the political and cultural life of their communities, their experience will reveal the contours of America's emergent ethnic structure. Their experience will show us whether, and under what conditions, the children of black, Latino, and Asian immigrants will merge with native minorities, maintain their ethnic distinctiveness, or become "socially white."

Of course, today's immigrants and their children face an American society that is different in many ways from the one that confronted their predecessors in the early to midtwentieth century. When it comes to the question of race, two historical changes stand out. The first is that while the earlier immigrants did, by and large, assimilate into American society (see Alba and Nee 2003), they also changed and broadened that society in the process. The shift from what Milton Gordon (1964) described as the "Anglo-conformity" model of incorporation dominant in the late nineteenth century to the version of what Lawrence Fuchs (1982) called "civic pluralism" that had become dominant by the late 1960s greatly reduced the pressure toward cultural conformity experienced by newcomers. The second historical change was the African American civil rights movement and its aftermath, which, however partial its victories and unfulfilled its promise, did serve to delegitimate much of the de jure segregation and overt white supremacy that had been central facts of American life and law since the beginning of the Republic. This movement contributed a repertoire of ideas and organizational forms for challenging racial subordination. In some ways these built on the pluralist model of the European immigrants, but in other ways they stood in contradiction to it. The forms of political action that emerged from the struggle for African American empowerment provided different ways of thinking about racial and ethnic difference. Several developments point to the extension of the "African American model" to other groups: the extension of affirmative action programs to the children of immigrants; the emergence of ethnic studies programs on campus; the enforcement of the Voting Rights Act and other civil rights era legislation using blanket categories, such as "black" and "Hispanic," that render recent immigrants and their children indistinguishable from long-standing native minorities; and the general acceptance for so many official and legal purposes of what David Hollinger (1995) has called the "ethno-racial pentagon" of five "racial groups" in the United States. Yet just as the once-common extension of the "immigrant model" to African Americans and other nonwhites clearly missed the point about the experiences of racialized minorities,[1] today's application of the African American model to recent immigrants and their children risks obscuring much about their reality. Indeed, I would suggest that the incorporation of the new immigrants and their children is creating new ways of thinking about and negotiating ethnic and racial difference in U.S. society. What these new models will look like is still not entirely clear. Certainly they draw on both the experiences of European immigrants and those of native African Americans. Yet they are likely to be fundamentally different from both.

THE HERITAGE OF EUROPEAN AMERICAN ASSIMILATION

The discussion of second-generation incorporation today often begins with reference to the incorporation of earlier immigrants. The popular—and to a great extent the social-scientific—literature on immigration is, whether it is explicitly stated or not, almost always comparative. This is, of course, unfair. It is also probably inevitable. The incorporation of the European immigrants has been one of twentieth-century America's most celebrated achievements. The Statue of Liberty and Ellis Island have become shrines to what makes America unique, and more and more in the decades since World War II they have come to eclipse images of the American Revolution in our patriotic iconography. At the same time, America's proud history of incorporating immigrants— at least immigrants who came to be seen as "white"—stands in sharp contrast to the tragic history of America's relations with its "racial"—or perhaps more accurately *racialized*—minorities. It is also a comparison that, as Roger Waldinger (2002) notes, takes place within a "hall of mirrors." Myths about the past shape how we see the present. Concerns about the present are reflected back, reshaping our views of the past.

One thing we can say with relative certainty about the assimilation (or perhaps the "whitening") of the late-nineteenth- and early-twentieth-century European immigrants is that it *happened*. It did not, of course, happen without considerable struggle. Nor was it as preordained as it might look in retrospect. An excellent body of recent historical work has shown the extent to which the immigrant's status as a "white" American was far from initially self-evident. It was achieved as the result of considerable conflict, both between immigrants and white natives and between European immigrants and African Americans, Latinos, and Asians (see, for example, Roediger 1991; Jacobson 1998; Foner 2000; Foley 1997; Twine and Warren 1997). An earlier body of popular and sociological literature from the early 1970s documented and celebrated the supposed "miraculous" staying power of the "unmeltable ethnics" (Greeley 1976; Novak 1974) in the face of the assimilating force of American culture. Yet, valuable as they are, in both of these literatures there is a danger of missing the forest for the trees. Although the Europeans may not have been unambiguously "white" on arrival, by and large their second-generation children became unqualified white Americans in a fairly short period of time. As Richard Alba and Victor Nee (2003) demonstrate, assimilation, in almost every meaningful sense, was the overall trend. If the line turned out to be "bumpier" and more subject to stops and starts than predicted by the "straight line" assimilation theory of Robert Park and his contemporaries, the long-run direction has remained remarkably consistent (see Gans 1979).

This is not to imply that things usually turned out the way assimilation literature of the early to midtwentieth century predicted. This literature, it is now clear, was subject to a variety of conceptual confusions. Assimilation has often been one of those areas in which social-scientific description is closely tied to political prescription, and observers of the late-nineteenth-century and early-twentieth-century immigrants often saw assimilation as highly desirable. Writing at the midtwentieth-century height of American self-confidence, they tended to assume (as the popular use of term "assimilation" continues to assume) that incorporation into the dominant society was closely associated with adopting the *culture* of the dominant society (acculturation) and that both were correlated with upward mobility. They further assumed that whatever its psychic costs, becoming an American (by which they meant, although they rarely stated it, a "white" American) would "pay off" in tangible social and economic rewards. William Lloyd Warner and Leo Srole (1945, 145), for example, imply that the children of immigrants will be drawn to American ways in part because these ways have higher status in American society and in part because American culture is simply *better.* "In any judgements of rank, the American social system, being the most vigorous and having also the dominance of host status, is affirmed the higher."

Of course, many late-nineteenth- and early-twentieth-century immigrants were greeted with skepticism as to whether they *could* be assimilated. By the midtwentieth century this issue had been settled largely along racial lines. Asians were clearly seen as unassimilable—"forever foreigners" in Mia Tuan's (1998) memorable phrase. Black immigrants, although more numerous than usually remembered, were largely ignored in the discussion (for a rare exception, see Reid 1939). Latinos and Native Americans, central to the eighteenth- and nineteenth-century discussions of race, had come to be seen as a regional issue and thus marginal to the national debate.[2] By contrast, the large majority of turn-of-the-century immigrants, who were European, had come to be seen as assimilable by the second generation, if not always in the first. However much the "whiteness" of their parents had been initially contested, the second generation were clearly white Americans, with the privilege that status implies.

This outcome was shaped by a number of specific historical circumstances. The end of mass immigration in 1924, which stopped the flow of newcomers into most U.S. immigrant communities, gave the question of assimilation a decidedly generational caste. Soon even in communities where most adults were immigrants virtually all children were U.S.-born. The labor struggles of the Depression and the unifying of parts of the white working class in the Congress of Industrial Organizations (CIO) unions also played a role, as did the national bonding experience of World War II. The enthusiastic and prominent participation of Italian and German Americans in that war helped put to rest any residual fears about dual loyalties and stands in stark contrast to the internment of 110,000 Japanese Americans, two-thirds of whom were U.S.-born (Tuan 2002). Finally, the unprecedented upward mobility of the postwar period played a central part in shaping the adult lives of much of the last "second generation." Thus, by the mid-twentieth century the fears of turn-of-the-century nativists about the permanently unassimilable nature of eastern and southern Europeans seemed overblown and bigoted, or perhaps just silly. The second and 1.5 generations had not only become Americans but had embraced a vision of America. These children of immigrants had produced some of the most self-consciously "American" art, music, and theater ever created. Consider the music of Aaron Copeland and George Gershwin, the theater of Arthur Miller, Eugene O'Neill, William Saroyan, and Lee Strasberg, the painting of Mark Rothko and Frank Stella.[3] Even the sons of southern Italians, the most recent and marginally "white" of the early-twentieth-century "white" immigrants, could be "all-American boys" by the early 1940s. It is worth noting that Joe DiMaggio and Frank Sinatra achieved this status just as the United States went to war with Italy.

Yet if the second generation was becoming American in the midtwentieth century, it was also expanding the definition of what "American" meant. The expression of ethnic differences, at least in private, was legitimized even while, as John Murray Cuddihy (1978) argues, those aspects of ethnic and religious particularism that might give offense to the tolerant liberal consensus were self-consciously toned down. By the early 1960s, with a Catholic in the White House, a version of civic pluralism that celebrated the nation's immigrant heritage and ethnic diversity while also insisting on common political traditions and the public use of the English language had come to the fore. Non-European immigrants make only cameo appearances in the midtwentieth-century social-scientific literature. (The lack of attention paid to the wave of Mexican immigrants at the time of the Mexican Revolution by mainstream American social scientists is particularly striking.) Generally, studies of Latino immigrants and black immigrants and even most of the studies of Asian immigrants ended up in the "race relations" literature, not the immigration literature. As their numbers were relatively small and their experiences at odds with the dominant assimilation story, they were generally simply "defined" out of the picture.

What was true of social-scientific observers was perhaps even more true of American culture at large. The incorporation of the children of the late-nineteenth- and early-twentieth-century immigrants created a far more broadly inclusive "white society," one that was self-consciously pan-European rather than Anglo-Saxon in its origins. An assumed common Protestant heritage was replaced by newly invented "Judeo-Christian traditions" in religious life, while in the classrooms the details of English history now had to compete with something called "Western Civ." Yet this new pluralism hit a distinct limit at the color line. This was not, I would argue, because nonwhite immigrants represented a greater degree of cultural difference from American norms; nor was it because of the nonwhite immigrant's colonial origins, as was often argued in the 1970s (Blauner 1972). Shtetl Jews and Sicilian peasants could hardly have been more culturally different from nineteenth-century New Englanders, and Irish famine refugees had certainly known all the horrors of colonial oppression. Rather, the new pluralism hit the color line because the United States was still essentially a racial state in which democracy was fundamentally limited by white supremacy. Color, not difference, was the key distinction, a fact thrown into sharp relief when the United States is contrasted to western Europe. As George Fredrickson (1999, 40) notes: "A confusion between the need to overcome phenotypic racism, which remains a more basic problem in the United States than for France, and the need for cultural toleration, which is not so difficult a challenge for Americans, has at time muddied the debates over multiculturalism in both countries."

Thus, in the United States race and ethnicity have come to stand for two fundamentally different models of incorporation of minority populations. There is some confusion on this point caused by the fact that in the early twentieth century the term "race" was still often used in an older sense—to mean something close to what we would now call "nationality" (Banton 1987).[4] And of course, race is a shifting category. Henry Adams (1918/1931, 238) and many of his contemporaries did not consider those "furtive Yacoobs and Ysaac's" "reeking of the ghetto" and "snarling in weird Yiddish at the customs officials" to really be members of the same "race." It also is true that the racialization of Celtic and southern and eastern European immigrants was at some level at least intellectually connected to attitudes toward blacks and Asians, to whom nativists often compared them. Yet the more inclusive vision of a multiethnic *white* America—the vision that begins in the Progressive Era and ultimately becomes dominant after World War II—asserts that ethnic difference among the descendants of Europeans is compatible with "American-ness" and "white-ness" precisely because it is a different phenomenon than the "racial" differences imagined to separate Europeans from non-Europeans. Thus, Progressive Era celebrations of ethnic diversity usually simply ignored African Americans, despite their large numbers and long-standing presence in the society. For example, James Gavit, in his book *Americans by Choice* (1922), proudly states that "the American is a product of all races," but then goes on to explain that, by "all races" he means the "Saxon, Teuton, Kelt, Latin and Slav" (quoted in Glazer 1997, 105). Even the most inclusive of the early-twentieth-century visions of a multicultural or "transnational" America, such as those of Horace Kallen and Randolph Bourne, assumed European hegemony. As Nathan Glazer (1997, 111) notes, "[W]e search this modest literature in vain for any reference to American Blacks," who were then about 13 percent of the U.S. population.

It is worth noting that today we rarely use the word "assimilation" in connection with African Americans. This was not always the case. In the nineteenth century African American leaders openly advocated assimilation in opposition to racial separation, acceptance of segregation, and various colonization schemes. Rejecting spatial separation, no less a fighter for black rights than Frederick Douglass stated in 1883: "There is but one destiny, it seems to me, left for us, and that is to make ourselves and be made by others a part of the American people in every sense of the word. Assimilation, and not isolation, is our true policy and our natural identity. Unification is life, separation is death." This notion continued among many African American spokesmen in the midtwentieth century. E. Franklin Frazier (1939; 1942), in his debate with Melvin Herskovitz, pointedly argued for the essential American-ness of African Americans. Yet by and large, assimilation has been, both in theory and practice, a "whites only" concept. Indeed, by the early twentieth century blacks were excluded from assimilation by definition. Intermarriage—for most social scientists the ultimate indicator of assimilation—was illegal between blacks and whites in much of the country during most of the twentieth century, and the unique American tradition of "hypo-descent" (Harris 1964)—the "one drop rule"—essentially eliminated the possibility of assimilation. Thus, by the midtwentieth century there was considerable intermarriage between the children of white immigrants—albeit within some class, religious, and regional limits (producing the "eth-class," "triple melting pot," and other formulations). By the third generation many Americans considered themselves half-Italian and half-Irish, or half-German and half-Scandinavian. But no one was half-white and half-black. Rather, there were 100 percent black Americans, most of whom had some white ancestry or Native American ancestry that in no way ameliorated their "black" status.

THE SECOND GENERATION AND RACE TODAY

And what of today's largely nonwhite second generation? It is clear that the model of previous waves of immigration does not precisely fit their experience. Neither is their situation really analogous to that of America's long-standing "racial" minorities. With Fredrickson (1999, 40) we must ask: "Can a model of multiculturalism work both for non-European immigrants who have come recently and voluntarily and also for those who were brought much earlier in chains for forced labor?" For that matter, can a model of assimilation that emerged out of the experience of European immigrants now be expanded to non-Europeans in the face of the historical exclusion of non-Europeans from the assimilation process?

American life changed dramatically between the period when the last major cohort of second-generation immigrants came to assume adult roles (roughly the 1920s through the late 1950s) and the present. In no area were these changes more pronounced than in racial and ethnic relations. The context of reception faced by today's second generation is fundamentally different, in part because of the incorporation of the previous second generation, but also in part because of the changing role of race in American society in the wake of the civil rights movement of the 1950s and 1960s.

Perhaps the first question to address is whether today's immigrants and second generation are being incorporated at all. In light of today's relative ease of communication and transportation, many argue that migrants and their children are not really "immigrants" in the traditional sense. Rather, they are "transnationals" or "transmigrants" living in social worlds that cross national borders. For nonwhite migrants, it is sometimes theorized, this transnational option can be particularly attractive. Why, after all, would one give up ties to communities and nations in which one is part of the ethnic majority to become part of a downtrodden minority if one does not have to? Rather than accept racialized minority status, refusing to be socially incorporated into U.S. society, even while functioning within its economy, might seem a reasonable mode of resistance.

This notion was articulated by Linda Basch, Nina Glick Schiller, and Cristina Szanton Blanc in their influential 1994 book *Nations Unbound*. International migrants, they maintain, are increasingly active politically, socially, and economically in two or more societies at the same time, necessitating a major rethinking of categories of nationality and citizenship. This concept has been expanded theoretically by the recent work of the sociologist Alejandro Portes (1999; 2001) as well as the empirical studies of ethnographers such as Robert Smith (2003) and Peggy Levitt (2001). While each has his or her own version of transnationalism, all would agree that the "do they or don't they" model of assimilating into U.S. society is outmoded in today's world of global labor markets and instant communication.

For those who are concerned about the supposed balkanization of contemporary American society, this transnationalism is a particular cause for concern. Yet the issue is hardly new. During the nineteenth century and the first decades of the twentieth century, nativists frequently invoked the specter of "dual loyalties" and complained about immigrants refusing to cut ties to their previous societies. Catholic schools, German American bilingualism, Jewish distinctive dress, all were seen by some as threats to American unity. On the other hand, those who welcomed immigration assumed that with time home-country ties would either fade or at least mutate into an "ethnic" culture that would be different from the mainstream but nonetheless a distinctly American creation, with less and less relationship to the cultural and political life of the home country.

By and large, these latter predictions were borne out. By the midtwentieth century fears that the children of European immigrants would be anything less than 100 percent American seemed overblown. To be sure, Irish immigrants and their American-born children remained concerned about Irish independence, and Jews remained active in efforts to create a Zionist homeland in Palestine. Yet efforts such as these were rarely seen as being at odds with loyalty to the United States. When immigrant and American identities *did* come into sharp conflict—as happened to German Americans when the United States entered World War I—it was almost always the ethnic identity that disappeared. German American bilingualism, which had flourished for three generations, was dropped almost overnight, German newspapers shut their doors, and thriving German American organizations were suddenly disbanded. By World War II, few questioned or even noticed the irony in the fact that the war against Germany was led by a general named Eisenhower. (Of course, the children of Japanese immigrants were suspected of congenital loyalty to Japan even after three generations!) For the Europeans, who constituted the overwhelming majority of immigrants before the 1960s, ties to ancestral lands, while not forgotten, rarely played a central role in their daily lives after a generation or two.

Today's immigrants face very different conditions that make the possibility of sustained transnational ties far more viable. Travel is now cheap enough that even working-class immigrants (if perhaps not the very poor) can return to the home country with some frequency; what used to be a once-in-a-lifetime trip is now often an annual event. Immigrant neighborhoods are jammed with businesses selling low-cost phone calls and instant money transfers to some of the most remote parts of the globe. Video- and audiotapes allow immigrants to "participate" in weddings and village festivals in the Andes, Iran, or West Africa, sometimes only a day or two after they take place. The Internet increasingly makes it possible to do so in "real time." Sending-society governments, which until recently tended to ignore their communities abroad, are now encouraging those communities to participate economically and politically in the home country, and many now grant dual citizenship rights to emigrants in the United States. Indeed, some "deterritorialized nation-states" (Basch, Glick Schiller, and Szanton Blanc 1994) now encourage their nationals abroad to become U.S. citizens and lobby their American representatives on behalf of their home country. Paradoxically, as studies by the sociologist Douglas Massey (2002) have recently shown, naturalization may actually encourage immigrants to return to their homelands and invest money there; if things do not work out, they know they have the "insurance policy" of an American passport that will always allow them to return.

Yet just how transnational the second generation will remain is less clear (see Levitt and Waters 2002). In their study of high school students in San Diego and Miami, Alejandro Portes and Rubén Rumbaut (2000) confirm what many anecdotal accounts have already suggested. Although the children of immigrants often express a strong ethnic identity (indeed, it becomes stronger as high school goes on), most prefer English to their parents' native language. This finding raises the question of how much the second generation will truly participate in a transnational social sphere. Many other indicators of transnational connections, such as political participation, are probably mainly elite phenomena. For some groups with strong village-based identities (the rural Mexicans, for example), strong connections to home villages seem to be sustained into the next generations. For others, however, transnational social ties may be destined to be more a matter of "roots tourism" than real, ongoing social participation.

If, however, the new second generation is going to be American, what sort of Americans will they become? In 1992 the sociologist Herbert Gans turned traditional assimilation theory on its head by proposing what he termed the "second-generation decline" scenario. Gans speculates that those second-generation immigrants who are restricted by a lack of economic opportunities and by racial discrimination to poor inner-city schools, bad jobs, and shrinking economic niches will experience *downward* mobility relative to their immigrant parents. Like traditional observers of assimilation, Gans assumes that substantial acculturation is taking place—the children of immigrants are indeed coming to share many of the values and outlooks of their American peers. This acculturation, Gans suggests, will lead the children of immigrants to refuse to accept the low-level, poorly paid "immigrant jobs" held by their parents. Lacking other opportunities, however, they may become caught in downward mobility. The other possibility is that the children of immigrants will refuse to "become American" and will stay tied to their parents' ethnic community. This might lead to better economic outcomes but less assimilation. "The people who have secured an economically viable ethnic niche are acculturating less than did the European 2nd and 3rd generation," Gans (1992, 188) writes, "and those without such a niche are escaping condemnation to dead end immigrant and other jobs mainly by becoming very poor and persistently jobless Americans."

Alejandro Portes and Min Zhou (1993) make a similar argument in their often cited article on "segmented assimilation," a notion that Portes and Rumbaut expanded on in their 2000 book *Legacies*. Perhaps the most influential of these "revisionist" perspectives, the concept of segmented assimilation describes the various outcomes of different groups of second-generation youth and argues that the mode of incorporation for the first generation gives the second generation access to different types of opportunities and social networks. Those who are socially closest to American minorities may adopt an oppositional, "reactive" ethnicity. Those groups that come with strong ethnic networks, access to capital, and fewer ties to U.S. minorities experience a "linear" ethnicity that creates networks of social ties and may provide access to job opportunities while reinforcing parental authority and values and forestalling acculturation.

The segmented assimilation model has now inspired a number of studies, all pointing out ways in which "becoming American" may have a negative impact on immigrants and holding on to the immigrant culture may have positive results. Mary Waters (1999) points out that, in the case of black immigrants, for whom "acculturation" literally means incorporation into the ranks of America's most consistently downtrodden and racialized native minority, ethnic identification may be both a way of preserving immigrant advantages *and* a way of establishing distance from American blacks. Along similar lines, Milton Vickerman (1998) has examined the tensions that black immigrants feel between distancing themselves from black Americans and the identification they come to feel with native blacks in the face of U.S. racism.

The most through examination of the downsides of assimilation is found in the work of Rubén Rumbaut (1999). Assimilation, Rumbaut argues, *if* it happens at all, may in many ways prove a hindrance to upward mobility and be bad for the quality of life and even the physical well-being of contemporary immigrants. In many spheres, he argues, immigrants come with cultural advantages that are lost as they "become American." Thus, acculturation may be associated with *downward mobility*. Rumbaut also looks at the health outcomes of immigrants and their children. Second-generation immigrants, he argues, become progressively less healthy the longer they stay in the land of opportunity. Along with acquiring the high-fat diet of the American poor, the second generation in Rumbaut's studies seem to have assimilated a host of American habits. They smoke, abuse drugs, eat junk food, and experience stress more than their immigrant parents, and the result is worse health outcomes on a variety of measures, most notably neonatal health and birthweight. Nor is this trend purely the result of poverty. Rumbaut (1999, 177) notes that "for immigrants food choices deteriorated as income *increased*." Rumbaut also notes the paradoxical effect of mass media. The greatest single acculturating device in modern American society is the television. Most American children watch it about seven hours a day. Surely television viewing could pull young people into the American culture faster than anything that existed in the early twentieth century. Yet, unfortunately, television watching is inversely correlated with school performance. Thus, the young people at the most distance from one acculturating institution (television) are liable to do better in another (school).

Min Zhou and Carl Bankston's (1998) work on Vietnamese youth in New Orleans makes perhaps the clearest case for the preservation of home-country ties, even at the expense of acquiring connections with the dominant society. They see language retention as an advantage, because it facilitates participation in the ethnic economy, where opportunities may exceed those in the mainstream economy. Yet here one is struck by how fundamentally pessimistic the segmented assimilation argument is. American culture, at least in its ghetto variant, is seen as utterly corrosive to one's ability to perform in American society. The fact that the research took place in New Orleans only underlines the issue—clearly the black proletariat of New Orleans has historically made enormous contributions to American, and indeed to world, culture. Earlier generations of immigrants in that city took up aspects of New Orleans black street culture and, in turn, influenced that culture as well. The resulting cultural hybrids were unequal in many ways: white immigrants often benefited from African American innovation. Nevertheless, black-immigrant interaction in early-twentieth-century New Orleans created one of the central moments of creativity in American cultural history. That immigrants feel a need to cut themselves off from even hearing black culture points out what is lost in even the most successful segmented assimilation scenarios.

Of course, the idea that assimilation has costs and paradoxes is hardly unprecedented, as Rumbaut (1999) has taken care to note. Early-twentieth-century immigrants and those who wrote about them often expressed concern about intergenerational conflict and the heartache it produced (see in particular Thomas and Znaniecki 1927). Leonard Covello, a leading educator in New York's Italian American community in the midtwentieth century, famously recalled of his own second-generation childhood: "We were becoming Americans by learning how to be ashamed of our parents" (quoted in Iorizzo and Mondello 1980, 118). Years later, as principal of an East Harlem high school, Covello introduced the Italian language into the curriculum of the New York City public schools specifically as a means of preserving ethnic heritage and keeping assimilation partially at bay. Nor is there anything particularly new about the complaint that the children of immigrants were becoming the "wrong kind" of Americans. As Bonnie Kahn (1987, 244) notes, as early as 1906 *The Outlook* magazine warned "against rushing Italian children into the 'streetiness' and 'cheap Americanism'" that "so overwhelms Italian youngsters in the cities." Even the notion that a dense "ethnic enclave" could provide a bulwark against the worst effects of the American streets is fore-shadowed in studies of early-twentieth-century New York's Jewish community. These studies often made the case that juvenile delinquency among boys and sexual promiscuity among girls were both a direct result of Americanization and most common among the most assimilated youth in the community (for examples, see Landesman 1969; Prell 1999).

Yet if most of the arguments made in segmented assimilation literature were made as the last great migration produced the last large second generation, voices skeptical of the promise of assimilation were at that time still very much in the minority among intellectuals, among social scientists, and in the immigrant communities themselves. It was still, as Kahn (1987, 244) notes, "an age when people believed they could successfully become American." And it was a promise by and large made good in the mass upward mobility of postwar America. Today, against a background of falling real wages, rising income inequality, and continuing racial conflict, belief in both the possibility and value of assimilation seems considerably less pervasive.

Thus, the growing number who see acculturation as detrimental to upward mobility—who argue that he who assimilates least incorporates best—are expressing a general lack of faith in the economic ability of the contemporary United States to provide upward mobility on the scale that it did for earlier immigrants. They seem also to believe that contemporary American culture will undermine the ability of the children of immigrants to "make it" in American society—a new case of the well-known "cultural contradictions" of capitalism (Bell 1976). To be sure, most of these critics point to the destructive effects of racialization into "ghetto" or "underclass" culture. But the aspects of that culture they point to—individualism, nihilism, materialism, the high rate of marital breakup, the low rate of saving, the low value it places on education, the high degree of penetration by mass media—are hardly unique to any real or imagined "culture of poverty." They are precisely the supposed aspects of "ghetto" life that most closely approximate, albeit in extreme form, the ways of the broader society.

A MOVING COLOR LINE?

Largely missing from the segmented assimilation model is the notion that there could be benefits as well as costs to identifying with African Americans or of adopting African American–inspired models of racial difference and racial politics. Standing the traditional assimilation model on its head, segmented assimilation argues, in effect, that assimilation cannot happen for much of today's second generation, both because the U.S. economy has changed and because they will be seen by mainstream American society as nonwhite. What this may underestimate is the extent to which the role of race in the United States has changed in the wake of the struggles of the 1960s.

This is not to argue that the color line has ceased to play a central role in American society. Indeed, most evidence would seem to reveal that the African American experience remains poles apart from that of other groups in the United States. In many parts of the country, African Americans were as residentially segregated in 2000 as they were in 1980, and while black-white intermarriage has grown rapidly, the rate is still so much lower than for other groups that it hardly seems to be the same phenomenon (see Perlmann and Waters, this volume). Yet while for immigrants of African descent the color line still seems to play a major role in shaping the context of their reception, assimilating into black America may not be the universally negative experience that segmented assimilation theory implies (see Neckerman, Carter, and Lee 1999; Kasinitz,

Battle, and Miyares 2001; Zéphir 2001). Even in earlier times identification with the larger African American community had benefits as well as liabilities for second-generation West Indian immigrants, who often used the educational and social institutions of that community and in many cases became part of its professional and political leadership (Kasinitz 1992). Since the 1960s, affirmative action and black political advances have greatly expanded opportunities within the African American sphere—opportunities that second-generation West Indians and African immigrants are often well positioned to take advantage of.

For the children of nonblack, nonwhite immigrants, however, it is important to remember that race is mutable and the color line may be moving. The central cleavage in American life was once clearly between whites and nonwhites. Today there is some evidence that it is between blacks and nonblacks. This has tremendous salience for much of the second generation. The changing position of Asian Americans—once as racially excluded as anyone—on most indicators of acculturation and assimilation in the last two decades should remind us that there is nothing permanent about race. Perhaps in the next century the ties of language will make of the children of Colombians, Ecuadorans, Cubans, and Mexicans (along with the grandchildren of Puerto Ricans and the great-great-great-grandchildren of southwestern "Hispanos") a single "Latino" race. But this is hardly the only possible outcome, or even the most likely one, given the consistent finding that many of the second-generation children of Latino immigrants prefer to use English.

Prior to the 1960s, there was little reason for immigrants to identify with, much less emulate, African Americans. Indeed, for the children of Irish and southern and eastern European immigrants, the establishing of "whiteness" absolutely required distancing themselves from blacks. Even dark-skinned immigrants, such as New England's Cape Verdeans, worked hard at maintaining that distance for generations, only to do a turnaround in the 1960s (see Halter 1993). When immigrants did identify with African Americans, it was usually in cultural forms, and those doing so were usually among young people assuming an oppositional stance by identifying with the ultimate outsider, often to the chagrin of their elders. The Mexican American youth who took up the African American zoot suit as a symbol of rebellion in the 1940s are a case in point.[5] It is interesting to note that while rebellious Mexican youth were making a black cultural style very much their own on the streets of Los Angeles, middle-class Mexican American civil rights groups were still fighting segregation on the grounds that they were, in fact "white."

Since the 1960s, however, the African American model has been far more salient for nonblack, nonwhites in the United States; it provides a real alternative to the mode of incorporation of the European immigrants. This is often true even for those with little social connection to African Americans. Most of the second-generation Asian American professionals studied by Min and Kim (2002, 177), for example, report that they feel more "comfortable with" whites and have "more in common" with them than with blacks or Latinos. Yet they still report feeling "moderate levels of kinship with African Americans and Latinos" because "these minority communities provide role models in fighting white racism" that many perceive as missing in their own immigrant-dominated communities (see also Rodriguez 2002; Espiritu 1992).

During the 1960s the heroic model of the civil rights movement was taken up by other racialized minorities. Both mainstream civil rights groups and street-fighting Black Panthers inspired Latino, Asian, and Native American equivalents. Black studies on campus quickly spawned Chicano studies, Puerto Rican studies, and Asian American studies—to say nothing of Jewish, Middle Eastern American, and gay and lesbian studies. Affirmative action for African Americans quickly expanded to other protected categories, including women as well as racial minorities (and even, at my university, Italian Americans). At least one major second-generation Mexican American writer, Richard Rodriguez (2002, 25–26), has caused some controversy by making his discomfort with this mode of incorporation a major theme. "As a young man," he writes, "I was more a white liberal than I ever tried to put on black. For all that, I ended up a minority, the beneficiary of affirmative action programs to redress black exclusion." He goes on to note that now, as a writer, "I remain at best ambivalent about those Hispanic anthologies where I end up; about those anthologies where I end up the Hispanic . . . [yet] the fact that my books are published at all is the result of the slaphappy strategy of the northern black Civil Rights movement." Of course, what no one could have predicted in the 1960s was the enormous expansion of the nonblack, nonwhite population—the parents of today's second generation—due to massive immigration.

One need not subscribe to William Julius Wilson's (1977) view that the significance of race in American is "declining" to share his insight that, for African Americans, racial oppression is multidimensional. It includes overt racist practices, covert racist practices and assumptions within the culture, and residual disadvantage that is the result of *past* racist practices. The civil rights movement greatly reduced, although by no means eliminated, the first element of racial oppression. It was less successful against the second. The original, individualistic language of "civil *rights*" was generally not equipped to address the present-day effects of past discrimination. Affirmative action policies are an effort to do just that, although their record in doing so is mixed at best. Much of today's second generation has also been profoundly affected by the changes of the civil rights era. For many, their very presence in this country is in large part the result of one important piece of civil rights legislation, the 1965 Hart-Celler Act immigration reforms, which ended national origins quotas. However, as the children of immigrants mostly from societies in which they were part of the racial majority, the second generation is far less encumbered by the residue of past discriminatory practices. Although covert racist practices and assumptions obviously do affect the lives of second-generation immigrants (the second-, third-, or fourth-generation Asian American professional "complimented" on his command of English or asked when she is "going home" are the archetypical examples), I suspect that such practices and assumptions are less pernicious and less pervasive than those confronting minorities whose castelike subordination has been central to the formation of American identity.[6] Ironically, the children of nonwhite immigrants may have been better positioned to benefit from the delegitimation of the overt white supremacy and de jure racism that the civil rights struggles achieved than were long-standing U.S. minorities—particularly African Americans.[7]

In some cases these relative newcomers may be unaware of the extent to which they have benefited from the largely African American struggle for equality, or the degree to which people who "look like them" were excluded in the past. In other cases they may be well aware of this history but consider it irrelevant to their lives. Most of the second-generation Korean Americans interviewed by Dae Young Kim (2001) knew about the history of anti-Asian racism. Many in this largely college graduate population reported having taken Asian American studies classes. For most, however, this history was just that: history. Although most reported having personally experienced racism and a politically mobilized minority saw race as a central factor in their lives, the majority saw discrimination as a minor concern. (To be sure, like most second-generation adults, the people in Kim's study were young—in their twenties and early thirties. Deborah Woo [2000] argues that there are "glass ceilings" in their futures, which is certainly possible.) Socially and phenotypically closer to African Americans, the Caribbean immigrants studied by Flore Zéphir (2001), Mary Waters (1999), and Milton Vickerman (1998) were extremely aware of and concerned about discrimination. They also identified with the struggles of African Americans, which they saw as also being their own (see also Kasinitz 1992). However, for more upwardly mobile second-generation West Indians, this awareness often led to attempts to distance themselves from African Americans, whom they saw as suffering from both white racism, a problem they noted that West Indians shared, and the heritage of past discrimination, which they often insisted West Indians did not share.

The situation is even more complicated for members of groups—Mexican Americans, the largest second-generation group in the United States today, are the clearest example—who include both the descendants of long-standing, clearly racialized populations whose forebears have been in this country for many generations and very recent immigrants, as well as a large second-generation population. Scholars should probably be paying more attention to how these differences in generation and immigration history are thought about and discussed within this community. In the Mexican American discourse about group identity, racial models, immigrant-ethnic models, "conquered peoples" models, and transnational notions of border identity all come into play, as do significant regional differences in both immigration history and the history of political activism.[8]

Whether or not the second generation is aware of how much the struggles against antiblack racism have affected their lives, the second generation is often well positioned to take advantage of the reforms put in place to remedy past discrimination against African Americans. Douglas Massey's (2002) study of higher education reveals that immigrants are generally overrepresented among the nation's black college students, and this is most true at high-status institutions. Indeed, in many of America's elite colleges the majority of the "black" students are immigrants, the children of immigrants, or biracial. Similarly, imprecise definitions have often meant that programs designed for Mexican Americans, Puerto Ricans, and long-standing Asian American communities have been utilized by the children of recent Asian immigrants and an ever-broadening category of recent "Latino" immigrants. The replacement of "justice" with "diversity" as a rationale for affirmative action on campus and elsewhere has greatly facilitated this trend, and many elite institutions have happily gone along with it. It is, after all, far less wrenching to admit the children of dark-skinned but middle-class, often college-educated immigrants than to truly confront the heritage of America's racial past. However, I suspect that the perception that affirmative action has become a "bait and switch"—with the benefits going to the children of often elite immigrants rather than to impoverished African and Latino Americans—bears some responsibility for the erosion of the always weak support for such programs among whites.

If affirmative action and other institutional reforms coming out of the civil rights era have benefited the second generation in some contexts, the civil rights model has proved a poor fit in others, particularly in electoral politics. The Voting Rights Act and other reforms that seek to redress the history of minority political exclusion tend to assume African American levels of residential concentration (and for that matter endogamy), generalizing from the most extreme case. As a result, efforts to carve out "Latino" super-majority electoral districts have often linked distant communities with few common interests into districts that have either failed to elect Latinos or failed to pass constitutional muster. The Chicago congressional district that linked distant Puerto Rican and Mexican neighborhoods or New York's "Bullwinkle" district—so named because the map of the three-borough patchwork of Dominican, Puerto Rican, and South American neighborhoods resembles a large antlered moose—are but two examples. Among Asian Americans, whose level of racial segregation is even lower and whose out-marriage rates are higher, attempts to create "Asian American" districts have been even more problematic. Further, in places where aging and declining African American (or Mexican American) populations now manage to politically dominate immigrant Latino or West Indian majorities, owing to the latter's youth and lack of citizenship, the voting rights model provides no obvious remedy.

On the whole, however, African American (and to a lesser extent Mexican American and Puerto Rican) institutional structures and modes of organization have provided new models and institutions for this second generation that were not present for the children of immigrants in earlier times. For better or ill, the children of nonwhite immigrants have often taken up these models, and this represents a major change in U.S. society. For one thing, it means that institutions dominated by African Americans and Latinos now face ethnic succession struggles. Amy Foerster (forthcoming), for example, writes about the difficulties encountered by the largely older leaders of a professional trade union, who are African American and veterans of the civil rights movement, in understanding the concerns of the union's much younger, largely West Indian and Latino second-generation membership. Alex Trillo's (forthcoming) study of a community college in New York shows the changing role of a Puerto Rican studies course now that the student body is largely made up of immigrant and second-generation South Americans and Dominicans. Once envisioned as a way for Puerto Rican students to learn "about themselves," Puerto Rican studies became a place to learn how to become (Latino) American—in addition to fulfilling a social science distribution requirement.[9]

It is possible to exaggerate the contrast between the post–civil rights model of ethnic politics and the civic pluralism practiced by the children of the last great wave of immigrants. Ethnic politics was not invented by African Americans. Indeed, the civic pluralist model might with equal justice be termed the political machine model. Ethnically balanced tickets and ethnic divisions of patronage were facts of life in many American cities in the midtwentieth century. Ethnic preferences in hiring in both the private and public sectors were widely accepted long before the phrase "affirmative action" was coined. The type of ethnic collective action seen in the civil rights movement in many ways built on precedents established by the white ethnics (see Perlmann and Waldinger 1999). Still, the shift in ideology seems undeniable. The earlier second generation fought for inclusion despite being members of previously racialized and excluded groups. The current second generation at least has the option of fighting for inclusion precisely because they are members of (or resemble members of) previously excluded groups.

THE SECOND GENERATION AND HYBRID CULTURE

Finally, it should be remembered that the new second generation—the children of people who have come to this country since the mid-1960s—are still young. This generation's oldest members are now in their midthirties. It is thus not surprising that their racial identity, like so much else about their identity, is still a work in progress. So far the evidence is less clear on who or what they are than it is on who or what they are not.

They clearly are not immigrants. The notion that the most successful of them would cling to their parents' ethnic enclaves seems to have little empirical support. A study of the second generation in metropolitan New York study shows that economically, even among groups with high rates of parental business ownership, few seek to work within the ethnic economy (Kasinitz, Waters, et al. 2002; for an even stronger finding among Koreans, see Kim, forthcoming). There is some support for the idea that the least successful of the second generation would fall back into the immigrant jobs of their parents—the enclave less a springboard than a safety net—but even there the numbers are small. More important perhaps, they are not immigrants culturally. Having been raised in the United States, most of them accept norms of behavior, language, and gender roles that often create a profound disconnect with the world of their parents. As Rumbaut and Portes (2001, 302) note, "[T]he second-generation youths who loudly proclaim their Mexicanness or Haitianness often do so in English and with a body language far closer to their American peers than to anything resembling their parents' culture." And yet many of them, particularly those who are seen as nonwhite, feel that they are also not "American"—or as one of Tuan's (2002, 212) informants put it, "not American enough." As Yen Le Espiritu (2002, 40) notes in the case of Filipino Americans, the emergence of a second-generation identity is creating a culture that is "distinct," one that is "neither an extension of the 'original' culture nor facsimile of 'mainstream' America" (see also Kasinitz 2000).

The content and boundaries of these new identities also seem to be in flux. Some are panethnic (Espiritu 1992) and to an extent racialized, such as "Asian American" or "Latino." Yet the second-generation Chinese and Korean college students in Nazlie Kibria's (2002) study report discomfort at the obviously synthetic, artificial, and often politicized nature of the Asian American category. Will panethnicity be the new "triple melting pot"? Are the children of Koreans and Chinese really becoming "Asian Americans"? Or is this just a way station on the road to total incorporation? The South Americans interviewed in the second generation in metropolitan New York study (Kasinitz, Mollenkopf, and Waters 2002) clearly have a sense of themselves as members of a group larger than their parents' ethnic background. They see themselves as not white—but are equally certain that they are not Puerto Rican! These children of Colombian, Peruvian, and Ecuadorean immigrants seem to be struggling for a name for this new racial category, which they most often describe (fully aware of the inaccuracy) as "Spanish." In addition, the question of racial and ethnic identity seems increasingly crosscut by gender. Nancy Lopez (2003), for example, reports that Dominican and Haitian second-generation girls are both far more educationally oriented and upwardly mobile *and* more tied to their families' immigrant communities than their brothers, who are far more enmeshed in a street culture that is in large part African American and Puerto Rican. Among second-generation members of every Asian group (and many Latino groups, although to a lesser extent), women out-marry at rates much higher than men do. What this will mean in terms of the intersection of race and gender, particularly for the third generation, has yet to be fully understood. Finally, we should remember that while the new second generation confronts North American models of racial difference, they often bring with them a knowledge of the more flexible and multidimensional racial structures of their parents' homelands. What impact the immigration of millions of people who take for granted the norms of "mestizo" or "creole" cultures will have on a "one drop rule" society is still not clear.[10]

My own reading of the literature on racial identity and the current second generation suggests that we often underestimate the fluidity in the ways people acquire and use these identities. All too often assimilation is seen as a zero-sum game—the more ethnic you are, the less you are a member of the dominant culture. What this perspective misses is the possibility of multiculturalism, not of balkanized groups but of cultural pastiche and interaction—less a "gorgeous mosaic" than a pointillist painting where the edges of the distinct colors blur together in new and eclectic mixtures. The current discussion of second-generation incorporation also often sounds as if there is one clearly defined majority culture into which people do or do not "assimilate." Of course, we know things are more complicated than that. The cultural and political life of New York, Los Angeles, and Miami has been transformed by immigrants, even as the immigrants are transformed themselves. It is really not a question of "preserving traditions" versus "becoming American." As in the Progressive Era, American identity is being renegotiated. Further, much of the real action of acculturation takes place not just between immigrants and some monolithic "majority culture," but between the different immigrant groups and, although more problematically, between immigrants and long-standing native minorities, particularly African Americans, whose own struggle for equality and their cultural practices provides alternative models for thinking about race. As noted by the Palestinian American poet Suheir Hammad, author of a book entitled *Born Palestinian, Born Black* (1996): "I grew up around rhymes and break dance . . . [we] created our own minority group. Asians, blacks, Caribbeans, we were all minority" (quoted in Dinitia Smith 2003, E9).

I am not implying any new undifferentiated multiracial melting pot. The color line clearly remains a central fact shaping the life chances of those children of immigrants of sufficiently African descent to be thought of as "black." And yet, if there is any hope for deconstructing America's pernicious racial categories, it may lie in the daily life practices of the large number of young people, like Hammad, now growing up in multiethnic neighborhoods and cities with no clear racial majority. Their experience is new, and while they confront both the white immigrant pluralist model and the African American post–civil rights model, we should not ignore the possibility that they are creating something quite different from both, something whose parameters are not yet clearly defined. Thus, as we think about race and the new second generation, it behooves us to pay close attention to the popular culture these young people are creating. In the end that culture may prove far more fluid and dynamic than the advocates of renewed assimilation recognize, and less corrosive than the predictors of segmentation and second-generation decline now fear.

NOTES

1. The boldest statement of this position is probably Irving Kristol's (1972) essay "The Negro Today Is Like the Immigrant of Yesterday," first published in 1966. Nathan Glazer and Daniel Patrick Moynihan's 1963 classic *Beyond the Melting Pot* provides another example of the application, with some caveats, of the immigrant model to African Americans. Interestingly, by 1970 events had convinced the authors that this analogy was increasingly problematic, as the long essay that introduces the book's second edition makes clear.

2. The discussion of assimilation in the early and midtwentieth-century United States is colored by a strong East Coast–Midwest bias. Of course, that is where most Americans lived

during this period. The growing population and increased cultural centrality in American life of the Southwest and the West Coast, with their very different racial histories, is one of the factors that make the current situation different.

3. Often at the expense of immigrant parents in the case of O'Neill's work. *Long Day's Journey into Night* contains a chilling confrontation between the immigrant father and the second-generation son. In a heated argument, the son insults what he sees as the father's Irish peasant ways. The father retorts that the son should not be insulting Ireland "with the map of it on your face." The son replies, "Not after I wash my face."

4. Of course, in the midnineteenth century "race" was used even more broadly. In "Bartleby the Scrivener" (1856), for instance, Herman Melville refers to scriveners as a "race."

5. On the East Coast during this period, rebellious young white "hipsters," many of them second-generation, also wore zoot suits, listened to jazz, experimented with drugs, and generally tried to become, in Norman Mailer's (1957) words, "white Negroes." In most cases this was a matter of emulating what they imagined African Americans to be, as few knew any personally. A few white second-generation members did become more or less "socially black"—such as the Jewish American jazz musician Mezz Mezrow and the Greek American rhythm and blues impresario Johnnie Otis—yet these cases are so rare as to have become almost legendary. Most of the time, like today's hip-hop-listening suburban "wiggers," second-generation hipsters and beats took up a stereotyped image of blackness as a form of short-lived, youthful rebellion against assimilation into a mainstream they were destined to join.

6. Claire Kim (2000) and Mia Tuan (1998) have argued that anti-Asian racism differs from antiblack racism qualitatively rather than just in degree; the former emphasizes congenital exoticness, permanent foreignness, and unassimilability rather than inferiority, they argue. Although this clearly has historically been the case, the high rates of intermarriage and economic upward mobility among contemporary second-generation Asian Americans leave me skeptical about the permanent outsider status of the children of post-1965 Asian immigrants.

7. Indeed, I would argue that many sorts of minority groups—immigrants, gays, possibly Jews—have benefited as much if not more from the changes in U.S. society since the civil rights movement as have African Americans.

8. I was recently in a meeting with a group of Mexican American (their term) intellectuals and academics in San Antonio, Texas, discussing their city's relationship to the border as well as the long-standing Tejano community's complex feeling about recent arrivals from Mexico. One professor stood out from the group in her use of a racial language to describe the situation and in her insistence on describing herself as a "Chicano." Later, with this professor out of earshot, it was explained to me—the Jewish outsider from New York—why this difference in language was to be expected: "You have to understand. She's from California."

9. Trillo reports that the class was taught by a Cuban. There was not a Puerto Rican in the room.

10. Glazer and Moynihan's unfortunately stereotypical 1963 account of New York's Puerto Ricans does strike one strangely optimistic note. They observe that Puerto Ricans, for all of their other problems, generally lack the phenotypic racism of North Americans. Thus, they wonder, might not the incorporation of such a large group of people who do not conform to North American racial norms actually serve to help undermine those norms? Unfortunately, this turned out not to be the case. Rather than deconstruct racial categories by example, New York Puerto Ricans ended up being racialized, often despite phenotype, as a sort of "virtual blacks." Still, today things could work out differently.

REFERENCES

Adams, Henry. 1938. *The Education of Henry Adams.* New York: Modern Library. (Orig. pub. in 1918.)

Alba, Richard, and Victor Nee. 2003. *Remaking the American Mainstream: Assimilation and the New Immigration.* Cambridge, Mass.: Harvard University Press.

Banton, Michael. 1987. *Racial Theories.* New York: Cambridge University Press.

Basch, Linda, Nina Glick Schiller, and Cristina Szanton Blanc. 1994. *Nations Unbound: Transnational Projects, Postcolonial Predicaments, and Deterritorialized Nation-States.* New York: Gordon and Breach.

Bell, Daniel. 1976. *The Cultural Contradictions of Capitalism.* New York: Basic Books.

Blauner, Robert. 1972. *Racial Oppression in America.* New York: Harper & Row.

Cuddihy, John Murray. 1978. *No Offense: Civil Religion and Protestant Taste.* New York: Scribner.

Douglass, Frederick. 1883. "Address of the Hon. Frederick Douglass, Delivered in the Congregational Church, Washington, D.C., April 16, 1883, on the Twenty-first Anniversary of Emancipation in the District of Columbia." In *African American Perspectives: Pamphlets from the Daniel A. P. Murray Collection: 1818–1907.* http:/lcweb2.loc.gov.

Espiritu, Yen Le. 1992. *Asian American Panethnicity: Bridging Institutions and Identities.* Philadelphia: Temple University Press.

———. 2002. "The Intersection of Race, Ethnicity, and Class: The Multiple Identities of Second-Generation Filipinos." In *Second Generation: Ethnic Identity Among Asian Americans,* edited by Pyong Gap Min. New York: Altamira Press.

Foerster, Amy. Forthcoming. "Isn't Anyone Here from Alabama? Solidarity and Struggle in a Mighty Mighty Union." In *Becoming New Yorkers: The Second Generation in a Global City,* edited by Philip Kasinitz, John Mollenkopf, and Mary C. Waters. New York: Russell Sage Foundation.

Foley, Neil. 1997. *The White Scourge: Mexicans, Blacks, and Poor Whites in Texas Cotton Culture.* Berkeley: University of California Press.

Foner, Nancy. 2000. *From Ellis Island to JFK: New York's Two Great Waves of Immigration.* New Haven, Conn., and New York: Yale University Press and Russell Sage Foundation.

Frazier, E. Franklin. 1939. *The Negro Family in the United States.* Chicago: University of Chicago Press.

———. 1942. "Rejoinder" [to Melvin Herskovits]. *American Sociological Review* 8(August): 402–4.

Fredrickson, George. 1999. "Mosaics and Melting Pots." *Dissent* 46(3, Summer): 36–42.

Fuchs, Lawrence. 1982. *The American Kaleidoscope: Race, Ethnicity, and the Civic Culture.* Hanover, N.H.: University Press of New England.

Gans, Herbert. 1979. "Symbolic Ethnicity: The Future of Ethnic Groups and Cultures in America." *Ethnic and Racial Studies* 2(1, January): 1–20.

———. 1992. "Second-Generation Decline: Scenarios for the Economic and Ethnic Futures of the Post-1965 American Immigrants." *Ethnic and Racial Studies* 15(2): 173–93.

Gavit, James. 1922. *Americans by Choice.* New York: Harper.

Glazer, Nathan. 1997. *We Are All Multiculturalists Now.* Cambridge, Mass.: Harvard University Press.

Glazer, Nathan, and Daniel Patrick Moynihan. 1963. *Beyond the Melting Pot: The Negroes, Puerto Ricans, Jews, Italians, and Irish of New York City.* Cambridge, Mass.: MIT Press.

Gordon, Milton. 1964. *Assimilation in American Life: The Role of Religion and National Origins.* New York: Oxford University Press.

Greeley, Andrew. 1976. "The Ethnic Miracle." *The Public Interest* 45: 20–36.

Halter, Marilyn. 1993. *Between Race and Ethnicity: Cape Verdean Americans 1860–1965.* Urbana: University of Illinois Press.

Hammad, Suheir. 1996. *Born Palestinian, Born Black.* New York: Writers and Readers Press.

Harris, Marvin. 1964. *Patterns of Race in the Americas.* New York: W. W. Norton.

Hollinger, David. 1995. *Post-Ethnic America: Beyond Multiculturalism.* New York: Basic Books.

Iorizzo, Luciano J., and Salvatore Mondello. 1980. *The Italian Americans*. Boston: Twayne.

Jacobson, Matthew. 1998. *Whiteness of a Different Color: European Immigrants and the Alchemy of Race*. Cambridge, Mass.: Harvard University Press.

Kahn, Bonnie M. 1987. *Cosmopolitan Culture: The Gilt-Edged Dream of the Tolerant City*. New York: Atheneum.

Kasinitz, Philip. 1992. *Caribbean New York: Black Immigrants and the Politics of Race*. Ithaca, N.Y.: Cornell University Press.

———. 2000. "Children of America: The Second Generation Comes of Age." *Common Quest* 4(3): 32–41.

Kasinitz, Philip, Juan Battle, and Ines Miyares. 2001. "Fade to Black? The Children of West Indian Immigrants in South Florida." In *Ethnicities: Coming of Age in Immigrant America*, edited by Rubén Rumbaut and Alejandro Portes. New York and Berkeley: Russell Sage Foundation and the University of California Press.

Kasinitz, Philip, John Mollenkopf, and Mary C. Waters. 2002. "Becoming American/Becoming New Yorkers: The Experience of Assimilation in a Majority Minority City." *International Migration Review* 36(4, Winter): 1020–36.

Kasinitz, Philip, Mary C. Waters, John Mollenkopf, and Mehr Anil. 2002. "Second-Generation Transnationalism in New York Today." In *The Changing Face of Home: The Transnational Lives of the Second Generation*, edited by Mary C. Waters and Peggy Levitt. New York: Russell Sage Foundation.

Kibria, Nazlie. 2002. *Becoming Asian American: Second-Generation Chinese and Korean American Identities*. Baltimore: Johns Hopkins University Press.

Kim, Claire Jean. 2000. *Bitter Fruit: The Politics of Black-Korean Conflict in New York City*. New Haven, Conn.: Yale University Press.

Kim, Dae Young. 2001. "Entrepreneurship and Intergenerational Mobility Among Second-Generation Korean Americans in New York." Ph.D. diss., City University of New York.

———. Forthcoming. "Leaving the Ethnic Economy: The Rapid Integration of Second-Generation Korean Americans in New York." In *Becoming New Yorkers: The Second Generation in a Global City*, edited by Philip Kasinitz, John Mollenkopf, and Mary C. Waters. New York: Russell Sage Foundation.

Kristol, Irving. 1972. "The Negro Today Is Like the Immigrant of Yesterday." In *Nation of Nations: The Ethnic Experience and the Racial Crisis*, edited by Peter Rose. New York: Random House. (Orig. pub. in 1966.)

Landesman, Alter F. 1969. *Brownsville: The Birth, Development, and Passing of a Jewish Community*. New York: Bloch.

Levitt, Peggy. 2001. *The Transnational Villagers*. Berkeley: University of California Press.

Levitt, Peggy, and Mary C. Waters, eds. 2002. *The Changing Face of Home: The Transnational Lives of the Second Generation*. New York: Russell Sage Foundation.

Lopez, Nancy. 2003. *Hopeful Girls, Troubled Boys: Race and Gender Disparity in Urban Education*. New York: Routledge.

Mailer, Norman. 1957. *The White Negro*. San Francisco: City Lights Books.

Massey, Douglas. 2002. *The River: The Social Origin of Freshmen at America's Selective Colleges and Universities*. Princeton, N.J.: Princeton University Press.

Min, Pyong Gap, and Rose Kim. 2002. "Formation of Ethnic and Racial Identities: Narratives by Asian American Professionals." In *Second Generation: Ethnic Identity Among Asian Americans*, edited by Pyong Gap Min. New York: Altamira Press.

Neckerman, Kathryn M., Prudence Carter, and Jennifer Lee. 1999. "Segmented Assimilation and Minority Cultures of Mobility." *Ethnic and Racial Studies* 22(6): 945–65.

Novak, Michael. 1974. "The Seventies: The Decade of the Ethnics." In *Race and Ethnicity in Modern America*, edited by Richard J. Meister. Lexington, Ky.: Heath.

Perlmann, Joel, and Roger Waldinger. 1999. "Immigrants, Past and Present: A Reconsideration." In *The Handbook of International Immigration: The American Experience*, edited by Charles Hirschman, Philip Kasinitz, and Josh DeWind. New York: Russell Sage Foundation.

Portes, Alejandro. 2001. "Introduction: The Debates and Significance of Immigrant Transnationalism." *Global Networks* 1(3, July): 181–94.

Portes, Alejandro, and Rubén Rumbaut. 2000. *Legacies: The Story of the New Second Generation.* Berkeley: University of California Press.

Portes, Alejandro, and Min Zhou. 1993. "The New Second Generation: Segmented Assimilation and Its Variants." *Annals of the American Academy of Political and Social Science* 530: 74–97.

Prell, Riv-Ellen. 1999. *Fighting to Become American: Jews, Gender and the Anxiety of Assimilation.* Boston: Beacon Press.

Reid, Ira de A. 1939. *The Negro Immigrant: His Background, Characteristics, and Social Adjustment: 1899–1937.* New York: Columbia University Press.

Rodriguez, Richard. 2002. *Brown: The Last Discovery of America.* New York: Viking.

Roedinger, David R. 1991. *The Wages of Whiteness: Race and the Making of the American Working Class.* New York: Verso.

Rumbaut, Rubén. 1999. "Assimilation and Its Discontents: Ironies and Paradoxes." In *The Handbook of International Immigration: the American Experience,* edited by Charles Hirschman, Philip Kasinitz, and Josh DeWind. New York: Russell Sage Foundation.

Rumbaut, Rubén, and Alejandro Portes, eds. 2001. *Ethnicities: Coming of Age in Immigrant America.* New York and Berkeley: Russell Sage Foundation and University of California Press.

Smith, Dinitia. 2003. "Arab-American Writers, Uneasy in Two Worlds." *New York Times,* February 19.

Smith, Robert C. 1997. "Transnational Migration, Assimilation, and Political Community." In *The City and the World: New York's Global Future,* edited by Margaret E. Crahan and Alberto Vourvuoulias-Bush. New York: Council on Foreign Relations.

———. 2003. "Diasporic Memberships in Historical Perspective: Comparative Insights from the Mexican, Italian, and Polish Cases." *International Migration Review* 37(143): 724–59.

Thomas, William I. and Florian Znaniecki. 1927. *The Polish Peasant in Europe and America.* New York: Alfred A. Knopf.

Trillo, Alex. Forthcoming. "Panethnicity and Educational Trajectories Among Latino Community College Students." In *Becoming New Yorkers: The Second Generation in a Global City,* edited by Philip Kasinitz, John Mollenkopf, and Mary C. Waters. New York: Russell Sage Foundation.

Tuan, Mia. 1998. *Forever Foreigners or Honorary Whites?: The Asian Ethnic Experience Today.* New Brunswick, N.J.: Rutgers University Press.

———. 2002. "Second-Generation Asian American Identity: Clues from the Second-Generation Experience." In *Second Generation: Ethnic Identity Among Asian Americans,* edited by Pyong Gap Min. New York: Altamira Press.

Twine, France Winddance, and Jonathon Warren. 1997. "White Americans, the New Minority? Nonblacks and the Ever-Expanding Boundaries of Whiteness." *Journal of Black Studies* 28(2): 200–18.

Vickerman, Milton. 1998. *Cross Currents: West Indian Immigrants and Race.* New York: Oxford University Press.

Waldinger, Roger. 2002. "The Remaking of America and Immigrants: Old and New." New York: New York University, Henry Hart Urban Policy Forum.

Warner, William Lloyd, and Leo Srole. 1945. *The Social Systems of American Ethnic Groups.* New Haven, Conn.: Yale University Press.

Waters, Mary C. 1999. *Black Identities: West Indian Dreams and American Realities.* New York: Russell Sage Foundation.

Wilson. William Julius. 1977. *The Declining Significance of Race.* Chicago: University of Chicago Press.

Woo, Deborah. 2000. *Glass Ceilings and Asian Americans: The New Face of Workplace Barriers.* New York: Altamira Press.

Zéphir, Flore. 2001. *Trends in Ethnic Identification Among Second-Generation Haitian Immigrants in New York City.* Westport, Conn.: Bergin and Garvey.

Zhou, Min. 1997. "Growing Up American: The Challenge Confronting Immigrant Children and Children of Immigrants." *Annual Review of Sociology* 23: 69–95.

———. 2000. "Contemporary Immigration and the Dynamics of Race and Ethnicity." In *America Becoming: Racial Trends and Their Consequences*, edited by Neil Smelser, William Julius Wilson, and Faith Mitchell. Washington, D.C.: National Academy Press.

Zhou, Min, and Carl L. Bankston III. 1998. *Growing Up American: How Vietnamese Children Adapt to Life in the United States*. New York: Russell Sage Foundation.

Part V

Intergroup Relations

John Lie

Chapter 14

The Black-Asian Conflict?

Who now reads Allport? Not so long ago, whatever one's scientific or political predilection, the contact thesis dominated the way in which we understand and explain interethnic relationships in the United States. In Gordon Allport's (1979, 9) view, manifestations of intergroup conflict—from anger and hatred to discrimination and violence—ultimately stem from prejudice, which "is an antipathy based upon a faulty and inflexible generalization." In this line of reasoning, racial or ethnic prejudice—however faulty and inflexible a generalization it may be—can be corrected and rendered flexible by the experience of interethnic contact, especially if groups are of equal status. Or as Allport (1979, 281) put it: "Prejudice . . . may be reduced by equal status contact between majority and minority groups in the pursuit of common goals." Thus, if we could expunge the evil of segregation and the obstacle of social distance, then people of distinct backgrounds would come to live in harmony and make, presumably, correct and flexible generalizations about each other (see, for example, Sigelman et al. 2001). Although Allport and his followers focused on black-white relations, the contact thesis has been applied to other interethnic relations. Along with the concept of assimilation, it expressed the post–World War II consensus that predicted the eventual accommodation and acculturation of immigrant groups. In this view, assimilation and harmony mark the trajectory and teleology of immigrants.

In concert with the widespread rejection of assimilation—both as a concept and a reality—many social scientists have also come to criticize the contact hypothesis. On the one hand, the vast amount of social-psychological research on intergroup contact has raised more questions than confirmations (see Pettigrew 1998; Oskamp 2000). Allport can be faulted for reducing group relations to individual psychologies and prejudices. Furthermore, the contact thesis has relied on evidence gathered in experimental or highly restricted social contexts, such as housing projects and college classrooms. Most embarrassingly, the very notion of contact remains underspecified: How frequent does contact between groups have to be? How deep and intimate?

On the other hand, many social scientists have simply rejected the contact thesis and embraced what I call the conflict thesis. Instead of consensus and harmony, conflict and discord characterize this view of interethnic relations. For example, rather than viewing segregation as the root cause of conflict and discord, Susan Olzak (1992, 3) argues that desegregation has increased ethnic conflict. In a related vein, H. D. Forbes (1997) roundly criticizes the Allport thesis for its empirical and theoretical failings. Indeed, the contemporary social-scientific vocabulary to describe and explain ethnic and racial relations—the exploitative middleman minority, the divide-and-conquer strategy, resource competition, and so on—makes conflict seem all but inevitable (see Horowitz 1985, 2001). That is, the presumption of conflict shapes many social scientists' vision of interethnic relations. Those who cite Allport today therefore often do so to criticize the contact thesis.

The very interest in the black-Asian conflict is predicated on the popularity of the conflict view. The suspicion of pervasive interethnic tension between African Americans and Asian immigrant groups generates calls for solutions, or at least academic analyses and conferences (see, for example, Kwang Chung Kim 1999 and Claire Jean Kim 2000), such as the Columbia University conference on blacks and Asians in November 2000 and the Boston University conference on "Black-Asian Conflict" in April 2002. The Columbia conference website discusses the salience of political, economic, and social tensions between the two groups and highlights the importance of the black-Korean conflict, which had in fact become a journalistic commonplace in the early 1990s.[1] On their 1991 album *Death Certificate*, Ice Cube raps in "Black Korea" that "your [Korean] chop suey ass will be a target/Of a national boycott." Their incendiary line "we'll burn your store right down to a crisp" seemed to be confirmed in the smoldering reality of the 1992 Los Angeles riots. Pundits ranging from Mike Davis to Richard Rodriguez highlighted the black-Korean conflict as one of the keys to the 1992 riots (Abelmann and Lie 1995). Yet the putative problem of the black-Korean conflict in particular or the black-Asian conflict in general hardly merited a footnote a mere decade ago. Although the leading African American intellectuals, ranging from James Baldwin to Henry Louis Gates Jr., bell hooks, and Cornel West, have propounded on the black-Jewish problem (Berman 1994), their concern with the black-Asian issue has been negligible. In fact, the received wisdom—to the extent that it exists—has emphasized black-Asian solidarity. Scholars have pointed in this regard to the existence of the African American critique of late-nineteenth-century anti-Chinese agitation (Okihiro 1994), some American policymakers' fear of African American support for Japan during World War II (Lipsitz 1998), or the impact of the Black Power movement on the Asian American ("yellow power") movement in the 1960s (Wei 1993).

In this chapter, I criticize the conflict thesis in general and question the salience of the black-Asian conflict in particular. In so doing, I scrutinize several presuppositions that animate the conflict thesis. I adduce case studies of Chinese immigrants and African Americans in the late nineteenth century and Korean immigrants and African Americans in the late twentieth century to illustrate my argument.

THE CONFLICT THESIS AND ITS DISCONTENTS

Because immigrants inevitably arrive in a populated land, they generate a distinction between insiders and outsiders, or established residents and newcomers. Whether for dogs or human beings, priority spells, at least initially, primacy. No dog owner could fail to observe the comical situation of minute dogs lording over their gigantic newcomer counterparts in a dog park. Similarly, regardless of wealth or beauty, power or prestige, the established assert their indefinable supremacy over the arrivistes. Indeed, it is a mode of formal sociation that is a cultural—possibly mammalian—universal.[2] Furthermore, the usual scarcity of housing, jobs, and other resources engenders competition and conflict. In this line of reasoning, the established seek to protect their territoriality and belonging, while the outsiders attempt to encroach on them; those attempts, in turn, generate intergroup competition and conflict. To be sure, material plenty or economic growth may alleviate and even eliminate competition and lead to accommodation and possibly assimilation. However, in the conflict view, population movement is rife with the possibility of interethnic conflict.

Whether informed by social Darwinism or evolutionary psychology or reports of racism and genocide, contemporary Americans are wont to highlight ethnic tension and conflict. The temptation is almost irresistible when two groups, such as African Americans and Asian Americans, seem so distinct in the American racial common sense. The ideologically antipodal minorities—the urban underclass against the model minority—seemed ripe for conflict (Abelmann and Lie 1995). Sure enough, the early 1990s brought the specter of the black-Korean conflict, most visibly in the aftermath of the 1992 Los Angeles riots. In turn, the black-Asian conflict buttressed the conflict thesis.

The most powerful riposte to the conflict hypothesis is empirical. Given the sheer ubiquity of immigration in modern life, we would expect to witness, if the received view is correct, numerous instances of interethnic conflict. Yet, by and large, interethnic conflicts are newsworthy precisely because of their relative rarity. For every well-publicized boycott or deadly riot, the mundane reality of accommodation, however tinged with tension, reigns around the world. And this is certainly the case with black-Asian relations, whether in the early twenty-first century or the late nineteenth century.

Beyond its empirical plausibility, the conflict model is predicated on several dubious assumptions. First, it presumes the salience of racial, ethnic, or national relations. The purely formal character of insider-outsider sociation is not necessarily, or even all that commonly, characterized as interracial, interethnic, or international relations. On the one hand, the relation may reflect the formal sociation between the old and the new. Even if all the new dogs in a dog park should turn out to be Chows and all the long-term users are Chihuahuas, we would be remiss to describe the ensuing sociation as fundamentally interbreed relations. Rather, they simply represent the old and the new, which in turn accounts for the particular pattern of sociation (for example, the dominance of the old over the new). On the other hand, we should not assume the primacy of racial, ethnic, or national identities. Why should canine sociology privilege breed but not sex or size? As for human beings, why discount or dismiss the importance of educational, occupational, political, or other differences? Should we dismiss classic British works on colonial immigrants (Rex and Tomlinson 1979; Castles and Kosack 1973/1985) that sought to analyze them through the prism of class relations? The primacy of race, ethnicity, or nation is something that must be proved rather than presumed.

Second, the conflict model assumes that immigrants arrive with ready-made racial, ethnic, or national identities. Certainly, we would not impute breed consciousness to dogs. Although many people in the United States today are highly conscious of their ethno-racial identity, would we be right to assume their universality across cultures, places, and periods? In general, until the dissemination of peoplehood identity[3] in the twentieth century, most migrants did not arrive in a new land with a strong sense of racial, ethnic, or national identity and probably did not even think of themselves as migrants or transplants (Lie 2001a; 2004; cf. Foner 2000). We can be fairly certain of the fundamentally religious—Protestant or Puritan—self-definition of the first European Americans for whom contemporary racial (white) or ethnic (English) identities would have been either alien or incidental (Delbanco 1989). Although the Puritan fashioning of the self may have informed later understandings of the American self, it should not be mistaken as an articulation of American national identity. Rather than exclusively highlighting peoplehood identity, we should also recognize the salience of religious, familial, and other identities. Although we speak of Polish immigrants to the United States or Irish immigrants to Australia, their fundamental self-definition was probably familial rather than ethno-national. According to William I. Thomas and Florian Znaniecki (1918–20, i, 303), "[A]ll the peasant letters can be considered as variations of the fundamental type . . . to manifest the persistence of family solidarity in spite of the separation." In a similar fashion, David Fitzpatrick (1994, 615) describes Irish immigrants in Australia: "[W]hen Irish Australians spoke of 'home,' they called to mind a social environment peopled by relatives or neighbours." Most Jewish immigrants to the United States in the late nineteenth century had vague inklings of Jewish ethnic or national identity (Howe 1976). Similarly, nineteenth-century Chinese immigrants, albeit hailing principally from a few regions, were linguistically and culturally diverse (see Chan 1986).

In a similar fashion, we should question the solidarity of the receiving community. Why should we assume that the established are any more homogeneous or self-conscious than the newcomers? Here we should take a hint from the historiography of nationalism and of whiteness. If there is any consensus in recent writings on nationalism, it is that national identity is a modern phenomenon (Hobsbawm 1992; Calhoun 1997). Certainly American (that is, U.S.) national consciousness is a nineteenth-century achievement. Even when it emerged belatedly after the American Revolution, the core American identity was urban, industrial, and northern (Appleby 2000); excluded were not only American Indians and African slaves but also many others, including rural, agrarian, and southern Americans. John Higham's (1955/1963) identification of three major strands of nativism in the 1850s—anti-Catholicism, antipolitical radicalism, and antipathy toward non-Anglo-Saxons—suggests that the norm of Americanness in the nineteenth century was Protestant, politically moderate, and Anglo-Saxon. This line of argument has recently been explored with great fanfare in whiteness studies, which reveal the prevalence of what we would call ethnic exclusions and even racism against people deemed white today, ranging from Italians to Russians (Saxton 1990; Roediger 1991). The belated emergence of inclusionary whiteness makes sense of early-twentieth-century immigration restriction legislation, which targeted non-western Europeans (Jacobson 1998).

These insights can also be applied to African Americans. In spite of being conflated as a homogeneous group with an essentialized identity, linguistic and ethnic heterogeneity, as well as migration experience, divided African Americans (see Littlefield 1981). Mass or popular black nationalism, after all, is an early-twentieth-century phenomenon that developed when many North-bound blacks were every bit as immigrant as Chinese (Spear 1967). In spite of the widespread diffusion of black collective consciousness in the early twenty-first century, plural identities continue to characterize the black population (Waters 1999).

In general, the nominalist temptation to conflate category and reality is rife in the social sciences. In what would otherwise be an admirable salvo against psychologism and individualism, many social scientists unwittingly embrace essentialism that presumes the holistic and organic solidarity of groups, categories, and even societies. From Montesquieu and Durkheim to the culture-and-personality school and national character studies, some social scientists discuss groups or societies as personality writ large, thereby eliding significant divisions of class or culture, gender or generation. Perhaps holism is warranted in certain times and places, but this needs to be shown, rather than dogmatically asserted.

Consider in this regard the classical theoretical trap that many Marxists fell into. The teleology of class conflict presumed the existence, however latent it may often be, of class consciousness or identity. Hence, few Marxists bothered to define or describe class (see Przeworski 1977). Instead, they falsely assumed the existence of class consciousness or identity and predicted class conflict or struggle. (If people feel exploited, after all, why shouldn't they at least identify themselves as the exploited and possibly agitate against the exploiters?) As their certainty about the future guided the equally certain ethnography of the present, every instance of suboptimal work performance became evidence of conscious resistance and class conflict. To be sure, recalcitrant reality drove some to highlight the distinction between class-in-itself and class-for-itself and to seek historical accounts of the emergence (or absence) of class consciousness. It would be enormously condescending to belittle the then-revolutionary insight that class is made, not given. Yet, in retrospect, a conceptual history illustrates the widely divergent meanings ascribed to class over the centuries and the hollowness of the orthodox Marxist conviction about the ontology of class and class-consciousness (Cannadine 1999). My intention is not to condemn the category or concept of class in toto. For example, the historical characterization of twentieth-century Britain as a class society has an analytical utility with a fairly solid basis in contemporary experience and consciousness (McKibbin 1998). Nonetheless, as much as we wish to use class as an analytical concept, we cannot assume its existence as a relevant category of experience and consciousness for all times and places.

Needless to say, few social scientists and fewer historians now confound the potential analytic utility of class categories with an unreflexive belief in the existence of class-consciousness. Yet many who delightfully deride the Marxist pieties confidently presume the isomorphism of peoplehood categories and identities. Why should we assume race, ethnicity, and nation to be transhistorical and transcultural categories? Just as class identity cannot be presumed, peoplehood identity should not be presumed. When Italy barely existed as an entity or even an idea—recall Massimo d'Agelio's classic statement after the Risorgimento: "[W]e have made Italy, now we have to make Italians" (Hobsbawm 1992, 44)—we can only talk of "Italian" emigrants as an analytic category (that is, as "population") rather than as a concrete or conscious group (as "people"). When I say that the existence of peoplehood identity cannot be presumed for all times and places, I mean that ethnicity-in-itself (as an analytic category) may be used transhistorically and transculturally as a heuristic idea, but ethnicity-for-itself does not (as a category of lived experience or collective consciousness) exist in all times and places. Although we can write a history of Italian emigration in the nineteenth century, we should not confuse our analytical exercise with the existence of widespread Italian ethno-national consciousness in the nineteenth century.

Finally, the conflict model highlights the potential primacy of interracial or interethnic conflict, but the reverse—the potential for consensus and integration—is a priori just as plausible. As I noted, the weight of empirical evidence seems to tilt heavily toward the likelihood of nonconflictual coexistence. Does interethnic contact lead to consensus or conflict? Such an articulation of dichotomous outcomes is problematic. As many critics of the contact thesis have pointed out, the very notion of contact needs to be specified. A similar point can be made about conflict. If an ethnic group does not demonstrate a high level of ethnic solidarity and identity, then why wouldn't it be possible for some members of the group to be in conflict with members of another group while others are in harmony? Even in the mechanistic universe of two atoms colliding, we would want at least to know mass, velocity, friction, and other variables. Why should we expect the social world to be so much simpler? In the world of post-Newtonian physics, atoms may very well split or transmogrify. Similarly, I take it as a given that ethnic groups are not homogeneous bodies organized along the line of Durkheimian mechanical solidarity. Surely, interethnic relations encompass heterogeneous entities, divides, and identities that defy simple generalizations. That is, the very articulation of the conflict thesis (or for that matter, the contact thesis) is not a well-formulated question. What we call interracial or interethnic conflicts comprise a variety of outcomes and conflicts.

Indeed, the conflict thesis risks misunderstanding an effect for a cause. Rather than a well-formed identity giving rise to conflict (or consensus), it may very well be that conflict gives rise to identity. Racist conflation is frequently the basis of political mobilization and identity formation, whether for African Americans or Asian Americans. That is, identification qua a racial, ethnic, or national minority may form precisely because of conflict.[4] If we reify the effect (identity formation) and treat it as the cause of interracial or interethnic conflict, then we may indeed heighten ethnic tension and conflict. What is intended as descriptive may well become prescriptive. It may even spread knowledge about group distinction and group hatred and thereby become a self-fulfilling prophecy.

TWO CASE STUDIES

To buttress my argument, I offer two instances of interethnic relations as illustrative case studies. Both concern what might be regarded as examples of the black-Asian conflict. The first deals with Chinese immigrants in the second half of the nineteenth century and their relations with African Americans. The second focuses on the widely publicized conflict between Korean immigrants and (especially poor urban) African Americans.

I focus on national rather than pan-national or pan-racial grouping for Asian immigrants. If my argument about the recent and belated emergence of peoplehood identity is correct, then it should be all the more true for the highly aggregated category of the Asian American. After all, the categories of "Orientals" or "Asians" resulted from the racist conflation of "inscrutable and somnolent" people (Hunt 1987, 69), reaching something of an ideological apogee as the "yellow peril" in the early twentieth century (Daniels 1962). The national distinction between Chinese and Japanese immigrants became especially pressing during World War II, but as with African Americans, the mainstream classification largely bypassed it. The putative solidarity of Asian Americans long remained the conviction of nativist and exclusionary forces in the United States, but its existence was at best inchoately intuited by Asian Americans themselves. As a historian of the Asian American movement, William Wei (1993, 70), puts it: "The underlying impetus for the Asian American Movement was the search for identity and the creation of a new culture. Unlike European Americans, who could incorporate their ethnic identity into their sense of being American, Asian Americans had to create an entirely new identity: the Asian American." He locates its origin in the 1960s in the crucible of the anti–Vietnam War movement and the Black Power movement. In other words, the Asian American as a peoplehood identity is of recent vintage (see Espiritu, this volume). Despite significant forces that seek pan-Asian identities (Espiritu 1992), the common consciousness of Asian identity remains—as one quip has it—most effervescent on college campuses. As Herbert Barringer, Robert Gardner, and Michael Levin (1993, 320) have mundanely but correctly concluded: "Asian Americans do not represent a single block of persons about whom one can generalize easily."

The second case exemplifies the black-Asian conflict and requires no lengthy justification. As I noted, the black-Korean conflict became probably the most widely disseminated account of interracial or interethnic conflict in the early 1990s. For historical comparison, however, a compelling case cannot be made for analyzing Korean immigrants. Not only did they constitute a very small group in the nineteenth century, but they were concentrated largely in Hawaii. Although plantation managers' conscious "divide and conquer" strategy is interesting (Takaki 1983), it deals with relations among new immigrant groups rather than relations among new and established groups. In any case, Hawaii was not an integral part of the United States in the nineteenth century. Therefore, I consider Chinese immigrants, the most numerous and the most widely discussed Asian immigrant category in the late-nineteenth-century United States. Critical of the nominalist temptation, the dictate of the past-present comparison forces me to conform to it.

Case 1: Chinese Immigrants and African Americans in the Nineteenth Century

The history of Chinese immigration to the United States seems tempestuous precisely because of the anti-Chinese movement of the late nineteenth century. As John Higham (1955/1963, 25) writes: "No variety of anti-European sentiment has ever approached the virulent extremes to which anti-Chinese agitation went in the 1870s and 1880s" (see Saxton 1971). The indisputable proliferation of racist rhetoric and the existence of racially motivated violence seem to seal the conclusion that Chinese immigrants experienced constant conflict. Yet the existence of the anti-Chinese movement does not prove the presence of widespread ethnic conflict. After all, it was a nationwide phenomenon when the Chinese presence was largely restricted to the Pacific Coast (Miller 1969). Whether we locate its source in organized labor (Miller 1969) or electoral politics (Gyory 1998), anti-Chinese sentiments expressed a political response to the perceived, largely symbolic, threat. Furthermore, in spite of the racist veneer that we are wont to highlight, the contemporary rhetoric often highlighted nonracial elements. In particular, if we take labor-inspired opposition to Chinese immigration seriously, then the impulse behind anti-immigration agitation followed the logic of capital-labor conflict. M. B. Starr's *The Coming Struggle* (1873, 7) is symptomatic: "It is now generally understood and believed that a powerful combination of capital is systematically organized to bring into the midst of the most civilized portions of the world vast hordes of the debased, ignorant, and corrupt heathen races." Although he was discussing the threat posed by Chinese immigrants, Starr could have been talking about any group. Deployed as strikebreakers, Chinese workers faced the wrath of labor union organizers and activists. Interestingly, many Chinese workers in turn used the language of workers and capitalists to describe their lives in the United States (see Nee and Nee 1973, 43–48).

To put it polemically, anti-Chinese racism existed relatively independently of the existence of Chinese immigrants. Anti-Chinese agitation was not motivated solely by racism. Instead, we need to consider the significance of labor opposition or electoral strategy that contributed to late-nineteenth-century anti-Chinese agitation. Not surprisingly, the repeal of the Chinese Exclusion Act also occurred in the context of national-level pressure groups and international concerns that had very little to do with Chinese immigrants themselves (Riggs 1950; cf. McKenzie 1927, 181).

More important for my purposes, few now or then focused on the black-Chinese conflict. Far from expressing a high level of solidarity and consciousness, Chinese immigrants entered an interethnic universe that was far from conflict-ridden. Gunther Barth (1964, 145) describes San Francisco in the 1860s: "Negroes and Chinese frequented the same dance halls. The Chinese also found other groups sharing their life. Americans entered their employ, Germans occupied their dormitories, tents, and log cabins, Frenchmen sat at their tables, and Mexicans guided their pack horses through the Sierra. All these nationalities intermarried with the Chinese." The mundane reality undoubtedly included numerous instances of tensions and conflicts—bias was certainly expressed on occasion (Chen 2000)—but they did not amount to a widespread interethnic conflict. In any case, black leaders did not support the anti-Chinese agitation and exclusion (Okihiro 1994).

Beyond the cosmopolitan city of San Francisco, the fate of Chinese immigrants can hardly be reduced to constant rejection and contestation. Consider some 1,200 Chinese who settled in the Mississippi Delta around 1870. Unlike most Chinese immigrants of the nineteenth century, they became shopkeepers (see Chan 1986). In other words, they became the middleman minority who often seem to be the structural source and the spark plug of interethnic conflict. James Loewen (1971) argues that they were initially classified as black but eventually became white over the course of the twentieth century. Be that as it may, in spite of their predominant occupation as small grocers—the classic middleman minority—the interracial relationship was free of overt conflict, and the number of black-Chinese interracial families increased (Loewen 1971). The interracial relationship became ridden with tension only after Chinese became "white" and blacks became "black" after the rise of the Black Power movement in the 1960s (Loewen 1971). The recent influx of Chinese immigrants highlights the illusory character of racial or ethnic solidarity. As one of the descendants of the original Chinese settlers, Patricia Wolf, speaks of recent Chinese immigrants: "They look like us but that's about it. . . . We don't have much in common" (Sengupta 2000).

More damaging to the conflict thesis is the influx of Chinese in Louisiana in 1866. According to the historian Roger Shugg (1939, 254), planters made a conscious effort to recruit Chinese workers from Cuba and the Philippines: "Competition between Chinese and Negroes, it was claimed, would teach the latter to be industrious and thrifty." The choice of Cuban and Filipino Chinese was dictated by their Catholic background, which presumably rendered them "industrious and thrifty." The well-planned ethnic competition and conflict failed even to generate sustained sociation. Like Marx's famous description of Wakefield's colonization scheme, the model proletariat "soon deserted the plantations to become independent fishermen and truck farmers for the New Orleans market" (Shugg 1939, 255). That is, ethnic competition and conflict failed to materialize even when it was the intended outcome.

In summary, the cases of Chinese immigrants in the second half of the nineteenth century fail to corroborate the conflict thesis. We have no compelling evidence that they were engaged in sustained conflict with African Americans. The anti-Chinese movement, to be sure, conflated not only Chinese immigrants but all Orientals. In so doing, however, it promoted not so much the solidarity of Asian Americans as the unity of whites and the idea of white supremacy (Saxton 1971). In spite of the paucity of systematic evidence, the racially inspired attacks on Chinese followed, rather than preceded, the anti-Chinese movement (Coolidge 1909). That is, conflict in the form of racism and racist agitation generated identities that contributed to racial tension and violence. Like the Black Power movement of the 1960s in Louisiana, the white power movement was the predominant source of identity formation and ethnic violence.

Case 2: The Black-Korean Conflict in the 1990s

Let me shift to the near past: the specter of black-Korean conflict haunted urban America in the 1990s. After the 1992 Los Angeles riots—perhaps the most destructive civil violence in the twentieth-century United States—pundits often seized on the centrality of the interracial competition between long-term African American residents and recent Korean immigrants. For example, Richard Rodriguez (1992) wrote in the *Los Angeles Times*: "[O]ne of the most important conflicts in the 1992 L.A. riots was the tension between Koreans and African Americans."[5]

Unlike the nineteenth-century Chinese immigrants, twentieth-century Koreans have a well-honed national consciousness that it would be foolhardy to deny. However recent the popular dissemination of Korean national consciousness (Lie 2001b), most post-1960s Korean immigrants arrived with a distinct and strong sense of their national identity. Furthermore, the strength of black identity was undeniable by the 1990s. Indeed, few would question the strength of in-group feelings among Korean Americans and African Americans or the solid boundaries that divided them.

Nonetheless, the conflict thesis offered misleading prognostications. First, the bases of conflict were less than robust. Whether we consider employment, housing, or politics—the usual loci of resource conflict—we find little or no presence of interracial competition or conflict between African Americans and Korean Americans. Quite simply, the two groups by and large did not vie for the same type of jobs, seek the same housing, or fight for political representation. In each instance, Chicanos or Latinos posed a much more compelling threat for African Americans, whether for jobs at hotels, in housing in South Central Los Angeles, or in city politics.

Second, there was no compelling evidence to sustain the conflict thesis. Although fifty-eight people died during the 1992 Los Angeles riots, no one died as a result of interracial violence. That is, Korean Americans did not kill African Americans, nor did blacks kill Koreans. Some African Americans may have targeted Korean-owned stores, but only one-third of the destroyed businesses in South Central Los Angeles were Korean-owned when Korean Americans accounted for roughly 40 percent of the dry cleaning businesses and 50 percent of small grocery stores in the area. Indeed, the extensive destruction in South Central Los Angeles and the neighboring area of Koreatown was due in large part to propinquity to rioters and looters and to the police protection of other areas (or lack of protection in Koreatown).

Interviews that Nancy Abelmann and I conducted with blacks and Koreans revealed expressions of prejudice and ethnic tensions, but they did not amount to a state of pervasive interethnic conflict. As a young Korean American man told us:

> The media attributed the black-Korean conflict as the underlying factor of the violence [the riots]. To justify their point, images of crying Korean merchants damning the looters and angry African American bystanders asserting that Koreans received what they deserved flooded the media. Unfortunately, people's sense of judgment became anesthetized after a while, so that many accepted conflict between Koreans and African Americans as a motivating factor for the violence.

Many working-class Korean Americans actively resisted the suggestion that there was an interracial conflict, and some even explicitly claimed the existence of class solidarity between black and Korean workers. Only a few Korean Americans accepted the existence of the conflict, usually in order to acknowledge the antiblack prejudice among Korean Americans. Similarly, many African Americans, while aware of interracial tensions, resisted giving significance to the black-Korean conflict. A young African American gang member told us: "It's not the Korean-black thing; the merchants were there, there were problems, but it's a way for us to not think about the real problem, which is the oppressor [white]." An owner of a restaurant in South Central Los Angeles went so far as to praise Korean immigrants and claimed that he sought to protect his Korean American neighbors during the riots. As I noted, black intellectuals largely bypassed the topic of the black-Korean conflict.

To the extent that conflict existed, it often signaled something other than black-Korean racial conflict. The 1991 Red Apple boycott in Flatbush, New York, was often cited as a major manifestation of black-Korean conflict. However, it was initiated by Haitian immigrants. Although "black" in the dominant U.S. racial vocabulary, Haitians are not synonymous with long-established African Americans, as evinced by the black-Haitian conflict in Miami (Portes and Stepick 1993). The Bulls riots in Chicago featured shopkeepers and looters who were both ethnically diverse (Rosenfeld 1997); Arab American merchants, far more than Korean Americans, were the central target during that disturbance. The Los Angeles riots were, of course, not triggered by black-Korean conflict but by popular anger against the "not guilty" verdict for the four police officers who had beaten up Rodney King, an African American. It would certainly be a huge leap to locate black-Korean conflict as the source of the largest civil disturbance of the twentieth-century United States.

Needless to say, I am not denying the existence of individual altercations or group-level prejudices. However, reports of racial tension between African Americans and Korean Americans have focused almost exclusively on the realm of merchant-customer relations (Min 1996; Yoon 1997). There have been frequent reports of African American clients complaining about rude Korean American merchants as well as Korean American merchants bemoaning the frequency of African American shoplifters. There is a grain of truth to the middleman minority thesis that political movements by inner-city African Americans demanded the encouragement of black merchants and the collateral resistance to immigrant entrepreneurs. Hence, in the early 1990s there were newspaper reports on the black-Palestinian conflict in Cleveland, the black-Laotian conflict in Philadelphia, the black-Arab conflict in Chicago, the black-Chinese conflict in Washington, D.C., and the black-Vietnamese conflict in Los Angeles. It is possible to conclude that African Americans are in conflict with virtually every ethnic group or that all immigrant groups are prejudiced against African Americans. It would be more reasonable, however, to seek the source of these conflicts in the economic and political efforts by urban African American groups to demand economic empowerment and social dignity. In any case, these manifestations of merchant-customer tensions in poor areas do not necessarily point to the general existence of a simmering interracial conflict (see Gold, this volume).

To the extent that the Los Angeles riots were significant for interracial relations, the causal arrow went the other way from that predicted by the conflict thesis. The widespread report of the conflict heightened the identity and mobilization of both groups. African American as well as Korean American organizations sought racial identification and promoted putative racial interests (see Kim 2000). Rather than well-established identities leading to conflicts, it was the presumed existence of a conflict that seemed to entrench ethnic-based identities. Once reified, however, the news of the black-Korean conflict spread as a matter of fact.

CONCLUSION

In this chapter, I have criticized the conflict thesis, especially its articulation as the black-Asian conflict. Just as social scientists have rejected the class nominalism and essentialism associated with Marxism, I argue that we should avoid ethno-racial nominalism and essentialism. We simply cannot assume the existence at all times and places of ethnic or national identities and therefore the possibility of describing group relations as simple phenomena (though even relations between two individuals can be exceedingly complex). Neither should we assume the inevitable existence of ethnic tensions or conflicts.

The very discussion of the black-Asian conflict would constitute a height of unhealthy abstraction. Yet we should be wary of merely reversing the conflict thesis and asserting black-Asian racial harmony. In countering the notion of black-Asian conflict, the Columbia University historian Gary Okihiro (1994, 34) writes: "[Y]ellow is a shade of black, and black a shade of yellow. . . . We are a kindred people, African and Asian Americans. We share a history of migration, interaction and cultural sharing, and commerce and trade. We share a history of European colonization, decolonization, and independence under neocolonization and dependency. We share a history of oppression in the United States." I am not an expert on colors, but I do know that Japan and Thailand—two indisputably Asian nations—were never colonized by Europeans, and Korea and China were colonized principally by Japan. I also know that in Hawaii—a topic of one of Okihiro's books—Asian immigrants were part and parcel of European colonization, however exploited they may have been.

Well-intended abstractions, though platitudinous, may promote interracial or interethnic harmony. However, romantic abstractions strike me as the stuff out of which destructive demagogues and mass murderers empower themselves. After all, the very expression of interracial conflict reifies identities and strengthens boundaries that may in turn lead to interethnic conflict. By mistaking effect for cause, the contingent power grab—such as the brutal Serbian regime that sought to justify state power and expansion in the name of Serbian nationalism and anti-Bosnian racism—is articulated as interethnic conflict, a nearly natural state of affairs (Lie 2004). Wrong analysis, in other words, contributes to the particular form in which savage hatred wreaks havoc.

Here Henri Tajfel's (1981) striking work lends some empirical support. He argues that it is not contact per se but the establishment of crosscutting social ties that deconstructs, as it were, the solidity of categories and identities. That is, interracial or interethnic harmony is achieved precisely by attenuating, rather than articulating and reinforcing, racial and ethnic boundaries and consciousnesses. In this regard, we might take a leaf from an early Marx essay in which he inveighs against the Young Hegelians for talking of freedom of religion rather than freedom from religion. In our desire to eliminate the blight of racism, we should not become trapped in the prison-house of race.

NOTES

1. See the website for the Columbia University conference "Blacks and Asians: Revisiting Racial Formations" (November 9–10, 2000), Institute for Research in African-American Studies

(IRAAS), www.columbia.edu/cu/iraas/htm/iraas_ events_ 11_ 09_ 2000.htm (accessed July 30, 2002).

2. "Sociation," following Georg Simmel's (1908/1992, ch. 4) pioneering analysis, refers to formal and generic modes of social interaction. See Elias and Scotson (1965/1994) for the sociation of established and outsiders.

3. "Peoplehood" is a generic term to refer to racial, ethnic, or national group; see Lie (2004).

4. The thesis that conflict generates identity—rather than identity generating conflict—may appear mechanistic and simpleminded. However, construction is perforce never de novo, and the thesis points to the general strengthening and dissemination of an identity that may have been inchoately intuited by the populace. For a suggestive case study, see Turits (2003, ch. 5).

5. This section is a revised articulation of the argument in Abelmann and Lie (1995, ch. 6). All of the references and evidence can be found therein.

REFERENCES

Abelmann, Nancy, and John Lie. 1995. *Blue Dreams: Korean Americans and the Los Angeles Riots.* Cambridge, Mass.: Harvard University Press.

Allport, Gordon W. 1979. *The Nature of Prejudice.* 25th anniversary edition. Reading, Mass.: Addison-Wesley. (Orig. pub. in 1954.)

Appleby, Joyce. 2000. *Inheriting the Revolution: The First Generation of Americans.* Cambridge, Mass.: Harvard University Press.

Barringer, Herbert, Robert W. Gardner, and Michael J. Levin. 1993. *Asians and Pacific Islanders in the United States.* New York: Russell Sage Foundation.

Barth, Gunther. 1964. *Bitter Strength: A History of the Chinese in the United States, 1850–1870.* Cambridge, Mass.: Harvard University Press.

Berman, Paul, ed. 1994. *Blacks and Jews: Alliances and Arguments.* New York: Delacorte Press.

Calhoun, Craig. 1997. *Nationalism.* Minneapolis: University of Minnesota Press.

Cannadine, David. 1999. *The Rise and Fall of Class in Britain.* New York: Columbia University Press.

Castles, Stephen, and Godula Kosack. 1985. *Immigrant Workers and Class Structure in Western Europe.* 2nd ed. Oxford: Oxford University Press. (Orig. pub. in 1973.)

Chan, Sucheng. 1986. *This Bittersweet Soil: The Chinese in California Agriculture, 1860–1910.* Berkeley: University of California Press.

Chen, Yong. 2000. *Chinese San Francisco 1850–1943: A Trans-Pacific Community.* Stanford, Calif.: Stanford University Press.

Coolidge, Mary Roberts. 1909. *Chinese Immigration.* New York: H. Holt.

Daniels, Roger. 1962. *The Politics of Prejudice: The Anti-Japanese Movement in California and the Struggle for Japanese Exclusion.* Berkeley: University of California Press.

Delbanco, Andrew. 1989. *The Puritan Ordeal.* Cambridge, Mass.: Harvard University Press.

Elias, Norbert, and John L. Scotson. 1994. *The Established and the Outsiders.* London: Sage Publications. (Orig. pub. in 1965.)

Espiritu, Yen Le. 1992. *Asian American Panethnicity: Bridging Institutions and Identities.* Philadelphia: Temple University Press.

Fitzpatrick, David. 1994. *Oceans of Consolation: Personal Accounts of Irish Migration to Australia.* Ithaca, N.Y.: Cornell University Press.

Foner, Nancy. 2000. *From Ellis Island to JFK: New York's Two Great Waves of Immigration.* New Haven, Conn.: Yale University Press.

Forbes, H. D. 1997. *Ethnic Conflict: Commerce, Culture, and the Contact Hypothesis.* New Haven, Conn.: Yale University Press.

Gyory, Andrew. 1998. *Closing the Gate: Race, Politics, and the Chinese Exclusion Act.* Chapel Hill: University of North Carolina Press.

Higham, John. 1963. *Strangers in the Land: Patterns of American Nativism 1860–1925*, 2nd ed. New York: Atheneum. (Orig. pub. in 1955.)

Hobsbawm, Eric J. 1992. *Nations and Nationalism Since 1780: Program, Myth, Reality*. 2nd ed. Cambridge: Cambridge University Press.

Horowitz, Donald L. 1985. *Ethnic Groups in Conflict*. Berkeley: University of California Press.

———. 2001. *The Deadly Ethnic Riot*. Berkeley: University of California Press.

Howe, Irving. 1976. *World of Our Fathers*. New York: Harcourt Brace Jovanovich.

Hunt, Michael H. 1987. *Ideology and U.S. Foreign Policy*. New Haven, Conn.: Yale University Press.

Jacobson, Matthew Frye. 1998. *Whiteness of a Different Color: European Immigrants and the Alchemy of Race*. Cambridge, Mass.: Harvard University Press.

Kim, Claire Jean. 2000. *Bitter Fruit: The Politics of Black-Korean Conflict in New York City*. New Haven, Conn.: Yale University Press.

Kim, Kwang Chung, ed. 1999. *Koreans in the Hood: Conflict with African Americans*. Baltimore: Johns Hopkins University Press.

Lie, John. 2001a. *Multiethnic Japan*. Cambridge, Mass.: Harvard University Press.

———. 2001b. "Diasporic Nationalism." *Cultural Studies—Critical Methodologies* 1: 355–62.

———. 2004. *Modern Peoplehood*. Cambridge, Mass.: Harvard University Press.

Lipsitz, George. 1998. *The Possessive Investment in Whiteness: How White People Profit from Identity Politics*. Philadelphia: Temple University Press.

Littlefield, Daniel C. 1981. *Rice and Slaves: Ethnicity and the Slave Trade in Colonial South Carolina*. Baton Rouge: Louisiana State University Press.

Loewen, James W. 1971. *The Mississippi Chinese: Between Black and White*. Cambridge, Mass.: Harvard University Press.

McKenzie, Roderick Duncan. 1927. *Oriental Exclusion: The Effect of American Immigration Laws, Regulations, and Judicial Decisions upon the Chinese and Japanese on the American Pacific Coast*. New York: Institute of Pacific Relations.

McKibbin, Ross. 1998. *Classes and Cultures: England 1918–1951*. Oxford: Oxford University Press.

Miller, Stuart Creighton. 1969. *The Unwelcome Immigrant: The American Image of the Chinese, 1785–1882*. Berkeley: University of California Press.

Min, Pyong Gap. 1996. *Caught in the Middle: Korean Communities in New York and Los Angeles*. Berkeley: University of California Press.

Nee, Victor G., and Brett de Bary Nee. 1973. *Longtime Californ': A Documentary Study of an American Chinatown*. New York: Pantheon.

Okihiro, Gary Y. 1994. *Margins and Mainstreams: Asians in American History and Culture*. Seattle: University of Washington Press.

Olzak, Susan. 1992. *The Dynamics of Ethnic Competition and Conflict*. Stanford, Calif.: Stanford University Press.

Oskamp, Stuart, ed. 2000. *Reducing Prejudice and Discrimination*. Mahwah, N.J.: Lawrence Erlbaum Associates.

Pettigrew, Thomas F. 1998. "Intergroup Contact Theory." *Annual Review of Psychology* 49: 65–85.

Portes, Alejandro, and Alex Stepick. 1993. *City on the Edge: The Transformation of Miami*. Berkeley: University of California Press.

Przeworski, Adam. 1977. "Proletariat into a Class: The Process of Class Formation from Karl Kautsky's 'The Class Struggle' to Recent Controversies." *Politics and Society* 7(4): 343–401.

Rex, John, and Sally Tomlinson. 1979. *Colonial Immigrants in a British City: A Class Analysis*. London: Routledge & Kegan Paul.

Riggs, Fred W. 1950. *Pressures on Congress: A Study of the Repeal of Chinese Exclusion*. New York: King's Crown Press.

Rodriguez, Richard. 1992. "Multiculturalism with No Diversity." *Los Angeles Times,* May 10, p. M1.

Roediger, David. 1991. *The Wages of Whiteness: Race and the Making of the American Working Class*. London: Verso.

Rosenfeld, Michael J. 1997. "Celebration, Politics, Looting, and Riots: A Microlevel Analysis of the Bulls Riot of 1992 in Chicago." *Social Problems* 44(4): 483–502.

Saxton, Alexander. 1971. *The Indispensable Enemy: Labor and the Anti-Chinese Movement in California*. Berkeley: University of California Press.

———. 1990. *The Rise and Fall of the White Republic*. London: Verso.

Sengupta, Somini. 2000. "Delta Chinese Hang on to Vanishing Way of Life." *New York Times*, November 1, A18.

Shugg, Roger W. 1939. *Origins of Class Struggle in Louisiana: A Social History of White Farmers and Laborers During Slavery and After, 1840–1875*. Baton Rouge: Louisiana State University Press.

Sigelman, Lee, Susan Welch, Timothy Bledsoe, and Michael W. Combs. 2001. *Race and Place: Race Relations in an American City*. Cambridge: Cambridge University Press.

Simmel, Georg. 1992. *Gesamtausgabe, band 11: Soziologie*, edited by Otthein Rammstedt. Frankfurt am Main: Suhrkamp. (Orig. pub. in 1908.)

Spear, Allan H. 1967. *Black Chicago: The Making of a Negro Ghetto 1890–1920*. Chicago: University of Chicago Press.

Starr, M. B. 1873. *The Coming Struggle; or What the People of the Pacific Coast Think of the Coolie Invasion*. San Francisco: Excelsior Office, Bacon & Co.

Tajfel, Henri. 1981. *Human Groups and Social Categories: Studies in Social Psychology*. Cambridge: Cambridge University Press.

Takaki, Ronald. 1983. *Pau Hana: Plantation Life and Labor in Hawaii, 1835–1920*. Honolulu: University of Hawaii Press.

Thomas, William I., and Florian Znaniecki. 1918–20. *The Polish Peasant in Europe and America: Monograph of an Immigrant Group*, 5 vols. Boston: G. Badger.

Turits, Richard Lee. 2003. *Foundations of Despotism: Peasants, the Trujillo Regime, and Modernity in Dominican History*. Stanford, Calif.: Stanford University Press.

Waters, Mary C. 1999. *Black Identities: West Indian Immigrant Dreams and American Realities*. Cambridge, Mass.: Harvard University Press.

Wei, William. 1993. *The Asian American Movement*. Philadelphia: Temple University Press.

Yoon, In-Jin. 1997. *On My Own: Korean Businesses and Race Relations in America*. Chicago: University of Chicago Press.

Steven J. Gold

Chapter 15

Immigrant Entrepreneurs and Customers Throughout the Twentieth Century

Since the late nineteenth century, conflicts between immigrant business owners and their customers have been common in American society, especially in inner cities and isolated rural regions. Because such conflicts are often destructive of human lives, property, and public order, they have been the subject of periodic investigation by politicians, journalists, and social scientists. The resulting body of literature is voluminous but narrow, focusing on the most violent incidents in big cities and limited almost exclusively to the interactions of three ethnic groups—Jews, Koreans, and African Americans—during specific historical periods (the 1930s through the 1960s for Jews and blacks; the 1980s and 1990s for Koreans and blacks).

A detailed examination of the historical record reveals several problems with this characterization. A significant flaw is that the vast majority of interactions involving immigrant entrepreneurs and their customers have been free from conflict (Horowitz 1985; David 2000; Lee 2002; Lie, this volume). Business owners and customers realize their mutual dependence and generally make efforts to maintain civility (Ong, Park, and Tong 1994; Levine 2001; Lee 2002, 84). On many occasions when immigrant businesses have been attacked or looted, they were simply accessible targets during times of social disorder—associated with political discord, power outages, or uncontrolled celebrations—rather than the focus of public outrage (Yoon 1997). Further, only small fractions of most implicated groups are actually involved in urban entrepreneurship or heated conflicts with local merchants. Accordingly, such clashes seldom reflect the sentiments of the broad ethnic categories described in popular accounts (Lie, this volume; Sonenshein 1996; Gates 1993).[1]

Many more groups besides Jews and Koreans are represented among the ranks of immigrant entrepreneurs, and African Americans are not the sole market served by these merchants. Finally, many of the most powerful forms of restriction and vengeance imposed on immigrant and ethnic entrepreneurs come not from the hands of ghetto teenagers but rather from the social, economic, and legal actions of society's power holders—its leading companies and ruling institutions. As Gunnar Myrdal (1944) and St. Clair Drake and Horace Cayton (1945) argued almost sixty years ago, a society's racial problems and the position, conduct, and "entire flow of life" of oppressed minority groups are the product of the conditions imposed on them by the dominant group (Wright 1945/1962, xxix). What is more, elites' interpretations of interracial conflicts have played a central role in characterizing racial-ethnic groups and justifying their repressive treatment.

Consequently, this analysis does not focus solely on interpersonal violence between ethnic entrepreneurs and minority customers but also considers forms of coercion, discrimination, disinvestment, and the like through which major groups and institutions define the economic niches and locations of ethnic groups in American society (Wacquant 1998). Actions and programs initiated by white elites—such as the Jim Crow laws in the South that restricted black entrepreneurship, the internment of Japanese Americans during World War II, the exclusion of immigrant populations from education and employment, and the financial exploitation of inner-city residents by major corporations—are considered as factors that have shaped conflicts between immigrant/ethnic entrepreneurs and their customers. In the long view, conflicts between entrepreneurs and customers are more often a result of broader patterns of inequality, prejudice, and alienation in American society than the cause of them.

In terms of conflicts themselves, my review of case studies and the analytic literature from throughout the twentieth century suggests that while locally specific circumstances and events contribute to discord between merchants and customers, other conditions that have been recognized by existing social science research as heightening tension, competition, and hostility between identifiable groups have played a central role in initiating most disputes (Coser 1956; Blumer 1958; Olzak and Nagel 1986; Bobo and Hutchings 1996; Horowitz 1985). Following Ewa Morawska (2001), I maintain that circumstances that contribute to intergroup dissension are of two interrelated types. The first involves structural conditions, such as configurations of political and economic opportunity, patterns of uneven development, demographic transformations that enhance competition for scarce and valued resources, and changing racial and ethnic categories and relationships within the larger society. The second range of factors consists of phenomenological reactions to these and other issues fomented by the media, political or social movements, and communal activists (Morawska 2001, 48; Dahlke 1961; Lieberson and Silverman 1965; Johnson and Oliver 1994; Sears 2000; Gooding-Williams 1993).

PROPENSITY TOWARD BUSINESS OWNERSHIP

To examine relations between immigrant and ethnic entrepreneurs and their customers, we need to account for the differential propensity of ethnically defined groups to become self-employed (see Light and Gold 2000; Waldinger 1996; Portes and Bach 1985; Light and Rosenstein 1995; Fairlie 1999). Although the theoretical and descriptive literature on this question is far too large to be addressed here, basic findings adapted from Light (1984) and Light and Gold (2000) can be summarized (see table 15.1).

Self-employment has long been glorified in American culture, and the Horatio Alger myth has been remarkably durable. Nevertheless, a sociological analysis of self-employment attributes the practice to a reaction to disadvantage. Among other factors, Max Weber traced the invention of modern capitalism to the Calvinists' need to support themselves, since they could not obtain jobs in the civil service or armed forces (Light and Gold 2000, 195). Of course, while disadvantage provides a group with the motive for self-employment, running a successful business requires resources, such as investment capital and management skill. Because disadvantaged groups often lack these, disadvantage alone is an inadequate explanation for a group's involvement in self-employment. Ethnic groups characterized by a combination of disadvantages and resources are those with the highest rates of self-employment.

TABLE 15.1 Motives and Resources for Self-Employment Among Native and Immigrant Groups

	Comparison Groups			
	Middleman Minorities[a]	Foreign-Born	Native Blacks	Native Whites
Co-ethnic business resources (capital, labor, advice, goods)	x			
Business experience	x			
Unpaid family labor	x	x		
Wage differentials (compared to the United States)	x	x		
Labor force disadvantage	x	x	x	
Ineligible for public welfare	x	x		
Language barrier	x	x		
Special consumer demand	x	x	Some	
Political resources (yield influence, jobs)			x	x
State-imposed discrimination	Some	Some	High levels prior to 1970s	

Source: Adapted from Light (1984, 210, table 3).
[a]Refers to first generation.

Sources of Disadvantage

Economic disadvantages that may encourage a group's entry into proprietorship include being foreign-born, lacking English-language proficiency, lacking knowledge of and connections to the larger society, being without U.S. citizenship, having low levels of education or having a credential or degree from an unrecognized foreign institution, being a member of a low-status ethnic or racial group (and consequently being seen as an undesirable employee or as subject to low wages), being subjected to discrimination, and being ineligible for welfare benefits. These economic disadvantages generally apply to native-born minority group members, including African Americans and Latinos, as well as the foreign-born. Few, if any, apply to the mass of native-born, non-ethnic whites.

Resources for Entrepreneurship

Although members of immigrant and minority groups are often characterized by economic disadvantages, at the same time their ethnic culture, their experience in the country of origin (for migrants), and their affiliation with a strong co-ethnic community or overseas social ties sometimes provide resources that can be beneficial in creating or running businesses. Of course, like native-born whites, immigrant and minority group members can also deploy class resources, such as education and money, toward self-employment.

Those ethnic groups called "middleman minorities" are associated with high rates of self-employment and are noted to be especially well endowed with entrepreneurial resources (Bonacich 1973; Zenner 1991). Their assets include co-ethnic sources of capital, labor, salable merchandise, business advice, and customers; business experience, education, marketable skills, and access to unpaid family labor; and the increased level of U.S. earnings in comparison to those available in the country of origin. In addition, some ethnic groups maintain norms of family or communal cooperation and money sharing—including rotating credit and savings associations—that facilitate self-employment (Light and Gold 2000).

Groups characterized by a combination of both disadvantages and resources are especially well suited for self-employment. For example, as a group, Korean immigrants are highly educated, but owing to their difficulty with English and their foreign degrees, they have trouble obtaining professional jobs in the United States. Having sold their homes prior to migration, many arrive with substantial financial resources. Their establishment in business is further facilitated by their access to co-ethnic sources of advice and salable goods, family norms that mandate the labor of wives and children in a business enterprise, and wage differentials between the United States and Korea that provide a higher standard of living than was available in Korea (Kim 1981; Light and Bonacich 1988; Yoon 1997; Min 1996).

In contrast, native-born whites who lack disadvantages in the labor market generally have rates of self-employment close to or sometimes below the average in the United States. The same is true for immigrant groups that have high levels of American-style education and speak English, such as Canadians, French, Filipinos, and Indians (Portes and Rumbaut 1996, 72; Yoon 1997, 20). Finally, groups characterized by economic disadvantages but lacking entrepreneurial resources, such as African Americans, Puerto Ricans, and Mexicans, have low rates of self-employment.

It should be noted that this model offers a broad and general explanation for rates of ethnic self-employment, which varies considerably according to historical period, location, and other contextual factors. For example, during the early twentieth century, Japanese had a high level of self-employment in the western United States but far fewer were self-employed in Hawaii (Takaki 1989). Similarly, as discussed in greater detail later in the chapter, after the 1880s increases in residential segregation and competition from European immigrants resulted in a significant reduction in black entrepreneurship (Butler 1991).

ENTREPRENEUR-CUSTOMER CONFLICT IN HISTORICAL CONTEXT

In this section, I summarize several patterns of conflict between immigrant and ethnic entrepreneurs and their customers that occurred over the course of the twentieth century in order to document general trends and illustrate bases of conflict.

African Americans as Entrepreneurs and Middlemen

A common explanation for conflict between immigrant entrepreneurs and native minority customers emphasizes blacks' low rates of self-employment as a central factor.

However, as John Sibley Butler (1991; Harris 1936/1968; Woodard 1997) and others have noted, from the antebellum era until the Great Depression, African Americans did have a small yet accomplished business class. "The total value of all free Black-owned establishments and personal wealth in the U.S. in 1860 was at least $50 million dollars—half of which was based in the slave South" (Marable 1983, 141). Prior to the full implementation of Jim Crow laws, many of these enterprises catered to white as well as black customers. Consequently, Butler (1991) describes their owners as middleman entrepreneurs. The existence of these many black-owned businesses prior to the twentieth century points to the fact that discrimination, hostile legislation, and competition have contributed significantly to low rates of black entrepreneurship since that time.[2]

Before the twentieth century, blacks owned a variety of enterprises that served a multiracial clientele (Butler 1991; Woodard 1997). Most involved the provision of domestic services such as barbering, catering, tailoring, and clothes washing—occupations that native whites disdained. However, there were notable exceptions in more prestigious and lucrative fields, including lumberyards, furniture manufacturing, the professions, and the ownership of prestigious restaurants, like Thomas Downing's eating house near Wall Street, "which catered to the leading members of New York's professional and commercial classes" (Butler 1991, 72).

In *The Philadelphia Negro*, W.E.B. Du Bois (1899/1967) noted that blacks owned the city's leading catering firms and sailmakers (cited in Bates 1997, 145). In Cleveland, as in many northern cities, this pattern lasted until almost 1920. "On the eve of the Great Migration," Kenneth L. Kusmer (1976) observed, "a small group of Negro tailors, caterers, barbers, and merchants continued to serve a predominantly White clientele." Black professionals also had white as well as black customers. As late as 1915 Cleveland's black lawyers served more white than co-ethnic clients, and many of the city's African American doctors had integrated practices as well (Kusmer 1976, 81). Because they provided valued goods and services in a growing economy, there was relatively little conflict between black entrepreneurs and white customers during this period.[3]

However, shortly before the turn of the twentieth century, several factors had the effect of reducing the number of black businesses that served whites. With President Rutherford B. Hayes's rollback of Reconstructionist policy and the Supreme Court rulings in *Hall v. De Cuvis* (1877) and *Plessy v. Ferguson* (1896), the separate-but-equal doctrine became the law of the land. As a consequence, "[s]egregation laws restricted Blacks from competing against any other entrepreneur in an open market" by restricting the location of black-owned businesses to black neighborhoods (Woodard 1997, 16).

And just as blacks' ability to trade with whites was being limited to black neighborhoods, millions of job-seeking Europeans arrived in the United States. They constituted a "large immigrant work force that was responsible for driving Blacks out of barbering" and other entrepreneurial niches that they had previously occupied (Kusmer 1976, 76). In 1870, 43 percent of Cleveland's barbers were black; in 1890 this figure had slipped to 18 percent. In 1910 fewer than one in ten were black, and it is likely that these were serving co-ethnics rather than the more lucrative white clientele (Kusmer 1976, 76). Italians took over the previous black niche of cutting white people's hair, while the Irish occupied formerly black jobs in construction. White privilege (including customers' preferences) and the immigrants' ability to cut prices below prevailing standards allowed these groups to occupy what had previously been black niches.

Although they were granted more privileges than blacks, immigrant groups were nevertheless subject to forms of social control that prevented them from challenging the social and economic domain of native whites. Hence, many focused on the underserved black customer. For example, Jean Ann Scarpaci (1972, 246–51, 254) describes several instances in Louisiana in the late nineteenth century of economically competitive Sicilian merchants and laborers being lynched or driven out of town by angry white mobs, with the complicity of the legal system. Stereotypes concerning Italians' "inherent criminality" were used to justify such brutality.

Owing to immigrants' competition and Jim Crow laws, there was a "gradual disappearance of Black businesses that catered to a predominantly White clientele" in all northern cities during the late nineteenth and early twentieth centuries (Kusmer 1976, 76). In addition to economic competition, black entrepreneurs now also faced more violent confrontations in many locations. For example, the prosperous "Black Wall Street" of Greenwood in Tulsa, Oklahoma, was the victim in 1921 of a pogrom by jealous whites, who had support from police and the National Guard. Almost four hundred people died, and fourteen hundred homes and businesses were destroyed (Light and Gold 2000; Morris 1999). Similar attacks on blacks and their communities occurred in Springfield, Illinois, in 1908, in St. Louis in 1917, and in Chicago in 1919 (Drake and Cayton 1945).

Reduced in their ability to trade with white customers, a new black middle class in both northern and southern cities developed a variety of businesses in the 1920s to service the growing population of newly arrived rural southern black migrants. Paradoxically, this was made possible by the deterioration in race relations at the end of the nineteenth century, as evidenced by residential discrimination and concentration, and the refusal of white insurance and banking companies to service blacks. "Real estate dealers, undertakers, newspaper editors, insurance agents, bankers and a plethora of small businessmen relied on Black consumers" (Kusmer 1976, 81). There were also opportunities for self-employed black professionals, including ministers, doctors, dentists, and nurses. Lawyers and engineers, however, had less success, since there was little co-ethnic demand for their services.

In his historical analysis of black entrepreneurship, Butler (1991) concludes that the great obstacles confronted by black entrepreneurs severely restricted their ability to enhance African American economic advancement. At the same time, however, this group made significant and long-lasting economic, cultural, institutional, and educational contributions to African American life.

Immigrant Entrepreneurs and Ethnic Customers

The middleman minority analogy suggests that ethnic entrepreneurs "naturally" gravitate toward underserved and risky business locations, but historical evidence indicates that patterns of social and economic contact between immigrant entrepreneurs and customers evolved over time and varied according to place, economic structure, and local racial norms. It was in the racially segregated and economically backward regions of the agricultural South that Italian, Jewish, and Chinese immigrant entrepreneurs first began to service black consumers.

For many immigrants, self-employment offered the only viable avenue for upward mobility, since discrimination and union policies excluded migrants from jobs in existing firms. In Louisiana, immigrants who did the same work as blacks—such as Sicilian laborers in the sugar industry—were derided by local whites as "Negroes with White skin" (Scarpaci 1972, 222). To enhance their status, they sought to distinguish themselves from blacks, but the local economy offered few alternative jobs. By becoming self-employed as farmers, saloon keepers, or shop owners, increasing their levels of consumption, and adopting prevailing white attitudes about race, the Italians became more acceptable to local whites. Hence, selling to blacks offered a route not only to economic survival but to approbation by native whites. Although they had to endure epithets and even lynchings along the way, by 1912 "the transition from agricultural proletarian to entrepreneur seemed complete" for Italian immigrants in Louisiana (Scarpaci 1972, 193).

Businesses directed toward black customers played a central role in this transition. In 1902 sugar planters who had recruited Sicilians as farm laborers complained that it was difficult to retain this workforce for more than two seasons, since by that time, "they have laid by a little money and are ready to start a fruit shop or a grocery store at some cross-roads town. Those who do not establish themselves thus strap packs and peddle blue jeans, overalls and red handkerchiefs to the Negroes" (Scarpaci 1972, 211).

From the 1870s on, Mississippi Chinese adopted a similar pattern of male migrant laborers developing businesses that catered to black customers. Expected by their families back home to remit earnings, the Chinese found that the southern sharecropping system was incapable of generating abundant revenue. The domestic service occupations in which immigrant Chinese found employment in other regions of the United States were unavailable in Mississippi, where blacks already occupied such positions. Like the Louisiana Italians, the Chinese saved and borrowed funds from co-ethnics and relatives to start small shops—as little as $100 was needed in the early decades, and only $400 as late as the 1940s. The store building served as both residence and business (Loewen 1971, 32–33). Until the advent of supermarkets in the post–World War II era, Chinese had a near-monopoly over the grocery business in the Mississippi Delta, especially with regard to black shoppers. Indeed, almost 97 percent of Chinese in the region were employed in this single occupation.

Jews also ran numerous businesses in small southern towns. In *Caste and Class in a Southern Town*, John Dollard (1937/1957, 129) describes the virtual monopoly of Jewish store owners during the 1930s over the retail sale of dry goods; their shops were frequented by both black and white consumers. The Jews were especially successful in selling to African Americans. "The Jews have treated the Negroes with courtesy, or at least without discourtesy in strictly business relations." Immigrant entrepreneurs found little competition for this captive market. Native whites were castigated for trading with blacks and found the level of frugality maintained by immigrant entrepreneurs to be unacceptable while blacks themselves were largely excluded from business ownership through poverty, lack of experience, Jim Crow laws, and discrimination by banks, wholesalers, and distributors (Scarpaci 1972; Loewen 1971, 52). Chinese, Italian, and Jewish business owners encountered some difficulty in negotiating their ambiguous position between black customers and the white elite. However, relations were generally without extensive conflict.

If migrant entrepreneurs in the South directed their businesses toward black customers, those in northern settings initially catered to foreign and native-born white consumers. (The African American population in many northern cities was minuscule prior to the late 1910s, making them a limited market.)[4] In some cases, merchants retained economic relationships that had been established prior to migration. For example, in *The Ghetto*, Louis Wirth (1928, 229) notes that Jewish immigrants in Chicago kept the uneasy but familiar patterns of trade with Poles that they had developed in eastern Europe.

These two groups detest each other thoroughly, but live side by side. . . . A study of numerous cases shows that not only do many Jews open their businesses on Milwaukee Avenue and Division Street because they know that the Poles are the predominant population in these neighborhoods, but the Poles come from all over the city to trade on Maxwell Street because they know that there they can find the familiar street-stands owned by Jews. These two immigrant groups, having lived side by side in Poland and Galicia, are used to each other's business methods.

Despite their common European origins and shared immigrant status, business relations among (and sometimes even within) white immigrant groups were often risky, tense, and violent. In pre–World War I Detroit, the Jewish Peddlers Union formed in 1900 as a self-defense organization to resist sometimes-fatal attacks by Polish and Irish ruffians. Suggesting the importance of economic conditions in yielding conflict between merchants and customers, hostility was magnified during the depression of 1893 to 1894, when unemployment, the eastern European Jews' high visibility, and age-old stereotypes of Jews as exploiters and Shylocks led to their being targeted (Rockaway 1986, 20, 90). John Bukowczyk (1984, 70–71) notes that during a series of strike-related riots in 1915 and 1916, the largely Polish workforce sacked Bayonne, New Jersey, businesses owned by Jews and Irishmen. The *Jewish Daily Forward* described a 1902 incident involving discord between entrepreneurs and customers of the same background. Outraged by the high prices charged by kosher butchers, Jewish women on the Lower East Side mounted a boycott. The protesters clashed with co-ethnic meat vendors, enlisted the support of local rabbis to their cause, and sustained their boycott by citing religious passages that permitted the consumption of nonkosher meat during dire emergencies (Green 1998, 120–22). Rhonda Levine (2001) describes the case of German Jewish cattle merchants in upstate New York who enjoyed generally better relations with Gentile customers (for whom they provided a vital service) than with established Russian Jews who did not own cattle.

It was only after ethnic entrepreneurs had first serviced immigrant whites that many began to sell to African Americans, who were moving to northern cities as part of the Great Migration. Black migrants from the South entered the same Chicago neighborhoods—on the South and West Sides—where overseas immigrants settled. Seeking profits and ignorant of or willing to ignore the predominant racial codes, Jews sought out these new arrivals. "Unlike the White landlords and residents in other parts of the city, the Jews have offered no appreciable resistance to the invasion by the Negroes. . . . The prevailing opinion of the merchants on the near West Side is that the Negro spends his money freely, and usually has some to spend, and thereby is a desirable neighbor" (Wirth 1928, 230). One of the earliest accounts of Jews selling to African Americans in New York appeared under the headline "The New Ghetto" in *Harper's Weekly* in 1897. The article, its text laden with stereotypical descriptions of both Jews and blacks, explains that Polish Jews moved from Baxter Street to Manhattan's West Side and now outnumber the black residents toward whom their businesses are directed (Emerson 1897).[5]

Immigrant entrepreneurs found little competition from native whites in selling to blacks within black neighborhoods. Outside of ghettos prior to the 1940s, however, white store owners in the South as well as in northern cities, including New York, Cleveland, and Chicago, offered limited service or altogether refused to sell to blacks in order to maintain patterns of racial segregation. Department stores would not allow blacks to try on clothes and would not hire black salespeople, even when they were located in black neighborhoods. Movie theaters, transit companies, and hospitals limited blacks' access or banned them outright. If and when businesses served African Americans or landlords rented to them, they were overcharged (Kusmer 1976; Rockaway 1986). Given this racial and economic climate, some blacks valued the presence of immigrant shop owners in their neighborhoods, if they treated blacks well.[6] Because immigrants' shops were often better capitalized than those run by blacks, the former were often seen as more prestigious, less expensive, and better stocked than African American firms (Drake and Cayton 1945; Loewen 1971; Lee 2002; Silverman 2000).

At the same time, immigrant entrepreneurs often found more opportunity and acceptance among black than white customers. Of Harlem during the war years, Roi Ottley (1943/1968, 128) avowed, "Negroes have never been associated with any overt forms of anti-Semitism, such as the 'Buy from Christians' movement, though attempts have been made to enlist their support." Hence, at least in some cases immigrant entrepreneurs and customers enjoyed a symbiotic rather than conflict-ridden relationship. A degree of shared interest brought the two groups together.

Activist Challenges to Ethnic Businesses: The Depression Era and World War II

Declining economic conditions during the Depression, coupled with new levels of political activism, focused and intensified conflicts between immigrant entrepreneurs and their customers during the 1930s and 1940s. In the East and Midwest, blacks used boycotts and protests to demand jobs and better treatment from businesses and public services that relied on their patronage. On the West Coast, whites used the wartime political climate to eliminate the competition presented by Japanese American entrepreneurs.

During the Depression, because economic competition and social exclusion limited the ability of immigrants to find jobs in existing firms or to run businesses in white communities, they increasingly directed their efforts toward black customers.[7] Some white ethnic entrepreneurs intentionally sought out racial minority customers. Others—in Harlem, South Chicago, Newark, Detroit, the Bronx, Glenville, and Boyle Heights—retained their shops as the neighborhood changed from Jewish, Greek, or Italian to black or Latino (Myrdal 1944, 308). Whatever the reasons for their presence, white merchants sometimes collectively dropped their prices to drive black competitors out of business (Silverman 2000).

Popular stereotypes identify Jews as the leading entrepreneurs in black neighborhoods of the 1930 and 1940s, but other ethnic populations had shops there as well. For example, Italians owned 75 percent of the saloons and cabarets in Harlem during the 1930s. A 1934 jobs campaign by a Harlem activist targeted white-run shops, which included 151 Greek- and 242 Jewish-owned stores on 125th Street that did not hire blacks (Hunter 1977, 187). The Harlem journalist Roi Ottley (1943/1968, 53–55) noted a significant number of Chinese stores on Harlem's Lenox Avenue during the 1940s and also observed that Chinese had cordial relations with blacks and participated in black culture and that interracial marriages were not infrequent.

Illustrative of the limited employment opportunities available in white-run firms that relied on black patronage, in 1934 only 13 of 2,791 jobs on Harlem's 125th Street were in the hands of blacks (Hunter 1977, 191). Similarly, of 3,000 stores in Cleveland's black community in 1935, blacks owned only 50, and these employed only about 100 persons, usually as porters or janitors (Hunter 1977, 245). When requested to hire African Americans, the manager of one Cleveland grocery responded that he would "rather die and go to hell before I employ a Negro in my store."[8]

It was in this climate that the "don't shop where you can't work" campaign developed (Greenberg 1991, 117). Inspired by the writings of W. E. B. Du Bois, the campaign took shape in Chicago in 1929 and spread to major black communities throughout the country, including New York, Cleveland, Detroit, Toledo, Pittsburgh, Philadelphia, and Newark (Harris 1936/1968, x; Hunter 1977, 286). Although national in scope, the specific nature of the campaign reflected the conditions, personalities, and interest groups of the city in which it was located. A comprehensive review reveals that these campaigns elicited diverse reactions from the black populace. The central goal was to obtain jobs for black workers in ghetto shops, not ownership per se. Accordingly, boycotts and protests were just as often directed at corporate outlets like Rexall, the A&P, or Woolworth's as they were at stores owned by ethnic entrepreneurs. Progressive blacks supported these campaigns, as did black store owners, who saw in them a means of reducing competition from white rivals. The conservative black elite, leftists, and newspaper publishers were less enthusiastic. Nevertheless, when skillful political leaders, such as Adam Clayton Powell Jr. or Cleveland's John Holly, were able to overcome factional disputes and mobilize an inclusive social movement, results were impressive. Of the efforts to obtain jobs for blacks in New York City, Roi Ottley (1943/1968, 116) wrote: "Harlem supported the drive, loudly and wholeheartedly. Everyone in the community, it seemed, participated in the boycott, even to giving social affairs to raise funds. Business dropped to the vanishing point." Over time the organizers of boycotts became increasingly sophisticated and were able to mobilize extensive community backing. Having ensured employment opportunities for some blacks in ghetto stores, the movement went on during the late 1930s and early 1940s to open up positions in utilities, transit companies, hospitals, dairies, and other enterprises dependent on black patronage.

Some dimensions of the "don't shop where you can't work" movement did intensify antagonism between ethnic entrepreneurs and African Americans. Certain movement leaders, including Sufi Hamid (active in both Chicago and New York), frequently and pejoratively mentioned that Harlem's white merchants were of Jewish extraction as they asserted the need for black employment and community self-determination. Jews, however, were not the only targets of ethnic slurs. Hamid derided Italian entrepreneurs as "spaghetti slingers" and "wops," Greeks as "goat herds," and middle-class blacks as "uppity niggers." Some Harlem residents responded positively to the chorus of epithets. Others condemned them as echoing "every Hitleresque charge against the Jewish community" and joined forces to appoint alternative representatives for the jobs campaign (Ottley 1943/1968, 119). At the same time, the store owners' ethnic groups showed little restraint in applying their own brands of racial abuse. They used political influence as well as red-baiting and accusations of fascism to derail the activists' campaign.[9] Bitterness and frustration among community members erupted into violence in the Harlem Riots of 1935 and 1943. When the smoke cleared, the impact of the movement's influence was clear. Those stores that refused to hire blacks were the most heavily vandalized (Hunter 1977, 194).

In retrospect, the "don't shop where you can't work" campaign had many important impacts. It gave blacks a degree of control over the employment in their neighborhoods and made great progress in getting blacks jobs in public utilities, transport companies, and a wide array of public and private firms, often at higher levels than had previously been available. In his study of the movement, Gary Hunter (1977, 284) concluded: "Outside the federal government, no other organization during the depression was responsible for bringing more employment to the Black community than job campaigning." In addition, the campaign developed blacks' political skills and, accordingly, their representation.

As the Depression years flowed into the World War II era, economic and legal conditions in inner-city communities were remade. The growing need for wartime labor, coupled with the draft, increased the demand for workers. Flush with their relative success in the "don't shop where you can't work" campaigns and empowered by New Deal legislation that furthered their organizational and economic opportunities, many black activists focused their efforts on obtaining government jobs for their community.[10] Accordingly, conflicts between ethnic entrepreneurs and customers received less attention during this period than they had during the Depression years. Nevertheless, during 1943 two significant riots occurred—in Harlem and Detroit—resulting in the widespread destruction of ethnic businesses.

In New York the uprising was instigated when a uniformed black serviceman was arrested in a white-owned shop (Greenberg 1991). Observers claimed that the riot reflected the fact that blacks' opportunities and living conditions showed few signs of improvement despite the booming wartime economy. In Detroit the riot was a consequence of racial conflicts that developed as thousands of black and white rural migrants sought jobs, housing, and social space in the crowded industrial neighborhoods of the Motor City. Jewish merchants occupied an uneasy location between the combatants. White groups blamed the Jews—who had been involved in interracial dialogue—as instigators and supporters of black activism, while Jewish merchants, as the only white presence in the poorest black neighborhoods, were visible targets for the community's resentment toward an unjust system (Bolkosky 1991). As a consequence of the riots, numerous white ethnic entrepreneurs abandoned their businesses in both New York and Detroit.

Finally, the World War II era witnessed perhaps the harshest governmentally implemented act of control over ethnic entrepreneurs in American history—the wholesale internment of 120,000 Japanese Americans. Long the object of white hostility on the West Coast because of their highly competitive business practices, the Japanese had been targeted by a number of restrictive laws that impeded their ability to do business, made them ineligible for citizenship, and prohibited the foreign-born from owning land. By restricting the range of economic opportunities available to the Japanese, these laws actually furthered the group's economic dominance over the handful of enterprises—small grocery stores, restaurants and hotels, and truck farming—in which they could find employment (Light 1972). Having excluded the Japanese from all but these few occupations, whites then tried to remove the remaining options. Toward this end, in San Francisco the Anti-Jap Laundry League, formed in 1908 by white and "French" laundry workers and owners, used anti-Japanese boycotts as well as pressure on politicians in an effort to deny Japanese the opportunity of running laundries (Light 1972, 72).

Despite white efforts to limit Japanese economic advancement, the Japanese prevailed. On the eve of World War II, Japanese, who constituted a mere 2 percent of California's population, were producing one-third of all truck crops in the state and up to 90 percent of certain commodities. They also owned many laundries, grocery stores, restaurants, hotels, and gardening businesses (Jiobu 1988, 359; Light 1972). Hence, when calls for the mass incarceration of Japanese were heard at the start of the war, white agricultural groups actively supported the cause. In early 1942 the anti-Japanese coterie included the Grower-Shipper Vegetable Association, the Western Growers Protective Association, and the California Farm Bureau Federation (Takaki 1989, 189). Following their release from the internment camps, many Japanese returned to their entrepreneurial occupations. But they would never enjoy the degree of entrepreneurial concentration they had maintained prior to the war.

Popular stereotypes and strident editorials often condemn racial minorities for their hostility to ethnic entrepreneurs (Kim 2000; Banfield 1974). In retrospect, however, we see that nonwhite entrepreneurs serving native white customers—including nineteenth-century black middlemen and West Coast Japanese—have been the victims of the harshest antimerchant campaigns in U.S. history. What is more, these were carried out not by angry mobs but by government agencies. In addition, various forms of discrimination by large firms, unions, public employers, colleges and universities, and other institutions served to limit job possibilities and consequently to direct Jews, Italians, and other immigrants to high rates of self-employment in minority neighborhoods (Gordon 1949; Glazer and Moynihan 1963).

In sum, the Depression and World War II period was a turning point in relations between ethnic entrepreneurs and customers. Activist groups and government agencies took multiple and dynamic roles in shaping interactions between ethnic businesses and their customers. Some developments of the period contributed to the well-being of racial minority customers. These included government spending on social services as well as pro-union and antidiscrimination laws. On the other hand, the period also featured harsh measures that restricted the actions of minorities, culminating in the mass incarceration of a nonwhite group that just happened to be especially successful in business. Finally, urban rioting in New York introduced a new pattern—one involving black attacks on ethnic businesses in response to police brutality rather than turf battles between white and black adversaries—that would become predominant during the 1960s and after (Light 1972; Hirsch 1983).

The Postwar Era

The late 1940s until the mid-1960s witnessed relatively few conflicts between immigrant entrepreneurs and their customers. However, the urban landscape was restructured during this period by economic growth, a gradual expansion of social, political, and economic opportunities for blacks, and the movement of whites—and with them, economic and communal institutions—away from urban centers. Hence, the era had contradictory effects on urban and minority communities.

Urban renewal and highway building programs—devised by white elites with little input from minority and working-class groups—were intended to revive declining cities during the 1960s and 1970s (Jackson 1985). As a consequence, they often had negative impacts on ethnic neighborhoods and especially on black entrepreneurs. Such policies displaced established businesses as well as residents and failed to provide the resources necessary to reopen in a new location (Woodard 1997). Joe Darden and his colleagues (1987, 170) cite the case of Detroit's Elmwood Park Phase I program of the 1960s. While a few larger businesses with a citywide clientele survived and even benefited from relocation, about half of all those in the area folded.

> The effect on most businesses, however, was devastating; 69 percent of the 64 businesses in Elmwood Park Phase I were small, neighborhood convenience stores, mainly oper-

Immigrant Entrepreneurs and Customers 327

ated by owners who depended on surrounding residents for customers. Half of the businesses were owned by Blacks, and all but two Black businesses were local convenience stores. Fifty seven percent of the businesses owned by Blacks did not survive relocation. The small, Black-owned barbershops, grocery stores, and pool halls, which were so unlikely to survive relocation, were also important community institutions. The majority performed non-economic functions that greatly helped neighborhood cohesion: They extended credit, supervised juveniles, and served as centers of communication and contact. Many of these businesses simply could not survive as neighborhood establishments once their neighborhoods were destroyed. Some former proprietors remained bitter years after their relocation. Urban renewal had killed a large pocket of viable minority enterprises.

At the same time, new freeways provided easy access to those who wished to live in the suburbs or shop in suburban malls, thus contributing to further urban decline in many localities (Vergara 1995). Finally, from the 1930s to the 1970s government-sanctioned redlined loan policies destabilized urban regions characterized by racial and class diversity and concentrated the poor and minorities in cities while driving more affluent whites to new suburbs. Between 1940 and 1950, 7 million people moved to the suburbs, with millions more following in the years after (Weaver 1966, 335). "The lasting damage done by the national government was that it put its seal of approval on ethnic and racial discrimination and developed policies which had the result of the practical abandonment of large sections of older, industrial cities" (Jackson 1985, 217).

A series of ghetto revolts occurred in cities large and small between 1964 and 1969. A national advisory commission tabulated 164 such riots during the first nine months of 1967, and 1,893 between 1964 and 1969 (Light 1972, 2; Porter and Dunn 1984, 175). The single largest event of the era occurred in Detroit and resulted in the death of 33 persons, the looting of 2,700 businesses, and $50 million worth of damage to property; some 5,000 persons were left homeless, most of them black (Darden et al. 1987, 72). Not all events, however, took place in major cities such as Detroit or Los Angeles. Small towns like York, Pennsylvania (1970 population: 50,000), were also rocked by racial violence (CNN 2001). James Loewen (1971, 174–75) describes how long-established Chinese- and white-owned grocery stores in small Mississippi Delta towns were also targeted by violence and boycotts during the late 1960s.

A broad literature has addressed the 1960s uprisings and identified a wide range of contributing factors. They include the black baby boom generation entering its teens and early twenties; blacks' feelings of frustration at their difficulty in achieving middle-class status and equality (especially in contrast to the images of affluence displayed on increasingly available television); various social movements of the 1960s—civil rights, antiwar, Black Power, and anticolonialism—that catalyzed demands for community control; the public condemnation of police brutality; the apparent willingness of the Kennedy and Johnson administrations to respond to black demands; and later, the race-baiting law-and-order agendas of Nixon-Agnew, George Wallace, and the like (Banfield 1974; Sears 2000; Blauner 1972; Skrentny 2000).

Two specific outcomes of this period are worth mentioning because they would continue to shape the business environment of urban communities in the coming years. The first was the large-scale exit of businesses—be they owned by corporations or by individual entrepreneurs—from inner cities. A 1969 survey of three hundred merchants (four-fifths of whom were Jewish) in Boston's black ghettos found that 25 percent had liquidated their operations and another 50 percent intended to do so (Weisbrod and

Stein 1970, 81). Similarly, as a result of the riots that swept through Chicago's West Side after the assassination of Dr. Martin Luther King Jr., the North Lawndale neighborhood lost 75 percent of its business establishments. In 1986 the community, with a population of almost 70,000, had only one bank and one supermarket (Wilson 1996, 35). Businesses left because of fear of crime, inability to obtain insurance, and drastic reductions in local bases of employment—and hence customers.

Although the decision to leave was ultimately made by the business owner, co-ethnic communities sometimes encouraged niche abandonment. For example, in 1966 articles appeared in *National Review* and *Conservative Judaism* suggesting that the larger Jewish community both assist and compel Jewish inner-city merchants and slumlords to sell their holdings to blacks in order to advance black self-sufficiency and diffuse a major source of black-Jewish tension (Teller 1966; Geltman 1966; Weisbrod and Stein 1970, 81). Further reflecting Jewish dissension on relations with blacks was a 1959 CORE demonstration against a segregated, Jewish-owned department store in Miami. When the protesters, who included a contingent of "Jewish radicals," took their positions, "the employees working behind the luncheon counter responded to the interracial sit-in with anti-Semitic remarks. 'Which nigger is the Jew?' they taunted" (Dash-Moore 1994, 171). These actions, as well as those of African American and Korean American activists in the 1980s and 1990s, reveal that participants in ethnic conflicts do not maintain a reflexive and unified position with regard to ethnic conflicts. Instead, they exhibit internal dissonance, often associated with generational and class differences (Sonenshein 1996; Kim 2000).

A second major outcome of the urban riots of the 1960s was a series of attempts by government and major foundations to diffuse ethnic tension by helping blacks to establish their own businesses, either directly with loans and technical assistance, or indirectly by broadening access to education and jobs. According to Timothy Bates (1997), William Julius Wilson (1978), and Michael Woodard (1997), the economic impacts of civil rights era programs intended to increase business ownership by disadvantaged minority groups varied according to social class. Middle-class racial minorities already in possession of skills, education, and personal savings encountered growing opportunities in existing firms, the public sector, and entrepreneurship (Morawska 2001; Wilson 1978). At the same time, with some reductions in residential segregation, members of the black middle class were increasingly able to move away from urban ghettos to either integrated neighborhoods or black middle-class enclaves (Wilson 1978; Gates 1993). However, fewer possibilities opened up for blacks who lacked class resources. In fact, many of the latter found their condition worsen owing to deindustrialization and cutbacks in social services (Wilson 1996; Johnson and Oliver 1994). And after the late 1980s conservative attacks against set-aside programs resulted in a drastic reduction of the support available for minority businesses by government (Gold and Light 2000).

Local events, like the 1960s riots, were but one of the factors making conditions difficult in urban neighborhoods. Additional sources of decline had global origins. These included the two oil shocks of the 1970s and the rise in international economic competition. Their result was to reduce demand for U.S.-made products, thus yielding massive layoffs. Among the industries most directly affected were the unionized manufacturing concerns that provided a large fraction of the best jobs to inner-city residents (Wilson 1987, 40). For example, between 1970 and 1984 New York City lost almost 500,000 jobs requiring less than a high school education, while Philadelphia lost over 150,000 such positions. From 1978 to 1989, South Central Los Angeles lost nearly 200,000 jobs (Johnson et al. 1992, 359, 362).

As a consequence, despite the effects of civil rights, antipoverty, and urban renewal programs enacted during the 1960s and 1970s, by the early 1980s many inner-city areas were more racially concentrated and had fewer jobs, fewer viable institutions, fewer government services, and fewer chain stores than had been the case decades earlier (Hacker 1992, 229). Nevertheless, the welfare state continued to provide minimal income to residents, much of which would be spent in local stores. In this environment, inner-city areas were seen as risky and undesirable locations for businesses, although they continued to sustain a sizable consumer demand (Light and Bonacich 1988; Silverman 2000).

Post-1980s: Ethnic and Economic Transformations

Since the middle 1960s, the urban United States has been the destination of millions of immigrants. The presence of these new arrivals has altered urban life and the relations between ethnic entrepreneurs and their customers. Even when recent immigrants open few businesses, the competition rendered by their presence is sometimes associated with violence. Indeed, the most destructive riots to occur in the United States since 1980 have taken place in Miami and Los Angeles, locations where large numbers of international migrants settled in or near traditionally African American neighborhoods, increasing competition for jobs, business ownership, government services, housing, and political power (Portes and Stepick 1993; Johnson et al. 1992; Ladner et al. 1981).

Although the mere presence of immigrants can increase tension, migrants' entry into urban entrepreneurship has often resulted in discord with native black customers. Following the riots of the 1960s, white ethnic entrepreneurs sold their shops to black owners. A decade later, many blacks resold them to immigrants (Cho 1993). As a result, during the late 1970s and early 1980s new immigrant entrepreneurs, including Arabs, Chaldeans, and Koreans, had become the major business owners in many cities. By 1991 Koreans owned one thousand businesses on Chicago's South Side (Silverman 2000, 95). Min (1996, 67) cites 1992 figures that indicate 80 percent of businesses in South Central Los Angeles were owned by Koreans. In the 1990s Koreans held nine thousand businesses in New York City, including five thousand in the Bronx and Brooklyn. Korean business growth is facilitated by vertical integration, as Koreans also own the importing firms, distributors, food wholesalers, and garment manufacturers that supply goods to co-ethnic retail businesses (Yoon 1997; Min 1996). Gary David (1999; 2000) estimates that Chaldeans own 80 to 90 percent of the businesses in Detroit and notes that grocers' and gas station owners' associations are largely Chaldean in membership.

In many of these settings, black residents have had significant conflicts with the newly arrived ethnic entrepreneurs. In some cases, conflicts are exacerbated because at least initially shop owners do not speak English, are unfamiliar with American customs, and prefer to employ family members, co-ethnics, or other migrants rather than established locals. Moreover, inner-city businesses often rely on the sale of profitable but socially destructive products like liquor, cigarettes, drug paraphernalia, and lottery tickets, while charging high prices for staples such as bread, milk, and cleaning supplies (Sonenshein 1996). Local residents feel that ethnic businesses encourage addictions and attract undesirables to the store vicinity. William Julius Wilson (1996, 35) cites the case of a Chicago neighborhood: home to seventy thousand residents in 1986, it had only one bank and one supermarket, but forty-eight state lottery agents, fifty currency exchanges, and ninety-nine licensed liquor stores and bars. Ethnic business owners are often blamed for the sale of such unsavory products. However, it is important to note that this development is also linked to the actions of more powerful groups. The California State Legislature, for example, permitted ten times the number of liquor licenses per square mile in South Central Los Angeles than were allowed in other neighborhoods of Los Angeles County (Sonenshein 1996, 718). Alcohol and tobacco companies manufacture and market special brands of malt liquor, fortified wine, and cigarettes to inner-city residents while state lotteries encourage gambling as a leisure activity (Light and Bonacich 1988; Bonacich 1994).

Since the 1980s, antagonism between inner-city residents and immigrant shop owners has been extensively reported in both mainstream and ethnic media, dramatized in popular music, films, and videos, and treated ideologically by ethnic activists (Johnson and Oliver 1994; Min 1996; Angel 2001). As a consequence, business-related ethnic conflicts became linked to broader discussions of racial solidarity, community control, and battles to redefine one's group and oneself in what Manuel Castells (1997) describes as leaderless but widely accessible, identity-based social movements.[11]

From the 1930s until the late 1970s, contending ethnic business owners and customer groups simultaneously developed political skills and resources and refined their use of political, legal, and media contacts as means to achieving collective ends (Ottley 1968; Hunter 1977; Waldinger 1996). Although there was competition, there was also a degree of political equality, collaboration, and common interest (Weisbrod and Stein 1970). Raphael Sonenshein (1996, 734) asserts: "It is particularly unrealistic to expect the relationship between Blacks and Korean Americans to match the long history of coalition between Blacks and Jews in Los Angeles. Blacks and Jews in Los Angeles met as political equals—outsiders in a political system dominated by hostile conservatives."

Since that time, migrant entrepreneurs have often been at a disadvantage in conflicts with customers, since their groups are numerically small, non-English-speaking, noncitizens, and generally unfamiliar with the American legal system.[12] Accordingly, mobilized customer groups sometimes use the legal and political system to exert a degree of control over entrepreneurs (Min 1996; David 1999; Bailey 1999).

Ethnic leaders publicize their conflicts with immigrant entrepreneurs, making relatively isolated incidents the focus of national and even international attention. Community activists have used political organizing to challenge ethnic business owners in inner-city settings through local elections, store boycotts, zoning regulations, environmental impact reviews, the withholding of liquor licenses, lawsuits, and demands for the punishment of shop owners who have injured customers (Sonenshein 1996; Yoon 1997; Min 1996; David 1999). For example, Al Sharpton has mobilized the National Action Network, which is involved in a nationwide campaign to improve the treatment of black customers in inner-city stores (Kurth and Patterson 2001). Whites too have used political action to limit the presence of Asian businesses and real estate developments in several cities (Foner 2000; Gold 1994a; Horton et al. 1995). As a result of these conflicts, migrant entrepreneurs increasingly realize that they need to improve their political skills and initiate coalitions to defend their interests. They have developed fund-raising campaigns and begun to support political candidates, form self-help organizations, make political contributions, establish dialogues with other groups, and rely on American-educated and English-speaking co-ethnics to expand their power base in the United States (Min 1996; Kim 2000).

With recent migrants constituting a large fraction of the population in urban areas—including both entrepreneurs and customers—ethnic conflicts frequently involve multiple foreign-born groups. Although led by homegrown activists like Al

Sharpton and Sonny Carson, New York City boycotts of inner-city grocery markets in 1991 generally ensnarled Korean entrepreneurs and Caribbean customers (Min 1996). In a like manner, the Los Angeles riot of 1992 was labeled as the nation's first multiethnic civil disorder and involved the destruction of businesses owned by Koreans, Middle Easterners, blacks, other Asian groups, whites, and Latinos, as well as arrests of members of various groups for looting and violence (Johnson et al. 1992). Despite the devastation experienced by Korean entrepreneurs during the Los Angeles riot, 40 percent of destroyed businesses were owned by Latinos, and the one business owner killed during the melee was Thanh Lam, the twenty-five-year-old Chinese-Vietnamese proprietor of a Compton shop (Chang and Diaz-Veizades 1999, 26; Merina 1992).

Although conflicts between native minority customers and recent immigrant entrepreneurs are often explosive, several observers have noted that immigrant customers tend to get along somewhat better with immigrant entrepreneurs. For example, Chang and Diaz-Veizades (1999, 81) cite the case of Brenda Hughes, the seventeen-year-old daughter of Salvadoran immigrants who was shot and killed in a car in the Highland Park neighborhood of Los Angeles by Jo Won Kim, a Korean store owner, who suspected her companions of shoplifting (Ellington and Kang 1996). The Hughes event did not appear to have a major impact on Latino-Korean relations. In contrast, the case of Soon Ja Du—a Korean shop owner who shot and killed Latasha Harlins, an African American teenager accused of stealing, and received no jail time—greatly increased tension between blacks and Koreans in Los Angeles and is seen as a major antecedent of the 1992 Los Angeles riot.

Several explanations account for the relatively benign relations between immigrant entrepreneurs and foreign-born customers. Lucie Cheng and Yen Le Espiritu (1989) hypothesize that these groups see each other as fair competitors rather than hostile exploiters. Immigrant customers have fewer feelings of ownership or "rights" in U.S. society. They are less concerned with their relative group position than are native blacks and also have less political power and savvy, so they have fewer options to act on their discontent through political and legal channels (Yoon 1997; Min 1996; Sears 1994; Morawska 2001).[13] Because neither owners nor customers feel a strong sense of agency and ownership within the host society, they regard commercial interactions in a generally businesslike manner. This contrasts with the symbolic importance that native-born groups often attribute to their group's position in terms of limited community control and business ownership (Blumer 1958; Bobo and Hutchings 1996; Kasinitz and Haynes 1996; Morawska 2001).[14] Another reason for the relatively easy relations between immigrant entrepreneurs and immigrant customers is that migrant entrepreneurs commonly prefer immigrants to native-born whites or blacks as employees. Hence, for migrants, prospects for employment in ethnic shops are relatively good (Gold 1994a; 1994b; Kim 1999; Waldinger 1994).

Although they are marked by social, economic, linguistic, and legal disadvantages, even impoverished, undocumented, and recently arrived migrant groups—including Haitians (at least in Miami), Central Americans, Dominicans, Mexicans, and Senegalese—appear to maintain higher levels of entrepreneurship (albeit sometimes through very small-scale, informal businesses) than do most U.S.-born minority groups (Glazer and Moynihan 1963; Stepick 1998; Pessar 1995; Mahler 1995; Guarnizo 1998; Babou 2001). Although these entrepreneurs face many problems, including raids by police and shakedowns by co-ethnic gangs, their businesses do offer goods and services, provide training, yield earnings, and help groups develop a feeling of connection to their local environment (Light et al. 1994; Katz 1988; Vélez-Ibañez 1983; Light and Gold 2000).

Finally, although both native blacks and low-income nonwhite migrants often reside in segregated neighborhoods, rates of isolation from whites are considerably lower for most Latinos and Asians than for blacks, and intermarriage with whites is much more frequent. Moreover, a considerable body of evidence suggests that the Asian and Latino migrants' pattern of concentration is to a large extent voluntary and hence is not regarded simply as a form of ill treatment at the hands of the host society, as is commonly the case among native and foreign-born blacks (Scott 2001). Accordingly, local business owners—regardless of their ethnicity—are seen by some migrants simply as merchants rather than as the most visible representatives of an unjust and oppressive society. It remains to be seen whether these migrant populations will continue to maintain relatively benign relations with local merchants, or whether, over time, their conflicts will begin to resemble those between native-born populations and ethnic entrepreneurs.

The Current Scene

The years of economic growth during the 1990s witnessed some economic improvements in inner-city areas (*Chicago Tribune* 2001). Corporate and franchise businesses began locating branches in these areas, providing jobs for local residents and competition for ethnic entrepreneurs (Gallagher 1998). For example, the expansion of doughnut chains like Dunkin' Donuts and Krispy Kreme have displaced Cambodian entrepreneurs who formerly controlled this ethnic niche in Los Angeles (Ballon 2002). At the same time, ethnic entrepreneurs located in urban settings have quickly tired of the hostile environment and of doing business behind inch-thick Plexiglas. Several reports suggest that Korean, Chaldean, and other ethnic business owners are selling off their inner-city shops to open businesses in more benign locations (Ong, Park, and Tong 1994; Abelmann and Lie 1995; David 1999; Porter and Dunn 1984). Concurrently, when available, customers increasingly favor malls and superstores over ethnic convenience shops, thus reducing tension between local residents and immigrant entrepreneurs (Riccardi 1996).

Although some corporate and franchise businesses provide jobs, good service, and competitive prices to inner-city consumers, the corporate return to the inner city is not without its downside. Chains of pawn shops, loan companies, rent-to-own furniture stores, and other enterprises that are subsidiaries of Nationsbank, Transamerica Corporation, American Express, and other firms traded on Wall Street have recently opened in inner-city neighborhoods, where conventional banks and stores remain rare. They are cleaner and more presentable than ethnic shops of days gone by, but these companies use misleading advertising to lure customers and charge exorbitant interest rates to those with few alternatives. Several have been the target of government investigations and class-action lawsuits for their exploitative practices (Hudson 1994; 1996). According to Manning Marable (1983, 164, emphasis in original), corporate interest in black customers has a largely negative effect.

> Historically, rapid Black business growth occurred *only during the period of rigid racial segregation*, when relatively few White corporations made any attempt to attract Black consumers. The Civil Rights Movement and desegregation permitted the White private sector to develop a variety of advertising strategies to extract billions in profits from Black consumers, all in the name of "equality." The net result was the increased marginalization of the Black entrepreneur, the manipulation of Black culture and social

habits by White corporations, and a new kind of economic underdevelopment for all Blacks at all income levels.

Finally, racial minority groups, including blacks and Latinos, have become more stratified by class than has been the case in the past (Wilson 1996; Bates 1997; Hochschild 2000; Ortiz 1996; Omi and Winant 1993). As a consequence, low-income ethnic group members are increasingly circumspect about lending their support to co-ethnic enterprises as a means of improving communal conditions. The business journalist Earl Ofari Hutchinson (1994, 268) writes: "There is also the danger that Black business, given its inherent capitalist nature, will create greater wealth for a small Black elite. The resultant deepening of class divisions among African Americans would simply perpetuate the exploitation of African American workers and the poor."

CONCLUSIONS

Conflicts between ethnic entrepreneurs and their customers have stimulated extensive investigation by academics, policymakers, journalists, and social activists. The resulting studies are richly detailed, but they are generally lacking in a broadly comparative perspective and often focus on especially volatile incidents—ones often associated with major race riots—between a limited number of marginal groups, largely ignoring the full array of features that underlie most conflicts between ethnic entrepreneurs and their customers. This focus makes these studies ill suited for the generation of comprehensive theory.

I have taken a more comparative approach. Over the course of the last century the nature of inner-city communities has changed, as have the groups of customers and merchants who carry on economic relations within them. Further, a variety of policies intended to address urban inequality—ranging from welfare to urban renewal to micro-enterprise development to welfare reform—have been implemented, evaluated, and often abandoned.

This well-documented history of changing social and economic circumstances and applications of public policy stands as a natural experiment from which insightful observers have been able to foretell the conditions that are most often associated with civil versus violent relations between merchants and customers. This summary suggests that over the long term conflict between shop owners and customers tends to be aggravated by periods of dramatic demographic change, social disruptions that enhance conflict over scarce resources, increased levels of police brutality, and social movements that heighten intergroup antagonism. Yet despite a general awareness that such circumstances provoke violence between merchants and customers, those charged with maintaining safe and civil environments remain unwilling or unable to take corrective action. As a consequence, a century-old pattern of discord between merchants remains with us.

As long as the prevailing systems of racial, ethnic, and economic stratification and boundary maintenance endure in American society, at least some fraction of entrepreneurs and their customers are likely to be embroiled in conflicts. Group-specific, local, and contextual issues certainly contribute to these conflicts, but such events are also significantly shaped by the social, economic, and political concerns that originate in and involve the larger society and over which neither merchant nor customer have much control. Accordingly, conflicts between entrepreneurs and customers are often the consequence of broader patterns of inequality, prejudice, and racial-ethnic alienation in American society rather than the cause of them.

The popular notion that conflicts between merchants and their customers are confined to violent acts between Jews, Koreans, and blacks residing in ghettos is not just historically inaccurate. More important, it reinforces questionable notions about how American society functions. For if violent and unethical business transactions are confined to othered groups and locations, then the larger society and its majority citizens can absolve themselves of responsibility for such events and attribute these problems to the groups involved rather than to the policies and interest groups that have helped to create a context ripe for hostility (Davies 1990).

NOTES

1. For example, according to Edward Chang and Jeannette Diaz-Veizades (1999, 36), only about 10 percent of all Korean businesses in Los Angeles are located in predominantly African American areas, while 48 percent of such businesses are in white neighborhoods. Similarly, while Jewish businesses in inner-city neighborhoods were highly visible from the 1930s until the 1960s, such enterprises accounted for only a relatively small fraction of all Jewish-owned companies (Weisbrod and Stein 1970; Waldinger 1996; see also n. 4). Similarly, data for both the Detroit riot of 1967 and the Los Angeles riot of 1992, indicate that arrested rioters consisted of "[a] truly deprived group very nearly at the bottom of the opportunity structure"—generally jobless young males with low educational achievement (Singer, Osborn, and Geschwender 1970, 68).

2. A survey of American blacks conducted by the Urban League in 2001 found that two-thirds want to run their own business and would prefer self-employment to joining a law firm, medical practice, or established corporation (Holland 2001).

3. Booker T. Washington (1907, 14–15, cited in Butler 1991, 67) wrote: "I have been repeatedly informed by Negro merchants in the South that they have as many White patrons as Black and the cordial business relations which are almost universal between the races in the South proved . . . there is little race prejudice in the American dollar."

4. In 1910 there were 44,000 blacks and nearly 800,000 foreign-born whites in Chicago (Drake and Cayton 1945, 8).

5. In 1900, 61,000 blacks lived in New York City. During the same year, approximately 240,000 foreign-born Jews resided there (Glazer and Moynihan 1963, 318).

6. Survey data collected over a long period reveal that a fairly large fraction of black customers had positive views toward immigrant entrepreneurs. For example, in a 1964 survey of 873 blacks living in New York, Atlanta, Chicago, and Birmingham, 82 percent said that they had never been treated unfairly by a Jewish store owner (Marx 1967, 161). Similarly, in a 1992 survey Pyong-Gap Min (1996, 97) found that fewer than 15 percent of blacks in the New York City area agreed that blacks should not shop in Korean stores, and only about one in four (27 percent) supported the 1990 to 1991 boycott of Korean stores organized by New York activists.

7. From the 1920s until the 1950s, help wanted ads throughout the United States often specified "Christian Only" or "No Jews," thus limiting employment opportunities for Jews and compelling their entry into the ethnic economy (Bolkosky 1991). In the early 1950s studies of the job markets in Los Angeles and Chicago found that between 17 and 20 percent of all job openings requested non-Jewish applicants (Waldman 1956, 211–14).

8. Following a boycott, the store owner sold his store and left town. Its new owner agreed to employ African Americans (Hunter 1977, 249).

9. The sociologist Peter Rose (1997, 81) asserts that whispered jibes about "the shvartzes" were standard fare in small talk and nightclub acts from the Catskills to L.A. "Jews," he notes, "so sensitive to slights and stereotypes themselves, were not—and are not—exempt from criticism for their own prejudices."

10. In 1941 President Roosevelt signed Executive Order 8802 that prevented discrimination by companies receiving government contracts (Greenberg 1991, 200).

11. Nationwide rioting of the late 1960s form did not follow the Los Angeles riot of 1992. However, the late 1980s and early 1990s were characterized by a coast-to-coast occurrence of conflicts between immigrant entrepreneurs and customers.

12. One exception is Miami's Cuban American community, which has become politically powerful in short order (Portes and Stepick 1993).

13. During the Los Angeles riot of 1992 more immigrants—mostly Latinos—were arrested for violence and looting than were blacks (Petersilia and Abrahamse 1994). However, this number may not reflect actual rates of criminality. Rather, observers suggested that police were reluctant to arrest African Americans because, as English-speaking U.S. citizens, they were more likely to resist the criminal justice system than undocumented Latinos who had few options for recourse (Petersilia and Abrahamse 1994).

14. Of this, Harold Cruse (1968, 238–39, quoted in Blauner 1972, 86–87) wrote: "[W]hen we speak of Negro social disabilities under capitalism . . . we refer to the fact that he does not own anything—even what is ownable in his own community. Thus to fight for Black liberation is to fight for his right to own."

REFERENCES

Abelmann, Nancy, and John Lie. 1995. *Blue Dreams: Korean Americans and the Los Angeles Riots.* Cambridge, Mass.: Harvard University Press.

Angel, Cecil. 2001. "Gasoline Boycott Initiated: Blacks Asked to Avoid Arab-American Stations." *Detroit Free Press*, August 1.

Babou, Cheikh Anta Mbacke. 2001. "Brotherhood Solidarity, Education, and Migration: The Role of the Dahira in the Economy of the Murid Immigrant Community of New York." *Les Journées de l'IISM: l'Internationalisation du religieux, Réseaux et politiques de l'Islam Africain* (Écoles des Hautes Études en Sciences Sociales, Paris) 1, 2, 3(March).

Bailey, Ruby L. 1999. "Tensions Between Arab and Black Communities Fuel Protest Against Reopening Gas Station Where Man Was Killed." *Detroit Free Press*, October 5.

Ballon, Marc. 2002. "A Hole in Their Dreams; Ambitious Immigrants Found Success with Doughnut Shops, but Now Big Chains Are Eating Away Their Profits." *Los Angeles Times*, April 7.

Banfield, Edward C. 1974. *The Unheavenly City Revisited.* Boston: Little, Brown.

Bates, Timothy. 1997. *Race, Self-employment, and Upward Mobility: An Illusive American Dream.* Baltimore: Johns Hopkins University Press.

Blauner, Robert. 1972. *Racial Oppression in America.* New York: Harper & Row.

Blumer, Herbert. 1958. "Race Relations as a Sense of Group Position." *Pacific Sociological Review* 1: 3–7.

Bobo, Lawrence, and Vincent L. Hutchings. 1996. "Perceptions of Racial Competition in a Multiracial Setting." *American Sociological Review* 61(6, December): 951–72.

Bolkosky, Sidney. 1991. *Harmony & Dissonance: Voices of Jewish Identity in Detroit, 1914–1967.* Detroit: Wayne State University Press.

Bonacich, Edna. 1973. "A Theory of Middleman Minorities." *American Sociological Review* 38(5): 583–94.

———. 1994. "Thoughts on Urban Unrest." In *Race and Ethnic Conflict: Contending Views on*

Prejudice, Discrimination, and Ethnoviolence, edited by Fred L. Pincus and Howard J. Ehrlich. Boulder, Colo.: Westview Press.

Bukowczyk, John J. 1984. "The Transformation of Working-Class Ethnicity: Corporate Control, Americanization, and the Polish Immigrant Middle Class in Bayonne, New Jersey, 1915–1925." *Labor History* 25(1): 53–82.

Butler, John Sibley. 1991. *Entrepreneurship and Self-Help Among Black Americans*. Albany: State University of New York Press.

Castells, Manuel. 1997. *The Power of Identity*. Malden, Mass.: Blackwell.

Chang, Edward T., and Jeannette Diaz-Veizades. 1999. *Ethnic Peace in the American City: Building Communities in Los Angeles and Beyond*. New York: New York University Press.

Cheng, Lucie, and Yen Le Espiritu. 1989. "Korean Business in Black and Hispanic Neighborhoods: A Study of Intergroup Relations." *Sociological Perspectives* 32(4): 521–34.

Chicago Tribune. 2001. "The Renaissance of Black Chicago." March 11.

Cho, Sumi K. 1993. "Korean Americans Versus African Americans: Conflicts and Construction." In *Reading Rodney King, Reading Urban Uprising*, edited by Robert Gooding-Williams. New York: Routledge.

CNN. 2001. "Mayor Pleads Innocent in 1969 Race Riot Death." CNN.com, July 24.

Coser, Louis. 1956. *The Functions of Social Conflict*. New York: Free Press.

Cruse, Harold. 1968. *Rebellion or Revolution*. New York: Morrow.

Dahlke, Otto H. 1961. "Race and Minority Riots: A Study in the Typology of Violence." In *Sociology, the Progress of a Decade: A Collection of Articles*, edited by Seymour Martin Lipset and Neil Smelser. Englewood Cliffs, N.J.: Prentice-Hall.

Darden, Joe T., Richard Child Hill, June Thomas, and Richard Thomas. 1987. *Detroit: Race and Uneven Development*. Philadelphia: Temple University Press.

Dash-Moore, Deborah. 1994. *To the Golden Cities: Pursuing the American Dream in Miami and L.A.* Cambridge, Mass.: Harvard University Press.

David, Gary. 1999. "Intercultural Relations Across the Counter: An Interactional Analysis of In Situ Service Encounters." Ph.D. diss., Wayne State University.

———. 2000. "Behind the Bulletproof Glass: Iraqi Chaldean Store Ownership in Metropolitan Detroit." In *Arab Detroit: From Margins to Mainstream*, edited by Nabeel Abraham and Andrew Shryock. Detroit: Wayne State University Press.

Davies, Christie. 1990. *Ethnic Humor Around the World: A Comparative Analysis*. Bloomington: Indiana University Press.

Dollard, John. 1957. *Caste and Class in a Southern Town*. 3rd ed. Garden City, N.Y.: Doubleday Anchor. (Orig. pub. in 1937.)

Drake, St. Clair, and Horace Cayton. 1945. *Black Metropolis*. Chicago: University of Chicago Press.

Du Bois, W. E. B. 1967. *The Philadelphia Negro*. New York: Schocken. (Orig. pub. in 1899.)

Ellington, Ken, and K. Connie Kang. 1996. "A Student, A Shopkeeper, and a Moment of Tragedy Slaying." *Los Angeles Times*, November 23.

Emerson, Edwin. 1897. "The New Ghetto." *Harper's Weekly*, January 9, 44.

Fairlie, Robert W. 1999. "The Absence of the African-American Owned Business: An Analysis of the Dynamics of Self-employment." *Journal of Labor Economics* 17(1): 80–108.

Foner, Nancy. 2000. *From Ellis Island to JFK: New York's Two Great Waves of Immigration*. New Haven, Conn.: Yale University Press.

Gallagher, John. 1998. "Rite Aid Plans Ten Detroit Stores." *Detroit Free Press*, June 17.

Gates, Henry Louis, Jr. 1993. "Two Nations . . . Both Black." In *Reading Rodney King, Reading Urban Uprising*, edited by Robert Gooding-Williams. New York: Routledge.

Geltman, Max. 1966. "The Negro-Jewish Confrontation." *National Review* (June 28): 621–23.

Glazer, Nathan, and Daniel Patrick Moynihan. 1963. *Beyond the Melting Pot*. Cambridge, Mass.: MIT Press.

Gold, Steven J. 1994a. "Chinese-Vietnamese Entrepreneurs in California." In *The New Asian Immigration in Los Angeles and Global Restructuring*, edited by Paul Ong, Edna Bonacich, and Lucie Cheng. Philadelphia: Temple University Press.

————. 1994b. "Patterns of Economic Cooperation Among Israeli Immigrants in Los Angeles." *International Migration Review* 28(105): 114–35.

————. 1995. *From the Workers' State to the Golden State: Jews from the Former Soviet Union in California.* Boston: Allyn and Bacon.

Gold, Steven J., and Ivan Light. 2000. "Ethnic Economies and Social Policy." *Research in Social Movements, Conflicts, and Change* 22(Summer): 165–91.

Gooding-Williams, Robert, ed. 1993. *Reading Rodney King, Reading Urban Uprising.* New York: Routledge.

Gordon, Albert I. 1949. *Jews in Transition.* Minneapolis: University of Minnesota Press.

Green, Nancy L., ed. 1998. *Jewish Workers in the Modern Diaspora.* Berkeley: University of California Press.

Greenberg, Cheryl Lynn. 1991. *Or Does It Explode? Black Harlem in the Great Depression.* New York: Oxford University Press.

Guarnizo, Luis Eduardo. 1998. "The Mexican Ethnic Economy in Los Angeles: Capitalist Accumulation, Class Restructuring, and the Transnationalization of Migration." Working paper. Davis: California Communities Program, University of California, Davis.

Hacker, Andrew. 1992. *Two Nations.* New York: Scribner.

Harris, Abram L. 1968. *The Negro as Capitalist: A Study of Banking and Business Among American Negroes.* Gloucester, Mass.: Peter Smith. (Orig. pub. in 1936.)

Hirsch, Arnold R. 1983. *Making the Second Ghetto: Race and Housing in Chicago, 1940–1960.* Cambridge, U.K.: Cambridge University Press.

Hochschild, Jennifer L. 2000. "Rich and Poor African Americans." In *Multiculturalism in the United States: Current Issues, Contemporary Voices,* edited by Peter Kivisto and Georganne Rundblad. Thousand Oaks, Calif.: Pine Forge Press.

Holland, Gina. 2001. "Poll: Blacks Want to Run Businesses." *Los Angeles Times,* July 21.

Horowitz, Donald. 1985. *Ethnic Conflict.* Berkeley: University of California Press.

Horton, John, with the assistance of Jose Calderon, Mary Pardo, Leland Saito, Linda Shaw, and Yen-Tseng Fen. 1995. *The Politics of Diversity: Immigration, Resistance, and Change in Monterey Park, California.* Philadelphia: Temple University Press.

Hudson, Michael. 1994. "Robbin' the Hood: How Wall Street Takes from the Poor and Gives to the Rich." *Mother Jones* (July-August), available at: www.motherjones.com/news/feature/1994/07/hudson.html.

————, ed. 1996. *Merchants of Misery: How Corporate America Profits from Poverty.* Monroe, Me.: Common Courage Press.

Hunter, Gary Jerome. 1977. "Don't Buy from Where You Can't Work: Black Urban Boycott Movements During the Depression 1929–1941." Ph.D. diss., University of Michigan.

Hutchinson, Earl Ofari. 1994. "Black Capitalism: Self-Help or Self-Delusion?" In *Race and Ethnic Conflict: Contending Views on Prejudice, Discrimination, and Ethnoviolence,* edited by Fred L. Pincus and Howard J. Ehrlich. Boulder, Colo.: Westview Press.

Jackson, Kenneth T. 1985. *Crabgrass Frontier: The Suburbanization of the United States.* New York: Oxford University Press.

Jiobu, Robert M. 1988. "Ethnic Hegemony and the Japanese of California." *American Sociological Review* 53(3): 353–67.

Johnson, James H., Jr., Cloyzelle K. Jones, Walter C. Farrell Jr., and Melvin L. Oliver. 1992. "The Los Angeles Rebellion: A Retrospective View." *Economic Development Quarterly* 6(4): 356–72.

Johnson, James H., Jr., and Melvin L. Oliver. 1994. "Interethnic Minority Conflict in Urban America: The Effect of Economic and Social Dislocations." In *Race and Ethnic Conflict: Contending Views on Prejudice, Discrimination, and Ethnoviolence,* edited by Fred L. Pincus and Howard J. Ehrlich. Boulder, Colo.: Westview Press.

Kasinitz, Philip, and Bruce Haynes. 1996. "The Fire at Freddy's." *CommonQuest* 1(2): 24–34.

Katz, Jack. 1988. *Seductions of Crime.* New York: Basic Books.

Kim, Claire Jean. 2000. *Bitter Fruit: The Politics of Black-Korean Conflict in New York City.* New Haven, Conn.: Yale University Press.

Kim, Dae Young. 1999. "Beyond Co-ethnic Solidarity: Mexican and Ecuadorian Employment in Korean-Owned Businesses in New York City." *Ethnic and Racial Studies* 22(3): 581–605.

Kim, Illsoo. 1981. *New Urban Immigrants: The Korean Community in New York*. Princeton, N.J.: Princeton University Press.

Kurth, Joel, and Delores Patterson. 2001 "Boycott Targets Arabs." *Detroit News*, August 1.

Kusmer, Kenneth L. 1976. *A Ghetto Takes Shape: Black Cleveland 1870–1930*. Urbana-Champaign: University of Illinois Press.

Ladner, Robert A., Barry J. Schwartz, Sandra J. Roker, and Loretta S. Titterud. 1981. "The Miami Riots of 1980: Antecedent Conditions, Community Responses, and Participant Characteristics." *Research in Social Movements, Conflict, and Change* 4: 171–214.

Lee, Jennifer. 2002. "From Civil Relations to Racial Conflict: Merchant-Customer Interactions in Urban America." *American Sociological Review* 67(1, February): 77–98.

Levine, Rhonda F. 2001. *Class, Networks, and Identity: Replanting Jewish Lives from Nazi Germany to Rural New York*. Lanham, Md.: Rowman and Littlefield.

Lieberson, Stanley, and Arnold R. Silverman. 1965. "The Precipitants and Underlying Conditions of Race Riots." *American Sociological Review* 30(6): 887–98.

Light, Ivan. 1972. *Ethnic Enterprise in America: Business and Welfare Among Chinese, Japanese, and Blacks*. Berkeley: University of California Press.

———. 1984. "Immigrant and Ethnic Enterprise in North America." *Ethnic and Racial Studies* 17(2): 195–216.

Light, Ivan, and Edna Bonacich. 1988. *Immigrant Entrepreneurs: Koreans in Los Angeles*. Berkeley: University of California Press.

Light, Ivan, and Steven J. Gold. 2000. *Ethnic Economies*. San Diego: Academic Press.

Light, Ivan, and Carolyn Rosenstein. 1995. *Race, Ethnicity, and Entrepreneurship in Urban America*. New York: Aldine de Gruyter.

Light, Ivan, Georges Sabagh, Mehdi Bozorgmehr, and Claudia Der-Martirosian. 1994. "Beyond the Ethnic Enclave Economy." *Social Problems* 41(1): 65–80.

Loewen, James W. 1971. *The Mississippi Chinese: Between Black and White*. Cambridge, Mass.: Harvard University Press.

Mahler, Sarah J. 1995. *Salvadorans in Suburbia: Symbiosis and Conflict*. Boston: Allyn and Bacon.

Marable, Manning. 1983. *How Capitalism Underdeveloped Black America: Problems in Race, Political Economy, and Society*. Boston: South End Press.

Marx, Gary T. 1967. *Protest and Prejudice: A Study of Belief in the Black Community*. New York: Harper & Row.

Merina, Victor. 1992. "A Story of Refugee Success Ended Tragically in Riots." *Los Angeles Times*, August 17.

Min, Pyong-Gap. 1996. *Caught in the Middle: Korean Communities in New York and Los Angeles*. Berkeley: University of California Press.

Morawska, Ewa. 2001. "Immigrant-Black Dissension in American Cities: An Argument for Multiple Explanations." In *Problem of the Century: Racial Stratification in the United States*, edited by Elijah Anderson and Douglas Massey. New York: Russell Sage Foundation.

Morris, Jim. 1999. "Tulsa Panel Seeks Truth from 1921 Race Riot." CNN.com, August 3.

Myrdal, Gunnar. 1944. *An American Dilemma*. New York: McGraw-Hill.

Olzak, Susan, and Joane Nagel, eds. 1986. *Competitive Ethnic Relations*. Orlando, Fla.: Academic Press.

Omi, Michael, and Howard Winant. 1993. "The Los Angeles 'Race Riot' and Contemporary U.S. Politics." In *Reading Rodney King, Reading Urban Uprising*, edited by Robert Gooding-Williams. New York: Routledge.

Ong, Paul, Kye Y. Park, and Yasmin Tong. 1994. "Korean-Black Conflict and the State." In *The New Asian Immigration in Los Angeles and Global Restructuring*, edited by Paul Ong, Edna Bonacich, and Lucie Cheng. Philadelphia: Temple University Press.

Ortiz, Vilma. 1996. "The Mexican-Origin Population: Permanent Working Class or Emerging Middle Class?" In *Ethnic Los Angeles*, edited by Roger Waldinger and Mehdi Bozorgmehr. New York: Russell Sage Foundation.

Ottley, Roi. 1968. *New World A-Coming*. New York: Arno Press/New York Times. (Orig. pub. in 1943.)

Pessar, Patricia. 1995. *A Visa for a Dream: Dominicans in the United States*. Boston: Allyn and Bacon.

Petersilia, Joan, and Allan Abrahamse. 1994. "A Profile of Those Arrested." In *The Los Angeles Riots: Lessons for the Urban Future*, edited by Mark Baldassare. Boulder, Colo.: Westview Press.

Porter, Bruce, and Marvin Dunn. 1984. *The Miami Riot of 1980: Crossing the Bounds*. Lexington, Mass.: D. C. Heath.

Portes, Alejandro, and Robert Bach. 1985. *Latin Journey: Cuban and Mexican Immigrants in the United States*. Berkeley: University of California Press.

Portes, Alejandro, and Rubén G. Rumbaut. 1996. *Immigrant America: A Portrait*. 2nd ed. Berkeley: University of California Press.

Portes, Alejandro, and Alex Stepick. 1993. *City on the Edge: The Transformation of Miami*. Berkeley: University of California Press.

Riccardi, Nicholas. 1996. "Shops Under Siege." *Los Angeles Times*, November 27.

Rockaway, Robert A. 1986. *The Jews of Detroit: From the Beginning 1762–1914*. Detroit: Wayne State University Press.

Rose, Peter I. 1997. *Tempest-Tost: Race, Immigration, and the Dilemmas of Diversity*. New York: Oxford.

Scarpaci, Jean Ann. 1972. "Italian Immigrants in Louisiana's Sugar Parishes: Recruitment, Labor Conditions, and Community Relations, 1880–1910." Ph.D. diss., Rutgers University.

Scott, Janny. 2001. "Rethinking Segregation Beyond Black and White." *New York Times*, sect. 4, July 29.

Sears, David O. 1994. "Urban Rioting in Los Angeles: A Comparison of 1965 with 1992." In *The Los Angeles Riots: Lessons for the Urban Future*, edited by Mark Baldassare. Boulder, Colo.: Westview Press.

———. 2000. "Urban Rioting in Los Angeles: A Comparison of 1965 with 1992." In *Multiculturalism in the United States: Current Issues, Contemporary Voices*, edited by Peter Kivisto and Georganne Rundblad. Thousand Oaks, Calif.: Pine Forge Press.

Silverman, Robert Mark. 2000. *Doing Business in Minority Markets: Black and Korean Entrepreneurs in Chicago's Ethnic Beauty Aids Industry*. New York: Garland.

Singer, Benjamin, Richard W. Osborn, and James A. Geschwender. 1970. *Black Rioters: A Study of Social Factors and Communication in the Detroit Riot*. Lexington, Mass.: Heath Lexington.

Skrentny, John David. 2000. "The Origins and Politics of Affirmative Action." In *Multiculturalism in the United States: Current Issues, Contemporary Voices*, edited by Peter Kivisto and Georganne Rundblad. Thousand Oaks, Calif.: Pine Forge Press.

Sonenshein, Raphael J. 1996. "The Battle over Liquor Stores in South Central Los Angeles: Management of an Interminority Conflict." *Urban Affairs Review* 31(6): 710–37.

Stepick, Alex. 1998. *Pride Against Prejudice: Haitians in the United States*. Boston: Allyn and Bacon.

Takaki, Ronald. 1989. *Strangers from a Different Shore: A History of Asian Americans*. Boston: Little, Brown.

Teller, Judd L. 1966. "Negroes and Jews: A Hard Look." *Conservative Judaism* 21(1): 13–20.

Vélez-Ibañez, Carlos. 1983. *Bonds of Mutual Trust: The Cultural System of Rotating Credit Associations Among Urban Mexicans and Chicanos*. New Brunswick, N.J.: Rutgers University Press.

Vergara, Camillo Jose. 1995. *The New American Ghetto*. New Brunswick, N.J.: Rutgers University Press.

Wacquant, Loïc J. D. 1998. "Negative Social Capital: State Breakdown and Social Destitution in America's Urban Core." *Netherlands Journal of Housing and the Built Environment* 13(1): 25–40.

Waldinger, Roger. 1994. "The Making of an Immigrant Niche." *International Migration Review* 28(105): 3–30.

———. 1996. *Still the Promised City? African-Americans and New Immigrants in Postindustrial New York*. Cambridge, Mass.: Harvard University Press.

————, ed. 2001. *Strangers at the Gates: New Immigrants in Urban America*. Berkeley: University of California Press.

Waldman, Lois. 1956. "Employment Discrimination Against Jews in the United States—1955." *Jewish Social Studies* 18: 208–16.

Washington, Booker T. 1907. *The Negro in Business*. Chicago: Hertel, Jenkins and Co.

Weaver, Robert C. 1966. "Class, Race, and Urban Renewal." In *Racial and Ethnic Relations*, 2nd ed., edited by Bernard E. Segal. New York: Thomas Y. Crowell Co.

Weisbrod, Robert G., and Arthur Stein. 1970. *Bittersweet Encounter: The Afro-American and the American Jew*. Westport, Conn.: Negro Universities Press.

Wilson, William J. 1978. *The Declining Significance of Race*. Chicago: University of Chicago Press.

————. 1987. *The Truly Disadvantaged*. Chicago: University of Chicago Press.

————. 1996. *When Work Disappears: The World of the New Urban Poor*. New York: Alfred A. Knopf.

Wirth, Louis. 1928. *The Ghetto*. Chicago: University of Chicago Press.

Woodard, Michael D. 1997. *Black Entrepreneurs in America: Stories of Struggle and Success*. New Brunswick, N.J.: Rutgers University Press.

Wright, Richard. 1962. "Introduction." In *Black Metropolis: A Study of Negro Life in a Northern City* by St. Clair Drake and Horace R. Cayton, vol. 1. New York: Harper Torchbooks. (Orig. pub. in 1945.)

Yoon, In Jin. 1997. *On My Own: Korean Businesses and Race Relations in America*. Chicago: University of Chicago Press.

Zenner, Walter P. 1991. *Minorities in the Middle: A Cross-Cultural Analysis*. Albany: State University of New York Press.

Neil Foley

Chapter 16

Straddling the Color Line: The Legal
Construction of Hispanic Identity in Texas

The last few decades have witnessed the creation of a new identity for peoples of Latin American descent in the United States that is likely to be with us for some time to come. Used by the 1980 census to designate a free-floating ethnic category of any race, the term "Hispanic" has taken on a life of its own. Mexican Americans, Puerto Ricans, African Americans, whites, Asian Americans, and other groups use the term because it simplifies the problem of making distinctions among the numerous peoples of Latin America who reside in the United States.

The term "Hispanic" has also given us another new category that is used frequently in news media, government reports, and academic studies—"non-Hispanic whites." This is the catchall category for all those who identify as whites but whose ancestry does not include a Spanish-speaking nation. After decades of hearing and seeing these terms in the media to describe the two major categories of whites in the United States, Hispanic and non-Hispanic, we sometimes forget that the nation's largest group of Hispanics, Mexican Americans, were rarely accorded status as white people in the Southwest until after World War II. For over a century—since 1836 in Texas and after 1848 in the rest of the Mexican Southwest—the word "Mexican" denoted a race as well as a nationality. A fifth-generation Mexican American was still a "Mexican" rather than an American in the eyes of most Anglos. Anglos do not call Mexican Americans "Mexicans" anymore. They have become "Hispanic," a term that carries little of the racial freight of the past; it is a post-1960s, post–civil rights term that unites Mexican Americans to other groups who trace their heritage to Spanish-speaking countries.[1]

How did the color line get redrawn to put Latinos, a racially mixed people, on the white side of the line? Why is it not plausible for an African American to identify as white on the census the way almost half of all Latinos do? Why does the phrase "non-African American whites" seem odd and strangely absurd to us but not the phrase "non-Hispanic whites"? Why, in other words, does the phrase "African American white" strike us as paradoxical, if not outright contradictory? Granted that the category of white would be existentially meaningless without the category of black, what is gained by enlarging the circle of whiteness to include practically all groups except those whose ancestry can be traced to Africa and Asia? Although it is not the purpose of this chapter to point out the arbitrary and historically constructed categories of white, black, and Hispanic (that much, thankfully, has been done by many other scholars), I do want to examine specific moments in Texas history in which the courts have ruled on the racial status of Mexican-descent people involving three issues that lie at the heart of American democracy and national identity: naturalization, jury representation, and school segregation.

Beginning in the 1930s, most state courts acknowledged Mexicans as whites in desegregation cases, but in cases involving discrimination in jury selection the courts generally ruled that Mexicans could not invoke the equal protection clause of the Fourteenth Amendment, as had African Americans, because Anglos and Mexicans were both members of the white race. Mexican Americans in Texas faced a dilemma after World War II: official recognition of their status as whites in state and federal courts was not a guarantee that Anglos would treat them as whites, while their legal status as whites made it difficult for them to claim racial discrimination, since Anglos and Mexicans were accorded equal racial status in the law.

How Mexican Americans and other Latinos have come to identify themselves and be identified in the law—as an "identifiable minority group" also has important implications for Hispanic and African American relations, particularly in light of the fact that almost one-half of all Hispanics identified themselves as white in the census of 2000. Thus, on the one hand, the media focuses on the rising number of Hispanics in Texas and elsewhere in a nation that may one day be "majority minority," while on the other hand, the census, by grouping Hispanics and non-Hispanic whites together, illustrates that whites are the fastest-growing group in the nation. The ambivalence and ambiguity of Latino identity reflect the historical tension and legal uncertainty surrounding the racial status of Mexican Americans in a nation that draws the color line between whites and blacks.

This chapter examines key court cases in Texas that demonstrate the reluctance of Texas courts to acknowledge Mexican Americans as a separate race in Texas, even as the federal courts often ruled in favor of Mexicans in naturalization, jury selection, and school segregation cases. Mexican American civil rights attorneys sought to have the courts apply the same Fourteenth Amendment protections to Mexican Americans that the courts had applied to African Americans in cases involving jury selection. And after 1954, Mexican Americans sought to have Texas courts rule that *Brown v. Board of Education* applied to the segregation of Mexican Americans as well as to African Americans. Since the 1930s Mexican Americans had argued in court that they represented a distinct class of "other whites," but in desegregation cases in the 1960s and 1970s Mexican Americans argued that, like African Americans, they were an "identifiable minority group." Their legal status as whites had become a liability after the *Brown* decision, when school boards in Texas during the 1960s desegregated predominantly black schools by busing Mexican "whites" to black schools while leaving predominantly Anglo-white schools alone. Having positioned themselves in the courts for decades as both whites *and* members of an "identifiable minority group," Mexican Americans and other Latinos thus straddle the color line and rival African Americans as the nation's most numerous minority group. Latinos have come to occupy an uneasy relationship with African Americans, who regard them suspiciously as a newcomer minority group—or more accurately, legally at least, as whites of a different color.

NATURALIZATION

After the Texas Revolution in 1836 and the Mexican-American War in 1848, Mexican citizens were incorporated into the United States as citizens entitled to all the protections and privileges enjoyed by other citizens of the nation. But only a small number of

Mexican-descent people were ever accorded privileges generally reserved for whites, such as voting, serving on juries, holding elected offices, and sending their children to white schools. The vast majority of Mexican-descent people were regarded as non-white, though rarely were they relegated to the status of African Americans. It is difficult to generalize about the status of Mexicans in the United States, both citizens and noncitizens, because their racial status differed from region to region, from state to state, and often from town to town. Unlike African Americans, whose racial status was not questioned either in the courts or in society at large, Mexican Americans experienced a range of racial treatment—sometimes white, sometimes not.

The first court case concerning the racial status of Mexicans occurred in Texas in 1893 when Ricardo Rodríguez filed his intention to become a naturalized citizen with the Bexar County clerk. Thirty-five years old, Rodríguez had immigrated from Guanajuato, Mexico, in 1883 and settled in San Antonio. Floyd McGown, one of the attorneys who filed a brief opposed to the naturalization of Rodríguez, described him as "a pure-blooded Mexican, having . . . dark eyes, straight, black hair, chocolate brown skin, and high cheek bones" (*In re: Rodríguez*, 81 F. 345, 1897). The Naturalization Act of 1790 (ch. 3, sect. I;) held that only "free white persons" were entitled to become naturalized citizens, and after the Civil War and the enactment of the Fourteenth Amendment, the law was amended (Naturalization Rev. Stat. of 1870, sect. 2169) to include persons of African ancestry. McGown and the other attorneys filing briefs, A. J. Evans and T. J. McMinn, sought to deprive Mexicans of their right to vote by making it impossible for Mexicans to become naturalized citizens. If the court ruled that Mexican immigrants of Indian ancestry were ineligible for citizenship, McMinn maintained, then one-third of the Mexican voters of Bexar County would be disfranchised. Although the Fourteenth Amendment stipulated that "all persons born or naturalized in the United States . . . are citizens of the United States," McMinn contended that a woman was not "a person"—"from the suffrage standpoint"—and neither were "Indians, Mongolians, or Aztecs." Mexicans desiring to become naturalized citizens would thus no longer be able to vote once the courts ruled that Mexicans were ineligible for citizenship.[2]

McGown cited numerous naturalization cases in which naturalization was denied to persons judged to be "nonwhite." In the case of *In re: Ah Yup* (1 F. Cas. 223, 1878), a California court had ruled that the Chinese were not white and therefore were ineligible for citizenship. In Oregon a court ruled in *In re: Camille* (6 F. 256, 1880) that a native of British Columbia who was half-Indian and half-white was ineligible for citizenship because "Indians have never, ethnologically, been considered white persons. . . . From the first our naturalization laws only applied to the people who had settled the country, the European or white race." To be considered a white person, according to this court ruling, a person would have to be three-quarters white. And in *In re: Kanaka Nian* (21 Pac. 993, 1889), Nian, a native of Hawaii of Kanaka ancestors, was held to be nonwhite and ineligible for citizenship.[3]

Although courts had ruled on the ineligibility of Chinese, Hawaiians, and mixed-race Indians, no court had ruled on the eligibility of Mexicans to become citizens until the *Rodríguez* case in 1897. Up until this time, U.S. immigration inspectors were required to list all aliens admitted to the United States according to their original country of residence and their "race or people." Since no court decisions or departmental regulations had defined "Mexican race," inspectors on the U.S.-Mexico border generally listed light-skinned immigrants as belonging to the "Spanish race" and those with dark skin who appeared to be mixed with Indian ancestry as belonging to the "Mexican race." It was understood that "Spanish" was a marker of whiteness and that "Mexican" meant "mixed-blood" or Indian. McGown hoped to persuade the court that Rodríguez, judging from his skin color and appearance, was a descendant of the Indian races of Mexico, since in the United States American Indians could not become naturalized citizens.[4] McGown cited a study by a French anthropologist who classified race into categories of color by which "the varieties of human skin may be followed from the fairest hue of the Swede, and the darker tint of the Provençal, to the withered leaf brown of the Hottentot, the chocolate brown of the Mexican, and the brown black of the West African." McGown concluded that Rodríguez's brown skin, straight black hair, and high cheekbones made it clear that he was "not a white person . . . in the sense in which these words are commonly used and understood in the every-day life of our people" (*In re: Rodríguez*, 81 F. 346).

A. J. Evans hammered home the point made by McGown that Rodríguez was a "native Mexican" and, more to the point, "one of the 6,000,000 Indians of unmixed blood" in Mexico (*In re: Rodríguez*, 81 F. 347). In arguing that Rodríguez was an Indian Mexican, Evans cited an 1884 Supreme Court case in which an Indian, John Elk, attempted to register to vote in a municipal election in Omaha, Nebraska. The registrar denied the application on the grounds that Elk was an Indian and therefore neither a citizen nor a person eligible to become a citizen. Elk claimed that his right to vote derived from the Fourteenth Amendment, which stated that "all persons born or naturalized in the United States, and subject to the jurisdiction thereof, are citizens of the United States and of the state wherein they reside." Furthermore, Elk stressed, he had voluntarily separated himself from his tribe and "taken up his residence among the white citizens of a state." The majority of the Supreme Court disagreed with Elk's contention and insisted that "Indian tribes, being within the territorial limits of the United States, were not, strictly speaking, foreign states; but they were alien nations . . . with whom the United States might . . . deal, as they saw fit, either through treaties . . . or through acts of congress." Indians were, in short, equivalent to foreigners living in the United States who were barred, for racial reasons, from becoming naturalized citizens (*Elk v. Wilkins*, 112 U.S. 94).[5]

Evans anticipated the argument that all Mexican citizens, regardless of whether they were "Indians" or not, were entitled to become U.S. citizens by article VIII of the Treaty of Guadalupe Hidalgo, which had ended the Mexican-American War in 1848. Evans insisted that "no treaty can be found with Mexico that makes her citizens citizens of the United States, or that extends to her citizens the rights of naturalization when they come to the United States, for the simple and cogent reason that the power of naturalization is in congress, and not in the treaty-making power, i.e., the president and the senate" (*In re: Rodríguez*, 81 F. 347). McGown ended his brief by asserting that Mexican Indians were originally of Asiatic or Mongolian descent, having crossed into North America from Asia by a chain of islands, and therefore, like the Chinese, were barred from becoming citizens.

The court briefs on the eligibility of Rodríguez to become a naturalized citizen focused almost exclusively on the racial status of Mexicans who could not pass as "Spanish" and were thus, like Asians and Indians, rendered ineligible for citizenship. Judge Thomas S. Maxey, however, drew a distinction between tribal Indians living in the United States and Mexican citizens, regardless of their Indian heritage, who wanted to become naturalized U.S. citizens. He cited the terms of the Treaty of Guadalupe Hidalgo in 1848 protecting the rights of Mexicans who remained in the conquered territory for one year without signaling their intention to retain Mexican citizenship.

These Mexicans automatically became U.S. citizens after one year, regardless of their "color" or racial status. Judge Maxey also cited a treaty between Mexico and the United States concluded in 1868, contemporary with the deliberations over the Fourteenth Amendment, that clarified the application of U.S. law to Mexicans with respect to naturalization. The treaty required the United States to recognize the naturalization of U.S. citizens in Mexico and for Mexico to recognize the naturalization of Mexican citizens in the United States. Maxey acknowledged that "if the strict scientific classification of the anthropologist should be adopted, he [Rodríguez] would probably not be classed as white." Nevertheless, Maxey ruled, whatever Rodríguez's racial status might be "from the standpoint of the ethnologist," Mexican citizens were "embraced within the spirit and intent of our laws upon naturalization" (*In re: Rodríguez*, 81 F. 349, 354–55). Rodríguez was thus eligible to become a naturalized citizen, thwarting the attempt by McMinn and Evans to disfranchise Mexican immigrants on the grounds that they were not white.

The *Rodríguez* case was important because an immigrant's eligibility for citizenship depended on his racial status as a "white" or "person of African ancestry." By ruling that Mexicans were eligible for citizenship, the court was in effect ruling that Mexicans were to be naturalized as if they were "whites" without actually having ruled one way or the other on the complicated issue of Mexican racial status. For Mexican Americans, however, achieving virtually the same status as whites for the purpose of naturalization did not change their racialized status in Texas and elsewhere in the Southwest as non-whites relegated to second-class citizenship. The racial status of Mexicans thus fell somewhere between that of whites and blacks, though the courts regarded Mexicans as whites even in cases of discrimination. The problem for Mexican Americans, many of whom themselves claimed to be white, was to persuade the courts that the equal protection clause of the Fourteenth Amendment applied to them as well as to blacks in cases involving discrimination. The issue of whether the Fourteenth Amendment could be invoked by one group of whites claiming discrimination against another group of whites raised interesting questions for the courts as well as for Mexican Americans themselves. Was it possible, in other words, for Mexican Americans to insist that they were white and at the same time claim that they were subject to racial discrimination by "non-Hispanic whites"?

JURY SELECTION

Slightly over fifty years after the *Rodríguez* case, the Supreme Court ruled in 1954, two weeks before the historic decision in *Brown v. Board of Education*, that a Mexican American did not receive a fair trial when tried by an all-Anglo jury—not on the ground that the jury was all Anglo but on the ground that Mexican Americans had been systematically excluded from jury service. In *Hernandez v. Texas* (251 S.W. 2d 531, rev'd, 347 U.S. 475, 1954), two Mexican American civil rights organizations, LULAC (League of United Latin American Citizens) and the American GI Forum, challenged lower court rulings that Mexican Americans had not been systematically excluded from juries.[6] Pete Hernandez was indicted for the murder of Joe Espinosa by a grand jury in Jackson County, Texas, in 1951. He was convicted and sentenced to life imprisonment. Prior to the trial, the attorneys for Hernandez, Gus García and Carlos Cadena, offered motions to quash the indictment and the jury panel. When the district court denied the motions and convicted Hernandez, they appealed the case to the Texas Court of Criminal Appeals. The appeals court upheld the lower court ruling, which held that because Mexican Americans were members of the "white race" and the members of the jury were all white, no cause for discrimination existed, and that the equal protection clause of the Fourteenth Amendment could not be invoked because the amendment applied only to "Negroes" and "whites" (*Pete Hernandez v. State of Texas*, Texas Court of Criminal Appeals, no. 25,816, 1952, opinion by Judge Davidson at 6).

The Supreme Court, however, had frequently ruled that when jury commissioners failed to locate and select qualified African American jurors in counties with qualified black citizens, then discrimination resulted, "whether accomplished ingeniously or ingenuously" (Appellant's Brief, *Pete Hernandez v. State of Texas*, Court of Criminal Appeals, no. 25,816, 8–9).[7] Texas courts claimed that in the "absence of express discrimination," a jury drawn in accordance with the law was not obliged to select members of a nationality group, such as Mexicans; however, if the petitioner had been a "Negro," a different standard of proof would have been applied. In other words, the absence of blacks on a jury where qualified blacks eligible for jury service could be identified constituted a violation of the Fourteenth Amendment. Attorneys García and Cadena hoped to persuade the appeals court that "it cannot impose a heavier burden of proof on this appellant than it imposes on Negroes under like circumstances, and attempt to justify its action on purely racial grounds" (10). The heavier burden no doubt stemmed from the numerous court rulings that Mexicans were members of the white race.

Only a few years before the *Hernandez* case, in 1951, the Texas Court of Criminal Appeals had rejected the idea that Mexican Americans had been discriminated against in jury selection because "Mexican people . . . are not a separate race but are white people of Spanish descent" (*Sanchez v. State*, 243 S.W. 2d 700). García and Cadena did not object to the court's ruling that Mexican people were whites. Indeed, the Mexican American civil rights organizations providing financial support for the case, LULAC and the American GI Forum, had long maintained that Mexican Americans were white (see *Sanchez v. State*, 1951; Gutiérrez 1995, 81–90; García 1989, 46–53; Márquez 1993, 30–34). What they objected to was the refusal of the court to extend the protections of the Fourteenth Amendment to nationality groups within the white race where it could be shown that they had been "intentionally, arbitrarily, capriciously, and systematically excluded from service as grand jury commissioners and as grand jurors" (Appellant's Brief, *Pete Hernandez v. State of Texas*, Court of Criminal Appeals, no. 25,816, 13).[8] If corporations, "those raceless offspring of the law," sought "sanctuary within the sheltering provisions of the Fourteenth Amendment," then surely, García and Cadena argued, "discrimination against a person of Mexican descent is as violative of the Fourteenth Amendment as is discrimination against a corporation" (13) (see also *County v. Southern Pac. R.R.*, 118 U.S. 394, 1886).

Until the *Hernandez* case, the Supreme Court had not ruled on the question of discrimination against Mexican Americans. Lower courts in Texas, California, and elsewhere in the Southwest, however, had held that discrimination against schoolchildren of Mexican descent violated the Fourteenth Amendment by denying to these children the equal protection of the laws, as well as by depriving them of liberty without due process of law (*Mendez v. Westminster School District*, 161 F. 2d 774, 1947; *Gonzales v. Sheely*, 96 F. Supp. 1004, 1951).[9] In *Lopez v. Seccombe* (Supp. 71, 1944) it was held that the exclusion of Mexican-descent people from city swimming pools in California was a violation of the Fourteenth Amendment.[10] In Texas the San Antonio Court of Civil Appeals held that courts could not enforce a restrictive covenant prohibiting the sale of land to persons of Mexican descent, since such action would amount to a denial of equal protection of the laws (*Clifton v. Puentes*, 218 S.W. 2d 272, 1948; Appellant's Brief, *Pete Hernandez v. State of Texas*, Court of Criminal Appeals, no. 25,816, 15).

In citing these cases, the attorneys for Hernandez argued that the Fourteenth Amendment forbids all kinds of discrimination, not just discrimination based on racial grounds (that is, discrimination involving only blacks and whites). The exclusion of blacks from juries had a long legal history, and in cases where no blacks had been included in jury service, the courts almost always ruled that jury commissioners were obligated to familiarize themselves with the qualifications of all eligible jurors of the county, most especially Negroes (*Cassel v. Texas*, 339 U.S. 288–89, 1950). Not so in the case of Mexican Americans, the Texas court ruled, because Mexican Americans were not a separate race; they were members of the white race, and according to the Texas Court of Criminal Appeals, the Fourteenth Amendment contemplated and recognized only two classes: "the white race, comprising one class, and the Negro race, comprising the other class" (opinion of Judge Davidson, *Pete Hernandez v. State of Texas*, Court of Criminal Appeals, no. 25,816, 6).

In their brief, García and Cadena strenuously objected to the appeals court judge's ruling: "If, then, this Court holds that, while such statutes forbid exclusion of Negroes [from jury service], they allow exclusion of persons of Mexican descent because the latter are members of the white race, the Court is in effect saying that the statutes protect only colored men, and allow discrimination against white men" (Appellant's Brief, *Pete Hernandez v. State of Texas*, Court of Criminal Appeals, no. 25,816, 16). In a motion for a rehearing, García and Cadena accused the court of giving preference to black citizens in its rulings on jury exclusion:

> There exist, in the State of Texas, one rule of evidence for Negroes, and a different rule for persons of Mexican descent. . . . It requires the latter to show express discrimination, and it states frankly that persons of Mexican descent must bear this more onerous burden solely because they are not Negroes; i.e., because they are white. . . . Thus, it becomes patent that the Court has denied to this appellant a means of proving discrimination which is available to Negroes; and that this denial is based solely, exclusively and expressly on the fact that appellant is not a Negro. To put it in simpler terms, this Court has set up a classification based solely, exclusively and expressly on race (16).

Here was the central paradox: Mexican Americans themselves insisted on their status as whites. The courts then ruled that they could not claim discrimination at the hands of whites, as could African Americans, since the Fourteenth Amendment, the lower courts held, contemplated only two classes: "Negroes" and "whites." Mexican American civil rights attorneys responded by stating that, "for all practical purposes, about the only time that so-called Mexicans—many of them Texans for seven generations—are covered with the Caucasian cloak is when the use of that protective mantle serves the ends of those who would shamelessly deny to this large segment of the Texas population the fundamental right to serve as jury commissioners, grand jurors, or petit jurors" (Appellant's Brief, *Pete Hernandez v. State of Texas*, Court of Criminal Appeals, no. 25,816, at 17).

But if county officials insisted on the witness stand that Mexicans were whites "for the purpose of judicial convenience," as García and Cadena claimed, it also had to be recognized that Mexican American civil rights leaders insisted on their status as whites for the purpose of social convenience. As whites, they could, theoretically, attend white schools, swim in white-only swimming pools, and vote without being harassed or having impossible literacy standards imposed on them. The problem—and the paradox—of insisting on their whiteness was that Mexican Americans could not easily claim that they were being racially discriminated against even though all the evidence they adduced in the case was of a "racial" nature. No signs, for example, appeared in restaurant and café windows that read "No Germans Served" or "No Bohemians Served," unlike the ubiquitous "No Mexicans Served" signs observed throughout the Southwest from the early part of the twentieth century until well after World War II (see Foley 1997; Gutiérrez 1995; Montejano 1987). Mexican-descent children, whether U.S. citizens or not, whether English-speaking or not, were arbitrarily segregated in "Mexican schools." School segregation, as we will see, became the true test of whether a group was considered a race or an ethnic subcategory of white, such as Czech, German, Irish, and so forth.

Even when the evidence pointed overwhelmingly to racial discrimination, none of the courts, including the Supreme Court, were willing to recognize Mexicans as a separate racial group. Perhaps the courts felt that it was not within their jurisdiction to change the official roster of races listed in the 1950 census: white, Negro, American Indian, Japanese, Chinese, Filipino, and other (Lee 1993, 78; Nobles 2000). The question for the Supreme Court was how to overturn the lower courts by acknowledging that Mexicans had been unconstitutionally excluded from jury service without, at the same time, acknowledging that Mexicans had been discriminated against as a separate race. In weighing the evidence of discrimination against Mexican-descent people, the Supreme Court ruled that persons of Mexican descent constituted a "separate class" distinct from whites in Jackson County, Texas, and therefore could claim relief under the provisions of the Fourteenth Amendment.

The evidence was compelling. Persons of Mexican descent had rarely participated in business and community groups in the county; for many years children of Mexican descent were required to attend a segregated school for the first four grades; at least one local restaurant prominently displayed a sign announcing "No Mexicans Served"; and on the courthouse grounds, where the trial was originally held, there were two men's toilets, one unmarked and the other marked "Colored Men" and "Hombres Aqui" ("Men Here"). García and Cadena included in their briefs demographic data indicating that 14 percent of the county were persons with "Latin American surnames" and that over a period of twenty-five years there was no record of any person with a Mexican or Latin American name having served on a jury commission, grand jury, or petit jury in the county (*Hernandez v. Texas*, 251 S.W. 2d 531, rev'd, 347 U.S. 475, 1954).

That not a single person of Mexican descent had served on a jury in Jackson County in over twenty-five years, García and Cadena argued, "betrays the existence of a master plan." They further claimed that the number of cases in which the Texas courts had sanctioned the practice of excluding Mexicans from jury service demonstrated that Mexican Americans occupied an inferior legal status, as well as inferior social and economic positions. While the Texas courts maintained its "two-class" theory of races, Mexican Americans in Texas, the attorneys argued, were treated as a "third class—a notch above Negroes, perhaps, but several notches below the rest of the population" (Brief for Petitioner, U.S. Supreme Court, *Hernandez v. State*, 28). When persons of Mexican descent sought relief from discrimination in the courts, they were chided by judges as "members of the dominant class" who were seeking "special privileges." As García and Cadena put it, Mexican Americans "are told that they are assured of a fair trial at the hands of persons who do not want to go to school with them, who do not want to give them service in public places, who do not want to sit on juries with them, and who would prefer not to share restroom facilities with them, not even at the Jackson County court house" (29). The attorneys concluded their brief in these words: "All of the talk about 'two classes'; all of the verbal pointing with alarm at a 'special class' which seeks 'special privileges' cannot obscure one very simple fact which stands out in bold relief: the Texas law points in one direction for persons of Mexican descent . . . and in another for Negroes" (30). Mexican Americans wanted to be accorded the same treatment as African Americans, at least where the law and the Fourteenth Amendment were concerned.

In overruling the lower courts, the Supreme Court did not support the view of the state of Texas that there were only two classes—white and Negro—within the contemplation of the Fourteenth Amendment. Justice Earl Warren, writing for the unanimous Court, ruled that "community prejudices are not static, and from time to time other differences from the community norm may define other groups which need the same protection." These other differences included, but were not limited to, language, cultural practice, and religious beliefs. The Court noted, for example, that an attempt to exclude Roman Catholics from jury service was a violation of the equal protection clause of the Fourteenth Amendment. "When the existence of a distinct class is demonstrated, and it is further shown that the laws, as written or as applied, single out that class for different treatment not based on some reasonable classification," Justice Warren wrote, "the guarantees of the Constitution have been violated. The Fourteenth Amendment is not directed solely against discrimination due to a 'two-class' theory— that is, based upon differences between 'Negro' and 'white'" (*Hernandez v. Texas*, 251 S.W. 2d 531, rev'd, 347 U.S. 475, 1954).[11]

In successfully convincing the justices that Mexican Americans had been systematically excluded from jury service in Jackson County, García and Cadena relied on the pattern of proof established in *Norris v. Alabama* (294 U.S. 587, 1935). In that case, evidence that African Americans constituted at least 7 percent of the population of a county, that at least thirty blacks in the county qualified for jury service, and that none had been called for jury service in a generation, was held to constitute prima facie proof of the systematic exclusion of African Americans from jury service (Brief for Petitioner, U.S. Supreme Court, *Hernandez v. State of Texas*, 21). If the absence of blacks from jury service in counties where numbers of qualified blacks resided constituted evidence of discrimination regardless of the intention of jury commissioners, then the attorneys for Hernandez expected the courts to view the absence of Mexican Americans from jury service as no less discriminatory.

The lower court had ruled, however, that Mexican Americans could not have it both ways: insisting that Mexican Americans were white and, at the same time, arguing that a Mexican American could not receive a fair trial from a jury of all whites. In overruling the lower Texas courts, Chief Justice Warren cited as evidence of discrimination the fact that white residents of Jackson County regularly distinguished between "whites" and "Mexicans"; the fact of segregation of Mexican children in schools; and the failure of the county to appoint a single Mexican American juror in twenty-five years in a county whose population of Mexican Americans stood at about 14 percent. "It taxes our credulity," Warren wrote, "to say that mere chance resulted in there being no members of this class among over six thousand jurors called in the pool in 25 years" (*Hernandez v. Texas*, 347 U.S. 475, 482, 1954).

The *Hernandez* ruling established the legal precedent of extending the protections of the Fourteenth Amendment to Mexican Americans on the grounds that they constituted a "distinct class" of whites who had been denied equal protection of the laws governing jury selection. But it also created a dilemma: Mexican Americans, legally white, sought to protect their rights both as whites and as a "distinct class" that had suffered discrimination at the hands of whites. Their white racial status, even if only in the legal context, opened the door for social and economic advantage, but it proved to be a liability in court cases involving school desegregation.[12]

SCHOOL DESEGREGATION

Two weeks after the Supreme Court made its ruling in the *Hernandez* case, it made the historic ruling in *Brown v. Board of Education* (347 U.S. 483, 1954) that "separate but equal" segregation of blacks and whites was unconstitutional and thus overturned *Plessy v. Ferguson* (1896), which had made segregation the law of the land for over half a century. The ruling ended de jure segregation in schools and other public places, particularly in the South, where the color line was rigidly enforced.[13] In the Southwest, however, Mexican Americans sought to have *Brown* apply to them as well, even though they had been segregated by custom rather than by statutory authority. "Mexican schools," as they were called, were established throughout the Southwest from the late nineteenth century—allegedly for pedagogical reasons, which is what school officials had invariably claimed in courts in Texas, California, New Mexico, and Arizona since 1930. Mexican American children, these officials claimed, could not be educated in the same schools with Anglo children because Mexican-descent children had special language needs that could be met only in segregated classrooms. The problem was that school officials arbitrarily assigned all Mexican American children to these schools even though some were English-language dominant or spoke no Spanish at all. In Texas alone, by 1943, separate schools for Mexican Americans were maintained in 122 school districts in 59 counties across the state (Rangel and Alcala 1972, 314).

To avail themselves of the equal protection clause and *Brown*, Mexican Americans needed to win judicial recognition as an "identifiable minority group," similar to the ruling in *Hernandez* that Mexican Americans represented a "distinct class" of whites who had been systematically discriminated against. In that case, the Supreme Court had accepted evidence of community prejudice in the school segregation of Mexican American children as prima facie evidence that they were a distinct class, or an identifiable minority group, with regard to jury selection. From the earliest desegregation cases involving Mexican Americans, civil rights attorneys had argued that segregation of Mexican-descent children was unconstitutional in the absence of state law authorizing segregation of Mexican Americans.

In 1930 Mexican American parents in Del Rio, Texas, brought the first desegregation suit in Texas, *Independent School District v. Salvatierra* (33 S.W. 2d 790). They charged school officials with enacting policies designed to accomplish "the complete segregation of the school children of Mexican and Spanish descent . . . from the school children of all other white races in the same grade." The parents did not question the quality of the instruction or the condition of the separate schoolhouse; their suit was aimed exclusively at the school district's policy of separating Mexican American children from Anglo children. The Texas Court of Criminal Appeals upheld the lower court ruling, stating that "school authorities have no power to arbitrarily segregate Mexican children, assign them to separate schools, and exclude them from schools maintained for children of other white races, merely or solely because they are Mexicans." The arbitrary exclusion of Mexican American children from "other whites," the court ruled, constituted "unlawful racial discrimination" (795) (see San Miguel 1987, 78–80; Allsup 1979). Nevertheless, the court allowed for the segregation of Mexicans in the first three grades for those students whose English fluency was minimal, but only if such separation was applied with equal force to both white and "Mexican race" students.

No other school desegregation cases were brought before the Texas courts until after World War II, when returning veterans, like Dr. Hector García, founder of the American GI Forum, organized opposition to segregation of any sort, especially since there were no state laws mandating segregation of Mexican Americans as there were for African Americans. In 1947 a California federal court ruled in *Méndez v. Westminster School District* (64 F. Supp. 544, S.D. Cal. 1946, 161F. 2d 774, 9th Cir., 1947) that segregation of Mexican-descent children, in the absence of state law mandating segregation of Mexicans, deprived them of "liberty and property without due process" and "denied them the equal protection of the laws." Judge Albert Lee Stevens noted that California law authorized segregation of children belonging "to one of or another of the great races of mankind," which Stevens identified as Caucasoid, Mongoloid, and Negro. Stevens further noted that California law permitted segregation of Indians and "Asiatics" (as well as blacks), but that no state law authorized the segregation of children "*within* one of the great races" (emphasis added). Although Euro-Americans, or Anglos, rarely regarded Mexican Americans as "within" the white race, in the eyes of the law Mexican Americans were "Caucasoids" who could not be arbitrarily segregated from "other whites." In other words, the Court of Appeals for the Ninth Circuit ruled in favor of the Mexican American children on the ground, not that the "separate but equal" provision of *Plessy* was invalid, but that there was no California statute that mandated the segregation of Mexican Americans.

In 1948 Gus García, the able attorney in the *Hernandez* case, brought suit against four separate school districts in central Texas that segregated children of Mexican descent from "other white children." In *Delgado v. Bastrop Independent School District* (Civil No. 388, W.D. Tex., June 15, 1948), García used the "other white—no state law" strategy that had succeeded in previous desegregation suits, and the court enjoined the districts from segregating children of Mexican descent. The superintendent of public instruction, L. A. Woods, issued an order forbidding the segregation of Mexican-descent children on the ground that Mexicans were not, as far as the courts were concerned, "colored": "The reference to colored children . . . has been interpreted by the Texas courts and the Texas Legislature as including only members of the Negro race or persons of Negro ancestry. The courts have held that it does not apply to members of any other race" (quoted in Rangel and Alcala 1972, 337).[14] In Texas at least, the "Mexican race" was not considered "colored."[15]

Six years after the *Delgado* ruling, the Supreme Court ruled in *Brown v. Board of Education* (1954) that the segregation of blacks and whites was unconstitutional. But what about the segregation of Mexican Americans in public schools? Did *Brown* apply to them? In most places in the South, including Texas, desegregation meant eliminating the formerly de jure dual school system and instituting a unitary one that included both blacks and whites. In Texas, unlike the rest of the South, desegregation came to mean the dismantling of the tri-racial school system in which both blacks and Mexicans had been segregated into separate schools.

In 1968 African American and Mexican American parents of children in the Corpus Christi Independent School District filed a class-action desegregation suit, *Jose Cisneros v. Corpus Christi Independent School District* (1970), alleging that the school district operated a racially segregated school system in violation of the Fourteenth Amendment. More specifically, besides allegations of discrimination in boundary lines, construction policies, faculty assignments, and so forth, the parents accused the school district of desegregating predominantly black schools by integrating black and Mexican American students without substantially affecting the predominantly Anglo schools.[16] State officials, in other words, began using the "other white" argument to justify grouping black and Hispanic children to fulfill integration. *Cisneros v. Corpus Christi Independent School District* recognized Mexican Americans as an "identifiable minority group" and replaced the "other white" argument based on *Hernández v. State of Texas*. Specifically, Mexican Americans asked the court to rule on whether *Brown* applied to Mexican Americans as well as to African Americans. District Judge Woodrow Seals found that Mexican Americans and blacks were segregated in all levels of the school system as the direct result of state action: "The Court is of the opinion that . . . placing Negroes and Mexican-Americans in the same school does not achieve a unitary system. As contemplated by law, a unitary school district can be achieved here only by substantiated integration of the Negroes and Mexican Americans with the remaining student population of the district" (*Jose Cisneros v. Corpus Christi Independent School District*, 324 F. Supp. 599, S.D. Tex., 1970). Judge Seals further made it clear that *Brown* applied to Mexican Americans:

> This court reads *Brown* to mean that when a state undertakes to provide public school education, this education must be made available to all students on equal terms, and that segregation of any group of children in such public schools on the basis of their being of a particular race, color, national origin, or of some readily identifiable, ethnic minority group, or class deprives these children of the guarantees of the Fourteenth Amendment as set out in *Brown*. . . . Although these cases speak in terms of race and color, we must remember that these cases were only concerned with blacks and whites. But it is clear to this court that these cases are not limited to race and color alone. In this case, if the proof shows that the Mexican-Americans in the Corpus Christi Independent School District are an identifiable, ethnic-minority group, and for this reason have been segregated and discriminated against in the schools in the manner that *Brown* prohibits, then they are certainly entitled to all the protection announced in *Brown*. Thus *Brown* can apply to Mexican-American students in public schools.

The ruling in the *Cisneros* case was cited by the Court of Appeals for the Fifth Circuit in overturning a ruling made in a district court in Houston, *Ross v. Eckels* (468 F. 2d 649, 5th Cir., 1972), in which the judge maintained that "Mexican-American citizens resident within this school district historically have been and are now considered as if they were members of the white race and have never been considered or treated as a separate race or group with respect to any scholastic policy of the school district." The circuit judges cited an Austin desegregation case that came to the same conclusion that Judge Seals reached in the *Cisneros* case:

> No remedy for the dual system can be acceptable if it operates to deprive members of a third ethnic group of the benefits of equal educational opportunity. To dismantle the black-white segregation system without including the third ethnic group in the desegregation process would be to deny to that group all of the benefits of integrated schooling which the courts of this nation have been protecting for twenty years. To exclude Mexican-Americans from the benefits of tri-partite integration in the very act of effecting a unitary system would be to provide blacks with the benefit of integration while

denying it to another (and larger) group on the basis of ethnic origin. This in itself is a denial of equal protection of the laws.[17]

Mexican Americans in Corpus Christi had won their case to be integrated with whites, but not *as whites*. As an "identifiable ethnic-minority group," many Mexican Americans in the 1970s renounced their status as whites and claimed to be "brown," partly as a legal strategy but mostly as a consequence of the Chicano movement's emphasis on the Indian and mestizo heritage of Mexican people. Their legal status as "other whites" meant, as far as many Texas school boards and lower courts were concerned, that busing Mexican Americans to predominantly African American schools effectively desegregated these schools. Mexican Americans were careful not to imply that they objected to being educated alongside of blacks. Rather, they believed that Mexican Americans constituted an "identifiable minority group" despite prior court rulings that they represented a "separate class" of whites and that therefore, as members of a "third ethnic group," they should not be used to integrate predominantly African American schools.

The paradoxical nature of Mexican American identity, as an identifiable minority group and a separate class of whites, derives both from court rulings in the United States and from cultural notions in Mexico, like "mestizaje," in which mestizos comprise both white (Spanish) and nonwhite (primarily Indian) identities. The legal and cultural confusion over Mexican American identity stems in part from the fact that the United States has repudiated the idea of racial hybridity for most of its history and consequently has no cultural or legal context for understanding the racial place of mestizo peoples. When the census, for example, discontinued the use of the category "mulatto" after 1920, all racially mixed black-white offspring thus became "black." And antimiscegenation laws have long played a part in enforcing cultural as well as legal proscription against interracial intimacy (see Moran 2001).[18] The result is that Mexican Americans, or Latinos in general, are sometimes thought to be white and sometimes not. A case in point is the way in which our colleges and universities break down "diversity" by reporting the percentages of African Americans, whites, Asian Americans, Native Americans, and Hispanics on their campuses. This classification scheme is no different than the one used by the media and state agencies, which renders the category of "Hispanic" on a par with—and separate and distinct from—black and white. At the same time, the media uses the phrase "non-Hispanic whites" to distinguish them from Hispanics who identify themselves as white.

The creation of the Hispanic identity in the 1980 census reified this racial antinomy: Hispanics are a minority group (even when they are the majority), and they can choose to be white (see, for example, *Austin American-Statesman* 2002).[19] To add to the confusion, the media regularly alludes to the "browning" of America in its reports on the changing demographics of the United States, particularly in states like California, Texas, New York, Florida, and Illinois. The 2000 census, however, reveals that 48 percent of all Latinos in the United States chose "white" as their race, while 42.2 percent chose "some other race" besides white, black, Asian, or Native American. If almost half of all Latinos claim white racial status, then media hype about the browning of America notwithstanding, whites constitute the fastest-growing group in the nation.

The equivocal racial status of Mexican Americans continues to the present day and has influenced both the legal strategies and the court rulings in numerous cases involving issues of race and discrimination with respect to jury selection and school desegregation. And were it not for the Treaty of Guadalupe Hidalgo in 1848 guaranteeing the right of Mexicans to become U.S. citizens, the status of Mexicans as "white" for purposes of naturalization would certainly have been contested throughout the twentieth century, as the *Rodríguez* case amply illustrates.[20]

Finally, the relatively recent legal construction of Hispanic identity as both a minority group and a distinct class of whites has complicated the relationship between Mexican Americans and African Americans. In Texas and elsewhere in the Southwest, especially in recent decades, African Americans often find themselves in direct competition with Latinos for representation on school boards, city councils, and other local arenas of power in cities where Latinos have recently outnumbered African Americans (Davis 2001). And it appears that this competition will likely only get worse: recent census reports confirm that Hispanics have become the nation's largest minority group, raising troubling questions for African Americans, whose percentage of the population in many cities is actually declining. Will Latinos attempt to displace African Americans from positions of power locally? Will courts continue to back Hispanics who claim "minority" status over issues of affirmative action, equal employment, and jury selection? Will Hispanics insist on their whiteness in social and political contexts involving African Americans? This chapter cannot answer these and other questions like them, but if the continued growth of the Hispanic population in Texas and the ambiguity of their white-nonwhite racial status are any indication, then tensions between African Americans and Latinos throughout the nation will continue to complicate relations between these two groups for the foreseeable future.

NOTES

1. "The dark father of Hispanicity," according to the author Richard Rodriguez (2002, xii, 108), was Richard Nixon, for it was he "who drafted the noun [Hispanic] and who made the adjective uniform." See also Stavans (2002). I use the terms "Latino" and "Hispanic" interchangeably. See Rodriguez (2002, 103–23).

2. Mexican immigrants were entitled to vote after filing their intention to become naturalized citizens; see De Leon (1979, 1–2).

3. See also *In re: Saito*, 62 F. 126 (1894), *In re: Rodríguez*, 81 F. 345, Haney Lopez (1996), and Menchaca (2002, 282–85).

4. Besides *In re: Camille*, see also *In re: Burton*, 1 Alaska 111 (1900), *In re: Para*, 269 F. 643 (1919), *Elk v. Wilkins*, 112 U.S. 94 (1884), and Taylor (1929, 242–44).

5. Not until 1924 (Act of June 2, 1924, ch. 233, Stat. 253) did Congress pass an act conferring citizenship on all Native Americans in the United States.

6. In *Sanchez v. State*, 243 S.W. 2d 700 (1951), the Texas court held that "Mexican people are not a separate race but are white people of Spanish descent." Recent writings on the *Hernandez* case include Haney Lopez (1998) and Sheridan (2003).

7. See also *Smith v. Texas*, 311 U.S. 132 (1946), *Hill v. Texas*, 316 U.S. 403–5 (1942), and *Cassel v. Texas*, 339 U.S. 288–89 (1950).

8. In 1886 the Supreme Court extended the protection of the Fourteenth Amendment to the Chinese; see *Yick Wo v. Hopkins*, 118 U.S. 356, 369 (1886).

9. See also *Del Rio Independent School District v. Salvatierra*, 33 S.W. 2d 790 (1930), for the first case involving the segregation of Mexican-descent children in Texas.

10. But see *Terrell Wells Swimming Pool v. Rodríguez*, 182 S.W. 2d 824 (Tex Civ. App. 1944), in which Texas courts upheld a proprietor's right to deny Mexican Americans admittance to privately owned city swimming pools.

11. Justice Warren also cited an earlier case, *Hirabayashi v. United States* (1943, 320 U.S. 81), in which a Japanese American was indicted for failing to comply with curfew laws imposed on citizens of Japanese ancestry: "Distinctions between citizens solely because of their ancestry are by their very nature odious to a free people whose institutions are founded upon the doctrine of equality."

12. W. E. B. Du Bois (1903/1993, 9) coined the term "two-ness" to describe the duality—and the dilemma—of being an American and a Negro in America.

13. For the definitive history of the five cases that collectively came to be known as *Brown v. Board of Education of Topeka* (347 U.S. 483, 1954) and the politics of the process by which the case was decided, see Richard Kluger's magnum opus (1975). For more recent assessments of *Brown*, see Patterson (2001), Tushnet (1994), and Klarman (1994).

14. An exception was made for children in the first grade with language difficulty, but only if they were segregated on the same school grounds as Anglo students and only after such a determination had been made from the results of standardized tests.

15. While in Texas "colored" meant having "Negro ancestry," in Mississippi "colored" took on a broader, more inclusive meaning. In 1927 the Supreme Court upheld a Mississippi court ruling that allowed school officials to classify Chinese American schoolchildren as "colored" to prevent them from enrolling in the white-only school; see *Gong Lum v. Rice,* 275 U.S. 78 (1927).

16. See Brief for United States, U.S. Court of Appeals for the Fifth Circuit, *Jose Cisneros v. Corpus Christi Independent School District*, box 1, folder 2, Hector García Papers, Texas A&M University Archives, Corpus Christi, Texas. See also U.S. Commission on Civil Rights (1977). For a recent article on this case and other desegregation cases in Texas, see Wilson (2003).

17. Two years earlier, two of the three Fifth Circuit Court judges had upheld the Houston lower court decision that ruled that Mexican Americans were white for the purpose of desegregation, allowing Houston school officials to pair blacks with Mexican Americans while leaving Anglo schools largely unaffected; see *Ross v. Echols*, 434 F. 2d 1140 (5th Cir., 1970); see also San Miguel (2001).

18. On interracial sex in colonial New Mexico, see Gutiérrez's pathbreaking work (1991). For a review of recent scholarship on racial mixing, see Johnson and Burrows (2003).

19. Two-thirds of the 28 million foreign-born residents of the United States identified themselves as "white" on the 2000 census, compared to only half in 1990.

20. On the historical origins of racial ambivalence among Mexican Americans, see Foley (1998; 2003). For an important work on the formation of a Chicano identity in California during the 1960s and 1970s, see Haney Lopez (2003, 205–29).

REFERENCES

Allsup, Carl. 1979. "Education Is Our Freedom: The American GI Forum and the Mexican American School Segregation in Texas, 1948–1957." *Aztlan* 8: 27–50.
Austin American-Statesman. 2002. "Choosing to be 'White': Newcomers Expand Traditional Census Definitions." September 1. A-17.
Davis, Mike. 2001. *Magical Urbanism: Latinos Re-invent the City*. Rev. ed. London: Verso.

De Leon, Arnoldo. 1979. *In Re Rodríguez: An Attempt at Chicano Disfranchisement in San Antonio, 1896–1897.* San Antonio, Tex.: Caravel Press.

Du Bois, W. E. B. 1993. *The Souls of Black Folk.* New York: Alfred A. Knopf. (Orig. pub. in 1903.)

Foley, Neil. 1997. *The White Scourge: Mexicans, Blacks, and Poor Whites in Texas Cotton Culture.* Berkeley: University of California Press.

———. 1998. "Becoming Hispanic: Mexican Americans and the Faustian Pact with Whiteness." In *Reflexiones: New Directions in Mexican American Studies,* edited by Neil Foley. Austin: University of Texas Press.

———. 2003. "Partly Colored or Other White: Mexican Americans and Their Problem with the Color Line." In *Beyond Black and White: Race, Ethnicity, and Gender in the U.S. South and Southwest,* edited by Stephanie Cole and Alison M. Parker. College Station: Texas A&M Press.

García, Mario T. 1989. *Mexican Americans: Leadership, Ideology, and Identity, 1930–1960.* New Haven, Conn.: Yale University Press.

Gutiérrez, David G. 1995. *Walls and Mirrors: Mexican Americans, Mexican Immigrants, and the Politics of Identity.* Berkeley: University of California Press.

Gutiérrez, Ramón A. 1991. *When Jesus Came, the Corn Mothers Went Away: Marriage, Sexuality, and Power in New Mexico, 1500–1846.* Stanford, Calif.: Stanford University Press.

Haney Lopez, Ian F. 1996. *White by Law: The Legal Construction of Race.* New York: New York University Press.

———. 1998. "Race, Ethnicity, Erasure: The Salience of Race to LatCrit Theory." *California Law Review* 85(5, January): 1143–1212.

———. 2003. *Racism on Trial: The Chicano Fight for Justice.* Cambridge, Mass.: Harvard University Press.

Johnson, Kevin R., and Kristina L. Burrows. 2003. "Struck by Lightning? Interracial Intimacy and Racial Justice." *Human Rights Quarterly* 25(2, May): 528–62.

Klarman, Michael. 1994. "How *Brown* Changed Race Relations: The Backlash Thesis." *Journal of American History* 81(1, June): 81–118.

Kluger, Richard. 1975. *Simple Justice: The History of* Brown v. Board of Education *and Black America's Struggle for Equality.* New York: Vintage Books.

Lee, Sharon M. 1993. "Racial Classifications in the U.S. Census: 1890–1990." *Ethnic and Racial Studies* 16(1, January): 75–94.

Márquez, Benjamin. 1993. *LULAC: The Evolution of a Mexican American Political Organization.* Austin: University of Texas Press.

Menchaca, Martha. 2002. *Recovering History, Constructing Race: The Indian, Black, and White Roots of Mexican Americans.* Austin: University of Texas Press.

Montejano, David. 1987. *Anglos and Mexicans in the Making of Texas, 1836–1986.* Austin: University of Texas Press.

Moran, Rachel F. 2001. *Interracial Intimacy: The Regulation of Race and Romance.* Chicago: University of Chicago Press.

Nobles, Melissa. 2000. *Shades of Citizenship: Race and the Census in Modern Politics.* Stanford, Calif.: Stanford University Press.

Patterson, James T. 2001. Brown v. Board of Education: *A Civil Rights Milestone and Its Troubled Legacy.* Oxford: Oxford University Press.

Rangel, Jorge C., and Carlos M. Alcala. 1972. "Project Report: De Jure Segregation of Chicanos in Texas Schools." *Harvard Civil Rights–Civil Liberties Law Review* 7(March): 307–91.

Rodriguez, Richard. 2002. *Brown: The Last Discovery of America.* New York: Viking.

San Miguel, Guadalupe, Jr. 1987. *"Let All of Them Take Heed": Mexican Americans and the Campaign for Educational Equality in Texas, 1910–1981.* Austin: University of Texas Press.

———. 2001. *Brown, Not White: School Integration and the Chicano Movement in Houston.* College Station: Texas A&M University Press.

Sheridan, Clare. 2003. "'Another White Race': Mexican Americans and the Paradox of Whiteness in Jury Selection." *Law and History Review* 21(1, Spring): 109–44.

Stavans, Ilan. 2002. "The Browning of America." *The Nation*, June 17, 30–32.

Taylor, Paul S. 1929. "Mexican Labor in the United States: Migration Statistics." *University of California Publications in Economics*, vol. 6. Berkeley: University of California Press.

Tushnet, Mark V. 1994. *Making Civil Rights Law: Thurgood Marshall and the Supreme Court, 1936–1961*. New York: Oxford University Press.

U.S. Commission on Civil Rights. Texas State Advisory Committee. 1977. *School Desegregation in Corpus Christi: A Report*. Washington: U.S. Commission on Civil Rights.

Wilson, Steven H. 2003. "*Brown* over 'Other White': Mexican Americans' Legal Arguments and Litigation Strategy in School Desegregation Lawsuits." *Law and History Review* 21(1, Spring): 145–94.

Albert M. Camarillo

Chapter 17

Black and Brown in Compton: Demographic Change,
Suburban Decline, and Intergroup Relations in a South
Central Los Angeles Community, 1950 to 2000

In the wake of the civil disturbances that rocked Los Angeles in the spring of 1992, many social scientists hurriedly compiled demographic, socioeconomic, and attitudinal data on persons who lived within the South Central Los Angeles region where the destruction of private property and loss of life were concentrated. To the surprise of many scholars and the public at large, the racial and ethnic group composition of this area of metropolitan Los Angeles was different from what was expected. Indeed, many of the communities in the corridor stretching from downtown Los Angeles to Long Beach had changed significantly during the last quarter of the twentieth century. The once predominantly African American communities of South Central Los Angeles, the initial studies of riot-torn areas revealed, were in the throes of a demographic transformation. The three days of civil strife in Los Angeles over a decade ago also revealed the tensions and hostilities between members of the long-established black community and more recent residents of the area, including Korean immigrants and the new Latino majority. Further research in the aftermath of the riots pointed to many underlying sources of frustration among residents in these rapidly changing communities, especially declining occupational opportunities, increasing poverty, and cultural misunderstanding.

As a site of interracial and interethnic contact, the "City of Angels" and dozens of other cities across the nation changed profoundly over the course of the twentieth century. The nation's largest cities in particular and their expansive metropolitan areas were transformed over the past one hundred years. Suburban populations skyrocketed, city infrastructures expanded, and millions of native-born and foreign-born people alike moved in, out, and around the metropolises. But cities in different regions of the nation experienced different patterns of urban development and population change. For example, a snapshot of the principal cities in the northeast quadrant of the United States a century ago would reveal urban societies experiencing dynamic industrial growth and population expansion as millions of European immigrants migrated to those cities seeking occupational opportunities and affordable housing. At the same time, new urban transportation networks opened the door to suburban development, attracting upwardly mobile native-born whites and the children of immigrants who, over time, increasingly opted to leave ethnic communities for better housing. In their place, a growing migrant stream of African Americans from southern states ushered in the "Great Migration" beginning around World War I; they eventually changed the face of northern urban America. In the southwest quadrant of the nation, by contrast, a different type of urbanization process unfolded in a region characterized by different patterns of spatial growth, economic development, and ethnic-racial diversity. Here, intergroup relations during the first half of the twentieth century unfolded differently, as Latinos—primarily Mexican in origin—and Asian and European immigrants shaped the urban ethnic landscape. Not until World War II did blacks in large numbers figure prominently as urban dwellers in western cities. However, during the second half of the twentieth century in the Southwest and in the Northeast, a host of economic and demographic factors set in motion patterns of ethnic and race relations that were significantly different from those of previous decades. In the early decades of the century, intergroup relations in the nation's largest cities were largely defined by contact between native-born whites and European immigrants (and their offspring) and, increasingly over time, by black-white relations. The patterns in the final decades of the century, by contrast, were earmarked more by interactions between nonwhite groups in cities, especially urban areas where minorities were beginning to form majorities. Indeed, this pattern was clearly revealed in 1990 U.S. census data: racial and ethnic minorities had achieved majority population status in seven of the ten largest cities in the nation and approached near-majority status in two others (O'Hare 1992, 25). Consequently, relations between people of color increasingly defined a new racial frontier in intergroup relations in the American metropolis and in many metropolitan suburbs.

The city of Compton, a community located at the southern end of South Central Los Angeles, provides a window for viewing some of the changing dynamics of intergroup relations on the American urban scene and serves as an example of how economic, demographic, and social-cultural changes have altered much of suburban Los Angeles in the second half of the twentieth century. This chapter broadly outlines a process of suburban decline that has affected communities in South Central Los Angeles. Focusing on Compton, I examine the demographic changes that fundamentally transformed the city's population after 1950, setting in motion by the 1990s a new era of intergroup relations between blacks and Latinos. Although new intergroup relations manifested themselves in tensions among leaders over institutional resources and political inclusion, some initial evidence suggests that cooperation and more amicable relations exist at the neighborhood street level of local society. Interactions between people of color, as reflected in Compton, it can be argued, will increasingly characterize ethnic relations in the Los Angeles metropolitan region and in other cities where historic minorities now constitute contemporary majorities.

LOS ANGELES, SUBURBAN DECLINE, AND RACIAL INEQUALITY

Until recent years, Los Angeles and other western cities have not received ample attention because the literature on the origins of the so-called urban underclass and urban crisis has focused for the most part on the geographic isolation of African Americans in the deteriorating areas of older northeastern industrial centers. The work of urban historians, most notably Thomas Sugrue (1996), and a number of sociologists, William Julius Wilson (1987) and Douglas Massey (Massey and Denton 1993) foremost among them, provides insight into the variety of forces—racial attitudes, changing occupational opportunities, housing policies, and so on—that help explain why certain groups of poor blacks became trapped in urban core areas. Although there is debate about when the urban crisis began—whether in the pre– or post–World War II era—the literature clearly points to structural conditions in cities that gave rise to patterns of economic marginalization and the residential segregation of black urbanites. The analyses employed by scholars writing in this genre of literature are extremely useful in considering any case study, but they are generally less concerned with the relations between inner-city residents than they are with describing urban inequality and the status of the underclass. Furthermore, this literature does not examine changes that affect minority populations in suburban areas, a phenomenon that defines the Los Angeles experience for most groups.

Not until after the social upheaval that gripped Los Angeles in the early 1990s did many scholars begin to turn serious attention to this metropolis and its unique ethnic and racial group formations. *The Los Angeles Riots*, edited by Mark Baldassare (1994), was among the first publications to examine demographic, economic, attitudinal, and other perspectives that provided much-needed context for understanding the civil disorders in the spring of 1992. Two years later another anthology, *Ethnic Los Angeles*, edited by Roger Waldinger and Mehdi Bozorgmehr (1996), offered additional analyses of the many groups that predominate in this city and its environs. More recent publications have focused on particular case studies of communities in the Los Angeles metropolitan area that have been significantly changed as a result of population shifts among different ethnic groups (see, for example, Saito 1998). The most important publication, a recent volume edited by Lawrence Bobo and his colleagues (2000) entitled *Prismatic Metropolis: Inequality in Los Angeles*, provides a foundation for exploring the broad contours of racial inequality in contemporary Los Angeles County. Focusing on a variety of important topics, contributors to this volume point to several factors that help explain the relationships between the restructuring of urban-metropolitan economies, employment opportunities, residential isolation, poverty, and demographic change, especially as a result of immigration. A brief description of some important trends in Los Angeles County during the 1980s and 1990s, as examined by the contributors to *Prismatic Metropolis*, provides useful background here for explaining many of the changes that affected South Central Los Angeles communities at that time, including the city of Compton.

Although the diverse economy of the Los Angeles region did not go through the same type of deindustrialization that had such a severe impact on the older Rust Belt cities in the Northeast, some important changes occurred in the county since the 1970s. As the largest industrial center along the Pacific Coast, some of the durable manufacturing sectors in Los Angeles (for example, auto, rubber, glass, and steel industries) declined significantly after 1970, taking with them thousands of unionized blue-collar jobs. But the location of defense industries in the area buffered Los Angeles from precipitous downturns in the manufacturing sectors through the 1980s. Over the same period, other sectors of the economy expanded, such as professional services, retail trade, nondurable goods manufacturing (for example, garment and furniture industries), construction, business and repair services, and recreation and entertainment services. Over the twenty-year period from 1970 to 1990, the percentage of white-collar jobs increased and, with the exception of burgeoning service-sector jobs, the proportion of blue-collar occupations declined (Grant 2000, 51–56).

Shifts in the regional and local economies also reflected changes in the labor force, changes that mirrored larger demographic trends that altered the population profile of Los Angeles County in the last third of the twentieth century. Two patterns in particular had great bearing on changes in South Central Los Angeles communities, including Compton. First, the occupational structure in the county is still substantially stratified along certain racial, ethnic, and gender lines, although substantial progress occurred for many groups. For example, although the proportion of white, Asian, and black women in higher-paying jobs increased significantly between 1970 and 1990, and their proportion in the lower-paying jobs fell, Latinas, by contrast, continued to be heavily overrepresented in the worst-paying jobs. This development was directly related to the large-scale entrance of foreign-born Latinos into the labor market during these decades. Second, white men in 1990 continued to be overrepresented in the top-paying occupations and significantly underrepresented in the lower-paying jobs. Their Asian counterparts were more evenly distributed throughout the occupational structure, though they too tended to be overrepresented in the higher-paying jobs and underrepresented in the lower-paying positions. Black men, who as a group in 1970 were heavily underrepresented in six out of ten occupational categories, achieved a more even distribution among the higher-, medium-, and low-paying jobs in the labor market in 1990. However, black males with low levels of education who lived in high-poverty areas with correspondingly high crime rates were far more likely than their white or Latino counterparts to experience low levels of labor market participation. Finally, Latinos were the only group to show few signs of occupational advancement outside of the lowest-paying jobs at the bottom of the occupational ladder (Grant 2000, 57–59). Clearly, massive immigration from Mexico and other Latin American countries since the 1970s depressed the occupational achievement of Latinos as a group. In the context of these changes in the structure of the economy and corresponding changes in the labor force, Latinos and blacks who found themselves living in South Central Los Angeles neighborhoods and in Compton during the last two decades of the twentieth century faced enormous disadvantages.

With regard to demographic patterns, the population profile of Los Angeles County has been fundamentally refashioned by immigration from Latin America and Asia, white out-migration, and higher fertility rates among certain groups over the past thirty years. The county's population increased by almost two million between 1970 and 1990, but the number of white residents declined by 1.4 million. Proportionately, the decline was tremendous: in 1970 whites constituted 71 percent of the total population in the county, but by 1990 they were only 41 percent. Those who departed the county during these years included upper- and middle-income people who wished to move farther away from the expanding communities of immigrants and minorities as well as those with less education and fewer job skills who may have competed with immigrants for lower-paying jobs. In contrast to the sharp decline in the number of whites, the population of immigrants and their children has skyrocketed since the 1970s. This is especially true for Latinos and Asians, groups with larger families and a higher proportion of younger adults in the labor market. By 1990 foreign-born Latinos and Asians in the county had eclipsed the population of native-born within their respective populations. Latinos born outside the United States outnumbered their native-born counterparts three to one, while the ratio of foreign-born to native-born Asians was six to one. The population of Latinos and Asians in the county increased 238 percent and 426 percent, respectively, between 1980 and 1990. The stunning population growth of these two groups in particular continued unabated during the 1990s. Meanwhile, the population of African Americans remained stable over the last decades of the century as natural increase and in-migration of new residents helped offset a significant out-migration, especially from South Central Los Angeles neighborhoods. In 1970 blacks made up 10 percent of the county's population, a percentage they maintained in 1990 and in 2000 (U.S. Department of Commerce 2000; Grant 2000, 51–54).[1]

For black and Latino residents of South Central Los Angeles who could not afford to move to better housing areas in adjacent or distant suburbs, their economic conditions deteriorated during the 1980s and 1990s. Nowhere were signs of inequality and poverty more noticeable in Los Angeles County than in this area. A survey conducted by the United Way in 1998 estimated that the median household income in the South Central Los Angeles area was $18,673, and in Compton it was $29,083; the median income for all Los Angeles County households was $43,942. The percentages of persons below the poverty level in the South Central neighborhoods and in Compton that same year were 43 percent and 37 percent, respectively. Thirteen percent of persons sixteen years or older in Compton and 15 percent in South Central were unemployed in 1998; the unemployment figure for Los Angeles County was 7 percent overall (United Way of Los Angeles 1999, tables 6.6, 6.9, and 6.10). By any measurement, communities in South Central Los Angeles and Compton during the last two decades of the twentieth century manifested many of the characteristics closely associated with what social scientists have labeled the "urban crisis," but in the case of these areas, it was a "suburban crisis."

"SUBURBAN" SEGREGATION IN LOS ANGELES

Driving through the sprawling neighborhoods of South Central Los Angeles and Compton, it is difficult to imagine these communities in the same way one envisions Harlem, Chicago's South Side, or North Philadelphia. In contrast to many of the older industrial cities of the Northeast, where communities of immigrants and racial minorities were characterized more by population density in a vertically built environment during the first half of the twentieth century, the minority communities of Los Angeles fanned out in suburbs spreading east and south from the city's center. The suburban nature of Los Angeles and other cities of the West provides the geographical landscape for ghettos and barrios that have very different profiles from their counterparts in Rust Belt cities. For example, although Mexicans, historically the city's largest ethnic group, were initially concentrated in the old pueblo plaza downtown district early in the 1900s, tens of thousands of new immigrants from Mexico settled in working-class suburbs east of the Los Angeles River, where a variety of other immigrants also lived (Sánchez 1993, 63–83). By the 1960s, however, as native-born whites and European immigrants and the their offspring steadily relocated to suburbs on the west side, the sprawling east side barrios and smaller barrios in the Los Angeles area contained the second-largest Mexican-origin population outside of Mexico City and Guadalajara. Over 600,000 Spanish-surnamed people lived in the Los Angeles metropolitan area in 1960 (see Grebler, Moore, and Guzman 1970, 114–17). The barrio that took root in the Compton-Willowbrook area beginning in the 1920s was part of the metropolitan region where Mexican American communities dotted an expanding suburban landscape.

There were obvious reasons why Mexicans tended to concentrate in the sprawling east side barrios and in the smaller residentially segregated barrios scattered throughout the Los Angeles basin. Certainly social, cultural, and linguistic ties attracted growing numbers of residents to these Spanish-speaking communities, and the cost of housing was far more reasonable in barrios. But even those Mexicans with the means to live elsewhere, in predominantly white residential areas of Los Angeles, could not do so because of prevailing real estate practices and customs that forbade minorities from living in restricted districts. As the number of racial minorities increased in the Los Angeles area in the first half of the century, so too did the use of the ubiquitous restrictive real estate covenant. In the 1920s it was estimated that about 20 percent of the municipalities in Los Angeles County utilized restrictive covenants excluding non-whites altogether or segregating them into particular sections of the cities. By the mid-1940s the percentage was estimated to have climbed to about 80 percent.[2]

African Americans who settled in Los Angeles during and after World War II in large numbers were perhaps more deeply affected by restrictions based on race than any other minority group. The emergence of black neighborhoods south of downtown Los Angeles and their steady growth and concentration along a south central corridor gave rise in the postwar era to the largest black urban population in the West. Drawn to Los Angeles by prospects of good-paying jobs and a less hostile environment than that faced by their counterparts in other regions of the nation, the black population increased significantly over time (Grant, Oliver, and James 1996, 380–82; de Graaf 1970).[3] These same conditions were also responsible for luring a second great wave of immigrants from Mexico to Los Angeles and a migration of Mexican Americans from Texas and other states in the Southwest during the 1940s and 1950s. By 1970, although African Americans and Mexican Americans together numbered close to two million people in Los Angeles County, they lived in separate sections of the metropolitan area for the most part (Sabagh and Bozorgmehr 1996, 88; Grant 2000, 51–54). But during the last third of the twentieth century, economic and demographic trends changed these spatial patterns and set in motion a new era of black-Latino relations.

FROM WHITE TO BLACK IN COMPTON: THE FIRST RACIAL TRANSFORMATION

The city of Compton, incorporated in 1888, was like many of the suburban communities established in the late 1880s and early 1900s in Los Angeles County that attracted hundreds of thousands of people who relocated in southern California from other states. Jobs were plentiful in the expanding light industrial areas that sprouted up between the port of Los Angeles, near Long Beach to the south, and the growing commercial and transportation centers in and near downtown Los Angeles to the north (now known as the "Alameda corridor"). Workers in the "hub city" of Compton, located in the heart of the metropolitan area, had easy access to abundant employment opportunities across the region using the extensive urban electric railway system that was established long before freeways and autos utterly transformed transportation networks in the region. The boom of the war years and the stimulus brought about by the military-industrial economy fueled a population explosion throughout the county. Compton was no exception. From a small community of about sixteen thousand in 1940, the city's population expanded nearly threefold during the 1940s. Like most suburban municipalities in the southern and western sections of Los Angeles County, Compton at midcentury was home to a mostly white working-class and middle-class population. In 1940, 93 percent of Compton's residents were white (U.S. Department of Commerce 1942, table 32, 615).[4] With the exception of a small Mexican American barrio of several hundred people, established in the 1920s and located in the north-central area of the city that bordered the unincorporated Los Angeles County areas known as Watts and Willowbrook, few minorities lived elsewhere in the city (Camarillo 1971).

The residential segregation of Mexican Americans and the presence of only a small number of black residents scattered along Compton's northernmost boundaries was not a coincidence. Since the 1920s, realtors in Compton had rigorously controlled the sale of property through real estate covenants that prevented blacks from entering the city and relegated most Mexican Americans to a well-defined barrio area. In 1927, for example, researchers associated with the University of Chicago, who were interested in the residential segregation of minorities in California cities, distributed a survey to local real estate boards throughout the state. Compton's realty board president matter-of-factly reported, in response to a question about the city's segregation of residents by race, that "[a]ll subdivisions in Compton since 1921 have restrictions against any but the white race. . . . We have only a few Mexicans and Japanese in the old part of the city." In answering a question on the survey regarding how realtors could best deal with the problem of minorities in the city, he replied, "Advocate and push improvements and the Mexicans will move." "Sell the undesirables' property to a desirable," he added. "Never sell to an undesirable."[5] By the early 1950s, however, changes were under way that fundamentally altered the racial composition of Compton over the next twenty years. In 1950 the U.S. Census Bureau reported that 4.8 percent of the approximately 48,000 residents of Compton were African American. Within two years their proportion of the population had increased to 10.8 percent (U.S. Department of Commerce 1962, table 34, 5–98; Institute of Government and Public Affairs 1970). Middle-class and working-class blacks seeking better housing away from the growing congestion and deteriorating housing stock in South Central Los Angeles neighborhoods began to buy homes from whites wanting to flee areas of Compton that bordered encroaching black neighborhoods. Departing from their usual practices of racial restrictions, and in an environment where they could capitalize on the fears of whites, some real estate agents participated in "block-busting" efforts that facilitated rapid demographic change in west Compton. In other examples of block-busting, liberal white friends purchased homes in all-white neighborhoods and then quickly resold the homes to blacks, precipitating a rapid departure of white neighbors (*Los Angeles Times*, May 5, 1990, B-10). As whites fled to east Compton neighborhoods or to cities east of Compton that adhered to real estate restrictions based on race, such as nearby Lynwood, sections of northwest and central Compton were in the process of transition from white to black.

The 1960 census revealed that whites constituted only 60 percent of the city's population and that one-third of all residents, mostly blacks, had moved into Compton within the previous two years. By the mid-1960s Compton was geographically divided by race, with blacks predominating on the west side, most Mexican Americans clustered in their historic barrio on the north side, and whites on the east side. The light industrial manufacturing area located along Alameda Boulevard separated white from nonwhite Compton (Franklin 1962, 22).

The process of demographic change, already under way in the 1950s and early 1960s, gave way to a white exodus after 1965—the year of the Watts riots. What began with a routine arrest of a black motorist on a hot summer night in a community located about a mile north of Compton escalated into one of the most destructive race riots in American history up to that time. The civil chaos in Watts signaled to Los Angelenos, and to the nation as a whole, that pent-up frustrations and anger among blacks, in reaction to their unequal status in society, could erupt into violence, death, and massive destruction of property. For white residents in Compton, it ushered in a fear prompting an urgency to relocate, and indeed they did, in wholesale fashion. Within five years of the riots, the white population of the city had precipitously declined to only 16 percent. In 1970 African Americans composed 71 percent of Compton's residents, while Mexican Americans formed 13 percent of the city's population. Whites had all but abandoned Compton by the early 1970s, taking with them many, if not most, of the retail establishments and services that stretched along the downtown business center (U.S. Department of Commerce 1972, table P-1, Los Angeles–Long Beach SMSA; Camarillo 2001, 24–25; Cohen and Murphy 1966).

Touted as the first municipality west of the Mississippi River exclusively in the hands of black elected officials, Compton's new African American majority could rejoice in securing the reins of political power in a city where whites had previously shut them out of city hall and government jobs. Problems loomed on the immediate horizon, however, as newly elected officials grappled with a city treasury depleted by declining business revenues and a shrinking property tax base. As early as 1962, the author of a report for the Los Angeles Welfare Planning Council indicated that "[c]onditions fostering the growth of a deteriorating slum ghetto are present, and a potentially 'explosive' situation is bound to develop if left unchecked" (Franklin 1962, 22). Although the explosion occurred in Watts rather than in Compton in 1965, the report clearly pointed to structural problems that only grew worse through the 1970s and into the 1980s. Boarded-up storefronts in the old downtown area and the closure of banks and medical-dental facilities reflected increasingly dire economic conditions in the city. The Compton public schools also began to suffer from a lack of resources. Many school facilities, some of which were constructed in the 1930s and 1940s, were falling into disrepair. To make matters worse, the crime rate against people and property increased considerably, straining the ability of the local police department to manage a city that gave rise in the 1970s to infamous street gangs such as the Crips and Bloods. The introduction of crack cocaine into Compton and other South Central communities and the associated gang violence over the profitable trade in drugs sent Compton into a downward spiral of violence and further decline. National attention focused on the city by the late 1980s and early 1990s when it gained notoriety as the "murder capital" of the nation—the city that surpassed Washington, D.C., with the highest per capita homicide rate—and as the birthplace of "gangsta rap" music.

Black and Brown in Compton:
The Second Racial Transformation

Since 1970 an unprecedented number of immigrants from Latin America—especially from Mexico—came to the United States, and to California in particular. These new immigrants, the fourth and largest wave of Spanish-speaking immigrants to arrive in the twentieth century, and a high fertility rate among Latinos largely account for a demographic change of enormous proportion in Los Angeles County. The number of Latinos in the county increased from 3.3 million in 1990 to over 4.2 million in 2000. In 1990 they constituted 37 percent of the county's total population, a figure that increased to over 45 percent in 2000 (U.S. Department of Commerce 2000; Grant 2000, 52). Latinos continued to reside in the huge barrios in East Los Angeles but began to spread out into communities in the San Gabriel Valley, San Fernando Valley, Southeast Los Angeles, South Central Los Angeles, and southern Los Angeles County. Perhaps the most striking changes were neighborhoods in South Central L.A. where Latinos settled. Within two decades or so, many historic black neighborhoods were transformed into majority Spanish-speaking communities. African Americans with the means to do so moved to nearby communities to the west (Inglewood and Hawthorne, for instance) and to cities in adjoining counties to the east. Between 1980 and 1990 the black populations of San Bernardino County and Riverside County increased by 134 percent and 99 percent, respectively. Some, especially retirees, opted to return to their states of origin in the South, a movement that also included tens of thousands of African Americas from northern cities. The violence and destruction that occurred in April 1992 prompted others to leave their neighborhoods behind. In their place, Latinos, mostly immigrants, moved into the available, low-cost housing. Working-class and poor blacks in South Central L.A. communities during the 1980s and 1990s found themselves, for the first time, living next door to or near large numbers of Latino neighbors who were steadily becoming the majority residents in many areas (Morrison and Lowry 1996, 28–29; Camarillo 2001, 27; Rocco 1996).[6] This same process played itself out in Compton with unusual speed after 1970.

The small but stable barrio of Mexican Americans, located on the northern-central boundary between Compton, Watts, and Willowbrook (both of which are unincorporated areas of Los Angeles County), continued to make up about 10 percent of the city's total population through the 1940s and 1950s. Even as the dramatic demographic shift from the majority white to a majority black population in Compton unfolded with amazing rapidity during the 1960s, the Latino population (almost exclusively of Mexican origin) increased its proportion of the city's total to 13 percent. During the 1970s, however, the start of a massive and continuous movement of people from Mexico to the United States, and to southern California cities in particular, portended changes that would soon transform Compton in ways similar to what was happening in communities throughout South Central Los Angeles and beyond. Legal immigrants as well as a growing percentage of undocumented people composed this migration that, over time, has become one of the largest continuous international migration movements in United States history. The 1980 census revealed that Latinos were 21 percent of Compton residents while the African American majority population peaked at 73 percent. A decade later the 1990 census enumeration (despite what was obviously a substantial undercount of undocumented immigrants and a problem with the census form that affected the designation of race-ethnicity for Hispanics) indicated that the ethnic transformation of Compton had accelerated. Latinos had increased their share of Compton's population to 39 percent while the percentage of African Americans dipped to 49 percent. The pace of in-migration of Latinos, predominantly Mexican-origin people, and the out-migration of blacks from Compton did not slow down during the 1990s. Indeed, 2000 census data show that the population shift continued unabated: Latinos are now at least 57 percent (53,143) of the city's total population of about 93,000, though the actual percentage is probably closer to 60 to 62 percent. The corresponding decline of black residents in Compton during the 1990s reduced their proportion of the population to 40 percent (37,369) in 2000 (U.S. Department of Commerce 1993; 2000; Camarillo 2001, 26).[7]

Prior to 1970, the only visible features of things Mexican in Compton were located in the heart of the historic barrio where two small "mom-and-pop" grocery stores and a few retail shops had existed for at least two generations. Thirty years later, despite an out-migration of many middle-class Mexican Americans, Spanish-language storefront signs for Mexican restaurants, taquerias, auto repair shops, bakeries, barbershops, and a host of other retail trade establishments and services dot the city's landscape in conspicuous ways. New Latino residents are still most heavily concentrated in and around the historic barrio, but as the number of newcomers increased over time they inhabited most areas of the city by 1990. The northwest neighborhoods of Compton are the only sections of the city where blacks still outnumber Latinos, but even here the population is in a state of flux. The neighborhoods near the old barrio contain relatively few African American residents. But outside these two areas of the city, Compton has become a cultural, ethnic, and racial borderland where Latinos and African Americans meet on a daily basis. For the first time in the twentieth century in Los Angeles, black and brown people are living among one another in large numbers. Their interactions, both in public and in private spheres, are shaping a new frontier in ethnic and race relations in California (Kern County Superintendent of Schools 1999, figures 6 and 7).

LATINO-BLACK RELATIONS IN
CHANGING COMMUNITIES

The historical literature on intergroup race relations has focused primarily on black-white conflict. Residential dislocations, competition for jobs and housing, episodic uprisings, and the effects of negative racial attitudes tell much of the story about the historical tensions and conflict between whites and blacks. We know far less about conflict between various immigrant groups and racial minorities. Unlike historians who utilize archival documents and other primary sources to describe past relations between different ethnic groups, sociologists employ survey research and interviews to form perspectives about contemporary race and ethnic relations. These surveys attempt to gauge how people view others and how attitudes (including group stereotypes) influence perceptions. Survey researchers, like historians, are also interested in learning about the effects of neighborhood and demographic change and about tensions that arise over economic competition between various groups. Other scholars have examined how conflict and cooperation can be forged between groups as they focus attention on gaining influence in local politics.[8]

The few studies that examine black-brown relations point to several factors for explaining conflict and tension between African Americans and Mexican Americans and, to a lesser extent, other Latino groups. Melvin L. Oliver and James H. Johnson Jr. (1984, 84–85) were the first to analyze intergroup relations between Latinos and blacks in South Central Los Angeles in the early 1980s. The authors premised their survey research on the effects of the "urban crisis" in Los Angeles, an economic restructuring that led to changing occupational opportunities and demographic changes—especially the increase of the Latino population—in South Central neighborhoods. Using various sociological frameworks to describe intergroup relations, Oliver and Johnson conclude that the "survey data revealed that black and Latino expressions of antagonism toward each other are not that great, especially when compared to whites." "Whites," they add, "still express considerable antagonism and hostility toward both blacks and Latinos." They also conclude that though extreme antagonism does not characterize black-brown relations, there is some evidence identifying sources of ethnic tension. They find, for example, that the persistence of stereotyping and other negative perceptions affect social relations, especially when respondents are asked questions about competition over jobs, political power, and attitudes about one's neighbors. These potential sources of intergroup conflict, the authors suggest, are more highly correlated to younger, less-educated residents of both groups, individuals who are most likely to experience the consequences of the "urban crisis" in their respective neighborhoods (Oliver and Johnson 75–87). A decade after the Oliver and Johnson study was published, another survey of race and ethnic relations in greater Los Angeles, conducted by Lawrence Bobo and Devon Johnson (Bobo and Johnson 2000), came to similar conclusions with regard to perceptions about competition and negative attitudes about the group behavior of blacks and Latinos. Here again, however, the authors find no extreme racial polarization. In addition to these two survey research-based studies on attitudes and perceptions, there are a few case studies that describe black-brown conflict in other U.S. cities (Browning 1994; Mohl 1997; Castañeda 1989; Ericksen 1980; West, Klor de Alva, and Shorris 1996); they tend to focus on issues of competition over declining local resources, both economic and political.

In the case of Compton, the research on intergroup competition helps explain much of the interaction and reaction between African Americans and Latinos who coexist in rapidly changing neighborhoods. What is usually left out of these various analyses are examples of cooperation and coalition building that may help to ameliorate the tensions and conflict between Latinos, blacks, and other groups.[9] A case study of Compton clearly locates tension and conflict between the local African American and Mexican American leadership, especially concerning access to political representation and institutional resources. However, preliminary oral history research suggests that cooperation and positive interactions are also occurring between Latinas and their black women counterparts in some neighborhoods. Ironically, while struggles were taking place among group leaders over politics, power, and control of various institutions—issues that received widespread public exposure in the media—more positive interactions between blacks and Latinos were also taking place in neighborhoods. Furthermore, some efforts that are under way to build interracial cooperation and civic participation suggest possible future developments that may signal a different path for Latino–African American relations in Compton.

Mention the city's name and even the occasional reader of metropolitan and local newspapers or casual viewer of nightly television newscasts in Los Angeles will conjure up at least three principal images of the city of Compton: a gang-infested place, a city plagued by violence and political scandals involving municipal leaders, and an area with a deteriorating school system that required state intervention and administration. To these news-grabbing stories was added another in the 1990s: tensions and conflict between Latinos and blacks. Indeed, intergroup tensions surfaced among leaders from both groups over political representation and related issues, but these tensions are old ones that commonly arise when newer groups vie for political power with more established groups. The unique aspect of the conflict in Compton was that it involved issues of racial discrimination and calls for affirmative action to answer the claims not of nonwhites against whites, a pattern that largely defined race relations in the twentieth century, but instead of one minority against another. This interesting new twist on an old story of racialized politics reflected tensions that manifested themselves in other institutional settings in Compton's society.

It is clear that the rapid demographic shifts and neighborhood displacement of blacks by Latinos since 1970 contributed to concerns among black political leaders that a surging Latino population might threaten their local political control. But in the opinion of several black and Latino leaders, more was at play than simply the increasing number of Latinos in Compton. By the early 1990s questions had surfaced publicly for the first time about the absence of Latino representation in municipal politics and in other areas of the city, issues that help to explain the foundations on which tensions developed. For veteran black leaders in Compton who recalled the bitter civil rights struggles of African Americans a generation earlier, and for younger leaders who came of age in Compton when their leaders had wrestled control of local politics from whites, the issue of inclusion of Latinos into the body politic was one of "paying dues." In other words, to some black leaders, Latinos had no right to claims of political representation because they were latecomers who had not engaged in the struggles to win the right to vote. Why, some black leaders asked, should Latinos share in the political rewards that African Americans who had experienced discrimination in all aspects of local life had fought hard to obtain when Compton was predominantly white? In reaction to Latinos who were critical of the city's lack of representation of their group at all levels of municipal politics and in visible jobs, the flamboyant and controversial former mayor Omar Bradley reportedly said: "I see this as a well-constructed attempt to utilize the historical context of the African American civil rights movement for the benefit of a few people, who in fact probably don't even consider themselves nonwhite." Claiming that he had "no hostility toward Latino people," Bradley went on to say, "They have to organize. They have to strategize the way we strategized" (*Los Angeles Times*, April 16, 1998, A-8). Maxy D. Filer, a longtime leader in the local NAACP and Compton city councilman, put the matter in a similar context. "I have walked many picket lines in Compton," he said, recalling the days when blacks were routinely discriminated against in the 1950s and 1960s. "I have yet to have one Latino walk the picket line with me. . . . They crossed it many times. . . . They called me some names even the whites didn't call me" (*Los Angeles Times*, May 7, 1990, B-1).

In a similar refrain, after a group of Latinos claimed that Compton officials needed to create an affirmative action plan for hiring Latinos for city and school district jobs, Compton Unified School District Board trustee John Steward reportedly said that affirmative action was created as reparations for black slavery and was "not based on going back and forth across the [U.S.-Mexico] border 10 or 15 times a year," an obvious jibe at local Mexican residents who were immigrants (*Los Angeles Times*, May 7, 1990, B-1). Although there were some African American leaders who believed otherwise, enough comments were made by high-profile politicians to reinforce in the minds of Latinos that blacks were intent on keeping them out. Recoiling from what they considered to be comments that bordered on the offensive, some Latino leaders, such as Arnold Alatorre, vice president of the Latino chamber of commerce in the city, offered a different interpretation of how blacks gained political power. "Did they [blacks] really fight to get where they are now, or was it more or less that white people left and they were just here and took it [local politics] over?" "It was the white flight, it was the Watts Riots . . . when they [whites] left," Alatorre concluded, and "you guys [blacks] stepped in."[10] Clearly what had developed during the 1990s was a significantly different orientation among black and Latino leaders about why Latinos lacked political representation.

Speaking before the Compton city council in 1998, a Latina activist commented on the absence of a single Latino elected official, offering a reminder to the all-black council of their own recent history. "It was not that many years ago when black people were at this podium saying the same things to a bunch of white folks," she claimed. "How could you forget?" she asked the council rhetorically (*Los Angeles Times*, April 16, 1998, A-1). Two years later the frustration among some Latinos continued, as expressed by another local Mexican American who complained that "[t]here's no one to represent the Latino community. . . . The mayor is black. . . . The city council is black. . . .

There is not a single Latino representative on the council" (*Los Angeles Times*, February 13, 2000, D-1). In response to these types of criticism from Latinos, Mayor Omar Bradley quipped: "Representation is not based on population. . . . [It] is based on participation. . . . And for the large part of the last three decades, Latino participation has not been extremely high" (*Los Angeles Times*, February 13, 2000, D-1). In one important respect, the mayor was accurate, since a large percentage of Latinos in the city are immigrants and cannot vote. Latinos themselves recognize this problem in much the same way longtime resident Gloria Miranda put it: "We haven't politically mobilized, and you have a large number of residents who are not citizens. . . . We have not come together."[11] On the other hand, as Miranda was quick to note, under the leadership of Mayor Bradley in the 1990s she "saw a bigger divide, a bigger chasm emerge," between Latinos and African American leaders. This political chasm prompted a *Los Angeles Times* reporter to comment in 1990 that "blacks control every public and quasi-public institution in Compton—the schools, City Hall, the Compton Chamber of Commerce, the Democratic Party machine—and show no sign they intend to share their power" (*Los Angeles Times*, May 7, 1990, B-1).

Pedro Pallan, a longtime owner of a Mexican bakery in the city, was an important local Latino leader who grew disaffected in his pursuit of a city council seat as a result of being rebuffed by black officials. He was one of the Latino spokespersons who asked the city council to create a hiring committee in 1990 to increase the appointment of Latinos to municipal jobs and who pressed the local school district to appoint Latinos to positions in Compton's schools. As the first Latino appointed to the personnel commission of the school board, Pallan was taken aback by the unresponsiveness of his black colleagues on the commission who, he argues, resisted the hiring of Latinos. "One of the requirements seemed that you had to be black to be able to get the jobs here in the school district," Pallan states. "They kept telling me Latinos don't apply." "That is not true," he said emphatically. "I see them at the office applying for these jobs."[12] Exasperated with the political climate, which he and others saw as discriminatory, Pallan concluded: "Here we are, a truly minority community and the blacks are not giving us an affirmative action committee in either the city [government] or the school district" (*Los Angeles Times*, May 7, 1990, B-1). This fact seemed to him particularly ironic since Latino students already constituted a large majority of pupils in the district.[13]

In addition to the rift over representation in municipal politics, the handling of the public school district became another source of tension between Latino advocates and black leaders during the 1990s. The Compton schools were yet another example of the consequences of suburban decline and a changing population. The demographic shift in Compton during the 1950s and early 1960s had resulted in schools that were increasingly segregated by race—the east side schools were predominantly white, and the west side schools were primarily black. However, after 1965, as the city experienced a massive out-migration of whites and a corresponding in-migration of blacks, the student profile of Compton's schools abruptly changed. In 1950, for example, blacks made up only 19 percent of the district's student body, but a decade later they constituted 53 percent of the district's enrollment. By 1968 they made up the overwhelming majority of students in all district schools (Regional Planning Commission of Los Angeles County 1968, 9–10).

As a result of white flight, African Americans inherited five independent school districts operating within the city, but the Compton city council decided in 1970 to unite all schools under a single unified district. Nearly all of the newly appointed members of the Compton Unified School District Board of Trustees were African Americans. As they took control, a new accountability system of communication between the community, parents, and school administrators ushered in what they hoped would be a more efficient management of the schools. By the late 1970s and early 1980s, however, it was becoming apparent that the school district was facing mounting problems. Much in the same way municipal leaders were grappling with reduced revenues and mounting costs for city services, the Compton Unified School District also experienced financial woes related to the city's eroding property and business tax base. Without sufficient funds for repairs, upgrades, and the building of new schools in an increasingly over-crowded district, the Compton schools began to show signs of distress. Several questionable building revitalization projects and costly "sweetheart" construction contracts further exacerbated the financial condition of the district, a school system that state investigators later found suffered from gross mismanagement. The cumulative effect of these problems was that the school district faced enormous debt by 1992 and could no longer operate without additional aid from the state. Unable to meet payroll and financial obligations that amounted to $10.5 million in 1992–1993, the Compton school board requested emergency assistance from Sacramento. The state legislature granted the emergency loan, but with huge strings attached—Compton lost local control of its schools in 1993 as state receivership resulted in an administrator being appointed by the state superintendent of public instruction to oversee all operations of the district. To make matters worse, the state-appointed administrator reported that an additional $9.5 million was necessary to keep the district afloat the following academic year. Compton thus had the dubious distinction of being the first district in California history to be taken over entirely by the state, a status that lasted for ten years (Kennedy 1973, 1–15; Fiscal Crisis and Management Assessment Team 1999).

Not surprisingly, the state takeover of Compton's schools attracted widespread media attention that focused on the dilapidated buildings, leaking classrooms, and crumbling infrastructure of the city's public educational system in general. To the surprise of many, however, the new media spotlight on Compton schools in the early 1990s revealed that the large majority of students were not African American but Latino. The school crisis in Compton coincided with the period when the demographic shift in Compton's population from black to Latino was in its most rapid stage of transition. As recently as 1985, for example, African American pupils constituted 60 percent of the students in the district while Latinos formed 37 percent of the student body. By 1997 the proportions had reversed: Latinos composed about 63 percent of the student body while the proportion of black students had declined to 36 percent (Kern County Superintendent of Schools 1999, 9).

The swift change in the school population in Compton swamped a district ill prepared to handle the special needs of Spanish-speaking pupils. Consequently, issues arose among Latino parents and leaders about the educational neglect of their children. The issues at stake mirrored many of those that characterized the political arena in the 1990s. In 1999, for example, the state-appointed Fiscal Crisis and Management Assessment Team reported that many Latino parents and some schoolteachers and staff complained that district officials were reluctant to allocate funds for limited-English proficient (LEP) students, who accounted for over 41 percent of all students in Compton's schools (Fiscal Crisis and Management Assessment Team 1999, ii). Some Latino parents complained that black teachers, who constituted the great majority of Compton's teaching corps, stereotyped their students or were culturally biased. "They see all Latinos as dropouts and gang bangers. . . . It's the way they project us," said a Latina mother whose five children were enrolled in local schools (*Los Angeles Times*, May 7, 1990, B-8). Another Latino parent commented, "This problem has been going on for many years." "If you speak English, they listen to you," he concluded, "but if you don't speak English, school officials don't bother to do anything" (*Los Angeles Times*, June 8, 2000, B-1). Some of Compton's Latino leaders joined a chorus of criticism as they objected to what they saw as a major problem between the district's majority Latino student population and the gross underrepresentation of school personnel able to handle Latino children effectively. They pointed to the fact that in 1990 there were over eight thousand pupils in Compton schools who spoke little or no English, yet there were only forty-six certified bilingual education teachers districtwide (Fiscal Crisis and Management Assessment Team 1999, ii). Part of the problem of providing adequate educational services to a large LEP population was one of resources in a district caught in an untenable situation of limited resources and loss of local control. A native-born Latina, a principal at one of the district's elementary schools, admitted: "The things we have to do to teach Latino kids cost money . . . [and] we don't have enough bilingual materials" (*Los Angeles Times*, February 13, 2000, D-1). This type of explanation was plausible when Latino parents heard this statement coming from a Latina principal, but what parents and leaders reacted to negatively were statements made by black district leaders that infuriated them. One such statement came from a school board trustee: "I have no respect for the language issue." "This is America," he declared. "Because a person does not speak English is not a reason to provide exceptional resources at public expense" (*Los Angeles Times*, May 7, 1990, B-8). These types of statements embodied what many Latino parents and leaders considered to be an environment in the Compton schools that had a negative impact on their children. It led some to file a complaint with the U.S. Department of Education, citing reports that "school staff and administrators made racially disparaging remarks about students and/or treated students differently on the basis of race." The department's Office of Civil Rights concluded a two-year investigation in 2000 by asking the district to take appropriate steps to resolve these and other sensitive problems (*Los Angeles Times*, June 8, 2000, B-1).

In the wake of the 1990s, a decade marked by ethnic and racial tensions in at least two important institutional settings in the city of Compton—municipal politics and the school district—there are signs that the most troubling times in intergroup relations may be on the decline. A recent change in political leadership at the mayoral level, the appointment of a Latino to the school board, and a greater effort to pay more attention to the special needs of Latino students may signal a future characterized by improved relations between leaders and advocates from both groups, though lingering resentment dies slowly. At a different level of local society, preliminary evidence suggests that tensions and disputes in the political arena between black and Latino leaders may not necessarily transfer to intergroup conflict at the neighborhood street level. Oral accounts from a number of local citizens, both Latino and African American, hint at a cooperation and understanding that augurs well for future interaction between residents from very different backgrounds. Walter Cleveland, for example, a longtime African American resident of the city, sees the need for Latino representation in local government and welcomes political sharing between the two groups.[14] A young Latina, Claudia Soto, mother of a grade school pupil, agrees. "It's not a race thing with me," she remarks. "I support Latino candidates, but I also support people who do the right thing. They could be Chinese, they could be African American, whoever, as long as they do their job" (*Los Angeles Times*, April 16, 1998, A-8). Mr. Cleveland further states that he observes a sense of cooperation on many streets in Compton neighborhoods despite the language barriers that may exist. On his street, Cleveland reports, he witnesses daily examples of black and Latina mothers looking after each other's children playing on the streets and neighbors cordially greeting each other. In a different section of Compton, Ramona Corral, who lives among her black neighbors, comments that neighbors from both groups share a common goal of keeping their street clean and free of crime and drugs, a problem that once plagued the area. Despite simmering tensions and cultural misunderstandings, she has noted signs of positive change.[15] In a different example of personal intergroup sensitivity, a tearful scene at a Compton city council meeting demonstrated a level of concern in which women seem to be leading the way. City council meetings have been the site of many intense confrontations in recent years, but at a meeting of the council in June 2000, Jeffrey Camarillo (2001, 85), a project researcher, witnessed a different scene.

> During the portion of the meeting for audience comments, a Mexican American woman shared a heartfelt story about the murder of her husband and how she felt betrayed by the city because they provided her with no type of assistance after her husband's death and during her pregnancy. The woman's story was part of a plea to the mayor and city council to not disband the Compton Police Department for fear that more murders would occur as a result. Toward the end of her story, the woman completely broke down, crying and desperately yelling at Mayor Bradley to listen to her story. During her breakdown, two elderly African American women, who attended every city council meeting that I attended, left their seats in the audience and went to console the Mexican American woman. First, they hugged and held the woman as she was unable to hold back tears, and then they helped the woman back to her seat and sat next to her the rest of the meeting and comforted her.

Only additional research will determine whether these few personal accounts of intergroup cooperation and caring reflect a better climate of interaction between Latinos and African Americans outside of the political realm. One thing is certain in Compton, in both the spheres of one-on-one interpersonal relations and the realm of politics and education—more and more contact will occur between these groups. The challenge of intergroup relations in Compton was concisely stated by Martin Chavez, a longtime Mexican American resident: "We have a chance to really pull ourselves together and show how struggling groups can struggle together and not with each other" (*Los Angeles Times*, May 7, 1990, B-8).

Although the history of ethnic succession in neighborhoods has long been associated with the changing demography of urban America, suburban decline in Los Angeles and many other western cities in the United States has altered long-standing patterns of intergroup relations. To be sure, tensions and conflict over resources and institutional power, as they manifest themselves in cities such as Compton, are part of a long history of intergroup interactions. But these tensions are occurring in a vastly different environment where opportunities for upward mobility for some groups at the bottom of the economic hierarchy have constricted over the past twenty-five years. It is an environment where racial inequality, affecting certain segments of communities of color, is no longer confined to inner cities. It is, in addition, an environment where the dynamics of intergroup relations are being played out in the post–civil rights era with competing orientations among different groups of people of color about issues of equal opportunity and inclusion. Compton is one of many communities in California and elsewhere in the nation that stand at the crossroads of a new era of ethnic and race relations, where majorities of minorities will encounter one another with increasing frequency and where the seeds of coalition building and ethnic tensions may coexist.

NOTES

1. The proportion of blacks in Los Angeles County dropped slightly in 2000 to 9.8 percent.

2. For a report to the Los Angeles County Board of Supervisors regarding the use of racial restrictive real estate covenants, see John Anson Ford Collection, Huntington Library Manuscripts, box 68, Huntington Library, San Marino, California.

3. For a number of topical essays on blacks in California, including Los Angeles, see de Graaf, Mulroy, and Taylor (2001). For descriptions of blacks in cities of the West, including Los Angeles, see Taylor (1998).

4. The best available overview of ethnic and racial change in Compton is provided in Camarillo (2001).

5. See "Survey of Race Relations," box 2, Hoover Institution Library and Archives, Stanford University.

6. For a description of black out-migration from Los Angeles County, see Grant et al. (1996, 402–5).

7. Undercounts of minority groups, especially undocumented immigrants, are acknowledged by the U.S. Census Bureau. For example, it was estimated that 5 percent of all Hispanics and 4.4 percent of African Americans were missed in the 1990 census enumeration. See U.S. Department of Commerce (1992, table 2).

8. For a good overview of racial attitudes and surveys, see Bobo (2001). On the topic of coalition building between different groups in Los Angeles, see Regalado (1994) and Sonenshein (1994).

9. For one of the few studies that focuses on coalition building between blacks and Mexican Americans, see Marquez (forthcoming) and Pulido (1996).

10. Arnold Alatorre, interview with Albert Camarillo and Jeffrey Camarillo, Compton, Calif., August 2, 2000.

11. Gloria Miranda, interview with Ilda Jimenez y West, Torrance, Calif., August 7, 2000.

12. Pedro Pallan, interview with Albert Camarillo and Jeffrey Camarillo, Compton, Calif. August 3, 2000.

13. For a general treatment of intergroup relations in Compton, see Chavez (1998).

14. Walter Cleveland, interview with Jeffrey Camarillo, Compton, Calif., August 10, 2000.

15. Ramona Corral, interview with Jeffrey Camarillo, Compton, Calif., August 4, 2000.

REFERENCES

Baldassare, Mark, ed. 1994. *The Los Angeles Riots: Lessons for the Urban Future*. Boulder, Colo.: Westview Press.

Bobo, Lawrence D. 2001. "Racial Attitudes and Relations at the Close of the Twentieth Century." In *America Becoming: Racial Trends and Their Consequences*, vol. 1, edited by Neil Smelser, William Julius Wilson, and Faith Mitchell. Washington, D.C.: National Academy Press.

Bobo, Lawrence D., and Devon Johnson. 2000. "Racial Attitudes in a Prismatic Metropolis: Mapping Identity, Stereotypes, Competition, and Views on Affirmative Action." In *Prismatic Metropolis: Inequality in Los Angeles*, edited by Lawrence D. Bobo, Melvin L. Oliver, James H. Johnson Jr., and Abel Valenzuela Jr. New York: Russell Sage Foundation.

Bobo, Lawrence D., Melvin L. Oliver, James H. Johnson Jr., and Abel Valenzuela Jr., eds. 2000. *Prismatic Metropolis: Inequality in Los Angeles*. New York: Russell Sage Foundation.

Browning, Jeremy D. 1994. "Intergroup Conflict in Chicago: The Intersection of Ethnicity and Economic Restructuring at the Neighborhood Level." Ph.D. diss., University of Illinois at Urbana-Champaign.

Camarillo, Albert. 1971. "Chicano Urban History: A Study of Compton's Barrio, 1936–1970." *Aztlan* 2(2, Fall): 79–106.

Camarillo, Jeffrey Benjamín. 2001 "In and Out of Compton: The Impact of Demographic Change and Urban Decline in a Los Angeles Community: A Case Study of Compton." Senior honors' thesis, University of Pennsylvania, Urban Studies Program.

Castañeda, Ruben. 1989. "L.A. Job Fight: A Bitter Struggle or an Alliance?" *California Tomorrow: Our Changing State* 4(1, Winter): 7.

Chavez, Roberto. 1998. "A Historical Analysis of Race Relations Between Blacks and Mexicans/Latinos in Compton, California, 1960–1996." Master's thesis, California State University at Northridge.

Cohen, Jerry, and William Murphy. 1966. *Burn, Baby, Burn! The Los Angeles Race Riot, August 1965*. New York: Dutton.

de Graaf, Lawrence B. 1970. "The City of Black Angels: Emergence of the Los Angeles Ghetto, 1890–1930." *Pacific Historical Review* 39: 323–52.

de Graaf, Lawrence B., Kevin Mulroy, and Quintard Taylor, eds. 2001. *Seeking El Dorado: African Americans in California*. Seattle: University of Washington Press.

Ericksen, Charles. 1980. "Brown and Black: Collision or Coalition?" *Nuestro* 4(6, September): 17–20.

Fiscal Crisis and Management Assessment Team. 1999. "AB52 Assessment and Recovery Plans—Compton Unified School District." Sacramento, Calif.: California State Assembly (February 1).

Franklin, David. 1962. *Compton: A Community in Transition*. Los Angeles: Los Angeles Welfare Planning Council.

Grant, David M. 2000. "A Demographic Portrait of Los Angeles County, 1970 to 1990." In *Prismatic Metropolis: Inequality in Los Angeles*, edited by Lawrence D. Bobo, Melvin L. Oliver, James H. Johnson Jr., and Abel Valenzuela Jr. New York: Russell Sage Foundation.

Grant, David, Melvin Oliver, and Angela D. James. 1996. "African Americans: Social and Economic Bifurcation." In *Ethnic Los Angeles*, edited by Roger Waldinger and Mehdi Bozorgmehr. New York: Russell Sage Foundation.

Grebler, Leo, Joan W. Moore, and Ralph C. Guzman. 1970. *The Mexican-American People: The Nation's Second Largest Minority*. New York: Free Press.

Institute of Government and Public Affairs. 1970. "Report of the Compton-UCLA Urban Research and Development Project." Los Angeles: University of California, Institute of Government and Public Affairs (July).

Kennedy, Frederick A. 1973. *An Analysis of the Effect of Decentralization upon Groups of Affected People in the Compton Unified School District*. Los Angeles: University of Southern California Press.

Kern County Superintendent of Schools. 1999. "A Community in Transition: A Comparative Analysis of Demographic and Education Statistics, Compton Unified School District 1990–1998." Bakersfield, Calif·: Kern County Superintendent of Schools Research Services (January).

Marquez, John D. Forthcoming. "Rethinking Black-Brown Relations: Racial Violence and Unexpected Coalitions in Baytown, Texas." Ph.D. diss, University of California at San Diego.

Massey, Douglas S., and Nancy A. Denton. 1993. *American Apartheid: Segregation and the Making of the Underclass*. Cambridge, Mass.: Harvard University Press.

Mohl, Raymond A. 1997. "Blacks and Hispanics in Multicultural America: A Miami Case Study." In *The Making of Urban America*, by Raymond A. Mohl. Wilmington, Del.: Scholarly Resources.

Morrison, Peter A., and Ira S. Lowry. 1996. "A Riot of Color: The Demographic Setting." In

Ethnic Los Angeles, edited by Roger Waldinger and Mehdi Bozorgmehr. New York: Russell Sage Foundation.

O'Hare, William P. 1992. "America's Minorities—The Demographics of Diversity." *Population Bulletin* 47(4, December). Washington, D.C.: Population Reference Bureau, Inc.

Oliver, Melvin I., and James H. Johnson Jr. 1984. "Interethnic Conflict in an Urban Ghetto: The Case of Blacks and Latinos in Los Angeles." *Research in Social Movements, Conflict, and Change* 6: 57–94.

Pulido, Laura. 1996. "Multiracial Organizing Among Environmental Activists in Los Angeles." In *Rethinking Los Angeles*, edited by Michael Dear, H. Eric Schockman, and Greg Hise. Newbury Park, Calif.: Sage Publications.

Regalado, James A. 1994. "Community Coalition Building." In *The Los Angeles Riots: Lessons for the Urban Future*, edited by Mark Baldassare. Boulder, Colo.: Westview Press.

Regional Planning Commission of Los Angeles County 1968. "Compton Unified-Enrollment and Projection Analysis." Los Angeles: Regional Planning Commission of Los Angeles County.

Rocco, Raymond A. 1996. "Latinos in Los Angeles: Rethinking Boundaries/Borders." In *The City: Los Angeles and Urban Theory at the End of the Twentieth Century*, edited by Allen J. Scott and Edward W. Soja. Berkeley: University of California Press.

Sabagh, George, and Mehdi Bozorgmehr. 1996. "Population Change: Immigration and Ethnic Transformation." In *Ethnic Los Angeles*, edited by Roger Waldinger and Mehdi Bozorgmehr. New York: Russell Sage Foundation.

Saito, Leland T. 1998. *Race and Politics: Asian Americans, Latinos, and Whites in a Los Angeles Suburb*. Urbana-Champaign: University of Illinois Press.

Sánchez, George. 1993. *Becoming Mexican American: Ethnicity, Culture, and Identity in Chicano Los Angeles, 1900–1945*. New York: Oxford University Press.

Sonenshein, Ralph J. 1994. "Los Angeles Coalition Politics." In *The Los Angeles Riots: Lessons for the Urban Future*, edited by Mark Baldassare. Boulder, Colo.: Westview Press.

Sugrue, Thomas J. 1996. *The Origins of the Urban Crisis: Race and Inequality in Postwar Detroit*. Princeton, N.J.: Princeton University Press.

Taylor, Quintard. 1998. *In Search of the Racial Frontier: African Americans in the West 1528–1990*. New York: Norton.

United Way of Los Angeles. 1999. *Los Angeles County Service Planning Area, SPA 6–Databook*. Los Angeles: United Way of Los Angeles.

U.S. Department of Commerce. U.S. Bureau of the Census. 1942. "Characteristics of the Population—California: 1940." Washington: U.S. Government Printing Office.

U.S. Department of Commerce. U.S. Bureau of the Census. 1962. "Characteristics of the Population—California: 1960" Washington: U.S. Government Printing Office.

U.S. Department of Commerce. U.S. Bureau of the Census. 1972. *Census of the Population and Housing: 1970: General Characteristics of the Population*. Washington: U.S. Government Printing Office.

U.S. Department of Commerce. U.S. Bureau of the Census. 1992. "Assessment of Accuracy of Adjusted Versus Unadjusted 1990 Census Base for Use in Intercensal Estimates: Report of the Commission on Adjustment of Postcensal Estimates" (August 7). Washington: U.S. Government Printing Office.

U.S. Department of Commerce. U.S. Bureau of the Census. 1993. *Census of the Population-1990, California 040, Compton 160*. Washington: U.S. Government Printing Office.

U.S. Department of Commerce. U.S. Bureau of the Census. 2000. "Race, Hispanic or Latino, and Age: 2000." *Census 2000 Redistricting Data*, P.L. 94–171, Summary File.

Waldinger, Roger, and Mehdi Bozorgmehr, eds. 1996. *Ethnic Los Angeles*. New York: Russell Sage Foundation.

West, Cornel, Jorge Klor de Alva, and Earl Shorris. 1996. "Our Next Race Question." *Harper's* 292(1751, April): 55–63.

Wilson, William J. 1987. *The Truly Disadvantaged: The Inner City, the Underclass, and Public Policy*. Chicago: University of Chicago Press.

Index

Boldface numbers refer to figures and tables.